The Essential Jazz Records

Volume 1
Ragtime to Swing

The Essential
Jazz Records

VOLUME 1
Ragtime to Swing

Max Harrison, Charles Fox and Eric Thacker

A DA CAPO PAPERBACK

Library of Congress Cataloging in Publication Data

Harrison, Max.
  The essential jazz records / Max Harrison, Charles Fox, and
Eric Thacker.
  (A Da Capo paperback)
  Reprint. Originally published: London: Mansell, 1984.
  Contents: v. 1. Ragtime to swing.
  1. Jazz music–Discography. I. Fox, Charles, 1921-   . II.
Thacker, Eric. III. Title.
[ML156.4.J3H33 1988]
789.9′136542–dc19   88-16174
ISBN 0-306-80326-7 (pbk.: v. 1)   CIP

This Da Capo Press paperback edition of *The Essential Jazz
Records: Vol. I* is an unabridged republication of the edition
published in London in 1984. It is reprinted by arrangement
with Mansell Publishing Ltd.

Published by Da Capo Press, Inc.
A Subsidiary of Plenum Publishing Corporation
233 Spring Street, New York, N.Y. 10013

Contents

Introduction

Those who listen to jazz usually hold aloof from popular music. Certainly there are few links between the sophistication found, in varied forms, in most periods of jazz and the plausible crudities of rock'n'roll. Yet it was the enormous international impact of rock in the 1960s that dealt what, for a while, seemed like a fatal blow to jazz, drastically reducing the size of its audience, above all among the young. But jazz has withstood many crises, and although at the time of this book's publication rock is still with us, it is far past its peak. Not wholly unconnected with rock's decline is the fact that the flow of jazz recordings, new and reissued, which at one time almost stopped, gradually in the 1970s rose to flood levels. The 1980s have seen a continuation.

This material, partly because of its sheer quantity, is the subject of very little informed comment, and the present book is the first of two volumes that are intended to fill the vacuum by providing a critical guide to the entire field of recorded jazz. As such, the approach is highly selective, and this serves two purposes. The main one is to draw attention to the finest jazz that has survived on disc. But, secondly, an important task of criticism, as Egon Friedell points out in his *Cultural History of Modern Times*, lies 'in clear division and classification, in order to make the totality accessible and understandable'. Which is to say that a thorough knowledge of the specific performances analysed here should lead to comprehension of jazz as a single, indivisible entity, and may well provide insights about other, quite different, forms of music. Further, while this is, of course, a book of record reviews, not a history, the choice of recordings dealt with and the order in which they are set imply definite attitudes, some of them quite fiercely revisionist, to the way this music has developed. The book is decidedly in opposition to much received opinion on the subject, and this arises partly from its undertaking a number of tasks which hitherto had been evaded.

Perhaps the most important of these is its evaluation of the jazz of the 1930s, which occupies by far the longest chapter. This phase of the music, although the focus of much energetic propaganda, has received little critical attention. Scarcely less neglected by the established histories, however, have been the New York school of the later 1920s, dealt with in the second section of Chapter 3, or the enlightening early performances found in the 'New Orleans' section of Chapter 1. Often, standard attitudes towards famous jazz recordings are the result of their being listened to in comparative isolation. Once they are heard in context with a substantial body of related, allegedly subsidiary, material a new perspective can emerge. The choice presented here is the fruit of persistent and very wide listening carried out over many years. That is not to suggest there were no disagreements between the three authors. In fact these occurred fairly often, and there has been no editorial attempt to suppress their expression in the text. At one point, indeed, evidence of a strong difference of opinion occurs in two adjacent reviews! The issue here is that although this work may identify the best jazz, and perhaps discuss it in a helpful way, ultimately the reader should make his own evaluations.

Most of the contents of the present volume are LP collections of 78 rpm recordings, and such assemblages, particularly those dating from the earlier years of the microgroove era, have been put together with extremely varied degrees of understanding. An important task, therefore, was to find the most perceptively chosen compilations. In doing so the net was cast widely, and the scope of this book is international, which in turn reflects the nature of the record world. The flood of jazz LPs comes from several countries in Western Europe, plus the United States and Japan. They are produced by a very large number of companies, many of them small and with limited areas of general distribution. This means that a considerable proportion of the issues recommended here are not easy to obtain, except from retail outlets concentrating on jazz records. The market for such music has in fact defined itself more clearly in recent years than hitherto, and in parallel with this trend, jazz LPs, both of new and reissued material, have increasingly been designed for specialist collectors.

Yeats reminds us that 'only dead sticks can be tied into convenient bundles', and we are dealing here with the branches of a tree that is very much alive and still growing, despite regular announcements of its démise. The classification of the chosen material adopted here may at some points be found surprising, but it is designed to suggest the network of relationships, many of them generally unacknowledged, which unite the many strands of this music. It was not easily arrived at.

A more technical question that persistently arose was that of the pitch of reissues, and, in the case of earlier items, of the original recordings. It was a long time before the companies were able to get their turntables rotating at an even speed and one that was consistent from session to session. Consequently, many of the classics of early jazz (and contemporaneous recordings of other music, of course) were cut at a variety of slightly wrong speeds. The problem is compounded by their often being remastered for microgroove reissue fractionally above or below the original pitch. It was decided, however, that it would be tedious to comment repeatedly on such variations in the main text, although the matter is one that ought to be surveyed in detail elsewhere.

There is little point in listing the many other problems faced during the preparation of this book, though a further one may be mentioned. This was the difficulty of obtaining information from American sources. With the exceptions, gratefully acknowledged herewith, of Shirley Klett, Jerome Shipman, Dan Morgenstern of the Institute of Jazz Studies, and Frank Driggs, no U.S. institution or individual ever replied to any of our requests for information or comment, even when these were repeated several times. In rather noticeable contrast, nearly all European individuals and organizations answered promptly, in full, and often with enthusiastic offers of further help. Typical was the case of Jacques Lubin of Barclay Records, who at one point, for example, sent a French MCA catalogue carefully annotated by hand with a mass of further information.

But the person to whom the present volume owes most is Derek Langridge. He acted as what might be termed its research and development officer, and located many of the most advantageous LP embodiments of the chosen material. Without the very many ideas he contributed and his prodigious quantity of work, which included making the indexes, this book would have taken a different, almost certainly inferior, form, and might not have been completed at all.

Max Harrison

Abbreviations

Instrumental and Related Abbreviations

acc	piano accordion	fl	flute
ah	alto horn	g	guitar
alt	alto saxophone	gfs	goofus
ban	bandoneon	har	harmonium
bar	baritone saxophone	hca	harmonica
bh	baritone horn	hfp	hot fountain pen
bj	banjo	hps	harpsichord
bj-mand	banjo-mandolin	hrp	harp
bs	string bass	jg	jug
bs clt	bass clarinet	kz	kazoo
bs d	bass drum	mand	mandolin
bsn	bassoon	mar	maraccas
bs sx	bass saxophone	mel	mellophone
cap	comb and paper	mrm	marimba
cel	cello	ob	oboe
ch	chimes	p	piano
cls	celeste	perc	percussion
clt	clarinet	picc	piccolo
C-mel	C melody saxophone	sar	sarrusophone
cnt	cornet	sl w	slide whistle
cond	conductor	sop	soprano saxophone
cym	cymbal	spch	speech
d	drums	tbn	trombone
eng h	english horn	ten	tenor saxophone
eu	euphonium	th	tenor horn

timp	timpani	vib	vibraharp
tpt	trumpet	vla	viola
tu	tuba	vln	violin
vcl	vocal	v-tbn	valve-trombone
vcl gr	vocal group	wbd	washboard
vcl		wdbl	woodblock(s)
intrjc	vocal interjection(s)	xylo	xylophone

Discographical Abbreviations

After records' label names the country of origin is indicated as follows:

(A)	United States of America	(F)	France
(Ar)	Argentina	(G)	Germany
(Au)	Australia	(H)	Holland
(Cz)	Czechoslovakia	(It)	Italy
(D)	Denmark	(J)	Japan
(E)	Great Britain	(Sd)	Sweden
(Eu)	Europe	(Sw)	Switzerland

An asterisk (*) before a second label name at the top of a discographical heading indicates a record whose contents are only partially—though usually substantially—the same as those of the record actually discussed, whose number appears first. In such cases no exactly equivalent issue exists elsewhere.

Warning

Although every effort has been made to ensure the correctness of record numbers, neither the publisher nor the authors hold themselves responsible for purchases made with reference to this book.

1

Origins

Prelude:
the Afro-American Background

This is a restricted selection from the vast range of musics, related yet often very different, which both preceded jazz and ran parallel to it.

1 **Savannah Syncopators**
CBS (E) 52799

Elder Richard Bryant's Sanctified Singers: Bryant, possibly Bessie Johnson, B. Taylor, Sally Sumler (vcl); Will Shade (hca); unidentified mand, g, jg, wbd (probably members of the Memphis Jug Band). Memphis, Tenn., 28 February 1928.
Lord, Lord, He sure is good to me

Lonnie Coleman (vcl, bj); unidentified g. Atlanta, Georgia, 12 April 1929.
Wild about my loving

Walter Roland (p); Lucille Bogan, Sonny Scott (spch). New York City, 19 July 1933.
Jookit jookit

Blind Darby (vcl); Will 'Casey Bill' Weldon (g); probably Peetie Wheatstraw (William Bunch) (p). Chicago, 25 March 1935.
Meat and bread blues (Relief blues)

Robert Johnson (vcl, g). Dallas, 20 June 1937.
Stop breaking down blues

Butch Cage (vcl, vln); Willie 'Preacher' Thomas (vcl, g); Mrs Thomas (d). Zachary, Louisiana, 9 August 1960.
44 blues

Hassan Danlado Griots: Danlado (garaya two-string lute); five other garaya players; five calabash rattle players; female singers. Kantche, Niger, 26 February 1963.
Bako

Maikai (vcl, gouroumi three-string lute). Dogondoutchi, Niger, 7 March 1963.
Babai

Ladzekpo and Ewe Drum Orchestra: Ladzekpo (atsimeru master d); two kidi d, two sogo d, gong-gong clapperless bell. Legon, Ghana, 30 April 1964.
Agbekor

Kunaal (vcl, calabash rattle); Sosira (vcl, gourd two-string vln). Nangodi, Ghana, May 1964.
Praise song

Lanyare and Lobi Tribesmen: Lanyare (gil xylo); another gil xylo, pot-ring dale d, upright kor, log d, iron clappers. Lawra, Ghana, May 1964.
Sabere

Mamprusi Tribesmen: master drummer (calabash d); flutes, rattles, dancers. Navrongo, Ghana, May 1964
Ring dance

Thiam Sy Griots: Sy (halam five-string chordaphone); another halam. Dagana, Senegal, c. 1965.
Halam improvisation

Orchestra of Bour Fode Diouf: eight djoundjoungs (membrane d); players and singers. Kaone, Senegal, c. 1965.
Wong

Como Drum Band: Napoleon Strickland (vcl, fife); John Tyrus (snare d); Other Turner (bs d). Como, Mississippi, 5 September 1968.
Oh, baby

George 'Bongo Joe' Coleman (vcl, oil d, rattle-drumsticks). San Antonio, Texas, 7 December 1968.
Eloise

The Afro-American fusion, which led to jazz and blues as well as other genres outside the scope of this book, remains an historical fact yet a shadowy, only half-explained event, largely because gramophone recording was not invented in time, and musicologists, even early folklorists, were not really concerned about what was happening on the underside of American society. Scholarship has since rolled back some of the mystery, but even jazz and blues historians tend to be cautious about equating the culture of the transplanted slaves with what had been left behind in Africa. It is no longer good enough, everyone agrees, to generalize about 'Africa', or even 'West Africa', ignoring the complexities that exist within even quite smallish parts of that continent. This lack of hard information led the British blues writer, Paul Oliver, to produce a short but valuable book, *Savannah Syncopators* (see Bibliography), based on first-hand experience of both West Africa and the American South. What Oliver discovered was that the drum orchestras of the coastal rain forests had nothing in common with the buoyant swing of jazz or blues. A likelier source, he suggested, lay northward, in the savannah belt, where large trees — and consequently large drums — were scarce, and where a variety of stringed and wind instruments were played by griots, a class of hereditary musicians. This LP, compiled by Oliver to illustrate his theory, includes a number of field recordings he made himself in Ghana, Senegal and Niger. But as well as proffering an argument, the disc also constitutes a valuable anthology of musical practices which seem — just from listening to them, anyway — to surface both in Africa and in black communities of the American Deep South.

After an archetypal country blues from Blind Darby, there are three examples of drumming: elaborate overlaying of rhythms by the Ewe ensemble with their big drums, a ring dance by Mamprusi tribesmen, and — very African in stance and style — some fife playing and drumming from Mississippi. The high, strained voices of the Senegalese singing a war chant is paralleled by the approach of 'Bongo Joe' Coleman, who performed in the streets of Galveston and San Antonio, playing an oil drum and singing about the age-old theme of sexual rejection – though with a bawdy riposte near the end. The griot band of Kantche perform in praise of a renowned hunter, but in a manner that is echoed by Elder Bryant's Sanctified Singers, whose use of jug and washboard also reflect something of the griot tradition. Especially striking is the similarity between the savannah griots, Kunaal and Sosira, and the Louisiana duo of Butch Cage and Willie Thomas. It is not only the violin playing, but the way Cage and Thomas sing — just like the griots — in voices pitched higher than for normal speech. Similarly, there seems to be an obvious link between the five-string halam, as used by the Senegalese griots, introducing short riffs, even something akin to blues feeling, and the way Lonnie Coleman handles his banjo, an instrument that is almost certainly descended from the halam. Less convincing is Oliver's attempt to link West African xylophone playing — demonstrated by Lanyare and other Lobi tribesmen — with boogie woogie piano playing (the older theory about borrowed guitar patterns seems just as likely). But perhaps the most remarkable pairing occurs on the last two tracks, where the griot singer and gouroumi player, Maikai, uses the same sort of repeated vocal patterns and rhythmic phrases as Robert Johnson from Mississippi, one of the greatest of all bluesmen.

C.F.

2   Negro Church Music
Atlantic Special (E) 590.029, Atlantic (A) 1351

Recording made by Alan Lomax in the summer of 1959.
Vera Hall (vcl). Livingston, Alabama.
Death, have mercy
James Shorty (vcl); Fred McDowell (g). Northern Mississppi.
I want Jesus to walk with me
Mrs Mary Lee and congregation (vcl).
Jesus is real to me
Rev. R. C. Crenshaw and congregation (vcl).
I love the Lord · I'm going home on the morning train
Rev. G. I. Townsel and congregation (vcl).
A sermon fragment
Madam Mattie Wigley and congregation (vcl).
Power
Viola James (vcl); Ed Young (cane fife); Lonnie Young (bs d). Tyro,
Mississippi.
On that rock
Viola James, James Shorty and congregation (vcl). Tyro, Mississippi.
Jesus on the main line · This little light of mine
Henry Morrison and the St Simon's Island Singers (vcl). Georgia.
I'm gonna sail like a ship on the ocean
Bessie Jones, John Davis and the St Simon's Island Singers (vcl).
Georgia.
Blow, Gabriel
Felix Dukes (vcl); Fred McDowell (g). Northern Mississippi.
Motherless children
Bernice McClellan and congregation (vcl).
What do you think about Jesus? (He's all right)

> 'Oh death, have mercy,
> Oh death, be easy . . . '

Vera Hall's fluid, domestic voice dwells on mortality with little
hint of the transcendent hope evident in most gospel songs. Her
plea is not to God, but to death, an impersonal but threatening
watcher. Is this poetic convention, or a kind of polytheistic hint?
Examples of ritual music in **1**, such as *Ring dance* and *Praise
song*, may show that some of the vitality of black religious music
in America was derived from African attitudes to life and death.
There are few other verbal hints in this sequence of Lomax
recordings, but there is frequent drawing upon extra-Christian
sustenance. In *I love the Lord*, the rasped nasal roar of R. C.
Crenshaw's 'sacred voice' may seem to have more in common with
the hortatory tones of the Senegal war chant leader than with
anything that would normally be described as preaching. But it

taps more mysterious springs, for it is the universal earth-shaking voice of the shaman or conjur' man — a notion which probably would scandalize the preacher and his people. The savage tone-distortion suggests an almost visceral tradition which evokes natural and non-human sounds to achieve super-natural ends; and it seems to be this god-voice which was fed, by whatever ladle, into the growling, mute-distorted horns of the Ellington and other bands, just as the much simplified call-and-response patterns were transmitted, partly by piano ragtime conventions, into jazz orchestral arrangements.

In *I love the Lord*, voices shift pitch and interweave out-of-tempo, for this is not so much singing as it is a strange combination of crude melody and the wailing of heightened emotion. This more familiar rhythmic antiphon appears in songs like *What do you think about Jesus?* and *Power*. In these, and in *I'm going home on the morning train*, a deal of quite expert singing is mixed with more spontaneous sounds, and there are also percussion instruments and an organ on some tracks. There could be some jazz feedback here, yet the interaction of voices and instruments which is heard on some of the West African record-ings certainly became a feature of ritual music in post-slavery America. In *I'm going home on the morning train* and *Power* the excitement, for jazz ears, is enhanced by the way in which the chorus attacks phrases, precise as an orchestral section; and, in the former song, a similar sophistication may prompt the later exchange of roles between lead singer and chorus. The unison phrasing in the Mamprusi *Ring dance* from Ghana (1) provides an instructive comparison.

The Georgia sea-island songs are ostensibly much simpler, but closer listening reveals subtle intricacies. *I'm gonna sail like a ship on the ocean* and *Blow, Gabriel* may hint at musical commerce with the Bahamas, where nautical themes and the imagery of 'blowing spirits' crop up in anthems and spirituals. In the first of these the singers respond to the leader by joining their voices to his in improvised harmonies and phrase variations, whereas *Blow, Gabriel* is more antiphonal and, in its accelerating frenzy, approximates to the wildness of a ring shout. Clapping and stomping patterns become especially complex in *Blow, Gabriel*. Once, hands, feet and meeting-house floor were drum substitutes; now they are integral to the expression, even in those more organized services where conventional percussion instru-ments are used.

All these recordings, from Alabama, Mississippi and Georgia, are valuable for their clear hints of the sounds which must once have influenced southern jazz musicians. There are related performances on **3**, e.g. Fred McDowell's guitar playing, a unison voice rather than an accompaniment in the normal sense; other examples of the styles of Vera Hall, Viola James, Lonnie and Ed Young; a magnificent white spiritual; and, in the baptizing scene, an instance of spirit-possession which exhibits the violence of feeling which is frequently conveyed here in more musical ways.

The relation between religious fervour and musical expression is not easy to write about. It seems clear that the singers on most of these tracks are more immediately concerned with what they feel than with the form their expression takes. Usually a pretty rudimentary form will suffice. In the two items involving Pastor Crenshaw, the charismatic chant somehow retains a coherence which depends partly on the basic alternations between tonic and dominant or tonic and flattened third, and partly on the logic of shared emotion. There is little on the other tracks which goes further in melodic complexity, but of rhythmic, melodic and harmonic variation in the spontaneous paraphrasing of themes there is more than enough to keep any keenly listening mind busy.

Though much of this flexibility may flow from African springs, two things should be remembered. The first is that much of the West African music typified by examples on **1** has passed a formal rather than an emotional legacy to its American offspring. The second is that, independently of tradition, religious enthusiasm has often encouraged musical spontaneity. Eighteenth- and nineteenth-century evangelical singers, in England and elsewhere, were much given to florid ornamentation of tunes, and the Great Revival obviously carried this penchant over into American fields. In the white *Sacred Harp* tradition (*cf. Windham* on **3**), the process of 'southernization' — making drab harmonic parts more animated — went on for decades, and ornamentation, both written and improvised, was endemic. So techniques of variation were fostered and developed consciously; though such emphases were stronger amongst the white congregations with their specialized didactic systems. Fervour prevails over form more readily amongst the black singers. 'Yes, God is real,' sang the New Orleans-born Mahalia Jackson, 'because I feel Him in my soul.' This is the antithesis of classical theology, but remains the essence of the black gospel singer's approach to faith and song. Simple means suffice, for 'the Spirit gives life'; and it is the resultant musical fluidity which had the profoundest effect on the spirit of jazz — though seldom in the most obvious ways.

Instances of what is often called church influence in jazz styles will emerge later in this book, but it will always be easiest to comment where the gift is a formal one (as in, say, James P.

Johnson's *Carolina shout* in **171** or Fletcher Henderson's *Down south camp meeting* in **127**), and countless bequests of impetus and fervour will go unnoticed because they have become so integral to the inheriting music.

One might remark, finally, that *Down south camp meeting* sounds extremely tame in comparison with *I'm going home on the morning train*, which has a far more convincing echo in Henderson's *Hotter than 'ell* (also on **127**). Theological speculation on this point is probably best avoided. E.T.

3 **Sounds of the South**
Atlantic (E) 590.092, Atlantic (A) 1346
Recordings made by Alan Lomax in the summer of 1959.
Neil Morris (vcl); Charles Everidge (mouth bow[1]); unidentified g[2].
Mountain View, Arkansas.
Banks of the Arkansas · *Wave the ocean*[1] · *Jesse James*[2]

Lonnie Young (vcl, bs d); Ed Young (cane fife); Lonnie Young jnr (snare d). Northern Mississippi.
Hen duck

Estil C. Ball (vcl); unidentified g. Rugby, Virginia.
The farmer's curst wife

Vera Hall (vcl). Livingston, Alabama.
Boll weevil holler · *Trouble so hard*

Mountain Ramblers: Cullen Galyen (vcl, vln, bj); Charles Hawks (bj); James Lindsay (g) or Eldridge Montgomery (g, vcl); unidentified mand; Thurman Pugh (bs, vcl). Galax, Virginia.
Jesse James

Bob Carpenter (vcl, g). Galax, Virginia.
Kenny Wagner

Viola James and congregation. Tyro, Mississippi.
Is there anybody here that loves my Jesus?

Rev. W. A. Donaldson and congregation. Huntsville, Alabama.
Baptising scene

Alabama Sacred Harp Singers (mixed choir). Fyffe, Alabama.
Windham

Fred McDowell (vcl, g). Northern Mississippi.
Keep your lamps trimmed and burning

Sid Hemphill (pan pipes); Lucius Smith (d). Senatobie, Mississippi.
Come on, boys, let's go to the ball

Charley Higgins (vln); Wade Ward (bj); Charley Poe (g), West Virginia.
Paddy on the turnpike

John Davis and group.
Join the band

Ed Lewis (vcl) with group[1]. Parchman, Mississippi.
Lucky holler · *I be so glad when the sun goes down*[1]

Further material collected in 1959 can be found on six companion LPs, each with a specific theme, that were released at the same time in the *Southern Folk Heritage series*. *Sounds of the South*, however, attempts to give an overall picture of the range of both white and black musics. Understandably, a proportion of the contents are not immediately relevant to this book. Those are the songs and dances of the white mountain folk, their traditions still close to Anglo-Saxon or Scots roots, any contact with Afro-American practices — in these examples, anyhow — minimal or non-existent. Which is a pity, for there are plenty of instances of the overlapping of white and black styles in the South, particularly the adoption of blues by singers such as the phenomenally popular Jimmy Rodgers [1]*. Instead, we get ballads sung by Estil C. Ball and Bob Carpenter (Kenny Wagner, it seems, was a murderer who was captured by a woman sheriff), and square dance patterns played by Neil Morris (who passes on his grandfather's recollections of Jesse James), the Mountain Ramblers, and — most impressive of all — the banjo player Wade Ward. But the most remarkable performance must be that by the Alabama Sacred Harp Singers. *Windham* is to be found in Sankey's *Sacred Songs and Solos*, but the approach here is that of the shape-note singers, whose repertoire is drawn from the 461 pieces in the *Sacred Harp* hymnal, all notated in squares, rounds, diamonds and triangles. Perhaps the vigour and passion of this music is related to the looseness of that harmonic method. Certainly the result has much in common — emotionally rather than formally — with black gospel singing.

Black gospel singing itself provides more links (of the kind outlined under 1) with African practices. For example, the interaction between the Rev. W. A. Donaldson and his congregation, projecting a high level of intensity into the ritual of baptism. Excitement of a different order is provided by Viola James and her congregation, the latter building up repeated patterns like big band riffs, buoyant and swinging; an open-ended performance, unlike the hermetic pressures of the previous tracks. *Trouble so hard* ('Don't nobody know my trouble but God') is a spiritual sung unaccompanied by Vera Hall, who transcends the normal conventions, existing in an aesthetic dimension where any division between form and content appears meaningless. A superb artist. Her *Boll weevil holler* is, as its title suggests, a field holler, that solitary cohort of the worksong and precursor of the blues. Ed Lewis's *Lucky holler* falls into the same category, although Lewis lacks Vera Hall's spiralling virtuosity. Lewis and

* Numbers in square brackets refer to the Notes listed on page 553 ff.

a group of fellow prisoners at Parchman Farm contribute an instance of the worksong itself, its rhythm related to the job in hand, very much a group effort, with the role of the lead singer akin to that of a preacher exhorting his congregation, another example of the call-and-response patterns so often cited as an African survival.

The African tinge is also evident in the pan pipes and drum duet of Sid Hemphill and Lucius Smith, and in the work of the Young family of Mississippi. Ed Young plays a cane fife more or less in tandem with the drumming, repeating the same phrases, while Lonnie Young sings in a slightly casual fashion. But the drumming here sounds in some ways more military than African, another instance of how hard it is to be sure about origins or influences. What must be beyond dispute, however, is the quality of Fred McDowell's singing and playing. Voice and guitar can rarely have cohered so intimately as they do in *Keep your lamps trimmed and burning*, even to the extent of half a line being sung, then completed by the guitar. C.F.

4 Great Jug Bands
Historical (A) HLP36

Dixieland Jug Blowers: Lockwood Lewis (alt); Clifford Hayes (vln); Cal Smith, Emmett Perkins, Curtis Hayes (bj); Earl McDonald (jg, vcl[1]); H. Clifford (jg). Chicago, 12 October 1926.
Florida blues · *Skip skat doodle-do*[1] · *Louisville stomp*

Earl McDonald's Original Louisville Jug Band: personnel probably as above with H. Clifford absent; vcl by McDonald. Atlanta, 30 March 1927.
Rocking chair blues

Memphis Jug Band: Will Shade (hca); Vol Stevens (g, vcl, spch); Will Weldon (g); Ben Ramey (kz); Charlie Polk (jg). Memphis, 13 February 1928.
Papa long blues

Cannon's Jug Stompers: Noah Lewis (hca, vcl); Elijah Avery (g); Gus Cannon (bj, jg); probably Hosea Woods (kz). Memphis, 20 September 1928.
Viola Lee blues

Jed Davenport and His Beale Street Jug Band: Davenport (hca); unidentified vln; probably Joe McCoy (g, vcl[1]); unidentified mand[2]; unidentified jg; Davenport or Memphis Minnie (refrain vcl[3]); comments by band[4]. Memphis, February 1930.
Beale Street breakdown[2,4] · *You ought to move out of town*[1,3] · *The dirty dozen*[5] · *Save me some*[1,3]
[5]unidentified 12-string g added.

Phillips' Louisville Jug Band: Hooks Tilford (alt); unidentified fl, g, jg. Chicago, *c.* early August 1930.
Soldier boy blues

Cannon's Jug Stompers: Lewis (hca); Woods (vcl, g); Cannon (bj, jg).
Memphis, 24 November 1930.
Bring it with you when you come
Memphis Jug Band: Shade (hca); Jab Jones (p, vcl); Charlie Burse
(mand); Robert Burse (perc). Chicago, 6 November 1934.
Mary Ann cut off
Charlie Pierce (vln); probably Shade (g); Charlie Burse (ten g);
Jones (jg); Robert Burse (perc); probably Shade, Burse (scat vcl). Chicago,
8 November 1934.
Memphis shakedown

Like the performances on 1–3, the above recordings were made at
a time when jazz was in a quite advanced state of development,
yet they refer back to a period long before it existed. Though jug
band music took many forms, and so anthologizes well, a rough
separation may be proposed into 'country' and 'jazz' categories,
and that division is followed by the two sides of this disc. Both
kinds of group, however, occupied territory between, although
adjacent to, blues and real jazz, and were country and urban folk
bands. Another common denominator was the use of unorthodox
instruments, specifically the jug, played by blowing across the
aperture to produce a booming noise. Also met with is the kazoo, a
sausage-like tube with a membrane inside which vibrates when
sounds are vocalized into the instrument, the washtub bass, and
the washboard, played by scraping the corrugations with fingers
wearing thimbles. Such devices must date from a time when
instruments were scare, but more conventional resources were
eventually used in combination with them and, indeed, the great
clarinettist Johnny Dodds recorded with one of the groups
represented here, the Dixieland Jug Blowers, in 1926 and used a
washboard on several of his sessions (see **38–40**).

Performances like those on the above disc are no more
recreations of a distant past style than were the band recordings
made in New Orleans during the 1940s, and they contain, in fact,
references to other near-contemporary music. For example, Tilford's contributions to *Soldier boy blues* by Phillips' Louisville
Jug Band evoke his playing on Ma Rainey's 1925 *Army camp
harmony blues*, and Cannon's Jug Stompers' *Bring it with you
when you come* partially resembles *Waiting for a train* by Jimmy
Rodgers. Davenport's *Beale Street breakdown* and *The dirty
dozen*, an instrumental version of the familiar insult game, are
classic instances of the music of such groups, especially the
former; but perhaps the Dixieland Jug Blowers, with alto
saxophone, violin, three banjos and two jugs, best exemplify their
heterogeneous instrumentation. Lockwood Lewis is a more capable altoist than some heard on mid-1920s orthodox jazz dates.

The jugs are a raucously disruptive element in the otherwise rather sedate *Louisville stomp* but fit well into *Skip skat doodle-do*, a nonsense song. The interplay of Clifford Hayes and Lewis on *Florida blues*, a remake of this group's 1924 *Hatchet head blues*, and that between Tilford and the unidentified flautist on *Soldier boy blues*, should be compared to the counterpoint with Dodds on **39**.

Although the minstrel-evoking banjos are replaced by softer-voiced guitar and mandolin, the Memphis Jug Band has more of a folk character than some of the groups here, especially as harmonica and, sometimes, kazoo are present. *Memphis shakedown*, one of the best tracks, features remarkable violin playing by Pierce, and although the jug sometimes attempts a boogie bass, there is something of the *alfresco* air of country dance music to this, as there is to the Beale Street Jug Band titles. In *Mary Ann cut off* it takes on more the ambience of a blues band, with prominence given to Jones's barrelhouse piano playing, which is aptly complemented by harmonica, mandolin and miscellaneous percussion. Another notable performance is *Viola Lee blues* by Cannon's Jug Stompers, a prison song which features moving vocal choruses by Noah Lewis.

The sleeve's claim that none of these pieces had before appeared in microgroove is incorrect, more than half of them having been reissued on LPs in the RBF, Origin, Roots and other catalogues. Also recommended is Origin (A) OJL4, which has the same title as this disc.   M.H.

Ragtime

Ragtime was the most identifiable precursor of jazz. Although thought of by contemporaries as mainly a vocal form [2], subsequent developments were influenced by the best of piano ragtime.

5 **Heliotrope Bouquet: Piano Rags 1900–1970**
Nonesuch (A) H71257

Ragtime nightmare (Tom Turpin) · *Heliotrope bouquet* (Louis Chauvin –Scott Joplin) · *The easy winners* (Joplin) · *Ethiopia rag* (Joseph Lamb) · *Pegasus* (James Scott) · *Wall Street rag* (Joplin) · *Pork and beans* (Luckey Roberts) · *Graceful ghost* (Bolcom) · *Sea biscuits* (Bolcom) · *Brass knuckles* (Bolcom-William Albright)
William Bolcom (p). New York City, 1970.

It is an encouraging sign of the diversity of which jazz and related musics were capable nearly from the start that while the folk craft of barrelhouse piano playing evolved in red-light districts, others strove to produce a body of consciously artistic keyboard music, almost free of any hint of the blues spirit (despite exceptions such as the third strain of Joplin's *Pineapple rag* on **6**) or of improvisation. Though in some ways paralleling Sousa's determinedly optimistic marches (**11**) and the exultant glitter of Gottschalk's virtuoso piano works, ragtime can have had few models [3]. One, though, was minstrel show banjo music, as can be heard both in Turpin's fairly primitive *Ragtime nightmare* of 1900 and in Scott's more sophisticated *Pegasus* of almost two decades later. It is fascinating to study this music's texture, its adaptation of banjo figures to the keyboard, which parallels Scarlatti's earlier use of guitar (or vihuela) phrases in his harpsichord pieces. Metric regularity enhances the eupeptic vigour of each rag, and if the persistent syncopations do not create tension in the long term that is because the formal outlines are so clear. Yet structural control arises because there *is* something to control, and within these strict patterns, with strongly contrasted sections instead of the continuity of the blues, considerable discoveries were possible.

Joplin's *Easy winners*, for example, though written in 1901, already goes, with its chromatic passing-notes and contrapuntal dissonance, some way beyond Turpin's rather despairing use of diminished sevenths. The first two sections of *Heliotrope bouquet* (1907) were notated by Joplin from Chauvin's playing, and they have a refined Gallic piquancy that recalls Jelly Roll Morton, a Creole like Chauvin. Joplin's programmatic *Wall Street rag* (1909) is a more satisfying achievement than his overtly experimental *Euphonic sounds* (**6** and **7**), pointing to the heightened fusion of popular and more complex elements which he might have brought off had he lived longer — and forged himself a fuller compositional technique.

But Lamb's *Ethiopia rag*, from the same year as *Wall Street*, and Roberts's *Pork and beans* (1913) show, in any case, that all sorts of pianistic and expressive possibilities were suggested to the next generation and, particularly in the latter piece, that barrelhouse elements could be intensified by ragtime's lucidity. To be sure, the point was made more conclusively by James P. Johnson (e.g. his *Carolina shout* of 1921 on **171**) and by Morton (e.g. the 1923 *Kansas City stomps* on **45**). And whatever its limitations, ragtime, this reverse image of the blues, has a strange and sad poetry, which is fleetingly caught in Bolcom's own *Graceful ghost*, one of the three modern pieces which somewhat anachronistically pad out this programme. The poetry arises from ambiguity: does the music mock the formal devices it borrows, or does it mock the process of borrowing itself? Bolcom's performances, which exactly follow the original sheet music, take good account of such matters, and of the idiomatic differences between, say, Joplin's style, which is rooted in Missouri, and the more forceful big-city rhythms of Roberts. (This account of *Pork and beans* should be compared with the very different one recorded for the Circle label by the composer in 1946.)   M.H.

6 Scott Joplin: Ragtime Pioneer
Riverside (Eu) RLP8815

Original rags (1899) · *Maple leaf rag* (1899) · *Sunflower slow drag* (1901) · *The entertainer* (1902) · *Something doing* (1903) · *Weeping willow rag* (1903) · *The cascades* (1904) · *Fig leaf rag* (1908) · *Pineapple rag* (1908) · *Euphonic sounds* (1909) · *Stoptime rag* (1910) · *Scott Joplin's new rag* (1912) · *Kismet rag* (1913) · *Magnetic rag* (1914).

The above are all piano rolls; the dates refer to the original publication of the compositions, but may also correspond with the dates when the rolls were cut.

7 Piano Rags by Scott Joplin Vol. 1
Nonesuch (A) H71248

Maple leaf rag (1899) · *The entertainer* (1902) · *The ragtime dance* (1906) · *Gladiolus rag* (1907) · *Fig leaf rag* (1908) · *Euphonic sounds* (1909) · *Magnetic rag* (1914).

The dates refer to the original publication of the compositions.

Joshua Rifkin (p). New York City, 1969.

Joplin was always convinced that one day his music would be performed in concert halls around the world. To some extent that prophecy has been fulfilled, aided by the kind of approach that Rifkin brought to these pieces, with its coaxing of audiences hitherto innocent of ragtime's past. In his lifetime, however, Joplin owed at least part of his success — that early success which followed upon the publication of *Maple leaf rag* — to the fact that his rags could be rattled out on player-pianos, even if the trickier passages often sounded jerky. Those mechanical overtones surface quite frequently on the Riverside LP. Unfortunately, too many recordings of piano rolls display the lack of subtlety so evident here, the instrument being pedalled relentlessly, without regard for those variations of speed and dynamics — expression, in other words — that are called for in the sheet music and which a skilful operator can supply. Nevertheless, being able to hear these piano rolls provides an historical perspective.

Whether Joplin himself cut six of the rolls, as the sleeve note claims, seems debatable (even distinguishing between hand-played and mechanically cut rolls can be difficult). In any case, he was never a particularly gifted performer: the young pianists in St Louis delighted in getting him to play *Maple leaf rag*, then throwing it off themselves at a dizzy pace and with extravagant decoration. Six of these particular rags are also played by Rifkin, and several of them are discussed below. The others include *Original rags*, Joplin's first publication and unusual in having five strains instead of the four common to the majority of classic rags, and *The cascades*, a piece of programme music, intended to flow and ripple, written specially for the 1904 St Louis Exposition. *Sunflower slow drag, Something doing* (described on the sheet music cover as a 'ragtime march'), *Scott Joplin's new rag* and *Kismet rag* (three strains only) were collaborations between Joplin and Scott Hayden, a relative by marriage, whose only published rags were those he wrote with Joplin. Incidentally, the English issue omits *Kismet rag* from the sleeve, while *Euphonic sounds* — omitted from the record label — shares a track with *Pineapple rag* (whose third strain hints at jazz, even at the blues) following so closely upon it as to seem like a continuation of that piece.

Whether Rifkin rescued or romanticized Joplin's music depends on how you view his interpretations. Instead of the jazz-tinged versions common between the 1920s and 1960s, with their emphasis upon swinging (if the listener is lucky) rather than lilting, Rifkin reasserted the autonomy of classic ragtime, stressing the authority of the composer (nothing is played that is not in the score), treating the rags as piano music capable of standing up to performance in any concert programme. There has been adverse criticism (one writer claimed that Rifkin made Joplin sound like watered-down Schumann). Maybe Rifkin does not perform the livelier pieces, such as *Maple leaf rag*, with the kind of *brio* expected by jazz buffs, but his versions of the later, more ambitious rags afford extra insight into what Joplin was up to.

In many tight, small-scale musical forms there often occurs a moment when disciplines become strained by the expansion of the emotional content (Gesualdo's madrigals are one example of this kind of exhilarating imbalance). Something of that sort happened with Joplin's rags. Earlier compositions — notably the superb *Gladiolus rag*, not so rigidly two-beat as its predecessors — exemplify Joplin's strong melodic identity. But over the years the harmonies became bolder, culminating in the tonal shifts and implied rhythms of *Euphonic sounds* and *Scott Joplin's new rag*, but most of all in *Magnetic rag*, virtually his last composition. Like those two other rags, *Magnetic rag* uses rondo form, its opening strain returning at the end, but with the third and fourth strains (the third is twenty-four bars long, incidentally, instead of the customary sixteen) hinting at sonata form, going in for thematic and harmonic development rather than just presenting two more themes. All this is handled by Rifkin very capably. A pity, though, that he did not unbutton sufficiently to follow Joplin's instructions, on the sheet music, and stamp his foot on the floor during *The ragtime dance*. C.F.

8 **Pastimes and Piano Rags**
Nonesuch (A) H71299

James Scott: *Great Scott rag* (1909) · *Modesty rag — a classic* (1920). *Efficiency rag* (1917) · *New era rag* (1919) · *Troubadour rag* (1919). Artie Matthews: *Pastime rag No. 1 — a slow drag* (1913) · *Pastime rag No. 2 — a slow drag* (1913) · *Pastime rag No. 3 — a slow drag* (1916) · *Pastime rag No. 5 — a slow drag* (1918) · *Pastime rag No. 4 — a slow drag* (1920)

The dates refer to the original publication of the compositions. William Bolcom (p). New York City, 1973.

9 **Piano Rags by Joseph Lamb**
Genesis (A) GS1045

Sensation — a rag (1908) · *Excelsior rag* (1909) · *Ethiopia rag* (1909) · *American beauty rag* (1913) · *Reindeer — ragtime two-step* (1915) · *The ragtime nightingale* (1915) · *Top liner rag* (1916) · *Patricia rag* (1916) · *Alabama rag* · *Bird-brain rag* · *Blue grass rag* · *Cottontail rag* · *The old home rag* · *Thoroughbred rag* · *Toadstool rag* (all 1965)

The dates refer to the original publication of the compositions. John Jensen (p). New York City, 1974.

It will always be difficult, on random hearing, to mark important differences between Joplin, Lamb and Scott. It was the lure of Joplin's art and the fact of his direct tutelage that strengthened the similarities between his compositions and those of his younger disciples. All three are creative spirits of lasting attraction.

Lamb's music, played ably on **9** by Jensen, is, particularly in the early pieces, reliant on Joplin's techniques and turns of melody. *Sensation*, his first publication and not to be confused with Joplin's *Sensation rag*, also of 1908, has affinities with the older man's *Maple leaf rag* which are obvious enough in the repetitive melodic figures, as also are those in *Patricia rag*. Less obvious are the *Maple leaf* echoes in the famous *American beauty rag*, where the inversion of the first strain's initial motive in the second shows how subtle were the lessons to be learnt. So closely packed a style is ragtime that themes and devices are constantly recurring in different moods and guises, and the borrowings are legion. Self-borrowings, too: a comparison of the opening bars of *Reindeer rag* with those of *Cleopatra rag* and *Champagne rag* (neither included here) shows a typical slight reworking of almost identical phrases. But *Reindeer rag* also shows how lively and varied was Lamb's imagination. Hints of the influence of march music are there in the impetus of the second strain, and when the first strain returns to herald the song-like third, its rhythms are skippingly transformed. The languorous, nostalgic face of ragtime is heard in *The ragtime nightingale*, inspired, perhaps, by Scott's *Ragtime oriole*, but with a minor-key emphasis and a quite different mood; the sentiment determined by the use of a tune by Ethelbert Nevin, suitably adapted. This most melodious rag is, like *Heliotrope bouquet* (5), one of the treasures of the style. The likeness of *Patricia rag* to *Maple leaf* has been mentioned and, like the earlier piece, this belongs to that more strutting motion which invited the transformations of Morton, James P. Johnson and others; yet, rather oddly, an apparent purloining from Debussy's *La fille aux cheveux de lin* has been suspected of it.

Lamb's musical interests were clearly wide, and he was, with his New Jersey background, seemingly remote from the normal ragtime *milieu*. His composing heyday was brief — less than a decade — and it was only in the last years of his life that he emerged to revive and rework old and unfinished material and to record (Folkways (A) FG3562). It is remarkable that a musician so much outside the stream of popular ragtime activity should have become one of the three leading exponents of its classic style, no less genuine in his response to a peculiarly Midwestern muse than were his Negro peers. Like them, he tapped many sources of inspiration, and the mixture of dance rhythms — cakewalk, polka, schottische, etc. — was especially piquant in his music. The posthumous pieces heard on **9**'s second side are up to the earlier standard and even show some development in fluidity of line. The lyrical *Cottontail rag*, and *Blue grass rag*, with its comic trippings and unexpected touch of Spanish rhythm, are especially noteworthy.

A representative selection of compositions by Scott may be found on Biograph (A) BLP 1016Q, but there the deficiencies of player–piano reproduction have to be endured. The expressive Bolcom has made a small selection for **8**, and a comparison of his vigorous rendering of *Efficiency rag* with the lurching, inanely elaborated mechanical version on Biograph shows, first, how important to ragtime is skilful and sympathetic interpretation and, second, how woefully wrong is the still widespread belief that ragtime is an intrinsically 'mechanical' form. Bolcom has a sprightlier range of dynamics than Rifkin (**7**), and is more varied and sensitive than Jensen. His execution of the characteristic high-register echoings in *Efficiency rag* has all the brilliance called for. *New era rag* is attacked with the brassy accents which are typical of the Morton style, and has irresistible verve; while the choice of a somewhat brittle, rather than a sustained, touch in *Troubadour rag* proves that the occasional nostalgia need not be cloying. *Great Scott rag* struts firmly in a manner which shows aptly how this composer frequently transmuted 'white' material into a typically Negroid mode by linking it skilfully to black folk themes. If a choice has to be made, it is perhaps Scott, rather than Lamb, who most nearly rivals Joplin's pre-eminence, and his distinction from Joplin consists in his aptitude for a kind of thematic development, as against Joplin's choice of thematic contrast (though hear the latter's *Magnetic rag* on **6** and **7**). His music became more demanding of pianistic technique as time went on.

Whatever their publication dates, Matthews's *Pastime rags* appear to have been composed about 1913, and some companion pieces may have been lost. A widely experienced musician, he seems not to have taken smoothly to the ragtime idiom, and certainly he rejected it for more academic concerns later in life. Despite this, his *Pastimes*, though probably intended as rag 'exercises', are true and distinguished examples of an art which he had learnt from more famous mentors. They reflect a varied musical experience and, though the slow drag form dictates close similarity of tempo, the melodic and rhythmic fare ranges widely. *Pastime No. 4* employs chords which recall Matthews's association with the early commercial popularizing of the blues. Morton makes an approbatory reference to him in the course of the Library of Congress interviews (**21**), and Morton's application of the 'Spanish tinge' is forcefully brought to mind by the final track of this record.

Bolcom, assured as ever, brings out what he himself, in an exemplary sleeve note, calls 'the sure sense of theatre so evident in those five pieces'. E.T.

10 New Orleans Ragtime Orchestra
Arhoolie (A) 1058

New Orleans Ragtime Orchestra: Lionel Ferbos (tpt); Paul Crawford (tbn); Orange Kellin (clt); William Russell (vln); Lars Ivar Edegran (p); Frank Fields (bs); John Robichaux (d). New Orleans, 17 and 19 May 1971.

Creole belles · Black and white rag · Purple rose of Cairo · War cloud · Maple leaf rag · High society · The entertainer · The ragtime dance · New Orleans hop scop blues · My Maryland · The chrysanthemum · Panama

Despite its having been extensively recorded, starting in the cylinder days, by military bands (11) and banjo soloists, ragtime was later associated almost exclusively with the piano. This may have marked a return to the initial ideas of the best composers, yet small instrumental ensembles also had a role, and our understanding is increased when these pieces are heard in contemporary orchestrations. These emphasize that usually the line of attack was not through continuous variation, as in jazz, but rather in terms of thematic quality, calculated overall variety, immediate contrast. It must be admitted that the orchestrations, sometimes made by the composers themselves, do not especially highlight such features, do not use unexpected ensemble textures. Instead of being treated as occasions for further imaginative exploration, they are, their frequent gaiety notwithstanding, almost severely functional.

However, the instrumentation follows jazz band practice, even down to the violin which may be observed in photographs of some early jazz ensembles, and performances like those on the above record would have been familiar to pioneer jazzmen. Comparisons between this version of *High society* and King Oliver's (44), between this *New Orleans hop scop blues* and Jimmy Noone's (230), between *My Maryland* and Sidney Bechet's *Swing parade*, will yield striking indications of what was learnt and what was altered.

The New Orleans Ragtime Orchestra was founded in 1967 by Edegran to perform rediscovered orchestrations of such music, this material coming chiefly from Tulane University's Archive of New Orleans Jazz. Mainly they are played as written, although the tango rhythm of the *Panama* arrangement is changed and Kellin naturally includes the famous clarinet solo in *High society* [4]. Besides such jazz pieces and the rags, they also perform cakewalks like *Creole belles*, marches, blues and waltzes. Good stereo recording helpfully separates the parts and reveals the sometimes picturesque detail of these interpretations, such as

Russell's portamentos on *New Orleans hop scop blues* which echo the 'glide' and 'slide' of the lyrics. Joplin's *The ragtime dance* was first written as a twenty-minute ballet, but as this encountered the obvious commercial difficulties, he made a much shortened version for piano solo (**7**), and it is an orchestration of this which is played here. Regarding another Joplin piece, *Chrysanthemum*, it should be mentioned that, according to his publisher, Stark, this was inspired by *Alice in Wonderland*. On a somewhat different level, we may note that *War cloud* is better known as *Fidgety feet*, and a performance of it under the latter name, by the band in which its two composers won fame, can be heard on **12**.

Work of exploration similar to that of the New Orleans Ragtime Orchestra, though covering a wider repertoire, has been undertaken by such ensembles as the New Sunshine Jazz Band, as on *Too Much Mustard* (Biograph (A) BLP 12058). This Arhoolic LP appears here because it gives lively representation to several composers, including lesser lights such as J. Bodewalt Lampe, but for superior performances of the Joplin items hear *The Red-Back Book* by the New England Conservatory Ragtime Ensemble (Angel (A) S36060).   M.H.

Proto-jazz and the Earliest Recordings in New York

These are some of the first recordings of jazz (or jass) as it grew out of ragtime. They show that this new music was established far from New Orleans much earlier than is usually supposed.

11 Ragtime Vol. 2
RCA (F) PM42402

Unidentified band. Probably New York City, *c.* 1900.
Cakewalk

Metropolitan Orchestra: unidentified 2 cnt, tbn, picc, fl, clt, vln, p, tu, d. New York City, 28 September 1900.
Smokey mokes

Sousa's Band: collective listing of musicians known to have taken part in various of Sousa's recordings at this time — Walter Rogers, Harry Higgins, Bohumir Kryl, Rouss Millhouse, Herman Bellstedt, Herbert Clarke (cnt); Arthur Pryor, Frank Holton, Leo Zimmerman (tbn); Darius Lyons, Clement Barone, George Schweinfest (picc, fl); Louis Christie (clt); Simon Mantia (eu); Herman Conrad (tu); S. O. Pryor (d). New York City, 3 October 1900.
Whistling Rufus

The Victor Minstrels: unidentified players and singers. New York City, 13 December 1902.
The cakewalk

Victor Dance Orchestra: Rogers, Walter Keneke, Walter Pryor (cnt); Edward Wardwell (tbn); Lyons (picc, fl); Christie, A. Levy (clt); Frank Reschke (alt, vln); Charles d'Almaine, Theodore Levy (vln); Conrad (tu); S. O. Pryor (d). New York City, 10 April 1905.
Cakewalk in the sky

Victor Military Band: Rogers, T. Levy, Keneke, J. Fuch (cnt); Frank Schrader (tbn); Otto Winkler, H. Reitzel (ah, th); Barone (picc, fl); Christie, A. Levy (clt); Conrad (tu); William Reitz (d). New York City, 27 September 1911.
Alexander's ragtime band · *Slippery place rag*

Jim Europe's Society Orchestra: Crickett Smith (cnt); unidentified (tbn); Edgar Campbell (clt); Tracy Cooper, George Smith, Walker Scott (vln); Leonard Smith, Ford Dabney (p); 5 unidentified (bj-mand); Buddy Gilmore (d); Europe (cond). New York City, 29 December 1913.
Too much mustard · *Down home rag*

Charles Ford (cello), unidentified fl, bh added; 5 bj-mand absent. New York City, 10 February 1914.
You're here and I'm here · *The Castles in Europe* · *Castle walk*

The Six Brown Brothers: Tom Brown (sop, alt); Guy Shrigley (alt, ten); James 'Slap Rags' White (C-mel); Harry Cook (bar); Harry Fink (bs sx). Camden, New Jersey, 20 November 1914.
That moaning saxophone rag

Conway's Band: unidentified 3 cnt, 2 tbn, picc, fl, 4 clt, tu, d; Patrick Conway (cond). New York City, 10 July 1916.
Two-key rag

Victor Military Band: unidentified personnel with instrumentation similar to that for 1911 session. New York City, September 1916.
Medley: Joe Turner blues–St Louis blues

Earl Fuller's Famous Jazz Band: Walter Kahn (cnt); Harry Raderman (tbn); Ted Lewis (clt); Fuller (p); John Lucas (d). New York City, 10 September 1917.
A coon band contest · *Li'l Liza Jane*

Eubie Blake and His *Shuffle Along* Orchestra: Billy Hicks, Russell Smith (cnt); Calvin Jones (tbn); Sam Yearwood (fl); Bill Johnson (clt); Vess Williams (alt); Noble Sissle (vln); Blake (p); Leroy Vanderveer (bj); John Ricks (tu); George Reeves (d). New York City, 15 July 1921.
Baltimore buzz · *Bandana days*

This record contains the oldest performances dealt with in this book, although still earlier specimens do exist, notably by banjo soloists like Vess Ossman, who started in 1897. The absence of solo pianists is regrettable, but that instrument could not be satisfactorily recorded at the time. One piece, the Victor Minstrels' portrayal of a cakewalk competition, refers back to a still more remote era and is the earliest known instance of a recorded historical recreation. It gives off a strong period aroma, with the voluble master of ceremonies checking that none of the 'bad coons' present has a razor. Most of this music is unequivocally ragtime, but the later examples show it moving towards something different, as is implied by the LP's subtitle: *Cakewalks, Military Bands, Ragtime Orchestras, Coon Contests, Blues and Jass.*

Two divergent tendencies are evident in the quasi-military ensembles. Some, like the Victor groups, present conventional military band interpretations, offering reassurance through the discipline and regularity of their playing. Others, though in some cases recorded earlier, convey a sharp impression of the new music's energy. Among these are the Metropolitan Orchestra's *Smokey mokes* and, perhaps surprisingly, Sousa's *Whistling Rufus*; and they point directly to Jim Europe.

Deliberately tense, crammed with obsessive repetitions, Europe's headlong performances do everything possible to create immediate excitement. Such features as the rhythmic emphasis of the massed banjo-mandolins on the 1913 items or the drummer's evocation of a machine gun at the end of *Castles in Europe* and of pistol shots in *Castle walk* are crude yet effective. These pieces in their turn point towards the nervous brilliance of the Original Dixieland Jazz Band (12).

Although solo piano recordings from this period would have been enlightening, these performances outline well enough how ragtime changed and jazz grew out of it. The anthology also illustrates how genuinely progressive tendencies are both misinterpreted and ignored. Weakest among the many echoes set up by the ODJB were those of Fuller's group, who show no understanding of how the idiom works. More disappointing still are Blake's orchestra efforts which, although recorded considerably later, sound retrogressive beside Europe or even Fuller. There is nothing of ragtime, let alone jazz, here. M.H.

12 Original Dixieland Jazz Band
RCA (F) 730.703/4 (2 LPs), *RCA (A) LPV547

Nick LaRocca (cnt); Eddie Edwards (tbn); Larry Shields (clt); Henry Ragas (p); Tony Sbarbaro (d). New York City, 26 February 1917.
Livery stable blues · Dixie jass band one-step

Same personnel and location, 18 March 1918.
At the jazz band ball · Ostrich walk

Same personnel and location, 25 March 1918.
Skeleton jangle · Tiger rag

Same personnel and location, 25 June 1918.
Bluing the blues · *Fidgety feet* · *Sensation*
Same personnel and location, 17 July 1918.
Mourning blues · *Clarinet marmalade* · *Lazy daddy*
Benny Kreuger (alt) added; J. Russel Robinson (p) replaces Ragas. New York City, 1 December 1920.
Margie
Same personnel and location, 4 December 1920.
Palesteena
Same personnel and location, 30 December 1920.
Broadway rose · *Sweet mama*
Same personnel and location, 28 January 1921.
Home again blues · *Crazy blues*
Frank Signorelli (p) replaces Robinson. New York City, 3 May 1921.
Jazz me blues
Al Bernard (vcl) added. New York City, 25 May 1921.
St Louis blues · *Royal Garden blues*
Same personnel and location, 7 June 1921.
Dangerous blues
Bernard absent. New York City, 1 December 1921.
Bow wow blues
Robinson (p) replaces Signorelli; Kreuger absent. New York City, 25 September 1936.
Skeleton jangle
Same personnel and location, 10 November 1936.
Clarinet marmalade · *Bluing the blues* · *Tiger rag* · *Barnyard blues* · *Original dixieland one-step*

On turning from recordings like those on 11 to this band's early work, an immediate sharpening of focus is experienced. Preposterous claims to have 'invented' jazz advanced by LaRocca may have led to ridicule, but once it is heard in context the importance of this music becomes apparent. Most striking initially are its idiomatic consistency and integration of parts, these being paid for with a somewhat rigid stylization. Forceful performances such as *Sensation* and the little-known *Mourning blues* are perfect of their kind, yet although the sheer tension of its polyphony encourages us to listen to each piece as a whole, if we attend to separate instrumental lines in turn the music's origins are revealed in the many echoes of marching bands, ragtime and pre-jazz dance tunes which emerge. Like the composers of the first published rags, the ODJB achieved a formalization and synthesis of earlier and convergent tendencies.

It was crucial that in Sbarbaro they had a true jazz percussionist, as comparison with Buddy Gilmore's ragtime drumming on 11 will show. Shields was the most accomplished player, and his control can still seem exceptional — those very tricky downward portamentos, for instance — his breaks on *Clarinet marmalade* and particularly *Lazy daddy* being full of ideas. Edwards, though no soloist, was surprisingly active in the ensembles, and while far behind George Brunies of the New Orleans Rhythm Kings (**43**), he was superior to Honoré Dutrey in the Oliver Creole Band (**44**) and to most of Kid Ory's non-Morton work. The Bixian configuration of LaRocca's breaks on *Jazz me blues* and *Home again blues* points to an influence that has been widely noted. Like many later groups, the ODJB was at its best when playing members' own themes, and because some of them have been in the jazz repertoire since these recordings began to circulate, familiarity has bred the proverbial contempt. Yet as **63** shows, Beiderbecke found them suitable vehicles for some of his most daring explorations. At a less exalted level, they established enduring ensemble patterns, and Barney Bigard's part in the Ellington band's 1929 *Tiger rag* (**90**), for example, is essentially a virtuoso amplification of what Shields had recorded eleven years before.

This music is very different from either the stately polyphonic density of King Oliver's band or the fluid and melodious sensibility of the NORKs; it seems unlikely that its harsh brilliance, with joltingly displaced brass accents and searing clarinet runs, had much to do with New Orleans, and it might have crystallized in Chicago or even New York itself. Their delayed but eventually very great success may have been related to the violent reaction against Romantic conventions in music that was so prevalent after World War I.

The ODJB was the first significant jazz group to play outside America, and the records they made in London during 1919–20 (Riverside (A) RLP156/7, Music for Pleasure (E) MfP1106) are their last representative ones. Back in New York, they took on a saxophonist who could add nothing to ensemble textures that were already complete, and various abominable singers. The listlessness of *Margie*, which clocked-up huge sales, is all too typical. They reformed in 1936 and the later recordings obviously enable us to hear the band more clearly. But Shields and Sbarbaro had remained professionally active in music, not unaware of what had since happened to jazz, and so these performances are not the literal recreations of the ODJB's historic contributions which they were assumed to be. Rather, they point to a desire to perform anew in the older jazz styles which that same year was confirmed by Bob Crosby (**236**) and in the immediately succeeding years by many others. M.H.

13 New York Jazz Scene 1917–20
Riverside (Eu) RLP8801

Frisco Jass Band: unidentified tbn, clt, vln, p, bj, d. New York City, 10 May 1917.
Johnson jass blues

Same personnel and location, 2 August 1917.
Umbrellas to mend

Earl Fuller's Famous Jazz Band: Walter Kahn (cnt); Harry Raderman (tbn); Ted Lewis (clt); Fuller (p); John Lucas (d). New York City, 4 June 1918.
Jazzbo jazz

Same personnel and location, 13 June 1918.
Jazz de luxe

Louisiana Five: Charles Panelli (tbn); Alcide 'Yellow' Nunez (clt); Joe Cawley (p); Karl Burger (bj); Anton Lada (d). New York City, 14 April 1919.
Footwarmer · B-hap-e

Same personnel and location, 12 September 1919.
Clarinet squawk · Yelping hound blues

Lopez and Hamilton's Kings of Harmony Orchestra: Bob Effros (cnt); Slim Hamilton (tbn); Andy Hamilton (clt); Vincent Lopez (p); Eddie Shearer (d). New York City, 9 January 1920.
Peggy · Bluing the blues

Same personnel and location, 3 February 1920.
Patches

Same personnel and location, 5 February 1920.
Bo la bo

Because thousands of amateur groups learnt, several decades later, to play dixieland, we tend to forget that it was once the *avant-garde* style in jazz, as hard to grasp in the teens of our century as bop was just after World War II. The point is painfully underlined by many of the imitative bands which sprang up around the ODJB once their records became successful. Actually, performances by the anonymous Frisco Jass Band, although contemporaneous with the ODJB's earliest Victor and Aeolian discs, represent an older phase of the music. This is instrumental ragtime, with syncopated melodies exchanged between clarinet and violin, their rhythmic character determined chiefly by the banjo. There is no improvisation, although the trombone's portamentos in *Johnson jass blues* suggest contact with jazz, as to a lesser extent do the drums on *Umbrellas to mend*. These two tracks form a charming historical memento.

Though described elsewhere, without evident humorous intent, as 'an important transitional group' [5], Fuller's band offers the most feeble of all recorded ODJB imitations. Their travesties here mark no advance over the 1917 performances on **11**, the players still having no clear understanding of the role of each instrument within the ensemble.

The Louisiana Five are not copyists: the matter of instrumentation aside, Nunez had the clarinet chair in the ODJB before Shields. They do represent the same period in the music's development, however, and comparison between the alternative versions they recorded of some pieces shows that performances were thoroughly worked out leaving, as with the ODJB, little scope for improvisation. Like the Frisco Jass Band they lacked a cornet or trumpet, but the large-toned clarinet is sufficiently fluent and decoratively melodic to compensate for the rather too simple trombone bass lines. Another similarity with the ODJB is that the Louisiana Five's best material was composed by members of the band. There is nothing on the above LP, though, as good as their *Church Street sobbing blues* (Fountain (E) FJ101), later taken up by Eddie Lang (**68b**) and others.

Like the Louisiana Five, Lopez and Hamilton's Kings of Harmony included musicians from New Orleans, yet in neither case is there any sign of that feeling for the blues which is supposed to have distinguished players originating in the South from northerners. Not for the first time, recorded evidence contradicts the recollections of interviewees speaking decades after the event [6]. Lopez and Hamilton's group is at once closer to and further away from the ODJB than the others. With detailed differences in the clarinet and trombone parts, their *Bluing the blues* sensitively echoes the pioneers' version on **12**, but elsewhere something more formal is undertaken. There are some arranged sections — probably committed to memory rather than to paper — and such things as a *chalumeau*-register clarinet solo with subdued polyphonic backing on *Patches*. Though he subsequently became a society bandleader, Lopez plays respectable ragtime piano here, and on *Peggy*, as in *Bluing the blues*, there are keyboard chimes effects of the sort which several years later appeared on King Oliver's *Chimes blues* (**44**). There is real counterpoint between clarinet and cornet in *Patches* and between the two Hamiltons on *Bo la bo*; the drummer is pointfully active on woodblocks and the like. Such performances show that groups which, having taken their cue from the ODJB, struck out for themselves can still hold our interest, and this is confirmed by the next record. M.H.

14 The Original Memphis Five
Folkways (A) RBF26

Jazz-Bo's Carolina serenaders: Phil Napoleon (tpt); Miff Mole (tbn); Johnny Costello (clt); Rudy Wiedoeft (alt); Frank Signorelli (p); Jack Roth (d). New York City, April 1922.
Cuddle up blues

Original Memphis Five: Jimmy Lytell (clt) replaces Costello; Wiedoeft absent. New York City, 11 May 1922.
Lonesome mama blues

Ladd's Black Aces: Doc Behrendson (clt), Sam Lanin (d) replace Lytell, Roth. New York City, 25 May 1922.
Hopeless blues

Jazz-Bo's Carolina Serenaders: Costello (clt), Bill Lambert (d) replace Behrendson, Lanin. New York City, July 1922.
Yanky doodle blues

Original Memphis Five: Vincent Grande (tbn), Lytell (ctl), Roth (d) replace Mole, Costello, Lambert. New York City, 2 October 1922.
Ji-ji-boo

Mole (tbn) replaces Grande. New York City, November 1922.
Great White Way blues

Ray Kitchingman (bj) replaces Roth. New York City, 4 December 1922.
Railroad man

Roth (d) replaces Kitchingman. New York City, April 1923.
Memphis glide

Kitchingman (bj) added. New York City, 25 May 1923.
Pickles

Kitchingman absent. New York City, 20 June 1923.
Strutting Jim

Costello (clt) replaces Lytell. New York City, July 1923.
Shuffling Mose

The Tennessee Ten: Jules Levy (tpt), Gus Sharp, Loring McMurray (alt), John Cali (bj) added; Lytell (ctl) replaces Costello. New York City, 23 July 1923.
That big blond mama

Original Memphis Five: Levy, Sharp, McMurray, Cali absent. New York City, December 1923.
Snuggle up a bit

Same personnel and location, January 1924.
Lots o' mama

Same personnel and location, June 1924.
Red hot mama

Same personnel and location, 21 July 1924.
I'm going back to those who won't go back on me

The discographies show many short-lived ensembles such as the Original Georgia Five and the Original New Orleans Jazz Band whose names echo that of the Original Dixieland Jazz Band and who tried, often ineptly, to echo its music. Although both Lytell and Signorelli had played with the ODJB, the Original Memphis Five was a different case, having worked out an approach of its own in the course of much recording and while tackling a constant flow of new material. This was, indeed, the first of countless jazz groups that came into existence chiefly to make discs rather than to fulfil public engagements. Despite changes of personnel, instrumentation and recording name, it maintained a style that was clearly defined if less pungently assertive than that of the ODJB.

Napoleon and Signorelli were the band's founders and key members. The former, whose real name was Filippo Napoli, had a more percussive manner than many jazz musicians of Italian origin (e.g. Frank Guarente on **15**), and played a direct, simple kind of lead, well exemplified by *Snuggle up a bit*, which is a sober performance despite its title. Lytell achieved impressive linear independence in the ensembles, as on *Great White Way blues* or *Memphis glide*, and Mole's ease of movement, which permitted such things as the brief yet remarkable stop-time solo on *Lots o' mama*, always had a liberating effect on the others. These three, in fact, constituted the first outstanding recorded front line to be entirely composed of non-New Orleans musicians, and as such pieces as the very early *Lonesome mama blues* show, they were notably certain about their objectives. It is worth adding that all sixteen of the performances here were set down before Louis Armstrong's supposedly crucial appearance in New York with Fletcher Henderson's band.

Though ensembles dominate, the OM5 were concerned, in a way that earlier recorded groups were not, with varying the music's emphasis and tone colour. Notice, for example, the contrasting accompaniments given to Napoleon on *That big blond mama*, first by piano and then by banjo, this being followed by a clarinet and saxophone duet which looks forward to the partnership of Jimmy Noone and Joe Poston (**41**). Similarly there is a fine contrapuntal passage between trumpet and trombone with only keyboard support in *Ji-ji-boo*, and *Railroad man* starts with a passage for trumpet and banjo alone. There are a few unwelcome intrusions, such as Wiedoeft's slap-tonguing and 'laughing' effects on the initial *Cuddle up blues*, yet there are good solos too, as by Signorelli in *Shuffling Mose* and *Pickles*. In that distant time, with the idiom less exhausted, it was easier for such minor figures to make valid contributions than it later became. Another satisfying improvisation comes from Behrendson, over stop-time chords, on *Hopeless blues*, and the OM5's earliness in the field should again be noted, for this, as with Lytell's work on *Lonesome mama blues*, preceded Leon Roppolo's recordings with the New Orleans Rhythm Kings (**43**).

The sleeve of the above record is totally lacking in discographical information.

A comparable European reissued selection appears on RCA (F) 741.115.   M.H.

15 The Georgians
VJM (E) VLP12

Frank Guarente (tpt); Ray Stilwell (tbn); Johnny O'Donnell (clt, bs clt, alt); Dick Johnson (clt, alt, ten); Arthur Schutt (p); Russell Deppe (bj); Chauncey Morehouse (d). New York City, 1 December 1922.
Sister Kate · Chicago

Unidentified tu added. New York City, 22 December 1922.
Way down yonder in New Orleans · Nothing but

Same personnel and location, 27 January 1923.
Loose feet

Same personnel and location, 29 January 1923.
Aggravating papa

Same personnel and location, 13 February 1923.
You tell her — I stutter

Tu absent. New York City, 26 February 1923.
You've got to see mama every night

Johnson absent. New York City, 7 March 1923.
Farewell blues

Same personnel and location, 15 March 1923.
Snake hips

Johnson (clt, ten) returns. New York City, 27 April 1923.
Old King Tut · Barney Google

Same personnel and location, 16 May 1923.
Henpecked blues · Long lost mama

This is another group that hammered out an individual approach to the materials and techniques of its day, one that contained many hints of what followed. Guarente was the first significant jazz musician born outside the USA and, as with many players of Italian origin, there is a strong vocal aspect to his ideas. These are fluently melodious, his solos, as on *Long lost mama*, having many unexpected turns of phrase. As a technician exceptional for his period, though, he commanded several manners of expression, and the relatively 'dirty' playing in *You tell her* is quite different from his delicately muted *Chicago* solo. Again, he inserts a quasi-oriental passage into *Snake hips*, is Beiderbeckian before Bix on *Loose feet*, and in *Aggravating papa* establishes a vein of gentle, pastel-toned melancholy that was supposedly pioneered several years later by Arthur Whetsol of the Ellington band.

Though it is most obvious on *Henpecked blues*, this music often displays a southern accent which presumably resulted from the trumpeter's friendship in New Orleans with Oliver, and his introduction to *Nothing but* directly anticipates the Creole Band's *Jazzing babies blues* of the following year (**44**). Yet although Guarente's concept dominated the Georgians, their collective effort was the decisive factor, this being an inventive band whose performances are rich in significant detail. The briskly contrasted episodes of *Barney Google* confirm this, and the diverse ways that the concerted passages, intense yet always clear, are laid out parallel the variety of the leader's solos. The ensembles of *Nothing but*, for instance, sound different from those of *Loose feet*, while *Farewell blues* follows another path again. On this last, note that when the theme returns it undergoes a striking simplification, played against an active keyboard obbligato; from this emerges another affecting Guarente solo.

Stylistic consistency had been arrived at over a period, for six months before the earliest of the above performances were set down, these musicians had recorded as Specht's Jazz Outfit. The Georgians were, in fact, part of Paul Specht's commercial orchestra, the first band within a band, forebear of the Goodman small groups and many others.

Such preparation helps to account for the surprising finish and maturity of the sidemen's breaks and solos, especially O'Donnell's, which are comparable with those by the best Original Memphis Five men such as Jimmy Lytell. True, he echoes Roppolo's *Farewell blues* clarinet solo of the previous August (**43**), and his 'cool' alto playing had antecedents such as Loring McMurray's thirty-two bars on the California Thumpers' *Haunting blues* of June 1922; yet this version of *Way down yonder in New Orleans* sets an obvious precedent for Trumbauer (**64**). Regarding O'Donnell's bass clarinet passage in *Nothing but*, it might be pointed out that Rudy Jackson's use of this instrument on Ellington's 1927 *Song of the cottonfield* (**89**) was later to be hailed as an innovation.   M.H.

16 Eubie Blake: Blues and Rags — His Earliest Piano Rolls 1917–1921 Vol. 1

Biograph (A) BLP1011Q

Charleston rag (1917) · *Somebody's done me wrong* (February 1918) ·
Goodnight, Angeline (August 1919) · *Schubert Gaieties of 1919* (1919) ·
Gee, I wish I had someone (1919) · *Broadway blues* (January 1921) ·
Crazy blues · *Strut, Miss Lizzie* · *Home again blues* · *It's right here for you* · *Fare thee well honey blues* (all February 1921)
The above are all piano rolls; in brackets are the dates of issue.

This gives a more favourable impression of Blake than the orchestral performances on 11, yet one that is revealingly inconsistent. He started making rolls in 1917 and, coming from a time when keyboardmen cut few gramophone recordings, the results give an indication of what his early playing, and by implication that of some other New York pianists, was like. Most piano rolls had their limitations in preserving the nuances of a player's touch, the minute differences of stress and timing through which much of his individuality as a performer was conveyed. Yet even allowing for this, the executive capability suggested here seems extremely variable. *Charleston*, a ragtime piece which Blake supposedly wrote in 1899, is thrown off immaculately, yet the *Gaieties* selection is seriously hesitant in places, the pulse sometimes quite unsteady.

Such performances suggest him to have been less jazz-orientated than players like James P. Johnson or J. Russel Robinson, one each of whose rolls from the same period can be heard on 17. Thus, although the *Gaieties* include *Beale Street blues* (and something called *I'll be your baby vampire*), we also hear *I've made up my mind to mind a maid made up like you*, which is redolent of late-1890s vaudeville. Similarly, *Goodnight, Angeline* is merely a popular ballad of the time, though played with more spirit than the *Gaieties*.

The rest of Blake's rolls here were cut for the Aeolian company's Mel-O-Dee line and were subject to extensive editing. In practice, this meant that so as to produce a more elaborate fullness of sound, a 'third hand' was punched into the roll, presumably with the artist's collaboration, after the main (two-handed) part of the recording had been cut. This again makes it hard to determine just what Blake could do, yet the results were sometimes agreeable, conveying a full-hearted gaiety to which all should respond. *Broadway* and *Crazy blues*, which have in them nothing of the blues, are fine examples, and these, with *Strut, Miss Lizzie* and *It's right here for you*, are more positively slanted towards jazz. That is not to suggest Blake improvises new melodies on the chord sequences: rather does he, in the usual manner of the New York 'stride' school, permutate the original tunes through varied keyboard textures.

Such a method reached its highest application with Art Tatum (**181**, etc.), but if used without sufficient imagination it can decline into dependence on formulae. Blake is sometimes guilty of that here, the most blatant instance being the flattened-seventh ending to *Fare thee well*; the inclusion of *Home again*, too, a non-blues by Irving Berlin, marks a shift back to Tin Pan Alley. The point of this LP's presence here, though, is precisely that these performances demonstrate how in the early days jazz was closely juxtaposed with, and hence likely to be influenced by, other musics that we tend no longer to associate with it.

M.H.

17 Parlour Piano
Biograph (A) BLP1001Q

F. Morton, H. Connor (p duet). Chicago, c. April/May 1915.
One-step medley No. 2 (I'm on my way to Dublin Bay, Ruff Johnson's Harmony Band, Everybody rag with me, I want to go to Tokyo)

James P. Johnson (p). Newark, February 1918.
Eccentricity

J. Russel Robinson (p). Chicago, May 1918.
Dixie jass band one-step

J. Lawrence Cook (p). New York City, August 1923.
He used to be your man

Lemuel Fowler (p). New York City, August 1923.
You've got everything a sweet mama needs but me

Clarence Johnson (p). New York City, August 1923.
Gulf Coast blues

James P. Johnson (p). New York City, August 1923.
Railroad man

Luckey Roberts (p). New York City, August 1923.
Molasses

Fats Waller (p). New York City, August 1923.
Haitian blues

Cliff Jackson (p). New York City, September 1923.
Hock shop blues

Clarence Williams (p). New York City, January 1926.
Papa-de-da-da

Cow Cow Davenport (p). Cincinnati, April 1927.
Cow Cow blues

The above are all piano rolls; the locations and dates refer to the places they were cut and to their time of issue.

If these are heard after the more diverse endeavours of **16**, they give, if in a lesser degree, an impression of stylistic clarification, of a sense of direction having been established, comparable to that which arises from listening to the ODJB after the still more miscellaneous performances on **11**. The skill of these pianists may vary and the evidence be blurred by the player-piano's limitations, yet they are all related to a single, identifiable tradition. (Another part of that tradition, peremptorily dismissed in jazz commentaries as 'novelty' pianism, is illustrated by gramophone recordings of this period by such men as Jimmy Andrews, Rube Bloom and the remarkable Willie Eckstein on Biograph (A) BLP12047.) In fact, the rolls are heard under optimum conditions, sensitively pumped by Michael Montgomery, a long-established expert in this field, who also chose the tempos; the instrument was a 1910 Steinway, obviously in fine condition. The only direct comparison with a gramophone recording that can be made is of Davenport's *Cow Cow blues*, which he cut for OKeh in 1925 (Magpie (E) PY1814), and the roll, as reproduced here, survives well beside it. Elsewhere the lack of dynamic variety can be monotonous, and the left-hand parts sometimes have an insensitivity quite uncharacteristic of James P. Johnson, Roberts or Waller; but rolls have their historical place. They were an important means of disseminating this music, at one stage rivalling discs, and some of these men, particularly Robinson, Clarence Johnson and Cook, were prolific in their production.

Stylistically, the sole outsider is the *One-step medley*, a purely commercial venture. At this time, jazz was much involved with such material, as **16** shows, yet none of its characteristics are apparent here. The present writer does not believe that the F. Morton listed is Jelly Roll Morton: certainly the performance does not sound remotely like the authenticated Morton rolls of 1924–26 on Biograph (A) BLP1004Q. Sober pianistic craftsmanship is offered by Williams and Clarence Johnson, the latter's *Gulf Coast blues* having a touch of the boogie. Waller is caught too early for a typical performance, although *Haitian blues* (advertised as 'the latest blues sensation' in the month of this roll's issue) indicates his precocity in the Harlem keyboard style — which, on this evidence, influenced even bluesmen like Fowler. Robinson became pianist in the ODJB the year after making *Dixie jass band one-step*, a rare early case of a keyboard version of a band piece; it should be compared with the 1917 prototype on **12**, as should James P. Johnson's *Railroad man* with the Original Memphis Five reading on **14**.

The latter pianist's *Eccentricity* is an interesting venture into 3/4 time, quite characteristic of the New York players' musical

curiosity and somewhat ahead of Benny Carter's 1936 *Waltzing
the blues* (**99**). The full, mobile textures of Roberts and Johnson
are, indeed, expressive of lively imaginations as well as of rare
keyboard skill. There is no doubt that the paucity of recordings,
on disc or roll, by the former, a major figure in early piano jazz,
has resulted in a considerable gap in our knowledge (see **238**).

M.H.

New Orleans

Recordings such as **11–17** notwithstanding, New Orleans was the
home of the earliest known mature jazz style; there was a
continuing local style there up until almost the present.

Documentary recordings

These offer detailed later indications of several kinds of the
nature of the earliest jazz, and its background, before any records
were made.

18 New Orleans Joys: The Young Tuxedo Brass Band
Atlantic (E) 590.023, Atlantic (A) 1297

Andrew Anderson, John 'Pickey' Brunious, Albert 'Fernandez' Walters
(tpt); Clement Tervalon, Eddie Pierson (tbn); Wilbert Tillman (sar); John
Casimir (E-flat clt); Herman Sherman (alt); Andrew Morgan (ten); Paul
Barbarin (snare d); Emile Knox (bs d). New Orleans, 1958.
*Lead me, Saviour · Eternal peace · Medley of hymns (Flee as a bird;
Nearer, my God, to thee; Pleyel's hymn)*

Jim Robinson (tbn) replaces Pierson. Same date.
*Just a closer walk with thee · Bourbon Street parade · Lord, Lord,
Lord · Just a little while to stay here · It feels so good · Panama · Joe
Avery's piece · John Casimir's whooping blues*

Jung's singing kettle at Bollingen taught him the disconcerting
lesson that the borderline between the 'harmonious' and the
'contradictory and chaotic' is sometimes extremely hard to
discern. One recalls this whilst listening to the interweaving
strains of these New Orleans horns. By an unself-consciousness
which is not at odds with considerable expertise, these musicians
become possessed by spirits of creative joy and pathos which
transcend the aims of art.

But the art and its aims are worthy of careful note. The total
effect of the Young Tuxedo's collective improvising may be
unaccountable within normal analysis, but long melodic and
rhythmic traditions and exceptional immediate skill are its
contributaries. By 1958, the year of those recordings, the number

of players with direct links to the early brass bands must have been dwindling rapidly. In addition, several of these participants had long been playing with jazz groups — Brunious with Billy Eckstine and Jay McShann, the excellent Barbarin with Luis Russell and many more, Robinson (a non-reader) with Bunk Johnson, George Lewis and other bands. So the conditioning of more advanced styles occasionally shows, and the shades of turn-of-the-century bandsmen might find much of the phraseology rather outlandish beside their own more ragtime-influenced accents.

However, there is sufficient evidence that the inherited techniques of polyphony (heterophony is perhaps an alternative) had reached a similar overall effect at least forty years before these recordings were made. The exuberant collective in King Oliver's 1923 *Snake rag* (**44**) is clearly heir to the same legacy; and a revealing comparison may be made of Johnny Dodds's clarinet solo in Oliver's *Canal Street blues* with Casimir's solo in *Whooping blues* behind which the agile Tillman plays a bass line strikingly akin to that supplied by the banjoist accompanying Dodds.

Already Oliver was adapting and formalizing to a degree, but his basis was evidently music very close in form and spirit to that played by the Young Tuxedo (and by the fine Eureka Band on Atlantic (A) 1408). It seems remarkable that such coherent collective improvising can be achieved by so large an ensemble, having almost the dimensions of a big band. To the jazz-attuned ear, every strand and every combination of strands sounds right here, even though part of the satisfaction results from the amount of risk that is taken. The glory of this music-making shines at the culmination of *Lord, Lord, Lord* and *Just a little while*. At the end of Barbarin's *Bourbon Street parade* it almost flies apart in alarming savagery.

The pattern of this collection is based on the New Orleans funeral convention. The first three tracks are headed 'Going to the Cemetery' and the rest, which are marches, 'Coming Back'. The dirges at the beginning are of less jazz interest. They are closer to formal band music and involve the reading of parts. Accents of the blues do shape the instrumental voices, but Casimir's dominant clarinet lines sound more sentimental than his work in the marches. Not all the hymn tunes are in minor keys, but melancholy inhabits each one.

The solemn drum rolls and peremptory trumpet calls (which also deftly indicate the tune to be played next) are markedly similar to summoning devices in other wind-band traditions. Bullring bands in Spain and Mexico mark points of crisis in much the same way; yet if the wailing New Orleans band produces its own kind of *toque de muerte* at the graveyard gates, it is partly because it too has borrowed from a military heritage, and partly because it is involved in a similarly elemental communal emotion.

Louis Moreau Gottschalk's piano composition *Souvenir de Porto Rico* (1859) conjures up a festival march of the *jibaros*, and follows a familiar sequence — a hint of muffled drums, and then the inexorable movement from a sombre minor melody quickening into the major and achieving an ecstatic combination of dance and march rhythms, *mutatis mutandis*, essentially what the New Orleans groups create. So the tradition is wide and old. What makes this music distinctive is the spirit of the blues and ragtime, transmutant into the fluency of jazz.   E.T.

Bunk Johnson

19 Early Bunk 1942–43
Dan (J) VC4020

Johnson (tpt); Jim Robinson (tbn); George Lewis (clt); Walter Decou (p); Lawrence Marrero (bj); Austin Young (bs); Ernest Rogers (d). New Orleans, 11 June 1942.
Moose march (3 rehearsal tests) · *These drafting blues* (2 rehearsal tests)

Johnson (spch). San Francisco, 7 May 1943.
On Buddy Bolden · *On Pete Lala's and Dago Tony's* · *On Tony Jackson*
Johnson (p). Same date.
Baby, I'd love to steal you

Johnson (tpt); Bertha Gonsoulin (p). Same date.
Pallet on the floor (4 takes) · *Plenty to do*
Same personnel and location, 10 May 1943.
Basin Street blues · *St Louis blues*

Johnson (tpt); Robinson (tbn); Lewis (clt); Marrero (bj); Sidney Brown (tu); Edgar Mosley (d). San Francisco, May 1943.
Pacific Street blues

Though we have classified this LP as being of documentary interest, disclaimers must be made. The period of several years in the 1930s during which Johnson was absent from public music-making, which he filled with a heavy teaching schedule under the auspices of the Works Progress Administration, became magnified in the minds of researchers who introduced him to the jazz community until it seemed to them that he must have known the world before the Flood. In the early 1940s he recorded several interviews — always conducted by what sounded like totally credulous youths — in which he reminisced about early days in

New Orleans and particularly about Buddy Bolden, this music's supposed founding father.

Such details as emerged are enshrined in countless books, yet they are a greater contribution to the mythology than to the history of jazz. In one of the conversations included here, Johnson speaks of composing *Baby, I'd love to steal you* in collaboration with the legendary Tony Jackson, then plays it on the piano — and it sounds like Edwardian drawing-room music. More importantly, he claimed to have played with the still more legendary Bolden, and moved his birth date back about ten years to substantiate this [7]. His assertion is not supported by anyone else active in New Orleans during the early years of this century, and there is no reason to assume that his illustrations of Bolden's style, whether by whistling in the first interview or in the trumpet performances accompanied by Bertha Gonsoulin, are accurate as musicological reconstructions.

Yet it is with the four versions of *Pallet on the floor*, one slow, the others faster, that serious business starts. These are specifically claimed to be played as Bolden would have done, yet the style is the one already hinted at in Johnson's Jazz Man (Good Time Jazz (A) GTJ12048) and Jazz Information (Commodore (A) DL30.007) recordings of the previous year and which was further developed in his numerous American Music performances of 1944 and 1945 (**28** and **29**). The music is shaped by a formal, almost precise, sense of variation, the notes are attacked and quitted cleanly, there are very few of the slurs used by such players as Wooden Joe Nicholas (**25**). It is also excellent jazz, delivered with fluency and even verve, especially in the placing of syncopations. Some of the phrases heard in the whistling recur here.

No antiquarian claims are made for the other trumpet and keyboard performances. *Plenty to do* seems like a piece very much of non-jazz origin and Johnson does not quite succeed in transforming it. His readings of the two blues are naturally of interest, though again not altogether happy. 'Readings' may be the exact word, for it sometimes sounds as if he had got the music in front of him and had not seen it for a long time (Miss Gonsoulin knows both items thoroughly, however). He treats them, virtually, as set compositions, and his departures are usually tentative, though he does play more freely, if also rather insecurely, towards the end of *St Louis blues*.

The difference in standard between Johnson's playing on these three tracks and on the four accounts of *Pallet on the floor* is disappointing, as is the band performance of *Pacific Street blues*, which gives no hint of the forthcoming achievements of the

American Music dates. Likewise the rehearsal tests, from the Jazz Man session which produced his very first recordings, are too brief to have much significance.   M.H.

20 The Music of New Orleans Vol. 4 — The Birth of Jazz
Folkways (A) FA2464

Charlie Love (tpt); Emile Barnes (clt); Billy Huntington (bj); Albert Glenny (bs); Albert Jiles (d). New Orleans, 8 September 1952.
Maple leaf rag

H. J. Boiusseau (p, spch). New Orleans, July/August 1954.
Red rose rag · Take your big leg off me · Too much mustard

Louis Keppard (vcl). New Orleans, 21 August 1957.
Bucket's got a hole in it

Harrison Barnes (spch). Algiers, Louisiana, 26 August 1957.
On Buddy Bolden

Charlie Love (spch). Algiers, Louisiana, 25 February 1958.
On Buddy Bolden

Louis Keppard used to play the guitar in the ;ame band as his more famous brother, Freddy. What he does here is to give a vocal imitation of how that band sounded around 1910, alternating snatches of the lyrics of *Bucket's got a hole in it* with impersonations of a duet between cornet and trombone, and of clarinet, guitar and bass solos, as well as an approximation to the entire ensemble. (It would, in the circumstances, be pedantic to suggest comparing this one-man band performance to Freddy Keppard's recordings in the 1920s on **34**.) All in all, a valuable — and curiously affecting — recreation of how jazz bands sounded in the beginning, as tunes began to be embellished and ornamented. The change-over came with the development of instrumental ragtime, which was what Buddy Bolden's band was playing at the peak of its popularity in 1905. Harrison Barnes and Love both listened to that band (Love once lent Bolden his cornet during a performance) and give affectionate accounts of how the musicians dressed ('blue coats and caps and dark trousers, and always white shirts and bow ties') and of the various formal dance tunes that were played — mazurkas, polkas, two-steps, quadrilles — as well as the handful of pieces that were Bolden's specialities. The practical demonstration at the end of side 1 illustrates the way that ragtime was to be transformed into jazz. A quintet that includes Glenny, who played occasionally with Bolden's band, and two performers — Emile Barnes and Love — who were playing before 1910, works its way meticulously through *Maple leaf rag*, with Barnes's clarinet managing to quote from *Balling* *the jack* during the repeat of the third strain. It would be impossible for musicians recording in 1952 to remember exactly what musical liberties they were taking nearly half a century earlier, but there is nothing here to strain credulity. Indeed, it all sounds remarkably convincing.

Boiusseau, born in the 1890s, spent a good deal of his youth playing the piano for fun in the cabarets of Storyville. By 1954 his piano playing was a trifle rusty, and the piano he used something less than pristine. But the music comes second to Boiusseau's recollections, not just of the New Orleans brothels but of the rough Irish Channel district and of Milneburg (it had fishing boats, a dance hall, a merry-go-round and its own jail). There are fascinating sociological tidbits, including the distinctions of status between the sporting houses: the cheaper ones had player-pianos which took nickels, but the classier establishments — Josie Arlington's or Flossie Livingston's — employed their own ragtime professors ('always coloured') to play the patrons' requests. These reminiscences should ideally be supplemented by E. J. Bellocq's superb photographs of some of the girls in those houses [8], full of background details which, as one reviewer put it, suggest the prevailing tone to have been one of stuffy gentility rather than romantic squalor.   C.F.

Jelly Roll Morton
21 The Library of Congress Recordings
This entire series is on Classic Jazz Masters (Sd) CJM2-9, Riverside (A) 9001-12

Morton (p, vcl, spch). Washington, D.C., May–June 1938.

These were extracted from interviews and performances recorded over a five-week period commencing on 21 May 1938, in the Coolidge Auditorium of the Library of Congress, in response to questions from Alan Lomax, Curator of Folk Music.

Classic Jazz Masters (Sd) CJM2

Vol. 1 *Mr Jelly Lord* · *Boyhood memories* · *Original Jelly Roll blues* · *Alabama bound* · *King Porter stomp* · *You can have it* · *Tiger rag* · *Panama*

Classic Jazz Masters (Sd) CJM4

Vol. 3 *Buddy Bolden* · *Bill Johnson* · *Salty dog* · *If you was whisky* · *My gal Sal* · *Animule ball* · *Shooting the agate* · *See see rider* · *Pallet on the floor* · *The murder ballad*

Classic Jazz Masters (Sd) CJM6

Vol. 5 *Creole songs* · *Indian songs* · *Funerals* · *The Broadway swells* ·*The Marching bands*

Mr Jelly Lord appropriately sets the scene, the song of an amiable braggart whose musical accomplishments bid disconcertingly fair to endorse the claims of his rodomontade. Washington nightclub owner, once one of jazz music's most ostentatious and romantic characters, Morton, now a tired and disillusioned man in his mid-fifties, recalls his own elevation; and in the skilfully-phrased lyrics and the mixture of simple blues chords and sharp-fingered filigree of the piano accompaniment may be heard the subjective proof, the inventive brilliance which, when the echoes of comic self-dramatization have died, makes the mythic accolade eminently feasible. He came as near as anyone to personifying the desperate, sad, cockeyed and marvellously life-affirming pretension of jazz.

Even in this simple song, Morton's masterly control of tempo and rhythmic swing are evident. This was no 'folk artist', and Lomax must have known that as clearly as anyone, but a professional virtuoso, jealous of his skills and, in his heyday, a commercial success. Yet what Lomax seems to have sensed is that here was a musician for whom music and life were one, each reflecting the other, and whose career and personality had been such that to tap his well of reminiscence and to unloose his flow of easy talk would be to learn much about the early years of jazz — its venues, its musical sources, its half-forgotten *dramatis personae*. He was right. The eight LPs of reissued material from these sessions (spread more thinly over twelve discs in the American edition) preserve a fascinating account of jazz in its early formation — diverse, and full of colour and vitality, even though (or maybe because) the realities are filtered through the proud personality of one rather battered and defensive self-apologist. There is much talk, and extended listening can be something of an effort; but there is some splendid music, the hearing of which takes no effort at all. For the purposes of this book, only certain parts of the interviews can be reviewed; they consist of Vols. 1, 3 and 5. There will be incidental references to material from other volumes.

Volume 1 begins with *Mr Jelly Lord*, and then, prompted by Lomax, Morton begins to talk, in a calmly expressive voice, about his own family history and early childhood. He recalls the pleasures music had for his Creole relatives, his introduction to the French Opera, how he 'liked to play piano' and stuck to it, in preference to the guitar, undeterred by ridicule. He stresses the correctness of his musical conditioning 'under the Catholic tutelage', and briefly exemplifies his learning 'numbers like *Faust*, and tunes like that'. He dodges a question about

Gottschalk, and plays polite versions of the *Miserere* from Verdi's *Il Trovatore* and the Sextet from Donizetti's *Lucia di Lammermoor*. Exit from this gentility comes with the realization that musical ability could mean money in the Tenderloin district and amidst the 'hilarity' of The Frenchman's saloon.

During the 'till ready' introduction to *Jelly Roll blues*, he gives a version of the source of his nickname. The rocking, freely ornamented blues, originally called *Chicago blues*, is much more interesting than the tongue-in-cheek tale; but there is an example here of the technical crudity which creeps into these recordings quite frequently. There is a rough join, and fuzzy sound for the final strains; but when Morton slows the tempo to accompany the lyrics, the blithe bravado pierces all distortion:

'He's tall and chancey,
He's the ladies' fancy . . .'

And the metronomic foot-tapping, omnipresent in these recordings ('Everybody in the world who's ever heard of me remembers the foot!'), suffers hardly at all.

Side 2 of Vol. 1 begins with a double echo of the piano traditions of the first years of the century. References to the St Louis Exposition and to the honky tonk bars of the Gulf Coast, together with the testimony of accompanying chords, show that midwestern ragtime and southwestern barrelhouse blues were the most formidable styles. Morton was mastering them both and adding elements of his own. The song *Alabama bound*, gently rocking, provides an excuse for varied reminiscences, some inconsequential if typically flavoured. Much more to the point of the entire exercise, since, in the end, music is here more eloquent than words, is the magnificent fast rendering of *King Porter stomp*, composed in 1905 and named for 'a very dear friend', one of those numerous but otherwise forgotten pianists who won Morton's admiration in the early days.

While singing *You can have it, I don't want it*, he asserts the 'real fact' that he taught its composer, Clarence Williams (**57**), how to play, and talks about the battles of music which sharpened musical wits. There follows the celebrated and no doubt very personal analysis of *Tiger rag* in terms of its supposed sources in French dance music, and a volatile performance of the famous number full of imitative orchestral effects, as evident, but far more subtle than the tiger's savage elbow-roars. Similarly representative of Morton's orchestral style is the subsequent treatment of *Panama*, perennial favourite of New Orleans marching bands, which is splendidly played by the Young Tuxedo Brass Band on **18** in a manner which must recall the band music that captured this pianist's imagination long ago.

At the start of Vol. 3, *Buddy Bolden* is introduced as 'one of the earliest barrelhouse blues'. In the course of his commentary, which recalls the potency of Bolden's own playing, Morton claims that the melody of this blues was stolen from what he calls *St Louis tickler*; but the strain in Barney and Seymour's ragtime hit *St Louis tickle*, though certainly identical, also bears close relation to a song by Scott Joplin, to a levee rousters' ditty, a spiritual, and to who knows how many older manifestations?

Morton is emphatic on the point that Bolden ('New Orleans boy, light-complected Negro') was 'a ragtime player', and provides a string of lively anecdotes about the trumpeter which may be set beside the comments of Bunk Johnson on **19**. Hints of both ragtime and blues spice *Salty dog*; the piano part and lyrics are rudimentary but have the characteristic Morton bounce. There is a simple evocation of Bill Johnson's 'three-piece organization', and references to Freddy Keppard's Tuxedo Orchestra and to Keppard's and his own 'dixieland' debut in Chicago in about 1914. In his singing and playing of *If you was whisky* and *My gal Sal*, his flexible voice and brass-bright treble phrases evoke a style of entertainment that, whilst very much of its age, is made to transcend mere fashion by the permeation of blues feeling. He transforms the sentimental *My gal Sal* with a rather exaggerated jazzing technique, and throws in bits of ragtime and tango phrasing.

Advice on the true origin of scat singing — one Joel Sims is given the credit — is part of the presentation of *Animule ball*, one of those jungletown pieces which reflect the whimsy of ragtime publicity and the minstrel shows. The zest of his indulgence fits strangely with his oft-expressed Creole dislike of Negro characteristics. His own attempt at scat is just a wordless imitation of his own pianistic lines and has nothing of the grotesque *élan* of the 'old comedians'. The following track on this second side of Vol. 3 is given over to a description of sartorial, perambulatory and culinary fashions among the stylish fellows of New Orleans. A lazily swinging version of the blues *See see rider* and a plaintively whined, inconclusive *Make me a pallet on the floor* carry the nostalgic mood along. By the time he gets to *The murder ballad* the potent whisky with which Lomax is plying him is ravaging his voice.

Volume 5 contains recollections both concentrated and varied of the public conventions, carnival and funereal, of New Orleans. The reference to Creole songs is brief, and surely gives no adequate impression of the variety of songs which Morton must have heard. His evocation of the Indians' jug dance and *To-wa-bac-a-wa*, and his description of the social clubs, will satisfy a liking for the picturesque, but of greater relevance to jazz history are his long discourses on the funeral customs and the marching bands. The verbal scene-drawing is extremely effective here, but it has to be said that the musical examples attempted are disappointing, and the latter part of the marching band section suffers from serious sound distortion.

The things written under **45** regarding Morton's piano style would only have to be repeated in assessment of the solos heard throughout these Library of Congress volumes for, while the style maintained its flexibility, it achieved no real formal development between the pianist's 1923 recordings (examples of an already mature utterance) and the end of his career. Yet beyond the merely documentary, these historic records contain some of Morton's most accomplished and occasionally ecstatic keyboard music. Volumes 7 and 8 have superb versions of many of his better known compositions, a little more expansive in their executive assurance, perhaps, and certainly less restricted by time limits than were the earliest renderings. The elegantly steered *moderato* version of *King Porter stomp* seems, though equally exciting, quite different in mood and motive to the fast, passionately swinging performance of the same number in Vol. 1, which carries the final strain over into additional variations of extraordinary power. The 'discourse on jazz' included in Vol. 8 has the famous and highly accomplished transformation of Joplin's *Maple leaf rag*, perhaps the most penetrating bit of historical wisdom in the entire marathon, and a fine *Kansas City stomps* unlike any other recorded version because an inspired repetition of the first strain turns it into a rondo. The distinctive mood he drew from the tango craze is heard in a fine performance of *The crave* in Vol. 4.

It is hard to say how much can be learnt from Morton's attempts to reproduce the styles of unrecorded pianists. After the first few bars of each example his own ineluctable accents take over, and one's overwhelming temptation is not to care! It is the rounded style and artistic verve of this great music-maker that leave the most profoundly instructive counsels tarrying in the mind. The music itself encapsulates the crowded panorama of 'an angel with great big feet' who, in a delinquent youth, had 'used the piano as a decoy', and who can still, though long dead, entice the wary into willing captivation:

'Now at home, as well as abroad,
They call him Mister Jelly Lord.'

                                                                E.T.

The earliest recordings in New Orleans

Activity in New Orleans during the 1920s was poorly documented (and the situation was to be even worse in the 1930s). These LPs, however, give as clear an idea as can now be obtained of the sorts of jazz heard there in that decade.

A. J. Piron/Louis Dumaine/Jones–Collins

22 New Orleans
Collectors' Classics (D) CC45

Piron's New Orleans Orchestra: Peter Bocage (tpt); John Lindsay (tbn); Lorenzo Tio jnr (clt, ten); Louis Warnecke (alt); Armand J. Piron (vln); Steve Lewis (p); Charles Bocage (bj); Charles Seguirre (tu); Louis Cottrell (d). New York City, 11 December 1923.
New Orleans wiggle · *Mama's gone, goodbye*

Same personnel and location, 8 January 1924.
Do-doodle-oom · *West Indies blues*

Unidentified clt replaces Tio; Lindsay absent. New Orleans, 25 March 1925.
Red man blues · *Do just as I say*

Louis Dumaine's Jazzola Eight: Dumaine (cnt); Earl Humphrey (tbn); Willie Joseph (clt); Louis James (ten); Morris Rouse (p); Leonard Mitchell (bj, vcl[1]); Joe Howard (tu); James Milligan (d). New Orleans, 7 March 1927.
Pretty Audrey · *To-wa-bac-a-wa* · *Franklin Street blues*[1] · *Red Onion drag*

Jones–Collins Astoria Hot Eight: Lee Collins (cnt); Sidney Arodin (clt); Theodore Purnell (alt); David Jones (ten); Joe Robichaux (p); Emmanuel Sayles (bj); Al Morgan (bs, vcl[2]); Albert Martin (d). New Orleans, 15 November 1929.
Astoria strut · *Duet stomp*[2] · *Damp weather* · *Tip easy blues*

The photograph of Piron's Orchestra on the sleeve shows nine suave-looking men. In the middle sits the leader, holding a sheet of manuscript paper, doubtless explaining some subtlety in the score. The onlooker can draw only one conclusion: that these are musicians of genuine class, every man an expert reader. And Piron's Orchestra certainly had a reputation for being perhaps the most refined of New Orleans ensembles, much in demand at Creole society functions. When the band visited New York in 1923, their polish and — to use the contemporary expression — snappy rhythm much impressed Fletcher Henderson's musicians.

The listener is now struck by the orchestra's sedateness, but also by an underlying gaiety which kept breaking through. Most of Piron's tracks on this LP reflect something of what commercial white dance bands were doing at the time, yet nearly every performance concludes with at least a chorus of fairly loose improvisation — never distinguished but generally attractive. Peter Bocage was a founder-member, collaborating with Piron on several tunes (and possibly some arrangements), but his trumpet solos are correct rather than exciting. In fact, the band had no outstanding soloist. Tio, just like his father, was one of the leading teachers of the clarinet in New Orleans, yet he surfaces very rarely (whatever the sleeve, and the discographers, say, he is probably responsible for the sixteen-bar solo in *Red man blues*).

Much more astringent music is supplied by the band which Dumaine led regularly in New Orleans during the late 1920s. He had a good technique, excellent for playing lead, but no pretensions to being a jazz soloist. The most interesting of his musicians is the clarinettist, Joseph, obviously influenced by Johnny Dodds. Joseph's tone and phrasing sometimes seem a trifle exaggerated, yet he takes a passionate solo in *Franklin Street blues*, a moving performance despite the indifferent singing. Humphrey makes little impact in the ensemble, while the tenor saxophonist never seems sure of exactly what his function is supposed to be. Nevertheless, the overall impression is of rough, exciting jazz. (Incidentally, *To-wa-bac-a-wa* is another name for *Bucket's got a hole in it*, while the chord sequence of *Pretty Audrey* sounds very reminiscent of *Song of songs*, a grandiloquent pop tune of the 1920s.)

Much more finesse, and at least as much intensity is provided by the Jones–Collins Astoria Hot Eight, another regular New Orleans band. For the recordings, they added a white clarinettist, Arodin, making this the first mixed session to take place in a New Orleans studio. He remains an underrated soloist, unlucky not to have been recorded more often (he died, aged only 47, in 1948). Using a very incisive approach, Arodin often summons up a kind of sting that clarinettists of the day seemed to acquire in Chicago. He makes an admirable partner for Collins, a soloist with a ravishing tone and behind-the-beat phrasing. Collins sounds a bit like Armstrong in *Duet stomp*, even throwing in a long, sustained note; but he and Arodin are at their best in *Tip easy blues*, as moving as it is lyrical. The two saxophonists take their most creditable solos on this track; elsewhere they sound expendable, except when used in tandem (Jones was responsible for writing the handy little arrangements). Morgan was already one of the finest New Orleans bassists, and Sayles an adroit banjo player (it is worth comparing Sayles's solos in *Astoria strut* and *Damp weather* with those he improvised thirty-one years later on **32**).

C.F.

23 Jazz Sounds of the 1920s Vol. 2: Dixieland Bands
Parlophone (E) PMC1171, Swaggie (Au) S1254

Original Dixieland Jazz Band: Nick LaRocca (cnt); Eddie Edwards (tbn); Artie Seaberg (clt); Don Parker (sop); Henry Vanicelli (p); Tony Sbarbaro (d). New York City, 23 November 1922.

Some of these days · Toddling blues

Johnny DeDroit and His New Orleans Jazz Orchestra: DeDroit (cnt); Russ Papalia (tbn); Henry Raymond (clt); Rudolph Levy (alt); Frank Cuny (p); George Potter (bj); Paul DeDroit (d). New Orleans, 15 March 1924.

New Orleans blues

Same personnel and location, 16 March 1924.

No. 2 blues

Johnny Bayersdorffer and His Jazzola Novelty Orchestra: Bayersdorffer (cnt); Tom Brown (tbn); Charles Scaglioni (clt); Johnny Miller (p); Steve Loyacano (bj); Chink Martin (bs); Leo Adde (d). New Orleans, 17 March 1924.

I wonder where my easy rider's riding now · The waffle man's call

Original Crescent City Jazzers: Sterling Bose (cnt); Avery Loposer (tbn); Cliff Holman (clt, alt); Eddie Powers (ten); Johnny Riddick (p); Slim Hall (bj); Bob Marvin (bs); Felix Guarino (d). New Orleans, 17 March 1924.

Sensation · Christine

Anthony Parenti's Famous Melody Boys: Henry Knecht (cnt); Russ Papalia (tbn); Parenti (clt, alt); Tony Papalia (ten); Vic Lubowsky (p); Mike Holloway (bj); Mario Finazzo (bs); George Triay (d). New Orleans, 22 January 1925.

That's a-plenty · Cabaret echoes

Halfway House Orchestra: Albert Brunies (cnt); Joe Loyacano (tbn); Leon Roppolo (clt); Charlie Cordella (clt, ten); Mickey Marcour (p); Bill Eastwood (bj); Adde (d). New Orleans, 22 January 1925.

Pussy cat rag · Barataria

Brownlee's Orchestra of New Orleans: Sharkey Bonano (cnt); Brown (tbn); Harry Shields (clt); Hal Jordy (alt, bar); Norman Brownlee (p); Behrman French (bj); Alonzo Crumby (d). New Orleans, 23 January 1925.

Peculiar · Dirty rag

Original New Orleans Rhythm Kings: Paul Mares (cnt); Santo Pecora (tbn); Roppolo (clt); Cordella (ten); Glynn Long (p); Eastwood (bj); Martin (bs); Adde (d). New Orleans, 23 January 1925.

She's crying for me · Golden leaf strut

24 The Sound of New Orleans Vol. 3
CBS (E) BPG62234, Columbia (A) CL2104

Original New Orleans Rhythm Kings: personnel, location and date as above.
Golden leaf strut

Celestin's Original Tuxedo Orchestra: Oscar Celestin, Kid 'Shots' Madison (cnt); William Ridgely (tbn); Willard Thoumy (clt, alt); probably Paul Barnes (ten); Manuel Manetta (p); John Marrero (bj); Simon Marrero (bs); Abbey Foster (d). New Orleans, 23 January 1925.
Original tuxedo rag

New Orleans Owls: Bill Padron (cnt); Frank Neito (tbn); Benjie White, Pinky Vidacovich (clt, alt); Lester Smith (ten); Mose Farrar (p); Rene Geipi (bj); Dan LeBlanc (tu); Earl Crumb (d). New Orleans, 14 April 1926.
Tampeko

Joe Mannone's Harmony Kings: 'Wingy' Mannone (cnt, vcl); Jordy (clt, alt); Bob Sacks (ten); Miller (p); Steve Brou (g); Arnold Loyacano (bs); John Ryan (d). New Orleans, 11 April 1927.
Up the country blues

Sam Morgan's Jazz Band: Sam Morgan (tpt, vcl[1]); Isaiah Morgan (tpt); Jim Robinson (tbn); Andrew Morgan (clt, ten); Earl Fouché (sop, alt); Tink Baptiste (p); Johnny Dave (bj); Sidney Brown (bs); Nolan Williams (d). New Orleans, 14 April 1927.
Stepping on the gas · *Everybody's talking about Sammy*[1] · *Mobile stomp* · *Sing on*

Walter Decou (p), Roy Evans (d) replace Baptiste, Williams; band vocal[2]. New Orleans, 22 October 1927.
Short dress gal[1] · *Bogalusa strut* · *Down by the riverside*[2] · *Over in gloryland*

Celestin's Original Tuxedo Orchestra: Celestin, Richard Alexis or Guy Kelly (tpt); William Matthews (tbn); Clarence Hall, Robert Hall, Joe Rouson (saxes); Jeanette Salvant (p); Henry Kimbell jnr (bj); Simon Marrero (tu); Josiah 'Cié' Frazier (d). New Orleans, 25 October 1927.
It's jam up

Johnny Miller's New Orleans Frolickers: Bonano (tpt); Sidney Arodin (clt); Jordy (alt); Miller (p); Brou (bj); Martin (tu); Adde (d). New Orleans, 25 April 1928.
Panama · *Dippermouth blues*

Bunk's Brass Band: Bunk Johnson, Madison (tpt); Robinson (tbn); Isadore Barbarin (ah); Adolph Alexander (bh); George Lewis (E-flat clt); Joseph Clark (tu); Baby Dodds (snare d); Lawrence Marrero (bs d). New Orleans, 18 May 1945.
Oh, didn't he ramble?

An inappropriate start is made here with the ODJB, for their performances were taken down in New York; with Larry Shields gone, they show the band in steep decline. Either DeDroit's group, like the Crescent City Jazzers in *Sensation*, adapted ODJB procedures to a smoother rhythmic flow or they drew from the same basic sources. A similar comment applies to the resemblance of Celestin's *Original tuxedo rag*, on **24**, to the work of King Oliver's Creole Band (**44**). With DeDroit the clarinettist is outstanding, with Celestin nobody is, although his later *It's jam up* is looser-limbed. *No. 2 blues* is a slowing-down of the ODJB's *Tiger rag*.

Bayersdorffer's men are more enterprising. A fiery player, the cornettist was active in New Orleans for many years, but these are his only recordings, as they are Scaglioni's. This clarinettist possessed a fine contrapuntal sense and maintained unflagging melodic independence; he and Roppolo are the most creative improvisors on **23**. Padron's two solos on *Tampeko* with the New Orleans Owls are in a similar style to Bayersdorffer's, though more elegant; there is good clarinet here, too, from Vidacovich. Competent solos come, also, from the Crescent City Jazzers, although they do best in the final ensemble of *Christine*, which is dominated by Holman and Bose. The Parenti items are more formal yet have considerable variety, while Brownlee's tracks are notable for an early solo appearance of the baritone saxophone and a distinctly promising Bonano.

A return is made by Roppolo with the Halfway House Orchestra, on whose *Barataria* his solo is the main event, although the final ensemble has some intensity and there are some excellent breaks. The New Orleans Rhythm Kings' titles are less remarkable than the most characteristic of those on **43**, partly because the triumvirate of Mares, Brunies and Roppolo has been broken. The latter moves coolly and confidently through the ensembles, however, and takes a masterly solo on *She's crying for me*. *Golden leaf strut* (alias *Milneburg joys*) finds him in a very different mood, his solo being dark-toned yet spectral, introverted despite the fast tempo. This is a rarefied achievement of a sort not widely associated with early jazz. Bonano's promise is duly fulfilled in Miller's *Dippermouth blues* and *Panama*. The former is superior to Oliver's own 1926 Dixie Syncopators' remake as *Sugar foot stomp*, and this, indeed, was a disciplined yet freely flowing group which set precedents for Bob Crosby (**236**). Arodin is still another notable clarinettist (see **22**), and Jordy is, with Fouché of the Morgan ensemble, easily the best saxophonist on these two discs, playing solos that are agile yet concentrated, even if somewhat in the shadow of Frankie Trumbauer (**64**).

Though described by an easily misled *savant* as a 'marvellous anachronism' [9], Morgan's band marked an important stage in the development of New Orleans music. Comparison with the

1923 Creole Band suggests that Oliver took a rather conservative view of New Orleans jazz, and here the ensembles, the plangent sweetness of the saxophones notwithstanding, are more open, the rhythmic pulse lighter. The textures are extremely diverse, variation being achieved from one chorus to another by changes of density, volume, and so on. Quite often, as in *Mobile stomp*, the participants engage in simultaneous variations; the trumpets are less commanding, and the reeds sometimes carry the most important threads, as in some of Johnny Dodds's recordings without Oliver or Armstrong (**38–40**). Such elements as the freedom of the parts, the trumpets' wide vibrato, the use of spirituals, the playing of Fouché, which is something like that of John Handy on **33**, all point to the New Orleans recordings of the 1940s. That later stage is here ineffectively represented with Johnson's *Oh, didn't he ramble?*, although further and better material of that brass-dominated kind may be found on such records as **18**, on American Music, and on Dixie (E) LP107. The point is, however, that the Miller and Morgan recordings prove New Orleans jazz was still blowing hot and strong, and was still evolving, even if attention had shifted elsewhere. (Note also Kid Howard's *Sam Morgan Revisited* on Icon (A) 10.)   M.H.

Later New Orleans recordings

These are *not* recreations of early jazz but show, rather, the continuing development of the New Orleans style.

25 Wooden Joe Nicholas New Orleans Band 1945–49
Storyville (D) SLP204, Dan (J) VC4010

Nicholas (tpt); Albert Burbank (clt); Lawrence Marrero (bj); Austin Young (bs). New Orleans, 10 May 1945.
Shake it and break it
Jim Robinson (tbn) added. Same date.
Lead me on · Careless love
Josiah 'Cié' Frazier (d) added. Same date.
Artesan Hall blues · Tiger rag · Eh la bas[1] · *Up jumped the Devil · Don't go away nobody · I ain't got nobody*
[1] Vocal by Burbank and the ensemble. *I ain't got nobody* is spliced from two takes.
Nicholas (tpt, clt[2]); Louis Nelson (tbn); Burbank (clt); Johnny St Cyr (bj); Young (bs); Albert Jiles (d); Ann Cook (vcl[3]). New Orleans, 21 July 1949.
Clarinet blues[2] · *The Lord will make a way*[3]

Although never recognized as such, Nicholas was among the best New Orleans trumpeters of his time. Born in 1883, he was of the same generation as Oliver and Morton (both b. 1885), and we might have expected his playing, like theirs, to be shaped by a rather deliberate sense of variation, activated, as also in the case of Bunk Johnson, by ragtime syncopation. In fact, his music shows that arguing New Orleans jazz history by generations leads to deceptive simplifications.

Nicholas began as a clarinettist, and his work on that instrument, as in *Clarinet blues*, is primitive in the best sense, which is why he appears first in this section. It is something like 'Big Eye' Louis Delisle's playing on the American Music label, both men having apparently by-passed the innovations of Morton, Oliver and their contemporaries. In contrast, Nicholas taught himself the trumpet after working professionally as a clarinettist for many years, and his improvisations on that instrument have a freedom uncommon even among men substantially younger.

Incessant variation, on several musical levels, is the basis of his trumpeting, and this is quite different from the somewhat formal kind found in the jazz of his leading contemporaries. Phrasing and attack, for example, are changed from one chorus to another with astonishing variety of resource. Sometimes he will scoop up to a note from below, deliberately overshoot the next, and hit the following one squarely. His vibrato is intense but also subject to frequent alteration. Nicholas's sense of swing, too, is unusually fiery, and he delays and anticipates whole phrases besides single notes, shifting around the beat with a freedom that was supposedly brought to jazz by a much later generation. His note-values are extremely mixed, ranging from (usually bent) notes lasting a whole bar to long quaver runs; he is especially fond of descending runs, as in the beautiful *Careless love*. The phrase-lengths, also, are notably diverse, overlapping not only the usual two- and four-bar units but even the chorus divisions themselves.

These performances, then, have a greater freedom within the chorus than most such jazz, yet, while he departs from the melody quite drastically, even wildly, he nearly always manages to imply its outline. Partly because of this, his lead is strong in overall form, and this despite his leaving plenty of space for the other instruments. Nearly all the above pieces demonstrate these qualities, but *Shake it and break it* is especially remarkable, its power belying the four-piece instrumentation. *Eh la bas* and *Up jumped the Devil* should also be mentioned, for here Burbank takes the lead most of the time, allowing the trumpeter to play, if possible, with even greater daring than elsewhere.

Several of the other musicians found here, indeed, are of interest, and Burbank was a particularly good partner for Nicholas. He swings hard, creates strong rhythmic patterns, and develops his ideas continuously from one chorus to the next, and beyond. These improvisations are again exceptional for their disciplined polyphonic feeling, and Burbank produces more real counterpoint than some more celebrated clarinettists in this idiom.   M.H.

26 George Lewis 1944–45
Storyville (D) SLP201, Dan (J) VC4004

Lewis (clt); Lawrence Marrero (bj); Alcide 'Slow Drag' Pavageau (bs). New Orleans, 29 July 1944.
Burgundy Street blues

Kid Howard (tpt); Jim Robinson (tbn); Lewis (clt); Marrero (bj); Chester Zardis (bs); Edgar Mosley (d). New Orleans, 1944.
Careless love

Kid 'Shots' Madison (tpt), Pavageau (bs), Baby Dodds (d) replace Howard, Zardis, Mosley. New Orleans, 5 August 1944.
High society

Madison absent. Same date.
San Jacinto blues No. 1 · Ice cream

Lewis (clt); Marrero (bj); Richard Alexis (bs). New Orleans, 17 May 1945.
Hindustan

Bunk Johnson (tpt); Robinson (tbn); Lewis (clt); Marrero (bj); Pavageau (bs); Dodds (d). Same date.
Lonesome road

Lewis (clt); Marrero (bj); Pavageau (bs). New Orleans, 21 May 1945.
Over the waves · New Orleans hula · This love of mine · St Philips Street breakdown

Perhaps in his later years, Lewis made too many records for the good of his final reputation, but at the time the above performances were set down his output was far higher in quality and much better integrated in terms of expression and technique than it subsequently became. In organization, his playing was based on arpeggios yet rarely did he then just run up and down the chords. Instead, he was, in melodic terms, always going somewhere, his runs being extended motivically and never, in ensembles, lapsing into mere joins between the trumpet phrases. In *St Philips Street breakdown* his ideas flow across the chorus divisions, and his irregular phrase-lengths should be noted. This continuity is important, and from it comes the rhythmic interest of Lewis's work. On *Ice cream*, where almost throughout the clarinet line is in unflagging quavers, there is considerable variety in his placing of accents, a surprising proportion of them, considering the fast tempo, coming between the beats; also, they closely relate to Dodds's part and are grouped in tellingly contrasted patterns which are the key to Lewis's fine sense of swing.

Such sophistications, along with Howard's striking display of rhythmic variation and Robinson's independence of tailgate conventions, ought to have been enough to indicate that this was essentially a contemporary style. As such, it was, like other viable jazz developments, free to borrow from elsewhere, and the point is neatly demonstrated by *St Philips Street breakdown*, which adapts ideas from Woody Herman's *Chips boogie woogie* and Benny Goodman's *Gone with what wind?* (both 1940). It is no contradiction to say, however, that Lewis's was essentially a blues style, and this is no small matter if his playing be compared with that of older clarinettists such as 'Big Eye' Louis Delisle or Alphonse Picou, who were only marginally affected by the blues. (This becomes evident if Lewis's account of the traditional *High society* chorus included here is set beside Picou's 1940 recording on Riverside (A) RLP12-119.) The large number of blued notes, on which the accents often fall, explains, too, much of the intensity of his improvising, and *Burgundy Street* is a justly celebrated instance, being a poignant set of well contrasted yet firmly linked variations. More complex is the already mentioned *Ice cream*, a masterpiece of its kind, an involved sequence of contrapuntal variations wherein the two horns exchange roles with what may initially seem disconcerting frequency, their normal tasks being modified by the absence of a trumpet. (This process may be observed in slow motion in Lewis's moving *Two Jim blues* of the previous year (Blue Note (A) BST81206, Vocalion (E) LAE12005), where there is an additional melodic line from a tuba.)

The appeal of *San Jacinto* is very different, lying in its sustained and searing melodies; this, indeed, ranks with *Burgundy Street* as an instance of Lewis's blues playing. The opposite side of the coin is represented by the rather excessive sweetness of *This love of mine* and the 3/4 beginning to *Over the waves*. The full band tracks, also, are mixed. Much of *High society* is crippled by tensely muddled ensembles, but *Lonesome road* could scarcely be more different. In contrast with the tightly organized collective playing of, say, Oliver's Creole Band (**44**), the ensembles of this later phase of New Orleans jazz are loose and spacious, and *Lonesome road's* complex lucidity, beautifully maintained over the rhythm section's light yet deeply swinging pulse, is a magnificent example. In terms of swing, drive, and musical awareness, the Marrero–Pavageau–Dodds rhythm section was a great one, phrasing as a section in integrated contours, varying their parts so that several rhythmic lines developed simultaneously. M.H.

27 Kid Ory 1944–45

Good Time Jazz (E) LAG12104, Good Time Jazz (A) 12022

Kid Ory's Creole Jazz Band: Mutt Carey (tpt); Ory (tbn, vcl[1]); Omer Simeon (clt); Buster Wilson (p); Bud Scott (g); Ed Garland (bs); Alton Redd (d). Los Angeles, 3 August 1944.
Get out of here · South · Blues for Jimmy Noone · Creole song[1]
Scott (vcl[2]). Los Angeles, 5 August 1945.
Panama · Careless love · Do what Ory say[1] *· Under the bamboo tree*[2]
Darnell Howard (clt) replaces Simeon. Los Angeles, 8 September 1945.
1919 rag · Maryland, my Maryland · Down home rag · Didn't he ramble?[1]
Same personnel and location, 3 November 1945.
Original dixieland one-step · Maple leaf rag · Weary blues · Ory's Creole trombone

It was Coleridge, musing on the nature of poetry, who hit upon that phrase about the 'willing suspension of disbelief'. Something very like that kind of abnegation seemed to be demanded during the early days of the New Orleans revival; certainly for those seasoned buffs of 1930s and 1940s jazz, reared on the pursuit of originality, who were now suddenly confronted with what appeared to be the deliberate archaism of, say, Bunk Johnson's records. Ory's band, on the contrary, seemed much easier to believe in; some diehard revivalists, indeed, thought it a trifle slick. The truth was that for Ory the revival was largely a matter of picking up where he had left off (between 1933 and 1942 he had been out of music, working in the post office or rearing chickens). Yet before World War I, Ory was already one of the most distinguished New Orleans bandmasters, expecting high standards from his sidesmen. He went on doing so, a fact attested to by the tightness of the ensemble work on this LP, the way each performance has a shape and identity to it. Which is all the more remarkable because the session of August 1944 was really the work of an *ad hoc* group. True, Carey and Garland had played with Ory in the early years, while Scott was his companion in King Oliver's band in the mid-1920s. A very similar ensemble had appeared a few times on Orson Welles's radio show, though with Zutty Singleton on drums and Jimmy Noone playing clarinet. Singleton had his commitments, however, and Noone died in April 1944. Which was why, when Ory realized that Simeon would be in Los Angeles that August, playing in Jimmy Lunceford's reed section, he recruited him for the record date.

Simeon was one of the finest clarinettists in the Creole tradition, alternately lyrical and attacking. Not surprisingly, he is heard at his noblest in *Blues for Jimmy Noone*. Other outstanding clarinet solos are to be found in *Get out of here* (a *Tiger rag* variant) and

Panama, but Simeon's skills were just as evident when he was being one-third of the front line. Howard sounds more pedestrian as a soloist (though he sparkles in *Didn't he ramble?*), but, once again, he proved a good man to have in the ensemble. And these performances rely upon ensemble work — either crisply organized or collectively improvised — with only the clarinettists getting much solo space.

Carey had never seemed a particularly gifted soloist, but he was a fine lead player (his only lapse occurs during the tricky theme statements of *Maple leaf rag*). The rhythm section was livelier than those of the purely revivalist bands, able to swing but also able to operate as part of a marching band, not just in *Maryland, my Maryland*, but in *1919 rag* (rags always had a kinship with marches so far as their structures were concerned, so what was needed was a rhythmic shift) and what might be described as a jazz march, *Didn't he ramble?* As it happens, the material here is a bit short on blues, but does include Bob Coles's elegant hit song of 1902, *Under the bamboo tree*, later parodied, or pastiched, by T. S. Eliot in *Sweeney Agonistes*.

Ory sings *Creole song*, suitably enough, in Creole patois, the language he grew up speaking. He was indeed a quintessential Creole (his wife once upbraided the present writer for implying that her husband was 'a coloured musician'). The gusty aspects of his playing, especially his mastery of the tailgate style, have sometimes blinded commentators to the subtlety of his solos and ensemble work. The solo in *Careless love*, for example, shows how Ory could deploy the more abrasive elements of his trombone style yet still achieve a kind of tranquillity, accepting the brazenness of his instrument and turning it into a virtue.   C.F.

28 Bunk Johnson's Band 1944 with George Lewis
Storyville (D) SLP128, *Dan (J) 4008

Johnson (tpt); Jim Robinson (tbn); Lewis (clt); Lawrence Marrero (bj); Alcide 'Slow Drag' Pavageau (bs); Sidney 'Jim Little' Brown (tu); Baby Dodds (d). New Orleans, 29 July 1944.
Lowdown blues

Brown absent; Myrtle Jones (vcl) added. New Orleans, 31 July 1944.
My life will be sweeter one day

Jones absent. New Orleans, 2 August 1944.
Lord, Lord, Lord · Careless love · Panama

Same personnel and location, 3 August 1944.
We shall walk through the streets of the city · Sister Kate

Same personnel and location, 4 August 1944.
Sugar foot stomp

The more remarkable virtues of this music are not, perhaps, the obvious ones. They ask for a kind of attention which may only be achieved after certain obstacles have been overcome; not merely technical ones like poor recording balance and an occasional musical ineptness that, whilst not to be over-emphasized, is not the recondite archaic skill some pretended it was. There are psychological hurdles, too. Some people may still be under the impression that Johnson's re-emergénce and his teaming up with other veterans suddenly provided an opportunity to hear jazz exactly as it was played in some pre-gramophone golden age. It did not do that, although it certainly refreshed insight into the living reality of New Orleans music which had been muddied by both commercial and critical notions. Set aside the preconceived ideas that (a) there is an orthodox instrumentation for this music, and that (b) these veterans were automatically suited to each other, and the music will come to life in startling ways for the attentive ear.

Neither the instrumentation nor the choice of numbers really matches Johnson's own preference, and his adaptability and skill are shown by his lively artistic response to the romantic impositions of promoters and the variant styles and experience of his partners. All three horns, though, are firmly in the New Orleans tradition, even if affected by differing approaches and developments. They make a very personal response to the opportunity before them. Instead of the rigid ensemble roles which orthodoxy prescribes for each wind instrument, and the shibboleth of unvarying trumpet lead, one hears constantly shifting patterns of prominence. The lead is passed, sometimes to Lewis, sometimes to Robinson. Sometimes Johnson 'lays out' of the interplay altogether. Sometimes, too, he 'leads from below', suggesting the shape of the counterpoint with variations harmonic rather than melodic in relation to the theme. *Lord, Lord, Lord* and *Careless love* contain examples of this. He is sensitive to the styles of the clarinettist and trombonist, but his adaptation never conceals the fact that he is a more considerable musician, and in some ways, despite seniority, more modern in outlook than they. His formality shows in his fine solos on *Careless love* and *Sugar foot stomp*, and in much of his ensemble playing. Its origins in ragtime classicism may be evident, but equally evident is his ability to adapt and augment the style; and he contrives to swing in a way that frequently eludes the others.

Lewis, a singular musician not easily fitted into conventional categories of New Orleans clarinet playing, has a rather perpendicular approach which, agile as it is, contrasts sharply with Johnson's forward thrust and with Robinson's recklessly appropriate venturings. He plays a good *legato* solo, accompanied by Dodds's temple block figurations, in *Careless love*; he assumes a firm melodic lead in *Lord, Lord, Lord* and *We shall walk through the streets of the city*; and his normal ensemble role, if a little monotonous and often under-recorded, is always apt. Robinson is rather more versatile than his hazardous technique may suggest. When prominent, as in the later measures of *We shall walk through the streets*, and the obligatory passages of *Sugar foot stomp*, he moves confidently. The curious staccato passages which he injects into *Careless love* and his saxophone-like riffs in *Panama* should surprise those nurtured on the legend of the tailgate trombone.

But Johnson is the true *Spiritus Rector*. His mastery is clear throughout, even, paradoxically, in his self-effacements. He gives this music its impetus and prompts its shaping. Dodds's varied and appropriate drumming aids the excitement at many points. One wonders how needful the *Niflheim* clang of Marrero's banjo is to this sort of music, and suspects that it is addictive — Lewis used *two* banjos on other occasions. Pavageau's contribution is hard to comment on for reasons of aural balance, but Brown's tuba in *Lowdown blues* is only too audible, and becomes offensive. This latter piece proves that the leader's generally 'legitimate' tonal concept does not prevent him from blowing some forceful blue notes when such are required.   E.T.

29 Bunk Johnson 1945
Dan (J) VC4018

Johnson (tpt); Jim Robinson (tbn); George Lewis (clt); Lawrence Marrero (bj); Alcide 'Slow Drag' Pavageau (bs); Baby Dodds (d). New Orleans, 14 May 1945.
Sister Kate · All the whores like the way I ride · Margie · Amor Amor Amor

Same personnel and location, 15 May 1945.
High society · Shine · Slow Drag's boogie woogie

Noon Johnson (vcl) added; Robinson absent. New Orleans, 17 May 1945.
Noon's blues · The cat's got kittens

Robinson (tbn) added; Noon Johnson absent. Same date.
Lonesome road · Golden leaf strut · My old Kentucky home · Lady, be good · Old grey bonnet

Johnson may have juggled with dates to elevate his place in jazz history (see **19**), yet he never looked upon himself, musically speaking, as an historical figure. That was the fate his admirers reserved for him. It was they who were shocked when, at a session with the Lu Watters band, he wanted to record *Mairzy doats*, a then-popular hit. New Orleans jazz, as Johnson saw it, was a way of playing popular tunes, whether ragtime numbers or melodies of later vintage. So it is interesting to note that one of the items included here, *Amor Amor Amor* (not *Amour* as shown on the sleeve and in the discographies), was a Spanish import popular in 1944, while another is Gershwin's *Lady, be good*, a standby at prewar jam sessions but not usually classified as traditional material.

These recordings were made — in Lewis's house — just after Johnson had returned from working alongside Sidney Bechet in Boston, and not long before he took this particular band, plus a pianist, to play at New York's Stuyvesant Casino. The 14 May session suffers from very indifferent recording quality, with the interior balance often aggravatingly blurred. The playing, too, is more uneven, especially in *Margie*, than on later dates. *High society* sounds skimpy, with a slightly chaotic transition into the traditional clarinet solo (Lewis tackles it capably enough). But *Slow Drag's boogie woogie* demonstrates the variety of treatment which Johnson's band could bestow upon what was just a straightforward twelve-bar blues. Each of the seventeen choruses has a different character to it; particularly interesting is the use of riffs (anathema to the stricter New Orleans buffs), tucked behind Lewis in the ninth and tenth choruses, while the thirteenth chorus introduces what sounds suspiciously like the closing figure of *One o'clock jump*.

The most successful music was recorded on 17 May. Even the blues with Noon Johnson, a friend of the Lewis family who wanted to hear what he sounded like, allowed scope for plaintive improvising in the background, while in *Lonesome road* (a performance also included on **26**), *My old Kentucky home*, *Old grey bonnet* and *Lady, be good* the band establishes an admirable interior balance, the lines interweaving in a way that ensured buoyancy. Indeed, it is the collective effort which makes this music work. One drawback is the rigidity of the banjo playing (it even seems to stop *Amor* taking on any sort of Spanish tinge). Pavageau's bass, nicely flexible, is not treated kindly by the recording balance. Dodds, however, emerges as a master drummer in this area of music, using the whole kit, concerned not only to thrust the band forward, as a drummer in a slightly later style might be compelled to do, but nudging the ensemble along, shading the background, proffering a whole range of percussive effects.   C.F.

30 Bunk Johnson: Last Testament
Philips (E) BBL7231, Columbia (A) JCL829

Johnson (tpt); Ed Cuffee (tbn); Garvin Bushell (clt); Don Kirkpatrick (p); Danny Barker (g); Wellman Braud (bs); Alphonse Steele (d). New York City, 23 December 1947.

The entertainer · The minstrel man · Chloé · Someday

Same personnel and location, 24 December 1947.

Hilarity rag · Kinklets · You're driving me crazy · Out of nowhere

Same personnel and location, 26 December 1947.

That teasing rag · Some of these days · Till we meet again · Maria Elena

Despite the high quality of his finest American Music improvisations (**28** and **29**), Johnson was never satisfied with the players with whom he there appeared. During his famous 1945–46 engagement at the Stuyvesant Casino in New York he wanted, for example, to replace Jim Robinson with Sandy Williams (beside whom he had recorded, with Sidney Bechet, in March 1945 — **242**). The claim that these 1947 performances were the only ones that entirely met with his wishes is not quite true, as the 1944 San Francisco *Spicey advice/Arkansas Blues* date (VJM (E) VEP33), using such musicians as Floyd O'Brien and Red Callender, produced very similar results. Certainly on his 1947 sessions, in effect his last professional engagements, Johnson employed men with experience comparable to that of Williams rather than to that of Robinson or George Lewis. Bushell, for instance, had been with Chick Webb and Cab Calloway, Cuffee with Fletcher Henderson and Count Basie, Barker with the Blue Rhythm Band, Braud with Ellington.

This was a regular working group that had appeared at the Stuyvesant Casino earlier in the year and was thoroughly rehearsed. Although New Orleans warhorses are conspicuously absent, Johnson believed that a jazz band should be able to play anything, that interpretation was what counted, and so the repertoire ranges widely. It starts with rags like Arthur Marshall's *Kinklets* and James Scott's *Hilarity*, and moves on, via a cowboy song and a Tin Pan Alley rhumba, to then-current popular ballads such as *Out of nowhere*. This last undergoes as drastic a desentimentalization as that recorded the previous month by Charlie Parker. Of the rags Johnson said, 'this music is hot as written', and so that is how it is played here; everything else is improvised.

As usual with Johnson, clarity and variety of texture are sought at all times. Some of the music's greatest pleasures arise from the careful dovetailing of ensemble parts, as in *Till we meet again*, and the effect is rather different from that of the exciting

collisions which occur in the American Music collective improvisations. These ensembles take their cue, of course, from
Johnson's high-stepping yet deftly-placed lead parts, which are
considerably varied in emphasis — quiet in *Someday*, hard-blown
on *Hilarity*. There are many notable subsidiary details also, such
as the thematically-based piano riff behind the *Chloé* trombone
solo.

The solos vary in their intensity. Cuffee is usually sober but
dependable, as in *Maria Elena*. Barker's solo on this sounds a note
of intimacy not often heard in these fundamentally attacking
performances. In *You're driving me crazy* and *Till we meet again*,
Bushell plays with agility and invention, yet the most imaginative solos come from the leader, on *Chloé* and especially *Some of
these days*. Though it is instructive to compare, for example, *The
entertainer* with Mutt Carey's less aggressive version (**31**) and
with the one on **10**, this music has a character of its own. It
clarifies Johnson's extremely personal and often misunderstood
attitude towards jazz, as do the location recordings he made with
this same personnel at the Stuyvesant Casino the month before
the above sessions (Nola (E) LP3).   M.H.

31 The Legendary Mutt Carey
Esquire (E) 32-130, *Savoy (A) SJL2251 (2 LPs)

Carey (tpt); James Archey (tbn); Albert Nicholas (clt); Hank Duncan (p);
Danny Barker (g); George 'Pops' Foster (bs); Baby Dodds (d). New York
City, 18 November 1947.
*Shimme-sha-wabble · Slow driving · Ostrich walk · Cake walking
babies*
Edmond Hall (clt), Cliff Jackson (p) replace Nicholas, Duncan. New York
City, 27 November 1947.
*Sensation rag · Chrysanthemum · The entertainer · Fidgety feet ·
Indiana*

It seems unlikely that Carey was ever one of the great trumpeters. His recordings other than those with Kid Ory (**27**) are few,
the Sunshine items of 1922 tell us little, and we can only hope
that the titles cut during 1944–46 (not forgetting the Hociel
Thomas accompaniment on Circle) convey an adequate impression of his latter-day capabilities. He played an ensemble part
that was firm, usually decisively leading — even in *Cake walking
babies*, where the quick tempo was probably difficult for him —
and not so tied to the beat as to induce rhythmic monotony. He
never attempts on these recordings to dominate unduly, giving
clarinet and trombone plenty of room, and this, when seconded by
a drummer like Dodds, produced buoyant, airy ensembles of a

most refreshing kind. Carey took few solos on these sessions; the one in *Slow driving* finds him using stock phrases with real eloquence, but on *Indiana* he merely alters the theme without distinctive effect, and his *Ostrich walk* solo has the kind of tension created by insecure technical control rather than a taut musical design.

Although Dodds makes his presence felt in almost every bar of this LP, Nicholas commands the foreground on the earlier session. In both solo and ensemble he plays the clarinet, and this musical style, with an authority and emotion that were already rare in 1947. His solo on *Slow driving* is perhaps the most beautiful thing on this record, and this track has a scaldingly hot final ensemble, denser than those at faster tempos. Other fine Nicholas solos occur on *Ostrich walk* and *Cake walking babies*. On the following date, Hall is fluent and dependable, but his rather curious adaptation of ideas from Benny Goodman to a basically New Orleans mode of expression sounds a little artificial in this context on *Fidgety feet* and *Indiana*, significantly less so in the rags.

These were nearly Archey's first small combo recordings since his 1930 titles with King Oliver on **82** [10], and the first to impress his abilities on the jazz audience. Although not providing as solid a part as some other trombonists, Archey was unusual in being inventive both in solos and improvised ensembles. It should be added that these ensembles do sound improvised, and certainly do not adhere to dixieland stereotypes, even in *Fidgety feet* or *Indiana*. Archey's best work is in the latter and *Slow driving*.

At the time these recordings were made, band performances of rags were thought to be hazardous, or worse, as this was considered exclusively pianistic material. In fact, as the items heard on **10** and several comparable LPs show, the practice was almost as old as ragtime itself, and Carey's are very idiomatic, though freer than those by Bunk Johnson (**30**). They escape the stiffness of many later ragtime interpretations while also avoiding imparting to the music too many jazz rhythmic traits. It is, however, the jazz performances which are the most important here, bringing us a very agreeable version of one of the later New Orleans styles and adding, though not decisively, to our scant knowledge of Carey's contribution to jazz.   M.H.

32 New Orleans: the Living Legends 1960–61
Riverside (A) 9356/7 (2 LPs)

Love–Jiles Ragtime Orchestra: Peter Bocage (tpt, vln); Charlie Love (tpt); Albert Warner (tbn); Paul Barnes (clt); Emmanuel Sayles (bj); Auguste Lanoix (bs); Albert Jiles (d). New Orleans, 12 June 1960.
West Indies blues

Kid Thomas and His Algiers Stompers: Kid Thomas Valentine (tpt); Louis Nelson (tbn); Emil Barnes (clt); Joe James (p); Joseph Butler (bs); Samuel Penn (d). New Orleans, August 1960.
Jada

Jim Robinson's New Orleans Band: Ernest Cagnolatti (tpt); Robinson (tbn); Louis Cottrell (clt); 'Creole George' Guesnon (bj); Alcide 'Slow Drag' Pavageau (bs); Alfred Williams (d); Annie Pavageau (vcl[1]). New Orleans, 24 January 1961.
Take my hand, precious Lord[1] · *Yearning* · *Somebody else is taking my place*

Percy Humphrey's Crescent City Joymakers: Humphrey (tpt); Nelson (tbn); Albert Burbank (clt); Sayles (bj); Lewis James (bs); Josiah 'Cié' Frazier (d). New Orleans, 24 January 1961.
We shall walk through the streets of the city · *Rip 'em up, Joe* · *Climax rag*

Sweet Emma Barrett and Her Dixieland Boys: Percy Humphrey (tpt); Robinson (tbn); Willie Humphrey (clt); Barrett (p, vcl[2]); Sayles (g); McNeal Breaux (bs); Frazier (d). New Orleans, 25 January 1961.
St Louis blues[2] · *High society* · *Sweet Emma's blues*

Peter Bocage and His Creole Serenaders: Bocage (tpt); Homer Eugene (tbn); Cottrell (clt); Benjamin Turner (p); Sidney Pflueger (g); Breaux (bs); Williams (d). New Orleans, 26 January 1961.
Bouncing around · *Mama's gone, goodbye*

Louis Cottrell Trio: Cottrell (clt); Sayles (g); Breaux (bs). New Orleans, 27 January 1961.
Down by the riverside · *You don't love me*

Billie and Dédé Pierce: Dédé Pierce (cnt); Billie Pierce (p, vcl[3]); Jiles (d). New Orleans, 27 January 1961.
Billie's gumbo blues · *Good tonk blues*[3] · *Freight train moaning blues*[3]

Kid Thomas and His Algiers Stompers: Valentine (tpt); Nelson (tbn); Burbank (clt); Joe James (p); Homer Eugene (bj); Butler (bs); Penn (d). New Orleans, 29 January 1961.
Mack the knife · *Panama*

All but two of these tracks were recorded within the space of five days in 1961 at a New Orleans meeting hall (it belonged, appropriately enough, to the Société des Jeunes Amis). The idea was to get a representative selection of authentic local jazz. Projects of that sort have sometimes come up with woebegone performances by musicians who had lost their sense of key as well as their *élan*. Not so with most of these tracks. Robinson's band, in particular, is a splendidly integrated ensemble, placing the emphasis on collective improvising rather than individual solos. The drumming was not helped by the echo of the hall, but the playing is still flexible and relaxed. *Take my hand, precious Lord* suffers from insensitive singing, but the other two pieces — pop songs from different decades — bring out the best in this group. Robinson is decidedly the leader, prominent within the ensemble as well as taking a couple of solos. The clarinettist, Cottrell, performs lissomly enough, but gets more chance to show his skill as a soloist on two items by Bocage's Creole Serenaders. Bocage was co-writer with A. J. Piron of *Bouncing around* and *Mama's gone, goodbye* (Piron's 1923 band can be heard performing the latter on **22**). Compared with the rest of the music on these LPs, these tracks are relatively sedate, with Cottrell the only soloist of note. Perhaps the clarinettist concentrates too much upon the middle and lower registers in his trio recordings, attractive but a trifle disappointing. At his finest he is a fluent player in the classic New Orleans style, much more likely to give a flowing performance of the traditional *High society* clarinet solo than Willie Humphrey does on the version by Emma Barrett. Humphrey's interpretation is unusually staccato, but the tempo, for a start, is exceptionally brisk, too fast for any but a company of Gurkhas to march to; his approach, as exhibited in *St Louis blues*, is not far removed from that of a trumpet player, forceful in the way that Bechet's soprano saxophone was. That quirkiness works to the music's advantage in *Sweet Emma's blues* — slow, luxuriant, with Robinson interpolating a trombone solo of outstanding sobriety. Miss Barrett is a useful, if unspectacular, pianist, but performs without the bells — sewn on garters, skirt and beret — which used to enliven her in-the-flesh appearances.

Sayles plays guitar with the Barrett band and in the Cottrell Trio, but less effectively than he handles the banjo, on which he takes solos with both the Percy Humphrey and Love–Jiles ensembles. *West Indies blues*, by the latter group, sets out to recreate the lightness of bands like Piron's (whose version of this piece can also be heard on **22**). Sayles is probably at his best, however, on *Climax rag* — ragtime tunes suiting his style and instrument — otherwise a fairly fierce performance by Humphrey's band, much more rumbustious than Robinson's, and setting out, just as Kid Thomas's does, to offer excitement to the tourists. Percy Humphrey takes no solos himself, but leads with elasticity and power. Most solo playing (apart from Sayles's) is by Nelson, a docile-sounding trombonist compared with Robinson but also more of an improviser, and the clarinettist, Burbank, yet another pupil of Lorenzo Tio jnr but a musician who might be said to have modified the traditional Creole style, mixing the sweet with the sour, the angular with the *legato*, sometimes fitting uneasily inside the ensemble but always coming up with intriguing solos.

The exuberance of Humphrey's band is surpassed, if anything, by that of Kid Thomas's Algiers Stompers, helped by the drumming of Penn. Perhaps Burbank fits into these surroundings best of all. As for Kid Thomas, his approach to the trumpet is often melodramatic, full of growls, even roars, 'a pre-Armstrong style', as somebody once wrote, but the music he and his band make is packed with vitality as well as being loud and fiery. Most trumpeters on these sessions, of course, preferred to lead rather than play solos. The exception is Dédé Pierce, whose blues playing in what are virtually duets with his wife (Jiles keep a fairly low profile) is beautifully lyrical, often lagging behind the beat to ravishing effect. Billie Pierce plays the piano and sings in the classic blues tradition (her style is not all that different from Ida Cox's), throwing plenty of familiar stanzas into *Good tonk blues* and *Freight train moaning* — and pacing the latter with particular skill. Also warmly recommended are three earlier LPs, using material from the same dates: Kid Thomas — Riverside (A) RLP365; Jim Robinson — RLP369; Billie and Dédé Pierce — RLP370.   C.F.

Kid Thomas Valentine–Captain John Handy
33 The December Band Vol. 2
Jazz Crusade (A) JC2008

Valentine (tpt); Jim Robinson (tbn); Sammy Rimington (clt); Handy (alt); Bill Sinclair (p); Dick Griffith (bj); 'Mouldy Dick' McCarthy (bs); Sammy Penn (d). Stamford, Connecticut, 3 December 1965.
High society · Careless love · Handy's boogie · Uptown bumps · You tell me your dream · Just a closer walk with thee

The Traditional Jazz Club of Stamford, Connecticut, provided four local musicians to accompany four celebrated visitors from Louisiana, and the dedication with which the New Englanders had assimilated the New Orleans techniques assured a notable cohesion for the resulting group. The dancing vitality of *High society* owes more than a little to Griffith's use of rhythmic variety in the banjo's part, though there are plenty of times elsewhere at which he lapses into monotony. Sinclair's naïve, relentless piano style learnt its full-fistedness and exaggerated sustenance from revivalist heroes, but its rhetoric, as demonstrated, for example, in *You tell me your dream*, is a taste not all acquire. Rimington plays very well throughout, with hints of both

George Lewis and Willie Humphrey in his faster passages and more of the former's arpeggiated building in the slow. He makes an able enough companion to the veterans, who are all in fine form.

Valentine is a strong but not particularly adventurous trumpeter whose variations on *Careless love* contrast with his usual adherence to the melody and have nothing of the conciseness of a Bunk Johnson invention. Still, his voice is as distinctive as that of his near-contemporary Robinson, who is in strong form here and, as on other occasions, blithely shatters hidebound notions about the trombone's role in New Orleans jazz, as witness his high-register comments behind Rimington's traditional chorus in *High society* and his firmly swinging contribution to *You tell me your dream*. In the latter, Handy's alto solo shows rather more clearly than elsewhere the legacy of his former clarinet playing; yet this is but one element in the eclectic style of this surprising artist. That he should fit so well into the New Orleans scene must be a blow to the purists, for there is a great deal of both swing and rhythm-and-blues phraseology in his solos — the sixteen-chorus one on *Handy's boogie*, which starts more melodically, is a case in point — mixed with older elements such as the rough-toned, almost Bechet-like intensity of *Uptown bumps*.

By the time this record was made the New Orleans revival was over three decades old and had formed traditions of its own. The necessity of *Just a closer walk with thee*, if doubted, is proved by the cheers which hail its opening; but the choice of an old Mills Brothers number, *You tell me your dream*, and the happy acceptance of a heterodox performer like Handy, together with the irreverent antics of Robinson, are part of the evidence that New Orleans musicians are not the stern arbiters of orthodoxy some supposed.

The long solo on *Handy's boogie* is, in this sphere, a rare example of individual improvisation extended over more than a few measures — though it might be that King Oliver, unrestricted by recording time, would have 'played that thing' on *Dippermouth blues* (44) for several more choruses. The language of Handy's first four or five choruses is reminiscent of that which Johnny Hodges seems to have learnt from Bechet. There is a degree of development, and it might have been extended further, but in the sixth to ninth choruses he turns to the use of riffs. The manner is, however, anything but stereotyped, and there is, particularly in choruses eight and nine, the shaping of a lusty soliloquy of call-and-response. By the time the altoist reaches the cascading figures of chorus thirteen, the audience is egging him on loudly; but there is a certain lessening of tension as he seeks to return to more discursive variation, and the last two choruses fall somewhat between discourse and incantation. This is a solo of considerable intrinsic interest, and it bears an unexpected relation to the music of Handy's fellow New Orleans players. It is certainly not incongruous, but it emphasizes strongly the fact that for the survivors of the revival, preservation did not mean stagnation. Handy's muse is a much travelled lady; but if tradition is forward movement made surefooted by experience, then his music is as healthily traditional as that of his *confrères*.   E.T.

2

The Twenties

Variations on the New Orleans Style

The Chicago Version

During the 1920s jazz, particularly in Chicago, became the vehicle of more individual modes of expression. The extent to which these performances depart from earlier New Orleans conventions is a measure of the strength of the musical personalities involved.

34 **Freddy Keppard: Legendary New Orleans Cornet**
Smithsonian (A) R020, *Fountain (E) FJ107
Cooke's Dreamland Orchestra: Keppard, Elwood Graham (cnt); Fred Garland (tbn); Jimmy Noone, Clifford King (clt, alt); Joe Poston (alt); Jerome Pasquall (ten); Jimmy Bell (vln); Tony Spaulding (p); Stan Wilson (bj); Bill Newton (tu); Bert Greene (d); Doc Cooke (cond). Richmond, Indiana, 21 January 1924.
Scissor-grinder Joe · So this is Venice · Moanful man · Memphis maybe man · The one I love
Cookie's Gingersnaps: Keppard (cnt); Garland (tbn); Noone (clt, vcl[1]); Poston (alt, vcl[2]); Kenneth Anderson (p); Johnny St Cyr (bj). Chicago, 22 June 1926.
Messing around[1,2] *· High fever · Here comes the hot tamale man*
Cooke and His Dreamland Orchestra: Keppard, Graham (cnt); Garland (tbn); Noone (clt); Poston, King (clt, alt); Pasquall (clt, ten); Anderson (p); St Cyr, Robert Shelly (bj); Rudolph Reynaud (tu); Andrew Hilaire (d); Cooke (cond). Chicago, 10 July 1926.
Here comes the hot tamale man · High fever

Freddy Keppard's Jazz Cardinals: Keppard (cnt); Eddie Vincent (tbn); Johnny Dodds (clt); Arthur Campbell (p); Jasper Taylor (wbd); Papa Charlie Jackson (vcl[3]). Chicago, September 1926.
Stockyard strut · *Salty dog*[3] (2 takes)

Jasper Taylor and His State Street Boys: Keppard (cnt); Eddie Ellis (tbn); Dodds (clt); Tiny Parham (p); Taylor (wbd). Chicago, c. January 1927
Stomp time blues · *It must be the blues*

Perhaps Keppard's is not so much a Chicago variation on the New Orleans style as an indistinct echo of one of its earlier phases. Certainly these recordings offer incomplete, and sometimes contradictory, information on the way he played. The Cooke Dreamland tracks mainly follow publishers' unimaginative stock orchestrations, somewhat embellished. *Scissor-grinder Joe* shows Keppard rougher in expression than Graham, who is neat and nimble with the wa-wa mute [11]. He leads the ensemble quite impressively in the last sixteen bars of the over-arranged *Memphis maybe man*, but we must hope that it is not him, wa-wa muted, duetting with Noone in *So this is Venice*; more likely, he takes the very smart break after the second keyboard passage (*cf Stockyard strut* and take 2 of *Salty dog*). He is uninventive in his duet with Noone on *The one I love*, but in the fifth chorus of *Moanful man* (which, incidentally, should be compared with Noone's 1929 *My daddy rocks me*), between Graham's high-note passages, he plays more engagingly.

Performances by the Gingersnaps, the small band within Cooke's large band, have Keppard recorded well for the first time, and we hear him very plainly on *Messing around*. Besides the stentorian tone, the rips, flares and occasional growl-flutters, one notices a considerable variety of detail, especially in the rhythmic dimension, in his usually short phrases. He blows with power and some enterprise on *High fever* — which again follows a published orchestration as well as the instrumental resources allow — and plays an excellent lead in *Here comes the hot tamale man*, at first muted but sounding almost violent by the end.

Stockyard strut, from the only date recorded under the cornettists's own name, is based on part of *Tiger rag*, and underlines his concern with rhythmic variety in the placing of his small groups of notes; at the same time, an impression of extreme energy is conveyed here. This session crosses Keppard's ragtime-with Dodd's blues-based style, emphasizing the differences and reminding us that according to some of the older musicians this was the cornettist who sounded most like Bolden [12]. Assuredly there is nothing of the blues in his contributions to *Salty dog*, but divergences between the two versions should be noticed. The general outlines are the same yet there are many small but significant differences of nuance, of accent, which speak of a conscientious desire to 'make it new'.

The author of the voluminous notes which accompany the above Smithsonian issue, Larry Gushee, suggests Punch Miller, not Keppard, as the cornettist on the Taylor items. That seems most unlikely if a comparison be made with Miller's playing with Albert Wynn on **42** and with Tiny Parham on **58**. Obviously there are other, at least theoretical, possibilities. One is Bob Shoffner, to judge from his work for Jimmy O'Bryant's Washboard Band, particularly take 1 of *Everybody pile* (Gannet (A) GEN5486). This sounds like the man with Taylor, except that these performances date from 1925, and two years later, when the State Street Boys recorded, Shoffner was playing more like Armstrong.

A further problem is the difference between the cornet phrases on *Stomp time blues* and those on *It must be the blues*. The musician on the latter does not, in the final chorus and coda, sound altogether like the one on the Jazz Cardinals session or in *Stomp time blues*, being more *legato* in something like the manner of Lee Collins or Ed Swayzee — if it *is* Swayzee who solos on Morton's *Deep creek blues* (**47b**). The present writer would guess that it is in fact Keppard, bearing in mind how uneven this collection, and his few other recordings, show him to have been. Indeed, the imaginative set of breaks on *Stomp time blues* may be his best recorded claim to fame. Taken together, though, these performances invite the conclusion that he recorded only in his decline. There is little enough here to justify the high praise of Morton and others, particularly of his powers of invention. But Keppard in New Orleans and on tour with the Original Creole Band in the teens of our century may have been something different.   M.H.

35 Lovie Austin
Fountain (E) FJ105, *Riverside (A) RLP8802

Lovie Austin and Her Blues Serenaders: Tommy Ladnier (cnt); possibly Junie Cobb (clt); Austin (p). Chicago, November 1924.
Stepping on the blues · Travelling blues
Ladnier (cnt); Jimmy O'Bryant (clt); Austin (p); W. E. Burton (d); Priscilla Stewart (vcl[1]). Chicago, April 1925.
Charleston mad[1] (2 takes) · *Charleston, South Carolina*[1] · *Heebie jeebies · Peeping blues · Mojo blues*
Bob Shoffner (cnt); O'Bryant (clt); Austin (p); Burton (d). Chicago. August 1925.
Don't shake it no more · Rampart Street blues · Too sweet for words

Possibly Shirley Clay (cnt); Kid Ory (tbn); Johnny Dodds (clt); Austin (p); Burton (d). Chicago, April 1926.

Jackass blues · *Frog tongue stomp*

Shoffner (cnt); Ory (tbn); Dodds (clt); Austin (p); Eustern Woodfork (bj); Henry Williams (vcl²). Chicago, August 1926.

*Chicago mess around*² · *Gallion stomp* · *In the alley blues* · *Merry maker's twine*²

Lovie Austin (née Cora Calhoun) was actively involved in vaudeville, and may well have seen the bands she led as integral to that scene. The emphasis of the second of these groups upon the immensely popular charleston dance rhythm (including the archetypal number, surely James P. Johnson's least endearing creation, *Charleston, South Carolina*) is another pointer to show business motives. But none of this means that the leader was deaf to the subtler and more enduring spirit of the music her companions made. The musicians she chose for these bands were, the vocalists apart, capable jazzmen; two of them, Ladnier and Dodds, were minor geniuses.

She is, herself, a very interesting musician; at least as effective an ensemble pianist as Lil Hardin Armstrong, with an adequate and varied technique and strength of expression. Whether the music she (and, for that matter, Lil Armstrong) plays is a recognizable jazz piano style is not easy to say. Her robust support of the cornet and clarinet in *Stepping on the blues* and *Travelling blues*, with its varied bass line and agile sequences of chords, and the tantalizing snatch of solo playing in the charming *Frog tongue stomp*, prompt speculations which are possibly bootless. What is this style? Not so much jazz, perhaps, as a species of 'vaudeville circuit ragtime'. It is an accompaniment form which has few obvious graces when exposed in solo, but Miss Austin had a flair for composing lively numbers to suit the kind of jazz played by Ladnier, Dodds and the others. *Charleston mad* is one of the few which genuflect too deeply to popular gods, and the habanera ending of *Rampart Street blues* is one small indication of the lady's receptiveness to diverse strains, native and immigrant.

However, the music to be treasured is not hers. Ladnier at that stage clearly in fee to King Oliver, but with equally clear announcements of his own to make, lifts the first two of these sessions beyond the ordinary. He is well partnered by the Doddsian Cobb (if it is indeed he) on the first date, and in the one with the less fluent O'Bryant he almost, though not quite, conquers the naïve syncopations of the charleston.

In the last two sessions it is Dodds who captures, and deserves, most attention. His New Orleans-cum-Chicago style unifies many voices and, as will be seen later, was a decisive influence on a number of younger clarinettists. (It is also interesting to catch, just after Ory's rather lugubrious introduction to *In the alley blues*, a hint of the tone favoured by George Lewis.)

Jazz has often flourished better when not too self-conscious as 'art'. Defenders of its dignity may resent the sheltering of such musicians as these under a burlesque aegis; but the characteristic thematic material (Miss Austin is sole composer of nine items), related to both popular blues songs and ragtime, is musically richer than the attenuated riffs dominant in later times. Furthermore, jazz genius was able to burst the confines of wider proscenia than this world of Negro entertainment, whilst appearing to fit genially into them.   E.T.

36 Sidney Bechet Memorial
Fontana (E) TFL5087

Clarence Williams Blue Five: Thomas Morris (cnt); John Mayfield (tbn); Bechet (sop); Williams (p); Buddy Christian (bj). New York City, 30 July 1923.
Wild cat blues · Kansas City man blues

Same personnel and location, October 1923.
New Orleans hop scop blues

Same personnel and location, 10 November 1923.
Shreveport blues · Old fashioned love

Same personnel and location, 14 November 1923.
Mean blues

Louis Armstrong (cnt), Charlie Irvis (tbn) replace Morris, Mayfield; Bechet also plays clt. New York City, 17 October 1924.
Texas moaner blues

Aaron Thompson (tbn), Buster Bailey (sop) replace Irvis, Bechet; Eva Taylor (vcl) added. New York City, 6 November 1924.
Of all the wrongs you've done to me · Everybody loves my baby

Irvis (tbn), Bechet (sop, sar) replace Thompson, Bailey, New York City, 17 December 1924.
Mandy, make up your mind · I'm a little blackbird

Same personnel and location, 8 January 1925.
Cake walking babies

Bailey (clt, sop), possibly Don Redman (clt, alt) added. New York City, 4 March 1925.
Papa de-da-da

Bechet absent. New York City, 6 October 1925.
Just wait till you see my baby do the charleston · Living high

Same personnel and location, 8 October 1925.
Coal cart blues

Reputations in jazz often seem to depend upon the amount of influence exerted by a performer over his contemporaries, rather than the music he actually played. Otherwise, how could Bechet have remained so neglected until the 1940s? The only musician he influenced during that period was Johnny Hodges (indeed, when Hodges recorded *The sheik of Araby* with Ellington in 1932, he played, more or less note for note, the solo that Bechet finally recorded himself — as a counter-melody on tenor saxophone — in the one-man band version he made in 1941: see **225**). In addition, Bechet specialized in the soprano saxophone, an instrument which suited his musical personality but was rarely used by others. Finally, he spent no more than four years in the United States during the whole of the 1920s, bad tactics for anybody wanting to make a name in jazz. Even so, his apparent obscurity bewildered those of us who first came across his records towards the end of the 1930s. It seems even more startling now that items such as the above are widely available. For what gets demonstrated is that as early as 1923, when Armstrong was still playing second cornet in Oliver's Creole Band (**44**), Bechet was already a mature soloist, his style the same in nearly all particulars as that which was to become so familiar two decades later.

Wild cat blues and *Kansas City man blues* can still take the listener's breath away. Bechet dominates the performances from beginning to end; there are no hesitations, no descents into period bathos or naïvety. The sound is flaring, the vibrato wide, the phrasing full of blues slurs — his break in the penultimate chorus of *Kansas City man blues* sums it all up in just two bars. Above all, there is the sweeping melodic invention, the elaborate, incessant, exciting decoration. Bechet certainly believed in sticking to good solos when he had created them (his routine on *The sheik of Araby* is one example, that on *China boy* another), yet he was perfectly capable of improvising superb solos on the spot. The four other titles from 1923 find Morris and Mayfield asserting themselves a trifle more, but it is Bechet's presence which lifts this music out of its period.

Like Bechet, Williams came from New Orleans. By the start of the 1920s, however, he was active in New York as a publisher and composer, his piano playing decidedly subsidiary to those pursuits. In 1921 he had married Eva Taylor, who sings, competently but without much jazz or blues feeling, on all the tracks from November 1924 onwards. Williams remained faithful to the New Orleans front line, using it on nearly all his records. And when Armstrong arrived in New York to work with Fletcher Henderson's band, Williams promptly recruited him. The combination of Armstrong and Bechet, both, in 1924, head and shoulders above any of their contemporaries, resulted in the exhilarating *Texas moaner blues* and the equally inspired recordings that followed. *Cake walking babies* typifies the rhythmic vivacity these two musicians brought to jazz. So does *Mandy, make up your mind*, its commonplace theme translated — by accenting, paraphrase, thematic variation — into something much more subtle and challenging. And this despite Bechet's insistence on taking a solo with the sarrusophone, a cumbersome instrument he spotted on the way to the studio.

Odd though it may seem for an LP with the title this one bears, Bechet is absent from five of the tracks. All are notable, however, for powerful playing by Armstrong, while Bailey, one of the cornettist's colleagues in the Henderson band, made a surprisingly good job of stepping into Bechet's shoes. His sound, especially on the November 1924 date, almost convinces, but instead of Bechet's organic, authoritative sense of structure, Bailey offers what amounts to a series of rhetorical flourishes. By the autumn of 1925, Bechet was off once more, wandering round Europe, turning up in such unlikely spots as Kiev and Kharkov. Armstrong, of course, returned to Chicago, and embarked on the triumphs which are dealt with under **37** and **48**. In the meantime they had proved themselves the two foremost soloists in the jazz of their time.   C.F.

Louis Armstrong
37 Young Louis: the Sideman (1924–27)
MCA (F) 510.010, MCA (A) 1301

Fletcher Henderson and His Orchestra: Howard Scott, Elmer Chambers (tpt); Armstrong (cnt); Charlie Green (tbn); Buster Bailey, Don Redman (clt, alt); Coleman Hawkins (clt, ten); Henderson (p); Charlie Dixon (bj); Ralph Escudero (tu); Kaiser Marshall (d). New York City, 30 October 1924.
Words

Same personnel and location, 18 April 1925.
When you do what you do

Perry Bradford's Jazz Phools: Armstrong (cnt); Green (tbn); Bailey (clt); Redman (alt); James P. Johnson (p); Marshall (d); Bradford (vcl). New York City, 2 November 1925.
Lucy Long · I ain't gonna play no second fiddle

Erskine Tate's Vendome Orchestra: Armstrong, James Tate (tpt); Fayette Williams (tbn); Alvin Fernandez (clt); Stump Evans (alt, bar); Norval Morton (ten); Teddy Weatherford and another (p); Frank Ethridge (bj); John Hare (tu); Jimmy Bertrand (d). Chicago, 28 May 1926.
Static strut · Stomp off, let's go

Lil's Hot Shots: Armstrong (cnt, vcl[1]); Kid Ory (tbn); Johnny Dodds (clt); Lil Armstrong (p); Johnny St Cyr (bj). Chicago, 28 May 1926.
Georgia bo bo[1] · *Drop that sack*
Jimmy Bertrand's Washboard Wizards: Armstrong (cnt); Dodds (clt); Jimmy Blythe (p); Bertrand (wbd, wdbl). Chicago, 21 April 1927.
Easy come, easy go blues · *Blues stampede* · *I'm going hunting* · *If you wanna be my sugar papa*
Johnny Dodds's Black Bottom Stompers: Armstrong (cnt); Gerald Reeves (tbn); Johnny Dodds (clt); Barney Bigard (ten); Earl Hines (p); Bud Scott (bj); Baby Dodds (d). Chicago, 22 April 1927.
Weary blues · *New Orleans stomp* · *Wild man blues* · *Melancholy*

Judged by the standards of almost any other jazz musician, the cornet (or trumpet) solos on this LP would be considered outstanding, even major performances. But when the listener is aware of what was to follow, and particularly of Armstrong's majestic playing later in the 1920s (**48** and **52**), some of the music here seems a trifle lightweight, the work of a man moving towards maturity. The two Henderson items certainly demonstrate how superior Armstrong was — in a totally different class, to put it bluntly — to his companions; to such an extent that it is possible to overrate these solos. They are springy, exciting, full of curiosity, but lack the structural development that is such a feature of Armstrong's finest playing (the trumpet breaks and duet with trombone in *Words*, by the way, are probably the work of Chambers).

A contingent from Henderson's orchestra joined James P. Johnson (who might as well not have bothered to turn up for all we hear of him) for two tracks under the leadership of Bradford, a singer and pianist from Georgia who, like Clarence Williams (**36**), was setting up as a publisher and composer (Mamie Smith's 1920 recording of his *Crazy blues* (Columbia (A) C3L33) had sold over a million copies). Bradford's earlier career in minstrel shows and on theatre circuits makes itself apparent in *Lucy Long*, although there is excellent stoptime playing from all the front line, with Redman's alto saxophone nicely formal and Bailey sounding hotter, and less tied up with his technique, than he did a decade later. None of these New York recordings, however, is on a level with Armstrong's partnership with Bechet in Williams's Blue Five.

Static strut and *Stomp off, let's go* present Armstrong as he sounded to his contemporaries in Chicago in 1926 (his own Hot Five recordings from that period were deliberately aimed at those southern blacks living in the North who liked old-style New Orleans music). The other musicians of Tate's band were of variable quality, apart from Weatherford, who impressed even the youthful Hines; his solos here may be over-busy but are more adventurous, harmonically and rhythmically, than those of other pianists around at the time. But it is Armstrong — playing trumpet rather than cornet, incidentally — who is the focus of attention, taking a series of scintillating breaks in *Static strut* and sounding even more dominating in *Stomp off, let's go*. (It is a pity that the alternative take of the latter is not included here.) The impression is of a musician performing at the very edge of his technique, discovering what he can do, constantly surprising even himself (the same sort of nervous excitement can be detected in Roy Eldridge's playing a decade afterwards).

Later the same day Armstrong took up his cornet for two tracks under the leadership of his wife, the line-up exactly the same as that used for his own original Hot Five. Dodds plays with great intensity. Armstrong sings gruffly, and obscurely, in *Georgia bo bo*, a twelve-bar blues. *Drop that sack* is curiously unbalanced, beginning with Armstrong fluffing during the introduction and opening chorus, yet concluding with one of his most masterly solos.

The fact that Armstrong was under contract to another record company may have inhibited him on that session. It certainly did on the remaining tracks, especially those with Bertrand's Washboard Wizards, where he keeps an uncharacteristically low profile. Bertrand was Tate's drummer, decidedly second class, but not averse to featuring his washboard playing on his own records. The approach was casual, sometimes even sloppy. Nevertheless, Armstrong comes across majestically in *Blues stampede*, and there is an exhilarating rapport between him and Dodds in *I'm going hunting* and *If you wanna be my sugar papa*. Rather more curious was the session held the next day under Dodds's leadership. On two of the tracks, *Weary blues* and *New Orleans stomp*, Armstrong could be mistaken for any of the better New Orleans trumpeters — Punch Miller, say, or Lee Collins. Dodds himself contributes several admirable low-register choruses, but Bigard's tenor saxophone solos contrive to be either jerky or bathetic. Hines, playing on his first recording session with Armstrong, is splendidly concise in *Melancholy*, a solo that presages what was to come. Armstrong only assumes his true stature in *Wild man blues*, taking a sombre but affecting solo, very different in character from that he played when recording the same number with his Hot Seven just over a fortnight later (**48**). Improvising of this quality was certainly something that no other jazz trumpeter was capable of equalling.   C.F.

38a Johnny Dodds Vol. 1
MCA (F) 510.089, MCA (A) 1328

Jimmy Bertrand's Washboard Wizards: Junie Cobb (clt); Jimmy Blythe (p); Bertrand (wbd, wdbl). Chicago, 29 May 1926.
Little bits · Struggling

Johnny Dodds Trio: Dodds (clt); Lil Armstrong (p); Bud Scott (g). Chicago, 21 April 1927.
San · Oh, Lizzie (2 takes) *· Clarinet wobble · The new St Louis blues*

Johnny Dodds's Black Bottom Stompers: Louis Armstrong (cnt); Gerald Reeves (tbn); Johnny Dodds (clt); Barney Bigard (ten); Earl Hines (p); Scott (bj); Baby Dodds (d). Chicago, 22 April 1927.
Wild man blues · Melancholy

Jimmy Blythe's Owls: Natty Dominique (cnt); Johnny Dodds (clt); Blythe (p); Scott (bj); Baby Dodds (d). Chicago, 5 October 1927.
Weary way blues

Johnny Dodds's Black Bottom Stompers: George Mitchell, Reuben Reeves (cnt); Gerald Reeves (tbn); Johnny Dodds (clt); Charlie Alexander (p); Scott (bj); Baby Dodds (d); unidentified vcl[1]. Chicago, 8 October 1927.
Come on and stomp, stomp, stomp · After you've gone[1] · Joe Turner's blues · When Erastus plays his old kazoo

38b Johnny Dodds Vol. 2
MCA (F) 510.106

Jimmy Blythe's Owls: Dominique (cnt); Johnny Dodds (clt); Blythe (p); Scott (bj); Baby Dodds (d). Chicago, 5 October 1927.
Pouting papa · Hot stuff · Have mercy

Jimmy Blythe's Washboard Wizards: Dodds (clt); Blythe (p); W. E. Burton (wbd); unidentified vcl trio. Chicago, 30 March 1928.
My baby · Oriental man

Beale Street Washboard Band: Herb Morand (cnt); Johnny Dodds (clt); Frank Melrose (p); Baby Dodds (d, wbd). Chicago, 24 July 1929.
Forty and tight · Piggly wiggly

Johnny Dodds and His Chicago Boys: Charlie Shavers (tpt); Dodds (clt); Lil Armstrong (p); Teddy Bunn (g); John Kirby (bs); O'Neill Spencer (d, wbd, vcl[2]). New York City, 21 January 1938.
Wild man blues · Melancholy · 29th and Dearborn · Blues galore[2] · Stack o' Lee blues[2] · Shake your can[2]

Johnny Dodds and His Orchestra: Dominique (cnt); Preston Jackson (tbn); Johnny Dodds (clt); Richard M. Jones (p); Lonnie Johnson (g); John Lindsay (bs); Baby Dodds (d). Chicago, 5 June 1940.
Red Onion blues · Gravier Street blues

39   Johnny Dodds: Sixteen Rare Recordings
RCA (E) RD7983, RCA (A) LPV558

Dixieland Jug Blowers: Dodds (clt); Lockwood Lewis (alt); Freddy
Smith, Cal Smith (bj); Henry Clifford, Earl McDonald (jg). Chicago,
11 December 1926.
Carpet Alley breakdown
Clifford Hayes (vin), Curtis Hayes (bj) added. Same date.
Memphis shake · Hen party blues
Johnny Dodds Trio: Dodds (clt); Alexander (p); Bill Johnson (bs).
Chicago, 5 July 1928.
Blue clarinet stomp · Blue piano stomp
Johnny Dodds's Washboard Band: Dominique (cnt); Honoré Dutrey (tbn);
Baby Dodds (wbd) added. Chicago, 6 July 1928.
*Bucktown stomp · Weary city · Bull fiddle blues · Blue washboard
stomp*
Johnny Dodds's Orchestra: Lil Armstrong (p) replaces Alexander; Baby
Dodds plays d. Chicago, 16 January 1929.
Pencil papa · Hear me talking
Same personnel and location, 30 January 1929.
Sweet Lorraine · My little Isabel
Johnny Dodds's Hot Six: same personnel. Chicago, 7 February 1929.
Goober dance · Too tight
Johnny Dodds Trio: Dominique, Dutrey, Baby Dodds absent. Same date.
Indigo stomp

40   Johnny Dodds and Kid Ory
Philips (E) BBL7136, Epic (A) 16004

New Orleans Wanderers: Mitchell (cnt); Ory (tbn); Dodds (clt); Lil
Armstrong (p); Johnny St Cyr (g). Chicago, 13 July 1926.
Perdido Street blues
Joe Clark (alt) added. Same date.
Gate mouth · Too tight blues · Papa dip
New Orleans Bootblacks: same personnel. Chicago, 14 July 1926.
Mixed salad · I can't say · Flat foot · Mad dog
Chicago Footwarmers: Dominique (cnt); Johnny Dodds (clt); Blythe (p);
Baby Dodds (wbd). Chicago, 15 December 1927.
My baby · Oriental man
Dutrey (tbn), Johnson (bs) added. Chicago, 4 July 1928.
Brown bottom Bess · Lady love

Born in 1892, Dodds was immersed in the traditions of New
Orleans jazz, and gained his experience in those venues where
jazz was making its uncompromising case during the first two
decades of the twentieth century — dance halls, street parades,
minstrel shows, riverboats, cabarets. On his first recordings,
made with King Oliver in 1923 (**44**), may be heard, developed to a

considerable degree, the elements of a personal style of clarinet playing. Those elements were to remain, not changed markedly but used with increasing zest and skill, throughout a latterly rather circumscribed professional career. Consort of the great at an early stage, and particularly a far more than merely capable foil to Armstrong in some of his moments of genius, Dodds himself fell short of the highest jazz achievements, though his passionately forged style was to be the inspiration of clarinettists who attained larger and more facile celebrity. He played exclusively with small ensembles, and was closely associated with Chicago for the second half of his life; indeed, it could be said with some justification that Dodds's jazz voice is a pivotal utterance of Chicago style, tough, strident, rhythmically urgent, and relentlessly haunted by the blues.

Of the groups on these four LPs, those recorded during the 1920s are representative of the virile music popular in and around Chicago. A few of them exploit the craze for 'found' instruments — washboards, jugs, etc. — but they are by no means amateur or folk music groups (see 4). In *Little bits* and *Struggling*, Bertrand's unvaried rattle does not distract attention from the full-toned and rather straightforward clarinet playing or from Blythe's apt piano support [13]. The more interestingly manned Dixieland Jug Blowers may teach unintentional lessons to the jazz musicologist, as with the revelatory banjo breaks in *Carpet Alley breakdown* and Clifford Hayes's 'alley fiddle' in *Hen party blues* declaring its only half-suspected kinship to the blues-whining clarinet in matched solo and spikey counterpoint. In these, and amid the spooky drama of *Memphis shake*, Dodds ranges through his solo and ensemble skills.

In July 1926, Ory joined Dodds in the Wanderers and Boot-blacks sessions which produced some of the most beautifully controlled post-New Orleans ensemble jazz ever recorded. Ory himself is something of a musical enigma. He was well regarded as a leader, and the early presentation of New Orleans jazz appears to have gained greatly from his unalloyed enthusiasm. Yet he had limited solo capability and possessed a somewhat hazardous technique; but despite these restrictions he does merit, musically, the good reputation that remains his. The evidence of these Dodds tracks is that Ory mastered the trombone's role in this kind of music in an unusual way, lacking the facility of Brunies, not so easily tempted to portamento sentimentality as Dutrey, and developing an instinct for abbreviation which made possible ensemble support which seems balletic rather than acrobatic. *Gate mouth*, apotheosis of the tailgate style, and *Too tight blues* illustrate this skill excellently, together with the occasional mishaps of such brevity-amid-complexity.

Mitchell's strong cornet lead, besides being admirable in itself, allows what is — apart from him — a Louis Armstrong group to achieve a clearer collective identity. And through all this the distinctive voice of Dodds is heard, as full of interest in ensemble as in solo; soaring in *Perdido Street blues* to a full-throatedness worthy of Bechet; singing thoughtful lines in *I can't say*; interjecting breaks in *Papa dip* with popping precision.

The attraction of even smaller groups must have been strong for a soloist as confident as Dodds, and this setting will have its attractions for his admirers, too. Blythe's Washboard Wizards and the trio with Lil Armstrong and Scott give ample space for the evocation of a variety of musical moods, but with only Blythe serving anything like matching wit the overall effect is a bit unrelenting. Dodds seems to produce his best work when pitting his musical ingenuity against that of others, and with the 1927 Black Bottom Stompers he is alongside Louis Armstrong again, giving as spirited a deliverance of his soul as ever.

Dominique, partnering Dodds in Blythe's Owls, is a complementing voice. Later on, with the Chicago Footwarmers, this cornettist gives firm stimulus again, and Dodds attains some of his ablest utterances: sinuous and effervescent by turns in *Brown bottom Bess*, impishly ornamental in *Oriental man*, skipping at fast tempo in *My baby* and, in the same piece, creating some of the loveliest examples preserved of the old ensemble clarinet style.

The second version of the Black Bottom Stompers is a group plainly modelled on Oliver's Creole Band, with harmonized breaks for the cornets, but an ensemble style developed beyond the improvised collective to take account of developments in jazz arranging. This approach, more formal, less contrapuntal, is marked in *Come on and stomp, stomp, stomp* and *After you've gone*. It is rather less worthy of what has been called Dodds's 'proud seriousness' [14], and accentuates the fragile nostalgia of *When Erastus plays his old kazoo*. However, the improvised parts are of high quality, with Dodds an exultant craftsman in *Joe Turner's blues* and *Come on*, and Mitchell and Reeves fashioning an intertwined counterpoint in *When Erastus plays* such as Oliver and Armstrong had never attempted on record.

Blue clarinet stomp, Blue piano stomp and *Indigo stomp* are trio performances: there is greater subtlety from Dodds in the first two, and more variety of expression. His approach to rhythm is striking; in his more ardent improvisations, *parlando* phrases float across the beat (which is rather crudely stressed by the

pianist), and when hanging close to thematic material he incorporates the beat into his variations with irresistible thrust. Differing kinds of vocalization, riff-like simplicities and complex
melodies, emphasizings and disregardings of the beat are juxtaposed in rapid sequence, and it is of the essence of Dodds's minor
genius that his inspired imagination unifies these jostling
elements in a manner which leaves the variety apparent. A
characteristic device used in *Blue piano stomp* is the interjection
of a phrase, usually in descent, in double tempo, so as to serve
both ornamentally and rhythmically; oddly prophetic of far more
dexterous runs to be used similarly by Art Tatum.

The Dodds Washboard Band, Orchestra and Hot Six produced
some of the best-known Doddsian creations, the stomping style of
Bull fiddle blues with smeared, angular clarinet tumblings, stark
registral contrasts in the fine *Bucktown stomp*, and melodies
adeptly built out of those very contrasts in *Pencil papa* and *Weary
city*. The trio of improvising horns, though, shapes the collectives
less well than that including Mitchell and Ory, the fast *Blue
washboard stomp* particularly showing up the limitations of
Dominique and Dutrey even if the cornettist is elsewhere a
consistent leading voice. Dutrey is extravagant in ensemble,
frequently giving vent to trombonistic light baritone parlour
ditties a world away from the searing, crying, strutting treble
of Dodds who, whether improvising or negotiating the precise
punctuating harmonies, displays unfailing jazz capability.

Throughout the latter half of the 1920s he led a band at Kelly's
Stables, Chicago, a long engagement terminated in 1930. The
Depression brought obscurity, if not unemployment; and it was
not until 1938 that he recorded again, this time with a group
which, though it contained a restrained Lil Armstrong, was
obviously of a Harlem swing bent. The emphasis is on solos,
although Dodds manages some exchanges with Shavers which
can stand expressively beside the conversations he once had with
Dominique and Bertrand in the light-hearted context of Blythe's
Owls and the Beale Street Washboard Band.

On the New York date the clarinettist sounds adequately at
home, playing phrases at the beginning of *29th and Dearborn*
which validate his swinging legacy to others, and only now and
then, as in *Stack o' Lee blues* and *Shake your can*, sounding rather
the dignified stranger in contrast with Shavers's lavishness.
These two respect one another admirably, however, in *Blues
galore*, with Bunn, a guitarist bridging old and new styles,
supporting wonderfully.

The sad crudities of *Red Onion blues* and *Gravier Street blues*
were, at the time of issue, thought by some enthusiasts to betoken

an authentic archaism. Unfortunately they were only the signs of Dodds's physical decline; but, still, these recordings are not quite the broken memorial some think them. In one sense they provide a necessary complement to the 1938 music, for here, towards the end of *Gravier Street blues*, is that ecstatically shaken blues tone, which Dodds had modified considerably for the Chicago Boys date. It is perhaps as emphatic a reminder as we need of this steadfast musician's lifelong regimen.   E.T.

41 Jimmy Noone and Earl Hines at the Apex Club
MCA (F) 510.039, MCA (A) 1313

Jimmy Noone's Apex Club Orchestra: Noone (clt, vcl[1]); Joe Poston (clt, alt, vcl[2]); Hines (p); Bud Scott (bj, g); Johnny Wells (d). Chicago, 16 May 1928.
I know that you know · *Sweet Sue, just you* · *Four or five times* [1,2] · *Every evening* (2 takes)
Same personnel and location, 14 June 1928.
Ready for the river [1,2] · *Forevermore*
Lawson Buford (tu) added. Chicago, 23 August 1928.
Apex blues · *My Monday date* · *Blues my naughty sweetie gives to me*
Same personnel and location, 25 August 1928.
Oh sister, ain't that hot · *King Joe* · *Sweet Lorraine* (2 takes)

Musicians always admire craftsmanship. Above all, they esteem expertise on their own instruments, which is one reason why Noone exerted so much influence on his fellow clarinettists towards the end of the 1920s. Bigard, Nicholas, Simeon: all absorbed something of his fluency. So did Goodman, while Joe Marsala remained an unabashed disciple throughout his playing career. It was not just Noone's technical resourcefulness that attracted them, the seamless way in which he could move through the registers of the instrument, but also a rhythmic sophistication not to be encountered in the work of earlier New Orleans clarinettists, or even among the majority of his contemporaries. In many respects he represented the Creole clarinettist *in excelsis*, but sharpened up by having moved to the big city (indeed, he had arrived in Chicago as early as 1917).

Yet alongside those virtues must be set a number of flaws. Noone was celebrated for the sweetness of his playing (suitably enough, *Sweet Lorraine* illustrates this very clearly), but that approach was always in danger of lurching, as it occasionally did, into sentimentality. The trills that could punctuate a performance so dramatically became sadly trite when exploited for cheaper ends.

An interesting aspect of these tracks is Noone's individual

adaptation of the New Orleans ensemble. Although a very effective soloist, especially in blues (the 1936 recording of *The blues jumped a rabbit*, an outstanding example of this genre, can be found on **229**), he really needed a foil, the equivalent of a lead trumpet, to allow him to embark upon the decoration that was the essence of his style. But instead of the traditional three-piece front line, he preferred just two reeds, with Poston's alto saxophone providing that straight lead around which the clarinet could swoop and weave. (Both men can be heard trying it out two years earlier in the first chorus, after an introduction and sixteen-bar verse, of *Love found you for me* by Cookie's Gingersnaps (Herwin (A) 101); Mezzrow, another admirer of Noone's playing, probably had the formula in mind when he recorded with Bechet nearly two decades later: **243**.) When deployed contrapuntally, this partnership could sound deliciously light and nimble, but in passages where Noone falls back on playing a harmony part the timbre often becomes glutinous, examples occurring in *Sweet Sue* and *Sweet Lorraine*.

All the musicians in the band, which worked regularly at the Apex Club, came from New Orleans or nearby parts of the south, except for Hines, from Pittsburgh. The pianist's interventions constantly attract attention, even when he is not taking a solo, and the backing he provides in *Sweet Sue* is an outstanding example of his so-called 'trumpet style', with the treble octaves cutting through the ensemble. *I know that you know* was one of Noone's specialities, illustrating his brilliant control of dynamics; *Four or five times* contains passages which demonstrate how successfully he could use the trill, as well as his overall command of the clarinet; *Every evening* has him festooning Poston's lead excitingly and later taking a stoptime chorus. *Ready for the river* and *Forevermore* are less distinguished, the latter proving just how mawkish Noone could get: only Hines emerges from this disaster with much credit.

Apex blues was another of the clarinettist's famous numbers (once again the trills are used organically), a genuine blues, unlike *Blues my naughty sweetie gives to me*, which is the only track consisting entirely of solos, and which has some of his most luxuriant playing, an instance of how he could control tone and timing at the slowest of tempos. Hines composed *My Monday date*, had recorded it two months earlier with Armstrong's Savoy Ballroom Five (**48**), and was to do so again, as a piano solo, the following December (**49**). Noone's treacly version of *Sweet Lorraine* was much admired by fellow clarinettists, and Artie Shaw may have had it in mind when he recorded the tune with strings in 1936 (**145**); Hines comes through well, just as he does — and Noone too — in the more effervescent, and more satisfactory, *King Joe* and *Oh sister, ain't that hot.*   C.F.

42 Gutbucket Blues and Stomps
Herwin (A) 112

Jelly Roll Morton's Incomparables: possibly Ray Bowling (cnt); unidentified tbn, alt, ten, bj; Morton (p); Clay Jefferson (d). Richmond, Indiana, 23 February 1926.
Mr Jelly Lord

Luis Russell's Hot Six: George Mitchell (cnt); Albert Nicholas (clt, sop, alt); Barney Bigard (ten); Russell (p); Johnny St Cyr (bj); Ada Brown (vcl). Chicago, 10 March 1926.
Panama Limited blues · Tia Juana man

Kid Ory (tbn) added; Brown absent. Same date.
29th and Dearborn

Richard M. Jones (spch) added. Same date.
Sweet Mumtaz

Albert Wynn's Gutbucket Five: possibly Dolly Jones (cnt); Wynn (tbn); Bigard (sop, ten); Jimmy Flowers (p); Rip Bassett (bj); Lily Delk Christian (vcl). Chicago, 25 June 1926.
When · That Creole band

Levee Serenaders: Punch Miller or Bob Shoffner, Ed Swayzee (cnt); Zue Robertson (tbn); Joe Thomas, Paul Barnes (clt, sop, ten); Walter Thomas (ten, bar); Morton (p); Ike Robinson (bj); Hayes Alvis (tu); Walter Bishop (d); Frances Hereford (vcl). Chicago, 21 January 1928.
Midnight mama · Mr Jelly Lord

Lil Hardaway's Orchestra: probably Miller (cnt); Wynn (tbn); Lester Boone (alt); Hardaway (p); unidentified bj, d, vcl. Chicago, September 1928.
Milneburg joys

Albert Wynn's Creole Band: Miller (cnt, vcl[1]); Wynn (tbn); Boone (clt, alt, bar); William Barbee (p); Papa Charlie Jackson (bj); Sidney Catlett (d). Chicago, 2 October 1928.
Down by the levee[1] · She's crying for me

Albert Wynn's Gutbucket Five: Alex Hill (p) replaces Barbee; unidentified vcl[2]. Chicago, 9 October 1928.
Crying my blues away[2] · Parkway stomp[1]

Jimmy Wade and His Dixielanders: Wade (cnt); Miller (cnt, vcl[3]); Ike Cousington or Charles Lawson (tbn); unidentified reeds; Hill (p); Jackson or Stan Wilson (bj); unidentified tu; Clifford Jones (d, kz). Chicago, 10 October 1929.
Mississippi wobble · Gates blues[3]

Inventive endeavour vies with modishness in a number of these performances. The creativeness is self-identifying; the modishness is of more than one kind. There is the passion to present jazz as tough and defiant of convention, the laudable but occasionally rather slavish emulation of jazz figures who were currently making the musical running, and also the seemingly necessary inclusion of the kinds of vocal and instrumental novelty which aided commercial success.

The first two of the recordings from the Russell session feature unimaginative singing by Ada Brown. Most of the instrumentalists were later associated with the band which made King Oliver's first Vocalions. Here the cornettist is Mitchell, better known as a companion of Morton and Johnny Dodds, a player of unadorned forcefulness. *29th and Dearborn* (a faster version of *Riverside blues*: cf. 44) and the Latin-American *Sweet Mumtaz* achieve a freer, hotter atmosphere than Oliver's larger group was to exhibit. The opening of *Sweet Mumtaz* is an instance of the dilemma then presented by the presence of saxophones. Attempts were being made to integrate their tonal capabilities into the jazz ensemble in ways that had not been discovered by the New Orleans bands. With Russell, the attempt is only partially successful, since the reed scoring contrasts lamely with the freer counterpoint of the brass instruments. The abilities of Nicholas and Bigard on alto and tenor do not match their assurance as clarinet players and, indeed, much of the difficulty seems to lie in their tendency, as soloists, to play the saxophone as they would the clarinet in its *chalumeau* register. Attempts to find a distinctive saxophone style, such as the inelegant slap-tonguing indulged in by Bigard in Wynn's *That Creole band*, sound embarrassingly dated now, and considering the heights of Creole lyricism which this great musician was to attain later with Ellington, it is a little strange that he handles the soprano as clumsily as he does on the same number. But even such gaucheries are fascinating evidence of musical quest — of a desire to move beyond the bounds of the 'classic mode'.

Rather lightweight is the approach of the first two Wynn tracks, exploiting the popularity of others' achievements; and the almost universal admiration for Louis Armstrong, heard in the straight impersonation of the problematical Dolly Jones, is also a source of inspiration for Mitchell, and for the excellent Miller, whose playing is especially pleasing in the later Wynn performances. There seems little reason to doubt that it is he whose sprightly lead gives Lil Hardaway's *Milneburg joys* much of its impetus; and his work in *She's crying for me* and *Parkway stomp*, together with the much more liberated alto playing of Lester

Boone, makes for swinging jazz which is both reminiscent of the Armstrong small bands and prophetic of Harlemite groups yet to come. Morton's performances invite comparison both with each other and with the rest of this music. The first *Mr Jelly Lord*, by the obscure Incomparables, tries out various jazz devices that were apparently beguiling the popular ear, exaggerating them almost to the point of caricature. However much Morton may have been a party to this, he himself plays with the expected poise, an *avatar* amid dull mortals. Thankfully, he had disciples more sensible of his leadings when, two years later, he directed the Levee Serenaders in *Midnight mama*, and a greatly superior *Mr Jelly Lord* in which the accents so grossly attacked by the Incomparables are heard in just perspective to a series of contrapuntal episodes which contrive, as do all Morton's best endeavours, to be at once finely controlled and beautifully relaxed.   E.T.

The Classic Style

The collective ensemble style of New Orleans reached its aesthetically most satisfying expression, far from its place of origin, in the different yet complementary work of these two bands.

43 **The New Orleans Rhythm Kings 1922–23**
Classic Jazz Masters (Sd) CJM12/13 (2 LPs), Milestone (A) M47020 (2 LPs)

Friars Society Orchestra: Paul Mares (cnt); George Brunies (tbn); Leon Roppolo (clt); Jack Pettis (C-mel, ten); Elmer Schoebel (p); Lew Black (bj); Arnold Loyacano (bs); Frank Snyder (d). Richmond, Indiana, 29 August 1922.
Eccentric · *Farewell blues* · *Discontented blues* · *Bugle call rag*
Same personnel and location, 30 August 1922.
Panama · *Tiger rag* · *Livery stable blues* · *Oriental*
New Orleans Rhythm Kings: Mares (cnt); Brunies (tbn); Roppolo (clt); Mel Stitzel (p); Ben Pollack (d). Richmond, Indiana, 12 March 1923.
Sweet loving man (2 takes) · *That's a-plenty* · *Shimme-sha-wabble* · *Weary blues*
Same personnel and location, 13 March 1923.
That da da strain · *Wolverine blues* (2 takes) · *Maple leaf rag* · *Tin roof blues* (3 takes)
Mares (cnt); Brunies (tbn); Roppollo (clt); Glen Scoville (alt, ten); Pettis (C-mel); Don Murray (ten); Jelly Roll Morton (p); Black (bj); Chink Martin (tu); Pollack (d). Richmond, Indiana, 17 July 1923.
Sobbing blues · *Clarinet marmalade* (2 takes) · *Mr Jelly Lord* (2 takes)

Kyle Pierce (p) replaces Morton. Same date.
Marguerite · *Angry* (2 takes)
Same personnel and location, 18 July 1923.
Mad

Morton (p) replaces Pierce. Same date.
London blues · *Milneburg joys* (2 takes)

The music of the New Orleans Rhythm Kings provides a bridge between that of the ODJB (**12**) and wholly midwestern groups like the Wolverines (**61**) and the Bucktown Five (**53**). But it must also be assessed in the light of its active relation to contemporary coloured musicians and groups; for this in some ways typically white New Orleans expression is jazz which displays a zeal for the more liberating and less commercially exploitable strains in black dance music, especially for the blues. Racially and musically, this ensemble bestrode two worlds and helped keep open a creative commerce between them. The band had its roots in New Orleans, but flourished in Chicago. Mares, Roppolo and Brunies were the New Orleans nucleus, augmented by midwestern players such as Pettis, Stitzel and Pollack. The three horns who take the leading roles in all these performances gained their skills in that city which nurtured both Nick LaRocca and King Oliver, with their respective bands. They acknowledge a debt to both but, while LaRocca was publicly denying black influence on his music, the NORKs were glorying in the Negro and Creole springs of jazz, and seizing the opportunity to record with Morton. The result of this community of intention is a small body of performances, set down within eleven months, which, despite acoustic reproduction, conveys to later ages much of the vitality of these young visionaries.

From the first strains, it is Roppolo who strikes the ear most compellingly with his beautifully directed, fluent clarinet phrases. His blues abilities emerge immediately in *Eccentric*, where they contrast quite sharply with the rather jerky breaks of Mares who, here and elsewhere, notably in the vaudevillian *Discontented blues*, disguises his undoubted lyricism by overuse of the plunger mute. Mares's admiration for Oliver is unconcealed. *Eccentric*, *Tiger rag* and *Livery stable blues*, though from the dixieland repertoire, have, in performance, parallels with Oliver's Creole Band (**44**) — evidence of the musical air to be breathed in Chicago, for the first recordings of that great ensemble were not made until the following year. The NORKs' advance upon the ODJB's formal achievements is gained not by developing anything intrinsic to that mode, but by matching the emotional commitment of a coloured group. The difference which this makes is excitingly shown in *Tiger rag*, which swings from the outset, with a more eloquent Mares sounding much like Oliver. Brunies, who provides the tiger's roar, displays his early-achieved mastery of the trombone's wide-ranging harmonic role, as a comparison of his work with Dutrey's for Oliver will reveal. Roppolo, mewling against a fiercely rocking rhythm, drives *Tiger rag* towards a fine ride-out chorus in which Mares attains to that desperate, crying tone so characteristic of Oliver.

The first 1923 sessions pare the ensemble down to what has come to be thought the perfect dixieland instrumentation. Rid of the saxophone, the remaining horns seem, in *Sweet loving man*, almost at once to gain an intensity and concentration of powers which had partially eluded them before. This does not invariably work towards freedom, because the interplay between improvisation and arrangement is not well contrived on all numbers. It is poor at the start of *That's a-plenty*. Stitzel's vamping adds nothing to the band's impetus, and Mares lapses into inelegance. The cornettist's peppery seasoning of a melodic solo in *Sweet loving man*, and the taut vigour leading the final chorus of *Tin roof blues* suit his ambition better. A typical ebullience saves the expert caperings of Brunies from sounding facile, but he has not travelled so far as the others from the melodic figures of ragtime and, if the blues are in his voice, they affect it in a smoother fashion. His breaks and solos in *That da da strain* and *Tin roof blues* occasionally suffer from maudlin tone and raggy phraseology.

In anticipation of later sessions, the Morton influence is heard in Artie Matthews's *Weary blues* and Morton's own *Wolverine blues*. In the former, Stitzel's ill-advised attempt at Morton imitation would have scuttled a less confident solo than Roppolo's; and in the latter, where the ensemble alternates between Oliverian and Mortonian passages, it is Stitzel again who threatens the good effect.

Pierce, who alternates with Morton in the July 1923 recordings, is another inadequate aspirant, and it only needs a moment of Morton's underpinning rhythm, in *Clarinet marmalade* (rather than *Sobbing blues*, which is marred by heavy percussion), to prove that the younger pianists were copying the wrong things.

Three Morton compositions and one Shields-Ragas piece are the vehicles for the most adventurous of these NORK essays. The freshness which Morton donates to the whole performance is unmistakable. His superb ensemble sense is never just a matter of accompaniment; rather is it a musical generosity which transmits its own *élan* to all the music's parts. He must have found Roppolo a peculiarly responsive partner. In *Clarinet mar-*

malade and *Mr Jelly Lord* their rapport is excellent. The arrangement of the latter, like a not too rudimentary sketch for Morton orchestrations yet to come, is competently played. The composer's subtlety is shown in the way that the rhythms of his accompaniment to Roppolo foreshadow the double-time section of the final chorus.

London blues (later to become *Shoe shiner's drag* — **47b**) is arranged too closely to the pianistic conception to allow much individual freedom. *Milneburg joys* has more elbow room and is more freely swinging. In its own way, it is no less formal than the 1928 version by McKinney's Cotton Pickers (**83**), in which Roppolo's NORK solo is scored for three clarinets in unison. Thumping drum beats and mooing saxophones mar the ending.

The less satisfactory, modish material in this collection (notably *Marguerite* and *Mad*) is far outweighed by fine music, and nothing ever quite conceals that these men had a tenacious thirst for the most invigorating fountains.   E.T.

44 The Saga of the King Oliver Creole Jazz Band

Kings of Jazz (I) NLJ18003/4 (2 LPs)

King Oliver's Creole Jazz Band: Oliver, Louis Armstrong (cnt); Honoré Dutrey (tbn); Johnny Dodds (clt); Lil Hardin (p); Bill Johnson (bj, vcl intrjc[1]); Baby Dodds (d). Richmond, Indiana, 31 March 1923.
Just gone · *Canal Street blues* · *Mandy Lee blues* · *I'm going away to wear you off my mind* · *Chimes blues*
Same personnel and location, 6 April 1923.
Weatherbird rag · *Dippermouth blues*[1] · *Froggie Moore* · *Snake rag*
Bud Scott (bj, vcl intrjc[2]) replaces Johnson; Baby Dodds doubles on sl w[3]. Chicago, 22 June 1923.
Snake rag · *Sweet loving man* · *High society* · *Sobbing blues*[3]
Same personnel and location, 23 June 1923.
Where did you stay last night? · *Dippermouth blues*[2] · *Jazzing babies blues*
Buster Bailey (clt), Johnny St Cyr (bj) replace Johnny Dodds, Scott; Stump Evans (C-mel) added. Richmond, Indiana, 5 October 1923.
Alligator hop · *Zulus' ball* · *Working man blues* · *Krooked blues*
Probably Ed Atkins (tbn), Jimmy Noone (clt) replace Dutrey, Bailey; Evans absent. Chicago, 15 October 1923.
Chattanooga stomp · *London café blues*
Same personnel and location, 16 October 1923.
Camp meeting blues · *New Orleans stomp*
Dutrey (tbn), Johnny Dodds (clt) replace Atkins, Noone; Charlie Jackson (bs sx) added. Chicago, c. 25 October 1923.
Buddy's habit[3] · *Tears* · *I ain't gonna tell nobody* · *Room rent blues*

Same personnel and location, *c.* 26 October 1923.
Riverside blues · *Sweet baby doll* · *Working man blues* · *Mabel's dream*
St Cyr absent. Chicago, *c.* 24 December 1923.
Mabel's dream (2 takes) · *The southern stomps* (2 takes) · *Riverside blues*

Allied to an increase in the recording of popular music, the number of jazz issues rose substantially in 1923, the most significant being Morton's piano solos (**45**), the Clarence Williams Blue Fives with Bechet (**36**), and these performances by Oliver's Creole Band. Remembering its specific achievement, it was important that this last had been together for a considerable time before reaching the studios, so that its ensemble method was fully crystallized, and not to be affected by the personnel changes shown above. Such consistency has resulted in a unique prestige, leading to bands that had the temerity to record comparable material at earlier dates being solemnly regarded as having copied the Creole Band!

In fact its ensemble integration fell shorter of perfection than is generally supposed, Dutrey being a notable culprit, with playing that is often out of tune (*The southern stomps*), and insufficiently rhythmic (*Buddy's habit*, *Sweet baby doll*); sometimes it sounds as if he is playing in a different band altogether (*Tears*, *Room rent blues*, *I ain't gonna tell nobody*). There are harmonic clashes between trombone and bass saxophone lines, and only on the second *Working man blues* does the latter instrument find an effective role. Mistakes in the harmony are, indeed, quite common, particularly by Miss Hardin, as on *Just gone*. Evans's C-melody saxophone confuses the ensembles of the 5 October session, and though Oliver usually chose and maintained excellent tempos, there was a tendency to slow down, as in *Sweet loving man* and *Sweet baby doll*.

However, this band's style was a triumph over the limited skills of most of its members, enabling the expressive content of its music to be projected through unified feeling and disciplined performance. The material is of three types: three-strain pieces such as *Snake rag* which resemble marches and rags and refer back to pre-jazz times: verse-and-chorus popular songs like *I ain't gonna tell nobody*; and blues such as *London café blues*. More important is that this music reconciles the collective emotions of marches and hymns with the solitariness of the blues and the equivocal optimism of ragtime. Like most comparable achievements in music, the result is conservative rather than revolutionary, a distillation of much that was best from what had gone into the jazz tradition up to this point, focused by the taste and outlook of one man.

The potentialities of the instrumentation Oliver favoured were further explored only by Johnny Dodds on his second Black Bottom Stompers date (**38a**), but such music casts shadows in several directions. Resemblances between *Jazzing babies blues* and the New Orleans Rhythm Kings' earlier *Tin roof blues (***43***)* have caused peculiar agitation among the Creole Band's admirers, and it is perhaps as well that it is less widely known that the first theme of *Canal Street blues* occurs on the Synco Jazz Band's 1922 *State Street blues*. Equally significant is that *Camp meeting blues* contains a theme later employed in Ellington's *Creole love call* (**87**), and that in the fourth chorus of *Jazzing babies blues* we hear from Oliver an earlier 'state' of an idea used by Armstrong not only in the second chorus of his *Muggles* solo (**48**) but decades later when he recorded *Black and tan fantasy* with Ellington in 1961. Also, Armstrong's *Chimes blues* solo, his first on disc, was echoed by Charlie Creath's 1924 *Market Street blues*. Oliver's *Dippermouth blues* solo, of course, was imitated by many trumpeters in the 1920s, 1930s and beyond.

At their best, the Creole Band's performances accommodate to the 'three-minute form' of ten-inch 78 rpm discs more comfortably than many which came later, and convey an impression of overall shapeliness rather than of being just strings of choruses. This does raise, however, the question of how much improvising went on. *New Orleans stomp* sounds as if it is at least influenced by a stock orchestration — presumably the Melrose one — and the two very similar versions of *Riverside blues* suggest a like origin. Again, aside from Johnny Dodds's two choruses accompanied by the piano, *Sweet loving man* has the same layout as the earlier NORKs performance. Sometimes differences arise more from changes in studio balance than anything else, as between the two *Snake rags*, where the first version is more closely recorded, with Dcdds and Dutrey more prominent. The June recording of *Dippermouth blues* separates the parts more clearly than the April, is very slightly faster, and more flowing. On the earlier one it is Oliver who leads the ensemble chorus which precedes his solo, while on the later it is Armstrong, this providing an instructive comparison. Despite considerable differences in their third choruses, there are more than enough similarities between Oliver's two accounts of his solo here to make it obvious that members of the Creole Band did not always improvise so much as is assumed. These stand, however, with Roppolo's poignantly introspective contributions to the NORKs' *Tiger rag* and *Wolverine blues* as the earliest really distinguished jazz solos to be recorded. Oliver builds around the flat third, whose exact pitch he shifts constantly, often placing the notes between, rather than on, the beats; the colour of the notes is varied, too, with the mute.

Again, some of the pieces are more coherently organized on the compositional level than might be expected, *London café blues*, with its repeatedly altered harmonies, being an example. Oliver's performance should be studied in conjunction with the versions Morton recorded (as *London blues*) in 1923 with the NORKs, as a piano solo in 1924 (**45**), and particularly the 1928 reworking as *Shoe shiner's drag* (**47b**).

Despite the Creole Band's virtues in terms of ensemble playing and formal organization, though, solos, whether predetermined or truly improvised, provide some of the finest moments. Instances are supplied by Oliver on *Jazzing babies blues*, by Dodds on *Canal Street blues* and by Armstrong on *Tears*, where his breaks are a quite remarkable step into the future. These three are by far this group's most creative players.

The Kings of Jazz issue shown above contains all known Creole Band titles, but for better reproduction of the March, April and 5 October dates, see Herwin (A) 106, and for those of June and the remaining October sessions, World Records (E) SH358. On these the recordings are heard more clearly than ever before, especially *Zulus' ball* and the first *Working man blues* [15].   M.H.

New Orleans Composer

In contrast with the collective syntheses of **43–44**, jazz performance is here, and for the first time, shaped by a composer's formal requirements.

45   **Jelly Roll Morton: Thesaurus of First Recordings**
Kings of Jazz (I) NLJ18007/8 (2 LPs), *Milestone (A) MLP2003

Jelly Roll Morton and His Orchestra: Tommy Ladnier or Bernie Young (cnt); unidentified tbn; Wilson Townes (clt); Arville Harris (alt); Morton (p); Jasper Taylor (wdbl). Chicago, June 1923.
Big foot ham (2 takes) · *Muddy water blues*

Morton (p). Richmond, Indiana, 17 July 1923.
King Porter stomp · *New Orleans joys* (2 takes)

Same personnel and location, 18 July 1923.
Grandpa's spells · *Kansas City stomps* · *Wolverine blues* · *The pearls*

Jelly Roll Morton Jazz Band: Natty Dominique (cnt); Zue Robertson (tbn); Horace Eubanks (clt); Morton (p); W. E. Burton (d). Chicago, October 1923.
Someday, sweetheart · *London blues*

Morton's Steamboat Four: Boyd Senter (clt); Morton (p); 'Memphis', Burton (kz). Chicago, April 1924.
Mr Jelly Lord (2 takes)
Morton's Stomp Kings: 'Memphis', Russell Senter (kz); Boyd Senter (bj, kz). Chicago, April 1924.
Steady roll (2 takes)
Morton (p). Chicago, c. April 1924.
Thirty-fifth Street blues · *Mamanita*
Same personnel and location, April–May 1924.
Froggie Moore · *London blues*
Morton (p). Richmond, Indiana, 9 June 1924.
Tia Juana · *Shreveport stomp* · *Mamanita* · *Jelly Roll blues* · *Big foot ham* · *Bucktown blues* · *Tom cat blues* · *Stratford hunch* · *Perfect rag*
Jelly Roll Morton's Kings of Jazz: Lee Collins (cnt); Roy Palmer (tbn); 'Balls' Ball (clt); Alex Poole (alt); Morton (p). Chicago, c. September 1924.
Fish tail blues · *High society* · *Tiger rag*
King Oliver (cnt); Morton (p). Chicago, c. December 1924.
King Porter stomp · *Tom cat blues*
Jelly Roll Morton's Jazz Trio: Volly DeFaut (clt); Morton (p); Burton (kz). Chicago, c. May 1925.
My gal
Burton absent. Same date.
Wolverine blues
Jelly Roll Morton's Incomparables: possibly Ray Bowling (cnt); unidentified tbn, alt, ten, bj; Morton (p); Clay Jefferson (d). Richmond, Indiana, 23 February 1926.
Mr Jelly Lord
Morton (p). Chicago, 20 April 1926.
The pearls · *Sweetheart o' mine* · *Fat meat and greens* · *King Porter stomp*

Morton was not simply the first real jazz composer; he was the first jazz musician to make his entire approach to the music compositional. Whether as a piano soloist, or as leader of orchestras over which he had undoubted control, he emerged, and will be chiefly honoured, as the creator of totally conceived jazz masterpieces. His grandiose claims as an innovator must not be allowed to obscure the fact that he was a virtually self-contained master of invention, the originator of orchestral jazz.

Only the initial aspect of this achievement is revealed in these his earliest recordings, but that aspect is marvellously determinative, consisting of twenty-three piano solos (not counting alternative takes) he recorded between the summer of 1923 and the spring of 1926. The first *King Porter stomp*, set down at the time of his memorable collaboration with the New Orleans

Rhythm Kings (**43**), must be regarded as one of the great revelatory moments in recorded jazz history. Yet here we are catching his genius at a point of maturity. In spite of his 'elucidations' made towards the end of his life (**21**), we can only guess at the phases through which his playing and thinking had passed prior to this, though it is reasonable to assume that his strongest influences had been the forms of Missouri ragtime and the barrelhouse blues styles of Gulf Coast towns. No mere amalgam of these variant modes could account for the brilliantly singular transmutation of ragtime and the piano blues which he waxed at Richmond and was later to make the basis of some of the most complex and exciting ensemble jazz ever created.

King Porter stomp follows, in its formal layout, a typical ragtime sequence — the syncopated development of those binary, ternary and rondo forms which came out of the baroque dance suites of seventeenth-century Europe by way of eighteenth- and nineteenth-century American adaptations of the gavotte and popular march. Other compositions which employ this system of relating, contrasting and extending different melodic strains are *Grandpa's spells*, a rollicking example of the elasticity which Morton was bestowing on ragtime; the cagily formal *Kansas City stomps*, with floating trio chords that were to prove so amenable to the mock-serious spookiness of a 1928 Red Hot Peppers realization (**47b**); *Froggie Moore*, in which the ragtime quaintness of the second strain is joshed by amazingly fluid syncopations in the finale; *Shreveport stomp*, a reckless exercise, not quite so skilfully executed here as in the later trio session; *Perfect rag*, one of the most adept of rag compositions, whose stomping final strain is pure jazz celebration. And there are others, further in spirit from ragtime, which, however, use compound form. Notable among these is *The pearls*, march-like and echoing instrumental counterpoint more formal even than the ragtime of the early New Orleans marching bands, and yet, despite a tempo which could easily become plodding, alive with subtle jazz accentuations. Again, the ragtimers' love of musical humour prompts the mock modulations of *Froggie Moore* and *Stratford hunch*, and the abrupt alternation of the fragile and the boisterous in *Sweetheart o' mine*.

Morton's approach to the blues involves a lusty formalism which may be sampled in the two versions of *New Orleans joys*, *Fat meat and greens*, and the rather less substantial *Thirty-fifth Street blues*. Strain developments enter into these pieces too, evidence of Morton's impatience with rudimentary forms. Spanish–Caribbean influence assists the aerodynamic lyricism of *New Orleans joys* and is borne over into many things. Even the earthy barrelhouse opening of *Fat meat and greens* displays an exuberant fascination with form, and one senses a constant strategy of skilful containment to outwit the anarchy of crude feeling. His control is magisterial, even when, as so frequently happens, a piece culminates in that personal kind of pianistic ecstasy which merits the Wagnerian phrase, 'apotheosis of the dance'.

A good deal has been written about Morton's 'orchestral' style of pianism, and about the relation of this to his recordings with the Red Hot Peppers. The conveyance of orchestral effects from the bands Morton heard in New Orleans is obvious in almost any of these keyboard pieces. Once the expressive range of the piano — and its predecessors — was realized, its potentiality for imitation was realized, too; and effects of this kind abound in baroque keyboard works. Emulations of trombone swoops (*A coon band contest*) and clarinet trills (*Smokey mokes*) were common enough in piano ragtime, but Morton's assimilation of such effects moved well beyond a desire for novelty. The trills are there, the trombone and tuba melodies in the bass, the impulsive trumpet rips — yes, and a few ghostly operatic voices, too, perhaps — but they have all become integral to his style. Further, it would be a mistake to suppose, because of the obvious similarities, that these piano recordings were preliminary sketches for later band versions. Morton's approach was always compositional — the putting together of all available elements — and whether he was expressing his vision through the keyboard or through a band of sympathetic musicians, there was normally full concentration upon the immediate means. Though spontaneous variation was allowed for in both piano and band realizations, it was always well contained within the overarching conception. Few if any of Morton's best orchestral pieces were merely enabling arrangements.

The keyboard solos can stand by themselves. So can the great Peppers interpretations, though the latter will inevitably be seen in the light of the former. We grasp Morton's orchestral motives better because of this pianistic genius — something which cannot be said of Ellington or John Lewis, two other masters of jazz composition, though it can possibly be said of Monk. Yet occasionally, as in the 1927 account of *The Pearls* and 1928 *Shoe shiner's drag* (*London blues*), the pianistic form *per se* does seem to impose itself upon the group expression.

Very little in the other recordings of this collection matches the genius of the solos. In *Big foot ham* and *Muddy water blues*, the compositional relationship has not yet been found, and although the Kings of Jazz titles show a little more of Morton's shaping influence, the results compare unfavourably with the NORKs sessions. As for the orgies of kazoo-blowing in *Mr Jelly Lord* and *Steady roll*, it may be indicative of his attitude to such amateurism that he does not even play on the second of these. The trio and duet involving DeFaut, a clarinettist of simple aims, are fairly inconsequential; and the same might almost be said of the somewhat unlikely meeting between Morton and Oliver, were it not for the incidental lessons to be learnt. The two great jazzmen were unsuited to each other, and since there is no real chance of spontaneous interchange, Oliver is reduced to emphasizing keyboard parts. But the choice of *King Porter stomp* and *Tom cat blues* adventitiously allows us to hear in sample statement the two chief formal elements which shaped the jazz of New Orleans and were fused in Morton's music, namely the ragtime figurations dominant in Oliver's reading of *King Porter* and the crying blue notes which almost permit the cornettist to assert his own freedom in *Tom cat.*

The four 1926 solos allow the piano style to be heard for the first time in undistorted reproduction. Comparison of *The pearls* and *King Porter stomp* with the 1923 versions and those made in 1938 (**21**) will reveal both the formality and the flexibility of this singular music. The riffing final choruses of *King Porter* dance tantalizingly on three steps — the dominant, the octave and, at last, above that, the insistent flattened third with which Oliver and those like him had bruited the death and transfiguration of ragtime.

(The Milestone LP shown above contains a selection of solo and band performances; Fountain (E) FJ104 reproduces all the solos with clearer sound than any previous issue.)   E.T.

46 **Jelly Roll Morton Vol. 1**
Gaps (H) 010

Jelly Roll Morton Jazz Band: Natty Dominique (cnt); Zue Robertson (tbn); Horace Eubanks (clt); Morton (p); W. E. Burton (d). Chicago, October 1923.
Someday, sweetheart · London blues

Unidentified cnt, tbn, clt/ten, p, bj, d. St Louis, 12 May 1926.
Soapsuds

Johnny Dunn and His Band: Dunn (tpt); Herb Flemming (tbn); Garvin Bushell (clt, alt); Morton (p); John Mitchell (bj); Harry Hull (tu); possibly Mort Perry (d). New York City, 13 March 1928.
Sergeant Dunn's bugle call blues · Ham 'n' eggs · Buffalo blues · You need some loving

Wingy Mannone and His Orchestra: Mannone (tpt); Dicky Wells (tbn); Artie Shaw (clt); Bud Freeman (ten); Morton (p); Frank Victor (g); Kaiser Marshall (d). New York City, 15 August 1934.
Never had no loving · I'm alone without you
Morton (p, vcl). Washington, D.C., May/June 1938.
Pallet on the floor.
Morton (p, vcl[1]). Washington, D.C., December 1938.
Finger buster · Creepy feeling · Wining boy blues[1] *· Honky tonk music*
Morton, Gabriell Heatter (spch). New York City, 30 September 1939.
Interview
Morton (p); unidentified band. Same date.
Tiger rag

This may appear a somewhat random collection, but in fact it usefully closes gaps in our knowledge of Morton's activities. True, *Pallet on the floor*, an extract from his Library of Congress recordings (**21**), is too brief to have significance, and *Soapsuds*, although traditionally regarded as a Morton item, is almost certainly no such thing. In terms of organization, it bears a few points of resemblance to typical band performances of his from this period, such as *The pearls* (**47a**), yet the playing is far below the standard of his contemporaneous work for the Victor company. What little can be heard of the piano in the ensembles is not unlike Morton, but there is no reason why at precisely the time he was making his greatest records in Chicago he should have journeyed to St Louis to set down this thoroughly undistinguished attempt. Admittedly, the melody is the one Morton later recorded as *Fickle Fay creep*, yet he borrowed material from several unexpected sources, the introduction to *Shreveport stomp* (**47b**), for example, coming from Rudy Wiedoeft's *Saxophobia*.

The 1923 Jazz Band titles add no more to our knowledge than the items done the previous June and noted under **45**. Morton's keyboard work on *London blues* is as characteristic as we should expect from his solo recordings of that year, but the ensembles confirm that he had not yet learnt how to shape a band to his compositional ends. Nor is there anything here to support the reputation of Robertson as an outstanding early trombonist, least of all his inept solo on *London blues* [16].

Blatantly energetic if rather on edge, the recordings under Dunn's name were the first in which Morton participated in New York. *Ham 'n' eggs* is really his *Big foot ham* (**45**) and *Buffalo blues* is the piece he recorded as a piano solo titled *Mister Joe* (a tribute to Oliver) in 1939, but all four are shaped on Dunn's rather than the composer's terms. Highly accomplished if also fairly stiff rhythmically, the former dominates the ensembles and is quite impressive with a wa-wa mute, as on *You need some loving*. This track also includes a fine solo from Morton, and there is creditable work elsewhere by Flemming and Bushell.

Mannone's session, which marked Shaw's recording debut as a soloist, was the only one in which Morton took part between the *Fickle Fay creep* date of 1930 and his 1938 marathon for the Library of Congress. Although the leader's playing is simple and effective — superior to his work later in the decade — the personnel could scarcely be more heterogeneous. Saddled by irreconcilable stylistic differences, the sidemen merely go through routine motions in their solos, although Morton's passage in *I'm alone without you* strikes a special note of incongruity.

His 1938 solos have tended, like his more numerous band and solo recordings of 1939–40, to be overshadowed in the Morton literature by his imposing Library of Congress sequence. They ought to be studied in conjunction with his 1939 solos for the General label: *Creepy feeling*, for instance, is close to *The crave* of 1939 (which in turn is close to the *Hacienda tango* recorded by Felix Arndt in 1914), and *Wining boy blues*, though faster and having partially different lyrics, anticipates the General version. *Finger buster*, fast and not convincingly furious, is more informative of Morton's technique than of his musical intentions, but *Honky tonk music* is a late yet authentic echo of barrelhouse blues styles.

The interview with Heatter is from a CBS *We, The People* radio programme. Morton tells entertaining fibs about how he invented jazz and then, to the faceless accompaniment of an unknown studio band, he elegantly decorates *Tiger rag*.   M.H.

47a The Complete Jelly Roll Morton Vols. 1–2
RCA (F) PM42405 (2 LPs), *RCA (A) LPM508, 524

Jelly Roll Morton's Red Hot Peppers: George Mitchell (cnt); Kid Ory (tbn); Omer Simeon (clt); Morton (p); Johnny St Cyr (bj); John Lindsay (bs); Andrew Hilaire (d). Chicago, 15 September 1926.
Black bottom stomp · Smoke house blues · The chant (2 takes)
Same personnel and location, 21 September 1926.
Steamboat stomp
Barney Bigard, Darnell Howard (clt) added. Same date.
Sidewalk blues (2 takes) · *Dead man blues* (2 takes)
Bigard, Howard absent. Chicago, 16 December 1926.
Grandpa's spells (2 takes) · *Original Jelly Roll blues* (2 takes) · *Cannonball blues* (2 takes)
J. Wright Smith, Clarence Black (vln[1]); Morton (vcl[2]). Same date.
Someday, sweetheart[1] (2 takes) · *Doctor Jazz stomp*[2]

Mitchell (cnt); Gerald Reeves (tbn); Johnny Dodds (clt); Stump Evans (alt); Morton (p, spch[3]); Bud Scott (g); Quinn Wilson (tu); Baby Dodds (d); Lew LeMar (vcl effects[4]). Chicago, 4 June 1927.

Hyena stomp[4] (2 takes) · *Billy goat stomp*[4] (2 takes) · *Wild man blues*[3] (take 1) · *Jungle blues* (2 takes)

LeMar absent. Chicago, 10 June 1927.

Beale Street blues (2 takes) · *The pearls* (2 takes)

Johnny Dodds (clt); Morton (p); Baby Dodds (d). Same date.

Wolverine blues (2 takes) · *Mr Jelly Lord*

47b The Complete Jelly Roll Morton Vols. 3–4
RCA (F) PM43170 (2 LPs), *RCA (A) LPM524, 546

Jelly Roll Morton's Red Hot Peppers: Mitchell (cnt); Reeves (tbn); Johnny Dodds (clt); Evans (alt); Morton (p, spch[3]); Scott (g); Wilson (tu); Baby Dodds (d). Chicago, 4 June 1927.

Wild man blues[3] (take 3)

Ward Pinkett (tpt); Geechie Fields (tbn); Simeon (clt); Morton (p); Lee Blair (bj); Bill Benford (tu); Tommy Benford (d). New York City, 11 June 1928.

Georgia swing · *Kansas City stomps* · *Shoe shiner's drag* · *Boogaboo*

Simeon (clt); Morton (p); Tommy Benford (d). Same date.

Shreveport stomp (2 takes)

Fields (tbn) added. Same date.

Mournful serenade

Jelly Roll Morton and His Orchestra: Ed Anderson, Ed Swayzee (tpt); William G. Kato (tbn); Russell Procope (clt, alt); Paul Barnes (sop); Joe Garland (ten); Morton (p); Blair (g); William Moore (tu); Manzie Johnson (d). New York City, 6 December 1928.

Red Hot Pepper stomp · *Deep creek blues*

Morton (p). New York City, 8 July 1929.

Pep · *Seattle hunch* (2 takes) · *Frances* · *Freakish* (2 takes)

Jelly Roll Morton and His Orchestra: David Richards (?), Boyd 'Red' Rosser (tpt); Charlie Irvis (tbn); George Baquet (clt); Barnes (sop); Walter Thomas (alt); Joe Thomas (ten); Morton (p); Barney Alexander (bj); Harry Prather (tu); William Laws (d). New York City, 9 July 1929.

Burning the iceberg (2 takes) · *Courthouse bump* (2 takes) · *Pretty Lil* (2 takes)

Same personnel and location, 10 July 1929.

Sweet Anita mine (2 takes) · *New Orleans bump* (2 takes)

Same personnel and location, 12 July 1929.

Down my way · *Try me out* · *Tank town bump* (2 takes)

Jelly Roll Morton and His Red Hot Peppers: Henry Allen (tpt); J. C. Higginbotham (tbn); Albert Nicholas (clt); Morton (p); Will Johnson (g); Pops Foster (bs); Paul Barbarin (d). New York City, 13 November 1929.

Sweet Peter (2 takes)

Success, Ellington once declared, is being in the right place, doing the right thing, before the right people, at the right time. In his case that was exactly how it happened. But where Ellington ended up being mourned throughout the world (there was even a memorial service at St Martin-in-the-Fields, London), Morton died, in Los Angeles in 1941, obscure and unhonoured. He had lacked at least one of the necessary components making up Ellington's axiom. For Morton the time was decidedly out of joint. When he began making his Red Hot Peppers recordings in Chicago in 1926, he was 41 (the age, incidentally, at which Ellington started making, in 1940, what many think to be his finest recordings — 153). But where Ellington moved with the current of jazz history, aided by the fashion for big bands and virtuoso soloists, Morton discovered himself to be something of an anachronism. What he excelled at was devising pieces which deployed the various elements of the New Orleans ensemble, dramatizing that style, demonstrating the variety of timbres and dynamics which the classic line-up could provide. Yet he did so at the very moment when that kind of jazz was becoming *demodé*. By the time interest in it had revived, he was no longer around.

In relation to the decade of his maturity, therefore, Morton was a conservative, even reactionary, artist. Yet, paradoxically, he was simultaneously a great innovator, nothing less than the first jazz composer, showing how a jazz ensemble could be shaped by an individual, just as Armstrong was showing how it could be dominated by a soloist. Morton, of course, had always been a composer. His piano solos (**45** and **46**) were not concerned with inventing variations upon familiar material, but with creating an overall entity. And those solos employed the piano as if it were a band, so that converting some of them — *Grandpa's spells*, *Kansas City stomps*, *The pearls*, *Jelly Roll blues* — into orchestral terms seemed perfectly natural, even logical. The compositions reflect the background that nurtured Morton, including his fondness for devising melodic (rather than abstract) blues and, most importantly of all, his very personal use of the structures of ragtime.

The first of the above sessions came as near perfection as Morton was ever to do. All three performances (and orchestrations) are classics, marvellous examples of the ideal balance between ensemble and solos, between the authority of the composer and the identities of the front-line musicians. Mitchell was exactly the right cornet player for Morton, a capable soloist yet still concerned with the responsibilities of leading the others. Simeon, significantly enough, remained Morton's favourite clarinettist (he even brought him from Chicago for the first of the New

York dates): formal, but flexible enough to come up with surprises. It was Simeon who recalled how Morton paid the musicians to rehearse for these sessions. Not at all a regular practice then or afterwards, this was an indication of Morton's seriousness and integrity. He may have been employing an *ad hoc* ensemble, yet the performers needed to be familiar with the compositions in order to make them flow naturally and effectively. That is one reason why the inclusion on these LPs of numerous alternative takes is revealing only to students of minutiae. In every case the structure stays the same; so do most of the solos — except in performances such as *Wolverine blues*, where Johnny Dodds thinks afresh each time — confirming that a strategy had been agreed upon. Sometimes a later take even shows a deterioration (Mitchell fluffing in *Dead man blues*, St Cyr forgetting the chord sequence during his *Cannonball blues* solo), although generally it is the process of polishing that comes across rather than new flaws or fresh insights.

Black bottom stomp encapsulates most of the practices that Morton was always urging other musicians to adopt: plenty of breaks and riffs, an obsession with dynamics, keeping, as he put it, the glass half full so that more could always be poured in. There is too — it happens most notably in *Grandpa's spells* — a parcelling out of instrumental groupings, a concern with the variation of texture not to be encountered again to quite this extent until, say Ellington's *Harlem airshaft* or Gil Evans's *Boplicity*. *Smoke house blues* (a theme by Charles Luke — not Morton, as shown on the sleeve and label) is not so much an orchestration as a series of solos, yet it communicates a lazy charm, concluding, as though the aesthetician was intent on overkill, with one break after another. Two additional clarinettists were added for *Sidewalk blues* and *Dead man blues*, enabling Morton to write for the latter a particularly effective trio, with trombone underneath, rather more reminiscent of what Ellington was to get up to later than what Don Redman was currently doing with Henderson's band. Adding two violinists for *Someday, sweetheart* had less happy results. Morton, in fact, provides a depressing example of the inability of early jazz writers, apart from Bill Challis, Paul Whiteman's best arranger, to incorporate strings within the melodic scope of their music.

The first two dates were notable for Lindsay's admirable bass playing. Not only did he impel the ensemble forward, but he also had the ability to make his absence felt. When he drops out, from behind the piano, then the clarinet, towards the end of *Grandpa's spells*, the effect is to emphasize his reappearance in the final chorus. Quite why Morton decided to use a tuba instead remains a mystery. But other changes took place on the session of 4 June 1928. Simeon was replaced by Johnny Dodds — reedier, more idiosyncratic, much more of a thoroughgoing blues player. A saxophonist, Evans, was introduced, sounding staccato and very out of place at first, yet fitting usefully into *Beale Street blues* and *The pearls*. Hokum had put in an appearance earlier. The repartee and sound effects in *Sidewalk blues, Steamboat stomp* and *Dead man blues* were harmless enough, but LeMar's animal impersonations occupied far too much space in *Hyena stomp* (actually, a rather interesting orchestration) and *Billy goat stomp*. *Mr Jelly Lord* is a fairly straightforward trio performance, but *Wolverine blues* (not a real blues at all) begins with Morton playing at least half the piece on his own, only to be joined later by the Dodds brothers — who give the piece an entirely new twist.

The implications of Morton's move to New York are not particularly apparent on the session of 11 June 1928, which produced four tracks that are at least comparable with the best of the Chicago recordings. Simeon was there to provide some continuity, but Fields snarled on his trombone much more than Ory or Reeves ever did, and so, at times, did Pinkett, a worthwhile deputy for Mitchell. What begins to emerge on this and subsequent dates is a shift towards the romanticism with which Ellington was beginning to be associated. It is most noticeable in *Mournful serenade*, a reworking of Oliver's *Chimes blues* (**44**). Deceptively simple, the opening keyboard passage leads to the sobriety of clarinet and trombone solos, followed by the subdued exuberance of the final two choruses. What started as a plain blues ends as a little tone poem, a forerunner, by about two years, of *Mood indigo* (**91**). The band used for that session was one that Bill Benford, the tubaist, led at the Rose Danceland, Morton and Simeon being the only outsiders. The group which recorded *Red hot pepper stomp* and *Deep creek blues*, however, included several musicians who went off with Morton on a four-month tour, notably Barnes, the soprano saxophonist. He is just one of a series of soloists who, in *Deep creek blues*, evoke a mood rather than build up an orchestral structure. Significantly enough, Morton called this ensemble, which had three saxophones, his Orchestra rather than his Red Hot Peppers.

The four piano solos of 8 July 1929 contain a few imperfections (Morton, like Ellington, was sometimes careless as a performer), but the pieces are fairly typical of the sort of compositions that he had been writing for over a decade. The dynamics of *Pep* contrast with the amassing of musical weight that goes on in *Frances* (also known, perhaps aptly, as *Fat Frances*), while *Freakish* makes use of what in 1929 must have seemed very daring harmonies. The three sessions which follow, however, show Morton getting to grips with a big band.

Interestingly enough, his clarinettist is the New Orleans veteran Baquet, living and working in Philadelphia at the time, whose playing now sounds quaint, even antique. Perhaps Morton felt the need for another Creole to cover his musical flank, a substitute for the much-missed Simeon. The sleeve note perpetuates a popular notion that Morton took only the piano solos on these tracks, the workaday playing being done by Red Rodriguez. Latterday scholarship tends to dismiss this theory; critical opinion, though, still takes a patronizing view of the actual music. In fact, Morton frequently uses the unfamiliar resources — those sections of brass and saxophones — quite cunningly, especially in *New Orleans bump* and the aggressive, exciting *Burning the iceberg*. An Ellingtonian ambience is conjured up by the former, and in one passage Baquet's fluttering clarinet recalls Bigard playing over rustling banjo chords in *Echoes of the jungle* (**130**).

In a way these performances are more successful than *Sweet Peter*, where is used a contingent from Luis Russell's band, all New Orleanians but mostly of a younger generation and often phrasing in a rhythmic style at variance with Morton's. Allen is the most original of them, and also the most out of place. Perhaps this track illustrates Morton's dilemma, that of a popular composer who was losing touch with his time, more poignantly than even those attempts at leading, and writing for, a big band.   C.F.

The Breakdown of the Collective Style

New Orleans collective playing was undermined by the individuality of solo performances which continued to expand the expressive and technical scope of jazz.

48 The Louis Armstrong Legend 1925–29
World Records (E) SM421-4 (4 LPs, boxed), *Columbia (A) CL851-3 (3 LPs)

Vol. 1 — Louis Armstrong and His Hot Five: Armstrong (cnt, vcl); Kid Ory (tbn); Johnny Dodds (clt); Lil Hardin Armstrong (p); Johnny St Cyr (bj). Chicago, 12 November 1925.
My heart · Yes, I'm in the barrel · Gut bucket blues
Same personnel. Dodds also plays alt. Chicago, 22 February 1926.
Come back, sweet pupa

Same personnel and location, 26 February 1926.
Georgia grind · Heebie jeebies · Cornet chop suey · Oriental strut ·
You're next · Muskrat ramble

Armstrong also plays sl w[1], Dodds alt[2]. Chicago, 16 June 1926.
Don't forget to mess around[2] · *I'm gonna gitcha · Dropping shucks ·*
Whosit[1]

Clarence Babcock (vcl[3]) added. Chicago, 23 June 1926.
King of the Zulus[3] · *Big fat ma and skinny pa*[3]

Vol. 2 — Same personnel, date and location.
Lonesome blues · Sweet little papa

May Alix (vcl[4]) added: Babcock absent. Chicago, 16 November 1926.
Jazz lips · Skit-dat-de-dat · Big butter and egg man[4] · *Sunset Café*
stomp[4]

Alix absent. Chicago, 27 November 1926.
You made me love you · Irish black bottom

Louis Armstrong and His Hot Seven: John Thomas or Gerald Reeves
(tbn) replaces Ory; Peter Briggs (tu), Baby Dodds (d) added. Chicago,
7 May 1927.
Willie the weeper · Wild man blues

Louis Armstrong and His Stompers: Armstrong, Bill Wilson (tpt);
Honoré Dutrey (tbn); Boyd Atkins (sop); Joe Walker (alt); Al Washington
(ten); Stump Evans (bar); Earl Hines (p); Rip Bassett (bj); Briggs (tu);
Tubby Hall (d). Chicago, 9 May 1927.
Chicago breakdown

Louis Armstrong and His Hot Seven: Armstrong (cnt, vcl); Thomas or
Reeves (tbn); Johnny Dodds (clt); Lil Hardin Armstrong (p); St Cyr (bj);
Briggs (tu); Baby Dodds (d). Chicago, 10 May 1927.
Alligator crawl · Potato head blues

Same personnel and location, 11 May 1927.
Melancholy blues · Weary blues · Twelfth Street rag

Vol. 3 — Same personnel and location, 13 May 1927.
Keyhole blues · S.O.L. blues

Same personnel and location, 14 May 1927.
Gully low blues · That's when I'll come back to you

Louis Armstrong and His Hot Five: Ory replaces Thomas or Reeves;
Briggs, Baby Dodds absent. Chicago, 2 September 1927.
Put 'em down blues · Ory's Creole trombone

Same personnel and location, 6 September 1927.
The last time

Same personnel and location, 9 December 1927.
Strutting with some barbecue · Got no blues

Lonnie Johnson (g) added. Chicago, 10 December 1927.
Once in a while · I'm not rough

Same personnel and location, 13 December 1927.
Hotter than that · Savoy blues

Louis Armstrong and His Savoy Ballroom Five: Armstrong (tpt, vcl);
Fred Robinson (tbn); Jimmy Strong (clt); Hines (p); Mancy Cara (bj);
Zutty Singleton (d). Chicago, 27 June 1928.
Fireworks · Skip the gutter · A Monday date
Same personnel and location, 28 June 1928.
Don't jive me
Vol. 4 — Same personnel, date and location.
West End blues · Sugar foot strut
Same personnel and location, 29 June 1928.
Two deuces · Squeeze me
Strong also plays ten. Chicago, 5 July 1928.
Knee drops
Louis Armstrong with Carrol Dickerson's Orchestra: Armstrong Willie
Hightower, Homer Hobson (tpt); Robinson (tbn); Bert Curry, Crawford
Wethington (alt); Strong (ten); Dickerson (vln); Hines (p); Cara (bj);
Briggs (tu); Singleton (d). Chicago, 5 July 1928.
Symphonic raps · Savoyagers' stomp
Louis Armstrong and His Savoy Ballroom Five: Armstrong (tpt, vcl);
Robinson (tbn); Strong (clt); Hines (p, cls[5]); Cara (bj, g[6]); Singleton (d).
Chicago, 4 December 1928.
No, papa, no[6] · Basin Street blues[5]
Don Redman (alt) added; Strong also plays ten. Chicago, 5 December
1928.
No one else but you · Beau koo Jack · Save it, pretty mama
Armstrong, Hines only. Same date.
Weatherbird
Louis Armstrong and His Savoy Ballroom Five: personnel as for
4 December 1928. Chicago, 7 December 1928.
Muggles
Redman (alt, spch[7]) added. Chicago, 12 December 1928.
Hear me talking to you · St James' Infirmary · Tight like this[7]
Louis Armstrong and His All-Star Orchestra: Armstrong (tpt); Jack
Teagarden (tbn); Happy Cauldwell (ten); Joe Sullivan (p); Eddie Lang
(g); Kaiser Marshall (d). New York City, 5 March 1929.
Knocking a jug

That day is long past in which enthusiasts believed that the
music of the Armstrong Hot Fives and Sevens represented a
pristine form of New Orleans jazz; and neither can similar claims
be made for Oliver's Creole Band nor the Red Onion Jazz Babies.
The style of such groups was doubtless imbued with the spirit of
New Orleans, and depended a great deal upon an ability to
improvise collectively; but, already, working in the different
environment of Chicago, motives more urgent and concentrated
were having their effect. Much of the impact of these early

ensembles under Armstrong's leadership is the result of careful working out of musical routines, and of the skilful way these simple but precise head arrangements are combined with forthright improvising. In fact, the routines followed in the earliest Hot Five sessions are freer and less involved, in terms of premeditation, than those used by the Red Onion group which carried to a greater degree of stylization trends evident in the Creole Band music (44). On those 1924 sessions the lyricism of Armstrong's solo style was revealing itself, and one is struck by the unforced assurance of his lead in some intricately timed stop-chord supporting passages, typical of which is that accompanying Buster Bailey's solo on *Santa Claus blues* (Fountain (E) FJ107); but the approach seems heavily influenced, in most of its aspects, by the Oliver conception.

From the very start of *My heart* (recorded almost exactly a year after the Red Onion performances) a new liberty is sensed. Not that the means are more revolutionary; on the contrary, they are even a little less ambitious in terms of basic resource. *My heart* and *Gut bucket blues* open with straightforward New Orleans-style improvised counterpoint, yet how much more mobile and uncluttered it sounds! Some credit for this must be given to improved sound recording, and it is also pretty obvious now that, with companions as schooled in the art as Dodds and Ory, Armstrong could hardly have failed to achieve the best at that level; but there should be no doubt in any percipient hearer's mind that the dazzlingly fresh character of these collective choruses flows from Armstrong's own playing. However much he may have been in fee to Oliver and others — and the extent of that will remain debatable — the twenty-five-year-old cornettist had by this point indubitably found his own voice. It is perhaps possible that the more formal experimentation and challenge to solo skills of his encounters with the Henderson band had furthered Armstrong's musical self-knowledge to a point at which he could return to a more intimate and traditional vehicle and steer it to his own purposes. The assurance is there from the start in the ripping accents, the superbly controlled cornet tone, and the wide variety of phrasing. There is little trace of an Oliver influence here, though there is, as there was with Oliver, the all-pervasion of the blues. The cloudy tone introducing *Yes, I'm in the barrel*, and the choked statement following Dodds's fine solo on the same number, are but one aspect of this influence; the cutting, sharply tongued opening phrases of *Come back, sweet papa* are another which, like the street-band rips of *Muskrat ramble*, recall the New Orleans training ground. But there are developing sophistications which are very much Armstrong's own, and even at this stage the comprehensiveness of his jazz imagination can be glimpsed.

Georgia grind is a better introduction than the rather jokey *Gut bucket blues* to something which is crucial to any understanding of Armstrong's art, and that is the relationship between his singing and playing. It is not possible, and might be bootless if it were, to say which is the strongest shaping influence. He is doing essentially the same thing in each, though there are plenty of occasions when voice clearly apes horn, and vice versa; and it would be tiresome to enumerate them. The exuberant, generally light-hearted, and frequently clownish singing is not to be judged as betokening the 'popular' as opposed to the 'artistic' Armstrong (whatever may be said about his later career). It is true that the singing seldom encompasses dignity and pathos, as his instrumental solos not infrequently do, but there will be numerous examples from the mid-1920s of the genuine *musical* genius of his vocal technique. It might not be far from the truth to claim that he invented jazz singing. Certainly, few of the vocalists who are specially featured in this book developed their styles independently of his promptings.

It is not only in the imitative scat singing that a jazz impetus is strong. Amongst these early numbers, both *Georgia grind* and *Big fat ma and skinny pa* show Armstrong manipulating words to serve both meaning and rhythm, using dentals, labials and gutterals as he would use tonguing in a cornet solo, and enlivening the vowel colours with abrasive flutterings of the throat. The usual triviality of the lyrics should hardly affect admiration of this shrewdness. But, of course, the instrumental mastery is the thing most to be applauded; for this is not just the fruit of remarkable vocalistic *savoir faire*. Armstrong was the first widely influential virtuoso in jazz, and his greatest work remains a yardstick, in creative as much as in technical terms, for all subsequent jazz virtuosity.

Even though he had not yet reached the peak of his creativeness, the variety of expression in these first Hot Five sessions is remarkable. The marvellous leaping introduction to *Cornet chop suey* voices a journeying certainty, and even though his solos do not always quite achieve what he imagines, his melodic zest is stunning as phrases cascade in a dance of ecstasy. Upon the operatic opening of *You're next* the cornet takes on an ingratiating tone such as will increasingly emerge in the voice in later times. It is entirely personal.

There is a wild spirit of discovery in these sessions which the thumping piano and occasionally ill-advised trombone bellowings never really threaten. Even the vaudeville hokum of *Heebie jeebies* and *King of the Zulus* is redeemed by undeniable jazz artistry. More good examples of the singing technique may be heard in *Don't forget to mess around*, as in *Dropping shucks* and *I'm gonna gitcha*. Here the folding-in of verbal phrases, affected to a degree by the exaggeration of a comedy motive (listen to just the single phrase 'Dropping shucks on me'), may hold the key to his singular cross-beat instrumental phrasing that was to increase in facility as time went on. At this stage the ease of phrasing tends to be more in the singing, and there are certain cornet essays, such as the end of *Dropping shucks*, which are not smoothly negotiated. There is still a strong relatedness to the beat, and the hot anticipations of *Big fat ma and skinny pa* only differ from Oliver's style in their firmer tone. By the time of the November 1926 sessions there is greater freedom still, and in *Jazz lips, Skit-dat-de-dat, Big butter and egg man* and *Sunset Café stomp*, Armstrong ranges through passages of rich emotionality, rasping *alfresco* peremptoriness, and particularly in *Big butter and egg man*, where his singing provides a merciful foil to May Alix's piercing declamations, improvised variations which involve the almost complete reshaping of themes.

The first Hot Seven recordings were made in May 1927. They include some unsurpassable jazz, though certainly the atmosphere changes a little and, with the addition of tuba and drums, the free-flying effect of the quintet is a little diminished. But in sheer joyousness of ensemble sound they are outshone only by Morton's Red Hot Peppers' titles of the previous September and December (47). Again it is the Armstrong genius which gleams through all, urging the ecstatic drama of *Willie the weeper*'s collective improvising, and pronouncing Morton's *Wild man blues* with blistering upper-register phrases and deft rhythmic multiplications. *Alligator crawl* opens with a Dodds clarinet solo of reckless disclosure, then, after a brief collective in which the trombone is heard hollering like a lamed beast, Armstrong plays authoritatively over a beat split between tuba and banjo. The variety of resource within this one solo is superb, and here, as in the celebrated stoptime choruses in *Potato head blues* and *Weary blues*, there is an emotional logic of melody building, exploiting linear and harmonic relationships with a strength which makes allowances for the rapid ornamenting phrases which punctuate the development. The relaxed, mellifluous tone and lazy phrasing in *Melancholy blues* radically challenges the quondam notion that lagging behind the beat is always inimical to the mood of hot jazz, and one remarks how here, just as in the more impetuous statements, Armstrong is moulding tone and phrase simultaneously.

The Stompers track, *Chicago breakdown*, is a slightly curious intervention, with some excellent work from Armstrong and Evans, otherwise of interest because it introduces the piano style of Hines, soon to become Armstrong's most controversial and catalytic partner.

Of the remaining Hot Seven tracks, *Twelfth Street rag* is a skilfully humorous interlude guying the jerkier accents of rag-time with melodramatic lurchings. Only Dodds — and even he is trying to seem sweet and prissy — sounds remotely righteous; and it may be convenient to acknowledge here the fine contribution which the clarinettist makes to these and the earlier Hot Five sessions. All that is said of him under **38–40** can be applied here. Though a less considerable artist than the leader, he is never put to shame, and his solos on *Once in a while* and *Hotter than that* rank not only amongst his own best achievements but amongst the most expressive clarinet solos which jazz recordings can offer. Ory, too, is a quite indispensable subscriber. Although his solos do improve somewhat in confidence and his gyrations in *Ory's Creole trombone* are memorable, it is the canny footwork of his ensemble playing that is worthiest of praise. He supports gloriously at the outset of *Strutting with some barbecue*, develops a kind of background soliloquy in *Potato head blues*, lends to the double-time section of *I'm not rough*, a siren song of delightful alarm, and, at the end of *Hotter than that*, maintains the temperature perfectly until Armstrong rises in full song like a skylark from the long grass. Such good things are typical.

Keyhole blues, *S.O.L. blues*, *Gully low blues* and *That's when I'll come back to you* complete the Hot Seven canon. There is a sense of slight distractedness as *Keyhole blues* starts, but there are some skilful harmonizings between Armstrong and Dodds, and an intense piece of scat improvisation which re-emphasizes the importance for the cornettist — and, as we shall later see, for Hines — of double-time interpolations as a species of impetuous ornamentation. *S.O.L. blues* has one of Armstrong's most swinging entries thus far, which is saying much, but *Gully low blues*, which is the same blues with different lyrics to it, is faster and even more swinging. There are some glistering high notes towards the end, yet the melody-building is chiefly in the collectives. The cornet soars only briefly at the close of *That's when I'll come back to you*, and most time is given to comic singing.

September and December 1927 saw a return to quintet

instrumentation. There is admirable freedom between parts in *Put 'em down blues*, with a beautiful vocal, passionate and satirical at once, and not above a little gentle guying of the nascent craze for crooning. The collectives between the *allez-oup* and somersaults of *Ory's Creole trombone* have an irresistible dancing quality, and in the midst of them, Ory, when not clowning, flies free. Armstrong's singing in *The last time* carries the arhythmic adventure even further, especially in the second of its choruses. The trumpet solos here and in *Put 'em down blues*, *Strutting with some barbecue*, *Once in a while* and *Hotter than that* are full of developments which seem apt and startling at the same time. Lonnie Johnson's contribution to the December tracks is pleasant but strange. He conveys a street-piano sound into *I'm not rough* and something of an Italianate strain into the seriously determined *Savoy blues*, wherein the riffs ride high alongside Ory's perfectly controlled rising portamentos. Armstrong's closing chorus in this latter piece is one of those many that prove beyond doubt his right to be considered as a serious musical creator.

A session of 26 June 1928 — not included here — had to give too much space to the baby-doll singing of Lily Delk Christian to allow a promising combination of Armstrong, Hines and Noone to be heard fairly, and most of their capable jazz was uttered *sotto voce* in a suggestion of conspiracy. Then, on the next three days, an important step was taken with the recording appearance of the Savoy Ballroom Five, made up of Dickerson associates. Strong, who introduces *Fireworks*, has a clarinet style somewhere between and below those of Noone and Dodds, and he plays no more than capably throughout these sessions. The difference in conception from the earlier group is obvious, and it is due in considerable measure to the pioneering approach of Hines, though an increased lightness of attack in Armstrong's playing is also important. In the faster numbers there is a more restless rhythmic ardency, and in general there is a movement away from the relaxed and humour-laden spirit which New Orleans still donated to the 1927 Hot Five. Strong is seldom called on to exercise Doddsian ensemble aptitudes, and Robinson's role is closer — allowing for inferior skill on his part — to that of Higginbotham with Luis Russell (**50** and **51**).

Musical experiment is in the air, and one senses the eagerness of discovery which animates the exchanges between trumpet and piano, as exemplified by the complex aerial manoeuvres of *Skip the gutter* and the unsupported duet on *Weatherbird*. Armstrong's lightsome singing of *A Monday date* over the pianist's own superb swing makes for another kind of duet. Everything else in these

1928 performances seems incidental to the excitement of the encounter between Hines and Armstrong, and the delights of their solos and exchanges are far too numerous to be listed here.

Hines's style is many-faceted. Solos like that in *Don't jive me* show the toughness of its rhythmic basis, as do his many accompaniments to others' solos; but it also gives free rein to a lyricism untouched by any pianist recorded earlier. The writers who compared the 'essential simplicity' of Lil Hardin Armstrong favourably with the 'floweriness' [17] of Hines cannot really have listened to the latter. Even the most complicated cascades and spirals of notes have a cohesion of conception which distinguishes them from the more dexterous but also more utilitarian complexities later indulged by Art Tatum. The light filigree of his famous solos on *West End blues* and *Muggles* is as expressive of pathos, in its own manner, as is the trumpet's full-throated song; and in the first of these numbers it is complemented miraculously by steely dance steps. A similar concatenation of modes will be heard in the magnificent *It's tight like that*, and this ability to embrace a wide variety of rhythmic and melodic concepts within one solo sometimes leads Hines into hair-raising technicalities. When this happens, a sense of unease is felt, partly because one realizes that the promise of this kind of daring could never be fulfilled in this particular musical context. It might even be debated whether the auguries of the counter-rhythms, contrapuntal suspensions, and dramatic pauses heard in *Skip the gutter*, and in the piano solos, *A Monday date* and *57 varieties* (Philips (E) BBL7185) cut a few days after *Weatherbird*, were fulfilled in his own later music — other than by being absorbed with greater assurance into a broader dialect. Such elements seem to suggest that the pianist's greatest future strength was to be in his role as a solo artist. Yet he was a fine ensemble pianist, and a witty one, as his comments behind the vocal in *Save it, pretty mama* show; and his gifts as a leader of big bands were soon to be proved (**79, 129** and **147**).

Armstrong's own lyricism becomes more vivid all the time, and the lightness of tone and ease of attack seem unsurpassable by this stage — though his limit of melodic creation had manifestly not been reached. The famous clarion call heralding *West End blues* and echoed in *Two deuces* leads to some wonderful blues playing; a warm tribute to the composer, Oliver, as is the reshaping of the latter's *Jazzing babies* solo in *Muggles*. *Two deuces* contains a fragile muted improvisation over rolling Hines chords, a solo built in rhythmic spurts with all kinds of temporal variations and melodic progressions in them, conveying, for all its inner liveliness, a soliloquial mood. The *High society* quote in the *Squeeze me* improvisation emphasizes by contrast the simplicity of the rest of that solo. *Basin Street blues* is justly admired for the dreamy nostalgia so artfully created and inwardly challenged. Here, as in *West End blues*, the final chorus building carries the trumpet variations through mid-register to high serenely, though *Basin Street* ends in breathy low-note seriousness and lonely celeste chords.

Weatherbird has its theme glancingly ushered in by Armstrong as Hines supports obliquely; then the pianist takes over the melodic burden with improvised comments from the trumpet, and this role-changing becomes more complex as the piece proceeds. In his longest solo passage, Hines drives forward with little indulgence in the double-time disquisitions of which he is so fond, but in the final argument both he and Armstrong are up to all their most tantalizing tricks. Compared to the emotional warmth of Oliver's Creole Band in this piece, the result sounds almost like an intellectual exercise in counterpoint. There is much more to it than that, of course: how much more, only listening will tell.

Knocking a jug has, in its general pattern, a more impromptu feeling than anything else in this long and varied sequence. It is a series of solo blues choruses, with simple rhythmic accompaniment, played by a sextet of fine instrumentalists associated musically with Chicago and New York. The rougher vocal declamations of the blues are evoked lustily in the opening measures by Teagarden, and the statements of Lang, Cauldwell and Sullivan sound tentative by comparison, though Lang's solo should be respected for its auguries of a guitar style which others (notably Django Reinhardt in the following two decades) were to fulfil in greater technical freedom. That Armstrong was regarded as the real master of the occasion is shown by the greater length of a solo developed with typical dramatic sophistication and rhythmic ease. Trombone and tenor attend his passionately-built climax with quiet sustained chords.

By the stage reached here he was already a stylistic influence of immense force. In most of his later recordings he will be heard to dominate almost entirely, so it is very important to study his earlier work, from the little statement in Oliver's *Chimes blues* to the golden *clarino* flights with Hines and the Russell and Dickerson bands, in order to see that this marvel did not evolve in a vacuum but was itself shaped and prompted by co-operation with voices whose creativeness had their own validity. Armstrong's own achievement would have been different had it not been for the unpretentious forcing-bed of these short-lived recording bands.   E.T.

49 Earl Hines 1928
BYG (F) 529090, Milestone (A) MLP2012

Deppe's Serenaders: Leon Smothers (tpt); Frank Brassfield (tbn); Vance Dixon (clt, alt); Harry Jackson (alt); Charles Stoner (ten); Emmett Jordan (vln); Hines (p); . . . Dison (bj); Joe Watts (tu); Harry Williams (d). Richmond, Indiana, 3 October 1923.
Congaine

Lois Deppe (vcl); Hines (p). Richmond, Indiana, 6 November 1923.
Isabel · Dear old Southland · Sometimes I feel like a motherless child · For the last time call me sweetheart

Hines (p). Long Island, New York 8 December 1928.
Blues in thirds · Off time blues · Chicago high life · A Monday date · Stowaway · Chimes in blues · Panther rag · Just too soon

Jazz *aficionados* have frequently displayed a puritanical distrust of technical curiosity as a motive for music-making. They prefer to think of a soloist communicating some kind of emotional message or mood. Hines is a performer who sometimes has fallen a victim to attitudes of that sort, suspected of being 'flashy' and therefore not to be taken seriously. It would be foolish, of course, to deny the emotional power of great blues players such as Dodds or Bechet (or of rhapsodists like Coleman Hawkins); when Hines settles down to playing a blues — *Off time blues, Blues in thirds, Chimes in blues* — his intention is not to embark upon any sort of soulful colloquy but to construct a musical abstract; in one of these instances his starting-point was a musical interval, in another a homely programmatic device. What the listener delights in is the contest that ensues, how the pianist solves his aesthetic problems: the daring melodic flights, the way the rhythm is shattered and reassembled.

Hines's first professional job was as accompanist to the singer (and occasional C-melody saxophonist) Lois Deppe. He was nineteen when, in 1923, he made his first recordings, and already the style was there in embryo, beginning to escape the rigidities of ragtime, the harmonic dullness of most contemporary popular music. Deppe's vocal recordings are worth listening to nowadays only because of Hines's presence: the pianist takes sixteen-bar solos in *Dear old Southland, For the last time call me sweetheart* (this song is as maudlin as its title suggests) and Luckey Roberts's *Isabel*. Hines composed *Congaine* and takes a brisk thirty-two-bar solo in what otherwise is a tedious performance, with the recording balance giving too much prominence to the banjoist. Regarding the latter, discographers plump for a half-anonymous Dison, but it is a pleasant reminder that jazz scholarship does not yet have everything cut and dried that a contemporary photograph of this band [18] shows somebody named Silas Brown. It was in this ensemble, Hines claimed, that the difficulty of making himself heard led him to playing the melody line in octaves, instead of hitting the keys harder, as a less astute pianist would have done.

He already had recorded with Armstrong and Noone when he set out for New York to record for QRS, a company that normally specialized in making player-piano rolls. Legend has it that Hines entered the studio with only the sketchiest notion of what he would do, but he has always been one of the most spontaneous improvisors, taking different solos every time he plays a theme. (An extreme instance of this occurred when he returned to this particular batch of material over forty years later: see **220**.) Understandably, *A Monday date* is here treated with more bravura than when he recorded it with Noone (**41**) or Armstrong (**48**). On this and elsewhere, notably *Chicago high life* and *Panther rag*, he makes passing use of chording and syncopations more customarily associated with Harlem 'stride' pianists: perhaps he was determined to show that he could outdo the local competition. *Panther rag* has a chord sequence taken from *Tiger rag*, a harmonic identity shared with *57 varieties*, which Hines recorded in Chicago four days later (Philips (E) BBL7185). This piece has affinities with novelty piano, a descendant of ragtime that is dismissed far too cursorily. That link is even more pronounced in *Stowaway*, which also juggles extensively with the metre. *Blues in thirds*, also known as *Caution blues*, is the simplest, and perhaps the most memorable, of the three blues.

C.F.

50 Luis Russell
CBS (Eu) S88039 (2 LPs), Columbia (A) KG32338 (2 LPs)

Luis Russell's Heebie Jeebie Stompers: Bob Shoffner (tpt); Preston Jackson (tbn); Albert Nicholas or Darnell Howard (clt, alt); Barney Bigard (ten); Russell (p); Johnny St Cyr (bj). Chicago, 17 November 1926.
Plantation joys · Please don't turn me down · Sweet Mumtaz · Dolly mine

Luis Russell's Burning Eight: Louis Metcalfe (tpt); J. C. Higginbotham (tbn); Charlie Holmes (clt, alt); Teddy Hill (ten); Russell (p); Will Johnson (g); Bass Moore (tu); Paul Barbarin (d); Fats Pichon (vcl[1]). New York City, 15 January 1929.
Savoy shout · Call of the freaks · It's tight like that[1]

The Jungletown Stompers: possibly as for 15 January 1929, but this may be a Clarence Williams date with Metcalfe (tpt); Henry Hicks (tbn); Holmes (clt, alt); Charlie Grimes (ten); Williams (p, cls); Elmer Snowden (bj); Bass Edwards (tu); unidentified d. New York City, 15 April 1929.
African jungle · Slow as molasses

Luis Russell and His Orchestra: Bill Coleman, Henry Allen (tpt); Higginbotham (tbn, vcl[2]); Nicholas (clt, alt); Holmes (sop, alt); Hill (ten); Russell (p); Johnson (bj, g); Pops Foster (bs); Barbarin (d). New York City, 6 September 1929.
Feeling the spirit[2] · *Jersey lightning*

Lou and His Gingersnaps: same personnel and location, 13 September 1929.
Broadway rhythm · *The way he loves is just too bad*

Luis Russell and His Orchestra: Otis Johnson (tpt) replaces Coleman. New York City, 17 December 1929.
Doctor blues

Same personnel and location, 24 January 1930.
Saratoga shout · *Song of the Swanee*

J. C. Higginbotham and His Six Hicks: Allen (tpt); Higginbotham (tbn); Holmes (alt); Russell (p); Johnson (g); Foster (bs); Barbarin (d). New York City, 5 February 1930.
Give me your telephone number · *Higginbotham blues*

Luis Russell and His Orchestra: Allen (tpt); Higginbotham (tbn); Nicholas (clt, alt); Holmes (sop, alt); Hill (ten); Russell (p); Johnson (g); Foster (bs); Barbarin (d); Jesse Cryor (vcl[3]); Andy Razaf (vcl[4]). New York City, 29 May 1930.
Louisiana swing (2 takes) · *Poor li'l me*[3] · *On revival day*[4]

Greely Walton (ten) replaces Hill; Cryor, Razaf absent. New York City, 5 September 1930.
Mugging lightly · *Panama* · *High tension*

Luis Russell and His Orchestra: Gus Aiken, Leonard Davies (tpt); Rex Stewart (cnt); Jimmy Archey, Nat Storey (tbn); Holmes, Henry Jones (alt); Walton, Bingie Madison (ten); Russell (p); Lee Blair (g); Foster (bs); Barbarin (d); Sonny Woods (vcl[5]); the Palmer Brothers (vcl[6]). New York City, 8 August 1934.
Darktown strutters' ball[5] · *My blue Heaven*[5] · *The ghost of the freaks*[6] · *Hokus pokus* · *Moods (Primitive)* · *Old man river*[5]

51 Henry 'Red' Allen Vol. 1
RCA (F) FXM1 7060, *RCA (A) LPV556

Henry Allen and His New York Orchestra: Allen (tpt); Higginbotham (tbn); Holmes (clt, sop, alt); Nicholas (clt, alt); Russell (p, cls); Johnson (g); Foster (bs); Barbarin (d, vib). New York City, 16 July 1929.
It should be you (3 takes) · *Biff'ly blues* (2 takes)

Hill (ten) added. New York City, 17 July 1929.
Feeling drowsy (3 takes) · *Swing out* (3 takes)

Allen (tpt); Pichon (p, vcl); Teddy Bunn (g). New York City, 19 September 1929.
Dogging that thing · *Yo-yo*

Henry Allen and His New York Orchestra: personnel as for 16 July 1929; the Four Wanderers (vcl[7]); Victoria Spivey (vcl[8]). New York City, 24 September 1929.
Make a country bird fly wild[7] · *Funny feathers blues[8]*

The varied items on **50** span eight years but include, however, two gaps. A juxtaposition of the first and last sessions represented — the Heebie Jeebie Stompers, whose style is close to that of King Oliver's contemporaneous Dixie Syncopators, and the Russell 1934 orchestra playing swing arrangements with an ease and momentum which equals, when it does not exceed, the vivacity of rival bands — allows us to glimpse the kind of development encompassed here.

Plantation joys, Please don't turn me down and *Sweet Mumtaz* mark what almost was the end of Russell's association with Chicago. They have the form and spirit of Oliver's recordings of the period for the uncomplicated reason that the pianist was playing and arranging for Oliver at that time and, apparently without permission, was using Oliver sidemen. Two comparisons suffice to indicate aims and influences. The ensemble style of *Please don't turn me down* has close similarity to that of Oliver's *Snag it No. 2* recorded two months earlier with most of the musicians involved here (Collectors' Classics (D) CC42). The version of *Sweet Mumtaz* by Russell's Hot Six (**42**) is by a group which differs only in having George Mitchell and Kid Ory in seats later occupied by Shoffner and Jackson. Its springy tempo and sense of enjoyment contrast rather sharply with the present account, cut only eight months later and perhaps affected by experience of Oliver's seriousness of purpose. (Tommy Benford, consulted in Britain during 1983, claimed trumpeting in *Dolly mine* for Dolly Jones. The style is close to that heard on Wynn's *When* and *That Creole band* (**42**), but not sufficiently distinct from the other three 1926 Russells to confirm Benford's avowal with certainty.)

Savoy shout announces further change. Here, compared to the 1926 session, is vivid strength and certainty. The firmly-voiced introduction owes much to Higginbotham, who also ushers in the famous *Call of the freaks*. There are fine solos in these two numbers, particularly from Metcalfe, Holmes and the lithe, powerful trombonist. A wry nostalgia seems to colour *It's tight like that*, the ensemble rather too readily accepting the retarding heaviness of the plodding tuba. Something of that mood extends into the April 1929 *African jungle* and *Slow as molasses* despite good solos including some growled remarks in the latter from Metcalfe, who earlier had exhibited the style with Ellington (hear *Take it easy* on **90**).

With Metcalfe replaced by Coleman and Allen, and Foster's

string bass ousting the tuba, *Feeling the spirit, Jersey lightning, Broadway rhythm* and *The way he loves is just too bad* gain both relaxation and impetus. Higginbotham dominates the ensembles far less and there is great emphasis on extended section scoring, with some peculiarly zestful saxophone passages. Coleman, with solos on *Feeling the spirit* and *Broadway rhythm*, shows no real portent of the skilful improvising of his 1930s European sojourn (**102, 103**, etc.). Here he is far outshone by Allen, who to a melodic dialect and rhythmic elasticity appropriated from Armstrong adds an impetuous tone and peppery edge of impishness distinctly his own.

The sessions under Allen's name on **51** were recorded in the same year. *It should be you, Biff'ly blues, Feeling drowsy* and *Swing out* were produced about the time Allen joined Russell upon Metcalfe's departure. In use is a typically Russellian line-up, freely co-operating in combinations of rudimentary arrangement and exuberant improvising which hark back in some ways to the aims of Armstrong's small groups of 1925–28 (**48**). The availability of several takes of each piece makes a study of improvising techniques possible. It became obvious from alternative versions of numbers by the NORKs (**43**), Oliver's Creole Band (**44**) and others that extemporized solo variation does not, in a recording studio, necessarily mean total reshaping of phrases from take to take. The general drift of solos remains much the same in most cases, having presumably been worked out in rehearsal. A comparison of solos in these July 1929 performances shows that while the melodic structure of the solos by Higginbotham, Holmes and Nicholas changes little, there is a fair degree of variation of incidental emphases, and always a strong sense of spontaneous delivery.

Study of this kind should take into account both the care with which preparation for recording sessions was made, the importance of hitting the right standard of performance for eventual issue, and the concentration demanded by the brief duration of 78 rpm discs. It must be added that Allen's solos show considerably more development, and often increase in emotional commitment also. This sort of progression is particularly noticeable in *Swing out*, a number which also typifies the tension, even in a loosely marshalled group like this, between the twin urges to improvise and to enhance ensemble impetus by the use of riffs. Such tension was already influencing the development away from small co-operative bands towards larger sectional ensembles needing disciplined orchestration and a consequent restriction of solo playing.

In *Dogging that thing* and *Yo-yo*, Allen demonstrates his

aptitude as an accompanist in abetment of the farcical Pichon, and does so wittily with help from the reliable Bunn. On *Make a country bird fly wild*, with the vocal group mimicking band sounds, and *Funny feathers blues*, with Victoria Spivey's assured singing, the same band as that assembled in July is able to stretch itself in a spirited succession of solos, Allen being particularly expressive on the blues. In November of that year the same basic ensemble, with Morton on Russell's stool, recorded, as the Red Hot Peppers, three fine pieces, one of which may be heard, in two takes, on **47b**.

Higginbotham's imposing tones are prominent, on **50**, in *Give me your telephone number* and *Higginbotham blues*, the latter containing much sonorous bowing from Foster and a splendid stop-time chorus from the trombonist. The approach in these shows a swing of the pendulum back towards small band feeling. With *Louisiana swing* and the other performances of May and September 1930 through to *High tension*, there is a move to more ambitious scoring which takes advantage of the band's instrumental resources. There are interesting exercises in sectional counterpoint and the kind of extended unison variations which recall Benny Carter's work. *Louisiana swing, Mugging lightly, Panama* and *High tension* are full of essays of this kind which allow for a number of capable solos.

But with the leap forward to August 1934, and a substantially altered personnel, another world is entered. From the very first bars of *Darktown strutters' ball*, a completely new feeling appears; and the change is felt rather than heard. A physical, dance-like feeling informs the movement of ensemble parts, and it differs markedly both from the nervous frenzies of some of the 1930 arrangements and from the politeness of the mid-1931 efforts. Relaxation is not always maintained, and a certain jerkiness returns in *Hokus pokus*; where the new ease *is* retained it can degenerate into mere suavity, as in passages of *My blue Heaven*. The rapid tempos of *Old man river* and *Moods* prompt some disciplined but swinging work from the band. There are attractively skilful statements from Stewart, the best of the new soloists, and *Old man river* rides out passionately in simple riffs which conceal the tune and its mood entirely.

Stewart soon quit to join Ellington, and the fortunes of the Russell orchestra were shortly to be bound up with Louis Armstrong's stellar career. Like Armstrong, the group had left the co-operative genius of the small bands behind; they were helping to introduce the period of big band swing.   E.T.

Louis Armstrong/Jack Purvis

52 Satchmo Style
Parlophone (E) PMC7045, Swaggie (Au) S1267

Louis Armstrong and His Savoy Ballroom Five (*sic*): Armstrong (tpt, vcl); J. C. Higginbotham (tbn); Albert Nicholas, Charlie Holmes (clt, alt); Teddy Hill (ten); Luis Russell (p); Lonnie Johnson (g); Eddie Condon (bj); Pops Foster (bs); Paul Barbarin (d). New York City, 5 March 1929.
I can't give you anything but love

Louis Armstrong and His Orchestra: Henry Allen, Otis Johnson (tpt) added; Will Johnson (bj, g) replaces Condon, Lonnie Johnson. New York City, 10 December 1929.
I ain't got nobody · Dallas blues

Hoagy Carmichael (vcl[1]) added. New York City, 13 December 1929.
St Louis blues · Rocking chair[1]

3 unidentified vln, unidentified d added; Barbarin switches to vib. New York City, 24 January 1930.
Song of the islands

William Blue (clt) replaces Nicholas; vlns absent; Barbarin returns to d. New York City, 1 February 1930.
Bessie couldn't help it · Blue, turning grey, over you

Jack Purvis and His Orchestra: Purvis (tpt); John Scott Trotter (p); Gene Kintzle (g); Paul Weston (bs); Joe Dale (d). New York City, 17 December 1929.
Copying Louis · Mental strain at dawn

Purvis (tpt); Higginbotham (tbn, vcl[2]); Castor McCord (ten); Adrian Rollini (bs sx); Frank Froeba (p); Johnson (g); Charles Kegley (d). New York City, 4 April 1930.
Dismal Dan · Poor Richard · Down Georgia way

Greely Walton (ten) replaces McCord. New York City, 1 May 1930.
What's the use of crying, baby? · When you're feeling blue · Be bo bo[2]

By now, so far as Armstrong's vein of jazz was concerned, there was no longer any question of a collective method for improvisation. These performances show him as an unequivocally featured star soloist, accompanied by two editions of Luis Russell's band. Following the innovations of the later recordings considered under **48**, such a development was inevitable and this was to be his role for many years. Often the bands were poor, but Russell's ensemble was a perceptive (or lucky) choice, for its members shared Armstrong's musical background and they provided a matching vitality.

The best collaboration here is *St Louis blues*, whose uncompromising and abrasive splendour owes nearly as much to Allen and particularly Higginbotham as to Armstrong. (The climax was interestingly adapted by the Casa Loma Band for their 1934 *Stomping around*.) *Song of the islands*, a venture into Tin Pan

Alley exoticism, makes a strange contrast except that like all the other tracks it ends with a magnificent trumpet solo. Armstrong's mastery in these improvisations is complete and we can only lament their brevity, especially as the perfect formal control they usually display suggests that he was able to construct equally satisfying larger wholes. The variety of his ideas is remarkable, and even moments of seeming virtuoso extravagance are reconciled to the requirements of balanced overall design. The duet with Carmichael on *Rocking chair* was the first of several that Armstrong recorded on this piece, usually with Jack Teagarden; a 1947 version can be heard on **241**. *Mahogany Hall stomp*, the session-mate of *I can't give you anything but love*, appears on **68a** and **113**.

-This LP was obviously included chiefly for the Armstrong performances and, although Higginbotham provides a connecting link, Purvis's recordings are not strictly relevant at this point, and could not easily fit into any other category. But although they are a curiosity they are a valuable one. The title *Copying Louis* is partly misleading and perhaps deliberately so. Armstrong's influence is plain yet the detail is different and often surprising in its aggressive elegance, the degree of rhythmic freedom being rare for the period. Purvis had abundant agility and power, and his stinging attack galvanizes the ensembles of, for example, *Dismal Dan* and *Be bo bo*. All the themes are his, and he possessed considerable flair both for composition and arrangement, the ensembles putting the unusual combination of tenor and bass saxophones without any upper reed voices to quite imaginative use. In solo, the fervour of McCord and Higginbotham is an apt foil to Purvis's incisiveness, and there are good exchanges between McCord and Rollini in the mock funereal *Poor Richard*. Outstanding, however, is Froeba, some of whose best recorded work is found here. He was the finest of the Hines-influenced pianists, though scarcely recognized as such, and his solos on *Dismal Dan*, *What's the use of crying, baby?* and especially *Poor Richard* are striking. Purvis's memoirs, had they been written, would have made sensational reading, and one can only regret that his picaresque life took him so much away from jazz [19].   M.H.

The 'Second Line': the Chicagoans

Inspired partly by Oliver's Creole Band and Armstrong, partly by the New Orleans Rhythm Kings and Beiderbecke, the Chicagoans still found a route of their own, and their music pointed to many later developments.

53 Muggsy Spanier 1924–28
Fountain (E) FJ108, *Riverside (A) RLP12-107

Bucktown Five: Spanier (cnt); Guy Carey (tbn); Volly DeFaut (clt); Mel Stitzel (p); Marvin Saxbe (bj, g, cym). Richmond, Indiana, 25 February 1924.
Steady roll blues · Mobile blues · Really a pain · Chicago blues · Hot mittens · Buddy's habit · Someday, sweetheart

Stomp Six: Joe Gish (tu), Ben Pollack (d) added; Saxbe absent. Chicago, c. July 1925.
Why can't it be poor little me? · Everybody loves my baby

Charles Pierce and His Orchestra: Spanier, Dick Fiege (cnt); Frank Teschemacher (clt, alt); Pierce (alt); Ralph Rudder (ten); Dan Lipscomb (p); Stuart Branch (bj); Johnny Mueller (bs); Paul Kettler (d). Chicago, c. February 1928.
Bull frog blues · China boy

Charlie Altier (cnt), Maurie Bercov (clt, alt) replace Spanier, Fiege, Teschemacher. Chicago, c. March 1928.
Jazz me blues · Sister Kate

Spanier (cnt), Teschemacher (clt, alt) replace Altier, Bercov; Jack Reid (tbn) added. Chicago, c. April 1928.
Jazz me blues · Sister Kate · Nobody's sweetheart

Jungle Kings: Spanier (cnt); Teschemacher (clt); Mezz Mezzrow (clt, ten); Joe Sullivan (p); Eddie Condon (bj); Jim Lannigan (tu); Gene Krupa (d); Red McKenzie (vcl). Chicago, 5 April 1928.
Friars Point shuffle · Darktown strutters' ball

The Wolverines (**61**) were the practical heirs of the New Orleans Rhythm Kings, but their style was not so clearly a development beyond the NORKs' musical manner as was that gradually adopted by the groups associated with Spanier. To be sure, the Bucktown Five is very much in the dixieland mould. Spanier, a devotee of Oliver and Armstrong as his playing in the first tracks readily shows, seems to be girding against the style's confinement. There are some springing, Armstrong-like runs in *Hot mittens*, and his muted solo on *Buddy's habit* welds together the voices of the two great tutelary spirits of the Creole Jazz Band. So what Spanier had imbibed from that quarter is clear enough and assures these performances of serious attention; but it has to be said that his desired flights are hampered by his companions. Carey only occasionally manages to play appropriate jazz phrases, and DeFaut, on this showing, is a rather functional clarinettist.

Almost the same personnel forms the Stomp Six. A slight change of mood emerges, however, and the ensemble in *Why can't it be poor little me?* drives forward by dint of more purposeful arrangement in a fashion prophetic of astringencies yet to come. The continuing presence of Carey raps up the dixieland ghost again, but the final chorus of *Everybody loves my baby* gains a new toughness, even using the charleston rhythm effectively to urge matters towards the slithering double ending. In these 1925 recordings, Spanier has grasped an authority affecting the cohesion of the group he leads.

The most immediately striking aspect of the first two Pierce tracks is the acid voice of Teschemacher, whose reedy, rasping smears and frequent staccato doublings of the beat lend a new flavour to the proceedings. His playing on *Bull frog blues* is a good instance both of those things which link him to Dodds and Noone, and those which make his approach singular. In *China Boy* one hears his ability to search obliquely into the harmonic structure of a theme taken at fast tempo, and also his edgy tuning and fiercely concentrated tone, a taste for which may have to be acquired after the mellower sounds of Leon Roppolo have become favoured fare.

The second *Jazz me blues* has a different spirit from the first. Progress is held up somewhat by lacklustre saxophone scoring, yet Spanier and Teschemacher are discovering a fruitful rapport, and the famous Chicagoan ensemble yell heralds the final chorus. A lyrical muted cornet solo graces *Sister Kate*, around whose final ensemble are stitched both lazy and savagely impetuous clarinet threads.

There is a more balanced concentration of talents in the Jungle Kings. During *Friars Point shuffle*, Spanier fashions a solo of deep indebtedness to Armstrong; and there is Sullivan, the first really acceptable pianist in this collection, equally indebted to Hines and consequently introducing a flexibility of which Stitzel and Lipscomb were hardly capable. Lannigan's tuba occasionally militates against this elasticity.

Survivors of this period were to revert to music closer to dixieland, and some of the conventions of 'Chicago style' found their way into big swing bands in the 1930s. But the seven tracks exhibiting the interwoven sounds of Spanier and Teschemacher show how their partnership helped to ignite one of the first real movements forward from the post-New Orleans classic form.   E.T.

54 That Toddling Town: Chicago 1926–28
Parlophone (E) PMC7072, *Columbia (A) 632

Merritt Brunies and His Friars Inn Orchestra: Merritt Brunies (cnt);
Harry Brunies (tbn); Volly DeFaut (clt); unidentified alt, ten/bar; Marty
Freeman (p); unidentified bj; Jules Cassard (tu); Bill Paley (d). Chicago,
2 March 1926.
Up jumped the Devil

Sol Wagner and His Orchestra: Nate Bold (cnt); Hub Henning (tbn);
Jimmy Lord (clt, alt); Milton Neal (clt, ten); Harry Podolsky (vln);
Wagner (p); Sid Pritikan (bj); Frank Wasika (tu); Harry Weinstein (d);
the Brown Sisters and Green (vcl). Chicago, 13 May 1927.
You don't like it, not much

Red McKenzie and His Music Box: Joe Venuti (vln); Eddie Lang (g);
McKenzie (cap, vcl). New York City, 21 June 1927.
There'll be some changes made · My syncopated melody man

McKenzie and Condon's Chicagoans: Jimmy McPartland (cnt); Frank
Teschemacher (clt); Bud Freeman (ten); Joe Sullivan (p); Eddie Condon
(bj); Jim Lannigan (tu); Gene Krupa (d). Chicago, 9 December 1927.
Sugar · China boy

Mezz Mezzrow (cym) added. Chicago, 16 December 1927.
Nobody's sweetheart · Liza

Miff Mole and His Little Molers · Red Nichols (tpt); Mole (tbn);
Teschemacher (clt); Sullivan (p); Condon (bj); Krupa (d). New York City,
6 July 1928.
One step to Heaven · Shimme-sha-wabble

Eddie Condon's Quartet: Teschemacher (clt, alt); Sullivan (p); Condon
(bj, vcl); Krupa (d). New York City, 28 July 1928.
Oh, baby · Indiana

Eddie Condon and His Footwarmers: McPartland (cnt); Jack Teagarden
(tbn, vcl[1]); Mezzrow (clt); Sullivan (p); Condon (bj, vcl[2]); Art Miller (bs);
Johnny Powell (d). New York City, 30 October 1928.
I'm sorry I made you cry[2] *· Making friends*[1]

Bud Freeman and His Orchestra: Johnny Mendel (tpt); Floyd O'Brien
(tbn); Bud Jacobson (clt); Freeman (ten); Dave North (p); Herman Foster
(bj); Johnny Mueller (bs); Krupa (d); McKenzie (vcl[3]). Chicago,
3 December 1928.
Crazeology · Can't help loving that man[3]

55 Chicago Jazz Vol. 1
Classic Jazz Masters (Sd) CJM31, *Decca (A) DL9231

Chicago Rhythm Kings: Muggsy Spanier (cnt); Teschemacher (clt);
Mezzrow (ten); Sullivan (p); Condon (bj); Lannigan (tu, bs); Krupa (d);
McKenzie (vcl[4]). Chicago, 8 April 1928.
There'll be some changes made[4] *· I've found a new baby*

Frank Teschemacher's Chicagoans: Teschemacher (clt, alt); Rod Cless(alt);
Mezzrow (tcn); Sullivan (p); Condon (bj); Krupa (d). Chicago,|28 April 1928.
Jazz me blues

Chicago Rhythm Kings: Spanier (cnt); Lannigan (tu) added; Condon (vcl); Cless absent. Chicago, 2 May 1928.
Baby, won't you please come home?

Wingy Mannone and His Club Royale Orchestra: Mannone (cnt, vcl); Wade Foster (clt); Freeman (ten); Jack Gardner (p); Krupa (d). Chicago, 4 September 1928.
Downright disgusted · Fare thee well

Teschemacher (clt), George Snurpus (ten), Art Hodes (p), Augie Schellange (d) replace Foster, Freeman, Gardner, Krupa; Ray Biondi (g) added. Chicago, 17 December 1928.
Trying to stop my crying · Isn't there a little love?

Danny Altier and His Orchestra: Spanier (cnt); Johnny Carsella (tbn); Maurie Bercov (clt); Altier (alt); Phil Robinson (ten); Jess Stacy (p); Biondi (g); Pat Pattison (tu, bs); George Wettling (d); Frank Sylvano (vcl[5]). Chicago, 22 October 1928.
I'm sorry, Sally[5] · My gal Sal

Elmer Schoebel and His Friars Society Orchestra: Dick Fiege (cnt); Jack Reid (tbn); Teschemacher (clt); Floyd Townes (ten); Schoebel (p); Charlie Barger (bj); John Kuhn (tu); Wettling (d). Chicago, 18 October 1929.
Copenhagen · Prince of wails

Cellar Boys: Mannone (cnt); Teschemacher (clt); Freeman (ten); Charles Melrose (acc); Frank Melrose (p); Wettling (d). Chicago, 24 January 1930.
Wailing blues (2 takes) · *Barrelhouse stomp* (3 takes)

Studied critical neglect notwithstanding[20], the important jazz here is that by McKenzie and Condon's Chicagoans, the Chicago Rhythm Kings, Teschemacher's Chicagoans and the group led by Mole. And with Teagarden's, Nichols's and Freeman's main recorded work elsewhere, the most significant musician taking part, as on **53**, is Teschemacher. Dying young, he still achieved a highly individual mode of expression, an uncompromising musical personality being apparent on even his first sessions — those of December 1927, when he was twenty-one years old. Though an excellent saxophonist, his most characteristic playing was done with the clarinet, on which he spun angular, spare, yet melodically dense lines, explosive in effect and sometimes of almost obsessive intensity. Nothing puts Teschemacher off — not Krupa's clumsy and over-recorded drumming on the Condon Quartet date, nor even Melrose's accordion playing with the Cellar Boys; and he easily outclasses many of those with whom he recorded, such as Mannone, even when they appropriate an undue amount of space.

He had problems over intonation and, as with the young Armstrong, the daring of his ideas was such that a sprinkling of wrong notes was inevitable. But his rhythmic sense was sure, most noticeably in jagged quaver patterns with notes placed unexpectedly off the beat. The harsh, staccato emphasis of Teschemacher's phrases is as marked in ensembles, where he trod a strikingly independent path, as in solos and is underlined by a curiously deliberate use of blue notes. Indeed, he played a version of the blues all his own, perhaps best exemplified by Charles Pierce's *Bull frog blues* and the Jungle Kings' *Friars Point shuffle* on **53**. The amount of direct quotation from Beiderbecke and especially from Noone in his work has been much exaggerated. In fact, the alternative takes from the Cellar Boys' date — Teschemacher's last — furnish proof of how much real improvising he did. These slightly later recordings, notably the Schoebel session, illustrate the clarinettist's continuing and rapid development, particularly the unfamiliar yet unmistakeable logic with which his ideas connect.

An imaginative effort may now be required, however, to grasp why the 'official' Chicagoan recordings were once considered so controversial, although their departures from New Orleans othodoxy should be obvious. Teschemacher aside, they may even sound tentative in comparison with, say, the wholly achieved modernism of Nichols's 1926 *Washboard blues/That's no bargain* date (**70**). Yet they had an influence even on such established figures, as Nichols's *Nobody's sweetheart* (**70**) shows, with its shuffle rhythm, explosions and Teschemacher-like solo by Fud Livingston. The Mole session was, indeed, a remarkable meeting of minds, not least for Teschemacher's response to the presence of an especially agile trombonist and Nichols's and Mole's reactions to the driving Chicago rhythm section. This music has a hard yet imaginative brilliance that is particularly memorable.

Much less can be claimed for the remaining items, although Freeman's determinedly anti-rhapsodic contributions to the pair of tracks under his name should be heard. So should DeFaut's impressive fluency on the Brunies piece, anticipating aspects of Don Murray's work for Beiderbecke (**63**). McPartland does better in company with Teagarden, as in *Whoopee stomp* and *Dirty dog* on **73**. It might be noted that the absolutely straight Podolsky violin solos in Wagner's *You don't like it* serve to highlight Venuti's specifically jazz virtues on the two succeeding McKenzie tracks. As to Mezzrow's bathetic interventions, readers can only be directed to the large and entertaining literature that has accumulated in praise of his melodic indigence, rhythmic stiffness, execrable tone and myriad wrong notes.   M.H.

Billy Banks

56 The Rhythmakers
VJM (E) VLP53, *IAJRC (A) 4

Billy Banks and His Orchestra: Henry Allen (tpt, vcl[1]); Pee Wee Russell (clt, ten); Joe Sullivan (p); Eddie Condon (bj); Jack Bland (g); Al Morgan (bs); Gene Krupa (d); Banks (vcl[2]). New York City, 18 April 1932.
Bugle call rag · *Oh, Peter*[1] (take 1) · *Margie*[2]
Zutty Singleton (d) replaces Krupa. New York City, 23 May 1932.
Oh, Peter[2] (take 3) · *Spider crawl*[2] · *Who's sorry now?*[2] · *Take it slow and easy*[2] · *Baldheaded mama*[2]
The Rhythmakers: Allen (tpt); Jimmy Lord (clt); Russell (ten); Fats Waller (p); Condon (bj); Bland (g); Pops Foster (bs); Singleton (d); Banks (vcl[2]). New York City, 26 July 1932.
I would do anything for you[2] (2 takes) · *Mean old bed bug blues*[2] (2 takes) · *Yellow dog blues*[2] (2 takes) · *Yes suh!*[2]
Jack Bland and His Rhythmakers: Allen (tpt, vcl[1]); Tommy Dorsey (tbn); Russell (clt); Happy Cauldwell (ten); Frank Froeba (p); Condon (bj); Bland (g); Foster (bs); Singleton (d); Chick Bullock (vcl[3]). New York City, 8 October 1932.
Who stole the lock?[1] · *Shine on your shoes*[3] · *It's gonna be you*[3] · *Someone stole Gabriel's horn*[1]

When these recordings were originally issued on 78 rpm discs the labels credited them to such varied ensembles as Condon's Chicago Rhythm Kings and even the Harlem Hot Shots, as well as to Banks. That confusion may have arisen from commercial finagling (a cluster of small regional labels was involved), yet there was a similar ambiguity about the style of the music itself. Apart from Waller, Cauldwell and Banks, all the black performers hailed from New Orleans, even if by that time most of them were working in big bands — Allen and Foster with Luis Russell, Morgan with Cab Calloway, etc. A sizeable number of the white players — Sullivan, Lord, Bland, Condon, Krupa — were hardcore Chicagoans who had only recently moved to New York. The man in the middle, Russell, has often been linked with the Chicagoans, yet he was never a participant in their early activities. But the clarinet had a dominant role in Chicago-style ensembles, and after Teschemacher's death in March 1932, with Goodman obviously nursing other ambitions, it was to be Russell who gradually took over as a key figure in the Chicagoans' aesthetic strategy.

What impresses about the first eight tracks is the duetting — jousting might be a more accurate term — between Russell's clarinet and Allen's trumpet, both improvising but within neither the disciplines of New Orleans jazz nor the more free-and-easy routines of the Chicagoans. This partnership worked intuitively just as, a quarter of a century later, Ted Curson and Eric Dolphy achieved something comparable in Mingus's *Folk forms No. 1* (Candid (J) SMJ6178). If anything, it is Russell who seems disposed to take the lead, rather as 'Yellow' Nunez, one of his earliest models, did in the Louisiana Five (**13**). Russell is heard on tenor saxophone in isolated passages (*Margie, Who's sorry now?*), his phrasing slightly less agile, his sound decidedly blander. On the 26 July date, however, he played that instrument in a front line including Lord, keeping a low profile and taking no solos except obbligatos. These performances are slightly less successful, despite the authoritative presence of Waller who, rather like Jack Teagarden, had the gift for making his most familiar phrases come up sounding fresh. On the earlier sessions, the five-man rhythm section is dominated by Morgan's slapped bass, with Condon's banjo and Bland's guitar spasmodically contributing the so-called 'Chicago shuffle'; it turns up behind Banks's singing of *Baldheaded mama*, for instance, and again, much more monotonously, in *Yes, suh!*

Banks was a young nightclub singer whose ingratiating brightness was seldom dimmed, even when the lyrics indicated otherwise — for example, 'Oh, the graveyard sure is a mean ol' place (repeat)/They throw you down the hole and dump dirt in your face'. The bizarre exchanges of *Mean old bed bug blues* are explained by Banks's ability to double as a female impersonator. Bullock, a session singer of the period, performs breezily on a couple of tracks, meeting the banal lyrics head-on. Froeba's solos turn out to be more interesting than Sullivan's: less indebted to Waller, aiming — no doubt under the influence of Hines — at attractive, if sometimes too contrived, rhythmic variations. Cauldwell had obviously been listening to Coleman Hawkins, but his presence tended to clutter up the front line. The best solos come from Russell — nicely rueful in *Someone stole Gabriel's horn* — and Dorsey, a master of how to make the best use of sixteen bars.   C.F.

3

The Twenties

Styles other than New Orleans

Chicago and Harlem Small Bands of the Late 1920s

Ranging from Parham's careful orchestrations to Smith's virtuoso daring, these recordings illustrate still further aspects of jazz in Chicago and New York as the 1920s moved towards their close.

57 **Clarence Williams's Jazz Kings**
VJM (E) VLP37

Clarence Williams's Jazz Kings: Benny Moten and probably Benny Waters (clt); Williams (p); Leroy Harris (bj); Cyrus St Clair (tu). New York City, 25 January 1927.
Gravier Street blues · Candy lips

Ed Allen (cnt); Charlie Irvis (tbn); Albert Socarras (clt, sop, alt); Williams (p); Harris (bj); St Clair (tu). New York City, 18 August 1927.
I'm going back to bottomland · You'll long for me when the cold wind blows

Williams (p, vcl). New York City, 19 August 1927.
When I march in April with May · Shooting the pistol

Clarence Williams's Jazz Kings: Allen (cnt); Ed Cuffee (tbn); Buster Bailey (clt, alt); Coleman Hawkins (clt, ten); Williams (p); Harris (bj); St Clair (tu). New York City, 12 January 1928.
Dreaming the hours away · Close fit blues

Arville Harris (alt), Floyd Casey (d) added. New York City, 10 April 1928.
Sweet Emmalina · Any time

King Oliver (cnt) added; Socarras (clt, alt) replaces Bailey, Hawkins.
New York City, 29 May 1928.
Red river blues · I need you

Similar personnel. New York City, 1 August 1928.
The keyboard express · Walk that broad

Allen (cnt); Socarras (clt, alt, fl); Arville Harris (clt, ten); James P.
Johnson (p); Leroy Harris (bj); Williams (vcl, and possibly p on *If you like
me*). New York City, 5 February 1929.
If you like me like I like you · Have you ever felt that way?

The inclusion of this disc is rather more than a necessary tribute
to the talented Louisianian enthusiast who, as 'race' records
manager of OKeh in New York, directed or supervised hundreds
of sessions involving many of the greatest jazz players during an
important period of musical establishment. It is also a testimony
to the setting of a mood, to the strength of a cultural ambience
which both stimulated and, perhaps unreasonably, indebted jazz
music. There is a consistency of assurance throughout this music,
yet no performance here can be judged distinguished. It will
instructively be related to other jazz being played during the
same years, but such comparison — except in one small respect —
is not the purpose of these paragraphs. Williams's own motive
and spirit are discernible enough, and some appreciation of them
may be attempted.

A study of these performances, recorded for an associated firm,
Columbia, prompts the question: how much does spontaneity
matter in jazz? *Gravier Street blues* and *Candy lips*, with agile
clarinet duet, are examples of almost entirely premeditated
music with no real improvisation at all; yet they have great zest
and variety, and possibly exhibit the jazz spirit more engagingly
than the rather leaden performances of *I'm going back to
bottomland*, *You'll long for me*, *Dreaming the hours away* and
Close fit blues, in which the several sources of vigour — Allen,
Irvis, Cuffee, Bailey and Hawkins — tend to be pretty securely
tethered. Furthermore, the earlier ensemble shows better, within
its smaller resources, how lively was Williams's imagination in
exploiting the tonal combinations discovered in preceding years.
This was a period in which the small group, still dedicated to the
ideal of improvisation, was looking for ways to expand its powers
of expression. Williams donated little formally to such expansion,
but he brought together people who had the vision to seek it, and
also did something to determine the spirit in which the music
might move forward.

There is more openness in the group which produced *Dreaming
the hours away* and *Close fit blues*, but no great deal of inventiveness. Close marshalling of forces again keeps the improvising

down to a minimum and, here and in most of these numbers, there is reason to regret Williams's magnification of the role of St Clair, whose tuba frequently makes the ensemble tunes swivel about with the antique delicacy of a tramcar. (St Clair is an acceptable supporter in some King Oliver Dixie Syncopators sessions made in the same year, but kinder recording balance keeps him in his place. Williams may deliberately have given the tubaist prominence — as he does especially in the brontosaurian opening of *Red river blues* — and, though the musical skill is obvious, the artistic effect is regrettable.)

Emmalina and *Any time* exploit the vaudeville spirit and, like *When I march in April with May, If you like me like I like you* and *Have you ever felt that way?*, include some animated lyrics and scat singing from the leader. There is distinctive work by Oliver in the mid-1928 tracks, but the general spirit, as extracted from ostensible form, is that sportiveness which the bands of the period shared with shows such as *Shuffle Along* which bore ahead the comic genius of minstrelsy.

How important is spontaneity? In the broadest terms it is indispensable, and it need not load each moment with the burden of high creativeness. There is little, if any, 'great jazz' here, but there is an almost unfailing freshness which seems to be of jazz's essence. It owes more than a little to the infectious timing and uninhibited gaiety of professional merrymakers such as Williams. The gleefully dancing *Keyboard express* — St Clair and all — will instance the pleasure of all that as well as anything.   E.T.

58a Tiny Parham Vol. 1
Collectors' Classics (D) CC39

Tiny Parham and His Musicians: Punch Miller (cnt); Charles Lawson (tbn); Charles Johnson (clt, alt); Parham (p); possibly Sam Tall (bj); Quinn Wilson (tu); Ernie Marrero (d). Chicago, 2 July 1928.
Stuttering blues · Snake eyes · Jogo rhythm
Elliott Washington (vln) added: Ray Hobson (cnt); Mike McKendrick (bj) replace Miller, Tall. Chicago, 1 February 1929.
Voodoo · Stomping on down · Blue melody blues
Same personnel and location, 2 February 1929.
Subway sops · That kind of love · Blue island blues
Same personnel and location, 22 July 1929.
Lucky 3-6-9
Unidentified clt/alt/ten, Tommy Brookins (vcl[1]) added; Ike Covington (tbn), Milt Hinton (tu) replace Lawson, Wilson. Chicago, 11 November 1930.
Now that I've found you · My dreams[1] · After all I've done for you[1]
(2 takes)

58b **Tiny Parham Vol. 2**
Collectors' Classics (D) CC40

Hobson (cnt); Lawson (tbn); Johnson (clt, alt); Washington (vln); Parham (p); McKendrick (bj); Wilson (tu); Marrero (d).
Chicago, 22 July 1929.
Jungle crawl · Echo blues
Miller (cnt), unidentified clt/alt/ten replace Hobson, Johnson. Chicago, 25 October 1929.
Pigs' feet and slaw · Fat man blues · Steel string blues
Same personnel; Parham plays cls². Chicago, 3 December 1929.
Dixieland doings · Cathedral blues² · Black cat moan
Johnson (clt, alt) returns; Hobson (cnt), Covington (tbn), Hinton (tu) replace Miller, Lawson, Wilson. Chicago, 4 November 1930.
Rock bottom · Down yonder · Squeeze me · Back to the jungle · Nervous tension · Memphis Mamie

Parham was active in the Chicago area for some years as a bandleader, pianist and composer — nearly all the themes on the above records are his. He also arranged for King Oliver, Earl Hines, and it has been suggested that he helped Jelly Roll Morton with some of his orchestrations [21]. His music is quietly intelligent, embodies a consistent viewpoint, and is decisive in the achievement of its aims; it is also modest in tone, and this has led to its receiving little critical attention.

The performances are spirited yet cleanly executed, and the best of them, like *Dixieland doings*, approximate to the zest of Red Hot Pepper items of a few years before such as *Black bottom stomp* (47a). Parham was refreshingly independent of the conventions that had been established for scoring for bands like this, and many quietly unorthodox ensemble textures can be found here, for example on *Blue island blues*. Notice also the unlikely juxtaposition of violin and tuba in *Black cat moan*, the contradiction between a sweet alto saxophone and mildly abrasive trumpet on *Blue melody blues*, the tinkling celeste above sustained ensemble chords in *Cathedral blues*.

But this music retained contact with its roots, and the interplay of alto and violin in *Stomping on down* is reminiscent of the Dixieland Jug Blowers (4). This passage is followed by a solo from Hobson, clipped, concise and modern, then come Parham's echoes of the barrelhouse, an ensemble with unpredictable voicings, an aggressively pinging single-string banjo solo, Johnson's mixture of very long and short clarinet notes, a clownish tuba solo, another ensemble. And such variety is typical. Repeatedly the small ensemble creates a large sound, as in *Jungle crawl* or *Snake eyes*, and Parham's use of the tuba had a part in this. He was almost the only arranger of that time who regularly made positive use of its qualities (though see **81**), and the bass line in *Fat man blues* or *Squeeze me* is remarkably flexible.

At the piano, Parham accompanies and interjects astutely, as behind the trombone on *Cathedral blues*, and in *Blue island blues*, where his backing goes some way to redeem a weak violin solo. (Nothing can redeem the *vox humana* sentimentalities of Brookins's singing, although the skittish alto break which follows him on *After all I've done for you* seems like a fair comment on it.) Also effective are the leader's treble interjections amid the weighted ensembles of *Black cat moan*, and the wry little keyboard postlude to *Memphis Mamie*.

The ordering of solo sequences, in *Voodoo* or *Lucky 3-6-9*, is done with a canny regard to changing tone colours. Miller is admirably forthright on *Jogo rhythm* and *Stuttering blues*, decisively sparks *Pigs' feet and slaw* and *Fat man blues*. In *That kind of love* and elsewhere, Hobson produces work something like George Mitchell's for Morton (**47**), and on the basis of solos such as that in *Echo blues* his obscurity is undeserved. However, the cornet (or trumpet) on *Down yonder* and some other 4 November 1930 titles sounds too aggressive for Hobson, although this is not true of others. The present writer wonders if Miller and Hobson alternated in this marathon session (not all of which is included on the above LPs). It has been suggested that the unidentified clt/alt/ten is Omer Simeon but, to judge from his contemporaneous work in **59**, this seems most unlikely. The track labelled as *Fat man blues* on Vol. 1 is in fact an alternative take of *After all I've done for you*.   M.H.

59   Omer Simeon 1929–30
Ace of Hearts (E) AH97

Reuben Reeves and His River Boys: Reuben Reeves (tpt); Gerald Reeves (tbn); Simeon (clt, alt); Jimmy Prince (p); Harry Gray (g); Jasper Taylor (d); unidentified vcl[1]. Chicago, 23 May 1929.
River blues

Same personnel and location, 10 June 1929.
Parson blues

Same personnel and location, 19 June 1929.
Papa Skag stomp[1]

Same personnel and location, 25 June 1929.
Bugle call blues[1]

Simeon (clt); Earl Hines or William Barbee (p); Hayes Alvis (tu); Wallace Bishop (d). Chicago, 21 August 1929.
Smoke house blues

Simeon (clt); Hines (p). Chicago, 11 September 1929.
Beau koo Jack

Dixie Rhythm Kings: Shirley Clay, unidentified (cnt); Simeon (clt, alt); Cecil Irwin (clt, ten); Barbee (p); Claude Roberts (bj); Alvis (tu); Bishop (d). Chicago, 23 September 1929.
The chant · Congo love song

Alex Hill and His Orchestra: George Dixon (tpt); Kenneth Stewart (tbn); George James (clt, alt); Cecil Irwin (clt, ten); Hill (p); Ikey Robinson (bj); Silas White (tu); Sidney Catlett (d). Chicago, 20 December 1929.
Toogaloo shout

Same personnel and location, 8 February 1930.
Dying with the blues

Harry Dial's Blusicians: Clay (tpt); Irwin (clt, ten); Lester Boone (alt); Bill Culbreath (p); Eustern Woodfork (bj); Walt Wright (tu, bs); Dial (d, vcl[2]). Chicago, 15 May 1930.
Don't give it away[2] · *Funny fumble*

This anthology, though it is misleadingly titled, is of importance in showing how emulations of the classic jazz style (**43–47**) and response to the rougher gutbucket groups (**42**) enlivened the late 1920s Chicago scene. The Reeves group recalls the style of the Hot Five (**48**), the leader contriving a fairly successful impersonation of Armstrong, and Gerald Reeves and Simeon joining him in the familiar adaptation of New Orleans counterpoint. The shrillness of Simeon's clarinet on *Parson blues* and his double-time episode in *River blues* emphasize the Chicagoan spirit. His playing, like Johnny Dodds's, particularly in this period, was a mixture of the acid and the mellow. Reuben Reeves, though not an original player, led and improvised with ample skill. His bright-toned, dexterous work in *Bugle call blues*, wherein Simeon plays fine alto, is pleasing.

Simeon's shapely full chorus in *Papa Skag stomp* shows how he could build solos from sequences of descending phrases. That practice is even more marked on *Beau koo Jack*, which is a different sort of recollection, partly because of the theme, but more so because it is a duet worthy to be compared with those dazzling 1928 exchanges between Armstrong and Hines (**48**) Some personnel lists (including the sleeve of this record) give William Barbee as the pianist in *Beau koo Jack* and *Smoke house blues*; others give Hines for both sessions. There can be no doubt that it is Hines on the first, and little doubt that it is he on the second. None of his several imitators could have achieved that buoyant daring; and Barbee's playing with the Dixie Rhythm Kings instances both his aspiration and his failure.

Hines adds his own different genius to the conception of another pianistic giant in *Smoke house blues*. Simeon's playing is, if anything, a little less deliberate and more relaxed than that in his famous contribution to Morton's own version (**47a**), yet it is a similar testimony to the vocabulary he learnt from his tutor, Lorenzo Tio jnr. Another Morton comparison is invited by *The chant* (a slower version than its original, as *Smoke house blues* is faster). A feature of the two Dixie Rhythm Kings pieces is a rich antiphony in harmonized passages between cornets and clarinets. There is less solo interest in the Ellington-inspired *Congo love song*, and the best thing in *The chant* is the beautiful mid-register clarinet solo, with Simeon using the smeared blues phrases of his 1926 Morton solo in what amounts to a variation upon former thoughts.

The two Alex Hill performances include exuberantly fashioned music, but there are identification problems here too. The sleeve gives Jabbo Smith as the trumpeter; Rust has Bob Shoffner. Of greater moment is Rust's showing Darnell Howard where the sleeve gives Simeon. The list appearing above has the personal authority of Dixon and Stewart, and this means that the excellent muted trumpet work in *Toogaloo shout* and the firm lead in *Dying with the blues* are by Dixon, and that the clarinettist is Irwin — a musician scarcely noted in the jazz histories.

We are left with the lively efforts of Dial's Blusicians with Clay springingly in the vanguard — good ensemble improvising, some of which goes on behind the leader's 'jug band' singing on *Don't give it away*, and some capable arranged parts. It seems, however, that Simeon is again absent, and the acerbic clarinet insertions are likely to be the work of Irwin.

Of the Simeon statements, those in *Beau koo Jack*, *Smoke house blues* and *The chant* are outstanding. With the Hines band, and with Lunceford in the 1940s, his eclectic style persisted, but in subsequent decades the tougher emphases receded, and he appeared to settle for the role of an accomplished but perhaps faintly illicit New Orleans veteran.   E.T.

Jabbo Smith

60 **The Ace of Rhythm**

Ace of Hearts (E) AH165, *Melodeon (A) MLP 7326/7 (2 LPs)

Jabbo Smith and His Rhythm Aces: Smith (tpt, vcl[1]); Omer Simeon (clt, alt[2]); Cassino Simpson (p); Ikey Robinson (bj). Chicago, 29 January 1929.
Jazz battle

Hayes Alvis (tu) added. Chicago, 22 February 1929.
Little Willie blues · Sleepy time blues[1]

Same personnel and location, 23 February 1929.
Take your time · Sweet and low blues[1]

Same personnel and location, 1 March 1929.
Take me to the river[1] · *Ace of rhythm · Let's get together*[1,2] · *Sau sha stomp*[2]

Earl Frazier (p) replaces Simpson. Chicago, 30 March 1929.
Michigander blues[2]
Same personnel and location, 4 April 1929.
Decatur Street tutti[1,2] · *Till times get better*[1,2]

European jazz record collectors were once convinced that Smith was really two separate people. One was the menacing, half-phantasmal soloist to be glimpsed on Ellington's OKeh version of *Black and tan fantasy* (**91**), where Smith deputizes for Bubber Miley. The other was the impetuous performer, rather in the mould of the young Armstrong, who made records with his own little band in 1929. On the face of it, the styles seem very different, yet they share a dimension of theatricality, a compulsion to play both villain and hero. Smith was one of the very few trumpeters at the end of the 1920s whose technique could be compared with Armstrong's; but his methods also had something in common with those of trumpeters such as Henry Allen and Roy Eldridge who were, or would be, loosening-up the solo lines, broadening the structures. Like Allen and Eldridge, he liked to operate on the edge of his technique (*Take me to the river* is a rousing example), creating an atmosphere of nervous excitement where anything seemed likely to happen.

The initial inspiration, though, was Armstrong, which appears to be why American Brunswick signed Smith up in 1929 to make records that — at first, anyway — set out to compete with those by Armstrong's Hot Five and Seven (**48**). The absence of a drummer was compensated for by the springiness of Smith's own playing and that of Simeon (more versatile than Dodds), and the excellence of Robinson, both within the ensemble and as a soloist (*Take your time*, *Michigander blues* and *Decatur Street tutti* all have creditable single-string work), while Simpson's piano playing reflected, if in a simplified fashion, the influence of Hines, as did that of Frazier, who replaced him.

There are period touches about Simeon's alto playing, but his clarinet solos range from staccato, multi-noted excursions like that on *Little Willie blues* (one could almost deduce from this that Simeon and Frank Teschemacher lived in the same city at the same time) to the languishing, *legato* style to be heard on *Sweet and low blues*. But it is Smith, of course, who gives the performances their real character. His vocalizing in *Let's get together* is recitative, more or less in the tradition of Bert Williams, but elsewhere he scats in a style somewhere between Armstrong's gruff syllabics and the more roguish manner of Allen. His trumpet solos owe their architecture to Armstrong (the munificent laying-out of the theme of *Sweet and low blues*, the brilliant series of breaks in *Sau sha stomp*), yet the effect is not of imitation but of a kind of spirited impersonation: dramatic, daring and — paradoxically — original. C.F.

Midwestern jazz, Bix and the New Yorkers

If the Chicagoans built on transplanted New Orleans music, their contemporaries elsewhere created the first wholly independent style. This culminated in Beiderbecke, the most aesthetically radical jazz musician of the 1920s who, partly via his influence on the New Yorkers, had a profound effect on his successors in the 1930s.

Bix Beiderbecke

61 **The Complete Wolverines**
Fountain (E) FJ114, *Milestone (A) M47019 (2 LPs)

The Wolverines: Beiderbecke (cnt); Al Gande (tbn); Jimmy Hartwell (clt, alt); George Johnson (clt, ten); Dick Voynow (p); Bob Gillette (bj); Min Leibrook (tu); Vic Moore (d). Richmond, Indiana, 18 February 1924.
Fidgety feet · *Jazz me blues*

Gande absent; Johnson doubles on bar[1]; Gillette doubles on g[2]. Richmond, Indiana, 6 May 1924.
Oh, baby · *Copenhagen* · *Riverboat shuffle*[2] · *Susie*[1] (2 takes)

Same personnel and location, 20 June 1924.
I need some petting[1] · *Royal Garden blues* · *Tiger rag*

George Brunies (tbn, kz[3]) added. New York City, 16 September 1924.
Sensation · *Lazy daddy*[3] (2 takes)

Brunies absent; Beiderbecke doubles on p[4]. New York City, 7 October 1924.
Tia Juana[1] · *Big boy*[4]

Jimmy McPartland (cnt) replaces Beiderbecke; Dave Harmon (vcl[5]) added. New York City, 5 December 1924.
When my sugar walks down the street[5] · *Prince of wails*

As men who do not have much time always must, Beiderbecke matured early. In their best moments the cornet solos and even ensemble parts of these his first recordings show not only a striking technical assurance but a certainty of expressive aim, a clearly focused emotional content, that is almost disquieting in one so young. We catch a glimpse of the extraordinary impact, attested by many surviving accounts, that he had on his contemporaries, and although they were later refined to highly poetic effect, as the finest performances with Trumbauer on **64** demonstrate, all the elements of his style may be detected here.

He used, as later (**63**), items from the Original Dixieland Jazz

Band repertoire (12) but, in arrangements devised at the piano with Voynow and learnt aurally by the Wolverines, he smoothed-down and rendered more flowing the earlier ensemble's jumpy rhythms to serve greater melodic coherence, a more subtle linear construction with wider harmonic reference. Solos like the one on *Tiger rag* show a brilliant grasp of the potentialities of jazz improvisation, and his innovations, chiefly in terms of melody, harmony and tone, added significantly to this music's resources. His piano solo on *Big boy*, the first he recorded with that instrument, is, with its wayward use of dissonance, further evidence of an exploratory mind, and in the aesthetic sense Beiderbecke was the most radical of the great jazz soloists of the 1920s. There is almost nothing of the blues in his playing, and when he does use devices from that idiom they are transmuted into something fresh, a good instance being the beautifully controlled downward slides in pitch on *Riverboat shuffle*, which are entirely personal in effect.

There were obvious difficulties in finding other musicians who could adequately complement his work, but the Wolverines lent better support than he could then have found in many other places and, as pieces like *Copenhagen* prove, they were at least fluent. The alternative takes of *Susie* and *Lazy daddy* show how carefully they rehearsed, but the arrangements depended absolutely on Bix's forceful yet melodious lead, and the two pieces in which he is replaced by McPartland are disastrous cases of *Hamlet* without the Prince. Even the earliest date, recorded when he was only twenty, finds Beiderbecke avoiding the obvious to an extent that seems remarkable still, and the later sessions show him making a steady advance that was impossible for his companions, his inventive power growing, his ideas becoming more varied but also more tightly knit.

The American Milestone catalogue number given above refers to a two-LP set called *Bix and the Chicago Cornets* which includes all the items on the Fountain disc plus the Spanier material discussed under **53** and further important Beiderbecke pieces. The new kind of sensibility he brought to jazz, already evident in the brief *Royal Garden blues* solo, achieves a definitive statement in *Davenport blues*, recorded as by Bix and His Rhythm Jugglers in December 1924. This goes beyond the promise of *Tiger rag* or even *Sensation* towards real mastery, with unprecedented harmonic inflections and mercurial rhythmic grace subordinated to the needs of melody, emotion and a satisfying musical shape.

M.H.

Curtis Hitch/Hoagy Carmichael/Emil Seidel

62 **Indiana Summer**
Fountain (E) FJ109

Hitch's Happy Harmonists: Fred Rollison (cnt); Jerry Bump (tbn); Rookie Neal (clt, alt); Dewey Neal (bs sx); Hitch (p); Maurice May (bj); Earl McDowell (d). Richmond, Indiana, 19 September 1923.
Cruel woman · *Home brew blues*
Same personnel and location, 23 February 1924.
Steady stepping papa · *Baptistown crawl* · *Ethiopian nightmare*
Rollison (cnt); Harry Wright (clt); Maurice May (ten); Hitch (p); Arnold Hubbe (bj); Haskell Simpson (tu); McDowell (d). Richmond, Indiana, 19 January 1925.
Cataract rag · *Nightingale rag blues*
Carmichael (p) replaces Hitch. Richmond, Indiana, 19 May 1925.
Boneyard shuffle · *Washboard blues*
Hoagy Carmichael and His Pals: Andy Secrest, Bob Mayhew (cnt); Tommy Dorsey (tbn); Jimmy Dorsey (clt, alt); Mischa Russell (vln); Carmichael (p); unidentified g. Richmond, Indiana, 28 October 1927.
One night in Havana
Byron Smart (tpt); Carmichael (cnt, p); Oscar Rossberg (tbn); Gene Woods, Dick Kent (clt, alt); Maurice Bennett (ten); Emil Seidel (p); Dan Kimmell (bj, g); Paul Brown (tu); Cliff Williams (d). Richmond, Indiana, 31 October 1929.
Friday night · *Stardust*
Emil Seidel and His Orchestra: same personnel except that several unidentified violins are added, and Carmichael is absent. Richmond, Indiana, 11 November 1927.
The best things in life are free · *Down south* · *Together, we two*
Same personnel and location, 25 November 1927.
For my baby
Jimmy Fisher (vcl) added. Richmond, Indiana, 9 December 1927.
Counting the days
Carmichael's Collegians: Bud Dant (cnt); Carmichael (cnt, p, vcl); Harold Keating (ten); Eddie Wolfe (vln); Hubbe (bj); Jack Drummond (bs); Andy van Sickle (d). Richmond, Indiana, 5 May 1928.
March of the hoodlums · *Walking the dog*

Most significant early jazz bands tend to be treated in isolation by the history books, yet each of them was originally part of a larger pattern of activity which cannot usually be discerned from surviving records. The above compilation, however, informatively provides a context for the Wolverines (**61**), the first session, with its echoes of the New Orleans Rhythm Kings (**43**), predating their initial visit to the recording studio, the second being contemporaneous with it. Of particular interest is *Ethiopian nightmare*, which must be one of the earliest instances recorded of the later quite widespread practice of basing a jazz piece on the chords of a popular song, in this case those of *Alexander's ragtime band*.

On the January 1925 Happy Harmonists date the influence of Bix Beiderbecke, and of his arranging practices for the Wolverines, is especially clear, but on the session of the following May, where Carmichael replaces the leader at the piano, that influence is used more creatively (even if *Boneyard shuffle* employs a variant of a phrase from the NORKs' *Eccentric*). *Washboard blues*, also written by Carmichael, is both as a composition and arrangement well ahead of its time, and is (*pace* the sleeve note) the most significant performance here [22]. The composer's piano solo is close to the one he recorded on the Paul Whiteman/Beiderbecke version of two years later (RCA (F) 731.131), and contains the germ of *Lazybones*, a popular song he was to copyright in 1933.

A few animated and jazz-like passages notwithstanding, Seidel's orchestra played the commercial music of its day, and his five tracks, with their dreadful singing, do not justify their place here. But Carmichael's pieces, following on from that session with Hitch's band, have a pleasing eccentricity, are clearly the work of men determined to suit themselves rather than abide by the jazz conventions that were then rapidly being established. And idiosyncrasy has its rewards, for this account of *One night in Havana* (which has Bix's predecessor and successor in the jazz chair of Whiteman's trumpet section) is far superior to the 1930 version on the final Beiderbecke recording date (**65**). Also interesting is *Friday night*, with its cornet and trumpet duet and restless scoring.

The first recorded performance of *Stardust* is taken at a surprisingly brisk tempo yet one in accord with the composer's original intentions. Smart's playing of the verse shows the link between Carmichael's writing and Bix's improvisational lyricism, and the keyboard solo (unaccountably attributed to Seidel in some discographies) is close in style, not least harmonically, to Beiderbecke's piano compositions (**63, 116** and **178**). Other allusions may be found; for example, the keyboard passage before the scat vocal in *Walking the dog* is amusingly based on the main phrase of the first of Edward McDowell's *Woodland Sketches*, Op. 51. Note also the intriguing square-dance flavour of Wolfe's contribution to *March of the hoodlums*. These last two items should be compared with the versions that Carmichael recorded the following year with a contingent from Whiteman's band under Eddie Lang's name (**66**). M.H.

Bix Beiderbecke

63 **Bix and His Gang**
Parlophone (E) PMC1221, Swaggie (Au) S1271

Beiderbecke (p). New York City, 9 September 1927.

In a mist (Bixology)

Bix Beiderbecke and His Gang: Beiderbecke (cnt); Bill Rank (tbn); Don Murray (clt); Adrian Rollini (bs sx); Frank Signorelli (p); Chauncey Morehouse (d). New York City, 5 October 1927.

At the jazz band ball · Royal Garden blues · Jazz me blues

Same personnel and location, 25 October 1927.

Goose pimples · Sorry · Since my best girl turned me down

Izzy Friedman (clt), Min Leibrook (bs sx), Tom Satterfield (p), Harold McDonald (d) replace Murray, Rollini, Signorelli, Morehouse, New York City, 17 April 1928.

Somebody stole my girl · Thou swell

Lennie Hayton (p), Harry Gale (d) replace Satterfield, MacDonald. Chicago, 7 July 1928.

Old man river · Wa-da-da

George Marsh (d) replaces Gale; Roy Bargy (p) added; Hayton doubles on har and timp. New York City, 21 September 1928.

Rhythm king · Louisiana · Margie

These recordings include some of Beiderbecke's most brilliant cornet playing; and some of his most run-of-the-mill. They issue from a time of circumstantial change. The Jean Goldkette group (see **65**) disbanded between the recording of *In a mist* and the occasion which produced *At the jazz band ball*, *Royal Garden blues* and *Jazz me blues*, a session peopled by members of Rollini's ephemeral New Yorker band. Then, two days after recording the other three tracks on side 1 of this LP, Bix joined Whiteman in Indianapolis, and most of the musicians on the remaining tracks are Whiteman associates.

Beiderbecke produced better music in the 1927 performances. There is good and very characteristic work from the later sessions, but much of it is self-effacing and functional, especially in comparison with the daring flights essayed elsewhere. None of his associates comes near to matching Bix in creative terms. They are chiefly men with whom he had been used to playing, and they are all competent; but without Beiderbecke they could have produced nothing memorable. In the earlier recordings there is a sense of clarity and cohesion in the ensembles and solo sequences which, though sought for later, slips away in near-confusion. Murray and Rollini are the ablest supporting soloists; Rank's intentions are good, but he cannot quite encompass their shaping;

Friedman, like Murray, knows how to tune up and overblow in Teschemacher fashion; and he knows his post-dixieland ensemble role fairly well, though without Murray's (perhaps rather studied) control of form. Of the pianists, Signorelli is the best in jazz terms — which is not to say much, though he gives some evidence of having listened to Jelly Roll Morton.

The freedom allowed by the flexible roles of piano and bass saxophone is notable and, again, it comes off better in the first six Gang tracks, partly because the participants are abler, partly because of less modish arrangements. The music moves somewhat beyond the dixieland style, which is still, however, its underlying stimulus; and, in this connection, *Royal Garden blues* and *Jazz me blues* may be compared with the 1924 Wolverines recordings (**61**), wherein the ensemble style is naturally closer to the mode of the New Orleans Rhythm Kings, and Bix's solo and leading work, though distinctive, is some way short of the multifaceted genius shining in his brief 1927 creations. A solo like that on the later *Jazz me blues* ranging with apparent recklessness from the mellifluous to the violently laconic, the floating ensemble lead in *Goose pimples* and *Since my best girl turned me down*, punctuated with wild whoops of assault, the spectral, clarinet-like voice that suddenly emerges in *Wa-da-da*, and many other felicities in both solo and contrapuntal playing, frequently touch 'that strain . . . of higher mood' which is the token of singular inspiration.

In a mist is not to be regarded as an oddity, as the piece of radical modernism which, according to Eddie Condon, put Joe Sullivan into a state of hypnosis [23]; rather, it should be allowed to utter its small but important message about Beiderbecke's aspirations. The harmonies are no more outlandish than things incidental to many a Whiteman arrangement. It is no Debussian aberration, but a jazz composition, rather unusual for its time, and an amateur's creation in the best sense. Its melodic lines may teach something of the imagination that Bix wanted to express in more conventional surroundings, and they should be held in firm relation to his cornet playing. The other title, *Bixology*, may be more apt, suggesting an inner philosophy, never fully formed, but helping to explain to some extent the magic which makes Beiderbecke's work so unforgettable and fascinating.

Short-lived, he never found his true musical *milieu*. Perhaps he had no clear idea of what it ought to have been. He *was* ahead of his time. The probings of *In a mist* (and of the compositions played by Jess Stacy on **116** and **178**) have their echoes in his cornet lines, yet this 'modernism' is fitted into a conventional context — not too surprisingly perhaps, because, although his tone and his adventurous phrasing outsoar his companions, Bix had sufficient mastery of hot ensemble techniques to prove a stimulating and uniting leader. If, on the 1928 sessions, he is sometimes forced into a functional role and if frustration leads to some musical lapses, as notably at the end of *Margie*, it still can be said that shining moments abound. (An initially rejected take of *Thou swell* lately surfaced (Wolverine (A) 3), but it contains no instructive differences.)   E.T.

Bix Beiderbecke/Frankie Trumbauer

64 Bix and Tram 1927
Parlophone (E) PMC7064, Swaggie (Au) S1242

Frankie Trumbauer and His Orchestra: Beiderbecke (cnt); Bill Rank (tbn); Jimmy Dorsey (clt, alt); Doc Ryker (alt); Trumbauer (C-mel); Paul Mertz (p, arr); Eddie Lang (g); Chauncey Morehouse (d). New York City, 4 February 1927.
Clarinet marmalade · Singing the blues
Don Murray (clt, alt, bar), Itzy Riskin (p) replace Dorsey, Mertz; Bill Challis (arr) added. New York City, 9 May 1927.
Ostrich walk · Riverboat shuffle
Same personnel and location, 13 May 1927.
I'm coming, Virginia · Way down yonder in New Orleans
Adrian Rollini (bs sx), Seger Ellis (vcl[1]) added. New York City, 25 August 1927.
Three blind mice · Blue river[1] · There's a cradle in Caroline[1]
Bobby Davis (alt), Frank Signorelli (p) replace Ryker, Riskin; Joe Venuti (vln) added; Ellis absent. New York City, 28 September 1927.
Humpty Dumpty · Krazy Kat · Baltimore
Unidentified tpt, Irving Kaufman (vcl) added. New York City, 30 September 1927.
Just an hour of love · I'm wondering who
Pee Wee Russell (clt) replaces Davis; Murray doubles on ten instead of bar; unidentified tpt; Kaufman absent. New York City, 25 October 1927.
Crying all day · A good man is hard to find

Suavity can offer short-term advantages yet be an historical handicap. Trumbauer must have seemed as suave as it was possible for a jazz musician to be in the second half of the 1920s, abreast of everything considered to be modern, projecting an agreeable coolness after what must have seemed like a surfeit of calculated hotness. Yet if he had not collaborated with Beiderbecke (and, in passing, impressed Lester Young), it is doubtful if anybody would listen to his records today. The solos Trumbauer plays in *Singing the blues* and *Way down yonder in New Orleans* offer some interesting ideas, and they fit the context well. Yet taken in isolation the overwhelming impression is of quaintness, accentuated by the fact that they sit alongside two of the most exquisite solos ever recorded by a jazz musician.

Beiderbecke's playing seems classically objective, yet it also introduced a new kind of sensibility to jazz. He plays as if he was taking the listener into his confidence, reading a page or two out of his diary. The paradox is that Bix's earliest influence was Nick LaRocca, scarcely the subtlest of cornettists. And Beiderbecke's admiration of the Original Dixieland Jazz Band extended to recording some of their numbers, not only with his own Gang (**63**) but in the more upholstered surroundings of Trumbauer's orchestra, a pick-up group mostly recruited from Jean Goldkette's band (**65**). So there is a defiantly robust version of *Clarinet marmalade*, a performance of *Ostrich walk* that introduces a three-piece saxophone section, and — though one easily forgets that the ODJB originated the number — *Singing the blues*, the basis for what proved to be the first 'ballad' interpretation in recorded jazz. What grips the listener in this last performance is the sense of structure in Bix's playing, the inevitability in what was, after all, an improvised solo. The same qualities are found again in *I'm coming, Virginia*, which starts off once more with Trumbauer and Lang counterpointing one another.

Unlike Armstrong, who sometimes made mistakes because of the sheer effrontery of his genius, Beiderbecke aimed at perfection of detail as well as of overall plan. His approach corresponded to the enclosed lyricism to be found in classic ragtime (the kind of thing, too, that a good sonnet writer aims at), rather than the open-ended adventuring which goes, say, with taking innumerable choruses on a twelve-bar blues. (It is significant that Bix was never a blues player in the sense that Jack Teagarden or Pee Wee Russell undoubtedly were.) The effect is nearly always ravishing, and heightened, maybe, by the soloist's companions rarely getting anywhere near his musical level.

There were exceptions, of course. Lang is always impressive, as sympathetic a performer as it was possible to find; Rollini strengthened every session he played on, an anchor-man in every sense. But Rank tries too diligently to duplicate Miff Mole's slyness, frequently sounding more like somebody completing a jigsaw puzzle than a jazz solo. And the later sessions often disappoint. *Three blind mice* succeeds, despite a cluttered-up arrangement, yet *Blue river* and *Cradle in Caroline* are dull, and not helped by Ellis's warblings. *Just an hour of love* and *I'm wondering who* are even worse, rescued only by Beiderbecke's solos. *Humpty Dumpty* happens to be a more interesting theme, composed by Fud Livingston, one of the brighter talents of the decade, and Bix responds to the challenge by taking a smouldering chorus. *Krazy Kat*, arranged by Murray, has a calmer solo, while *Baltimore*, much looser, presents Beiderbecke, Rollini and Lang at their finest. *Crying all day* harks back to the first session, its theme based on the opening figure of *Singing the blues*. Bix comes up with a brand new solo — outstanding, of course, yet not impressing itself on the memory quite so indelibly as the classic he recorded nine months earlier. (A larger selection of Beiderbecke's 1927–30 recordings, in fact all his work from this period except that done for RCA, appears on World Records (E) SH413–6.)   C.F.

65 The Bix Beiderbecke Legend
RCA (F) 731.036/7 (2 LPs), *RCA (A) LPM2323

Jean Goldkette and His Orchestra: Fuzzy Farrar, Tex Brusster (tpt); Beiderbecke (cnt); Bill Rank, Tommy Dorsey (tbn); Doc Ryker, Don Murray, George Williams (saxes); Joe Venuti (vln); Paul Mertz (p); Howdy Quicksell (bj); Henry Irish (tu); Charles Horvath (d). Detroit, 24 November 1924.
I didn't know

Farrar, Ray Lodwig (tpt); Beiderbecke (cnt); Rank, Spiegle Willcox (tbn); Ryker, Murray, Frankie Trumbauer (saxes); Venuti (vln); Itzy Riskin (p); Quicksell (bj); Eddie Lang (g); Steve Brown (bs); Chauncey Morehouse (d); Bill Challis (arr); Keller Sisters and Lynch (vcl). New York City, 15 October 1926.
Sunday

Danny Polo (reeds) replaces Murray; Eddy Sheasby (vln) added; Lang absent. New York City, 1 February 1927.
My pretty girl (2 takes)

Murray replaces Polo; Venuti, Sheasby absent. Camden, New Jersey, 6 May 1927.
Slow river

Lloyd Turner (tbn) replaces Willcox; Venuti (vln), Lang (g) added. New York City, 15 September 1927.
Clementine from New Orleans

Paul Whiteman and His Orchestra: Henry Busse, Charles Margulis (tpt); Beiderbecke (cnt); Wilbur Hall, Tommy Dorsey (tbn); Jimmy Dorsey (clt, alt); Chester Hazlett, Hal McLean (alt); Charles Strickfadden (alt, bar); Nye Mayhew (ten); Kurt Dieterle, Mischa Russell, Matty Malneck,

Mario Perry (vln); Harry Perella (p); Mike Pingitore (bj); Brown (bs);
Mike Trafficante (tu); Harold McDonald (d); Bing Crosby, Harry Barris,
Al Rinker (vcl). Chicago, 22 November 1927.
Changes
Trumbauer (C-mel) replaces Mayhew; Tommy Dorsey doubles on tpt,
Hall on bj; Barris, Rinker absent. Chicago, 25 November 1927.
Mary
Rank (tbn) replaces Tommy Dorsey; Perry, Crosby absent. New York
City, 4 January 1928.
Lonely melody
Margulis (tpt); Beiderbecke (cnt); Jimmy Dorsey (cnt, clt); Rank (tbn);
Trumbauer (C-mel); Min Leibrook (bs sx); Malneck (vln); Challis (p, arr);
Carl Kress (g); McDonald (d). New York City, 12 January 1928.
San
Busse, Margulis (tpt); Beiderbecke (cnt); Boyce Cullen, Hall, Rank (tbn);
McLean (ob, clt, alt); Strickfadden (ob, clt, ten); Rube Crozier (clt);
Jimmy Dorsey (clt, alt); Hazlett (bs clt, sop, alt); Trumbauer (C-mel);
Dieterle, Russell, Malneck, Perry, Charles Gaylord (vln); Ferdé Grofé
(p); Pingitore (bj); Trafficante (tu); MacDonald (d); Challis (arr). Camden,
New Jersey, 28 January 1928.
Back in your own backyard
Crosby, Jack Fulton, Austin Young, Gaylord, Harris, Rinker (vcl) added;
Roy Bargy (p) replaces Grofé; Tom Satterfield (arr). New York City,
8 February 1928.
There ain't no sweet man that's worth the salt of my tears
Crozier, Perry, Gaylord, Crosby, Fulton, Young, Barris, Rinker absent;
Challis (arr). New York City, 9 February 1928.
Dardanella
Red Mayer (clt, ten), Fulton, Gaylord, Young (vcl) added. New York City,
10 February 1928.
Love nest
Barris (p) replaces Bargy; Crosby, Rinker (vcl) added; Dorsey switches to
cnt; McLean, Trumbauer absent. New York City, 13 February 1928.
From Monday on
Beiderbecke (cnt); Eddie Pinder (tpt); Rank (tbn); Izzy Friedman (clt);
Hazlett, Trumbauer (alt); Strickfadden (ten); Leibrook (bs sx); Bargy (p);
Pingitore (bj); Trafficante (bs); MacDonald (d); Irene Taylor, Crosby,
Barris, Rinker, Fulton, Gaylord, Young (vcl); Satterfield (arr). New York
City, 18 February 1928.
Mississippi mud
Margulis, Pinder, Busse (tpt); Beiderbecke (cnt); Cullen, Hall, Rank,
Fulton (tbn); Strickfadden (eng h, ten, bar); Hazlett (E flat clt, bs clt, alt);
Crozier (clt, bsn, sop, alt, bs sx); Friedman, Trumbauer (clt, alt); Mayer
(clt, ten); Dieterle, Russell, Malneck, Perry (vln); Bargy (p); Pingitore
(bj); Trafficante (bs); Leibrook (tu); MacDonald (d); Challis (arr). New
York City, 28 February 1928.
Sugar

Busse, Rank absent; 14-voice mixed chorus added; Satterfield (arr). New York City, 1 March 1928.

Selections from 'Show Boat'

Rank (tbn), Gaylord, Young, Barris, Rinker (vcl) added; Trumbauer switches to C-mel; Hall, Fulton, mixed chorus absent; New York City, 12 March 1928.

When

Hall (tbn), Crosby (vcl) added; Challis (arr). New York City, 15 March 1928.

Lovable

Busse (tpt), Hall, Rank (tbn), Fulton (tbn, vcl), Perry, John Bowman (vln), Lennie Hayton (p) added; Gaylord switches to vln. New York City, 23 April 1928.

Louisiana

Margulis, Pinder, Harry Goldfield (tpt); Beiderbecke (cnt); Cullen, Rank, Hall (tbn); Fulton (tbn, vcl); Crozier (fl, clt, ten); Hazlett (clt, bs clt, alt); Mayer (clt, alt, bar); Trumbauer (alt, C-mel); Strickfadden (ten, bar); Dieterle, Russell, Malneck, Perry, Bowman (vln); Gaylord (vln, vcl); Bargy, Hayton (p); Pingitore (bj); Trafficante (bs); Leibrook (tu); George Marsh (d); Crosby, Barris, Rinker, Young (vcl); Satterfield (arr). New York City, 25 April 1928.

You took advantage of me

Hoagy Carmichael and His Orchestra: Beiderbecke (cnt); Bubber Miley (tpt); Tommy Dorsey (tbn); Benny Goodman (clt); Arnold Brilhart (alt); Bud Freeman (ten); Venuti (vln); Irving Brodsky (p, vcl[1]); Lang (g); Harry Goodman (tu); Gene Krupa (d); Carmichael (arr, p[2], vcl[3]); Carson Robison (vcl[4]). New York City 21 May 1930.

Rocking chair[1,2,3] · *Barnacle Bill the sailor*[3,4]

Bix Beiderbecke and His Orchestra: Beiderbecke (cnt); Lodwig (tpt); Cullen (tbn); Goodman (clt); Jimmy Dorsey, Pee Wee Russell (clt, alt); Freeman (ten); Leibrook (bs sx); Venuti (vln); Brodsky (p); Lang (g); Krupa (d); Wes Vaughan (vcl). New York City, 8 September 1930.

Deep down south · I don't mind walking in the rain · I'll be a friend with pleasure (2 takes)

Hoagy Carmichael and His Orchestra: Beiderbecke (cnt); Lodwig (tpt); Cullen (tbn); Jimmy Dorsey (clt, alt); Russell (alt); Freeman (ten); Leibrook (bs sx); Venuti (vln); Brodsky (p); Lang (g); Chauncey Morehouse (d); Carmichael (arr, vcl). New York City, 15 September 1930.

Georgia on my mind · One night in Havana · Bessie couldn't help it (2 takes)

Whatever the taste of the jazz community may since have decided to the contrary, the Goldkette and especially Whiteman bands provided Beiderbecke's preferred settings. The above items were chosen in the light of his contributions, so the more original

Whiteman recordings, such as a 1928 *Sweet Sue* with anticipations of Ellington's 1931 *Mystery song* (RCA (F) 741.085), are not included. There are some rewards, however, for connoisseurs of inventive scoring, like Challis's arrangement of *Dardanella*, and of fine ensemble playing, such as the saxophone section's work on *Back in your own backyard*. Again, a few tracks, like Goldkette's *Sunday* and *My pretty girl*, have no Bix solos (although the latter includes a good thirty-two-bar passage from Polo), and the Goldkette band's never-issued *Stampede*, scored by Don Redman, might better have been selected.

Though he provides splendidly incongruous episodes in the 'Show Boat' selection and in *Barnacle Bill the sailor*, Bix's playing usually creates an indelible impression, be it with a masterly re-reading of the banal *Dardanella* melody, or with a small gem such as his nimble eight bars on *Lovable*. The earliest Goldkette performance, to which he contributes a precise yet spontaneous-sounding sixteen-bar solo, was set down only a month after his last recording session with the Wolverines (**61**). A stock arrangement is used and this band, like Ben Pollack's (**73**, **74**), never quite established its true personality on discs. Even so, Challis's score of *Slow river* proves he was well on course for his later achievements with Whiteman, and the ensembles of *My pretty girl* suggest the manner of Trumbauer's *Clarinet marmalade* (**64**), recorded three days later. The thoughtful craftsmanship of Trumbauer's *Slow river* solo is appealing, also, and it is altogether possible that this band was considerably more impressive in person than on any of its recordings. *Clementine* suggests as much.

This last is one of a number of performances which Beiderbecke completely dominates in spirit as well as instrumentally, his presence being felt even when he is not playing. Similar cases are *Mississippi mud* (some passages of which have regrettably been removed for this reissue) and *There ain't no sweet man that's worth the salt of my tears*, a memorable tune that ought to have become a jazz standard. In *Clementine* and again on *Lonely melody* the effect of his solos is enhanced by the ensemble's sustained background chords, a device rarely heard on his recordings with smaller groups. In general with Whiteman, though, Bix's solos are only one facet of orchestrations that are diversified imaginatively yet often with a busyness that is out of scale with the performances' brevity. An exception is *San*, which is on similar lines to those of his own Gang recordings (**63**). This is notable for the momentum created by his commanding lead and also for its investigations of ensemble textures. Of related character is the duet between Beiderbecke's cornet and Strickfadden's baritone saxophone on *Sugar*, although this is surpassed by the one with Trumbauer in *You took advantage of me*. Comparison between this version of *Louisiana* and the one from Bix's Gang is less to Whiteman's disadvantage than might be assumed, and both are musically superior to Ellington's account on **90**.

The last three sessions produced acutely depressing results, typified by the limp melodies chosen for the date under Beiderbecke's own name. Each prominently features appalling singing, and though Bix and Goodman have their moments these are sabotaged by Krupa's leaden drumming. The second Carmichael session, Beiderbecke's very last, was built round the leader's composing, arranging and singing, and the cornettist's role is subsidiary. He makes no attempt to dominate, as he would have done effortlessly a short while before, and in the following year he died. Yet Bix's influence long survived him and can be heard in many of the recordings dealt with on this book's later pages.   M.H.

Tommy Dorsey/Jimmy Dorsey/Eddie Lang
66 **Tommy, Jimmy and Eddie 1928–29**
Parlophone (E) PMC7133, Swaggie (Au) S1299

Boyd Senter and His Senterpedes: Mickey Bloom (tpt); Tommy Dorsey (tbn); Senter (clt); Jimmy Dorsey (alt); Jack Russell (p); Lang (g). New York City, 23 March 1928.
Sister Kate · Mobile blues

Charlie Butterfield (tbn) replaces Tommy Dorsey. New York City, 3 May 1928.
Stack o'lee blues

Vic Berton (d) added. New York City, 8 May 1928.
Chinese blues · Somebody's wrong

Tommy Dorsey and His Novelty Orchestra: Dorsey (tpt); Arthur Schutt (p); Lang (g); Jimmy Williams (bs, tu); Stan King (d). New York City 10 November 1928.
It's right here for you · Tiger rag

Frank Signorelli (p) replaces Schutt; Williams absent. New York City, 23 April 1929.
Daddy, change your mind · You can't cheat a cheater

Eddie Lang and His Orchestra: Leo McConville (tpt); Tommy Dorsey (tpt, tbn); Jimmy Dorsey (clt, alt); Schutt (p); Lang (g); Joe Tarto (bs); King (d). New York City, 22 May 1929.
Bugle call rag · Freeze and melt · Hot heels

Jimmy Dorsey and His Orchestra: McConville, Manny Klein (tpt); Tommy Dorsey (tbn); Jimmy Dorsey (clt[1], alt[2]); Alfie Evans (alt); Paul Mason (ten); Schutt (p); Lang (g); Tarto (bs); King (d). New York City, 13 June 1929.
Praying the blues[1] · *Beebe*[2]
Eddie Lang and His Orchestra: Andy Secrest, Charles Margulis (tpt); Bill Rank (tbn); Izzy Friedman (clt, ten); Bernard Daly, Charles Strickfadden (alt); Henry Whiteman (vln); Hoagy Carmichael (p, cls); Lang (g); Mike Trafficante (bs); George Marsh (d); Mildred Bailey (vcl[3]). New York City, 5 October 1929.
What kind of man is you?[3] · *Walking the dog* · *March of the hoodlums*

In view of the leadership Lang provides on the two dates under his own name here, solos such as those he contributes to *Hot heels* and *Walking the dog*, and his work on other records like **67** and **68**, it is amusing to recall such largely unchallenged assertions as that it was only 'with Charlie Christian the guitar found its jazz voice' [24]. These are in fact classic sessions, the earlier one, especially, being comparable with the great Lang–Venuti 1931 performances on **119**. The *Bugle call rag* breaks summarize the combined force and verve of this music, the point being confirmed by the immaculate solos which follow, particularly McConville's. A similarly unflagging invention is displayed on *Freeze and melt*, Jimmy Dorsey's stinging clarinet improvisation being especially admirable. And McConville again shines in the imaginative solo he fashions over the deeply swinging ground beat of *Hot heels*.

The other Lang date, using a contingent of Paul Whiteman's band, is more formal, being concerned with ensemble subtlety more than with individual expression, although in his *Walking the dog* and *March of the hoodlums* clarinet solos, Friedman gives a better account of himself than with Beiderbecke (**63** and **65**). In orchestral terms the results are independent both of the pioneer big bands of the 1920s and of the later swing groups, and it is regrettable that, as so often, we do not know who the arranger was, though an obvious possibility is Carmichael, who takes an interesting piano solo on *Walking the dog*. Carmichael's *March of the hoodlums*, like *Freeze and melt*, receives a performance well in advance of that recorded by Ellington the same year.

Further evidence of Jimmy Dorsey's qualities is found in *Praying the blues* and *Beebe*, which throughout are features for his clarinet and alto playing respectively. The blues were by no means central to the playing of this school, yet the former piece, far from being a collection of stock phrases, is an entirely convincing essay and revealingly expressive. It underlines Ornette Coleman's statement about Dorsey that 'not too many people realize his value' [25]. Less may be claimed for his brother's trumpeting, although *Tiger rag*, particularly, is a reminder of his sometimes overlooked powers as a jazz improviser.

Senter was, with Wilton Crawley, the man whom New Orleans revivalist and, later, trad clarinettists usually emulated when they imagined themselves to be sounding like Johnny Dodds. His five tracks are an unfortunate burden to this LP and present the embarrassing case, sometimes found in jazz, of performances in which everyone plays far better than the leader. *Somebody's wrong* indeed, and it is always Senter (then billed as 'The Jazzologist Supreme'). One cannot help wondering what Lang and the Dorseys thought of his tasteless and tuneless antics.

M.H.

67 Venuti–Lang 1927–28
Parlophone (E) PMC7091, Swaggie (Au) S1266

Joe Venuti (vln); Eddie Lang (g). New York City, 24 January 1927.
Wild cat · Sunshine

Arthur Schutt (p) added. New York City, 4 May 1927.
Doing things · Going places

Joe Venuti's Blue Four: Adrian Rollini (bs sx, hfp, gfs); Venuti (vln); Schutt (p); Lang (g). New York City, 28 June 1927.
Kicking the cat · Beating the dog

Same personnel and location, 13 September 1927.
Cheese and crackers · A mug of ale

Don Murray (clt, bar); Venuti (vln); Frank Signorelli (p); Lang (g); possibly Justin Ring (cym). New York City, 15 November 1927.
Penn Beach blues · Four-string Joe

Rube Bloom (p) replaces Signorelli. New York City, 28 March 1928.
Dinah · The wild dog

Same personnel: Bloom (vcl[1]). New York City, 14 June 1928.
The man from the south[1] · *Pretty Trix*

Jimmy Dorsey (clt, bar); Venuti (vln); Bloom (p, vcl); Lang (g); possibly Ring (d). New York City, 27 September 1928.
The blue room · Sensation

Italy did not witness much jazz activity until after World War II, yet Italian–Americans, beginning with Nick LaRocca (**12**), played quite a significant part in the development of the music during the years between the two world wars. Four of them appear on this LP, three — Venuti, Lang (his real name was Salvatore

Massaro) and Rollini — quite formidable, the other — Signorelli — a relatively minor figure. The instruments used by Venuti and Lang were, of course, traditional to Italy; although Lang was born in Philadelphia and Venuti aboard a ship entering New York harbour (they later went to school together), something of those traditions must have been present in the family backgrounds of the two musicians.

Venuti's style was rooted in a classical technique; there was nothing of the American country fiddler, black or white, about his music. Lang, on the other hand, was unusually adaptable, able to sound completely at home playing alongside Negro jazz and blues performers (he recorded with Clarence Williams, Bessie Smith, Victoria Spivey and — see **68** — King Oliver, Louis Armstrong, Lonnie Johnson and Texas Alexander). His partnership with Venuti, however, stressed European musical values, always witty and inventive, and rhythmically most relaxed, with Lang inclined to lie back on the beat rather than push it. In the duets it is Venuti who takes the dominant role, his playing full of devices that catch the attention. Lang was content to be an accompanist, yet one of such brilliance that the listener can find satisfaction just contemplating his use of harmony, his skill at providing a rhythmic impetus.

Most of the pieces move at medium pace, with only *The wild dog* going in for alternating tempos. Several compositions make at least passing references to the chord sequence of *Tiger rag*, perhaps the most popular harmonic standby of the period, while *Sunshine* hints at what Beiderbecke was already doing (Lang played alongside Bix on one of his most influential recordings, *Singing the blues* (**64**), less than a fortnight later). *A mug of ale* uses the chords of *Limehouse blues* while, rather more unusually, *Doing things* is based on one of Debussy's *Préludes*, *La fille aux cheveux de lin*, more evidence of how, like Beiderbecke, musicians of this sort were fond of toying with what was then regarded as 'modern harmony'.

A sophisticated harmonic instinct was what Rollini brought to any group he played in, together with the ability to perform on a cumbersome instrument, the bass saxophone, with astounding lightness. And he could play jokey, self-invented instruments such as the goofus or hot fountain pen with the right kind of seriousness; on the latter, a tiny one-octave clarinet, he even sounds rather like Pee Wee Russell. When he left for Britain to play with Fred Elizalde's orchestra (**97**), his deputies were Murray and Jimmy Dorsey, both adroit but lacking his elegant audacity. They both use baritone instead of bass saxophone, but their strategy was similar to Rollini's, the role half-rhythmic, half-melodic. Murray's clarinet playing is respectable rather than dazzling; Dorsey sometimes, in contrast, overdid the technical bravura; his *Blue room* solo is Noone-like in its use of trills. *Pretty Trix* is graceful as well as ingenious, but perhaps the most remarkable track by the Blue Four was *Sensation*, made just ten years after the Original Dixieland Jazz Band's recording. The whole performance translates a dixieland routine into what was, in 1928, the most up-to-date kind of jazz, with Bloom's singing (greatly superior to his inept work on his other two vocal tracks) deployed within the structure of the piece.   C.F.

Eddie Lang/Lonnie Johnson
68a
Blue Guitars Vol. 1
Parlophone (E) PMC7019, Swaggie (Au) S1209

Lang (g); Arthur Schutt (p). New York City, 1 April 1927.
Eddie's twister

Schutt absent. New York City, 26 May 1927.
A little love, a little kiss

Johnson (g). Memphis, 21 February 1928.
Playing with the strings · Stomping 'em along slow · Away down in the alley blues · Blues in G

Lang (g); Frank Signorelli (p). New York City, 29 March 1928.
Rainbow dreams · Add a little wiggle

Johnson (g) replaces Signorelli. New York City, 17 November 1928.
Have to change key to play these blues

Louis Armstrong and His All-Star Orchestra: Armstrong (tpt); Jack Teagarden (tbn); Happy Cauldwell (ten); Joe Sullivan (p); Lang (g); Kaiser Marshall (d). New York City, 5 March 1929.
Knocking a jug

Louis Armstrong and His Savoy Ballroom Five (*sic*): Armstrong (tpt); J. C. Higginbotham (tbn); Albert Nicholas, Charlie Holmes (clt, alt); Teddy Hill (ten); Luis Russell (p); Johnson (g); Eddie Condon (bj); Pops Foster (bs); Paul Barbarin (d). New York City, 5 March 1929.
Mahogany Hall stomp

Lang, Johnson (g). New York City, 8 May 1929.
Blue guitars

Same personnel and location, 9 October 1929.
Hot fingers · Midnight call blues · Deep minor rhythm · Blue room blues

68b
Blue Guitars Vol. 2
Parlophone (E) PMC7106, Swaggie (Au) S1276

Lang (g); Schutt (p). New York City, 1 April 1927.
April kisses
Schutt absent. New York City, 26 May 1927.
Prelude in C sharp minor Op. 3 No. 2
Signorelli (p) added. New York City, 21 November 1927.
The melody man's dream · *Perfect*
Same personnel and location, 27 September 1928.
I'll never be the same · *Jeannine*
Justin Ring (ch) added. New York City, 5 November 1928.
Church Street sobbing blues · *There'll be some changes made*
Texas Alexander (vcl); Lang, Johnson (g). New York City, 15 November 1928.
Work ox blues · *The rising sun*
Alexander absent. New York City, 17 November 1928.
Two tone stomp
Blind Willie Dunn's Gin Bottle Four: King Oliver (cnt); J. C. Johnson (p); Lang, Lonnie Johnson (g); Hoagy Carmichael (vcl, perc). New York City, 30 April 1929.
Jet black blues · *Blue blood blues*
Lang, Johnson (g). New York City, 7 May 1929.
Guitar blues · *Bullfrog moan*
Same personnel and location, 8 May 1929.
A handful of riffs

Johnson's has been called 'essentially a jazz technique rather than a blues one' [26]. He will be remembered especially for the contributions he made to jazz sessions, even though the majority of his later recordings feature his blues playing and singing. But it can hardly be denied that he fits rather curiously into jazz ensembles like those of Armstrong and Ellington (**91**), the distinctiveness consisting of his forthright blues phrasing. Superficially he appears a more accomplished technician than Lang, but he may well have owed the opportunity to play in a jazz setting to Lang's own enterprise in developing the guitar as more than a 'rhythm' instrument. In this respect, Lang was more influential than his fairly limited technical achievements may immediately suggest. And it should be recalled that his collaborations with Joe Venuti (**67**) were to pioneer a style which, though much copied, was not significantly built upon except in the solo work of Django Reinhardt (**104–106** and **107d**).

The differences between Lang and Johnson are clear in their assured duets. Lang's phrasing is squarer, more accentually tentative than Johnson's more flowing lines, and yet there is a searching quality to it, something which is perhaps a little less facile, a little more subtle in its use of blue notes. But they blend well, creating a body of work that, if a little unvaried in overall effect, is musically unique and a small landmark in jazz history.

In their solo work the differences are more stark. The worksong strokes of *Stomping 'em along slow*, the floating treble and piano-blues bass of *Away down in the alley* and *Blues in G* rather question the judgement quoted above, for this style is part and parcel of a pre-jazz expression. Lang, on the other hand, for all his sensitiveness to the blues, is conditioned by a sophisticated eclecticism which, in the solos accompanied by Schutt and Signorelli, when aspiring to jazz, combines blue-note embellishments with harmonic prospectings of a 'Bixological' tinge. The blues come through more surely in *Perfect* than in the well-known *Church Street sobbing blues*, and it is augmentation springing from that source, rather than any real gift for improvisation, that gives his treatments of songs like *There'll be some changes made* and *I'll never be the same* what distinction they have. A rather quaint formalism close to ragtime touches his other solo work, whilst *April kisses*, *Jeannine* and Rachmaninoff's *Prelude in C sharp minor* have no jazz or blues content at all.

Johnson's approach to jazz ensemble playing is typified in *Mahogany Hall stomp*, a performance characteristic of the Armstrong–Luis Russell sessions to be heard on **52**; while Lang's equally recognizable accompanying style, springing plangently from the beat, gives to the earlier choruses of *Knocking a jug* much of their memorable atmosphere. And let not his brief solo in that number be remembered just because it is familiar; its development of blues dialect has a nice element of the unexpected.

The duet style, somewhat modified, supports well the poignant lyricism of Texas Alexander. Then Johnson and Lang, the latter hiding none too effectually behind the *persona* of 'Blind Willie Dunn', support with equanimity both the dignified laments of Oliver and the palely loitering scat of Carmichael in *Jet black* and *Blue blood blues*.   E.T.

69 The California Ramblers Vol. 2
The Old Masters (A) TOM25, *Halycon (E) 8

California Ramblers: Frank Cush, Chelsea Quealey (tpt); Ivan Johnston (tbn); Bobby Davis (clt, sop, alt): Sam Ruby (ten); Adrian Rollini (bs sx); Al Duffy (vln); Jack Russin (p); Tommy Felline (bj); Herb Weil (d); Ed Kirkeby (vcl[1]). New York City, 29 March 1927.
Pardon the glove · Yes she do, no she don't[1]

Cush, Quealey (tpt); Edward Lapp (tbn); Davis (clt, sop, alt); Pete Pumiglio (clt, alt); Ruby (ten); Rollini (bs sx); Russin (p); Felline (bj, g); Weil (d); possibly Arthur Fields (vcl[2]); unidentified vcl[3]. New York City, 26 May 1927.
Lazy weather[2] · *Vo-do-do-de-o*[3]

Little Ramblers: unidentified tpt; possibly Davis (clt, alt); Ruby (ten); Rollini (bs sx, gfs); unidentified p; Felline (bj, g); Weil (d). New York City, 8 July 1927.
Play it, Red · Swamp blues

California Ramblers: Cush, Quealey (tpt); Al Philburn (tbn); Pumiglio (clt, alt); Bob Fallon (alt); Ruby (ten); Spencer Clark (bs sx); Duffy (vln); Russin (p, cls[4]); Felline (bj, g); Weil (d); Kirkeby (vcl[1]). New York City, 20 September 1927.
Nothing does[1,4] · *It was only a sunshower*[1]

Golden Gate Orchestra: Cush, Tommy Dorsey (tpt); Johnston (tbn); Jimmy Dorsey (clt, alt); unidentified alt; Ruby (ten); Clark (bs sx); Duffy (vln); Russin (p); Felline (bj, g); Weil (d); Fields (vcl[2]). New York City, 7 October 1927.
Make my cot where the cot-cot-cotton grows[2]

California Ramblers: Quealey, Bill Moore (tpt); Tommy Dorsey (tbn); Davis, Pumiglio (clt, alt); Ruby (ten); Duffy (vln); Lennie Hayton (p); Felline (bj); Jack Hansen (tu); Weil (d); Sammy Fane, Artie Dunn, Kirkeby (vcl trio). New York City, 15 December 1927.
Mine, all mine · Changes

Moore, Tony Gianelli (tpt); Carl Loffler (tbn); Pumiglio, Freddy Cusick (clt, alt); Ruby (ten); Clark (bs sx); Duffy (vln); Russin (p); Felline (bj, g); Weil (d); possibly Arthur Hall (vcl[5]). New York City, 14 January 1928.
What do you say?[5] · *Singapore sorrows*

Fred van Eps, Tony Russo (tpt); Reg Harrington (tbn); Pumiglio, Harold Marcus (clt, alt); Ruby (ten); Clark (bs sx); Joe LaFaro (vln); Chauncey Gray (p); Felline (bj, g); Weil (d) New York City, 10 February 1928.
The pay-off

Moe Selzo (tpt), Jimmy Mullen (tu), Chick Gordon (d) replace Russo, Clark, Weil; unidentified vcl trio added. New York City, 13 June 1928.
You're just a great big baby doll

Same personnel and location, 27 July 1928.
Bless you, sister

Like that of the Original Memphis Five (**14**), the California Ramblers' name covers a mass of recordings, made between 1921 and 1936, which received some attention in the early days of jazz commentary but has been virtually ignored ever since. The policy was always a dual one of catering, firstly, to a large public with excellently played versions of the latest popular songs and, secondly, to a more restricted audience with jazz performances. Naturally, these categories were no more than loosely separated, and quite often a strongly jazz-orientated performance, such as *Lazy weather* or particularly *Bless you, sister*, was let down by poor singing — not a circumstance unique to the California Ramblers. Again, there was a very considerable turnover among the musicians who played in the band, and this, together with the sheer quantity of sessions, the many different labels recorded for, the various pseudonyms used, means that it probably never will be possible to establish altogether definite personnels. What appears above, although the fruit of much listening and comparison, is tentative, and sometimes the instrumentation is larger than is implied. Only the names of those supposedly known to have been present are shown, but some of these are questionable. The saxophonists on the 20 September 1927 date, for example, are allegedly Pumiglio, Fallon, Ruby and Clark, yet the alto solo in *Nothing does* sounds quite like Jimmy Dorsey.

The Little Ramblers' are among the most obviously jazz-centred items here, with fine, if unidentified, trumpet, alto, and Rollini on both bass saxophone and goofus. The latter sounds like a harmonica but looks like a saxophone, its reeds being operated by saxophone keys. *Mine, all mine* also has bold trumpet, presumably by Moore, and one of several good Duffy improvisations in a style close to that of Venuti, if less incisive. The hottest performance, though, is probably *The pay-off*, which boasts propulsive ensemble work and a succession of inventive solos by Clark, presumably Pumiglio, and one of the trumpets — who is also heard to striking effect in *Bless you, sister. Pardon the glove*, a curious title, contains a further demonstration of Rollini's extraordinary articulateness on his monster saxophone and some remarkable alto from Davis. There is a notable solo by Philburn in *Nothing does*, a good alto and violin duet on *Changes* and a better one in *What do you say?*

Generally the arrangements are functional rather than ambitious, although there is much animated ensemble playing, as on *Vo-do-do-de-o blues*. There are occasional intriguing textures also, such as that of the alto passage on *Yes she do*, which is supported only by a banjo underscored by the bass saxophone; this piece has a noteworthy coda, too, the thread of which is deftly passed from one instrument to another. It is a pity that we do not know the names of the arrangers, especially in a case like

Singapore sorrows, which is perhaps the most atmospheric score here, with particularly effective writing for the saxophone section. Also deserving of praise are such features as the forceful series of exchanges between brass and reeds in *Make my cot*. The various singers, however, are best left in condign obscurity.

The sleeve of the above record is totally lacking in discographical information. M.H.

70a   Red Nichols and His Five Pennies Vol. 1
Coral (G) 97016

Red Nichols and His Five Pennies: Nichols (cnt); Jimmy Dorsey (clt, alt); Arthur Schutt (p); Eddie Lang (g); Vic Berton (d). New York City, 8 December 1926.
That's no bargain

Nichols, Leo McConville, Manny Klein (tpt); Miff Mole (tbn); Pee Wee Russell (clt); Fud Livingston (ten); Adrian Rollini (bs sx, gfs); Lennie Hayton (p, cls); Dick McDonough (g); Berton (d). New York City, 15 August 1927.
Riverboat shuffle · Eccentric

McConville, Klein absent. Same date.
Ida, sweet as apple cider · Feeling no pain

Carl Kress (g) replaces McDonough; Dudley Fosdick (mel) added; Rollini absent. New York City, 25 February 1928.
Avalon

Same personnel and location, 27 February 1928.
Nobody's sweetheart

Nichols, McConville, Klein (tpt); Jack Teagarden, Glenn Miller, Herb Taylor (tbn); Benny Goodman (clt, alt, bar); unidentified alt; Babe Russin (ten); Schutt (p); Kress (g); Art Miller (bs); Gene Krupa (d). New York City, 18 April 1929.
Indiana · Dinah

Nichols, Klein, Tommy Thunen (tpt); Teagarden, Glenn Miller, Taylor (tbn); Russell (clt); Bud Freeman (ten); Joe Sullivan (p); Tommy Felline (bj); Art Miller (bs); Dave Tough (d). New York City, 12 June 1929.
Rose of Washington Square

Nichols, Klein, Thunen (tpt); Teagarden, Miller (tbn); Dorsey (clt, alt); Babe Russin (ten); Rollini (bs sx); Jack Russin (p); Treg Brown (g); Jack Hansen (tu); Krupa (d). New York City, 14 February 1930.
Peg o' my heart · China boy · I want to be happy

Same personnel: Jack Teagarden, Brown also sing. New York City, 3 July 1930.
The sheik of Araby

70b Red Nichols and His Five Pennies Vol. 2

Coral (G) 97024, *Brunswick (A) 58008/9, 58027 (These three Brunswicks are partial equivalents to the two Corals.)

Red Nichols and His Five Pennies: Nichols (cnt); Dorsey (clt, alt); Schutt (p); Lang (g); Berton (d). New York City, 8 December 1926.

Washboard blues

Mole (tbn) added. New York City, 20 December 1926.

Buddy's habit

Joe Venuti (vln) added. New York City, 12 January 1927.

Bugle call rag

Phil Napoleon (tpt), Rollini (bs sx) added; Venuti absent. New York City, 25 June 1927.

Mean dog blues

Nichols, McConville, Klein (tpt); Mole (tbn); Fosdick (mel); Livingston (clt, ten); Murray Kellner (vln); Schutt (p); Kress (g); Miller (bs); Berton (d). New York City, 2 March 1928.

There'll come a time

Venuti (vln) replaces Kellner; McConville absent. New York City, 1 June 1928.

Imagination · Original dixieland one-step

Goodman (clt, alt), Hayton (p), Chauncey Morehouse (d) replace Livingston, Schutt, Berton; Rollini (bs sx) added; Venuti absent. New York City, 16 February 1929.

Allah's holiday · Roses of Picardy

Louisiana Rhythm Kings: Nichols, Thunen (tpt); Miller (tbn); Dorsey (clt, alt); Babe Russin (ten); Rollini (bs sx); Jack Russin (p); Weston Vaughan (bj, g, vcl[1]); Krupa (d). New York City, 20 January 1930.

Swanee · Squeeze me · Sweet Sue · The meanest kind of blues · I have to have you[1]

Nichols takes good solos here, sounding typically sure-footed in *Buddy's habit*, thoughtful in *Ida, sweet as apple cider*, close-knit in *China boy*, and stabbing out the phrases with surprising ardour in *I want to be happy*. But it was as an organizer of recording sessions which gave opportunities to more creative musicians that he made his chief contribution and, like some other leaders in the 1920s, he was allowed considerable freedom. These performances are, in various ways, strikingly exploratory with regard to material and treatment, while the best of the players are engaged in extending the range of improvisation and the jazz capabilities of their instruments. The above accounts of Hoagy Carmichael's *Washboard blues*, which takes further the musical implications of the composer's initial version of nineteen months before (**62**), and of the fast *That's no bargain* are delivered with remarkable clarity and decision, considering that this was some of the most advanced jazz of its time. (It is unfortunate that

Get a load of this (Fountain (E) DFJ110), recorded by Nichols, Lang, Schutt and Berton the previous month, and which is packed with harmonic audacities, is not included on the above LPs; a slightly later version, renamed *Eddie's twister*, appears on **68a**.) More conventional is *Buddy's habit*, although lively clarinet and alto playing by Dorsey is included. Venuti makes an interesting contribution to the ensembles of *Bugle call rag*, as does Berton, with timpani, to *The meanest kind of blues*.

The tracks with larger instrumentation offer a kind of Chicago-style big band music which, even if the earliest instances are dated August 1927, already looks towards the swing era. Some of them, like *China boy* and *Peg o' my heart*, were scored by Glenn Miller, who provides simple yet effective frameworks for improvisation. More impressive, though, is Livingston's *Imagination*, which is fully a piece of jazz writing, a 'composition for band'. It juxtaposes curiously with a treatment of *Original dixieland one-step* that seems ironic in its lightness of touch, though a finely shaped solo by the muted Mole is included. He has two particularly well argued trombone solos on *Avalon* as well, with Hayton's celeste passage, accompanied only by guitar, providing extreme contrast in between. Other departures include the strange little duet between trombone and Rollini's goofus in *Feeling no pain*, the ensemble led by bass saxophone which starts *Ida, sweet as apple cider* (a passage which impressed the young Gil Evans [27]), and, at a more conventional level, the trumpets' deft teamwork on *Eccentric*.

Although these and comparable sessions brought Goodman and Krupa together in the first stage of a partnership which had no little impact as the 1930s wore on, the presence of both Mole and Teagarden on these LPs is of more immediate significance, for each brought off a revolution in jazz trombone playing. The latter is discussed below (**73**, **74**, etc.) but these recordings include some of the first and best-recorded demonstrations of what he brought to jazz. Teagarden dominates most of the performances in which he takes part here, and the deference shown him is obvious. This no doubt arose in response, for example, to the musical intelligence with which he balances chromatic triplets against bold melodic statements in *Rose of Washington Square*, or his adventurous use of augmented and minor seventh chords on *Dinah* in conjunction with melodic blues ideas. The rhythmic fluidity of the introductory phrases he throws against the racing *China boy* ensemble is amazing also, and although the harsh ensemble accents of *I want to be happy* suggest a rather desperate gaiety, he mixes semiquaver triplets and trumpet-like phrases in his solo with seeming nonchalance.

That last track has admirable alto playing by Dorsey, and Russell's *Dinah* solo is a worthy successor to Teagarden's. Goodman, who was just then becoming himself, contributes well to *Indiana* and especially *China boy*. Russell again excels in *Riverboat shuffle* and *Avalon*, exploring the less obvious reaches of the harmonic structures. Nor did the clarinettists have it all their own way, and *China boy*, for instance, also boasts a solo by the fleet yet hard-stomping Sullivan. In fact, Teagarden was excellently seconded at many points.   M.H.

The Charleston Chasers

71 **Thesaurus of Classic Jazz Vol. 3**
Philips (E) BBL7433, Vol. 3 of Columbia (A) C4L-18

The Charleston Chasers: Red Nichols (tpt); Miff Mole (tbn); Jimmy Dorsey (clt, alt); Arthur Schutt (p, arr); Dick McDonough (g); Joe Tarto (tu); Vic Berton (d). New York City, 4 January 1927.
Someday, sweetheart · After you've gone
Same personnel and location, 25 February 1927.
Farewell blues · Davenport blues · Wabash blues
Same personnel and location, 18 May 1927.
My gal Sal · Delirium
Leo McConville (tpt) added; Fud Livingston (clt, ten, arr), Jack Hansen (tu) replace Dorsey, Tarto. New York City, 6 September 1927.
Five pennies · Sugar foot strut
Same personnel and location, 8 September 1927.
Imagination · Feeling no pain
Carl Kress (bj, g) replaces McDonough. New York City, 7 March 1928.
Mississippi mud

Some of the best results of the Nichols–Mole partnership were recorded not under either of their own names but under that of the Charleston Chasers. This LP gives the complete output of five almost consecutive 1927 sessions plus one item from 1928 and, as the band's membership was quite stable, the musical aims are more steadily focused than on the Nichols dates under **70** where the personnel and instrumentation varied so much. The trumpeter in particular shines more consistently than on those more ambitious recordings, improvising with real power over sustained ensemble harmonies on *Five pennies*, playing with exceptional feeling in *Someday, sweetheart*, and contributing especially well-formed solos and closing ensemble leads to *Wabash blues* and *My gal Sal*. Dorsey is excellent on this last, too, playing, as he also does on *Davenport blues*, a thoughtful, almost withdrawn solo that well contradicts his reputation as a mere trickster (the rhythmically dexterous break on the former piece notwithstanding). Still on alto saxophone, he is more outward-going in *Farewell blues*, his contribution again being finely shaped, as is his later clarinet solo and ensemble part.

Indeed, most of this music sounds as good as new, and Mole's pointed fluency and inventive wit are impressive in his breaks on *After you've gone* and *Davenport blues*, and in his solos on *Sugar foot strut* and *Wabash blues*. There are plenty of other good improvisations, such as Livingston's passage, evenly flowing yet with real ideas, in *Sugar foot strut*, and by Schutt on his own piece, *Delirium*. This last, though a less remarkable essay than Livingston's *Imagination*, is a true jazz theme and significantly gives rise to notable solos from nearly all participants. Although with *Imagination* the ensemble is supreme, there are instructive differences between this version and the one under **70b**, even if these are chiefly a matter of emphasis. There are more considerable divergences between this *Davenport blues* and the one recorded under Mole's name some days later (**72**), not least in Nichols's part. Sensitive playing by McDonough on *Farewell* and *Wabash blues* ought to be noted, as should the fact that concerted work asserts itself again in the final *Mississippi mud*, which, despite a brief if striking Livingston solo, is mainly well-conceived ensemble passages.   M.H.

Miff Mole

72 Thesaurus of Classic Jazz Vol. 2
Philips (E) BBL7432, Vol. 2 of Columbia (A) C4L-18

Miff Mole and His Molers; Red Nichols (tpt); Mole (tbn); Arthur Schutt (p); Dick McDonough (bj, g); Vic Berton (d). New York City, 26 January 1927.
Alexander's ragtime band · Some sweet day
Jimmy Dorsey (clt, alt), Joe Tarto (tu) added. New York City, 7 March 1927.
Davenport blues · Darktown strutters' ball
Fud Livingston (clt, ten), Adrian Rollini (bs sx) added. New York City, 1 September 1927.
My gal Sal · Honolulu blues · The new twister
Leo McConville (tpt), Dudley Fosdick (mel) added; Carl Kress (g), Stan King (d) replace McDonough, Berton. New York City, 27 July 1928.
Crazy rhythm
McConville, Manny Klein (tpt); Mole (tbn); Dorsey (clt, alt); Schutt (p); Eddie Lang (g); King (d). New York City, 19 April 1929.
I've got a feeling I'm falling · That's a-plenty
Phil Napoleon (tpt); Mole (tbn); Dorsey (clt, alt); Babe Russin (ten); Schutt (p); McDonough (g); Tarto (tu); King (d). New York City, 24 September 1929.
After you've gone

Lennie Hayton (p), Kress (g) replace Schutt, McDonough; Rollini (bs sx), Smith Ballew (vcl) added. New York City, 6 February 1930.
Navy blues

Mole's technical capabilities were considerable, and by his and the century's mid-twenties he was sufficiently master of his instrument's 'classic' jazz ensemble functions to give occasional vent to his dissatisfaction with the limitations of that role. Others were seeking greater liberty for the trombone: Teagarden, working in a similar *milieu*, was soon to perfect a style that was to outstrip Mole's in flexibility and variety, and J. C. Higginbotham was possibly, in the period considered, a more powerful and daring soloist than either of them. Yet one has only to listen to his skilful, glancing contribution to the infectiously hot *That's a-plenty* to sense a potentiality of imagination in Mole's searchings that might have led him to quite different but no less valid jazz discoveries. Unfortunately, the imagination was not sufficiently tenacious in improvisatory terms. He was clearly ill-content with the remnants of tailgate style, as can be heard in *Darktown strutters' ball*, but in his solos one frequently guesses what he is aiming for without actually hearing it achieved, and the element of daring needs to be applauded. Some of his phrases — those in the *That's a-plenty* solo and in *Some sweet day* are instances — may even suggest that his auguries were to find fulfilment much later in the elegancies of trombonists like J. J. Johnson and Frank Rehak.

Mole does not fall short because of limited instrumental skill. In *After you've gone* he vies with the clarinettist in agility and even anticipates some of his phrases. His introduction to *The new twister*, simple though it is on the surface, clearly indicates powers held in check, and it also demonstrates even more effectually than Nichols's work how pervasive the questing spirit of Beiderbecke was among groups of these kinds. Just as saxophonists seemed to be seeking a style suitable to the instrument by emulating clarinet modes (though Livingston and Russin are shown to be exceptions to this by their playing here), so trombonists may have been tempted to borrow trumpet phraseology. But Mole's choices are more volatile than that, as will be shown by a comparison of his very Bixian solo in *Crazy rhythm* with the one on *Navy blues* where the trombone is permitted to suggest its own dialect. In all premeditated parts he can be both zestful and precise — listen, for example, to the marvellously executed coda to *Crazy rhythm*. His least satisfying solos are those in which he seems to be unduly occupied with the theme. *I've got a feeling I'm falling* is not a tune that gives much scope for improvisation, but he might have responded more enterprisingly to the invitation of *Alexander's ragtime band*. In the latter piece, and in *Some sweet day*, there are some pleasantly skilful duets by Mole and Nichols.

Most of these performances contrive to be both purposeful and relaxed, and many of them reflect the contemporary movement towards a less complex ensemble style. The trumpet scoring in *That's a-plenty* and the swinging section contrasts aimed at in the arrangement of *Navy blues* seem, as heard in retrospect, to provide ready fodder for the big bands of a few years later.

With the exceptions of Livingston, Russin and the critically neglected Napoleon, Mole's companions are generally less interesting than he is on these sessions. Dorsey's sweet tone does not suit the double-time Chicagoan angularities which he attempts and, among the cornettists, only Napoleon, whose clarion lead to *After you've gone* is admirable, directs the mind beyond a simplified conception of the Beiderbecke legacy.   E.T.

Jack Teagarden
73 King of the Blues Trombone Vol. 1
Columbia (E) 33SX1545, Epic (A) SN6044

Goody and His Good Timers: Manny Klein (tpt); Teagarden (tbn); Jimmy Dorsey (clt, alt); Fud Livingston (ten); Matty Malneck (vln); Frank Signorelli (p); unidentified bj, tu, d; Irving Mills (vcl). New York City, November 1928.
Diga diga doo

The Whoopee Makers: Jimmy McPartland, Al Harris (tpt); Teagarden (tbn); Benny Goodman (clt, alt); Gil Rodin (alt); Larry Binyon (ten); Vic Breidis (p); Dick Morgan (bj); Harry Goodman (tu); Ben Pollack (d). New York City, November 1928.
Bugle call rag

Jimmy McHugh's Bostonians: Eddie Bergman (vln[1]), George Terry (arr[2]), Elliott Jacoby (arr[3]) added. New York City, 27 November 1928.
Baby[1,3] · *Whoopee stomp*[2]

Jack Pettis and His Orchestra: Bill Moore, Phil Hart (tpt); Teagarden (tbn); Goodman (clt, alt); Pettis (C-mel, ten, arr[4]); Al Goering (p, arr[5]); Dick McDonough (g); Merrill Klein (tu); Dillon Ober (d). New York City, 8 February 1929.
Freshman hop[4] · *Sweetest melody*[4] · *Bag o' blues*[5]

The Whoopee Makers: McPartland, Tommy Thunen (tpt); Teagarden (tbn, vcl); Benny Goodman (clt, alt); Rodin (alt); Binyon (ten); Bredis (p); Morgan (bj); Harry Goodman (tu); Ray Bauduc (d). New York City, April 1929.
Dirty dog

McPartland, Tommy Gott (tpt); Teagarden (tpt, tbn, vcl); Dorsey (clt, alt); Bud Freeman (clt, ten); Rodin (alt); Pee Wee Russell (ten); Breidis (p); Morgan (bj); Goodman (tu); Bauduc (d). New York City, 6 June 1929.
It's so good

Mills's Merry Makers: Ruby Weinstein, Charlie Teagarden (tpt); Jack Teagarden (tbn, vcl); Matty Matlock (clt, alt); Rodin (alt); Binyon (ten); Bergman, Alex Beller (vln); Bill Schuman (cel); Breidis (p); Morgan (bj); Goodman (tu); Bauduc (d); Jacoby (arr). New York City, 31 January 1930.
When you're smiling

Joe Venuti and His New Yorkers: Klein, Ray Lodwig (tpt); Teagarden (tbn); Izzy Friedman (clt, ten); Arnold Brilhart, Bernie Daly (alt); Min Leibrook (bs sx); Venuti (vln); Lenny Hayton (p, cls); Eddie Lang (g); Herb Quigley (d). New York City, 22 May 1930.
Dancing with tears in my eyes

Ben Pollack and His Orchestra: Weinstein or Charlie Spivak, Charlie Teagarden (tpt); Jack Teagarden (tbn vcl); Matlock (clt, alt); Rodin (alt); Babe Russin (ten); Beller (vln); Breidis (p); Morgan (bj); Goodman (tu); Bauduc (d). New York City, 23 June 1930.
If I could be with you one hour tonight

Jack Teagarden and His Band: Spivak, Sterling Bose (tpt); Teagarden (tbn, vcl); Dorsey (clt, alt); Rodin (alt); Eddie Miller (ten); Gil Bowers (p); Nappy Lamare (g); Goodman (tu); Bauduc (d). New York City, January 1931.
Loveless love

Ben Pollack and His Orchestra: Benny Goodman (clt, alt), Sam Prager (p) replace Dorsey, Bowers. New York City, 2 March 1931.
Sweet and hot

Jack Teagarden and His Orchestra: Bose, Charlie Teagarden (tpt); Jack Teagarden (tbn, vcl); Russell (clt, ten); Joe Catalyne, Max Farley (alt); Adrian Rollini (bs sx); Fats Waller (p, vcl); Lamare (g); Artie Bernstein (bs); Stan King (d). New York City, 14 October 1931.
That's what I like about you · You rascal, you

74 Jack Teagarden
RCA (E) RD7826, RCA (A) LPV528

Roger Wolfe Kahn and His Orchestra: Gott, Klein (tpt); Teagarden (tbn); Alfie Evans, Brilhart (alt); unidentified ten; Venuti, Joe Raymond (vln); Harold Brodsky (p); Tony Colucci (bj); Lang (g); Arthur Campbell (tu); Vic Berton (d, cls). New York City, 14 March 1928.
She's a great, great girl

Eddie's Hot Shots: Leonard Davies (tpt); Teagarden (tbn, vcl); Mezz Mezzrow (clt, C-mel); Happy Cauldwell (ten); Joe Sullivan (p); Eddie Condon (bj); George Stafford (d). New York City, 8 February 1929.
I'm gonna stomp, Mr Henry Lee · That's a serious thing

Ben Pollack and His Park Central Orchestra: Weinstein, McPartland (tpt); Teagarden (tbn); Benny Goodman (clt, alt); Rodin (alt); Binyon (ten); Bergman, Beller (vln); Schuman (cel); Breidis (p); Morgan (bj); Harry Goodman (tu); Bauduc (d); Pollack (vcl). New York City, 5 March 1929.

My kind of love

Mound City Blue Blowers: Teagarden (tbn); Condon (bj); Jack Bland (g); Al Morgan (bs); Frank Billings (d); Red McKenzie (cap, vcl[1]). New York City, 25 September 1929.

Tailspin blues · *Never had a reason to believe in you* [1]

Fats Waller and His Buddies: Davies, Henry Allen (tpt); Teagarden, J. C. Higginbotham (tbn); Albert Nicholas, Charlie Holmes (clt, alt); Binyon (ten); Waller (p); Will Johnson (bj); Pops Foster (bs); Kaiser Marshall (d). New York City, 18 December 1929.

Riding but walking

Ben Pollack and His Orchestra: Spivak, Bose (tpt); Teagarden, Ralph Copsey (tbn); Rodin, Matlock (clt, alt); Miller (ten); Beller, Raymond Cohen (vln); Bowers (p); Lamare (g, vcl); Jerry Johnson (bs); Bauduc (d). Chicago, 19 March 1933.

Two tickets to Georgia

Paul Whiteman and His Orchestra: Nat Natoli, Harry Goldfield, Charlie Teagarden (tpt); Bill Rank, Hal Matthews, Jack Teagarden (tbn); Charles Strickfadden (ob, clt, alt, ten; bar); Benny Bonacio (clt, bs clt, alt); John Cordaro (clt, bs clt, alt, bar); Frankie Trumbauer (clt, alt, C-mel); Roy Bargy, Ramona Davies (p); Mike Pingitore (g); Art Miller (bs); Larry Gomar (d, vib). New York City, 9 July 1935.

Nobody's sweetheart

Metronome All-Stars: Bunny Berigan, Harry James, Sonny Dunham (tpt); Tommy Dorsey, Teagarden (tbn); Goodman (clt, alt); Hymie Schertzer (alt); Miller, Arthur Rollini (ten); Bob Zurke (p); Carmen Mastren (g); Bob Haggart (bs); Bauduc (d). New York City, 11 January 1939.

The blues

Spivak (tpt) replaces James. Same date.

Blue Lou

Jack Teagarden's Big Eight: Max Kaminsky (tpt); Teagarden (tbn, vcl[1]); Peanuts Hucko (clt); Cliff Strickland (ten); Gene Schroeder (p); Chuck Wayne (g); Jack Lesberg (bs); Dave Tough (d). New York City, 14 March 1947.

A jam session at Victor · *Say it simple* [1]

Louis Armstrong and His All-Stars: Armstrong, Bobby Hackett (tpt); Teagarden (tbn, vcl); Hucko (ten); Dick Carey (p); Haggart (bs); Sidney Catlett (d). New York City, 24 April 1947.

St James' Infirmary

Bud Freeman's Summa Cum Laude Orchestra: Billy Butterfield (tpt); Teagarden (tbn, vcl); Hucko (clt); Freeman (ten); Schroeder (p); Leonard Gaskin (bs); George Wettling (d). New York City, 8 July 1957.

I cover the waterfront · *There'll be some changes made*

Jazz musicians became aware of Teagarden's major innovations during the late 1920s and early 1930s, and although they are best heard in conjunction with the Nichols performances in which he took part under 70, the above two widely-ranging anthologies document his contributions well. On a few tracks, such as *Whoopee stomp* and *Baby*, his appearances are brief, yet he always creates a distinct impression, never playing a perfunctory bar, and the majestic ease as well as the individuality of his performances implies years of development away from the supposed centres of jazz innovation before these recordings were made. Though his work on, say, *A jam session at Victor* demonstrates a casual mastery of then-contemporary 52nd Street procedures, Teagarden's style, just because it was so personal, was untouched by the ordinary tides of change in jazz, was as near to being timeless as anything in this music can be.

He belongs, indeed, to that restricted category of jazz musicians who go on actually to surpass brilliant early achievements, as is suggested by the poised yet highly expressive trombone solo on *Say it simple*. Relevant also are his free statement, rhapsodic yet oblique, of the *I cover the waterfront* melody and the way his suave elaborations on *There'll be some changes made* coalesce, seemingly by chance, into a satisfying musical design. Some of the earlier groups with which he appears here are of poor quality, at best only in part orientated towards jazz, and his sophisticated obbligato to Pollack's singing on *My kind of love* makes the passage seem like a juxtaposition of substance and shadow, his counterpoint to McKenzie's comb-and-paper noises in *Never had a reason* having a similar effect. On the hitherto unissued take of *She's a great, great girl* he parodies and plays against the band's stiffness. In fact, nothing seems to distract Teagarden, not Klein's sweet-toned interruption to his solo on *Dancing with tears in my eyes* nor even the Condon session's abysmal saxophone playing. As if to counteract the monotony of such assemblages, he likes to appear on a performance in more than one guise, as is shown by his open and muted *Diga diga doo* solos. On *It's so good* he plays trumpet besides trombone, although in view of his mobility on the latter instrument it is surprising that he bothered with the former.

Certainly his in some ways unorthodox technique gave him an ease and rapidity of movement demonstrated on every track here and a particular virtuosity in the upper register well exemplified by *The blues*. His consequent freedom from the beat, no matter how heavily stated, is shown on *Never had a reason* and *You rascal, you*; and in *Two tickets to Georgia* this is allied with harmonic adventure. Teagarden's ear for harmonic subtleties was in the late 1920s matched only by Coleman Hawkins, Bix Beiderbecke and a very few others, and his interpolation of ambiguous diminished chords and treating major triads as if they were minor are especially noteworthy. This last is related to his sensitive use of blue notes — flat sevenths as well as the commonplace flat thirds — and the authenticity of his feeling for this idiom is apparent in *Tailspin blues, Riding but walking* and, above all, *Dirty dog* and *St James Infirmary*, two of the best recordings of his career. On the latter in particular his phrases are highly detailed yet have an inevitability that only a master could impart. The communicative force of the two trombone solos on *Dirty dog* (an alternative and superior version of *Making friends* heard on **54**) is remarkable although, on another level, there is something pleasingly surrealistic about this beautiful yet sombre piece having been recorded by a band calling itself the Whoopee Makers. Another prominent feature of Teagarden's musical armoury is his fine singing, exemplified by a touching account of *I cover the waterfront*, an excellent late instance of his elegiac ballad style. Yet it is his architectural sense which unites all the elements in his expression, and though he has been enormously influential the lessons he had to teach in this last regard have been least well learnt.

While there is not much of interest in the collective performances here, the close of *You rascal, you* should be noted as a prompt response to the Casa Loma example (**121**), and the ending of *Sweet and hot* is well conceived and executed for driving ensemble and solo lines. Again, the unusually animated *Two tickets to Georgia* is the sort of venture that may have influenced Goodman when he formed his own permanent band. The clarinettist is several times audibly affected by the blues aspect of Teagarden's language, as in *My kind of love*, and there are good contributions from Waller, McPartland, Schroeder, Charlie Teagarden and Bose. On *The blues* and *Blue Lou* (a previously unissued take), Dunham's elaborate yet disciplined solos make an especially apt foil to the great trombonist. M.H.

The Early Big Bands

The size of some bands was growing, and a distinction became apparent between informal, blues-based ensembles from the south-west and those which more deliberately explored the musical potentialities of a larger instrumentation.

75 The Territory Bands
Parlophone (E) PMC7082

The Blue Ribbon Syncopators: Harry Tate (tpt); Herbert Diemer (alt, bar); George West (p); Gilbert Roberts (bj); Hurley Diemer (d). Buffalo, March 1925.
Blues in A minor · *My gal, my pal*

Eddie Heywood and His Jazz Six: Robert Cheek (cnt); Sweet Papa Jonas Walker (tbn); Edward Alexander (alt, bar); Heywood (p); Henry Waite (bj); Theo Johnson (d). New York City, 6 October 1926.
Trombone moaning blues

Jesse Stone and His Blues Serenaders: Albert Hinton, Slick Jackson (tpt); Druie Bess (tbn); Glenn Hughes (alt); Jack Washington (alt, bar); Elmer Burch (ten); Stone (p, arr); Silas Cluke (bj); Pete Hassel (tu); Max Wilkinson (d). St Louis, 27 April 1927.
Starvation blues · *Boot to boot*

Charles Creath's Jazz-O-Maniacs: Creath, Dewey Jackson (cnt); Albert Wynn (tbn); Thornton Blue, Horace Eubanks (clt, alt); William Rollins (ten); Burroughs Lovingood (p); Pete Patterson (bj); Cecil White (tu); Zutty Singleton (d). St Louis, 2 May 1927.
Butter finger blues · *Crazy quilt*

Troy Floyd and His Plaza Hotel Orchestra: Don Albert (tpt); Benny Long (tbn); N. J. Siki Collins (clt, sop); Floyd (clt, alt); Scott Bagby (clt, ten); Allen Van (p); John H. Braggs (bj); Charles Dixon (tu); John Humphries (d); Kellough Jefferson (vcl). San Antonio, 14 March 1929.
Wabash blues · *Shadowland blues*

Herschel Evans (clt, sop, ten) replaces Bagby; Willie Long (tpt) added; Jefferson absent. San Antonio, 21 June 1929.
Dreamland blues

J. Neale Montgomery and His Orchestra: Henry Mason, Karl Burns (tpt); unidentified tbn; George Derrigotte, . . . Puckett (clt, alt); . . . Brown (clt, ten); Montgomery (p); unidentified bj, g; Jesse Wilcox (tu); Ted Gillum (d); unidentified vcl. Atlanta, 14 March 1929.
Atlanta low down · *Auburn Avenue stomp*

Roy Johnson's Happy Pals: Percy Trent, Slim Harris, Ed Humes (tpt); Tyree Humes (tbn); Robert Smith, Emmett Johnson (clt, alt); James Fauntleroy (clt, alt, bar); Silas Johnson (clt, ten); Leroy Wyche (p); Edward Trent (bj); Louis Carrington (tu); Roy Johnson (d). Richmond, Virginia, 15 August 1929.
Savoy rhythm · *Happy pal stomp*

A knowledge of the territory bands will not necessarily enhance perception of essential jazz development during the middle and late 1920s, but it helps perspective in showing that jazz activity was by no means confined to the glamorized centres of New Orleans, Chicago and New York City. This representative collection includes groups that worked in areas as widely separated as Georgia, Texas, upstate New York, Missouri and Virginia. The term 'territory' entered critical parlance fairly recently, perhaps in emulation of the old practice of referring to areas not yet officially part of the United States as 'the Territories'. A chief reason why places like Atlanta, Buffalo and San Antonio remained outside the jazz 'Union' was lack of established local recording facilities. Aspiring bands were thus recorded only if they could afford to visit the main centres or if an enterprising company sent mobile equipment into their area. It should hardly be surprising that the music of the territory bands is of good professional character; it would not have been recorded otherwise. What is pleasantly surprising is the amount of genuine, and not just imitative, jazz that can be heard here.

Heywood's band was popular in Atlanta from the early 1920s and recorded there for OKeh as accompanists to the vaudeville duo of Butterbeans and Susie. *Trombone moaning blues* was recorded in New York City and may give an inadequate impression of the group's capabilities. Poor sound balance does particularly ill justice to the featured trombonist, and the intonation of the other wind soloists is rather hazardous. Cheek imitates King Oliver's crying tones, while the leader's energetic blues style prompts regret that his fame was so parochial. A vicarious reputation was provided by his son and pupil — also Eddie — whose polite skills achieved popularity in the 1940s and 1950s and may be heard briefly with Billie Holiday in 204 and 205.

Stone's ensemble has a full-blooded attack owing much to the blues-charged spirit of south-western jazz. There are lapses, such as the whinnying saxophones on *Starvation blues*, and, later, an abrupt recollection of a New Orleans street band, but in general the approach is inventive, with a particularly successful wedding of freedom and order in the ensembles. And there is some exciting collective improvising at the end of *Boot to boot*.

Creath's double cornet lead may invite comparisons with Oliver, but the overall sound of the group is lighter. There are some corny accents in *Butter finger blues* cheek by jowl with bits of scoring which augur much later modes. *Crazy quilt*'s rapid exchanges between reed and brass are very ably played, but with a slight touch of the old-fashioned even for that time, although there is some good solo cornet towards the close.

Wabash, *Shadowland* and *Dreamland blues* are the only recorded examples of Floyd's music. Again the emphasis is on the blues, and there are some competent soloists vying with occasionally laboured ensemble harmonies. Long's curiously-toned trombone mute and liking for simulated laughter in *Shadowland* seem like delicacy itself beside the stentorian blues caricatures of Jefferson, a vocalist mercifully absent from *Dreamland*. This band's most satisfying moments occur on this latter, during a rhythmically-searching tenor solo by the young Evans, one of a number of future stars hidden in these various groups — Washington's being the other obvious case.

Mason provides a strong trumpet lead, good solos, and composing and arranging skills for Montgomery's band. His muted excursion on *Atlanta low down* is praiseworthy. This band's voice is brassier and less finely honed than the Texan and Missourian groups', yet its two performances are amongst the most satisfying included here.

For the rest, Johnson's Happy Pals play big-band scores with non-dynamic dutifulness, and the Blue Ribbon Syncopators play a form of novelty ragtime which, as their technical competence suggests, must have been a matter of choice rather than of innocence of reality.

The questing vigour of the best of these territory bands, and their grasp of the contemporary movement away from collective improvising towards ensemble arrangements, clearly manifest, must be weighed against a general lack of distinctive solo work. The Stone, Floyd and Creath bands are of especial interest considering their lively links with what was happening both in Chicago (**42**) and in Kansas City (**77** and **78**).   E.T.

76 The Missourians
RCA (F) FPM17017

The Missourians: Roger Quincy Dickerson, Lamar Wright (tpt); DePriest Wheeler (tbn); William Blue, George Scott (clt, alt); Andrew Brown (clt, ten); Earres Prince (p); Morris White (bj); Jimmy Smith (tu); Leroy Maxey (d). New York City, 3 June 1929.
Market Street stomp · *Ozark mountain blues* · *You'll cry for me* · *Missouri moan*
Same personnel and location, 1 August 1928.
I've got someone · *400 hop* · *Scotty blues*
Same personnel and location, 8 August 1929.
Vine Street drag
Walter 'Foots' Thomas (alt, ten, bar) replaces Scott. New York City, 17 February 1930.
200 squabble · *Swinging dem cats* · *Stopping the traffic* · *Prohibition blues*

Originally from St Louis, this band arrived in New York City during 1924, where they played at the Cotton Club, recording as the Cotton Club Orchestra the next year. Having been replaced by Ellington, they toured with Ethel Waters and only on returning to New York in 1928 assumed the name of the

Missourians. Shortly after the last of the above sessions they were taken over by Cab Calloway, and several of the musicians were still in the band a decade later (**148**). The Missourians are the rare case of a territory band that long preserved something of its regional flavour. These 1929–30 recordings may seem crude beside what Armstrong and Hines were doing in 1928 (**48**), Beiderbecke and Trumbauer in 1927 (**64**) or Nichols in 1926 (**70**), but they demonstrate that survival of earlier modes of expression which is not allowed for in strictly evolutionist views of jazz history. They were supposed to have been influenced by Benny Moten (**78**), yet although Wright had once been a member of that band, the Missourians' treatments of their simple themes was affected more by Harlem groups like those on **81**; Hendersonian clarinet trios can also be heard, as on *Missouri moan* or *Scotty blues*, while *Prohibition blues* and the out-of-tempo introduction to *You'll cry for me* suggest that aspects of Ellington's work had been noted.

The richly-voiced final ensemble of this last track is the only passage which implies that the Missourians had an ensemble voice of their own, but several of the performances are well organized, particularly the later ones. *Prohibition blues* is a good example, with fiercely muted playing by Dickerson fore and aft, a fine contrast provided by Wright's vehemently sad contribution, and excellent baritone from Thomas. The trumpeters, one muted, one open, are responsible for a telling antiphonal sequence towards the close of *Ozark mountain blues*. This *Tiger rag* variant also has a slow, deliberately lugubrious introduction that is as humorous in effect as the odd conclusion, by the banjo alone, to *You'll cry for me*. Equally unexpected, though to a different purpose, is the abrupt coda to the brisk *Market Street stomp* with muted trumpets, and again slow.

Although the ensemble riffs of *I've got someone* and particularly *Vine Street drag* were somewhat ahead of their time, other facets of this music are irrevocably dated, and perhaps were at the time the recordings were made. Instances are the banjo solos of *Scotty blues* and *200 squabble*, which almost take us back to plantation days, and most of the reed playing, typified by Scott in *Vine Street drag*, Blue on *I've got someone* and Brown in *Ozark mountain blues*. Scott does better, with both clarinet and alto, on *Scotty blues*, yet the real exception is Thomas, as his alto in *Stopping the traffic* and baritone on *Swinging dem cats* show. Such playing would not have been out of place on records made several years later.

Again, Wheeler has the tone, but not the rhythmic fluency and still less the invention of J. C. Higginbotham (**50**, **51**, etc.), and all his solos are clumsy. In accord with the Missourians' strong mixture of good and bad points, however, this is compensated for by such things as Wright's outstanding open solo on *Scotty blues* or his muted one in *400 hop*. Dickerson, also, makes an interesting use of detached notes on *Market Street stomp*, adds fiery yet logical solos, open and muted, to *Swinging dem cats*, and two splendidly declamatory blues choruses to *Missouri moan*. Whatever its weaknesses, there is never any doubt of this band's essential vitality.   M.H.

Andy Kirk
77
Clouds of Joy
Ace of Hearts (E) AH105

Andy Kirk and His Twelve Clouds of Joy: Gene Prince (tpt); Harry Lawson (tpt, vcl[1]); Allen Durham (tbn); John Harrington (clt, alt); John Williams (alt, bar); Lawrence Freeman (ten); Claude Williams (vln); Mary Lou Williams (p); William Dirvin (bj, g); Kirk (tu, bs sx); Edward McNeil (d). Kansas City, 7 November 1929.
Mess-a-stomp · *Blue clarinet stomp*[1]

Same personnel and location, 11 November 1929.
Corky stomp · *Froggy bottom*

Edgar 'Puddinghead' Battle (tpt) replaces Prince; Billy Massey (vcl[2]) added. Chicago, 29 April 1930.
I lost my girl from Memphis[2] · *Loose ankles*[2]

Same personnel and location, 30 April 1930.
Snag it · *Sweet and hot* · *Mary's idea*

Same personnel and location, 1 May 1930.
Once or twice[2]

Same personnel and location, 9 October 1930.
Dallas blues[2] · *Travelling that rocky road* · *Honey, just for you*[2]

Kansas City bands, from Benny Moten's (**78**) to Harlan Leonard's and Jay McShann's (**250**), adopted a very functional approach. Quite a few were territory bands, touring the Southwest, catering for audiences that liked blues and riffs and expected to be able to dance to the music. Kirk's Twelve Clouds of Joy fulfilled all those demands. Oddly enough, the orchestra's outstanding musician, Mary Lou Williams, was not the regular pianist when the first recording session took place; she was deputizing at the shortest of notice. Nevertheless, she takes the best solo, Hines-like in its clarity, on *Mess-a-stomp*. At that time Harrington's clarinet playing was still too staccato and melodramatic (as it is again in *Blue clarinet stomp*); later on he shaped up into a very reliable performer, even acquiring something of the astringency one associates with Edward Inge. More unusually, the other soloist of quality was a violinist, Claude Williams. The band was also lucky in having an outstanding drummer in McNeil; between them, he and Miss Williams gave deftness to what was otherwise a slightly stodgy rhythm section.

As well as becoming the band's pianist, Miss Williams was also its regular arranger (*Mess-a-stomp* seems to have been the first score she wrote for them). The versions of *Corky stomp* and *Froggy bottom* are fairly functional. *I lost my girl from Memphis*, recorded nearly six months later, has a sharper rhythmic impact but rough section work from the saxophones. (According to Jerome Shipman [28], this performance was based on an orchestration by Archie Bleyer, 'one of the first stock arrangers to try and write the sounds being made by the big Harlem swing bands'.) Oliver's *Snag it* had been recorded by Henderson's band in 1927, and Redman's arrangement is echoed here in the chorus played by three clarinets. Redman's influence surfaces again at the start of *Travelling that rocky road*, the opening chorus for saxophones very obviously a spin-off from McKinney's Cotton Pickers' recording of that number. On the whole, these later pieces are much more compact, the solos folding neatly inside the arrangements, as in *Once or twice* and *Dallas blues*.

Exactly who takes which trumpet solos is something that seems to have confused earlier writers. Not that any of them is especially remarkable: just good examples of genre playing. Kirk, chatting with Frank Driggs in the 1950s [29], said that Lawson took most of them in that early band. But the arrival of 'Puddinghead' Battle — quite an aggressive soloist when he was with Willie Bryant in 1934 — makes one speculate whether the slightly fiercer playing in *Dallas blues* and *Travelling that rocky road* might not be his handiwork. Meanwhile, it seems excellent that ambiguities of this sort should continue to perplex us.   C.F.

78 Benny Moten's Great Band of 1930–32
RCA (F) FXM17062, RCA (A) LPV514

Benny Moten's Kansas City Orchestra: Ed Lewis, Booker Washington (tpt); Thamon Hayes (tbn); Eddie Durham (tbn, g, arr); Harlan Leonard (clt, alt); Woody Walder (clt, ten); Jack Washington (alt, bar); Count Basie (p); Leroy Berry (bj, g); Vernon Page (bs); Willie McWashington (d); Buster Moten (acc). Chicago, 23 October 1929.
Jones law blues · *Small black*

Same personnel and location, 24 October 1929.
New Vine Street blues

'Hot Lips' Page (tpt), Jimmy Rushing (vcl[1]) added. Kansas City, 27 October 1930.
Won't you be my baby? [1]

Same personnel and location, 28 October 1930.
Oh! Eddie · That, too, do[1]
Same personnel and location, 30 October 1930.
When I'm alone[1]
Same personnel and location, 31 October 1930.
Somebody stole my girl
'Hot Lips' Page, Joe Keyes, Dee Stewart (tpt); Dan Minor (tbn); Durham (tbn, g, arr); Eddie Barefield (clt, alt, arr); Washington (alt, bar); Ben Webster (ten); Basie (p); Berry (g); Walter Page (bs); McWashington (d); Rushing (vcl[1]). Camden, New Jersey, 13 December 1932.
Moten swing · Blue room · New Orleans[1] *· The only girl I ever loved · Milneburg joys · Lafayette · Prince of wails · Toby*

Ragtime, particularly its less positive aspects, survived longer in the Southwest than elsewhere, and though Moten's proved eventually to be the greatest band associated with that area, his recordings were for several years often stiff and heavy. Early attempts such as *Crawdad blues* (1923) show no affinity for the blues, notwithstanding that idiom's allegedly strong and early roots in the Southwest, and even much later, as in *Jones law blues*, the thumping off-beats tie the music down (despite the kind of Jelly Roll Morton influence found here, as in Tiny Parham's music on **58**). The pulse is lighter on *New Vine Street Blues*, which has a curious twenty-four-bar structure and shows Walder in a better light than usual. But retrogressive elements, such as the Lombardo-sweet saxophones of *It's hard to laugh or smile* and the frightful banjo plunking of *Justrite* (both 1928) persisted. These are further typified by the accordion's blowsy interventions, as on *Oh! Eddie* and *Small black*, yet finally they were eliminated and the band's finest music was caught at its last recording date.

The influence of Ellington, Henderson and others has been exaggerated, and by 1932 Moten had arrived at a style which instead of lagging behind developments in the east had won independence from them. It made an ensemble use of the new rhythmic ideas pioneered by Armstrong and the other great soloists of the late 1920s, pointed to the Basie band of the late 1930s, and hence to aspects of bop. The tautness and absolute certainty of aim which characterize this session are evident from the opening bars of *Toby,* but it may be that, due to the familiarity of its melody, *Blue room* provides the clearest illustration of how this style works. Notice the process of rhythmic intensification which starts behind Webster's solo, and that the tune is simplified into a series of highly propulsive riffs (though here as on other titles one could, in terms of recording, wish that the saxophones had been balanced more closely). Such passages should be compared with the riff ending of Luis Russell's *Old man river* of two years later (**50**).

Of particular interest is the re-ordering of *Milneburg joys*, as this is material which relates to an earlier phase of jazz. On *Moten swing* a virtually perfect integration of all elements is achieved, with Basie weaving in and out of the ensemble in a most striking manner. As the earlier *Small black* also shows, the pianist was then nearer to his formative influences, James P. Johnson and especially Fats Waller, and these are also met with on *Prince of wails*. We can hear these stride elements being broken up, however, by the flowing 4/4 pulse of the drums and Walter Page's bass, which are the root of this ensemble's remarkably sure swing, as on *Lafayette*.

As important were the chief arrangers, Durham and Barefield, who maintained an exemplary balance between ensembles and solos. On the latter count there is much original work here, for example from 'Hot Lips' Page, who in *New Orleans* plays with masterly conciseness — and unusual harmonic freedom. This track has particularly good Webster, who then sounded athletic yet personally expressive, far from his later tonal obesity and pointless attempts to ape Coleman Hawkins.   M.H.

79 Earl Hines 1929 Complete Recordings
RCA (F) FPM17023

Earl Hines and His Orchestra: George Mitchell (cnt); Shirley Clay (tpt); William Franklin (tbn, vcl[1]); Toby Turner (clt, alt); Lester Boone (clt, alt, bar); Cecil Irwin (clt, ten, arr); Hines (p, vcl[2]); Claude Roberts (bj); Hayes Alvis (tu, arr); Benny Washington (d). Chicago, 13 February 1929.
Sweet Ella May[1] (2 takes) · *Everybody loves my baby*[2] (3 takes)

Same personnel and location, 14 February 1929.
Good little, bad little you[1] (2 takes) · *Have you ever felt that way?*[2]

Same personnel and location, 15 February 1929.
Beau koo Jack (2 takes) · *Sister Kate*[2]

Same personnel and location, 22 February 1929.
Chicago rhythm (2 takes)

Hines (p). Chicago, 25 February 1929.
Glad rag doll (2 takes)

Previous band personnel. Chicago, 25 October 1929.
Grand piano blues · *Blue nights*

The neglect of Hines's role as a bandleader is one of the curiosities of jazz historiography, for he fronted important and often under-rated ensembles over many years. This initial venture began in 1928 as what in a later period would be known as a 'rehearsal band', one that played for its own pleasure, and only later did Hines find work for it. These recordings, most of them made in a space of ten days, show that his first orchestral endeavours were confused, if less so than Ellington's, because although the arrangements, mainly by Irwin and Alvis, are full of varied incident, they are stylistically inconsistent. Several passages in *Everybody loves my baby*, almost certainly scored by Irwin who had considerable formal training behind him, signal the band's musical ambition — as in a different way does the leader's frantic solo statement of the theme, especially on take 1. And it is hard to believe that the arranger of *Beau koo Jack* was unfamiliar with the Armstrong–Hines version, recorded only two months before. Mitchell and Clay snatch insecurely here, as well they might, at phrases that are based on what at the time was *avant-garde* jazz trumpeting. Against such progressive elements, however, must be set the banjo's anachronistic rattle and the lugubrious pumping of the tuba, both effectively contradicting Hines's exemplary, if under-recorded, work in the rhythm section. Nor can it be pretended that Franklin's matinée idol vocal noises have any connection with jazz.

As in his recordings with Armstrong (**48**) and Jimmy Noone (**41**), Hines undertakes to project the piano as a front-line instrument, but his detailed involvement with the ensemble in the closing moments of *Everybody loves my baby* and the second voice he adds to the sensitive Clay solo on *Have you ever felt that way?* merely hint at procedures later taken much further (see **129**). The uncertainty of Hines's orchestral aims at this point, which leads to our being reminded by turns of McKinney's Cotton Pickers (**83**), who had begun recording in Chicago the previous year, and Benny Moten's group from the Southwest (**78**), contrasts sharply with the absolute mastery of his solo keyboard work. The main value of the alternative takes of the band pieces lies in his different improvisations on them, particularly in the cases of *Sweet Ella May* and *Chicago rhythm* (which latter also has fine Clay on take 1).

Best of his band solos here are on *Blue nights* and his own theme, *Grand piano blues*. With no support beyond simple time-keeping from the drummer (as on Noone's *King Joe*), Hines shows that he already has advanced beyond the achievements of his 1928 OKeh and QRS solos (**49**). This is confirmed especially by his two accounts of *Glad rag doll*, where rhapsodic exuberance, channelled most acutely through rhythmic and harmonic adventure, is contained by a secure and often unpredictable sense of form. The second is slower, more deliberately breaks new ground, and the difference is symbolized in the endings. Take 1's final chord has a commonplace added sixth, but take 2's includes a flattened fifth, which was decidedly unusual for 1929. Hines was on his way to musical ideas well beyond the grasp of most members of this band. M.H.

Louis Armstrong

80 Louis and the Big Bands

Parlophone (E) PMC7074, Swaggie (Au) S1253

Carroll Dickerson's Savoyagers: Armstrong (tpt, vcl[1]); Homer Hobson (tpt); Fred Robinson (tbn); Jimmy Strong (clt, ten); Bert Curry, Crawford Wethington (alt); Earl Hines (p); Mancy Cara (bj); Pete Briggs (tu); Zutty Singleton (d). Chicago, 5 July 1928.
Symphonic raps · Savoyagers' stomp

Louis Armstrong and His Orchestra: same personnel except Gene Anderson (p) replaces Hines. New York City, 22 July 1929.
Black and blue[1] · *That rhythm man*[1] · *Sweet Savannah Sue*[1]

Same personnel and location, 10 September 1929.
Some of these days[1] (take A) · *Some of these days* (take B)

Same personnel and location, 11 September 1929.
When you're smiling[1] (take A) · *When you're smiling* (take B)

Same personnel and location, 26 November 1929.
After you've gone[1]

Armstrong (tpt, vcl[1]); Ed Anderson (tpt); Henry Hicks (tbn); Bobby Holmes (clt, alt); Castor McCord (clt, ten); Theodore McCord (alt); Joe Turner (p); Buck Washington (additional p[2]); Bernard Addison (g); Lavert Hutchinson (tu); Willie Lynch (d, vib). New York City, 5 April 1930.
My sweet[1,2] · *I can't believe that you're in love with me*[1]

Same personnel and location, 4 May 1930.
Indian cradle song[1] · *Exactly like you*[1] · *Dinah*[1] · *Tiger rag*

The band heard on the first two tracks is the one Dickerson led at Chicago's Savoy Ballroom. Besides fronting it on guest appearances at theatres and in clubs, Armstrong worked regularly with this ensemble and it provided the personnel for his recording group, the Savoy Ballroom Five; indeed, *Knee drops* (**48**) comes from the same session. *Symphonic raps* is less pretentious than its title suggests, while *Savoyagers' stomp* proves to be a reworking of the opening theme of *Muskrat ramble*. Armstrong plays with the freshness of a man aware of his virtuosity yet not shackled by it; in fact, it is Hines who dazzles most in this pair of recordings.

Except for Hines, the next eight tracks are by the same band after Armstrong had taken it to New York. By that time he was indisputably the leader. He was also moving from recording traditional material or specifically jazz pieces to using popular songs of the day. It could be called the debut of Armstrong the show business phenomenon. Three of the tunes — *Black and blue, That rhythm man, Sweet Savannah Sue* — were numbers Fats Waller had written for the *Hot Chocolates* revue at Connie's Inn, where Armstrong was appearing. (A fourth Waller melody from that score, *Ain't misbehaving*, Armstrong's first big hit, was recorded a few days before and can be found on **113**.) *Black and blue*, an outstanding example of Armstrong's new style, begins with a notable paraphrase of the melody, continues with singing that is at once wistful and audacious, and concludes with a short trumpet cadenza — even more affecting, perhaps, because of its brevity.

Particularly fascinating is the comparison that can be made between the vocal and non-vocal takes of *Some of these days* and *When you're smiling*. In each case the first, vocal, take is slightly slower. *Some of these days* begins with the saxophones quoting from *Rhapsody in blue*, and later the trumpet solo builds logically to a series of high notes, used legitimately to establish tension. *When you're smiling* has Armstrong playing the melody almost as written, yet with every note recognizably his work, a superb instance of placing and accenting. Typical of this period, too, is the saxophone chorus which opens the piece, reflecting Armstrong's liking for the saccharin textures of Guy Lombardo's Royal Canadians.

During the four-and-a-half months separating *After you've gone* from *My sweet*, Armstrong was accompanied by Luis Russell's band, and the tracks they made together can be heard on **52**. He then toured and recorded with what virtually was the Mills Blue Rhythm Band. On the whole, the soloists are more adventurous than Dickerson's, particularly the clarinettist, Holmes, and Hicks, a trombonist in the mould of J. C. Higginbotham, while Anderson's very competent trumpet playing gets a rare chance to be heard behind Armstrong's singing on *Indian cradle song*. By this time the trumpeter was responding to the tastes of a public that was wider, and less familiar with jazz, than that which he had known in Chicago. It explains the increasing showiness of the climaxes, like the six choruses which conclude *Tiger rag* and the three at the end of *Dinah*; another Gershwin quotation, incidentally, from *Lady, be good*, surfaces in the former. Yet, except for *Tiger rag*, conceived deliberately as an excuse for showing off, the virtuosity never gets out of hand. And Armstrong's singing in *Exactly like you* is among the most felicitous that he ever put on record.   C.F.

81 Charlie Johnson, Lloyd Scott and Cecil Scott
RCA (F) 741.065/6 (2 LPs)

Lloyd Scott's Orchestra: Kenneth Roane (tpt, arr); Gus McLung (tpt); Dicky Wells (tbn); Fletcher Allen, John Williams (clt, alt); Cecil Scott (clt, ten, bs sx); Don Frye (p, arr); Hubert Mann (bj); Chester Campbell (tu); Lloyd Scott (d). New York City, 10 January 1927.
Harlem shuffle (2 takes) · *Symphonic scrontch* · *Happy hour blues* (2 takes)

Charlie Johnson's Paradise Orchestra: Jabbo Smith, Sidney DeParis or Thomas Morris (tpt); Charlie Irvis (tbn); Ben Whittet (clt, alt); Benny Waters (alt, ten); Charlie Johnson (p); Bobby Johnson (bj); Cyrus St Clair (tu); George Stafford (d); Monette Moore (vcl). New York City, 25 February 1927.
Paradise wobble stomp · *Birmingham black bottom* (2 takes) · *Don't you leave me here* (2 takes) · *You ain't the one* (2 takes)

DeParis definitely present; Benny Carter (clt, alt, arr), Edgar Sampson (alt, vln) added. New York City, 24 January 1928.
The charleston is the best dance, after all (2 takes) · *Hot-tempered blues* (2 takes)

Leonard Davies (tpt), Jimmy Harrison (tbn) replace Smith, Irvis; Carter absent. New York City, 19 September 1928.
The boy in the boat (2 takes) · *Walk that thing* (3 takes)

George Washington (tbn), Billy Taylor (tu) replace Harrison, St Clair. New York City, 8 May 1929.
Harlem drag (2 takes) · *Hot bones and rice* (2 takes)

Cecil Scott and His Bright Boys: Bill Coleman (tpt); Frankie Newton (tpt, vcl); Wells (tbn); John Williams, Harold McFarran (alt); Cecil Scott (clt, ten, bs sx); Frye (p); Rudolph Williams (bj); Mack Walker (tu); Lloyd Scott (d). New York City, 19 November 1929.
Lawd, Lawd · *In a corner* · *Bright boy blues* · *Springfield stomp*

These recordings are important, partly for what they show of the early essays of a number of subsequently famous jazzmen — Carter, DeParis, Coleman, Wells, etc. — partly because they redress the critical balance, aiding perspective on the work of bands which operated in the shadow of Ellington, Henderson, Luis Russell, who were playing music developed from the styles of Morton's Hot Peppers and the later Oliver groups. The Johnson and Scott bands formed a not insignificant part of the movement that was adapting the small improvising ensemble into augmented groups attempting more sophisticated orchestration and extending the role of soloists.

The 1927 Charlie Johnson performances mix varying proportions of hot jazz and novelty dance music, and both ingredients are very much of that age when little if any popular distinction was made between them. Monette Moore's clearly enunciated but emotionally fragile singing fits the archaic 'soundscape' well, but there are things like Smith's urgent lead that cut through the nostalgia and speak more timelessly. *You ain't the one* and *The charleston is the best dance, after all* are almost Carter's first recorded arrangements and are, in their section scoring, anticipatory of later and more elegant achievements. Echoes of Henderson, Russell and Ellington sound frequently in the music of these three bands. Johnson's efforts as a bandleader foundered early, for non-musical reasons, but there are qualities of zest and cohesiveness which place his best efforts only a little way below the characteristic work of the more durable groups. His September 1928 and 1929 titles organize a variety of sectional sounds with exuberance; most of the breaks and short solos are played with relaxed competence. Harrison's trombone work on the fine *Boy in the boat* and elsewhere is memorable, and Wells, with the two Scott groups, shows how uniformly striking his earliest playing could be.

Cecil Scott's trundling bass saxophone in both Lloyd's (1927) and his own (1929) band dates the music pointedly. Yet the Bright Boys were a splendid, riding group, and their four numbers make up the most accomplished part of this collection. The collective vocal in *Lawd, Lawd*, led by Newton, could have been another dating element, but the Boys' punctuations of Newton's wild scatting are extremely swinging and have no air of self-conscious novelty about them.

Harlem shuffle, *Symphonic scrontch* and *Happy hour blues* by Lloyd Scott's band suffer from rather heavy rhythm in places, but there are eloquent voices to be heard. Wells speaks with forthrightness in *Symphonic scrontch*, where he largely reproduces the notes of Charlie Green's solo on Henderson's 1924 *Gouge of Armour Avenue* (Collectors' Classics (D) CC28) but plays them with more subtle rhythmic nuances. Also, the introduction was echoed by that of Ellington's 1928 *Yellow dog blues*. There is some lightsome saxophone scoring and devil-may-care trumpeting by Roane in *Harlem shuffle*. Cecil Scott's clarinet at the beginning of *Happy hour blues* is lucid but stilted; indeed, almost as 'old-fashioned' as his bass saxophone on the same number. Yet one occasionally senses a more lithe aspiration even through the jerked intervals and slap-tonguing. And right at the end of *Springfield stomp*, Walker's tuba has depth-lending sustained notes to play which, like Tiny Parham's use of this instrument on 58, make one wonder if Gil Evans and John Carisi really were in the late 1940s and early 1950s its liberators.

These two discs capture the seething vitality of Harlem in a time of transitional experiment which achieved art largely because its creative spirits were not encumbered by high-faluting artistic principles. E.T.

82 King Oliver in New York
RCA (A) LPV529, *RCA (F) PM42411

King Oliver and His Orchestra: Oliver, Dave Nelson (tpt); Jimmy Archey (tbn); Bobby Holmes (clt, alt); Glyn Paque (alt); possibly Charles Frazier (ten); Don Frye (p); Walter Jones or Arthur Taylor (bj); Clinton Walker (tu); Edmund Jones (d). New York City, 8 October 1929.
Too late · *Sweet like this* · *What you want me to do?*

Oliver (tpt); Nelson (tpt, vcl); unidentified tbn; possibly Paque (clt, alt); Hilton Jefferson (alt); possibly Frazier (ten); James P. Johnson (p); Taylor (bj); Walker (tu); Jones or Fred Moore (d). New York City, 6 November 1929.
I'm lonesome, sweetheart

Oliver, Nelson (tpt); Archey (tbn); Paque (alt); 2 unidentified saxes; Frye (p); possibly Taylor (bj); unidentified g; Roy Smeck (g, hca[1]); possibly Walker (tu); Jones or Moore (d). New York City, 30 December 1929.
Frankie and Johnny[1] · *New Orleans shout*

Oliver, Henry Allen, Bubber Miley (tpt); Archey (tbn); Holmes (clt, alt); Paque (alt); 2 unidentified saxes; Frye (p); Taylor (bj); Jean Stulz (g); Walker (tu); Frankie Marvin (vcl). New York City, 28 January 1930.
St James' Infirmary

Oliver, possibly Nelson (tpt); Archey (tbn); Holmes (clt); Paque, Jefferson (clt, alt); possibly Hank Duncan (p); Taylor (bj); Walker (tu); Moore (d). New York City, 18 March 1930.
Rhythm club stomp

Oliver, Nelson, Allen (tpt); Archey (tbn); Paque (clt, alt); Jefferson (alt); Walter Wheeler (ten); Frye or Norman Lestor (p); Taylor (bj); Walker (tu); Moore (d). New York City, 10 April 1930.
Edna · *Mule face blues*

Oliver, Nelson (tpt); Archey (tbn); Holmes (clt, alt); Paque (alt); Frazier (ten); Eric Franker (p); Taylor (bj); Walker (tu); possibly Moore (d). New York City, 22 May 1930.
Struggle buggy · *Don't you think I love you?* · *Olga*

Oliver, Allen, possibly Nelson (tpt); Archey (tbn); Paque, Jefferson (alt); Frazier (ten); Duncan (p); possibly Taylor (bj); unidentified tu; Moore (d). New York City, 10 September 1930.
Shake it and break it · *Stingaree blues*

Oliver, Nelson (tpt); Archey (tbn); Paque, Jefferson (alt); Frazier (ten); unidentified p, bj, tu, d. New York City, 19 September 1930.
Nelson stomp

One reason for the rapid turnover of phases and styles in jazz has been the parallel growth of technology, the way that radio and records have enabled the latest developments to be heard, almost instantaneously, all over America and Europe. That acceleration really began just after World War I, resulting in what virtually amounted to a new fashion for each decade. Younger musicians, naturally enough, could take this in their stride, but older players had trouble coping. When New Orleans music went out of favour towards the end of the 1920s, for instance, those Delta musicians still under thirty — Omer Simeon, Barney Bigard, Albert Nicholas, Henry Allen, for example — had little difficulty in adapting to big band disciplines. The over-thirties — Johnny Dodds, Jimmy Noone, Kid Ory, Jelly Roll Morton, King Oliver, etc. — found it harder, sometimes impossible.

As early as the winter of 1924–25, only a year after the final recordings by his Creole Jazz Band, Oliver was using three saxophones. It was a slightly unsatisfactory phase in the transition from collective improvising to the big band performances encountered on this LP. Although he was pre-eminently a New Orleans player, happiest in a small improvising ensemble, the music here is frequently better than commentators have been prepared to admit. Oliver had arrived in New York during 1927, and for these sessions he used pick-up groups, recruited mainly from three Harlem bands, those of Charlie Skeet, Harry White and Emmett Matthews. He occasionally employed some of these musicians for New York engagements, but only one group, that used for the session of 22 May 1930, went on the road with him for an extended tour (which turned out disastrously, with the players hardly earning enough to eat).

Most of the pieces were arranged by Nelson, Oliver's nephew. While no Don Redman or Benny Carter, he produced scores that were often more than workmanlike. True, the opening of *I'm lonesome, sweetheart* is embarrassingly reminiscent of Guy Lombardo, but outstanding writing for saxophones can be found in *Sweet like this* (a miniature classic) and *What you want me to do?* as well as on many later tracks such as *Edna, Mule face blues* and *Nelson stomp*. The most consistent soloist was Archey, his tone growing warmer and more vibrant as 1929 moved into 1930. All the tenor saxophonists sounded immature, not quite sure what they were up to; the alto players came off better, especially Jefferson (*Shake it and break it, Rhythm club stomp, Stingaree blues*) and the often underrated Paque, who in *Sweet like this* sounds remarkably like Frankie Trumbauer, an illustration of how black and white styles were already overlapping. Holmes's clarinet playing, a bit reedy, tinged with Dodds's example, has also something of Edward Inge's faintly ironic stance.

Oliver was already experiencing trouble with his teeth (pyorrhea had virtually ruined his playing by 1935), yet he takes excellent solos on most tracks. Some are forceful and open, like that in *I'm lonesome, sweetheart*, the kind of playing that had beguiled the impressionable young Armstrong. And there is delicate muted playing, like the cornet–tuba duets to be heard on *What you want me to do?* and *Frankie and Johnny*. A few solos which some discographers still credit to Oliver sound unconvincing, notably the wa-wa routines in *Shake it and break it* and *Stingaree blues*, both much too corny to be the work of a master of the plunger mute. Those two items, however, do contain brilliant trumpet solos by Allen, while *St James' Infirmary* has a stinging solo and obbligato by Miley.   C.F.

83 McKinney's Cotton Pickers
RCA (Ar) AVL3072, *RCA (F) PM42407

McKinney's Cotton Pickers: John Nesbitt, Langston Curl (tpt); Claude Jones (tbn, vcl[1]); Don Redman (clt, alt, vcl[2]); Milton Senior (clt, alt); George Thomas (clt, ten, vcl[3]); Prince Robinson (clt, ten); Todd Rhodes (p); Dave Wilborn (bj, g, vcl[4]); Ralph Escudero (tu); Cuba Austin (d). Chicago, 11 July 1928.
Four or five times[1,2,3,4] · *Put it there* · *Crying and sighing* · *Milneburg joys*

Jean Napier (vcl[5]) added. Chicago, 12 July 1928.
Cherry[5] · *Stop kidding* · *Nobody's sweetheart*[3] · *Some sweet day* · *Shimme-sha-wabble*

Jimmy Dudley (clt, alt) replaces Senior; Redman (vib); Austin (vcl[6]). Chicago, 23 November 1928.
It's tight like that[3,6] · *There's a rainbow round my shoulder*[4]

Same personnel. Camden, New Jersey, 8 April 1929.
It's a precious little thing called love · *Save it, pretty mama*[2] · *I found a new baby*[4] · *Will you, won't you be my baby?*

Same personnel. New York City, 9 April 1929.
Beedle-um-bum[1,2,3,4]

Names, as every jazz follower knows, are often wildly misleading. For example, by the time McKinney's Cotton Pickers assumed that title, their founder, William McKinney, had ceased to play any musical part in the band's affairs. Nor did any of the musicians hail from the south. This was, in fact, an orchestra formed in Ohio which found its feet in Detroit, becoming the only major big band in the inter-war years to achieve success without going to New York or Chicago. Its recording career began just after Redman had left Henderson to become the band's musical director. One advantage was that Redman could now deploy four saxophones instead of Henderson's three. This was quickly reflected in his scores, which include many bravura reed passages, anticipating some of Redman's achievements with his own orchestra a few years later (**123, 124**).

He might be described as a musical pragmatist, adapting his methods to the resources available. And the difference between the Henderson band and McKinney's Cotton Pickers was that while the former contained some of the most exciting new talents in jazz, the latter mostly consisted of musicians who were very competent sidemen but not outstanding soloists. The major exception was Jones, an adroit and pithy trombonist. Robinson was superior to most tenor saxophonists of the time — excluding Coleman Hawkins, already far ahead of everybody else — and had a pleasantly astringent style on the clarinet, though if he lost his poise, as in *Shimme-sha-wabble*, the result could be too squeaky for comfort. Redman's alto saxophone playing remained ornamental rather than organic, often, in *Milneburg joys* for example, reminiscent of one of Jimmy Dorsey's technical forays; nevertheless, his solo on *Stop kidding* is pleasingly bouncy. Nesbitt, a trumpeter who greatly admired Beiderbecke, is reputed to have been exciting in the flesh, yet on record he comes across as better at creating atmosphere than at developing ideas.

Before Redman arrived, Nesbitt had been the band's principal arranger. His work now became heavily influenced by Redman's style. Indeed, Redman has claimed that although he composed *Cherry*, it was Nesbitt who actually wrote the arrangement [30]. If true, that would indicate a remarkable command of Redman's manner. Elsewhere — *Crying and sighing, Stop kidding, There's a rainbow round my shoulder, It's a precious little thing called love, Will you, won't you be my baby?* — Nesbitt's scores tend to be slightly heavier-handed than Redman's, lacking their piquancy. *I found a new baby* comes off admirably, however, and Nesbitt went on to write for other bands, notably a dazzling version of *Chinatown, my Chinatown* for Henderson. Redman's arrangements leave plenty of scope for the soloists, yet he relied upon them less than in his days with Henderson. The manner, indeed, is more fulsomely orchestral. On most of their recordings the Cotton Pickers display a very clean ensemble style, while Austin's drumming and Escudero's tuba playing helped to make the rhythm section outstanding for its period. Occasionally a number was taken too fast, *There's a rainbow round my shoulder* being a model of peppy excess; but mistakes like that were rare.

A useful supplement to this LP is *McKinney's Cotton Pickers* (RCA (E) RD 7561), containing only one track — *Beedle-um-bum* — which overlaps. It includes all but one — *Plain dirt* — of the seven recordings that Redman made in New York in November

1929 with what had to be a pick-up version of the Cotton Pickers using, but only in brief solos, sidemen such as Coleman Hawkins and Fats Waller. Other tracks feature notable solo playing by Joe Smith, Benny Carter (especially good on clarinet in *Never swat a fly*) and Rex Stewart (splendidly truculent on *Rocky road* and *Do you believe in love at first sight?*). C.F.

84 The Chocolate Dandies
Parlophone (E) PMC7038, Swaggie (Au) S1249

Big Aces: Tommy Dorsey, Nat Natoli (tpt); Jack Teagarden (tbn); Don Redman (clt, alt, arr); Jimmy Dorsey (clt, alt); Frank Teschemacher (clt, ten); George Thomas (ten, vcl); Frank Signorelli (p); Carl Kress (g); Hank Stern (tu); Stan King (d, vib). New York City, 29 September 1928.
Cherry

Chocolate Dandies: Langston Curl, John Nesbitt (tpt); Claude Jones (tbn); Redman (clt, alt, vcl[1]); Milton Senior (clt, alt); Thomas (clt, ten, vcl[2]); Prince Robinson (clt, ten); Todd Rhodes (p); Dave Wilborn (bj, vcl[3]); Lonnie Johnson (g); Ralph Escudero (tu); Cuba Austin (d). New York City, 10 or 13 October 1928.
Paducah · *Stardust* · *Birmingham breakdown* · *Four or five times*[1,2,3]

Little Chocolate Dandies: Rex Stewart (cnt); Leonard Davies (tpt); J. C. Higginbotham (tbn, vcl[4]); Redman, Benny Carter (clt, alt, vcl[5]); Coleman Hawkins (ten); Fats Waller (p); unidentified bj; Cyrus St Clair (tu); George Stafford (d). New York City, 18 September 1929.
That's how I feel today · *Six or seven times*[4,5]

Chocolate Dandies: Bobby Stark (tpt); Jimmy Harrison (tbn, vcl[6]); Carter (clt, alt, arr[7], vcl[8]); Hawkins (ten); Horace Henderson (p); Clarence Holiday or Benny Jackson (g); John Kirby (bs). New York City, 3 December 1930.
Goodbye blues[7,8] · *Cloudy skies* · *Got another sweetie now*[6] · *Bugle call rag*[7] · *Dee blues*

Max Kaminsky (tpt); Carter (tpt[9], alt); Floyd O'Brien (tbn); Chew Berry (ten); Teddy Wilson (p); Lawrence Lucie (g); Ernest Hill (bs); Sidney Catlett (d). New York City, 10 October 1933.
Blue interlude · *I never knew*[9] · *Once upon a time*[9]

Mezz Mezzrow (d) replaces Catlett. Same date.
Krazy kapers[9]

The Big Aces' *Cherry* is an analogue of the McKinney's Cotton Pickers' version of the piece recorded two months earlier (**83**) but not then released. Accompanied by Thomas, Redman took the arrangement of his composition to the OKeh studios, where the Dorsey Brothers' Orchestra was completing a session, and recorded it with the members of that group. Thus it is possible to hear two virtually independent realizations of the same musical conception. The McKinney's version is taken at a slightly faster tempo than the present one and exhibits a more piquant energy; but the Big Aces' rendering also reflects Redman's directive spirit and has much to commend it. Thomas's singing of the homespun lyrics improves upon Redman's bland utterance in the other, but one regrets that Teschemacher was not given the solo space afforded to Senior in a section of the score omitted from the OKeh recording.

Redman then contracted with OKeh for a further session, which took place the following month. The band is, in fact, the Cotton Pickers plus the then ubiquitous Johnson. The four performances are well up to the best McKinney's standard, with some excellently timed negotiation of powerful ensemble writing. Ellington's 1926 and 1927 versions of *Birmingham breakdown* (**89**) may be compared with this Redman reworking, which is certainly not inferior to either of them in dynamic assurance.

The group assembled for the 1929 date still has strong McKinney associations, and the most notable newcomer, having later phases of this small saga in mind, is Carter, who introduces himself with typically elegant solos in *That's how I feel today*. In spite of fairly comprehensive scored passages, there is a more intimate sense to these offerings and a greater emphasis than before upon solos. With more elbow room, the redoubtable improvisers present create wonderful music for which honours can be equally distributed, one's only regret being that Waller is not more openly featured. The instrumental and vocal exchanges of *Six or seven times* become rather tedious, though one notes that the erotic ambition of *Four or five times* is exceeded here!

The 1930 *rendezvous*, under Carter's leadership, involves Fletcher Henderson personnel. The arrangements are simple but carry a sense of power judiciously reined, and again it is the expressiveness of the soloists which is memorable — a mark of the new ascendancy of the improvising jazz artist towards the end of a period dominated by searches for ensemble identity. Hawkins, having replaced an earlier brusqueness (*cf.* his solo and break in the 1927 *Whiteman stomp* on **86**) with a romantic flexibility, has fine things to say in *Got another sweetie now*, *Dee blues* and *Goodbye blues*; the foremost hazard of this new approach is heard, though, in the theme statement of *Cloudy skies*, where he uses an unfortunate cloying vibrato. Carter solos well throughout the session — a sinuous alto exploration on *Bugle call rag* and clipped low-register clarinet phrases in *Dee blues* are good examples — and Stark brings a bold grace to both solo and ensemble playing.

The remaining four numbers, recorded by a group John Hammond assembled in 1933, are freer still in conception, their cohesiveness depending upon the assurance of the individual participants as much as upon Carter's discreet control of ensemble support. Kaminsky and O'Brien fit as ably into this 'swing' context as into a more familiar 'Chicago' one, and the comparison between Kaminsky's simple forthrightness (*Blue interlude*) and Carter's romantic trumpet playing, especially in the beautiful *Once upon a time*, typifies a dual aspect of the Armstrong influence. Some of Carter's finest alto work is to be savoured in *Blue interlude* and *Krazy kapers*, and it is noticeable that, even at his most rhapsodic, he plays closer to the beat than has become customary in the Hawkins style echoed in the solos of Berry.

There is ample evidence here, too, of the skills of Wilson, skills that will be more fully considered under **176, 177**. The superb impetus of his melodic rebuilding of fast themes like *I never knew* and *Krazy kapers*, with dazzling runs overriding bass tenths, owes a good deal to Hines, though Wilson is a little less daring, at this stage, in his emulation of Hinesian inner contrast, being intent on developing his own kind of rhythmic consistency.   E.T.

Fletcher Henderson

85 Smack
Ace of Hearts (E) AH41, *MCA (A) 1310

Fletcher Henderson and His Orchestra; Russell Smith, Joe Smith, Tommy Ladnier (tpt); Benny Morton (tbn); Buster Bailey, Don Redman (clt, alt); Coleman Hawkins (clt, ten); Henderson (p); Charlie Dixon (bj); June Cole (tu); Kaiser Marshall (d). New York City, 8 December 1926.
Hot mustard

Jimmy Harrison (tbn) added. New York City, 22 January 1927.
Stockholm stomp · Have it ready

Morton absent. New York City, 19 March 1927.
Sensation

Russell Smith, Bobby Stark (tpt); Rex Stewart (cnt); Claude Jones, Morton (tbn); Russell Procope, Harvey Boone (clt, alt); Hawkins (ten); Henderson (p); Clarence Holiday (g); John Kirby (bs, tu); Walter Johnson (d); unidentified male vcl[1]. New York City, 10 April 1931.
I'm crazy 'bout my baby[1] · *Sugar foot stomp · Just blues · Singing the blues*

Edgar Sampson (clt, alt, vln) replaces Boone; Stewart (vcl[2]). New York City, 17 July 1931.
Low down on the bayou · House of David blues · Radio rhythm · You rascal, you[2]

For an ensemble destined to exert such a substantial influence on orchestral jazz during the 1920s, Henderson's very earliest band was remarkably stodgy and unenterprising. Interest generally focused — late in 1924 and throughout 1925, anyway — upon the solos that Armstrong played (see **37**). In fact, his impact on the orchestra was considerable, especially his rhythmic vivacity, a quality promptly copied by other musicians and reflected in the arrangements that Redman was concocting. *Hot mustard* is an outstanding example, even if the rapid alternation of different instrumental groupings, much admired at the time, now seems a trifle choppy. But a shaping intelligence was obviously at work, devising scored passages which sounded like jazz solos, but also using soloists as part of a composition, as Jelly Roll Morton had already done and as Ellington was about to do, even if the solo passages themselves were often very short. *Hot mustard* contains no solo longer than eight bars, apart from Henderson's own twelve-bar piano chorus.

The brass soloists dominated, particularly the two trumpeters — Joe Smith, with his lyrical phrasing and plaintive tone, and Ladnier, hotter and rougher. Charlie Green's place had been taken by Harrison, deploying a subtle, even faintly evasive style, one of a handful of players — Jack Teagarden and Miff Mole were two of the others — who liberated the trombone from its dixieland functionalism. The clarinet trio, used again and again by Redman, became so identified with the orchestra that it appears in *Have it ready*, scored, a bit too fussily, by Ken Macomber, a publisher's staff arranger. All three brass players take solos in *Sensation*, a reworking of the Original Dixieland Jazz Band's number. Here, too, Hawkins shows signs of the mastery he was to develop over the next few years. The phrasing is less rigid, the tone takes on an edge and buoyancy; in the final chorus he even throws in a two-bar break which hints at *The eel*, that saxophone figure which Bud Freeman was to make famous (**166, 231**).

Redman left Henderson in 1927, working first with McKinney's Cotton Pickers (**83**), then forming his own band in 1931 (**123, 124**). Henderson began using a number of writers, although *I'm crazy 'bout my baby* sounds like a stock orchestration while *Just blues* could be a 'head' arrangement, worked up by the musicians on the bandstand. *Sugar foot stomp*, of course, is another name for Oliver's *Dippermouth blues*; this 1931 version represents an updating, possibly by Henderson himself, of Redman's 1925 arrangement. Oliver's celebrated three twelve-bar choruses are played by Stark, an underrated trumpet soloist, who adds a pungency and impudence all his own. *Singing the blues*, frankly based upon the Beiderbecke–Trumbauer recording (**64**), was probably arranged by Bill Challis of the Paul Whiteman organization. Stewart, a great admirer of Bix, interprets the famous solo, giving it his own inflections and distinctly different rhythmic stance. Nat Leslie wrote *Low down on the bayou* and *Radio rhythm*, and both were recorded by the Mills Blue Rhythm Band the same year, although the latter never was released.

The former, its opening theme voiced rather attractively for saxophones, contains a couple of short solos by Stewart which demonstrate the spryness of his approach. *Radio rhythm*, despite its title, falls into the category of 'jungle style' novelty numbers so popular at that time, with lusty growling from Jones and Stark. Interestingly enough, the final chorus includes the same saxophone figure that Redman was to use three years later in his *Got the jitters* on **124**. Jones's playing is always neatly calculated, but the most exciting trombone solos come from Morton, displaying an adventurous looseness, both in phrasing and vibrato; each trombonist solos — Jones first and, briefly, Morton later, taking three twelve-bar choruses — on *Sugar foot stomp*.

Of the other soloists, Procope was a more flexible clarinettist than his predecessor, Buster Bailey, and is featured in a shapely alto saxophone chorus on *Radio rhythm*. Incidentally, a brass bass was still being used quite a bit of the time (played now by Kirby), yet the band swung with a deftness that compensated for the occasional raggedness of the section work. That swing had a lot to do with the playing of Johnson, rarely listed among the hierarchy of jazz drummers yet probably the first to move, as James Lincoln Collier puts it, 'the ground beat from the snare to the hi-hat cymbals'. Collier also points out that in *Radio rhythm* and *Low down on the bayou*, Johnson 'can be heard playing the so-called ride beat on the hi-hat' at a time when 'Jo Jones was an obscure twenty-year-old working in Lincoln, Nebraska, with Harold Jones's Brownskin Syncopators' [31].

But the musician who now bestrode this orchestra was Hawkins, whether stomping along enthusiastically in *You rascal, you*, *I'm crazy 'bout my baby* and *Sugar foot stomp* or exploiting, in *Just blues* and *House of David blues*, that rhapsodic manner which proclaimed him one of the music's first romantics. His harmonic anticipation produced solos that stretched ahead, creating, in retrospect, a remarkable sense of inevitability. Half a century on, the listener still finds himself catching his breath, that old magnificence as seductive as ever.   C.F.

86   A Study in Frustration Vol. 2
CBS (E) BPG62002, Columbia (A) CL1683

Fletcher Henderson and His Orchestra: Russell Smith, Joe Smith,
Tommy Ladnier (tpt); Jimmy Harrison, Benny Morton (tbn); Buster
Bailey (clt); Don Redman (clt, alt, vcl[1]); Coleman Hawkins (ten);
Henderson (p); Charlie Dixon (bj); June Cole (tu); Kaiser Marshall (d).
New York City, 21 January 1927.
Rocky mountain blues · Tozo[1]

Dixie Stompers: Carmello Jejo (alt) replaces Bailey. New York City,
23 March 1927.
St Louis shuffle

Fletcher Henderson and His Orchestra: Bailey (clt), Fats Waller (p)
replaces Jejo, Henderson. New York City, 11 May 1927.
Whiteman stomp · I'm coming, Virginia

Dixie Stompers: Henderson (p) replaces Waller. New York City, 12 May
1927.
Variety stomp · St Louis blues

Don Pasquall (alt, bar) replaces Redman. New York City, 24 October
1927.
Goose pimples

Fletcher Henderson and His Orchestra: same personnel and location,
4 November 1927.
Hop off

Bobby Stark (tpt) replaces Ladnier. New York City, 14 March 1928.
King Porter stomp · D-natural blues

Dixie Stompers: Rex Stewart (cnt) replaces Joe Smith; Russell Smith,
Morton absent. New York City, 6 April 1928.
Oh, baby · Feeling good · I'm feeling devilish

Fletcher Henderson's Happy Six: Stewart (cnt); Charlie Green (tbn);
Bailey (clt); Benny Carter (alt); Hawkins (bs sx); Henderson (p); Clarence
Holiday (bj). New York City, November 1928.
Old black Joe blues

Fletcher Henderson and His Orchestra: Stark (tpt); Stewart (cnt);
Harrison (tbn); Bailey, Carter, Hawkins (reeds); Henderson (p); Holiday
(bj); Cole (tu); Marshall (d). New York City, 12 December 1928.
Easy money

It may be doubted whether success will crown recent attempts to
redress the balance of respect for Henderson's contribution to
orchestral jazz. The picture is likely to remain confused, partly by
the disparate phases through which his career moved, partly by
his early dependence upon other musical minds, particularly
Redman's, and partly because he does not appear, in any of the
phases, to have been completely the master of his own destiny.
Nobody would claim for him more than capable workmanship as
a pianist, so his own orchestral skills never depended, as Jelly

Roll Morton's and, to a lesser extent, Ellington's did, upon a vision realized at the keyboard. His aptitude as an arranger developed late and, though one might be tempted to find his most assured contribution in the scores he provided for his mid-1930s band and later for Goodman (**141**), there are few elements in his work that were not common coin amongst the Harlem bands of almost a decade earlier. He certainly achieved assurance, and a fairly shrewd simplification of resources in that important period; but more of that under **126**, **127** and **141**.

Some of his early essays in arranging can be heard amongst the 1928 tracks above, yet of much stronger significance is the writing of Redman, heard in the first nine items. These show a marked advance upon Redman's earlier attempts to formalize classic jazz polyphony and to augment it with refinements taken rather uncritically from dance bands and concert bands on the fringe of jazz, and it is immediately obvious from the rapid section exchanges and rich harmonic passages of *Rocky mountain blues*, *St Louis shuffle* and *I'm coming, Virginia*, how Redman was able now to juggle a variety of devices in skilfully impetuous patterns. These convey the restless energy that was, no doubt, a large part of the music's incidental popularity in those days, and the fleeting sustenance afforded to any element, including solo expression, leaves an impression that the public image of jazz as a novelty music was still being at least nodded, if not bowed, to. Still, the band would sound rather less dated to modern ears were it not for the unimaginative use of the rhythm section which, with its relentless beat and mannered punctuations, tends to retard the movements towards more swinging concinnity in the ensemble.

The spirit of *Variety stomp*, *Tozo* (with lyrics that are a small treasure of the lucidrous) and *Goose pimples* is still that of the orchestral extensions of ragtime, an impression strengthened by Henderson's few piano solos, and even by Hawkins's half-chorus in *Tozo*. Raggy phrases played fast, with a four-beat emphasis, do not quite become jazz, but against this misconception are vying the more flexible dialects which are probably the legacy of Armstrong's vivifying stay with the band during 1924–25. Enduring jazz character is lent these 1927 creations more than anything else by the frequent Ladnier solos and the somewhat less frequent ones of Bailey and Joe Smith. These ensure that the accents of the blues, which are far from strong even in *St Louis blues*, are not crowded out by self-conscious jazziness.

Sophisticated eclecticism is certainly present in *Whiteman stomp*, the celebrated Waller composition which, despite some moments of portentous drama, Gershwinian piano runs and 'soft staircase' arpeggios, sounds like an attempt to apprise a respected contemporary of some of his shortcomings. Harrison shows more flexibility here than he is allowed to do in most of these Redman scores. *Hop off* has more relaxation, good solos from Ladnier, Hawkins, Harrison and Bailey, and some interesting ensemble dynamics developing towards the end.

The 1928 Henderson arrangements are mixed, reflecting the wideness of his borrowings. *D-natural blues* gets off to a laboured start and generally lacks sparkle and variety, yet it shows more promise than *Oh, baby, Feeling good, I'm feeling devilish* and *Old black Joe blues*, which fall back upon Redmanesque devices, rather lamely emulated, and lack the redeeming joyousness of the 1927 tracks. Stark and Stewart, replacing Ladnier and Joe Smith, play excellent solos, as do Bailey and Harrison; but some of these numbers suffer from bad recording quality. *Easy money*, a Carter arrangement, has some of its most hopeful scoring — for example, the lightly riffing saxophones behind Stark's first solo — sadly impeded by prominent banjo chords. Hawkins is plainly beginning to find his second, more expressive, self here.

Henderson and Redman demanded high accomplishment from the band's musicians, and it was in this period that a flexible method of reading scores — not dissimilar in motive from the baroque mode for *notes inégales* — was perfected [32]. The co-operative spirit thus encouraged is beautifully shown in the finest of all these performances, *King Porter stomp*, which is a head arrangement and by far the most swinging Henderson recording to date. He was to make it the basis of his famous realization of the piece for Goodman (**141**), and its importance as a harbinger of the swing era cannot be over-emphasized. But it is instructive in another direction, too. Its relaxed antiphonal riffs, if related to James P. Johnson's *Carolina shout* (**171**), appear to demonstrate that the call and response of the religious tradition were fed into swing style from the spoon of Harlem ragtime, a fact not hinted at in Waller's interjections in *Whiteman stomp*. If this provenance is coupled with the honour which Henderson's *King Porter stomp* is paying to its creator, Morton, it will be seen that a dependence upon the offshoots of ragtime did not inevitably lead to the perky mannerism criticized above. In this case, spirits from Harlem and New Orleans are discerned, urging a fine band towards fresh jazz discovery.   E.T.

Duke Ellington

87 **Flaming Youth**
RCA (E) RD8089, RCA (A) LPV568

Duke Ellington and His Orchestra: Bubber Miley, Louis Metcalfe (tpt); Joe Nanton (tbn); Harry Carney (clt, alt, bar); Rudy Jackson (clt, ten); Otto Hardwicke (sop, alt, bar); Ellington (p); Fred Guy (bj); Wellman Braud (bs); Sonny Greer (d); Adelaide Hall (vcl[1]). New York City, 26 October 1927.
Creole love call[1] · *The blues I love to sing*[1] · *Black and tan fantasy* · *Washington wobble*

Carney also plays sop. New York City, 19 December 1927.
Harlem River quiver · *East St Louis toodle-oo* · *Blue bubbles*

Arthur Whetsol (tpt), Barney Bigard (clt, ten) replace Metcalfe, Jackson. New York City, 26 March 1928.
Black beauty · *Jubilee stomp* · *Got everything but you*

Whetsol, possibly Freddy Jenkins (tpt); Nanton (tbn); Carney (clt, alt, bar); Bigard (clt, ten); Johnny Hodges (sop, alt); Ellington (p); Guy (bj); possibly Billy Taylor (tu); Greer (d); possibly Ozzie Ware (vcl[2]). New York City, 30 October 1928.
The mooche · *No, papa, no*[2]

Miley, Whetsol, Jenkins (tpt); Nanton (tbn); Carney (clt, sop, bar); Bigard (clt, ten); Hodges (sop, alt); Hardwicke (alt, bar); Ellington (p); Guy (bj); Braud (bs); Greer (d); Ware (vcl[2]); Irving Mills (vcl[3]). New York City, 15 November 1928.
Bandanna babies[2] · *Diga diga doo*[2,3] · *I must have that man*

Hardwicke absent. New York City, 16 January 1929.
Flaming youth

88 **Duke Ellington at the Cotton Club**
Camden (E) CDN119, Camden (A) CAL459

Duke Ellington and His Orchestra: Whetsol, Jenkins (tpt); Cootie Williams (tpt, vcl[4]); Nanton (tbn); Carney (clt, alt, bar); Bigard (clt, ten); Hodges (sop, alt); Ellington (p); Guy (bj); Braud (bs); Greer (d). New York City, 7 March 1929.
Hot feet[4] · *Stevedore storp*

Same personnel and location, 3 May 1929.
Cotton Club stomp · *Arabian lover*

Williams, Bigard (clt), Hodges (alt), Ellington, Guy, Braud, Greer only. Same date.
Saratoga swing

Full band personnel but with Jenkins absent; Juan Tizol (v-tbn), Teddy Bunn (g) added. New York City, 16 September 1929.
Haunted nights

Bunn absent; Jenkins (tpt) added. New York City, 4 June 1930.
Jungle nights in Harlem · *Shout 'em, Aunt Tillie*

Charlie Barnet (ch) added. Hollywood, 26 August 1930.
Ring dem bells[4]
Barnet absent. Camden New Jersey, 11 June 1931.
Creole rhapsody

'I am a man of the theatre', Ellington once declared, in front of
BBC television cameras. What he meant involved more than an
obvious liking for appearing on-stage before audiences. His music
has a theatrical dimension, soloists being deployed rather like
characters in a play, their comings and goings planned and
orchestrated. Indeed, Ellington's early development as a composer was closely linked with the strongest of those soloists: the
trumpeter Miley, the trombonist Nanton. True, there is sensuous
scoring for reeds behind Adelaide Hall's ululating voice at the
start of *Creole love call*, and saxophones can be heard answering
brass later, but the nub of this piece is the tigerish snarling of
Miley's trumpet; and *The blues I love to sing*, almost as good, has
Miley and Miss Hall duetting once again. Definitive performances by Miley and Nanton, simultaneously raw yet sophisticated, occur in *Black and tan fantasy*, far and away the finest of
the several versions recorded at the time. Paradoxically, Ellington's formal contributions — the second (sixteen-bar) theme,
stated with too much oiliness by Hardwicke's alto saxophone, and
the piano solo — are the weakest parts. Miley is listed as co-
composer, as he was of *Creole love call* and several later pieces,
yet neither he nor Nanton, extraordinary performers though they
were, would have sounded half so effective in a less theatrical
situation. Ellington's dramatic impulse was already at work. *East
St Louis toodle-oo* is jauntier, less menacing; similarly, Miley's
playing is not so violent in *Blue bubbles* which has, rather
unusually, Carney playing the alto saxophone solo and Hardwicke taking the one on baritone.

Jackson was a good workaday musician (more than that,
perhaps, in *Creole love call*), yet the arrival of Bigard in 1928
meant the orchestra now contained one of the finest New Orleans
clarinettists, able to exploit the felicities of his instrument, an
adroit, even affecting, soloist as well as a gifted ensemble player
whose pirouetting against sonorous brass was to provide a climax
for many Ellington compositions. Bigard's skill as a soloist comes
across in *Black beauty*, his relaxed approach contrasting with
Nanton's brusque chorus, and both set off by Whetsol's wistful
statement of the theme. It has been suggested that this performance contains Ellington's first good piano solo on record; his early
work inclined to overkill, using too many notes, flowery rather

than concise [33]. Another New Orleans musician was Braud. In those days most big bands revolved around their drummers, but Ellington's was an exception. Greer, an excellent percussionist, provided the kind of orchestral drumming that this music required, more a matter of colouring than of trying to thrust the band forward. The real impetus came from Braud's bass, frequently slapped, pushing the ensemble ahead, often achieving a special rapport with Miley or Nanton.

Quite why Ellington decided to record *The mooche* without Miley is a mystery, for in all the other contemporary versions his growling has a central role in what should sound like a Dionysian procession. On this occasion his deputy was Whetsol, whose virtues were of a totally different order, fragile and intimate. In the event, Whetsol could not summon up the aesthetic antagonism required, either in the main theme or in the twelve-bar chorus he shares with Hodges. The latter, of course, represented the arrival of a major saxophonist in a band previously dominated by brass and clarinet (Carney's baritone playing still being largely functional). Yet despite Hodges' presence, it is Carney who plays the alto solo in *No, papa, no*, a Victoria Spivey blues also recorded by Armstrong (48). To add to the oddness of the session, Braud's place was taken by Taylor, his tuba playing competent but underlining how much this band relied upon having a string bass.

This was the period when Ellington's orchestra was building its reputation at the Cotton Club, where the song-writing team of Dorothy Fields and Jimmy McHugh often devised numbers for the floor show, including *Harlem River quiver, Bandanna babies, Diga diga doo, I must have that man, Hot feet* and *Arabian lover*. Sixteen fluent bars from Hodges illuminate what otherwise sounds like a stock arrangement of *Bandanna babies. Diga diga doo* is treated gruffly, Nanton and Miley coping doughtily but within scoring that seems very routine, just as it does in *Flaming youth*, rescued by one of Miley's fieriest solos. He growled on a trumpet as if he thought that way, perhaps the purest virtuoso ever to specialize with plunger and wa-wa mutes. The same was true of Nanton, whose solos rarely moved outside an octave yet possessed both remarkable aptness and — despite familiar phrases — an air of being freshly created. But while Nanton remained with the band until the mid-1940s, Miley departed at the start of 1929 and died only three years later. His replacement, Williams, became a master of growl playing, though always sounding calmer and slightly more calculating than Miley ever did. At the start, however, he felt his way. If the solo in *Ring dem bells* represents an early triumph within these bizarre disciplines, an understanding of how to make them work for him, the vibrant open playing on *Saratoga swing* is a reminder that, unlike Miley, Williams could also excel in a more conventional style. Jenkins, on the other hand, was always erratic. He ripostes usefully to Williams's scat singing in *Hot feet*, then sounds much too four-square on *Cotton Club stomp*, going on to growl rather like a cockerel in *Jungle nights in Harlem*, the epitome of a number whipped up quickly for the Cotton Club dance-line. Bunn, who later worked with that superb novelty quintet, the Spirits of Rhythm (**167**), was, rather surprisingly, chosen to play single-string guitar solos and to duet with Bigard on *Haunted nights*, otherwise an undistinguished rehash of Ellington's by then famous blend of blues and 'jungle style' growling.

Creole rhapsody has been hailed as the first work in jazz where the composer takes complete control. That is to ignore what Morton had been up to with his Red Hot Peppers (**47**) and to be too dismissive of Ellington's own earlier output. Yet the soloists in *Creole rhapsody* certainly have a different status to that enjoyed by Miley and Nanton in *Black and tan fantasy*. In both the double-sided ten-inch 78 rpm version, recorded in January 1931 (**90**) and the double-sided twelve-inch 78 made six months later, the scoring takes precedence. Otherwise the two performances are so different as to constitute separate compositions [34]. The earlier recording holds to one tempo, gaining intensity and a sense of continuity through doing so. But the orchestral playing in the later version is much better, while Ellington's use of different tempos results in a greater variety and flexibility. Nevertheless, the effect is occasionally choppy, while the finale is marred by second-hand pretentiousness. The biggest gain is the addition of a slow thirty-two-bar theme, stated by Whetsol in his most plaintive manner. Whichever the version, the truth is that *Creole rhapsody* marked a significant step in the career of Ellington the composer, a sign that he was assuming a new authority within his orchestra.   C.F.

89 Toodle-Oo Duke Ellington
Vocalion (E) VLP4, Decca (A) DL9224

Duke Ellington and His Kentucky Club Orchestra: Bubber Miley, Louis Metcalfe (tpt); Joe Nanton (tbn); Rudy Jackson, Otto Hardwicke (clt, alt); Harry Carney (clt, bar); Ellington (p); Fred Guy (bj); Bass Edwards (tu); Sonny Greer (d). New York City, 29 November 1926.
East St Louis toodle-oo · *Birmingham breakdown*

Same personnel and location, 29 December 1926.
Immigration blues · *The creeper* (2 takes)

Jackson also plays bs clt[1]. New York City, 3 February 1927.
New Orleans lowdown · Song of the cotton field[1]
Same personnel and location, 28 February 1927.
Birmingham breakdown
Same personnel and location, 14 March 1927.
East St Louis toodle-oo
The Washingtonians: same personnel and location, 7 April 1927.
Black and tan fantasy
June Clark (tpt) replaces Miley. New York City, 10 April 1927.
Soliloquy
Duke Ellington and His Orchestra: Wellman Braud (bs) replaces
Edwards. New York City, 29 December 1927.
Red hot band · Doing the frog
The Washingtonians: Arthur Whetsol (tpt), Barney Bigard (clt, ten)
replace Clark, Jackson. New York City, 21 March 1928.
Take it easy · Jubilee stomp

90 Cotton Club Days Vol. 2
Ace of Hearts (E) AH89, *Decca (A) DL9245, 9241

The Washingtonians: Metcalfe, Whetsol (tpt); Nanton (tbn); Hardwicke
(clt, alt); Bigard (clt, ten); Carney (clt, bar); Ellington (p); Guy (bj); Braud
(bs); Greer (d). New York City, 21 March 1928.
Take it easy · Black beauty
Duke Ellington and His Orchestra: Miley (tpt), Johnny Hodges (sop, alt)
replace Metcalfe, Hardwicke. New York City, 17 October 1928.
Louisiana
Freddy Jenkins (tpt), Hardwicke (clt, alt) added. New York City,
9 January 1929.
Tiger rag
Six Jolly Jesters: Jenkins (tpt); Nanton (tbn); Hodges (alt); Ellington (p);
Guy (bj); Braud (bs); Greer (d). New York City, 25 October 1929.
Six or seven times
Cootie Williams (tpt), Teddy Bunn (g), Bruce Randloph (wbd) added.
New York City, 29 October 1929.
Oklahoma stomp
Duke Ellington and His Orchestra: Williams, Jenkins, Whetsol (tpt);
Nanton (tbn); Juan Tizol (v-tbn); Carney (clt, alt, bar); Bigard (clt, ten);
Hodges (sop, alt); Ellington (p); Guy (bj); Braud (bs); Greer (d). New York
City, 20 March 1930.
When you're smiling
Joe Cornell (acc), Dick Robertson (vcl[1]) added; Jenkins absent. New York
City, 22 April 1930.
Accordion Joe[2] *· Double check stomp*
Jenkins (tpt) added; Cornell, Robertson absent. New York City, 17
October 1930.
Running wild

The Jungle Band: Robertson, Benny Paine (vcl) added. New York City,
27 October 1930.
Wang wang blues
Duke Ellington and His Orchestra: Robertson, Paine absent. New York
City, 20 January 1931.
Creole rhapsody

91 Hot from Harlem
World Records (E) SHB58 (2 LPs)

Duke Ellington and His Orchestra: Jabbo Smith, Metcalfe (tpt); Nanton
(tbn); Carney (clt, alt, bar); Jackson (clt, ten); Hardwicke (sop, alt, bar);
Ellington (p); Guy (bj); Braud (bs); Greer (d). New York City,
3 November 1927.
What can a poor fellow do? · *Black and tan fantasy* · *Chicago stomp
down*
The Washingtonians: Miley (tpt), Bigard (clt, ten) replace Smith,
Jackson. New York City, 9 January 1928.
Sweet Mama (Papa's getting mad) · *Stack o'Lee blues* · *Bugle call rag*
Duke Ellington and His Orchestra: same personnel and location,
19 January 1928.
Take it easy · *Jubilee stomp* · *Harlem twist (East St Louis toodle-oo)*
Irving Mills (vcl[3]) added. New York City, 10 July 1928.
Diga diga doo[3] · *Doing the new low down*
Ellington (p). New York City, 1 October 1928.
Black beauty · *Swampy river*
Full band personnel but with Whetsol (tpt), Lonnie Johnson (g), Baby
Cox (vcl[4]) added. Same date.
The mooche[4] · *Move over* · *Hot and bothered*[4]
Whetsol, Miley, Jenkins (tpt); Nanton (tbn); Bigard (clt, ten); Hodges
(sop, alt); Carney (alt, bar); Ellington (p); Guy (bj); Johnson (g); Braud
(bs); Greer (d). New York City, 20 November 1928.
The blues with a feeling · *Going to town* · *Misty morning*
Harlem Footwarmers: Whetsol (tpt); Nanton (tbn); Bigard (clt); Carney
(clt, alt, bar); Ellington (p); Guy (bj); Braud (bs); Greer (d). New York
City, 2 August 1929.
Jungle jamboree · *Snake hip dance*
Whetsol, Jenkins, Williams (tpt); Nanton (tbn); Tizol (v-tbn); Carney (clt,
alt, bar); Bigard (clt, ten); Hodges (sop, alt); Ellington (p); Guy (bj); Braud
(bs); Greer (d). New York City, 20 November 1929.
Blues of the vagabond · *Syncopated shuffle*
Williams, Nanton, Bigard (clt), Carney (clt, bar), Ellington, Guy, Braud,
Greer only. Same date.
Lazy Duke
Whetsol (tpt) replaces Williams; Carney absent. New York City,
14 October 1930.
Big house blues · *Rocky mountain blues*

Same personnel and location, 30 October 1930.
Mood indigo
Full band personnel but with Williams (vcl[5]), Greer (ch[6]), Mills (vcl[3]).
Same date.
Ring dem bells[5,6] · *Three little words*[3] · *Old man blues* · *Sweet chariot*[5]
Memphis Hot Shots: Sid Garry (vcl[7]) added; Mills absent. New York City, 8 November 1930.
I can't realise you love me[7] · *I'm so in love with you*[7] · *Rocking in rhythm*

Ellington's beginnings as a creative musical thinker were laid strongly under the influence of Eastern ragtime and jazz through his early meetings with Harlem pianists such as James P. Johnson and Willie 'The Lion' Smith and, when he began seriously to form a band, through his by no means uncritical admiration of the Whiteman and Henderson orchestras. [It is worth noting that even in 1930 he thought fit (as Oliver had done in 1926) to follow the arrangement of *Wang wang blues* that Whiteman had recorded as early as 1920.] Johnson and Smith influences are clearly heard in his 1928 piano solos, *Black beauty* ('A Portrait of Florence Mills'), which suggests the Johnsonian halfway house between ragtime and formal blues, and *Swampy river*, which owes more, perhaps, to 'The Lion's' impressionistic moods (see **237**). If Ellington's mature keyboard style appeared to abandon the conventions of stride piano, it is clear that the spirit was subtly re-embodied, and *Swampy river* may here be the more significant harbinger. However, an early relation between keyboard and orchestral techniques is shown by the orchestration of *Black beauty* also recorded in 1928: there is a dependence upon pianistic conceptions that will diminish in later phases of Ellington's career.

He acknowledged a debt to Henderson during the period covered here, and the similarities of approach may be heard by comparing *The creeper*, in two intriguingly varied takes, with such Redman arrangements as *Tozo* and *Rocky mountain blues* (**86** — note that the latter is not the same piece as the Ellington one found on **91**). That the commerce was in both directions is indicated by the respectful 1928 rearrangement by Redman for the Chocolate Dandies (**84**) of *Birmingham breakdown*, which is here represented by 1926 and 1927 takes on **89**.

Formalism that would be at home in any fairly jazzy New York context of the time may be heard towards the middle sections of the three versions of *East St Louis toodle-oo* (one first issued as *Harlem twist*); but in the minor-key opening and closing sections things are occurring which point to what were to be abiding strands in the warp and weft of Ellingtonian tapestries for decades to come. These strands were the effect of a New Orleans brass tradition and, closely linked to that, the influence of Negro religious music. Ellington may have glimpsed a vision of jazz dignity in Whiteman's music and in the music of movie theatre bands, yet — since for him imitation trailed far behind inspiration — part of his greatness is that he allowed jazz to demonstrate its dignity by its own innate means. In so doing he may have fulfilled vicariously the frustrated ambitions of Oliver, whose characteristic muted voice is developed to a sharper pungency by Miley in *East St Louis toodle-oo, Immigration blues*, the second *Birmingham breakdown* and elsewhere. And Nanton perfected at a remarkably early stage plunger-muted vocalizations that, with the trumpet sounds of Miley's successors, would characterize the band throughout a major part of its history. Beyond emulation of Oliver, these sounds hark back to an older, rather more conjectural southern source in the playing of New Orleans trumpeters such as the unrecorded Chris Kelly who, according to Danny Barker [35], played like a preacher. No doubt Barker was referring to Kelly's ability to move his hearers, but that growling style, evidently the inspiration of Oliver, Miley and Williams, may be rooted as much in the speech-song techniques of black preaching as in blues expression. The final blurted trumpet phrases and shouted punctuations from the ensemble in *Black and tan fantasy* (Miley is more powerful in **89** than Smith in **91**) are obvious proof of this source, and subtle responses to the influence are found in passages too numerous to mention. (Examples of Negro church music, and comments on jazz links, will be found under **2**.)

Much of what was once regarded as melodramatic savagery from the cabaret jungle is really an inherently musical extension of an ancient sound-sorcery which has persisted in the voices of R. C. Crenshaw (**2**) Blind Willie Johnson (Fontana (E) TFE7052), and others on the borderline between blues and spiritual. Too much can, no doubt, be made of this where Ellington's music is concerned, and it is not to be denied that he responded to the requirements of Cotton Club primitivism with a certain degree of burlesque hocus-pocus; but he did not have to invent the mode to fit the floor show, for the basis had already been provided. One might say that Ellington's shouting brass section echoed the southern rural preacher as Basie's shouting brass section echoed the mid-western city blues singer (**133–134**).

The strength of New Orleans influences must have come also from Bechet's short flirtation with the band in 1925, an association possibly as catalytic as Armstrong's with Henderson a trifle earlier. Yet Bechet's direct influence is not easy to discern in the earlier phases of the period dealt with here [36]. It emerges in the soprano and alto style of Hodges and is also anticipated slightly in the Creole portamentos of Bigard's clarinet and in those of his predecessor, the Indianian Jackson — and echoed later in Ellington's and Billy Strayhorn's approach to reed-section voicings. Bechet's donation, together with Miley's, is an enthusiastically 'vocal' one that helps to explain the choral quality of many of the band's greatest mid-period orchestrations.

During the time from late 1926 to the end of 1930, with growing fame and active involvement in the show business world, Ellington and his men are looking for a style but are seemingly too busy to find it more than fleetingly. The numbers included here may be divided into three overlapping categories: (i) arrangements of non-Ellington material played close to the styles of other bands; (ii) themes by Ellington or his sidemen whose realization goes but a little way beyond the first category; (iii) performances of Ellingtonian or other material which approach the unmistakable consistency of the leader's subsequent compositions for orchestra.

Under (i) may be listed, from 1927: *Red hot band* and *Doing the frog* which, though early in the Cotton Club period, are run-of-the-mill scores; *What can a poor fellow do?* and *Chicago stomp down*; from 1928: *Sweet Mama*, *Stack o'Lee blues*, *Bugle call rag*, *Diga diga doo* and *Doing the new low down*; from 1929: *Jungle jamboree* and *Snake hip dance*, in which Fats Waller had a compositional hand, *Tiger rag*, *Oklahoma stomp* and *Six or seven times*; from 1930: *Running wild*, *Wang wang blues*, *Three little words*, *I can't realise that you love me*, *Accordion Joe* and *When you're smiling*.

Under (ii), from 1926: *Immigration blues* and *The creeper*; from 1927: *New Orleans low down* and Percy Grainger's *Song of the cotton field*, in both of which atmosphere is sought by somewhat exotic means; from 1928: *Going to town*; from 1929: *Lazy Duke*, *Blues of the vagabond* and *Double check stomp*; from 1930: *Big house blues*.

Under (iii), from 1926: *East St Louis toodle-oo* and *Birmingham breakdown*; from 1927: *Black and tan fantasy*, *Take it easy* and *Jubilee stomp*; from 1928: further versions of *Take it easy* and *Jubilee stomp*; also *The mooche*, *Move over*, *Hot and bothered*, *Blues with a feeling* and *Misty morning*; from 1929: *Syncopated shuffle*, with some of Ellington's most powerful 'stride' piano on record; from 1930: *Rocky mountain blues*, *Ring dem bells*, *Sweet chariot*, *Mood indigo* and *Rocking in rhythm*; and finally, from 1931, *Creole rhapsody*.

Controversial divisions, no doubt; and controversial inclusions. The 1928 piano solos and the strange, rather Bixian, *Soliloquy* of 1927 may need categories of their own; and there is, of course, other recorded material which goes unregarded here. There is no attempt in suggesting the categories above to make sweeping judgements upon excellence, for it is recognized that a remarkably high standard of jazz creation was achieved in a majority of these performances. That excellence is achieved, however, to a great extent by Ellington's soloists, starting with Miley, Nanton, Carney, Jackson, Hardwicke and Ellington himself, and moving on to Metcalfe, Bigard, Whetsol, Hodges, Jenkins and Williams. It is they who make the running in many of these lively creations and, whenever the composer's vision gleams for a moment, one senses that wisdoms sounded in the improvising voices are being heeded.

The brass section statements and the gliding harmonic accompaniments become more assured; but, even in the advanced tone-painting and dramatic variation of *Creole rhapsody*, a new and characteristic voice for the reed section still eludes him. This is probably because until the advent of Hodges, and in spite of hints which Bechet may have given, there were no saxophonists then available to Ellington who had moved sufficiently beyond the common conception of their instrument as a species of clarinet to prompt new voicings. The orchestra was served far better by its rhythm team than Henderson's was during the main part of this period. Greer and Guy are consistently discreet and skilful, and it is essential to observe the contributions made by Braud, which were as important in terms of musical character as those made much later by Blanton (**153**).

Considering what is said above about the increasingly vocal nature of Ellington's orchestration, it is strange that he was largely unfortunate throughout his career in his choice of singers. Of the few vocals scattered through these recordings, only those by Williams in *Ring dem bells* and *Sweet chariot* and from Baby Cox in *The mooche* and *Hot and bothered* express jazz skill. And they are decidedly part of that dialogue of mutual challenge going on between voice and instrument currently affecting the development of Armstrong's virtuosity as an improviser (**48**), and maybe pointing forward to the more subtle and artistic discoveries of Billie Holiday (**204, 205**).

At all events, this is a period of formation, full of fascinating auguries. *Creole rhapsody* ushers in a new time of experiment in which individual voices will be related more closely to the composer's shaping will. But we have not quite reached the stage at which Ellington can justifiably say that the orchestra is his true instrument. *Creole rhapsody* is a very important turning point, but it is Bigard's lyrical weavings that give this first version of the piece its most poignant jazz character. Perhaps that is to say nothing more than that the Ellington saga is a marvellously co-operative one from beginning to end.   E.T.

Blues Singers and Jazz

These are as much jazz as blues singers, and they owe their place here largely to the unequivocally jazz character of the improvised accompaniments they nearly always receive.

92 **Jazz Sounds of the 20s Vol. 4: the Blues Singers**
Parlophone (E) PMC1177, Swaggie (Au) S1240

Sara Martin (vcl) acc Clarence Williams's Blue Five: Thomas Morris (cnt); John Mansfield (tbn); Sidney Bechet (sop); Williams (p); Buddy Christian (bj). New York City, 11 August 1923.
Blind man blues · Atlanta blues

Margaret Johnson (vcl) acc Clarence Williams's Blue Five: Charlie Irvis (tbn) replaces Mansfield. New York City, 19 October 1923.
E flat blues · If I let you get away with it

Butterbeans and Susie (vcl) acc King Oliver (cnt); Williams (p). New York City, 15 September 1924.
Construction gang

acc Louis Armstrong and His Hot Five: Armstrong (cnt); Kid Ory (tbn); Johnny Dodds (clt); Lil Hardin Armstrong (p); Johnny St Cyr (bj). Chicago, 18 June 1926.
He likes it slow

Sippie Wallace (vcl) acc Cicero Thomas (cnt); possibly Hersal Thomas (p). Chicago, 20 November 1926.
Bedroom blues

Chippie Hill (vcl) acc Armstrong (cnt); Richard M. Jones (p). Chicago, 23 November 1926.
Pratt City blues · Pleading for the blues

Sippie Wallace (vcl) acc Armstrong (cnt); Artie Starks (clt); supposedly Thomas (p); Bud Scott (g). Chicago, 6 May 1927.
The flood blues

Victoria Spivey (vcl) acc Clarence Williams's Blue Five: Oliver (cnt); Ed Cuffee (tbn); Omer Simeon (clt); Williams (p); Eddie Lang (g). New York City, 12 September 1928.
My handy man · Organ grinder's blues

Cleo Gibson (vcl) acc her Hot Three: Henry Mason (tpt); J. Neal Montgomery (p); unidentified g. Atlanta, 14 March 1929.
Nothing but the blues · I've got Ford movements in my hips

Mamie Smith (vcl) acc possibly Bill Dillard or Ward Pinkett (tpt); Jimmy
Archey (tbn); Fred Skerritt (alt); Henry Jones or Bingie Madison (ten);
Gene Rogers (p); Goldie Lucas (g); Richard Fullbright (bs). New York
City, 19 February 1931.
Jenny's ball

When the blues became the rage in the 1920s, following upon the
huge popularity of Mamie Smith's 1920 recording of *Crazy blues*
(Columbia (A) C3L33), jazz was a beneficiary in a number of
ways. The most obvious advantage was the preference of leading
female singers for accompaniments in jazz style, often by bands
whose musicians were encouraged to improvise. Thus several
individual and collective careers were borne ahead upon the
inexorable if short-lived current of this craze.

The singing, which dominates this representative collection, is
of varying jazz (and, for that matter, blues) interest, much of it
belonging to a tragi-comic minstrel tradition and calling for no
great subtlety. Chippie Hill has a simple, rather serious style,
given what liveliness it has by the expressive colouring of vowel
sounds rather than by the rhythm of her phrasing. In both *Pratt
City blues* and *Pleading for the blues* (a 'fixed melody' blues song)
there is faultless accompaniment by Armstrong and Jones; and
Armstrong is also heard with his Hot Five supporting the genial
Butterbeans and Susie. *He likes it slow* and *Construction gang*
(the latter with tentatively phrased cornet from Oliver) are
worthy of more than passing attention. The fruity vocal inflections and the assured timing of sung and spoken exchanges
probably hint at the histrionic inspiration of Armstrong's own
much less predictable vocal skill (**48**).

E flat blues and *If I let you get away with it* are sung with
precocious enthusiasm by Margaret Johnson, a performer whose
stridency needs the powerful accompaniment provided here by a
group dominated by Bechet's soaring soprano saxophone.

Cleo Gibson's Hot Three are 'territory' musicians, represented
on **75**. They give convincing support to a singer whose tonal
potency, if not her control of phrasal subtleties, helps to explain
why *Nothing but the blues* and *I've got Ford movements in my hips*
were at one time suspected of being pseudonymous performances
by Bessie Smith. In *Blind man blues* and *Atlanta blues* the
slightly wistful edge of Sara Martin's voice is challenged
by Bechet's ruthless emotionalism and positively mocked by
Mansfield's trombone crudity. Miss Martin sometimes attempts
melodic ornament which she cannot quite encompass and Sippie
Wallace, a singer who retains more of the inner elasticity of the
rural blues, achieves greater interest by what seem, on the

surface, more straightforward means. (Regarding the Wallace accompaniments, if, as is supposed, Hersal Thomas died in 1926, the excellent pianist on *The flood blues* cannot be he; and his presence on *Bedroom blues* is very unlikely.)

Victoria Spivey, who, like Miss Wallace, was to survive as a performer into advanced age, has an expressive delivery and a fairly subtle sense of jazz timing. She has able and discreet companions on her 1928 session, with Lang making some pleasurable contributions. *My handy man* and *Organ grinder's blues* are forthright examples of the sexual *doubles-entendres* which enliven many a 'classic' blues recording. Yet, brash as the motive of such songs is, the mock-ingenuousness with which they are delivered here actually lends them a kind of innocence; and there is art in that. *Organ grinder's blues* may be a million miles from Schubert's dejected hurdy-gurdy player in *Der Leiermann*, yet the calculated formalism of the accompaniment, particularly in the hands of Williams and Lang, together with the controlled shapeliness of the vocal line, may bring this close to a sort of blues *Lied*.

The celebrated Mamie Smith, singing *Jenny's ball* in 1931 abetted by a relaxed team of Harlemites, shows the immense warmth and vigour which has lately been associated with show singers like Ethel Merman and Pearl Bailey. Perhaps she comes nearer to jazz than most of the others in her impulsive execution of verbal 'breaks' in what is a typical vaudeville song.

In addition to providing excellent opportunities for jazz players, the blues craze may well have fed into growing jazz styles, through the sustained tonal qualities of the singing itself, elements of expressiveness to counter the feverish hangover of ill-digested ragtime. That influence would go on being felt in instrumental music long after these lusty ladies had lost their popularity.   E.T.

93 Louis Armstrong and the Blues Singers
CBS (F) 64218

Maggie Jones (vcl) acc Armstrong (cnt); Fletcher Henderson (p). New York City, 9 and 10 December 1924.
Poor house blues · Thunderstorm blues · Anybody here want to try my cabbage?

Same personnel and location, 17 December 1924.
If I lose, let me lose · Screaming the blues · Good time flat blues

Clara Smith (vcl) acc Armstrong (cnt); Charlie Green (tbn[1]); Henderson (p). New York City, 7 January 1925.
Nobody knows the way I feel this morning[1] · Broken busted blues[1]

Same personnel and location, 3 April 1925
Shipwrecked blues · Courthouse blues · My John blues[1]
Sippie Wallace (vcl) acc Armstrong (cnt); Hersal Thomas (p). Chicago,
1 March 1926.
Special delivery blues · Jack of Diamonds blues
Nolan Welsh (vcl) acc Armstrong (cnt); Richard M. Jones (p). Chicago,
16 June 1926.
Bridwell blues · St Peter's blues
Sippie Wallace (vcl) acc Armstrong (cnt); Artie Starks (clt); supposedly
Thomas (p); Bud Scott (g). Chicago, 6 May 1927.
The flood blues

Anyone who is surprised that Armstrong ranks among the finest
accompanists in jazz has failed to understand the full range of his
talents. Reared, as most of us have been, on the bravura side of
his playing, or contemplating his ability, in the final stage of his
career, to steal a scene from Barbra Streisand, it is difficult to
imagine how such a forceful musical personality could adapt so
easily to a secondary role. But as these and other recordings on **92**
and **94** testify, he possessed the kind of sensitivity which allowed
him not only to anticipate what his colleagues were about to do
but also to fashion the most delicate obbligato or responses to the
vocal line. The passing of time has revealed very bleakly the gap
between his stature and that of most of the singers with whom he
worked, yet this in itself underlines the extent of his application
to the job in hand.

Except Nolan Welsh, whose style was closer to country blues,
all these vocalists qualify as 'classic' blues singers, accustomed to
appearing in theatres where histrionics could be as valuable as a
good voice. Maggie Jones is an example of an average performer,
her repertoire taking in the moral homilies of *Poor house blues*
('Spend my money, spend it on my so-called friends (repeat)/And
now I'm broke, that's where friendship ends'), the melodramatics
of *Thunderstorm blues*, complete with sound effects, or the
euphemistic overtures of *Anybody here want to try my cabbage?*
Yet the last-named piece contains an adventurous twelve-bar solo
from Armstrong (first eight, then four, with Miss Jones taking a
stop-time four in between). *Good time flat blues*, incidentally, will
be familiar to those who saw the film *New Orleans*, where it
turned up as *Farewell to Storyville*; the sentiments of the original
are much the same: 'The chief of police done tore my playhouse
down (repeat)/No use in grievin', I'm gonna leave this town'.

Clara Smith, on the other hand, was one of the best singers of
the period, her voice possessing a darker edge, less rigid in her
phrasing; notice how she spreads the lines in *Courthouse blues*.

Nobody knows the way I feel this morning has too repetitive a theme for the musicians to do much more than play the one-bar response. *My John blues* is another restrained performance, mainly of interest because Armstrong, uncharacteristically, goes in for wa-wa effects, possibly because of Green's presence. But *Shipwrecked blues* and *Courthouse blues* are outstanding, with Armstrong phrasing majestically, his tone at its purest; and he surprises the listener by starting off *Courthouse blues* in low register.

The Chicago sessions have a different ambience, probably because Armstrong's colleagues were more at home with the idiom. (Henderson, the pianist on all the New York titles, had, after all, to learn how to play the blues just as much as any Englishman or Japanese.) This acclimatization to the blues is most noticeable in Thomas's piano playing behind Sippie Wallace, another better-than-average singer. Armstrong utters the word 'Special!' in the hokum introduction to *Special delivery blues*; his cornet playing on this track, and even more markedly on *Jack of Diamonds blues*, is disappointing. *The flood blues* finds him back in form, but the backing group is larger and spends too much time trying to make the music programmatic. The singing on *Bridwell blues* has a grimness that points up Armstrong's drier tone and more expansive, almost leisurely, style. But perhaps Nolan Welsh achieved an accidental triumph, for *St Peter's blues* is sung in a very indifferent fashion, the performance rescued only by Armstrong's presence.   C.F.

Bessie Smith

94 **The Empress**
CBS (E) 66264 (2 LPs), Columbia (A) CG30818 (2 LPs)

Bessie Smith (vcl) acc Buster Bailey, Don Redman (clt); Fred Longshaw (p). New York City, 6 December 1924.
Sing Sing prison blues
acc Longshaw (p). New York City, 11 December 1924.
Follow the deal on down · *Sinful blues*
acc Bailey, Redman (clt); Longshaw (p). New York City, 12 December 1924.
Woman's trouble blues · *Love me daddy blues*
acc Charlie Green (tbn); Longshaw (p). New York City, 13 December 1924.
Dying gambler's blues
acc Louis Armstrong (cnt); Longshaw (p, har[1]). New York City, 14 January 1925.
Sobbing hearted blues · *St Louis blues*[1] · *Cold in hand blues* · *Reckless blues*[1] · *You've been a good old wagon*

acc Fletcher Henderson's Hot Six: Joe Smith (cnt); Green (tbn); Bailey (clt); Coleman Hawkins (ten); Henderson (p); Charlie Dixon (bj); Ralph Escudero (tu). New York City, 5 May 1925.
Cake walking babies · Yellow dog blues
acc Green (tbn); Henderson (p). New York City, 14 May 1925.
Soft pedal blues
acc Green (tbn); Bailey (clt); Longshaw (p); James T. Wilson (sound effects). New York City, 15 May 1925.
Dixie flyer blues
acc Armstrong (cnt); Green (tbn); Henderson (p). New York City, 26 May 1925.
Nashville woman's blues
Bessie Smith and Her Band: Smith (vcl) acc Joe Smith (cnt); Jimmy Harrison (tbn); Bailey, Hawkins (clt); Henderson (p); Dixon (bj). New York City, 2 March 1927.
Muddy water · There'll be a hot time in the old town tonight
Bessie Smith and Her Blue Boys: Smith (vcl) acc Joe Smith (cnt); Green (tbn); Henderson (p). New York City, 3 March 1927.
Trombone Cholly · Send me to the 'lectric chair · Them's graveyard words · Hot springs blues
acc James P. Johnson (p). New York City, 1 April 1927.
Sweet mistreater · Lock and key
acc Porter Grainger (p); Lincoln Conaway (g). New York City, 27 September 1927.
Mean old bedbug blues · A good man is hard to find
acc Ernest Elliott (alt); Grainger (p). New York City, 28 September 1927.
Homeless blues · Looking for my man
acc Tommy Ladnier (cnt); Henderson (p); June Cole (tu). New York City, 27 October 1927.
Dying by the hour · Foolish man blues
acc Demus Dean (cnt); Green (tbn); Longshaw (p). New York City, 9 February 1928.
Thinking blues · Pickpocket blues

Does an artist of such impressive stature merit comprehensive or merely representative treatment in a history of jazz? The dilemma posed by Bessie Smith is, it may appear, the very dilemma and paradox of the dubiously named 'classic' blues. Here is a singer who, like her distinguished mentor Ma Rainey, responded to the stimulus of good jazz accompaniment, but whose own repertoire and delivery, again like Ma Rainey's, reflected the early conditioning of a peripatetic theatrical career — the minstrel and tent shows, vaudeville theatres and cabarets. The vocal techniques developed by singers unaided by electrical amplification often led to stridency and exaggerated diction yet, though the power and clarity of Bessie Smith's voice owes much to a physical necessity, it does, quite marvellously, retain and enhance subtlety and variety of feeling.

Her right to be regarded as a jazz artist could be established superficially by her hummed imitation of a muted cornet at the end of *Sinful blues*, but there is more to the claim than that. Performances as different as *Cold in hand blues* and *A good man is hard to find* show how much there is of the jazz improviser's art in her approach to the songs which suit her style; and this discovery also highlights the difficulty inherent in any attempt to place her among the specialists of the vocal blues. Compared with Blind Lemon Jefferson's field-holler-like *Black snake moan* or the ingenuous simplicity of Memphis Minnie's *Me and my chauffeur* (both on CBS (E) 66218), even the elemental pathos of *Sing Sing prison blues* or *Follow the deal on down* has marked sophistication. It would be hard to imagine any rural singer or died-in-the-wool vaudevillean achieving the astounding expressiveness of *Reckless blues*, in which a single emphasized syllable (e.g. 'Now . . .' in the line 'Now I'm growin' old') can be fashioned into a moving melodic and rhythmic phrase. On the other hand, *Mean old bedbug blues*, with its rasped complaint over Conaway's dramatic guitar chords, might seem as good as any example of the transposition of rural techniques into an urban *milieu*.

In any of the five January 1925 songs the essential kinship of Miss Smith's singing and Armstrong's cornet accompaniment is clear at every moment. The sinuous vocal phrases of *Cold in hand blues* and *You've been a good old wagon* are complemented by the cornet's muted chattering and the piano's continually varied figurations. Reports that Miss Smith had little liking for Armstrong's style of support ring strange, especially if true, for she seems to respond to the relaxed expertise of both cornettist and pianist more inventively than she does to the premeditated and sometimes rather precious clarinet interjections of Bailey and Redman on the December 1924 dates. Expressive flexibility is also diminished when she is tied to a fixed melody as in *Muddy water*, *Them's graveyard words* or *There'll be a hot time in the old town tonight* (the latter marred — or enlivened, if you prefer — by uncertainties here and there about words and key). There are times, nevertheless, in these popular numbers when the need to reach a note outside her normal range uncovers unexpected purities in her voice.

That she is at her most artistically varied and persuasive in the most simply founded of blues songs, where the creation of melody is largely up to her, is exemplified well by *Reckless blues* and *Cold in hand blues*, and also by the 1927 *Homeless blues*, *Looking for my man*, *Dying by the hour*, *Foolish man blues* and *Thinking blues.* In these the multiplicity of shapings and shadings may hardly be apparent to superficial listening, since the basic means are so rudimentary; but to the ear well-attuned to the sensitivity of the best jazz musicianship, and to the emotional volatility of Negro song, the subtle musical satisfactions will remain manifold.

In addition, there is a number of songs, hovering halfway between traditional blues form and the popular song, in which Miss Smith is able to work within her best emphatic range — numbers like *St Louis blues, Yellow dog blues, You've been a good old wagon, Send me to the 'lectric chair, Dying gambler blues, Sweet mistreater* and *Lock and key.* In the last two named Johnson, who had a composing hand in these and other songs, accompanies with a vigorous grace that sounds rather formal in comparison with the playing of Longshaw, a pianist with a similar vocabulary uttered in looser expression. Henderson, another favoured accompanist, is more self-effacing; but the association with him is important for the involving of Joe Smith, a beautifully sensitive cornettist, and the naïve but well-loved Green. *Dying by the hour* and *Foolish man blues* have Ladnier suiting the mood with muted repartee which is a little uncharacteristic of him and, all in all, the instrumental backing throughout this collection is of high quality, with the numbers featuring Armstrong achieving peerless jazz distinction and those with Joe Smith, Johnson, Ladnier and Longshaw preserving supportive music to be cherished for its intrinsic worth.

Bessie Smith was, irrespective of musical source, one of the most emotionally compelling voices in the wide history of song. Drawing as it did upon the vivid wellspring of American Negro experience, and expressing a host of elemental themes in a style which never once betrayed the shaping genius of the blues, her singing had an incalculably beneficial impact on jazz. She must be judged to have exceeded jazz and the blues *per se.* A study of jazz that has no knowledge of her art will be seriously impoverished yet, even for that deprivation — and unbeknown — her effect upon the 'voices' of countless jazzmen will echo on. In the festive house of jazz hers was a short but devastating stay, and her departure was physically tragic; but it is evident that when — to quote *Lock and key* — 'the band crawled from behind the stand', they played on as dustier yet wiser men.   E.T.

95 Ethel Waters' Greatest Years
Columbia (A) PG31571 (2 LPs)

Ethel Waters (vcl) acc Joe Smith (cnt); Buster Bailey (clt); Fletcher Henderson (p). New York City, 29 April 1925.
Brother, you've got me wrong
unidentified bs sx added. New York City, 13 May 1925.
Sweet Georgia Brown
acc Horace Holmes (cnt); Pearl Wright (p); Bill Benford (tu). New York City, 28 July 1925.
Go back where you stayed last night
Alex Jackson (bs sx) replaces Benford; 'Slow Kid' Thompson (vcl intrjc) added. New York City, 25 August 1925.
You can't do what my last man did
acc by Her Plantation Orchestra: Holmes, Harry Tate (cnt); Joe King (tbn); unidentified reeds; Ralph 'Shrimp' Jones (vln); Lester Armstead (p); Maceo Jefferson (bj); Bill Benford (tu); Jesse Baltimore (d). New York City, 20 October 1925.
Sweet man
acc Wright (p) New York City, 23 December 1925.
Shake that thing
acc Smith (cnt); Henderson (p). New York City, 22 January 1926.
I've found a new baby
acc Maceo Pinkard (p). New York City, 20 February 1926.
Sugar, that sugar baby o' mine
acc Thornton Brown (cnt); Edward Carr (tbn); Lorraine Faulkner (p); unidentified d. New York City, 29 July 1926.
Heebie jeebies
acc Wright (p). New York City, 18 September 1926.
My special friend is back in town
Same personnel and location, 29 September 1926.
Jersey walk
acc James P. Johnson (p). New York City, 21 August 1928.
Lonesome swallow · Guess who's in town? · My handy man
acc Clarence Williams (p). New York City, 23 August 1928.
West End blues · Organ grinder's blues · My baby sure knows how to love
acc Bob Effros (tpt); Tommy Dorsey (tbn); Jimmy Dorsey (clt, alt); Ben Selvin (vln); Frank Signorelli (p); Tony Colucci (g); Joe Tarto (bs); Stan King (d). New York City, 7 June 1929.
True blue Lou
acc Selvin (vln) and unidentified personnel. New York City, 11 July 1929.
Waiting at the end of the road · Trav'ling all alone

acc Muggsy Spanier or Manny Klein (tpt); Selvin (vln); Signorelli (p); possibly Colucci (g); Tarto (bs). New York City, 1 April 1930.
Porgy

acc Klein (tpt); Tommy Dorsey (tbn); Benny Goodman (clt); Adrian Rollini (bs sx); Selvin (vln); Rube Bloom (p); New York City, 3 June 1930.
You brought a new kind of love to me

acc Klein (tpt); Tommy Dorsey (tbn); Jimmy Dorsey (clt, alt); Selvin (vln) plus other unidentified musicians. New York City, 18 November 1930.
Three little words

acc Klein (tpt); Tommy Dorsey (tbn); Goodman (clt); Selvin, Joe Venuti (vln); Bloom (p); Eddie Lang (g). New York City, 10 February 1931.
When your lover has gone · Please don't talk about me when I'm gone

Dick McDonough (g) replaces Lang; Venuti absent. New York City, 10 August 1931.
River, stay 'way from my door

acc probably Sterling Bose, Bunny Berigan (tpt); Tommy Dorsey (tbn); Jimmy Dorsey (clt, alt); unidentified alt; Larry Binyon (ten); Venuti, Harry Hoffman and others (vln); Fulton McGrath (p); McDonough (g); Artie Bernstein (bs); Stan King or Chauncey Morehouse (d); Victor Young (cond). New York City, 3 May 1933.
Love is the thing

acc probably similar personnel. New York City, 18 July 1933.
Don't blame me

acc Benny Goodman's Orchestra: Charlie Teagarden, Shirley Clay (tpt); Jack Teagarden (tbn); Goodman (clt); Art Karle (ten); Joe Sullivan (p); McDonough (g); Bernstein (bs); Gene Krupa (d). New York City, 27 November 1933.
A hundred years from today · I just couldn't take it, baby

acc by same personnel as for 3 May 1933. New York City, 30 March 1934.
Come up and see me some time · You've seen Harlem at its best

Jazz singers are hard to categorize. Blues singers — country, city, 'classic' — can be defined more easily, operating as they do within fairly precise traditions. The problem with jazz singing is that it has often inhabited that area where jazz overlaps the popular song. Ethel Waters, born in Philadelphia, began by singing blues in what was, after all, a period when blues were popular with Negro audiences. Writing in her autobiography [37] about her first encounter with Bessie Smith, she refers to 'my low, sweet and then new way of singing blues'. And, unlike a committed blues singer such as Bessie Smith who turned any popular song she sang into another kind of blues, Miss Waters could, when the time came, tackle that sort of material in her own way. The approach happened to include a sizeable amount of acting, of putting the emphasis upon telling a story, something which some 'classic' blues singers attempted to do also, but few so subtly. It was this, added to the fact that she possessed a remarkably expressive voice, a keen understanding of how language should come across in song, and a rhythmic flexibility very rare at that time, which made Ethel Waters the first important jazz singer.

This collection gives only a limited notion of her handling of formal blues. Indeed, only five of the numbers can be classed as blues at all: *Shake that thing*, *West End blues* and *Organ grinder's blues*, all twelve-bar songs, and two sixteen-bar pieces, *Go back where you stayed last night* and *You can't do what my last man did*. Apart from *West End blues*, these are really novelty numbers, either going with a dance (*Shake that thing*), exploiting salacious metaphors (*Organ grinder's blues*) or being smart enough to work in a reference to Ethel Barrymore (*You can't do what my last man did*). Much more significant is the way Miss Waters sings *Sweet Georgia Brown*. The year was 1925. Armstrong had still to record his first Hot Five session. There was, quite simply, no jazz singer on record performing with the kind of confidence — and the relaxed attitude to the beat — that is displayed here.

In a perceptive essay [38], Henry Pleasants comments on the importance of acting in her career — she became, of course, the first black woman to play a lead on Broadway — and its influence upon her singing. It emerges in her mastery of the 'point' number. And there are occasions, in *Trav'ling all alone* and *Love is the thing* for instance, when she could be accused of overdoing that approach. But, as with so many instinctive artists, the virtues and vices are complementary. She developed a style that worked for audiences in clubs and theatres. Later on, in the 1930s, this perhaps resulted in too determined an effort at holding attention through constant shifts of tempo, mood and style (*Don't blame me* is a typical example), yet the virtuosity still keeps the listener enthralled. Her diction is impeccable, and no doubt this helped in achieving success with white American and European audiences; yet she could moan and scat and adopt other Afro-American practices without stiffness or inhibition. Above all, she swings in a way no other singer had done before she came along. The really startling thing about the 1925 recordings is how modern they sound.

The diversity of the accompaniments can be explained by the fact that in her earlier period Miss Waters' records were released in Columbia's 14000 series, aimed at Negro record buyers. All the musicians on those were black, although none could be called outstanding except James P. Johnson and Joe Smith: Johnson plays admirably on three tracks, but Smith takes a disappointingly foursquare solo in *I've found a new baby*, and it is interesting to note that Horace Holmes sounds suspiciously like Smith on *Go back where you stayed last night* and *Sweet man*. On the whole, though, she tended to dominate her records, allowing little room for soloists. In 1929 she moved to Columbia's popular label, reaching a broader market, and now she was accompanied by white New York session men. They, too, got only limited opportunities to shine, with Goodman coming off best. (Incidentally, *A hundred years from today* and *I just couldn't take it, baby*, find her backed by the pick-up band, led by Goodman, which at the same session helped Billie Holiday to make her recording debut with *Your mother's son-in-law*, heard on **204**.) *Porgy* should not be confused with Gershwin's *I love you, Porgy*, even though both songs deal with life on Catfish Row. Written by Dorothy Fields and Jimmy McHugh for *Blackbirds of 1928*, *Porgy* enabled Ethel Waters to show off most sides of her particular genius including, at one point, paying a sidelong tribute to Armstrong by echoing the way he had sung *I can't give you anything but love*, another number from the same show.   C.F.

4

Jazz in Europe

The music soon found its missionaries, who between the world wars travelled principally across the Atlantic. Ever since then, jazz activity in Europe, by local players and visiting Americans, has steadily increased.

96 Arthur Briggs in Berlin
Black Jack (G) LP3006

Arthur Briggs and His Savoy Syncopators: Briggs (tpt, vcl intrjc[1]); Jean Naudin (tbn); George Jacquemont (clt, alt); René Dumont (alt, ten); Mario Scanavino (ten, vln); Gide van Gils (p); Harold Kirchstein (bj); Al Bowlly (g, vcl[2]); Hans Holdt (tu); Eugene Obendörfer (d); Bob Astor (vcl[3]). Berlin, February 1927.
Dulcinea

Same personnel and location, May 1927.
It made you happy when you made me cry[1,3]

Same personnel and location, August 1927.
Bugle call rag[1]

Same personnel and location, October 1927.
Song of the wanderer[2] · *Hallelujah*

Same personnel and location, November 1927.
Ain't she sweet? · *Do the black bottom with me* · *One o'clock baby* · *Yale blues*

Same personnel and location, December 1927.
Ain't she sweet?[2] · *Do the black bottom with me*[2] · *Among my souvenirs*[2] · *Since I found you*[2] · *I'm coming, Virginia*[2]

Although this record to some extent owes its place here to historical considerations, the listener, provided that he is not unduly put off by *Dulcinea*, which is pure *thé dansant* material, will be rewarded both with a glimpse of the early days of jazz in Europe and with a musical return to the city of *Goodbye to*

Berlin, albeit a little before Isherwood's time. Briggs, a pioneer jazz missionary, first came to Europe with the Southern Syncopated Orchestra (which also included Sidney Bechet) in 1919 [39], and was in Berlin during 1927–9, recording extensively. His band has a personnel of what appears to be international complexion and exerted a considerable influence on European jazz at the time. Indeed, the trumpeter himself, later domiciled in Paris, remained a guiding spirit for many years (see **105a, 107d** and Tax (Sd) m-8008).

Even at this early stage Briggs's technique was mature, and although on some pieces, such as *Among my souvenirs*, he merely decorates the melody, he more often syncopates it violently, as in the first *Ain't she sweet?*, or skitters across it obliquely, making only passing allusions, as on *Since I found you*. The record's best passages occur, however, when he spins an entirely independent line of his own, as on the first *Do the black bottom* and second *Ain't she sweet?*

Most of the rest of the weight is taken by the saxophones, who were a disciplined team in terms of ensemble if not of intonation, as *Hallelujah* or *It made you happy* well show. The sleeve note includes an entertaining extract from the writings of an East German jazz commentator who explains that Briggs employed saxophones in his band in conformity with the 'middle-class status' which this music had just then, apparently, acquired. In fact, some listeners may be offended by the blatant sweetness of these instruments as played here, even if it is contradicted by the matter-of-fact plunking of the banjo. Yet still the reed players gyrate with extreme liveliness in their solos, even if these are hit-or-miss. The rough treatment which is justly accorded *Song of the wanderer* provides good examples, and at least this animation is sympathetic to the buoyant confidence of Brigg's phrases on, for instance, *Yale blues*.

The leader's verbal appearances are confined to brisk announcements in English at the beginning of two pieces as indicated above. What the German buyers of the original 78 rpm discs made of these, and of the vocal interludes, it is hard to guess. More to the point, the effusions of Bowlly, the entertainer from Mozambique, stand as grim reminders of the circumstances under which these pioneers had to work.   M.H.

97 Jazz in Britain: the '20s
Parlophone (E) PMC7075

Original Dixieland Jazz Band: Nick LaRocca (cnt); Emile
Christian (tbn); Larry Shields (clt); Billy Jones (p); Tony Sbarbaro (d).
London, 8 January 1920.
My baby's arms

Billy Arnold's Novelty Band: Charles F. Kleiner (tpt); Billy Trittel (tbn);
Henry Arnold (clt, sop); Harry Johnson (alt); Billy Arnold (p); Chris
Lee (d). London, November 1920.
Stop it

Original Capitol Orchestra: unidentified cnt; Trittel (tbn); Murray
Barley (clt, alt); G. Webb (alt); Bud Sheppard (p); unidentified bj, d.
Hayes, Middlesex, 21 January 1924.
Tiger rag

Carolina Club Orchestra: Red Honeycutt, Monk Buie (tpt); Buck
Weaver (tbn); Ben Williams, Joe Gillespie (clt, alt); Hal Kemp (clt, ten,
bar); Slatz Randall (p); William Waugh (bj); Billy Wolfe (tu); Jimmy
Brooks (d). London, August 1924.
Ain't you ashamed?

Jack Hylton's Kit-Kat Band: Tom Smith, Edwin Knight (tpt); Ted
Heath (tbn); Al Starita, Jim Kelleher (clt, alt); George Smith (ten);
Hugo Rignold (vln); Sid Bright (p); Len Fillis (bj); Alfred Field (tu);
Eric Little (d). Hayes, Middlesex, 10 August 1925.
Milneburg joys

Devonshire Restaurant Dance Band: unidentified tpt, tbn, clt, alt;
Arthur Lally (clt, alt, bar); Bert Firman (vln); John Firman (p); Jack
Simmons (bj); unidentified tu; Jack Trebble (d). Hayes, Middlesex,
26 May 1927.
Sugar foot stomp

Fred Elizalde and His Cambridge Undergraduates: John d'Arcy, Dick
Battle (tpt); Manuel 'Lizz' Elizalde, Jack Donaldson (clt, alt); Dan
Wyllie (alt); Maurice Allom (ten, bar); Fred Elizalde (p); George
Monkhouse (bj); Bud Williams (tu); Eric J. Saunders (d). Hayes,
Middlesex, 22 June 1927.
Stomp your feet · Clarinet marmalade

Piccadilly Revels Band: Freddy Pitt, Andy Richardson (tpt); Bill
Hall (tbn); Ernie Smith, Phil Cardew (clt, alt); Ray Starita (clt, ten);
Eric Siday (vln); Donald Thorne (p); Jack Hill (bj); Clem Lawton (tu);
Rudy Starita (d, xylo). London, 6 October 1927.
Go, Joe, go

Same personnel and location, 20 October 1927.
Buffalo rhythm

Jack Hylton's Rhythmagicians: Jack Jackson (tpt); Lew Davis (tbn);
Edward O. Pogson (clt, alt); Billy Ternent (ten); Rignold (vln); Arthur
Young (p); Chappie d'Amato (g); Harry Robbins (d). Hayes, Middlesex,
15 December 1927.
Grieving for you

The Rhythmic Eight: Sylvester Ahola, Dennis Radcliffe (tpt); Perley Breed (clt, alt, bar); Johnny Helfer (clt, ten); John Firman (p); Joe Brannelly (g); Billy Bell (tu); Eddie Collis (d). Hayes, Middlesex, 6 February 1928.
There's a cradle in Caroline

New Mayfair Dance Orchestra: Norman Payne (tpt); Davis (tbn); Jack Miranda (clt, alt); Helfer (clt, ten); Leslie Payne (alt, bar, hfp); Siday, Rignold, Jean Pougnet (vln); Carroll Gibbons (p); Brannelly (bj); unidentified tu; Rudy Starita (d). Hayes, Middlesex, 20 March 1929.
Deep hollow

Fred Elizalde and His Music: Chelsea Quealey (tpt); Max Farley (clt); Bobby Davis (alt); Fud Livingston (ten); Adrian Rollini (bs sx); Elizalde, Billy Mason (p); Al Bowlly (g); Tiny Stock (bs); Ronnie Gubertini (d). London, 12 April 1929.
Nobody's sweetheart

Noble Sissle and His Orchestra: Pike Davis, Demus Dean (tpt); James Reevy (tbn); Buster Bailey, Rudy Jackson, Ralph Duquesne (clt, alt); Ramon Usera (ten); Juice Wilson, William Rosemand (vln); Lloyd Pinckney (p); Warren Harris (bj); Henry Edwards (tu); John Ricks (bs); Jesse Baltimore (d); Sissle (vcl). Hayes, Middlesex, 10 September 1929.
Kansas City Kitty · Miranda

Jazz in Britain is not the same as British jazz. The presence on this LP of the Original Dixieland Jazz Band, Arnold's Novelty Band, the Original Capitol Orchestra, Kemp's Carolina Club Orchestra, Elizalde's Music (but not, of course, his Cambridge Undergraduates) and Sissle's Orchestra, all of them using American sidemen, should make the distinction perfectly clear. Yet the good music is far from being exclusively the work of the Americans. Indeed, after a slightly sub-standard performance by the ODJB (the recording balance, alas, making it sound as if Shields is leading the group on clarinet), there is dull playing by Arnold's band (more of a ragtime than a jazz combo), the Original Capitol Orchestra (efficient but stylized) and the Carolina Club Orchestra (very staccato, though with forthright trombone playing). Hylton's *Milneburg joys* is better, particularly Heath's trombone chorus, yet the resonant recording quality lessens the impact. Firman's version of *Sugar foot stomp* may be a bit stilted, but remains very creditable for a British band in 1927, the unknown trumpeter copying King Oliver's three muted choruses (well, he strays a trifle during the third) and with lively all-in ensemble work at the end. Equally good are the tracks by Elizalde's Cambridge Undergraduates who included, as a matter of interest, a future peer and Minister of the Arts in Donaldson, and in Allom the only jazz musician who would take a hat trick in a Test Match and become President of the MCC. This is tidy jazz, with 'Lizz' Elizalde taking the alto solos and Fred showing himself to be more interesting harmonically than most jazz pianists in Britain at that time.

Ray and Rudy Starita were both Americans and the arrangements the Piccadilly Revels Band used were more adventurous than the average, especially for *Go, Joe, go*. And by now the influences on British soloists were obvious enough: trumpeters followed Red Nichols or Bix Beiderbecke, trombonists worshipped Miff Mole, saxophonists genuflected before Rollini, Frankie Trumbauer or Jimmy Dorsey. *Grieving for you* by Hylton's Rhythmagicians demonstrates this very effectively. Arranged by Ternent and d'Amato, this set out to provide a counterpart to the recordings of Nichols's Five Pennies — *Washboard blues* (**70b**) being especially popular with British musicians. The remarkable thing is that this performance suffers little by comparison. British players were much more successful, in fact, at coming to terms with the work of the white New York school — and often doing so with originality — than they were to be in the 1930s, when black players such as Armstrong, Coleman Hawkins and Roy Eldridge proved much more difficult to emulate. Some outstanding playing is heard from the American trumpeter Ahola in the Rhythmic Eight's *There's a cradle in Caroline*, and from Payne, a British trumpeter who was perhaps more flexible than Ahola, in the New Mayfair Dance Orchestra's *Deep hollow*. Davis also plays impressively here, and the band includes a distinguished trio of violinists.

Elizalde's imported Americans made *Nobody's sweetheart* one of the best jazz performances ever to have been recorded in Britain. Quealey is quietly melodic, Livingston has the rhythmic thrust of a Chicagoan (which he was not), while Rollini not only takes a fine solo but gives strength to the ensemble. It should also be noted that the rhythm section swings more and is altogether more 'modern' than any other on the LP. The worst things about the Sissle tracks are the leader's own singing and the fact that this was first and foremost a novelty band; almost a descendant of minstrelsy, even though its ranks had included, and would again, Sidney Bechet and would also take in, much later and very briefly, Charlie Parker. The best things are Bailey's clarinet passage in *Miranda* and excellent violin playing on both tracks by Wilson, certainly one of the finest jazz soloists on that instrument; he eventually settled in Malta, running a bar there throughout World War II.   C.F.

98 British Jazz in the '30s: Swinging Britain
Decca (E) DDV5013/4 (2 LPs)

The Embassy Rhythm Eight: Max Goldberg (tpt); Lew Davis (tbn);
Danny Polo (clt, alt); Billy Amstell (ten); Bert Barnes (p, arr); Joe
Brannelly (g); Dick Ball (bs); Max Bacon (d). London, 1 February 1935.
Hitchy koo · He's a rag picker

Same personnel and location, 5 February 1935.
Back home in Tennessee

Same personnel and location, 15 February 1935.
Where the black-eyed Susans grow

Lew Davis Trombone Trio: Davis, Ted Heath, Tony Thorpe (tbn);
Barnes (p); Sid Phillips (cls); Brannelly (g); Ball (bs). London
13 November 1935.
Three's company · Three of a kind

Tiny Winters and His Bogey Seven: Tommy McQuater (tpt); Andy
McDevitt (clt); Don Barrigo (ten); Ernest Ritte (bar); Monia Liter (p);
Archie Slavin (g); Winters (bs, vcl); Ronnie Gubertini (d). London,
22 April 1936.
How many times? · Frankie and Johnny

Leonard Feather and Ye Olde English Swynge Band: Archie Craig (tpt);
McDevitt (clt); Buddy Featherstonhaugh (ten); Eddie Macauley (p);
Eddie Freeman (g); Wally Morris (bs); Al Craig (d). London, 4 May 1937.
D'ye ken John Peel? · There is a tavern in the town

Danny Polo and His Swing Stars: McQuater (cnt); Polo (clt);
Macauley (p); Freeman (g); Ball (bs); Dudley Barber (d). London,
1 October 1937.
Stratton Street strut · More than somewhat · That's a-plenty

Sid Raymond (alt) added. Same date.
Blue murder

McQuater, Raymond, Freeman, Ball absent. Same date.
Money for jam · Mr Polo takes a solo · Home, sweet home

McQuater (cnt); George Chisholm (tbn); Polo (clt, ten); Macauley (p);
Norman Brown (g); Ball (bs); Barber (d). London, 11 January 1938.
*Jazz me blues · Don't try your jive on me · Mozeltov · If you were the
only girl in the world*

Leonard Feather and Ye Olde English Swynge Band: Dave Wilkins (tpt,
vcl[1]); McDevitt (clt, alt); Bertie King (ten); Will Solomon (p); Alan
Ferguson (g); Len Harrison (bs); Hymie Schneider (d).
London 12 September 1938.
Colonel Bogey · Widdecombe Fair[1]

Feather (p[2], cls[3]) added. Same date.
Early one morning[2] · Drink to me only with thine eyes[3]

George Chisholm and His Jive Five: McQuater (cnt); Chisholm (tbn);
Benny Winestone (clt, ten); Macauley (p); Winters (bs); Barber (d). London,
12 October 1938.
*Let's go · No smoking · Archer Street drag · Rosetta · You'll always be
mine*

Ferguson (g) added. London, 10 November 1938.
Penalty £5 · No smoking

Bearing in mind the distinction made above — that 'jazz in Britain
is not the same as British jazz' — it can be asserted that the music
here considered is the genuine home-grown product, for the few
distinguished immigrants involved had become firmly part of the
local scene. American influence can be taken for granted. In
addition to the visitors listed under **97**, of the companions Wilkins
sings about in Feather's *Widdecombe Fair* — 'Louis Armstrong,
Fats Waller, Benny Goodman, Benny Carter, Duke Ellington,
Teddy Wilson, old Uncle Tom Dorsey and all' — all but Goodman,
Wilson and Dorsey had appeared in Britain; and there had been
others too, notably, in the period under review, Coleman Hawkins.
There had also been the New York initiative of Spike Hughes (**128**),
and local leaders such as Ambrose, Jack Hylton and Lew Stone
were eager for American stimulus and participation. The best
British musicians were avid record hearers, and it might become
tiresome to list all the models they chose. The compliment of
imitation is by no means restricted to European jazzmen, for in jazz,
anywhere, emulation is one of the keys to progress — a truth,
indeed, for all music. Furthermore, the vivid character of much of
this British jazz actively discourages assessment in terms of mimic
success.

The style of the Embassy Rhythm Eight suggests that, in 1935,
swing innovations were not yet clearly heeded, for the rhythmic
emphases of Barnes's arrangements have a slight air of ragtime
filtered through the *palais de danse*. Barnes, as pianist, echoes early
Harlem 'stride', but there are freer solos in all four pieces, with
Goldberg and Davis working well up to the standard of the
American Polo.

Three's company and *Three of a kind* which are not well reproduced, recall the popularity of Ambrose's trombone section. The
muted trios do little more than underline the effectiveness which
this team had within the contrasting structures of big band music,
and the tempo changes in the first piece lend a sense of novelty.

There is relaxed riffing and snatches of dixieland in the accompaniments to Winters' pale-toned singing with his Bogey Seven,
and there are hints of the excellence of McQuater, McDevitt and
Barrigo. McDevitt is one of the more confident players on the 1937
session of Feather's group, yet he is exceeded by the thoroughly
Wilsonian Macauley in making free-flowing jazz out of the self-
consciously chosen and largely unsuitable traditional British
themes. The talents of the tenorist Featherstonhaugh loomed large
in those days, and his and Macauley's absence is felt in the 1938
Feather session, although the West Indians, Wilkins and King

(from Ken Johnson's band) make fine contributions and, taken as a whole, these dates testify to the liveliness of the activity centred upon the No. 1 Club.

By far the most consistent jazz is produced in the sessions of Polo's Swing Stars and Chisholm's Jive Five. The tighter and smoother styles of small recording groups like those of Goodman and Artie Shaw (emulated notably, some years on, by Harry Parry's Radio Rhythm Club Sextets) were not an allurement, and the approach of these 1938 groups is animated much more by the influences of Chicago and Harlem — in an amalgam favouring simple head arrangements and relaxed collective improvisation. Direct Chicago influence came in with Polo, an able if not highly original clarinettist and alto saxophonist who had joined Ambrose in the early 1930s. Polo's lower- and middle-register playing is a little expressionless, but he frequently climbs to high-note excursions more evocative of his Chicago heroes.

Stratton Street strut, More than somewhat, Blue murder and *That's a-plenty* have many delights, with Polo, McQuater and Macauley outstanding, though some ensemble passages suffer from faulty recording balance. Polo, exposed in the trio setting of *Money for jam, Mr Polo takes a solo* (based on Waller's *Squeeze me*) and *Home, sweet home*, is less derivative in style than Macauley, but somewhat less swinging too, and he sounds more straight-laced than the pianist, particularly in *Home, sweet home*.

Chisholm, like several of these musicians a member of the Ambrose orchestra, brings lithe robustness to Polo's January 1938 titles. His admiration for Jack Teagarden is not to be doubted, but neither is his early attainment of personal tone and inventive ability. The two dates with his Jive Five have him drawing fine co-operation from McQuater — a fellow Scot, and one of the best trumpeter/cornettists in the history of British jazz — and the inadequately honoured Macauley, and from Winestone, who is expressive on tenor and rivals Polo on clarinet.

The October version of the slow blues *No smoking* (first dubbed *Archer Street drag*) is issued for the first time on this LP and named after the November version. Polo's *Home, sweet home* is also released here for the first time. *Archer Street drag* proper is probably the Jive Five's most famous piece, but it does not exceed most of the other performances in worth. There is jazz skill and spirit here which has scarcely been surpassed by British bands and soloists in subsequent years.   E.T.

Benny Carter

99 Swinging at Maida Vale
Jasmine (E) JASM2010, *Everest (A) FS225

Benny Carter and His Orchestra; Max Goldberg, Tommy McQuater,
Duncan Whyte (tpt): Ted Heath, Bill Mulraney (tbn); Andy
McDevitt (clt, alt); Carter (clt, alt, ten); Edward O. Pogson (alt);
Buddy Featherstonhaugh (ten); Pat Dodd (p); George Elliott (g);
Al Burke (bs); Ronnie Gubertini (d). London, 15 April 1936.
Swinging at Maida Vale · Nightfall

Goldberg, Heath, Mulraney, Pogson absent. London, late April 1936.
When day is done · I've got two lips · Just a mood

Goldberg, McQuater (tpt); Leslie Thompson (tpt, tbn); Lew Davis,
Heath (tbn); Freddy Gardner, McDevitt (clt, alt); Carter (clt, alt, ten);
Featherstonhaugh (ten); Billy Munn (p); Albert Harris (g); Wally
Morris (bs); George Elrick (d). London, mid-June 1936.
Accent on swing · If only I could read your mind

Benny Carter and His Swing Quartet: Carter (tpt, alt, ten); Gene
Rodgers (p); Bernard Addison (g); Morris (bs); Elrick (d); Elisabeth
Welch (vcl[1]). London, 20 June 1936.
When lights are low[1] · Waltzing the blues

McQuater (tpt); Carter (clt, alt); Gerry Moore (p); Harris (g); Morris (bs);
Al Craig (d). London, 19 October 1936.
There'll be some changes made · Royal Garden blues

Benny Carter and His Orchestra: Thompson, McQuater (tpt); Davis,
Mulraney (tbn); Gardner, McDevitt (clt, alt); Carter (alt); George Evans,
Featherstonhaugh (ten); Eddie Macauley (p); Harris (g); Morris (bs);
Craig (d). London, mid-January 1937.
Gin and jive

100 Benny Carter: Holland, 1937
Decca (F) 154.062

Benny Carter and The Ramblers: George van Helvoirt, Jack
Bulterman (tpt); Carter (tpt, clt, alt, ten); Marcel Thielemans (tbn);
Wim Poppink, André van den Ouderaa (clt, alt); Sal Doof (ten); Freddy
Johnson (p); Jacques Pet (bs); Kees Kränenburg (d). Laren, Holland,
24 March 1937.
*Black bottom · Ramblers' rhythm · New Street swing ·
I'll never give in*

Benny Carter and His Orchestra: Sam Dasberg, Cliff Woodridge, Rolf
Goldstein (tpt); Carter (tpt, clt, alt); George Chisholm, Harry van Oven
(tbn); Louis Stephenson (alt); Bertie King, Jimmy Williams (ten); Freddy
Johnson (p); Ray Webb (g); Len Harrison (bs); Robert Montmarché (d).
The Hague, Holland, 17 August 1937.
Skip it · Lazy afternoon · I ain't got nobody · Blues in my heart

Carter (tpt, clt, alt); Chisholm (tbn); Williams (clt, alt); Coleman
Hawkins (ten); Johnson (p); Webb (g); Harrison (bs) Montmarché (d).
The Hague, Holland, 18 August 1937.
*Somebody loves me · Mighty like the blues · Pardon me, pretty baby ·
My buddy*

Jazz *aficionados* often have a disturbing penchant for equating
rawness with authenticity, or else discerning an emotional content only in what is palpably romantic. Musicians who communicate in less dramatic terms, aiming at more formal expression,
frequently come under attack. During the 1950s, 1960s and 1970s
the work of Lennie Tristano and his cohorts, of Paul Desmond, of
the Modern Jazz Quartet, even of Art Pepper and, more recently,
Anthony Braxton, has run up against this fundamentalism.
Similarly, in the 1930s, musicians such as Teddy Wilson sometimes were deplored as being too refined. History corrects such
absurdities, of course and never more starkly than when it gives
perspective to the playing, composing and arranging of Carter.
  Musicians always perceived his quality. And not just Americans. Many British saxophonists took him as their model; partly
because his formal approach was more accessible to emulation
than the playing — blues-rooted, Bechet-influenced — of Johnny
Hodges; partly because Carter spent thirteen months in Britain
(from March 1936 to March 1937), working as an arranger for
Henry Hall's BBC Dance Orchestra. The first of these records, **99**,
is a selection from the recordings he made during that visit, using
some of the best-known British players. The rhythm section, alas,
stayed too sedate; the ensemble, while reasonably accurate
(these, after all, were pick-up groups), sounds much too four-
square, lacking both the bite and the unself-consciousness of
Carter's Club Harlem Orchestra (**122**). That non-American ambience was accentuated both here and on the Dutch sessions,
particularly those at The Hague, by the recording balance,
involving so much echo that the musicians might as well be
performing at a public baths.
  Carter takes the majority of solos: most dexterously on alto
saxophone, of course, yet with almost as much felicity on trumpet
and clarinet. Only on tenor saxophone does he ever fall away.
Indeed, the best tenor solos are arguably those by Featherstonhaugh who, until he declined into being an out-and-out
imitator of Coleman Hawkins, was a player of considerable
originality (some of whose best work was done on recordings —
not all reissued on microgroove at the time of this book's publication — by Spike Hughes's British bands). Featherstonhaugh's

contributions to *I've got two lips, Gin and jive* and *When day is done* are worth hearing, although he fails to hold the interest in the dead-slow *Just a mood*. McQuater, a recent arrival in London from Glasgow, did not yet have his style — an attempted mixture of Berigan's magniloquence and Eldridge's bravura — properly under control; apart from his twenty-four bars in *Accent on swing*, he hurries too much.

That is a criticism, of course, which it would be impossible to make of Carter, whose poise was never exemplified more confidently than in the solo he takes immediately after McQuater's in *Gin and jive* (the eight bars of alto saxophone in the final chorus sound more like Gardner than Carter). Here and elsewhere, including on *Waltzing the blues*, a venture with two fellow-Americans, Rodgers and Addison, into what then was an unusual time-signature, Carter reveals himself as one of the great melodists of jazz, building his solos with a composer's grasp of form. And that extended to his writing, though he did not think orchestrally, as Ellington and Redman did, but considered a theme and its arrangement as separate elements, just as he tended, in his scoring, to keep brasses and saxophones apart.

Most of the orchestrations for the British bands were fairly simple, capable of being performed by *ad hoc* ensembles, although Carter's identity always comes through. *Accent on swing* is one of his most attractive themes, while *Just a mood*, on which his clarinet playing is especially pliant and beguiling, has some of the fragility, if not the early morning ennui, of *Mood indigo* (**91**).

If The Ramblers seem to possess more togetherness than the Britons, that is because the Dutch band was a regular working group. In addition, three of the pieces were composed and/or arranged by Dutch musicians and formed part of the band's repertoire. (Oddly enough, the opening and closing choruses of *Rambler's rhythm* are fairly reminiscent of the scores Spike Hughes wrote for his London recording band.) The exception was *I'll never give in*, credited to Johnson but the arrangement written by Carter. He plays excellently — it is hard to imagine him ever doing otherwise — yet his performances with The Ramblers are less distinguished than those by Coleman Hawkins (**101**).

For the session of 17 August 1937, Carter used the highly international band which he was leading that summer at the Kursaal in Scheveningen. The musicians perform what must have been familiar arrangements with *élan* as well as expertise. *Skip it* contains some adroit scoring for saxophones (always closest to Carter's heart), while the final chorus of *Lazy afternoon* has some of his most adventurous brass writing — before the saxophones round things off with a frilly coda.

What happened the following day in the studio was a jam session. Carter led on trumpet and takes alto saxophone solos in *My buddy* and *Pardon me, pretty baby*; but the dominating performer was Hawkins, displaying the same rhythmic boldness he had shown on his own Paris session four months earlier (**105a**). He plays one of his finest solos in *My buddy*; yet that is not as surprising as the fact that his *Mighty like the blues* solo, typically romantic and broad-ranging, is followed immediately by a muted trombone chorus from Chisholm that does not suffer by comparison. Chisholm, one of four British musicians in Carter's orchestra, possessed a distinctive style, sounding gruff, even pawky, already well aware of the importance of leaving notes out rather than cramming them in.   C.F.

101 The Hawk in Holland
Jasmine (E) JASM2011, Gene Norman Presents (A) GNP9003

Coleman Hawkins with The Ramblers: Henk Hinrichs, George van Helvoirt (tpt); Marcel Thielemans (tbn); Wim Poppink (clt, alt); André van den Ouderaa (clt, ten); Hawkins (ten); Theo uden Masman (p); Jacques Pet (g); Tonny Limbach (bs); Kees Kränenburg (d); Annie de Reuver (vcl[1]). The Hague, Holland, 4 February 1935.
Some of these days [1] · *After you've gone* · *I only have eyes for you*[1] · *I wish I were twins*

Jack Bulterman, van Helvoirt (tpt); Thielemans (tbn); Poppink (clt, alt); van den Ouderaa (clt, ten); Hawkins (ten); Nico de Rooy (p); Pet (g); Toon Diepenbroek (bs); Kränenburg (d). Laren, Holland, 26 August 1935.
Chicago · *Meditation* · *What Harlem means to me* · *Netcha's dream*

Sal Doof (alt), Frits Reinders (g) added; Pet switches to bs. Laren, Holland, 27 April 1937.
I wanna go back to Harlem · *Consolation* · *A strange fact* · *Original dixieland one-step* · *Smiles*

Bulterman, van Helvoirt, Thielemans, Poppink, Doof, van den Ouderaa absent; Freddy Johnson (p) replaces de Rooy. Same date.
Something is gonna give me away

These recordings can be heard, together with some found on **122**, as examples of a style which had reached its first great period of improvising genius. For Hawkins, the years between 1928 and 1933 seem to have made possible a crucial step forward, stylistic unification from which were created some of the most excitingly varied solos yet heard in jazz. The blending that was needed may be divined from a comparing of his 1929 *Hello, Lola* and *One hour* solos (**166, 192**), the first driving hard on the beat, the second searching for meditative relaxation. The desired combination of elements has been achieved in the recordings of 1933–4, and tonal modifications are evident, too.

The authority with which Hawkins announces his presence at the very outset of *Some of these days* (waxed, like the other February 1935 items, in an echoing hall) sets the tone for this whole series. Whatever qualities of zest and precision The Ramblers have are distorted by the physical setting, but their guest's rich tone and urbane vibrato are not marred. Neither are the tones of the inexpressive Annie de Reuver in this piece, nor in *I only have eyes for you*, wherein Hawkins ruminates skilfully upon the melodic line.

There is a small attempt at ensemble improvisation as *After you've gone* starts, but The Ramblers' aptitudes are other than that, and the crabbed riffing behind Hawkins's skipping final chorus in *Some of these days* and the rather stilted swing of *I wish I were twins* are not altogether typical of their response to the challenge of jazz orchestration. Better recording balance on the Laren dates helps one to judge the abilities of this enthusiastic group and of Bulterman, its arranger throughout, rather more confidently. *Chicago* is introduced firmly by the band. There is some mildly adventurous scoring in places, and a nice trumpet solo — perhaps by Bulterman.

Meditation and the 1937 *Consolation*, each a Bulterman theme, show an Ellington influence, with dry-toned harmonic scoring for reeds and muted brass. In both, Hawkins rejoices in the recollective mood, making his phrases in *Meditation* spring from unexpected areas of the chords and even throwing in a Hodges-like idea here and there; on *Consolation* he ranges through his instrument's registers with a kind of indolent ecstasy. The arrangement of his own theme, *Netcha's dream*, also has Ellington sounds in it, but the recording balance is not consistent and sometimes his lazily weaving line seems to be crowded by the ensemble. From the same date came *What Harlem means to me*, which opens with rare spoken comments from Hawkins. Like Bulterman's *I wanna go back to Harlem*, this latter is a novelty tune of an ephemeral mode, yet the tenorist pits intense and sophisticated mid-tempo musings against The Rambler's mainly trivial backing.

A strange fact could be regarded as something of a classic. It is certainly an intriguing performance, with Hawkins leading and interacting with the ensemble in an exhibition of mutual freedom that says much for Bulterman's sensitiveness to the visitor's musical thinking. The scoring and improvising of the final chorus build interestingly upon the first, and between these the tenor solos encompass fevered declamations, wiry spirallings and rhapsodies of the most beguiling sort. Sheer speed may make *Original dixieland one-step* sound the most swinging of these arrangements: the writing is not especially accomplished, but this is an exciting piece, with one exultant passage for brass over some of the springiest rhythm section work on the whole LP. Contrasted to his long, writhing phrases in the *One-step*, Hawkins's more subdued solo in *Smiles*, with its beautiful sequence of descending phrases and controlled undulations, has a detached air.

Johnson's simplified piano style adds little of interest to the quintet track from the same session. Hawkins's improvising comes up to normal expectations here, but it remains somewhere below the standard of those numbers in which he responds to the challenge of playing with an unusual band.   E.T.

102a   Bill Coleman in Paris Vol. 1
Parlophone (E) PMC7104, HMV (F) HTX40.328

Garnet Clark and His Hot Club Four: Coleman (tpt, vcl[1]); George Johnson (clt,, alt); Clark (p); Django Reinhardt (g); June Cole (bs). Paris, 25 November 1935.
The object of my affection[1] · *Rosetta*

Bill Coleman and His Orchestra: Coleman (tpt); Herman Chittison (p); Eugène d'Hellèmmes (bs). Paris, 31 January 1936.
After you've gone

d'Hellèmmes absent. Same date.
I'm in the mood for love

Edgar Courance (clt, ten), Oscar Aleman (g), d'Hellèmmes (bs), William Diemer (d) added; John Ferrier (p) replaces Chittison. Same date.
Joe Louis stomp · *Coquette*

Coleman (tpt); Stéphane Grappelli (vln, p[2]); Joseph Reinhardt (g); Wilson Myers (bs); Ted Fields (d). Paris, 12 November 1937.
Indiana[2] · *Rose room* · *Bill Street blues* · *The merry-go-round broke down*

Coleman (tpt); Christian Wagner (clt, alt); Frank 'Big Boy' Goudie (clt, ten); Emile Stern (p); Django Reinhardt (g); Lucien Simoens (bs); Jerry Mengo (d). Paris, 19 November 1937.
I ain't got nobody · *Baby, won't you please come home?*

Coleman (tpt); Courance (clt, ten); John Mitchell (g); Myers (bs, vcl); Tommy Benford (d). Paris, 28 September 1938.
Sister Kate · *Way down yonder in New Orleans*

102b Bill Coleman in Paris Vol. 2
Parlophone (E) PMC7105, HMV(F) CHTX240.628

Willie Lewis and His Orchestra: Coleman, Bobby Martin (tpt); Billy Burns (tbn); Lewis (clt, alt); Goudie (clt, ten); Johnson, Joe Hayman (alt); Chittison (p); Mitchell (g); Louis Vola (bs); Fields (d). Paris, April 1936.
Stomping at the Savoy · Christopher Columbus
Same personnel and location, 15 October 1936.
Sweet Sue · Organ grinder's swing
Alix Combelle and His Orchestra: Coleman (tpt, vcl); Combelle (clt, ten); David Martin (p); Roger Chaput (g); Myers (bs); Mengo (d).
Paris, 4 October, 1937.
Exactly like you · Alexander's ragtime band · Hangover blues
Bill Coleman and His Orchestra: Coleman (tpt); Grappelli (vln); Joseph Reinhardt (g); Myers (bs); Fields (d). Paris, 12 November 1937.
After you've gone
Coleman (tpt); Wagner (clt, alt); Goudie (clt, ten); Stern (p); Django Reinhardt (g); Simoens (bs); Mengo (d). Paris, 19 November 1937.
Big boy blues · Swing guitars
Eddie Brunner and His Orchestra: Coleman (tpt); Brunner (clt, ten); Combelle, Noël Chiboust (ten); Chittison (p); Aleman (g); Robert Grasset (bs); Benford (d). Paris, 13 June 1938.
In a little Spanish town · Montmartre blues · I double dare you · Margie

If Coleman's excellent contribution to the advance of jazz style has been consistently underrated, it is, ironically enough, not for any musical reason, but because he was for a long period an *emigré* largely forgotten by American pundits. His playing throughout these LPs shows him to be a trumpeter with a distinctive voice and an irrepressible vivacity in improvisation. As a young apprentice with Cecil Scott (**81**) and Luis Russell (**50**) he stumbled a little in the shadow of Frankie Newton and Henry Allen; but by the time he returned to France in 1935 with the dancer and musician Freddy Taylor he had achieved a technique and a range of expression worthy to be compared with those of more widely-lauded players.

Proof of this can be heard in the recordings with Clark. On *The object of my affection* and *Rosetta* his variations, muted and open, and his amiable singing are pleasingly complemented by the low-register clarinet weavings of the even more under-praised Johnson, whose solo in *Rosetta* has an attractive quiet vigour. From the start of the earlier *After you've gone*, Coleman exhibits, over the utilitarian vamping of Chittison, the remarkable plasticity, achieved by a characteristic pressure of tongue and lips, which makes his linking of syllables prognostic of postwar bop trumpeters. The slower tempo of *I'm in the mood for love*, a duet with Chittison, who plays more imaginatively here, gives his melodic gift even freer tether.

His association with the fine Lewis band spans this general period, and **103** deals with some of that leader's other European recordings. The four numbers here included, in addition to being of consistent musical worth, exemplify the style of jazz arrangement which was currently being exported from the States. The Henderson score of *Christoper Columbus* is used (and this performance should be compared with the much slower Goodman one on **141**); *Stomping at the Savoy*, Edgar Sampson's composition associated with both Chick Webb and Goodman, is played according to the Spud Murphy arrangement; *Organ grinder's swing*, popularized by Jimmy Lunceford, reflects the work of Sy Oliver. *Christopher Columbus* is played with zest, with Goudie's tenor threading its way through the riffs, and there are excellent solos from Johnson, Chittison and a slightly reserved Coleman. The inclusion of these Lewis pieces is useful in a context where small groups predominate, for they show (the relaxed *Sweet Sue* and ebullient *Organ grinder's swing* especially) how authoritative a voice his could be in a larger ensemble.

Joe Louis stomp and *Coquette* find Coleman again in a mixed company which includes the American Courance, playing well but within a limited emotional range, and the sensitive Argentinian guitarist Aleman. The twelve-bar riff theme of *Joe Louis stomp*, reminiscent of *Christopher Columbus*, invites and receives an effervescent approach with dancing statements from Coleman, and from Courance on tenor and clarinet. *Coquette* is similarly treated and has a graceful half-chorus from Aleman.

Exactly like you, Alexander's ragtime band and *Hangover blues* are from a group led by the expressive and highly regarded Combelle. There is a compulsive vigour in his solos which suitably complements what is some of Coleman's most powerful work; and there is nicely varied support from Martin, Chaput, Myers and Mengo. One finds a more unvarying rhythmic background to *Rose room, Bill Street blues, The merry-go-round broke down* and the later *After you've gone*. But the occasional heaviness is countered by the richness of Joseph Reinhardt's harmonies. Grappelli is generally in good form, chording with a tough impetus in the driving final chorus of *After you've gone*, though he gropes a little for the characteristic cadences of the blues, and is episodic and none too well related to Coleman's exuberant ideas in *The merry-go-round broke down*. The violin and trumpet solos in *Rose room* suggest telling cross-threads of influence, Grappelli's evincing the effect of a rhythmic approach typical of Coleman Hawkins, and Coleman's in their bouncing phrases, calling to mind the style of Pete Brown (heard in contemporary form with Jimmy Noone on **229** and with Frankie Newton on **185** and **228**) — possible evidence that Brown's alto saxophone vocabulary was trumpet-influenced.

Indiana, distinguished *confrères* notwithstanding, is Coleman's record. He sings an 'instrumentalist's vocal', using scat syllables to complete verbal phrases melodically, and follows this with a marvellously extrovert trumpet improvisation. *I ain't got nobody* has a jam-session spirit informing some enthusiastic collective choruses. Goudie, a man with a New Orleans background, plays a good tenor solo in the latter piece and some reedy clarinet in *Baby, won't you please come home?*, which has a lovely solo by the incomparable Django Reinhardt. A guitar solo of similar intellectual and emotional grace is heard in *Big boy blues*, wherein also Goudie, first in musical conversation with Coleman, then in an assured *chalumeau* chorus and finally in the collective, probably demonstrates the style he had formed with the Oscar Celestin orchestra more than a decade earlier. There is no solo work by Django in *Swing guitars*, a pleasant Reinhardt–Grappelli theme, although the performance is animated by his rhythm work; but there are good contributions from Goudie, on tenor, and from Wagner's huskily-toned clarinet. Coleman leads the ensemble athletically at beginning and end.

The compelling drummer on Brunner's session is Benford, best remembered for his playing with Jelly Roll Morton on a recording date almost precisely ten years before this (**47b**). The atmosphere is zealously charged, a rare moment of finesse coming from Aleman in *Montmartre blues*. The Swiss-born Brunner reflects the contemporary popularity of the clarinet as a leader's instrument, though he solos well on tenor in *I double dare you*. Of other tenor solos, Combelle takes the largest share, but his compatriot, Chiboust, improvises skilfully in the ensemble closing *Margie*. Coleman is more restrained during the September 1938 session, and the other musicians, Benford included, adapt themselves to intimacy, Courance soloing tunefully on both his instruments. Although *Sister Kate* and *Way down yonder in New Orleans* have come to be associated with dixieland treatment, the mood here is very much that of small band swing, and few better instances could be found to support Charles Fox's statement, in the sleeve notes for the British issue of Vol. 1, that Coleman is 'one of the most elegant and sensitive trumpet players to be found anywhere in jazz'.   E.T.

103 Willie Lewis and His Entertainers
Pathé (F) C054–11416

Willie Lewis and His Orchestra: Bobby Martin (tpt); Billy Burns (tbn); Jerry Blake (clt, ten); Lewis (alt, vcl[1]); Joe Hayman (ten); Herman Chittison (p. cls[2]); John Mitchell (g); June Cole (bs); Ted Fields (d). Paris, 23 April 1934.
Nagasaki

Alex Renard (tpt), Benny Carter (tpt, alt), Coco Khein (ten) added; George Johnson (alt) replaces Blake. Paris, 17 January 1935.
Stay out of love[2] · *Rhythm is our business*[1] · *Just a mood*[2] · *All of me* · *Stardust*

Bill Coleman (tpt), Frank 'Big Boy' Goudie (clt, ten), Louis Vola (bs) replace Carter, Khein, Cole; Renard; Hayman absent; Adelaide Hall (vcl[3]) added. Paris, 15 May 1936.
I'm shooting high[3]

Miss Hall absent. Paris, 15 October 1936.
Sing, sing, sing[1] · *Knock, knock — who's there?*[1]

Same personnel and location, 12 November 1936.
On your toes[1]

Jack Butler (tpt), Hayman (ten), Wilson Myers (bs) replace Martin, Johnson, Vola. Paris, 18 October 1937.
Old man river · *Swing, brother, swing,*[1] · *Doing the new low down* · *Swinging for a Swiss miss*

Lewis was in Europe with Sam Wooding's band during 1925–31, then led groups of his own in France, the Low Countries and Egypt, employing expatriate talent to sometimes impressive effect. For instance, the present writer was never fully convinced about Carter's trumpet playing until he encountered the relevant tracks here, which contain the best work Carter recorded with that instrument. In *Stardust, All of me* and *Rhythm is our business* he soars with exhilarating freedom above the ensemble; the phrases have an elegance comparable to that of his alto work yet, as is the nature of the trumpet, with a more assertive edge. There is some characteristic writing for the saxophone section by Carter here, performed creditably on *Stay out of love* and *All of me*, and rather better than that in *Stardust*. *Just a mood* is a Carter theme, given an enchantingly delicate treatment which includes a fine alto solo.

Most of the scores by hands other than Carter's do not have much character, being simple, functional and typified by *Swing, brother, swing* or *Old man river*. Lewis did not often aim at subtlety, but the energetic accuracy with which these arrangements are played is enjoyable. There is particularly good section work from the reeds on *Knock, knock — who's there?* and this may be due to the influence of Goudie, who takes excellent tenor solos in *On your toes* and *Swinging for a Swiss miss*. In fact, these recordings provide an instructive example of how a few gifted musicians can raise the level of an entire band, for the rank-and-file sidemen are in no way outstanding.

The performances are all eventful in their way, with highlights such as Blake's clarinet playing on *Nagasaki* and Adelaide Hall's charming singing in *I'm shooting high*. But Carter aside, the chief interest arises from the solos of Coleman and Chittison, the former contributing with notable impact, his adventurous phrases always mobile and dancing, on *Swing, brother, swing, Knock, knock – who's there?, Sing, sing, sing, Old man river* and *Swinging for a Swiss miss*. Every track benefits from Chittison's lucid and intelligent playing, and he is heard in solos on several tracks, such as *Stay out of love, Swinging for a Swiss miss* and *All of me*. *Doing the new low down* features him throughout to impressive, if rather self-consciously virtuosic, effect. The unaccompanied improvisations discussed under **107c** have, indeed, greater musical substance, although he is near his best on *Just a mood* here, playing celeste as well.   M.H.

Quintet of the Hot Club of France
104 Swing '35–'39
Eclipse (E) ECM2051

Quintet of the Hot Club of France: Stéphane Grappelli (vln); Django Reinhardt, Joseph Reinhardt, Pierre Ferret (g); Louis Vola (bs). Paris, 30 September 1935.
St Louis blues

Same personnel and location, 21 October 1935
Limehouse blues · I got rhythm

Tony Rovira (bs) replaces Vola. Same date.
I've found a new baby · It was so beautiful · China boy · Moonglow · It don't mean a thing if it ain't got that swing

Eugene Vées (g), Roger Grassnet (bs) replace Ferret, Rovira. Paris, 14 June 1938.
Billets doux · Swing from Paris · Them there eyes · Three little words · Appel direct

Ferret (g); Emmanuel Soudieux (bs) replace Vées, Grassnet. Paris, 21 March 1939.
Swing '39

By far the most creative European jazz musician of his generation, Django Reinhardt could easily have become isolated, and was fortunate in finding the above unlikely but appropriate instrumental context. This was the first non-American group to establish a distinct and lasting identity in jazz, and the surging excitement of performances such as *Appel direct* and *Them there eyes* is very much their own. The vehement yet sparkling brilliance of Reinhardt's improvising is obviously the central part of it, and the diversity of his ideas would not otherwise have been readily accommodated.

His best solos, with their wide range of gesture, their constantly shifting mixtures of note values, their interplay of sound and silence, of single-string and chordal ideas, of phrase-shapes and accentual displacements which cannot be anticipated, speak of his outstanding powers of invention. But passages like his thirty-two solo bars on *It don't mean a thing* illustrate a faculty for motivic variation that is not often remarked, and a subtle approach to harmony, with anticipations and chromatic alterations, which yields results that are logical yet, again, unpredictable, with every device cunningly exploited for expressive purposes alone. Despite such richness, Reinhardt sometimes, as in *Limehouse blues* and *Three little words*, did not allow the theme's outline entirely to disappear and, all the imperious elaborations notwithstanding, he achieved a melodic purity, in fact a stylistic purity, that is rare in jazz.

This last is most apparent here in *It was so beautiful*, *Moonglow* and at the start of *Billets doux*, where he plays with a most thoughtful tenderness and with a lovely tone which heightens the effect of his harmonic explorations. Such pieces show, indeed, another side of Reinhardt from the one that seems to be all astringent vigour, a side that became more prominent in his later years, as did his composing (although four of the themes here are his). Certain of these pieces, such as *China boy* and *Limehouse blues*, contain, however, some of the earliest of the many great improvisations that he recorded. The climax of the former is reached, after Grappelli's solo, with violently accented chords thrown across the beat, and the success with which tension is unrelentingly maintained here, in *Appel direct*, *Them there eyes* and some others, places these performances in a very high class. Some credit is due to Joseph Reinhardt for his rhythmic backing, and to Grappelli, whose solos may be fanciful rather than imaginative but which evoke a marvellously varied accompanimental response from the great guitarist.　　　　　　　　　　M.H.

105a Django and His American Friends Vol. 1
HMV (E) CLP1890, *Prestige (A) PR7593

Michel Warlop and His Orchestra: Arthur Briggs, Noël Chiboust, Pierre Allier (tpt); Guy Paquinet (tbn); André Ekyan, Charles Lisée (alt); Coleman Hawkins, Alix Combelle (ten); Stéphane Grappelli (p); Django Reinhardt (g); Eugène d'Hellèmmes (bs); Maurice Chaillou (d). Paris, 2 March 1935.
Avalon · *What a difference a day made*

Briggs, Chiboust, Allier, Paquinet, Ekyan, Lisée, Combelle absent. Same date.
Stardust

Garnet Clark and His Hot Club Four: Bill Coleman (tpt, vcl[1]); George Johnson (clt, alt); Clark (p); Reinhardt (g); June Cole (bs). Paris, 25 November 1935.
Rosetta · Stardust · The object of my affection[1]

Coleman Hawkins and His All-Star Jam Band: Benny Carter (tpt[2], alt); Combelle (clt[3], ten); Ekyan (alt); Hawkins (ten); Grappelli (p); Reinhardt (g); d'Hellèmmes (bs); Tommy Benford (d). Paris, 28 April 1937.
Honeysuckle rose · Crazy rhythm · Out of nowhere[2,3] *· Sweet Georgia Brown*[2,3]

Dicky Wells and His Orchestra: Bill Dillard, Shad Collins (tpt); Coleman (tpt, vcl[1]); Wells (tbn); Reinhardt (g); Dick Fullbright (bs); Bill Beason (d). Paris, 7 July 1937.
Bugle call rag · Between the Devil and the deep blue sea · I got rhythm
Dillard, Collins absent. Same date.
Sweet Sue · Hanging around Boudon[1] *· Japanese sandman*

105b Django and His American Friends Vol. 2
HMV (E) CLP1907

Eddie South (vln); Reinhardt (g). Paris, 29 September 1937.
Eddie's blues
Wilson Myers (bs) added. Same date.
Sweet Georgia Brown

Bill Coleman and His Orchestra: Coleman (tpt); Christian Wagner (clt, alt); Frank 'Big Boy' Goudie (clt[4], ten); Emile Stern (p); Reinhardt (g); Lucien Simoens (bs); Jerry Mengo (d). Paris, 19 November 1937.
I ain't got nobody · Baby, won't you please come home? · Big boy blues[4]
Wagner, Goudie, Stern, Simoens, Mengo absent. Same date.
Bill Coleman blues
South (vln); Reinhardt (g). Paris, 23 November 1937.
Somebody loves me
Paul Cordonnier (bs) added. Same date.
I can't believe that you're in love with me

Benny Carter and His Orchestra: Carter (tpt[2], alt); Bertie King (clt[5], ten); Fletcher Allen (alt); Combelle (ten); Yorke de Souza (p); Reinhardt (g); Len Harrison (bs); Robert Montmarche (d). Paris, 7 March 1938.
I'm coming, Virginia · Farewell blues · Blue light blues[2,5]

Rex Stewart and His Feetwarmers: Stewart (cnt); Barney Bigard (clt, d[6]); Reinhardt (g); Billy Taylor (bs). Paris, 5 April 1939.
Montmartre · Low cotton · Finesse[6] *· I know that you know · Solid old man*[6]

It was about halfway through the 1930s that Reinhardt turned into Europe's most celebrated jazzman: if not with the general public at least with his fellow musicians, and most significantly with American musicians. They were simultaneously dazzled by his technique (despite that mutilated left hand) and by the fact that he was the first non-American jazz player to come up with a style totally his own. For American musicians who visited Paris during the second part of that decade, it was almost as obligatory to record — or at least sit in — with Reinhardt as to inspect Versailles or take the lift up the Eiffel Tower. Not that this applied quite so markedly in 1935, when Warlop's band provided a rather sedate backing for Hawkins, although *What a difference a day made* contains one of Briggs's finest trumpet solos, nicely melodic. Neither track catches Hawkins on top form; nor does *Stardust*, recorded with a smaller group. Because *Stardust*'s melodic identity is stronger than its harmonic shape and because the harmonies and structure are unusual, few jazz musicians have improvised on it successfully. All he could do in 1935 was to decorate that melody. Indeed, Reinhardt's single-string solo now comes across as sounding more resourceful than Hawkins's embellishments.

And so, despite the occasional clinker, does Coleman's trumpet solo on Clark's version of *Stardust*. Clark, twenty-two years old at the time, had just arrived in Paris to join Willie Lewis's orchestra. His piano playing was bold, reflecting the influences of both Earl Hines and Fats Waller yet holding out the promise of developing into a very individual style. But in 1937 Clark was committed to a French asylum, where he died the following year. Curiously enough, Reinhardt takes no solos on this session. It is Coleman who dominates, vaulting from note to note with scarcely a pause, as mobile a player as Armstrong in his early Hot Five days.

Carter wrote scores for the four saxophonists to play on *Honeysuckle rose* and *Crazy rhythm*. Both tracks, however, find Hawkins towering above his companions, although Carter takes an airy solo in *Crazy rhythm*. By this time — 1937 — Hawkins had fashioned a more aggressive style for fast numbers, often employing riffs as part of his approach. In *Crazy rhythm*, for instance, he picks up a phrase Combelle played two choruses earlier, going on to deploy it with much more power. (Perhaps the most striking examples of Hawkins's new manner are some of the trio recordings he made in Hilversum a year later, especially *Swinging in the groove*, all to be found in *On the Loose* (H) OTL5.) *Out of nowhere* presents him in his more familiar and more bounteous guise of rhapsodist. Carter plays trumpet here, and in the slightly chaotic jamming that takes place on *Sweet Georgia Brown*.

Two months later came the date by a contingent from Teddy Hill's band (though with Coleman taking the place of the nineteen-year-old Dizzy Gillespie), offering some of the finest solos ever recorded by Wells and Coleman. The former's trombone playing was at its most imaginative, exploiting the instrument's quirkiness, the phrasing oblique yet logical, the approach akin to Pee Wee Russell's in its pursuit of the unexpected. As well as containing one of his very best trumpet solos, *Hanging around Boudon*, a slow blues, has Coleman scat singing (an outstanding instance of the genre) and Reinhardt takes a twelve-bar chorus that has its own exotic power. His blues playing may have lain closer to the Camargue than to the Mississippi Delta, yet the Gypsy undertones fit the emotional character of the music.

Coleman's own session finds the musicians performing the blues much better than the well-worn standards, where the solos are undistinguished. *Big boy blues* has Goudie on clarinet, which he plays with something of Bigard's languid fluency. Reinhardt takes one of his more dramatic solos, while *Bill Coleman blues* has him duetting with the trumpeter (still muted); another absorbing performance. But perhaps the most remarkable duets are those in which Reinhardt partners South. Possibly the finest jazz violinist, Smith combined classical poise with a warm, expressive sound and a capacity for lengthy improvisation. He had worked and studied in Budapest earlier in the 1930s, and perhaps it is not fanciful to discern in *Eddie's blues* a tzigane flavour contributed by both players. On this and other tracks, South demonstrates his skill at avoiding the obvious, constantly giving phrases an unexpected accent or rhythmic slant.

The Carter pieces are by a small band containing three of the musicians who had worked with him in Holland the previous summer (**100**). Once again the line-up was international, mixing Frenchmen and West Indians with an Englishman and two Americans. *I'm coming, Virginia* and *Farewell blues* both open with characteristic scoring by Carter. Apart from Reinhardt's chorus in the former, Carter is the only convincing soloist, and his two choruses on *Farewell blues* are a fine demonstration of how a solo can build upon its beginnings.

Reinhardt's role in most of these sessions was often functional. He took occasional solos, but also provided a rhythmic foundation (he was usually placed close to a microphone). Oddly enough, his rhythm playing now sounds more satisfying than it did in the 1930s, when European jazz *aficionados* expected local musicians to swing in the way that Americans did. A wider historical perspective now allows us to accept more easily what was a distinctively European manner. But Reinhardt's finest playing here occurs in the date with Stewart, recorded when the Ellington band was passing through Paris. Sonny Greer failed to turn up, so

Bigard is heard drumming in a couple of passages where Reinhardt would otherwise have had to take solos supported only by Taylor's bass. Stewart's half-valve technique projected its own kind of throttled eloquence, at once jaunty and dramatic; *Finesse* contains one of his most moving solos. But perhaps the finest playing by the American visitors came from Bigard: elegant, fluent, unruffled, epitomizing everything that was best in the New Orleans Creole clarinet tradition. Reinhardt played the only harmony instrument, his situation at once more vital and more exposed than on the majority of the other sessions. That he coped so splendidly, both in solos and within the ensemble, proves that by the end of the 1930s it was possible for at least one European to operate on the same level as the finest American players.   C.F.

106 The Legendary Django
World Record Club (E) T821

Eddie South, Stéphane Grappelli (vln); Django Reinhardt, Roger Chaput (g); Wilson Myers (bs). Paris, 29 September 1937.
Daphne
Michel Warlop (vln) replaces South; Myers absent. Same date.
You took advantage of me
Grappelli (vln); Django Reinhardt, Eugene Vées, Joseph Reinhardt (g); Louis Vola (bs). Paris, 14 December 1937.
My serenade
Django Reinhardt (g); Grappelli (p). Paris, 28 December 1937.
Sweet Georgia Brown
Grappelli switches to vln. Same date
Stéphane's blues
Vola (bs) replaces Grappelli. Same date.
You rascal, you
Django Reinhardt (g). Paris, 30 June 1939.
Naguine · Echoes of Spain
Pierre Ferret (g); Emmanuel Soudieux (bs) added. Same date.
I'll see you in my dreams
Grappelli (vln); Vées (g) added. Same date.
Stockholm · Younger generation
Hubert Rostaing (clt); Django Reinhardt, Joseph Reinhardt (g); Francis Luca (bs); Pierre Fouad (d). Paris, 1 October 1940.
Blues · Rhythme futur
Tony Rovira (bs) replaces Luca. 13 December 1940.
Vendredi 13

The secret of Django Reinhardt's almost independent aptitude for jazz improvisation may be divined in a freedom firstly inherent in his Gypsy tradition and later enhanced, or at any rate expanded, by his forthright response to the blues and to the free linear variations being achieved by Coleman Hawkins and others, The flamenco probings of *Echoes of Spain*, demonstrating a non-jazz form of improvisation, European but with Arabic roots, go a long way towards defining the quality which made Reinhardt's the first genuinely international voice that jazz produced. The savage flurries of chords and dramatic tremolos injected into many of his faster solos seem totally related to that Spanish source, and it is often difficult to say whether his 'bending' of single notes owes most to the same tradition or to the blues. But the larger part of the accomplished music heard here, and on **104** and **105**, is to be defined and appreciated in jazz terms and, in any case, the eclectic borrowings of jazz — including 'Spanish tinges' — were evident enough even in its earliest days.

Daphne immediately shows the guitarist's mastery and gives a rather daunting opportunity to identify the relative contributions of the violinists South and Grappelli. It is easier, perhaps, to distinguish Warlop's less Gallically mannered attack from Grappelli's work on *You took advantage of me*, in which Reinhardt, starting from a few bars of straight theme-quotation, spins an enchantingly varied solo with the building of related melodies, intricate double-tempo figures and tough, peremptory chords alternating with light threads of ornament — searching all the time with a magical combination of intensity and liberty. All these qualities can be heard in *Sweet Georgia Brown, You rascal you* and *Younger generation*, all performances with a similar approach. The early bars of his solos in *I'll see you in my dreams* and *Blues* show how rich and how superbly controlled his lower-register playing could sound.

The rhythmic support which he receives is generally good, though slight reservations may be expressed about the quality of Vola's bass tone in *You rascal, you*, The heavy pounding of the accompanying guitars in the curiously presented *Stockholm* is sufficiently moderated in *Younger generation* for this to be placed among the better ensemble tracks.

Blues, Rhythme futur and *Vendredi 13* feature the Bigard- and Goodman-influenced Rostaing, who plays attractively in all. *Vendredi 13* is a fast minor theme prompting one of Reinhardt's most compelling statements, whilst *Rhythme futur*, which has examples of his virtuosic octave lines, has an oblique Central European character.

Stéphane's blues may be Grappelli's response to *Eddie's blues* (**105b**) but, pleasant as it is, it certainly is no more successful than was South's effort in demonstrating that the violin is an instrument well suited to the blues. E.T.

107a
Swing Sessions Vol. 1 1937–39
Pathé (F) C054–16021

Teddy Weatherford (p, cls[1]). Paris, 23 June 1937.
I ain't got nobody · Tea for two · Weather-beaten blues[1] · Maple leaf rag

Dicky Wells and His Orchestra: Bill Dillard, Shad Collins (tpt); Wells (tbn); Howard Johnson (alt); Sam Allen (p); Roger Chaput (g); Bill Beason (d). Paris, 12 July 1937.
I've found a new baby · Dinah · Nobody's blues but mine.

Collins absent. Same date.
Hot club blues

Dillard, Johnson absent. Same date.
Lady, be good · Dicky Wells blues

Weatherford (p). Paris, 20 June 1937.
My blue heaven · Ain't misbehaving

Joe Turner (p); Tommy Benford (d). Paris 24 May 1939.
The ladder · Loncy

107b
Swing Sessions Vol. 2 1938–39
Pathé (F) C054–16022

Garland Wilson (p). Paris, 9 March 1938.
The blues got me · You showed me the way · The blues I love to play · Sweet Lorraine

Oscar Aleman, John Mitchell (g); Wilson Myers (bs, vcl[2]). Paris, 12 May 1939.
Russian lullaby[2] · Just a little swing · Dear old Southland[2] · Jeepers creepers[2]

Freddy Johnson and His Orchestra · Louis Bacon (tpt, vcl[3]); Alix Combelle (clt[4], ten); Johnson (p); Myers (bs); Benford (d). Paris, 28 June 1939.
Ain't misbehaving[3] · Big wig in a wigwam[4] · Blue room[4] · Jam with Bacon · Frenchy's blues[4] · Hi diddle diddle

107c
Swing Sessions Vol. 3 1938–39
Pathé (F) C054–16023

Herman Chittison (p). Paris, 13 June 1938.
My last affair/No more tears · I'm putting all my eggs in one basket · Melancholy baby · They can't take that away from me

Frank 'Big Boy' Goudie and His Orchestra: Jack Butler (tpt); André Ekyan (clt, alt); Goudie (ten); Turner (p); Norman Langlois (g); Myers (bs); Benford (d). Paris, 28 May 1939.
You and I, babe · You in my arms · Heebie jeebies · It's a sin to tell a lie · Who's sorry now?

Louis Bacon and His Orchestra: Bacon (tpt, vcl[3]); Eddie Brunner (clt, ten[5]); Albert Ferrari (clt[6], ten); Johnson (p); Chaput (g); Myers (bs); Benford (d). Paris, 30 June 1939.
Zumba · Sweet Lorraine[3] · Shine · Panama[5,6] ·Rhythm is our business

107d
Swing Sessions Vol. 4 1937–42
Pathé (F) C054–16024

Philippe Brun and His Swing Band: Brun, Gus Deloof, André Cornille (tpt); Josse Breyère, Guy Paquinet (tbn); Max Blanc, Charles Lisée (alt); Jacques Hélian, Combelle (ten); Stéphane Grappelli (p); Django Reinhardt (g); Louis Vola (bs); Maurice Chaillou (d). Paris, 28 December 1937.

College stomp

Philippe Brun and His Jam Band: Deloof, Cornille, Breyère, Paquinet, Blanc, Lisée, Hélian absent; Michel Warlop (vln) added. Same date.

It had to be you

Philippe Brun and His Swing Band: previous Swing Band personnel except that Noël Chiboust (ten) replaces Hélian. Paris, 9 March 1938.

Got a date in Louisiana

Fletcher Allen and His Orchestra: Pierre Allier (tpt); Allen, Lisée (alt); Combelle (ten); Ray Stokes (p); Marcel Bianchi (g); Tony Rovira (bs); Pierre Fouad (d). Paris, 15 March 1938.

What'll I do?

Allier, Allen, Lisée, Bianchi, Rovira absent. Same date.

Al's idea

Arthur Briggs and His Orchestra: Briggs (tpt); Christian Wagner (clt); Combelle (ten); Stokes (p); Django Reinhardt (g); Rovira (bs). Paris, 15 February 1940.

Melancholy baby · Sometimes I'm happy

Alix Combelle and His Swing Band: Allier, Brun, Al Piguilem, Alex Renard (tpt); Paquinet (tbn); Combelle (ten); Charlie Lewis (p); Django Reinhardt, Joseph Reinhardt (g); Marceau Sarbib (bs); H. P. Chadel (d). Paris, 20 February 1940.

Week-end stomp · Panassié stomp · Rock-a-bye Basie

Alix Combelle Saxophone Trio: Wagner (clt, alt); Hubert Rostaing, Combelle (ten); Django Reinhardt, Joseph Reinhardt (g); Rovira (bs); Fouad (d). Paris, 18 December 1940.

Onze heures vingt

Alix Combelle et Le Jazz de Paris: Aimé Barelli, Christian Bellest, Severin Luino (tpt); Maurice Gladieu (tbn); Blanc, Lisée (alt); Jean Luino, Rostaing, Combelle (ten); Paul Collot (p); Joseph Reinhardt (g); Rovira (bs); Fouad (d). Paris, 27 January 1941.

Sent for you yesterday

Same personnel and location, 31 January 1941.

Verlaine

Alix Combelle and His Orchestra: Raoul Coucoulle (tpt); George Galavielle, Michel Donray (alt); Combelle (ten, vcl); Jacques Dieval (p); Chaput (g); Lucien Simoens (bs); Armand Molinetti (d). Paris, 16 February 1943.

Oui

The first label entirely to specialize in jazz, Swing confirmed the interest which Europeans had taken in this music since the days of ragtime. At least to begin with, the sessions naturally centred round American visitors, and many fine performances were recorded. The above four LPs are the first of a series of ten selected therefrom, and further material from the Swing catalogue will be found on **102** and **105**.

Earliest to be set down of the music here were the first of Weatherford's solos. Although known as the energetically driving pianist of Erskine Tate's 1926 *Static strut* and *Stomp off, let's go* (**37**), he spent most of his time in the Far East, well out of the jazz limelight. Yet parts of *Blue heaven* explain why he was cited by some of the older Chicago musicians as an influence on Earl Hines [40]. Interesting, too, is the sometimes violent *Maple leaf rag*, which owes nothing whatever to ragtime style.

Wilson's heavy touch reminds one of Weatherford yet there is nothing like the same degree of vitality. *The blues I love to play* has good ideas, yet, despite an apparent injection from Hines, little rhythmic life; and *Sweet Lorraine* is the same. Stronger and more flexible bass patterns are heard from Turner, a representative of the New York 'stride' school. These two duos with Benford have an engaging optimism, yet he is heard to better effect on the band session led by Goudie a few days later.

All the pianists here, though, are outclassed by Chittison, a truly underrated musician. His talent and accomplishment are almost comparable to those of Art Tatum, and the full, smoothly-contoured textures of his solos, filled by a seemingly unstoppable flow of ideas, suggest that he was potentially a major figure in keyboard jazz. Each of his solos, its incidence of detail notwithstanding, is given a beautiful and unpredictable shape, and especially in *They can't take that away from me* one feels that a highly-elaborated plot has been acted out and brought to a satisfying conclusion. It is unfortunate that *My own blues* from this 1938 session was not included here, particularly as Chittison, despite a long and active career, made so few recordings. He can also be heard on **102** and **103**, however, and one of his few LPs appears under **216**.

If the Wells date is not quite so distinguished as that with a Reinhardt-powered rhythm section which appears on **105a**, it still gave rise to some of his most characteristic statements. Even though the accompaniment is far less sensitive than the soloist deserves, *Dicky Wells blues* stands out for the variety of its phrases and the unexpectedness of their contours. Wells's rhythm is supple, his tone dense yet highly expressive, sometimes with ironic inflections uncommon in jazz, especially at the ends of lines. There are neatly-phrased contributions from the trumpeters, too — Dillard on *I've found a new baby* and *Hot Club blues*, Collins on *Dinah* and *Nobody's blues but mine* (where he distantly echoes Bubber Miley on Ellington's *Black and tan fantasy* — **87** and **89**).

One of the minor discoveries of these sessions for many listeners will be Bacon's work, recorded both under his own name and with Freddy Johnson. This ex-Ellingtonian's playing is agile but full-toned, and there are some quite personal turns to his wide-ranging phrases, as in the switches of register on *Frenchy's blues*; at best it has a feeling of adventurous simplicity, well illustrated by the unappetizingly titled *Jam with Bacon*. Actually, despite some excellent clarinet playing from the little-known Brunner (also heard on **102b**) and a mildly intriguing swing version of *Panama*, the date led by Bacon himself yielded nothing quite so good as the sound of Combelle and the trumpeter in full cry together, as on *Hi diddle diddle*.

Aleman's pieces are a minor instance of jazz for strings alone, a European speciality at that time (see **104** and **106**), but a more rewarding session, comparable to those with Bacon, was that led by Goudie, a pioneer among American expatriate jazzmen. The rhythm section, sparked by Turner, is the best on these four LPs, and there are hoarse-toned but well sustained solos by the leader, exultant trumpet phrases from Butler and faithful echoes of Benny Carter from Ekyan (particularly on *You and I, babe*).

Volume 4 has a much smaller American presence, although note should be taken of the pieces by Briggs, some of whose earlier work is discussed under **96**. Both *Melancholy baby* and *Sometimes I'm happy* have fanciful, sure-footed, tirelessly mobile trumpet solos, and Wagner contributes excellent clarinet playing (as he does also to Combelle's *Onze heures vingt*). It is a pity that the other tracks from Brigg's session were not included here. However, the three led by Brun are well chosen, showing him in three quite different moods, though always athletic and attacking, a far cry from his Bixian solos with Grégor and His Grégorians (Wolverine (A) 3) and Ray Ventura (Wolverine (A) 4) of 1928–9. The main point, though, of Brun's *It had to be you* is Warlop's contribution, as on Allen's *What'll I do?* it is Allier's.

Combelle leads most of the other tracks and confirms his reputation as the best European tenor of that time. The big band pieces are in the Basie mould of the late 1930s (see **133–4**), with *Sent for you yesterday* (*Hier et aujourd'hui* on the original label!) hewing too close to its model. The others, however, have independent scores, alas unattributed, and cogent solos by Django Reinhardt, Allier, Brun, Lewis, Paquinet, Renard and Combelle himself. The closing ensemble of *Onze heures vingt* should be compared with that of *Honeysuckle rose* on **105a**, of which it is a variant and extension.

This LP is a sort of postscript to the previous three, demonstrating what French jazz musicians had learnt from their visitors. Also demonstrated is the fact that what may be termed the denationalization of American jazz was well under way. Besides **97–8**, it would be possible to cite comparable instances from several other parts of the Continent, and such music was the basis for European jazz's postwar achievements.   M.H.

5

Interlude

The Influence of Jazz
on European Composers

The musical richness of the best jazz was bound to interest younger composers in the 1920s and beyond. Although the works they wrote in response to it are not in themselves jazz, knowledge of some of the relevant pieces is essential to an understanding of the impact jazz has had on twentieth-century music.

108 **Jazz-Inspired Piano Compositions**
Recorded in Prague June 1972–March 1973
Supraphon (Cz) 1111721/2 (2 LPs)

Satie: *Jack-in-the-Box* (1899)
Jan Vrána (p)

Debussy: *Golliwogg's cakewalk* (1906–8)
Auric: *Adieu, New York!* (1920)
Peter Toperczer (p).

Hindemith: *Suite 1922* (1922)
Jan Marcol (p).

Schulhoff: *Rag-music* (1922) · *Esquisses de jazz* (1927)
Miloš Mikula (p).

Gershwin: *Preludes* (1926)
Emil Leichner (p).

Burian: *American suite* (1926)
Toperczer, Vrána (p).

Copland: *4 Piano blues* (1926–48)
Toperczer (p).
Martinů: *Preludes* (1929)
Leichner (p).

Some of the earliest successful European attempts to employ the jazz idiom compositionally made notable use of the piano. Following the recent initiatives of Bartók, which arose out of his investigations of Balkan folk music, the instrument was treated percussively and proved an apt vehicle for the studies in rhythm that are a main point of many of these works. Another guideline seized by nearly all the above composers was that of developing character pieces from the various dance genres, and it is encouraging that they all did this differently, producing sometimes unexpected results. Anyone who imagines, for example, that there is no such thing as a fugal foxtrot should hear the finale of Burian's *American suite*. Also surprising is Auric's combination of foxtrot and blues in *Adieu, New York!*, written in 1920 at a time when blues had only just begun to make an impression on the American commercial music and recording scenes. There are amusing hints of *mésalliance*, too, as in the title of the last movement of Schulhoff's *Rag-music*, 'Tempo di foxtrot à la Hawaii'.

Satie's *Jack-in-the-box* seems amazingly early, yet his period of work as a Paris cabaret pianist would have put him in touch with the most recent tendencies in entertainment music; and there was the precedent of Chabrier's use of popular idioms. In fact, to contemporary ears the lively *Jack-in-the-box*, now more familiar in Milhaud's orchestration, is redolent of music hall and vaudeville rather than jazz or even ragtime. In *Golliwogg's cakewalk*, ragtime is memorably seen through the eyes of one of the greatest composers of the century, and the result should be compared with Debussy's *Minstrels* and *Le petit Nègre*. Sophisticated humour is a consideration in *Golliwogg's cakewalk*, and the irreverence is heightened in the middle section with a syncopated quotation from Wagner's *Tristan und Isolde*.

Despite French celerity in these matters, other parts of Europe were not far behind and there was a quick response to jazz in, for example, Czechoslovakia, an uncommonly musical country, as the idiomatic performances on these LPs suggest. Confirmation of the point is offered by the works of Czech composers included here. Thus Schulhoff, a pupil of Debussy and a fine pianist active in the 1920s and 1930s in the performance of several kinds of new music, soon fused jazz with other contemporary idioms. He did so with real musical wit in *Rag-music*, with its very oblique allusions to popular favourites of the time — for instance to *Japanese sandman* in the first two movements. Still more verve is displayed in the later *Esquisses*. Burian, too, was much engaged in the contemporary music of his time, and whereas we in the West tend to think of Robert Goffin's *Aux Frontières du Jazz*

(Paris, 1932) as the first significant book on this subject, Burian's *Jazz* came out in Prague during 1928, a decade before anything of value appeared in America. His *American suite*, for two pianos, has greater textural elaboration than the other works here, especially in the direction of polyphony. More lyrical, though also possessed of much vigour, are the *Preludes* of Martinů, whose relation to jazz is discussed under **110**.

It is instructive to compare Martinů's, Burian's and Schulhoff's versions of blues and boston, of rag and foxtrot, with those in Hindemith's *Suite 1922*. In contrast with the ironic topicality of the latter's *Shimmy* movement, the Czech composers's music is more relaxed in its use of these genres, its appeal more melodic. There is a nearly manic harshness to Hindemith's *Ragtime*, and an acrid song of disillusionment echoes through his five movements; they are very much a statement from post-World War I Germany.

Gershwin and Copland, this anthology's American contributors, are likewise closer to the genres than Hindemith. Gershwin's *Preludes* show a strikingly individual sense of melody, his outer pieces being rapid-fire stomping dances, the middle one a touching evocation of the blues. Copland's *Blues* are variously dated from 1926 to 1948 and have an unexpected *alfresco* atmosphere: the blues out of doors. An exception is the last, which is a rapidly sidestepping ragtime dance.   M.H.

109 **Jazz-Inspired Compositions by Stravinsky**
Recorded in Prague, 1973
Supraphon (Cz) 50968

L'Histoire du soldat (1918)
Chamber Harmony; Libor Pešek (cond)

Ragtime for 11 instruments (1918)
Karel Krautgartner and His Orchestra.

Piano rag music (1919)
Jan Novotný (p).

Ebony concerto (1945)
Krautgartner and His Orchestra.

In the earlier pieces the influence is that of published commercial ragtime instead of jazz. As Stravinsky later said, 'My knowledge of jazz was derived exclusively from copies of sheet music, and as I had never actually heard any of the music performed I borrowed its rhythmic style not as played but as written. I *could* imagine jazz sound, however, or so I liked to think' [41]. Certainly the anticipations of jazz band instrumentation, both here and elsewhere in European music, are remarkable. *L'Histoire du soldat* employs cornet, trombone, clarinet, bassoon, violin, string bass and percussion, this having a precedent, unknown to Stravinsky at the time, in Satie's *Le Piège de Méduse of* 1913. Other popular genres are evoked, too, such as Spanish bullfight bands in the *Royal march* (see **18**), but there is a jazz-like emphasis on percussion throughout *L'Histoire*, and the concluding *Triumphal march of the Devil* in fact ends with a drum solo. Constantly the symmetry of phrases is broken up, and the score is rich in metrical counterpoint.

Adding flute, French horn, a second violin, viola and cimbalom to the above ensemble and subtracting the bassoon, *Ragtime for 11 instruments* takes further some of the ideas of the *Tango* and *Ragtime* movements of *L'Histoire*. Its writing has even more linear independence and the result, as Stravinsky's great contemporary Alban Berg said, is 'Something really very fine' [42]. In contrast with the steady 4/4 of this piece, much of *Piano rag music* is notated without barlines. Here the clusters of 'added notes' found in the *Ragtime* and *Tango* of *L'Histoire* are treated more expansively, and the work is turbulently rhapsodic, almost improvisatory in feeling. At the same time, and no doubt partly because it is a keyboard piece, it caricatures the clichés of Tin Pan Alley ragtime more drastically than his earlier contributions; and Novotný's performance underlines its indignant pungency.

Remembering the echoes of Broadway in his *Scènes de Ballet* (1944), Stravinsky's undertaking to write the *Ebony concerto* should have occasioned no great surprise [43]. It was designed, of course, for Woody Herman's virtuosic band of the mid-1940s, the so-called 'First Herd', and deployed the conventional big band instrumentation with extraordinary originality. No credit is due to jazz arrangers (excepting George Handy) for having ignored all the discoveries this score contains. However, if the *Ebony concerto* stands with *Ragtime for 11 instruments* as the best music on this LP, that is at least partly because in the former Stravinsky was astute enough not to emulate the more sophisticated diction of latter-day jazz too closely. Thus — and such features as the blue false relations in the harmony of the slow movement notwithstanding — the work's first subject is an ambiguously syncopated trumpet fanfare which is so deliberately corny that when it is developed on wryly conventional sonata-form lines the result sounds almost cynical, an ironic neo-baroque complement to the *Symphony in three movements* which Stravinsky was composing almost simultaneously. Herman's band recorded the *Ebony concerto* in 1946 but on his own later recording the composer set a notably faster tempo for the first movement; Krautgartner, however, makes the best of both worlds, retaining the urgency yet sounding more relaxed. In the central *Andante*, Herman's sidemen best relate to the composer's sidelong glances at the blues, while Krautgartner makes the finale's set of variations more a whole than anyone else.

It is unfortunate that Stravinsky's remaining jazz-influenced pieces, the *Scherzo à la Russe* written for Paul Whiteman (1943–4) and *Praeludium* (1936–7) could not be included here.

M.H.

110 **Jazz-Inspired Compositions by Martinů**
Recorded in Prague, 1972
Supraphon (Cz) 110.1014

Shimmy foxtrot (1922)
Prague Symphony Orchestra; Zbyněk Vostřák (cond)

3 skizzy moderné tanců (1927)
Zdeněk Jílek (p)

Kuchyňská revue (1927)
Václav Junek (tpt); Karel Dlouhý (clt); Jiří (bsn); Bruno Bělčík (vln); Miloš Sádlo (cel); František Bauch (p).

Le jazz (1928)
Prague Symphony Orchestra; Lubomír Pánek Singers; Vostřák (cond).

Jazz suite (1928)
Jílek (p); members of Prague Symphony Orchestra; Vostřák (cond).

Sextet (1929)
Jan Panenka (p); Prague Wind Quintet.

Martinů was quickly off the mark with a *Cats' foxtrot* written for the wind band of his home town in 1919. The above LP's earliest piece, the *Shimmy foxtrot*, one of several jazz episodes in his ballet *Kdo je ne světě nejmocnější?* (*Who is the Most Powerful?*), makes an uncommonly animated use of full symphony orchestra and is something of an achievement for its time. The *3 Sketches in modern dance rhythms* for solo piano — *Blues, Tango* and *Charleston* — have a surer stylistic touch, however, and the last movement's cross-rhythms are well pointed by Jílek.

Also dating from 1927 is *The kitchen revue*, another ballet, whose movements include what sounds like a brilliantly perceptive caricature of one of the Red Hot Peppers' stomps, with Junek outstanding in the 'George Mitchell' role. It seems extraordinary that Martinů should have composed this just when Morton was cutting his most characteristic records (47). It should be compared with the *Old Sir Faulk* and *Something lies beyond the scene* movements of Walton's *Façade* (1921–2). In the other movements of *The kitchen revue*, also, and as in Stravinsky's *L'Histoire du soldat* and *Ragtime for 11 instruments*, there is a clear parallel with early jazz bands in that blend is avoided and each instrument is made audaciously to stand off from the others.

In contrast, *Le jazz*, perhaps influenced by Paul Whiteman but more probably by one of his European imitators, is the weakest piece here, although its use of a saxophone section, banjo and jazz percussion in the symphony orchestra is of some interest. Far more engaging is the *Jazz suite* for chamber orchestra, which includes *Blues* and *Boston* movements. Of the European composers mentioned in this chapter, Martinů most frequently made room for jazz in his works — even including jazz episodes in three of his operas — and this piece, especially the lovely *Blues*, shows how closely jazz elements had become integrated with other aspects of his style, such as his increasingly complex harmonic vocabulary and elaborate textures. It is a pity that the piano is balanced too close in the above recording.

Latest of these works, and in some respects even finer than the *Suite*, is the *Sextet*. This is for piano and wind quintet, though with a second bassoon daringly substituted for the French horn usual in this instrumentation. Again there is a striking *Blues* movement, but the whole score displays a constant inventiveness within the personal version of the jazz idiom that Martinů had by now developed. It is regrettable that this could not have been a two-LP set so as to include his other jazz-influenced pieces.   M.H.

111 Milhaud/Weill
Recorded in New York City, 1973
Nonesuch (A) H 71281

Milhaud: *La création du monde* (1923)

Contemporary Chamber Ensemble: Allan Dean, Thomas Lisenbee (tpt); John Swallow (tbn); Paul Ingraham (Fr h); Paul Dunkel (picc, fl); Andrew Lolya (fl); George Haas (ob); Arthur Bloom, Stanley Walden (clt); Donald MacCourt, Bernadette Zirkuli (bsn); Al Regni (saxes); Jeanne Benjamin, Thomas Kornacker (vln); Fred Sherry (cel); Gilbert Kalish (p); Alvin Brehm (bs); Raymond des Roches, Robert Fitz (per); Arthur Weisberg (cond).

Weill: *Kleine Dreigroschemusik für Blasorchester* (1928)
Benjamin, Kornacker, Sherry, Brehm absent; Jay Berliner (bj, g), Toby Hanks (tu), Jerome Jolles (ban) added.

If one piece had to stand for all the music dealt with in this chapter it would be Milhaud's *La création du monde*, which embodies the most perceptive use of jazz idioms by a European composer during the period covered by this book. In one sense it was a predictable achievement, for Milhaud, a man of wide sympathies, had a real interest in popular culture, conveyed with poetic sensitivity in such works as *Carnaval à la Nouvelle-Orléans* (1947). This grew out of an early appreciation of the folk music of his native Provence, and it is perhaps not unduly fanciful to see a link between the tumbling, jagged shapes of the finale to *La création* and the Provençal landscape's noisy juxtaposition of colours. Again, the extended clarinet solo, beautifully executed here by Bloom, shows an amazing grasp of the essential character of jazz improvisation at a time when very little of it had been recorded [44]. There are oboe passages, too, which remarkably anticipate Gershwin.

Milhaud's piano solos *Caramel mou* and *Trois rag caprices* appeared in 1920 and 1922 respectively, and he made a version of the former for jazz band instrumentation. But he 'had the idea of using these rhythms and timbres in a piece of chamber music', and in 1922 visited New York. In Harlem he found 'Music completely different . . . the melodic lines, set off by the percussion, overlapping contrapuntally in a throbbing mixture of broken, twisted rhythms' [45]. Ballet, not chamber music, was the most advantageous framework for a sophisticated evocation of such performances, and Milhaud would have been aware of the precedent of Satie's ballet *Parade* (1917), which made use of ragtime.

In melodic inspiration, however, the music owes as much to the blues as to jazz, as in the subject and counter-subject of the fugal second section (played rather too fast in the above performance), with their variable major/minor thirds. The scenario of *La création* was by the one-armed poet Blaise Cendrars and was based on an African tribal myth of the creation of the world. Considering how new jazz was, the range of moods conveyed here is wide, the variety of gesture great, and Milhaud's compositional mastery adds a rare and subtle effect of 'distance' which intensifies this music's nostalgic beauty.

The Weill piece offers a selection of melodies from *Die Dreigroschenoper* happily divorced from the facile sentiments of Brecht's text. It is also a forceful composition in its own right whose instrumentation echoes, in for example the *Overture*, the tradition of marching bands; other movements such as *Pollys Lied* essay other veins of expression, however. Weill had used the jazz idiom in his earlier ballet-opera *Royal Palace* (1925–6) yet saw it from a further remove than Milhaud. Probably his situation was similar to that of another German composer of his generation, Ernst Křenek, who in connection with his own jazz opera, *Jonny Spielt Auf* (1925–6), later wrote, 'I tried to project the reflections of the image of jazz which I had formed in my mind' [46]. That Weill was on the right track is suggested by the fact that some of the textures of the *Kleine Dreigroschenmusik* echo early Paul Whiteman records like *I'll build a stairway to Paradise* (1922). And although his squarecut and sleazy melodies, such as the *Ballad of Mack the Knife*, may seem banal, they prove impossible to forget.   M.H.

112 Lambert, Bliss, Goossens and Walton
Recorded in London, 1975
HMV (E) ESD7164

Lambert: *Concerto for piano and 9 instruments* (1930–31)
Richard Rodney Bennett (p); members of English Sinfonia; Neville Dilkes (cond).

Bliss: *Bliss* (1923) · *The rout trot* (1927) · Goossens: *Folk tune* (1920) · Lambert: *Elegiac blues* (1927) · *Elegy* (1938) · Walton: *Old Sir Faulk* (1921–2)
Bennett (p).

Constant Lambert's *Concerto*, for piano, trumpet, trombone, flute (doubling piccolo), three clarinets (one each doubling the E flat and bass instruments), cello, double bass and percussion, could almost be taken as the chamber work that Milhaud did not write (see **111**). It is best heard in conjunction with his other main jazz-influenced pieces, *Rio Grande* and the *Sonata* for solo piano, although here the identifying musical characteristics of jazz are more fully absorbed into his own style, in fact into his technique of composition, and thus are less obvious. In fact, like Martinů in his *Sextet* and *Jazz suite* (**110**), Lambert was able to depart considerably from the conventions of jazz band instrumentation and texture without losing the jazz ambience; indeed, the special climate of feeling associated with that music is embodied in a particularly intense form in the *Concerto's* slow, elegiac finale.

The solo part is often busily toccata-like, this being complemented by skilful and varied writing for a considerable battery of percussion instruments. Unfortunately, in the above performance recording balance places the piano too far forward, but this does not conceal Lambert's constant textural inventiveness. There is much rhythmic interest, notably a telling use of irregular metres such as 7/4 and 11/8, and there is impressive long-term structural ingenuity. This latter gives rise to some striking transformations of themes, and it is worth following in detail, for example, the wide-ranging adventures of the central *Intermède's* blues melody. However, the music's strong emotional impetus is what makes this richly detailed score's diverse elements coalesce into a statement of dark urgency whose beauty has increased — or more fully emerged — as the decades have passed [47].

Among the piano solos on side 2 is Walton's *Old Sir Faulk*, one of several movements in that composer's *Façade* which show a precociously prompt grasp of jazz style. Also included is Lambert's *Elegiac blues*, which more than once the *Concerto's* finale draws close to quoting; it was prompted, like Ellington's *Black beauty* of the following year, by the death of Florence Mills. The two items by Arthur Bliss are examples of an energetically sophisticated, cosmopolitan post-ragtime music, the earlier one sufficiently so to allude to the proverbial 'Spanish tinge'. Like the *Night club scene* in Bliss's ballet *Adam Zero* (1946), they are an informative sidelight on one who later was appointed Master of the Queen's Music.   M.H.

6

The Thirties and Swing

The Early 1930s

Mainly, the recordings from this period are loosely organized, have an atmosphere different from that of the swing bands proper, large and small, and aims that were less uniform. Gradually solo virtuosity became more widespread, just as composers and arrangers exploited the resources of large ensembles in more varied ways.

113 **Louis Armstrong in Los Angeles**
Parlophone (E) PMC7098, Swaggie (Au) S1265

Louis Armstrong and His Savoy Ballroom Five (*sic*): Armstrong (tpt); J. C. Higginbotham (tbn); Albert Nicholas, Charlie Holmes (clt, alt); Teddy Hill (ten); Luis Russell (p); Lonnie Johnson (g); Eddie Condon (bj); Pops Foster (bs); Paul Barbarin (d). New York, 5 March 1929.
Mahogany Hall stomp

Louis Armstrong and His Orchestra: Armstrong (tpt, vcl); Homer Hobson (tpt); Fred Robinson (tbn); Jimmy Strong (clt, ten); Bert Curry, Crawford Wethington (alt); Carroll Dickerson (vln); Gene Anderson (p); Mancy Cara (bj); Pete Briggs (tu); Zutty Singleton (d). New York City, 19 July 1929.
Ain't misbehaving

Armstrong (tpt, spch); Buck Washington (p). New York City, 5 April 1930.
Dear old Southland

Louis Armstrong and His New Sebastian Cotton Club Orchestra: Armstrong (tpt, vcl); Leon Elkins (tpt); Lawrence Brown (tbn); Leon Herriford, Willis Stark (alt); William Franz (ten); L. Z. Cooper or Harvey Brooks (p); Ceele Burke (bj, g); Reggie Jones (tu); Lionel Hampton (d, vib). Los Angeles, 21 July 1930.
I'm a ding dong daddy · *I'm in the market for you*

Same personnel and location, 19 August 1930.
Confessing · If I could be with you one hour tonight

Armstrong (tpt, vcl); George Orendorff, Harold Scott (tpt); Luther Graven (tbn); Charlie Jones (clt, ten); Marvin Johnson (alt); Les Hite (alt, bar); Henry Prince (p); Bill Perkins (bj, g); Joe Bailey (bs); Hampton (d, vib). Los Angeles, 9 October 1930.
Body and soul

Same personnel and location, 16 October 1930.
Memories of you · You're lucky to me

Same personnel and location, 23 December 1930.
Sweethearts on parade · You're driving me crazy (2 takes) *· The peanut vendor*

Bailey switches to tu. Los Angeles, 9 March 1931.
Just a gigolo · Shine

114 Louis Armstrong V.S.O.P. Vol. 8
CBS(F) 62750, *Columbia (A) JEE22019

Louis Armstrong and His Orchestra: Armstrong (tpt, vcl); Zilner Randolph (tpt); Preston Jackson (tbn); George James (clt, sop, alt); Lester Boone (clt, alt); Albert Washington (clt, ten); Charlie Alexander (p); Mike McKendrick (bj, g); John Lindsay (bs); Tubby Hall (d). Chicago, 3 November 1931.
Lazy river · Chinatown, my Chinatown

Same personnel and location, 4 November 1931.
Wrap your troubles in dreams · Stardust

Same personnel and location, 5 November 1931.
You can depend on me · Georgia on my mind

Same personnel and location, 6 November 1931.
Lonesome road · I got rhythm

Same personnel and location, 25 January 1932.
Between the Devil and the deep blue sea · Kicking the gong around

Same personnel and location, 27 January 1932.
Home · All of me

Same personnel and location, 2 March 1932.
Love, you funny thing

Same personnel and location, 11 March 1932.
The new tiger rag · Keeping out of mischief now · Lawd, you made the night too long

115

Satchmo's Greatest, Vol. 1

RCA (F) 730.682, Bluebird (A) AZM2–5519

Louis Armstrong and His Orchestra: Armstrong (tpt, vcl); Louis Bacon, Louis Hunt, Billy Hicks (tpt); Charlie Green (tbn); Peter Clark (clt, alt); Edgar Sampson (alt); Elmer Williams (ten); Don Kirkpatrick (p); John Trueheart (g); Elmer James (tu); Chick Webb (d); Mezz Mezzrow (bells[1]). Camden, New Jersey, 8 December 1932.

That's my home (2 takes) · *Hobo, you can't ride this train*[1] · *I hate to leave you now* · *You'll wish you'd never been born*

Armstrong (tpt, vcl); Charlie Gaines and another (tpt); unidentified tbn; Louis Jordan, Arthur Davey (alt); Ellsworth Blake (ten); Wesley Robinson (p); unidentified (bj, g); Ed Hayes (tu); Benny Hill (d). Camden, New Jersey, 21 December 1932.

Medley of Armstrong hits (When you're smiling · *St James' Infirmary* · *Dinah* · *You rascal, you* · *Nobody's sweetheart* · *When it's sleepy time down south)*

Armstrong (tpt, vcl); Elmer Whitlock, Randolph (tpt); Keg Johnson (tbn); Scoville Brown, George Oldham (clt, alt); Budd Johnson (clt, ten); Teddy Wilson (p); McKendrick (bj, g); Bill Oldham (tu); Yank Porter (d). Chicago, 26 January 1933.

I've got the world on a string · *I've got a right to sing the blues* · *Hustling and bustling for baby* · *Sitting in the dark* · *High society* · *He's a son of the south*

Same personnel and location, 27 January 1933.

Some sweet day

Some jazz musicians need a sympathetic context for their talents to flower. But the very greatest performers seem able to excel in almost any circumstances. Charlie Parker outsoared those turgid strings. As for Armstrong, he was capable of taking control of almost any musical situation — an Hawaiian band, a close-harmony vocal group, even, as the present writer can testify, the Royal Philharmonic Orchestra — and emerge not only uncompromised but triumphant. Quite a number of tracks on these LPs exemplify that ability to transcend immediate surroundings — in this case dull arrangements and bands that frequently were downright sloppy. At the same time, few recordings demonstrate more strikingly Armstrong's greatness: his stature as a virtuoso trumpeter and the way he deployed that virtuosity to exhilarating, sometimes majestic, ends. Even in *The new tiger rag* he maintains his poise: the conception is bombastic, the trumpet solo studded — as forays of this sort often were — with quotations, particularly from the better-known operas; yet the apparent vulgarity is outweighed by the high spirits, the sense of fun.

But Armstrong, of course, was never trying to prove anything aesthetically. Although he must have realized how far ahead he stood technically, compared with other trumpeters of the 1920s and 1930s, it seems unlikely that he was ever aware of any disparity between the various tunes he improvised on, or was fussy about the variable qualities of the bands behind him. Which is why a slightly preposterous song such as *Sweethearts on parade* can be turned into a small masterpiece. It is, though, very much a single-handed victory, beginning with the muted trumpet paraphrase, proceeding through one of Armstrong's most audacious vocal choruses (the syntax is shredded, the musical logic remoulded), to conclude with what must, even by his exalted standards, be regarded as a quite superb solo and one summarizing almost everything he stood for at that point in jazz history.

The first three tracks are not at all typical. *Mahogany Hall stomp* has him backed by the Luis Russell Orchestra (plus Lonnie Johnson and Condon) in a simple yet bold performance. His sense of drama — and of structure — comes across in the way he sustains a single note for all but two bars of his second solo chorus and his repetition of a five-note phrase in the chorus that follows. *Ain't misbehaving* could fairly be described as Armstrong's first big hit, the number with which he stopped the show in the revue *Hot Chocolates* (its companion pieces, also written by Fats Waller, can be found on **80**). *Dear old Southland*, alas, operates at a much lower level than the duet Armstrong recorded with Earl Hines (**48**), lacking the give-and-take which made that performance so daring.

The remaining tracks on **113** present the band which supported Armstrong at Sebastian's New Cotton Club in Los Angeles. It contained two exceptional musicians in Hampton, then a drummer (although his earliest vibraharp playing on record can be heard in *Memories of you*), and Brown, very gifted yet capable — as became much plainer after he moved into Duke Ellington's trombone section — of sentimentality. Every bit as audacious as Armstrong's work in *Sweethearts on parade* are the closing choruses of *I'm a ding dong daddy*, especially the electrifying series of breaks, while his playing on *Memories of you* exhibits a gorgeousness of sound that no other trumpeter of the time could rival.

The band he led in Chicago in 1931 — assembled and rehearsed by Zilner Randolph — should have worked well, for it contained several well-known local musicians, including three New Orleans expatriates in Lindsay, Jackson and Hall. Yet the ensemble playing on many of these tracks (*You can depend on me*, for example) sounds woefully incompetent. Armstrong introduces the musicians one by one in *I got rhythm*, with almost everybody taking a solo; nothing could more starkly demonstrate the ascendancy the trumpeter had over all his colleagues. Only in *You can depend on me* does he descend to the surrounding level of mediocrity, reduced to playing what John Chilton has so accurately described as 'a series of incongruous siren-like effects' [48]. Yet only the day before Armstrong had set down a version of *Stardust* that undermines the present writer's theory (see the comments on **105**) about the apparently intractable problems this song poses for the improviser. In this performance — recorded, coincidentally, on the day of Buddy Bolden's death — Armstrong begins by disrupting the melody's rhythmic balance, goes on to a vocal chorus that scarcely impinges upon either the tune or words of the original, and concludes with a trumpet solo built around short phrases, a solo that develops in terms of itself rather than a Hoagy Carmichael's song.

Armstrong recorded the music to be found on **115** after spending the summer and autumn of 1932 in Europe. He also changed his record company, moving from OKeh to Victor. It is sometimes claimed that this shift, with a corresponding use of different recording acoustics, was responsible for the fact that the trumpeter's tone suddenly seems much fuller. Certainly that is the case in *That's my home*, a performance at once fiery and yet edged with grandeur. The band was Chick Webb's, playing with the accuracy to be expected from a regular ensemble of that stature; Green takes a nicely aggressive solo in *Hobo, you can't ride this train*. The *Medley of Armstrong hits* (originally issued as a twelve-inch 78 rpm disc) was recorded with a band under the leadership of Charlie Gaines, who can be heard playing distinctively lyrical obbligatos behind several of the vocal choruses. *St James' Infirmary* comes across as altogether more cheerful than Armstrong's original version (**48**), but the liveliest playing and singing occurs in the highly concentrated account of *Dinah*.

The group Armstrong worked with in Chicago in January 1933 was once again led by Randolph, yet it was generally superior to the one on **114**. This time it contained three quite exceptional musicians: Wilson, just at the start of his career and to be glimpsed fleetingly on the tracks included here, and the brothers Johnson, who both take worthwhile solos in *Some sweet day*. *High society* is a flurried attempt at performing what Armstrong refers to as 'one of them Creole arrangements', although the trumpeter's own performance is quite stunning: he leads the brass with great panache, then works up to a climax with a solo that always seems on the brink of dissolving into chaos, yet never does. The finest music, however, occurs in *I've got a right to sing the blues*, with a final chorus that is played in the upper register and which is technically startling yet aesthetically impeccable, a dazzling and at the same time curiously serene performance.   C.F.

116 Jazz in the 'Thirties
World Records (E) SHB39 (2 LPs)

Joe Venuti–Eddie Lang Blue Five: Jimmy Dorsey (tpt, clt, alt); Adrian Rollini (bs sx, gfs, p, vib); Venuti (vln); Phil Wall (p); Lang (g). New York City, 28 February 1933.
Ragging the scale · Hey young fella · Jigsaw puzzle blues · Pink elephants

Joe Venuti and His Blue Five: Dick McDonough (g) replaces Lang; Venuti doubles on bs[1], Rollini on kz[2]; Howard Phillips (vcl[3]) added. New York City, 8 May 1933.
Vibraphonia[1,2] · Hiawatha's lullaby[3]

Adrian Rollini and His Orchestra: Manny Klein (tpt); Tommy Dorsey (tbn); Benny Goodman (clt); Jimmy Dorsey (clt, alt); Arthur Rollini (ten); Adrian Rollini (bs sx, vib); Fulton McGrath (p); McDonough (g); Herb Weil (d); Phillips (vlc[3]); Irene Beasly (vcl[4]). New York City, 12 June 1933.
Blue prelude[3] · Mississippi Basin[4] · Charlie's home[3] · Happy as the day is long[3]

Joe Sullivan (p). New York City, 26 September 1933.
Honeysuckle rose · Gin mill blues · Little Rock getaway · Onyx bringdown

Joe Venuti and His Blue Six: Goodman (clt); Bud Freeman (ten); Adrian Rollini (bs sx); Venuti (vln); Sullivan (p); McDonough (g); Neil Marshall (d). New York City, 2 October 1933.
Sweet Lorraine · Doing the uptown lowdown · Jazz me blues · In de ruff

Benny Goodman and His Orchestra: Charlie Teagarden, Klein (tpt); Jack Teagarden (tbn, vcl); Goodman (clt); Art Karle (ten); Sullivan (p); McDonough (g); Artie Bernstein (bs); Gene Krupa (d); Arthur Schutt (arr). New York City, 18 October 1933.
I've got a right to sing the blues · Ain't cha glad?

Frank Froeba (p) replaces Sullivan. New York City, 27 October 1933.
Dr Heckle and Mr Jibe · Texas tea party

Joe Venuti and His Blue Four: Don Barrigo (ten); Venuti (vln); Arthur Young (p); Frank Victor (g); Doug Lees (bs). London, 20 September 1934.
Satan's holiday · Tea time · Hell's bells and hallelujah

Jess Stacy (p). Chicago, 16 November 1935.
In the dark · Flashes

Israel Crosby (bs), Krupa (d) added. Same date.
Barrelhouse · The world is waiting for the sunrise

Gene Krupa and His Chicagoans: Nate Kazebier (tpt); Joe Harris (tbn); Goodman (clt); Dick Clark (ten); Stacy (p); Allen Reuss (g); Crosby (bs); Krupa (d). Chicago, 19 November 1935.

The last round-up · Jazz me blues · Three little words · Blues of Israel

Bud Freeman and His Windy City Five: Bunny Berigan (tpt); Freeman (clt[5], ten); Claude Thornhill (p); Eddie Condon (g); Grachan Moncur (bs); Cozy Cole (d). New York City, 4 December 1935.

What is there to say? · The buzzard[5] · Tillie's downtown now · Keep smiling at trouble

Bunny Berigan and His Blue Boys: Berigan (tpt); Edgar Sampson (clt[6], alt); Eddie Miller (clt, ten); Cliff Jackson (p); Moncur (bs); Ray Bauduc (d). New York City, 13 December 1935.

You took advantage of me · Chicken and waffles[6] · I'm coming, Virginia · Blues

117 Benny Goodman: the Early Years Vol. 2
Sunbeam (A) SB139

Benny Goodman and His Orchestra: Charlie Teagarden, Shirley Clay (tpt); Jack Teagarden (tbn); Goodman (clt); Karle (ten); Sullivan (p); McDonough (g); Bernstein (bs); Krupa (d); Deane Kincaide (arr). New York City, 18 December 1933.

Love me or leave me · Why couldn't it be poor little me?

Klein, Charlie Margulis (tpt); Sonny Lee (tbn); Goodman (clt); Coleman Hawkins (ten); Schutt (p); McDonough (g); Bernstein (bs); Krupa (d); Mildred Bailey (vcl[7]). New York City, 2 February 1934.

Georgia jubilee · Junk man[7] (2 takes) · Old pappy[7] · Emaline[7]

Charlie Teagarden, George Thow (tpt); Jack Teagarden (tbn, vcl[8]); Goodman (clt); Hank Ross (ten); Teddy Wilson (p); Benny Martel (g); Bernstein (bs); Ray McKinley (d). New York City, 14 May 1934.

I ain't lazy[8] · As long as I live[8] · Moonglow · Breakfast ball

Russ Case, Jerry Neary, Sam Shapiro (tpt); Red Ballard, Jack Lacey (tbn); Goodman (clt, ten[9]); Hymie Schertzer, Ben Kantor (alt); Arthur Rollini (ten); Thornhill (p); George van Eps (g); Hank Weyland (bs); Sammy Weiss (d); Ann Graham (vcl[10]). New York City, 16 August 1934.

Take my word[9] · It happens to the best of friends[10] · Nitwit serenade · Bugle call rag (2 takes)

The sessions on **116**, mostly recorded for the British market during a period in which Americans were even less appreciative of jazz than usual, find the music growing in several directions. Typical are the new ensemble patterns of the Venuti–Lang date, which accommodate violin, vibraharp and bass saxophone as comfortably as trumpet or clarinet. Such features as the counterpoint between alto saxophone and violin towards the close of *Jigsaw puzzle blues* are as much to the point as the steadily inventive solos. Nor were these isolated endeavours, for the violin-led ensembles here and in Venuti's *Jazz me blues* or *Hell's* *bells and hallelujah* relate to textural explorations such as those of the Beiderbecke–Whiteman *San* (**65**). Also, the Blue Six instrumentation should be compared with that of Red Norvo's 1933 performances on **199** and the all-reed frontline of Reginald Foresythe's January 1935 New York session.

Goodman was present on most of these, and further instances of his musical curiosity are stylistic exercises like the Krupa date's *Last round-up*, a cowboy song done as a boogie piece; and, on **117**, *Nitwit serenade*, which proves to be a recomposition of King Oliver's *Dippermouth blues* (see **44**) done, if you please, in the Casa Loma idiom! This should, in fact, be compared with *Maniacs' ball* by the Casa Loma Band itself on Jazum (A) 32, although a parallel example is the Venuti–Lang updating of the ODJB's *Sensation* on **67**. Again on the outstanding Blue Six date, Goodman is involved with a less oblique version of *Dippermouth blues* called *In de ruff*, and the sense of adventure evident on such occasions was in a few years to lead him, though at the height of his fame as a swing band leader, towards recording Mozart and commissioning works from Bartók, Hindemith, Copland, Milhaud and other composers.

Doing the uptown lowdown has particularly incisive Venuti, and here Freeman, his efforts enhanced by Adrian Rollini's deeply plunging yet flexible bass line, reminds us, as he also does on *Sweet Lorraine*, that it was he and not Lester Young who first produced a significant alternative to Coleman Hawkins's approach to the tenor saxophone. On the 1935 session under his own leadership Freeman's dry, laconic phrases, on clarinet as well as tenor, provide an apt foil to Berigan's romanticism. This great trumpeter is heard on two dates, recorded nine days apart, and his every solo is concise, exactly to the point, notwithstanding a virtuosity that enables him to send phrases soaring complexly through the entire range of his instrument, their effect heightened by variety of timbre and attack, and a fine harmonic sense. Berigan's *Blues* should be equated with Krupa's *Blues of Israel*, two unadorned sequences of solos that make up communing performances wherein the participants seem to be playing for themselves rather than for us.

The piano solos composed by Bix Beiderbecke, *Flashes*, and *In the dark*, which Stacey interprets so perceptively, convey something of that feeling also. This musician took further some of their implications for the development of jazz in his later work, some of which is discussed on later pages (see **166**, **178** and **189**), yet above all in his long, meditative and perhaps admonitory solo on the otherwise garish *Sing, sing, sing* taken down at Goodman's

1938 Carnegie Hall concert (CBS (E) 66202), an instance of one man's blessed non-conformity that it would be hard to overpraise.

Solo Sullivan has always been in short supply, but his four 1933 pieces are admirable examples of his full-textured style (even if *Gin mill blues* borrows its introduction from the Whoopee Makers' 1929 *It's so good* on **73**) His playing was rooted in late-1920s Hines crossed with blues melody and the figurations of boogie and New York 'stride', yet it was always expressive of his own robust personality. Each of these solos, with their constantly varied incident, leaves a sense of completeness.

Both accounts of *Jazz me blues* include notable Goodman solos, and to the several dates under his own name he contributes aggressively leading clarinet playing of a particularly masterful kind. At several points his partnership with Jack Teagarden is renewed and they make music comparable to that recorded with Nichols on **70**, although, thanks to scores by Schutt and, on Sunbeam, by Kincaide, with a more decisive and hence clearer ensemble style. The trombonist's playing and singing rank with his very best on disc, and they are typified by the exquisitely lazy phrases thrown across the *Moonglow* ensembles; to this dialogue a third part is added by Wilson's racing piano, while Goodman's world-weary phrases and Charlie Teagarden's forthright blowing provide further contrasts. Wilson sounds more poised than with Armstrong on **115** the previous year, especially when he weaves round the ensemble as it accompanies Jack Teagarden's delightful singing on *As long as I live* and *I ain't lazy*.

Though Goodman is shown to have moved a stage nearer to the kind of big band with which he eventually would be identified, as heard on **141–143**, performances on **117** such as *Breakfast ball* also demonstrate the important contribution the Casa Loma Band made to swing (see **121**). Another identifying Goodman sound emerges, too, on the last Sunbeam date with Schertzer's lead playing, as in Benny Carter's four-part saxophone writing for *Take my word* (for further comments on this piece see **148**). The blistering yet previously unissued second take of *Bugle call rag*, besides being a fine instance of Goodman profiting from Casa Loma innovations, is also a remarkable anticipation of Basie's interlocking ensemble riffs (**133–135**). On other tracks, pleasures less predictable than Miss Bailey's singing include the telling accompaniment she receives from Schutt on *Emaline* and Klein's muted and effectively moody solos in *Georgia jubilee* and *Junk man*. On *Old pappy*, Hawkins's two solos are nicely positioned between the stomping and rhapsodic extremes of his style at that time.   M.H.

118 Featuring Jack Teagarden
MCA (E) MCFM2598

Johnny Mercer (vcl) acc Sterling Bose (tpt); Teagarden (tbn); Fulton McGrath (p); Dick McDonough (g); Hank Wayland (bs). New York City, 24 August 1934.

Lord, I give you my children · The bath tub ran over again

Adrian Rollini and His Orchestra: Manny Klein, Dave Klein (tpt); Teagarden (tbn); Benny Goodman (clt); Arthur Rollini (ten); Adrian Rollini (bs sx); Howard Smith (p); George van Eps (g); Artie Bernstein (bs); Stan King (d); New York City, 23 October 1934.

Sugar · Davenport blues · Somebody loves me · Riverboat shuffle

Dick Robertson and His Orchestra: Johnny McGee, Ralph Muzillo (tpt); Teagarden (tbn); Tony Zimmers (clt, ten); Frank Froeba (p); Dave Barbour (g); Haig Stephens (bs); Sammy Weiss (d); Robertson (vcl); New York City, 28 February 1938.

Goodnight, angel · Let's sail to dreamland · Drop a nickel in the slot · You went to my head

Teddy Grace (vcl) acc Teagarden (tbn); Billy Kyle (p); Barbour (g); Dalmar Kaplan (bs); O'Neill Spencer (d); New York City, 1 September 1938.

Love me or leave me · Downhearted blues · Crazy blues · Monday morning

Paul Whiteman and His Swing Wing: Charlie Teagarden (tpt); Jack Teagarden (tbn, vcl[1]); Sal Franzella (clt); Al Gallodoro (alt); Art Drellinger (ten); Walter Gross (p); Arthur Ryerson (g); Art Miller (bs); Rollo Laylan (d); Four Modernaires (vcl). New York City, 9 September 1938.

I'm coming, Virginia · Aunt Hagar's blues[1]

Paul Whiteman and His Orchestra: Bob Cusumano, Charlie Teagarden, Dan Moore (tpt); Jack Teagarden, José Gutierez (tbn); George Ford, Vincent Capone, Jack Bell (fl); Murray Cohen (ob); Franzella (clt, alt); Gallodoro (alt); Drellinger (ten); Roy Bargy (p); Ryerson (g); Miller (bs); Laylan (d). New York City, 20 September 1938.

My reverie · Heart and soul

Paul Whiteman and His Swing Wing: Cusumano, Charlie Teagarden (tpt); Jack Teagarden (tbn, vcl[1]); Franzella (clt, alt); Drellinger (ten); Frank Signorelli (p); Allan Reuss (g); Artie Shapiro (bs); George Wettling (d); Four Modernaires, Joan Edwards (vcl[2]). New York City, 8 December 1938.

Mutiny in the nursery[2] · Jeepers creepers[1]

As far as jazz is concerned, authenticity resides in the performer rather than his material, in the soloist not the setting, a proposition made abundantly plain by this LP, on which Jack Teagarden, one of the genuinely original voices of jazz, can be heard preserving his identity within what seem to be desperately uncongenial surroundings. Yet that might be to misunderstand the situation, for he was not a man to grumble about commercial restrictions. He worked with plenty of small jazz groups, but long stretches of his career were spent in the trombone sections of dance and show bands of the 1920s and 1930s. From December 1933 until December 1938, for instance, a time-span which includes all the sessions on this LP, he was a member of Whiteman's orchestra. The two performances by that ensemble — *Heart and soul* and Larry Clinton's *My reverie*, which sends Debussy clip-clopping off into the West — are of no jazz interest whatever, with Teagarden restricted to playing just the first trombone part. Whiteman's Swing Wing promises more yet offers cute arrangements (often with a quasi-dixieland flavour) and a vocal quartet, The Modernaires, who later defected to Glenn Miller. Yet Teagarden sings and plays potently enough in *Aunt Hagar's blues* and pops up more briefly elsewhere, as does his brother Charlie, a trumpeter of rare quality who deserved better — artistically, if not financially — than to become a session man.

Session men of a lesser calibre, clean and competent but unshakably derivative — the clarinet sounds like Goodman, the trumpet is sub-Berigan — take up most of the space on Robertson's tracks. Robertson, a freelance singer, undistinguished yet likeable, usually contrived to have some sort of jazz going on in the background. Unhappily, he was often saddled with second-rate songs, like the four here. But Teagarden's authority never seems to be diminished, even if he had only fifty-six bars to spread over the entire session. The velvety sound, the faintly lackadaisical phrasing, that taste for inserting curlicues and other decorative minutiae, even the fondness for well-loved routines: these surface even more defiantly on the performances with Teddy Grace, a singer who later worked with Bob Crosby's orchestra before sliding into obscurity. Like many white girls of her generation, she tried too hard in the blues, sounding energetic rather than emotional (her falsetto chirrup also becomes irritating); apart from the more casual *Monday morning*, the singing now sounds dated. But Teagarden's solos and obbligatos continue to rank among his finest performances on record, typical in the way he elaborates what basically is very simple material. (Billy Kyle seems to have been present strictly to make up the numbers; he takes no proper solos and even drops out of character by including a ginmill-style passage.).

The earlier tracks are mixed in quality. Mercer sings a mock-gospel number, full of exhortations for 'Brother Fiji McGrath' and the other musicians to step up front for solos, but *The bath tub ran over again* is inconsequential. Adrian Rollini, on the other hand, customarily provides something of interest. His playing of theme statements here is impeccable and resourceful, but a suggestion of artiness spoils the arrangements played by his little orchestra. The best performance is of *Riverboat shuffle*, with both Goodman and Teagarden in exuberant form. Yet in their way every one of these items apart from the two by the full Whiteman band attest to the palpability of Teagarden's music, the way a soloist of his stature merely has to play in order to survive.   C.F.

Joe Venuti

119 **Nothing But Notes**
MCA Coral (G) 622184

Eddie Lang–Joe Venuti All-Star Orchestra: Charlie Teagarden (tpt); Jack Teagarden (tbn, vcl); Benny Goodman (clt); Venuti (vln); Frank Signorelli (p); Lang (g); Ward Ley (bs); Neil Marshall (d). New York City, 22 October 1931.
Beale Street blues · After you've gone · Farewell blues · Someday, sweetheart

Joe Venuti and His Blue Five: Arthur Rollini (clt, ten); Adrian Rollini (bar, vib); Venuti (vln); Fulton McGrath (p); Frank Victor (g); Vic Angle (d). New York City, 20 March 1935.
Mellow as a cello · Mystery · Send me · Vibraphonia No. 2 · Nothing but notes · Tap room blues

Joe Venuti and His Orchestra: Bob Stockwell, Glenn Rohlfing (tpt); Charles Dahlsten (tbn); Wayne Songer, Charles Spero (alt); Elmer Beechler, Clark Galehouse (ten); Venuti (vln); Mel Grant (p); Victor (g); George Norvath (bs); Barrett Deems (d). New York City, 25 January 1939.
Flip · Something · Flop · Nothing

Although no longer widely recognized as such, the Lang–Venuti date is one of the great jazz recording sessions. Its four titles should be heard in conjunction with those made under the guitarist's name in May 1929 on **66**. Admirable though the Dorseys are there, Jack Teagarden and Goodman are deeper talents and this later music has greater expressive power. It relates to their 1933–4 collaborations on **116–117** and, like them, demonstrates the extraordinary consistency of Teagarden's playing and singing during these years. However, the point here is that the other participants attained a comparable standard, and he is less the star virtuoso, more a member of the band. On *Farewell blues*, for example, Venuti and Goodman play two of the best solos which they had thus far recorded, as does Charlie Teagarden on *After you've gone*. The casual mastery of the solos — Goodman's, again, after the *Beale Street* vocal, for instance — is deceptive, and their combined directness and concentration is matched with beautifully articulated ensembles. An interesting feature is the contrast between intimate textures, such as the Venuti–Lang sequence on *Beale Street* or the passage led by Goodman at the start of *After you've gone*, and the more stringent music for full ensemble.

Someday, sweetheart, too, foreshadows the swing era's quieter music, and the Blue Five session, with Adrian Rollini's vibraharp, provides ample precedents for the sound of Goodman's early small groups (his first quartet date, with Hampton, occurring seventeen months later — see **158**). The ensembles are quite richly detailed and most of the instrumental combinations made available by the Rollini brothers' doubling are used, instances being the counterpoint between violin and baritone on *Mystery*, and the alternations between tenor and baritone or clarinet and violin in *Send me*. Adrian Rollini's mastery of both vibraharp and baritone (instead of his usual bass saxophone) consolidates his already impregnable position as the premier multi-instrumentalist of jazz. His *Vibraphonia* solo is especially fine and here, also, his brother Arthur, a less strong musical character, achieves his best improvisation of the session, on clarinet. Adrian Rollini devised a more coherent style of accompaniment on the vibraharp than anybody else before Teddy Charles. Most of the themes are by him, also.

The Blue Five date caught some of Venuti's most characteristic playing of the period, though hardly his most celebrated. A main issue of the 1939 session is that he finds a variety of paths through the seemingly alien textures of the large ensemble. Here the themes are his own, the first three of them of strong melodic substance (the last is aptly named). It is a pity that the — in both senses — anonymous arranger could think of nothing better than to run through the standardized procedures of swing band scoring. Deems, playing far better than in his days with Armstrong's All-Stars, imparts some life to the proceedings, but they are considerably less distinguished than performances such as *Everybody shuffle* and *Moonglow* which Venuti recorded with a similar instrumentation in 1933 (RCA (F) FPM 17016).   M.H.

120   Ted Lewis's Orchestra
Biograph (A) BLP-C7

Ted Lewis and His Band: Dave Klein, Walter Kahn (cnt); George Brunies, Harry Raderman (tbn); Lewis (clt, alt, vcl); Sol Solinsky (vln); Frank Ross (p); Tony Gerhardi (bj, g); Bob Escamillo (tu); John Lucas (d); New York City, 22 November 1926.
When my baby smiles at me

Sol Klein (vln) replaces Solinsky; Don Murray (clt, bar) added. New York City, 16 July 1928.
Clarinet marmalade

Muggsy Spanier (cnt), Jack Aaronson (p), Harry Barth (tu, bs) replace Kahn, Ross, Escamillo. Los Angeles, 4 June 1929.
Lewisada blues

Jimmy Dorsey (clt, alt, bar) replaces Murray; Four Dusty Travellers (vcl) added. New York City, 10 January 1930.
Lonesome road

Four Dusty Travellers absent. New York City, 20 January 1930.
Aunt Hagar's blues

Same personnel and location, 18 April 1930.
Yellow dog blues

Same personnel and location, 24 April 1930.
Sobbing blues

Sam Blank (tbn); Benny Goodman (clt, alt); Fats Waller (p, vcl) replace Raderman, Dorsey, Aaronson; Louis Martin (alt, bar); Hymie Woolfson (ten); Sam Shapiro (vln) added. New York City, 5/6 March 1931.
Egyptian Elle · *Dallas blues*

Sol Klein, Shapiro absent. Same date.
I'm crazy about my baby · *Royal Garden blues*

Aaronson (p) replaces Waller; Sol Klein, Shapiro (vln) added. New York City, 13 April 1931.
Dip your brush in sunshine

Same personnel and location, 16 March 1932.
Sweet Sue · *Somebody loves you*

Slats Long (clt, ten) replaces Goodman. New York City, 19 April 1933.
The gold-diggers' song

Same personnel and location, 22 June 1933.
Rhythm

The French surrealist Robert Desnos once wrote that 'Ted Lewis, the King of Jazz, is never tiresome', but agreement about this has never been universal [49]. Erupting on most tracks, his vocal performances, with their laboriously homespun sentiments, sound horribly sincere. They warn us of the temptations moonlight can bring, extol the power of positive thinking ('think happy!'), and the remedial capacities of babies' smiles and of sunshine; their failure to mention mom's apple pie must be regarded as an oversight.

Yet among all this rubbish is a quantity of fine jazz which necessitated the inclusion in this book of a selection of Lewis recordings; indeed, Brunies's and particularly Spanier's appearances rank with their best work on disc. There is expressive blues playing from both of them, and from Dorsey on clarinet and alto, in *Aunt Hagar's blues*, while Dorsey, pointedly agile on clarinet and sober on baritone, virtually dominates *Yellow dog blues*. It is instructive to set performances like these beside his *Praying the blues* on **66**. The relaxed atmosphere here and on *Sobbing blues*, which is of similar quality, is typical, Lewis's hokum notwithstanding, and *Lonesome road*, done as a soporific revivalist meeting, suggests the man had a sense of humour. Again Spanier is prominent, and he is also heard at length in *The gold-diggers' song*. Fierce cornet and clarinet solos provide a welcome counterbalance on *Dip your brush in sunshine*, a typical Lewis title and performance, while Goodman alone, more elegant but still incisive, fulfils the same function in *Sweet Sue*.

There is an excellent sequence by Spanier, Goodman and Brunies on *Somebody loves you*, and in fact some of these items, particularly those recorded in March 1931, were done virtually as straight jazz performances, the leader's corn being thrust almost entirely aside. Nowhere is this more the case than during the *Royal Garden blues* improvisations of Goodman, Waller and Spanier, and on all four tracks Waller gives a masterful display of his powers as a band pianist. A solo from Brunies and deft ensemble clarinet by Murray lighten the effect of a dull collective performance on *Clarinet marmalade*, but such relief emphasizes that the orchestral writing, clearly a matter of no interest to Lewis, is the veriest hack work, a ragbag of the obvious. The borrowings from Ellington's *Black and tan fantasy* on *Lewisada blues* bore no fruit, although the leader's own clarinet playing on this does raise, if not at all insistently, the question of just how deliberate was the banality of his instrumental contributions elsewhere. Certainly we must regret that this anthology omits *Ho hum*, during a Goodman solo on which Lewis cries 'Play it, Ted!'.

M.H.

121 The Casa Loma Band
Bandstand (A) 7126

Glen Gray and the Original Casa Loma Band: Joe Hostetter, Frank Martinez, Bobby Jones (tpt); Pee Wee Hunt (tbn, vcl[1]); Billy Rauch (tbn); Gray, Ray Eberle (alt); Pat Davis (ten); Mel Jenssen (vln); Joe Hall (p); Gene Gifford (bj, g, arr); Stanley Dennis (bs); Tony Briglia (d). New York City, 11 February 1930.
San Sue strut

Kenny Sargent (ten, vcl[2]) replaces Eberle; Clarence Hutchenrider (clt, alt) added. New York City, 17 May 1932.
I never knew

Same personnel and location, 13 June 1932.
Indiana

Same personnel and location, 19 December 1932.
The lady from St Paul[1]

Same personnel and location, 31 January 1933.
Blue prelude · Wild goose chase
Same personnel and location, 30 December 1933.
I got rhythm
Same personnel and location, 9 May 1934.
Milneburg joys
Same personnel and location, 29 June 1934.
You ain't been living right[1]
Grady Watts (tpt), Sonny Dunham (tpt, tbn, arr) replace Martinez, Hostetter; Jack Blanchette (g) replaces Gifford, who continues arranging. New York City, 19 July 1934.
Moonglow[2]
Same personnel and location, 16 August 1934.
Corinne Corrina
Fritz Hummel (tbn), Art Ralston (alt, ob, bsn) added. New York City, 6 February 1935.
Who's sorry now?
Same personnel and location, 20 February 1935.
My dance[2]
Same personnel and location, 10 June 1936.
Bugle call rag

The Casa Loma Band's sentimental ballad recordings such as *Moonglow* were immensely popular, and the appeal of Sargent's singing, as in *My dance*, is still not altogether faded. But this group's jazz value lay in quite another direction and they struck their most original vein early on. This yielded generally fast instrumental pieces, typified by *White jazz, Black jazz* and *Maniacs' ball* (all dating from 1931, all on Jazum (A) 32), which marked a fresh orchestral departure. Virtually they are antimelodic as they depend on skilled deployment of riffs, elevated to a consistent method of ensemble writing. Whereas Ellington, say, was preoccupied with colour and texture, Gifford sought effects of line, mass, opposing pattern.

Played with headlong drive, *San Sue strut* is also representative, tension being increased relentlessly because each idea is slightly more propulsive than the last. A precise interlock between playing and writing explains the feeling of continuity which this music powerfully imposes, the performances being terse celebrations of ensemble virtuosity, as demonstrated by the saxes on *San Sue strut*, the trombones on *Bugle call rag* and the whole band in the tightly-concerted charge which brings *Corrine Corrina* to its precipitate yet exactly judged ending. These headlong interpretations demanded long rehearsal, but a fiery spontaneity is preserved. One can go further and say that by a paradox only possible in music and rarely exploited in jazz, such pieces sound both frantic and strictly controlled.

Shorn of any superfluous note, the scores' resulting austerity may partially have accounted for the band's consistently bad press [50]. Yet Gifford's writing embodied real discoveries and was strongly influential, particularly on bands more highly rated. Deeply in the Casa Loma shadow are Hines's 1932 *Sensational mood*, the Blue Rhythm Band's 1933 *Jazz martini* (Gaps (H) 110), and Lunceford's *White heat* (RCA (F) 741.045), Henderson's *Tidal wave* (**127**) and Goodman's *Cokey* (Nostalgia (A) CSM890/1), all of 1934. As with other original writers for the jazz ensemble, Gifford's procedures work best on his own material, but the elemental four-note theme of *I got rhythm* well suited him, while *Milneburg joys* is convincingly updated. His method was capable, too, of such things as the curious opposition of moods in *Wild goose chase*, where the character of the riffs changes after the passage topped by Hutchenrider's trill.

Blue prelude, sombre and richly varied, is unusual for this band, yet it emphasizes the singularity of the clarinettist's phrasing. Like Gifford, Hutchenrider seems to have contracted few debts elsewhere, and the personal quality of his ideas is confirmed on most of these tracks. Jones's solos, as on *Indiana*, represent, too, an individual line of endeavour, and *You ain't been living right* is one of many performances suggesting that Briglia is a seriously underrated drummer.

Not that this selection is ideal. It would have gained from the substitution of *Casa Loma stomp, Blue jazz, Nocturne* and the two-part *No-name jive*, possibly the band's masterpiece. Here, as in all the Casa Loma's finest performances, there is no compromise.

M.H.

122 Riding in Rhythm
World Records (E) SHB42 (2 LPs),
Prestige (A) 7643 and 7645

Duke Ellington and His Orchestra: Arthur Whetsol, Freddy Jenkins, Cootie Williams (tpt); Joe Nanton, Lawrence Brown (tbn); Juan Tizol (v-tbn); Harry Carney (clt, alt, bar); Barney Bigard (clt, ten); Johnny Hodges (sop, alt); Otto Hardwicke (alt, bs sx); Ellington (p); Fred Guy (g); Wellman Braud (bs); Sonny Greer (d); Ivie Anderson (vcl[1]). New York City, 15 February 1933.
*Merry-go-round · Sophisticated lady · I've got the world on a string[1].
Down a Carolina lane*

Mills Blue Rhythm Band: Wardell Jones, Shelton Hemphill, Ed Anderson, Eddie Mallory (tpt); George Washington, Henry Hicks (tbn); Gene Mikell (clt, alt); Joe Garland (clt, ten, bar, arr[2]); Crawford Wethington (alt, bar); Edgar Hayes (p, arr[3]); Benny James (g); Ernest Hill (bs); O'Neill Spencer (d); New York City, 1 March 1933.
Riding in rhythm[2] · Weary traveller[3] · Buddy's Wednesday outing

Benny Carter and His Orchestra: Shad Collins, Leonard Davies, Bill Dillard (tpt); Washington, Wilbur DeParis (tbn); Carter (clt, alt, tpt, arr, vcl[4]); Howard Johnson (alt); Chew Berry (ten); Rod Rodriguez (p); Lawrence Lucie (g); Hill (bs); Sidney Catlett (d); New York City, 14 March 1933.
Swing it[4] · Synthetic love · Six Bells stampede · Love, you're not the one for me[4]

Fletcher Henderson and His Orchestra: Henry Allen (tpt, vcl[5]); Russell Smith, Bobby Stark (tpt); Claude Jones, Dicky Wells (tbn); Russell Procope (clt, alt); Hilton Jefferson (alt); Coleman Hawkins (ten); Horace Henderson (p, arr[6]); Bernard Addison (g); John Kirby (bs); Walter Johnson (d); Fletcher Henderson (arr[7]); Will Hudson (arr[8]). New York City, 22 September 1933.
Queer notions[6] · It's the talk of the town[7] · Night life[8] · Nagasaki[5]

Coleman Hawkins and His Orchestra: Allen (tpt); J. C. Higginbotham (tbn); Jefferson (clt[9], alt); Hawkins (ten); Horace Henderson (p, arr[6]); Addison (g); Kirby (bs); Johnson (d). New York City, 29 September 1933.
The day you came along[9] · Jamaica shout[6] · Heartbreak blues

Horace Henderson and His Orchestra: Personnel as for 22 September. New York City, 3 October 1933.
Happy feet · I'm rhythm crazy now[6] · Old man river[5] · The anniversary of Minnie the Moocher's wedding day · Ain'tcha glad?[6] · I've got to sing a torch song

Benny Carter and His Orchestra: Mallory, Dillard, Dick Clark (tpt); Higginbotham, Fred Robinson, Keg Johnson (tbn); Carter (clt, alt, arr); Wayman Carver (alt, fl); Glyn Pacque (alt); Johnny Russell (ten); Teddy Wilson (p); Lucie (g); Hill (bs); Catlett (d). New York City, 16 October 1933.
Devil's holiday · Lonesome nights · Symphony in riffs · Blue Lou

Hawkins (ten); Buck Washington (p). New York City, 8 March 1934.
It sends me · I ain't got nobody · On the sunny side of the street

Hawkins absent. Same date.
Old fashioned love

Hawkins (ten); Stanley Black (p). London, 18 November 1934.
Lost in a fog · Honeysuckle rose

Albert Harris (g); Tiny Winters (bs) added. Same date.
Lullaby · Oh, lady be good

Meade Lux Lewis (p). Chicago, 20 December 1935.
Honky tonk train blues

Jack Hylton and His Orchestra featuring Coleman Hawkins: George Swift, Stan Roderick, Stanley Howard (tpt); Woolf Phillips, Jack Bentley (tbn); Benny Daniels, Leslie Gilbert (clt, alt); Freddy Schweitzer, Joe Crossman (clt, ten); Hawkins, Billy Ternent (ten); André Budegary, Reg Cole, Les Maddox (vln); Billy Hill (p); Al Thomas, Ulrich Neumann (g); Bruce Trent (bs); Lew Stevenson (d); Fletcher Henderson (arr). London, 26 May 1939.

Darktown strutters' ball · *My melancholy baby*

The most obvious link between the majority of these varied items is that they were recorded in 1933. Only the second Carter session, the Lewis piano solo, and Hawkins's recordings with Washington and in London came later. But there are more important links, comparisons and developments to be noted within a rather arbitrary selection of performances typifying a period of change at the start of the so-called swing era. The big-band tracks provide an opportunity to compare the styles of orchestration that were being essayed. The influence of Fletcher Henderson was strong, as creator or catalyst, even having its effect on the earlier progress of Ellington.

These Ellington tracks show the emergence of a completely distinctive harmonic voice. *Merry-go-round* (of which a later version appears on **131a**) arrests the ear with a rich yet astringent ensemble sound — an effect achieved by tonal juxtapositions that were daring at the time and scarcely surpassed even in the supposedly revolutionary days of bop and cool jazz. Chords wherein alto or clarinet would emphasize the flattened seventh against the tonic of muted trumpets, daringly positioned seconds and what sound like whole-tone descending phrases — these are devices which invited speculation about European borrowings, yet all of them can be accounted for within Ellington's personal response to the blues, and the germ of such ideas was in his own piano playing. Having said that, one admits that his keyboard essays in *Sophisticated lady* and *Down a Carolina lane* are both heavy and florid; and not all the orchestral writing is of such a distinguished order. Bigard's expanding role, not only as a soloist but also as an individual contributor to the ensemble textures, needs special mention.

The eleven tracks by the Henderson orchestra (whether Fletcher- or Horace-led) approach the standard of the excellent music in **127**, but they are not as consistently assured. Some of the most attractive writing is almost incidental, like the deft, rhythm-augmenting saxophone phrases beneath Allen's voice and horn on *Nagasaki*. Allen and Hawkins are the dominating soloists throughout, and the tenorist's lovely solo redeems the leaden dance band arrangement of *It's the talk of the town*.

Garland and Hayes are the identifiable arrangers for the commendable Blue Rhythm Band, and the former's treatment of *Riding in rhythm* shows panache, especially in the brass lines. Hayes's *Weary traveller* score does little to make more acceptable the mock 'Negro spiritual' modishness of the theme, while *Buddy's Wednesday outing* could be a Garland arrangement and includes an *Eel*-ish baritone solo by Wethington; it finds a better ensemble balance than the first piece.

Both Carter sessions reveal some of the strengths and weaknesses of this versatile musician's arranging style. *Swing it* and *Six Bells stampede* are better than the slow pieces for showing his singular gift for creating alternative melodies in the section writing. Something of his individual prowess on trumpet and saxophone (he introduces *Synthetic love* on the trumpet) shows in such scoring, but his pre-eminence as an alto stylist may be reflected in his greater success in writing for reeds. No one gets much chance for lengthy solo expression. Berry is heard to best advantage in *Six Bells stampede*, and it is ironic that Carter's best solo from this set serves chiefly to relieve the lugubriosity of *Love, you're not the one for me*, which also has one of several of the leader's vocal attempts to emulate Bing Crosby.

The 1934 Carters have a more lively and cohesive spirit. A good deal of the lift is due to the young Wilson, the best ensemble pianist in this whole collection, who is given his only full-chorus solo on the mid-tempo *Blue Lou*. *Devil's holiday* (one of Carter's best from a peak period), *Symphony in riffs* and *Blue Lou* all ride lightly upon Catlett's marvellous drumming, the most frequent soloists being Mallory, Higginbotham, Russell and Wilson. *Devil's holiday* has the added distinction of a quirky flute solo by Carver.

All to some degree marked by the self-consciousness of the 'rhythm' craze, these large ensemble performances hint at a vocabulary which some bands were to exploit beyond the threshold of tedium, and also at an increasing regimentation of soloists. Ellington would develop the co-operative spirit whilst virtuoso leaders and fashionable arrangers dominated elsewhere. And only those bands where solo creativity was honoured would keep the door open to genuine development.

Allen and Hawkins frequently bid fair to burst the seams of even the most congenial orchestral suit, and the freedom which Hawkins claims for himself and his companions in the September 1933 small band session — three numbers uniformly excellent — and with the small groups recorded in 1934 makes possible the finest jazz in this album. Sometimes the freedom is exercised in spite of its supposed abettors. Washington (better known as part of a dancing team, Buck and Bubbles) is a pianistic amalgam of Waller and Hines but has no real accompanying skill, so that his playing, especially in *It sends me* and *On the sunny side of the street*, sounds detached, as though played in another room. There is a suitable sophistication, if little originality, in Black's support for Hawkins, who is more relaxed here than with Washington. The two numbers played with the large and enthusiastic Hylton outfit, using Henderson scores, may serve as a small supplement to this book's chapter on Jazz in Europe.

Finally, *Honky tonk train blues* — a slightly later version than, though formally identical with, that heard on **169**, where the special characteristics and stylistic influence of boogie woogie are dealt with. It is an odd inclusion here, though perhaps justified as another sound beguiling the rhythm-conscious ear in the 1930s. All that can be said about it in this context is that whilst this fine, powerful blues may have inspired jazz emulations elsewhere, nothing even remotely like it can be heard in the groups represented here. E.T.

123 Big Bands Uptown
Decca (A) DL79242, *MCA (F) 510.070

Don Redman and His Orchestra: Langston Curl, Leonard Davies, Henry Allen (tpt); Claude Jones, Fred Robinson, Benny Morton (tbn); Edward Inge, Rupert Cole (clt, alt); Redman (clt, alt, arr, vcl[1]); Robert Carroll (ten); Horace Henderson (p); Talcott Reeves (bj); Bob Ysaguire (bs); Manzie Johnson (d); Lois Deppe (vcl[2]). New York City, 24 September 1931.
Chant of the weed · *Trouble, why pick on me*[2]
Same personnel and location, 15 October 1931.
Shaking the African[1] · *I heard*[1]

Claude Hopkins and His Orchestra: Albert Snaer, Sylvester Lewis (tpt); Ovie Alston (tpt, vcl[3]); Fernando Arbello (tbn); Fred Norman (tbn, arr); Ed Hall (clt, alt, bar); Gene Johnson (alt); Bobby Sands (ten); Hopkins (p); Walter Jones (g); Henry Turner (bs); Pete Jacobs (d). New York City, 14 September 1934.
Chasing all the blues away[3] · *King Porter stomp*
Same personnel and location, 22 October 1934.
Monkey business · *Zozoi*

Benny Carter and His Orchestra: Russell Smith, Bill Coleman, Shad Collins (tpt); Sandy Williams, Milt Robinson (tbn); Carter (clt, alt); George Dorsey, Carl Frye (alt); Stafford Simon, Sammy Davis (ten); Sonny White (p); Ulysses Livingstone (g); Hayes Alvis (bs); Keg Purnell (d). New York City, 20 May 1940.
Night hop · *Pom-pom* · *Okay for baby* · *Serenade to a sarong*

Lucky Millinder and His Orchestra: William Scott, Archie Johnson, Nelson Bryant (tpt); George Stevenson, Floyd Brady, Ed Morant (tbn); George James, Ted Barnet (alt); Simon (ten); Ernest Purce (bar); Bill Doggett (p); Trevor Bacon (g); Abe Bolar (bs); Panama Francis (d). New York City, 5 September 1941.

Apollo jump

Dizzy Gillespie (tpt), Joe Britton (tbn), Tab Smith, Billy Bowen (alt), Nick Fenton (bs) replace Johnson, Brady, James, Barnet, Bolar; Dave Young (ten) added; Morant absent. New York City, 29 July 1942.

Mason flyer · *Little John special*

Milton Fletcher, Joe Guy, Ludwig Jordan (tpt), Sam Taylor, Mike Hedley (ten), Ray Tunia (p), George Duvivier (bs) replace Scott, Gillespie, Bryant, Stafford Simon, Young, Doggett, Fenton; Frank Humphries (tpt), Gene Simon (tbn) added. New York City, 19 October 1943.

Shipyard social function

Frankly, the main points of interest here are *Chant of the weed*, recognized on its appearance as an exceptional piece, and Gillespie's solo on *Little John special*. Redman's never fully realized potential as a composer is evident in the former, and its mood of subdued aggression was unusual in jazz at that time, although the angular, whole-tone lines typify ideas that had for some years circulated in advanced jazz circles — e.g. *Brown sugar* recorded by Doc Cooke in 1926 (VJM (E) VLP27) and by the Red Heads (Phillips (E) BBL7434). It is instructive to set the two versions of *Chant of the weed* beside the two versions of Ellington's *Creole rhapsody*, the other outstanding jazz composition of 1931 (**88** and **90**). The second recording of Redman's piece, actually done in 1932, was issued as by Harlan Lattimore's Connie's Inn Orchestra (Columbia (A) C3L–33) and has a mistakenly slacker tempo which allows much of the score's nervous vitality to evaporate. Indeed, it says something about the different gifts of the two men that whereas Ellington used the opportunity of a second recording greatly to improve his piece, Redman did the opposite. The original *Chant of the weed* remains, however, one of the classics of recorded jazz.

Although Allen offers pleasingly dramatic and elaborate passages in *Trouble, why pick on me?* and *Shaking the African*, solos are more prominent, if often too short, in Hopkins's persistently neglected band. In particular, Hall on clarinet plays an earlier version of the *King Porter stomp* solo which he repeated under Zutty Singleton's leadership on **230**, and is excellent in *Chasing all the blues away* on baritone saxophone. The scores, mainly by Norman, are not distinctive but this band plays with a light and insistent swing.

With a personnel substantially different from that of his 1940 session discussed under **149**, Carter employs the conventions of his time yet does so in an individual way. He produces as personal a sound on clarinet as on alto saxophone, and there is some good trumpeting from Collins in *Pom-pom* and *Night hop*, and from Coleman in *Okay for baby*. It should be noted, however, that later in the year Jimmy Lunceford's band, using a Lonnie Wilfong arrangement, made a more impressive recording of this last item.

Millinder's group is a later edition of Mills's Blue Rhythm Band (see **122**) and, though recorded soon after Carter's pieces, the harder ensemble sound of this music indicates that it belongs to another phase of jazz. Mainly these are jivey riff affairs, yet Stafford Simon is heard to better advantage than with Carter, and the solo trumpet on *Apollo jump*, presumably by Johnson, is excellently integrated with the ensemble. There is a good Guy solo in *Shipyard social function*, and Smith blows with both power and sweetness on *Mason flyer* and *Little John special* (not to be confused with Fletcher Henderson's *Big John special*). Gillespie's contributions to these two make them more relevant to Chapter 8 than to this one, but it is on *Little John special* that he gives the clearer indication of things to come. Of course, his beautiful solo on this piece was at the time greeted with much consternation [51].   M.H.

124 Don Redman
CBS Realm (E) 52539

Don Redman and His Orchestra: Langston Curl, Shirley Clay, Sidney DeParis (tpt); Claude Jones (tbn, vcl¹); Fred Robinson, Benny Morton (tbn); Redman (clt, sop, alt, vcl²); Edward Inge (clt, alt); Rupert Cole (alt); Robert Carroll (ten); Horace Henderson (p); Talcott Reeves (bj, g); Bob Ysaguirre (tu, bs); Manzie Johnson (d). New York City, 26 February 1932.
*How'm I doin'? hey, hey?*²

Quentin Jackson (tbn) replaces Robinson. New York City, 6 June 1932.
*Hot and anxious*²

Harlan Lattimore (vcl³) added. New York City, 17 June 1932.
*I heard*²³ · *Reefer man*¹

Same personnel and location, 30 June 1932.
*Tea for two*³ · *I got rhythm*

Same personnel and location, 6 October 1932.
*Nagasaki*²

Don Kirkpatrick (p) replaces Henderson. New York City, 26 April 1933.
Sophisticated lady · *That blue-eyed baby from Memphis*³

Gene Simon (tbn) replaces Jones. New York City, 20 October 1933.
*That Dallas man*²

Henry Allen (tpt) replaces Curl; Jerry Blake (clt, bar) added. New York City, 9 January 1934.
Got the jitters[2]
Reunald Jones, Harold Baker, Otis Johnson (tpt); Jackson, Simon, Morton (tbn); Redman (clt, sop, alt); Inge (clt, alt); Cole (alt); Harvey Boone (alt, bar); Carroll (ten); Kirkpatrick (p); Clarence Holiday (g); Ysaguirre (bs); Sidney Catlett (d). New York City, 30 September 1936.
Bugle call rag
Gene Porter (ten), Bob Lessey (g) replace Carroll, Holiday. New York City, 28 May 1937.
Sweet Sue · *Exactly like you* · *On the sunny side of the street* · *Swinging with the fat man*

Just as horses are supposed to be picked for courses, so Redman devised arrangements which suited the particular styles of the bands for which he was writing. When he started his own orchestra in 1931, the music it played differed considerably from what he had been providing for Fletcher Henderson's band or McKinney's Cotton Pickers. Instead of the studied formality of those earlier scores, Redman's arrangements now set out to explore the timbres of his saxophone section, the textures to be drawn from mixing brass with reeds. The outstanding composition in this new style was *Chant of the weed*, discussed under **123** and setting out, just as Ellington did in *Creole rhapsody*, to use soloists as part of a larger orchestral entity. There are, as it happens, no out-and-out jazz solos at all in *How'm I doin'?*, on which Redman lavished some of his tightest and most delicate scoring (with a clarinet trio towards the end recalling a Henderson tradition that was largely Redman's creation). And his singing — whimsical, a soft-voiced recitation more than anything else — was to become part of the band's commercial appeal, as were the very different vocal contributions of Harlan Lattimore, an admirer, sometimes a frank imitator, of Bing Crosby, whose crooning had just become all the rage.

Not that the band was short of soloists. In Morton it possessed one of the most original jazz trombonists, his phrasing deceptively hesitant, while the clarinettist, Inge, a Kansas City musician, could soar against the brass, rather as Bigard did with Ellington, but also take solos which had a bitter edge to them. Yet the solos — on Redman's records, anyway — tended to be short, slotting inside the orchestration. An exception is *I got rhythm*, where Morton takes a full chorus (one of his finest recorded performances, beginning with the repetition of a single note, then expanding melodically and rhythmically) and Inge also contributes an outstanding solo. Redman wrote all the scores included on this LP except *Hot and anxious* (Horace Henderson), *That Dallas man* (Kirkpatrick) and *Swinging with the fat man*, a 'head' arrangement by the band of 1937. The present writer's copy of the 1938 edition of Charles Delaunay's *Hot Discography* contains a pencilled note implying that *Tea for two* was arranged by the British-born composer and bandleader, Reginald Foresythe. Foresythe was actually in America at the time — and writing for the Earl Hines and Paul Whiteman orchestras — but the musical evidence is far from conclusive: the overall sound is Redman's, especially the phrasing of the saxophones, yet some details of the orchestration are uncharacteristic. There is, on the other hand, no doubt about Redman's authorship of the arrangement of *Sophisticated lady*, far more interesting than Ellington's own recording of two months earlier (but then so was Jimmy Lunceford's version), while *That blue-eyed baby from Memphis*, although it features Lattimore's singing, is one of the band's most relaxed performances, with good solo playing from Inge and DeParis.

Redman's methods fell somewhere between Ellington's involvement of the total ensemble and Benny Carter's fondness for using one section at a time. He often used saxophones to state a theme, then counterpointed it with trombones and trumpets, but in a fashion much more intricate than the to-and-fro that went on in the Henderson band. That, at any rate, was the approach on most recordings up to 1934. The later pe.?ormances disappoint, relying too much upon clichés of the swing era. Any band with Catlett as its drummer was bound to possess some verve; and there are bright solos from Baker and Morton in an otherwise much too showy *Bugle call rag*. But these later tracks reflect a lack of commitment — and a resort to contrivance (*Sweet Sue* is embarrassingly pretentious) that Redman would have been quick to reject in earlier times.   C.F.

125 Chick Webb Vol. 1: A Legend 1929–36
MCA (F) 510.014, MCA (A) 1303

The Jungle Band: Ward Pinkett (tpt, vcl[1]); Edwin Swayzee (tpt); Jimmy Harrison (tbn); Hilton Jefferson (clt, alt); Elmer Williams (clt, ten); Louis Jordan (alt); Don Kirkpatrick (p); John Trueheart (bj); Elmer James or Lawson Buford (bs); Webb (d). New York City, 14 June 1929.
Dog bottom[1]

Robert Horton (tbn) replaces Harrison; Webb absent. New York City, 27 June 1929.
Jungle mama

Chick Webb and His Orchestra: Shelton Hemphill, Louis Hunt, Louis Bacon (tpt), Harrison (tbn); Benny Carter (clt, alt, arr); Jefferson (alt); Williams (ten); Kirkpatrick (p); Trueheart (bj); James (bs); Webb (d). New York City, 30 March 1931.
Heebie jeebies · *Soft and sweet*

Mario Bauza, Bobby Stark (tpt); Taft Jordan (tpt, vcl[2]); Sandy Williams, Claude Jones (tbn); Pete Clark (clt, alt); Edgar Sampson (alt, arr[3]); Wayman Carver (ten, fl); Elmer Williams (ten); Joe Steele (p); Trueheart (g); John Kirby (bs); Webb (d). New York City, 10 September 1934.
That rhythm man[2] · *Blue minor*[3]

Same personnel and location, 19 November 1934.
It's over because we're through[2] · *Don't be that way*[3] · *What a shuffle*[3] · *Blue Lou*[3]

Same personnel and location, 12 June 1935.
Down home rag

Dell Thomas (bs) replaces Kirby. New York City, 12 October 1935.
Facts and figures[3]

Nat Story (tbn) replaces Jones; Ella Fitzgerald (vcl[4]) added. New York City, 2 June 1936.
Go Harlem[3] · *A little bit later on*[4]

Webb, a diminutive hunchback who overcame marked physical and social disadvantages to achieve considerable musical stature, was born in Baltimore and died there thirty-seven years later of tuberculosis. For about a dozen of those years he was associated with the jazz scene in New York City, forming his own band in 1926. Johnny Hodges was in that group during 1927, as was Stark, a fine trumpeter who rejoined in 1934 and whose interim work with Fletcher Henderson can be heard on **85** and **86**. The propensity for swing that, as will be seen, the arrangers Carter and Sampson were able to utilize emerges in *Jungle mama* which, though it was recorded only two weeks later, shows a significant advance on the dated busyness of *Dog bottom*. There is some wild scatting in this latter from Pinkett, who also trumpets forcefully, sharing solo distinction with Swayzee, Harrison and Jefferson (on both alto and clarinet). The shaping of the strongly Ellingtonian *Jungle mama* may be largely the work of its composer, Webb, yet aural evidence suggests that he had no part in the actual performance [52].

The power of Webb's musical personality is easy to recognize, less easy to define. He was one of the finest drummers in jazz history, yet his solo essays were brief and infrequent, and his most telling achievement was the encouragement of chosen companions by his drumming and by his ability to attract congenial players and arrangers. Thus the music which drew the crowds to the Savoy Ballroom for many years was of a high order and exercised an influence which has not always been sufficiently noted.

Sampson's presence, as player and arranger, certainly assisted popularity. He was, during his stay, the main composer of a number of well-known swing standards, some of which he was later to rework for the Goodman orchestra (142). Of them, *Don't be that way* and *Blue Lou* are included here, together with other Sampson scores — *Blue minor, Facts and figures* and *Go Harlem*. Typical of Sampson's orchestral devices is the contrasting of flowing reed statements with staccato brass comments; and staccato inter-sectional counterpoint is sometimes used effectively, as in *What a shuffle*. In all the items mentioned, plus *That rhythm man*, Sampson's accomplished alto style is heard in solo. Other notable soloists in this 1934–6 period are Stark and Taft Jordan, whose contrasting styles are juxtaposed in *What a shuffle*, Sandy Williams, Jones and the little-remembered McRae who later led his own band and composed the Artie Shaw favourite, *Back Bay shuffle* (146). To *Blue Lou*, Steele contributes a whole chorus of Harlem 'stride' piano playing.

Carter arranged and played during 1931, and *Heebie jeebies* and *Soft and sweet* exhibit his variational scoring. He does not solo on either, but it is his clarinet which tops the reeds in the first chorus of the latter. Bacon, Hemphill, Harrison and Elmer Williams are prominent improvisers.

A little bit later on has the seventeen-year-old Ella Fitzgerald revealing more than the germ of that clarity of tone and flexibility of line that were to develop so powerfully during her years with Webb (who had discovered her in 1934 and whose band she led following his death) and for several decades afterwards as a solo artist (see **137**, which continues the Webb saga, and **203**).

Webb's own skill is tellingly but unobtrusively manifest, in his varied emphases of the beat, his use of bass drum and cymbals, his incisive breaks (hear the end of *Go Harlem*); his unfailing zest fires both ensemble and soloists. He may have 'led his regiment from behind', but lead it he did and, unlike the Duke of Plaza Toro, he undoubtedly found it and made it exciting enough.

E.T.

Fletcher Henderson

126
A Study in Frustration Vol. 4
CBS (E) BPG62004, Columbia (A) CL1685

Fletcher Henderson and His Orchestra; Rex Stewart (cnt); Bobby Stark, possibly Leora Henderson (tpt); J. C. Higginbotham, Sandy Williams (tbn); Russell Procope, Edgar Sampson (clt, alt); Coleman Hawkins (clt, ten); Fletcher Henderson (p); Clarence Holiday (bj, g); John Kirby (tu); Walter Johnson (d). New York City, 11 March 1932.
Blue moments

Russell Smith (tpt); Hilton Jefferson (alt), Freddy White (g) replace Leora Henderson, Sampson, Holiday; Kirby plays aluminium string bass; Katherine Handy (vcl[1]) added. New York City, 9 December 1932.
Honeysuckle rose · New King Porter stomp · Underneath the Harlem moon[1]

Smith, Stark, Henry Allen (tpt); Dicky Wells, Williams[2] (tbn); Procope, Jefferson (clt, alt); Hawkins (clt, ten); Fletcher Henderson (p); Bernard Addison (g); Kirby (bs); Johnson (d). New York City, 18 August 1933.
Yeah, man! · King Porter stomp · Queer notions[2] *· Can you take it?*[2]

Dick Vance, Joe Thomas, Roy Eldridge (tpt); Fernando Arbello, Ed Cuffee (tbn); Buster Bailey (clt, alt); Scoops Carry (alt); Elmer Williams, Chew Berry (ten); Fletcher and Horace Henderson (p); Bob Lessey (g); Kirby (bs); Sidney Catlett (d). Chicago, 27 March 1936.
Christopher Columbus · Blue Lou · Stealing apples

Vance, Smith, Emmett Berry (tpt); George Washington, Cuffee, Higginbotham (tbn); Jerry Blake (clt, alt); Jefferson (alt); Williams, Chew Berry (ten); Fletcher Henderson (p); Lawrence Lucie (g); Israel Crosby (bs); Johnson (d). New York City, 2 March 1937.
Rhythm of the tambourine

Same personnel and location, 22 March 1937.
Back in your own backyard

John McConnell, Albert Wynn (tbn), Peter Suggs (d) replace Washington, Higginbotham, Johnson. Chicago, 30 June 1937.
Chris and his gang

Ben Webster (ten) replaces Berry. New York City, 25 October 1937.
Sing, you sinners

Vance, Smith, Berry (tpt); Wynn, Cuffee, possibly George Hunt or Fred Robinson (tbn); Eddie Barefield (clt, alt); probably Budd Johnson (alt); Williams (ten); probably Webster or Franz Jackson (ten); Fletcher Henderson (p); Lucie (g); Crosby (bs); Suggs (d, vib). Chicago, 28 May 1938.
Moten stomp

The main difference between this band and the one Henderson was leading at the end of the 1920s (**85, 86**) lies in the fact that Don Redman's arrangements for that earlier group placed great emphasis upon the total pattern, with soloists often used as the equivalent of bit-part actors. After Redman's departure, however, those soloists came increasingly to the fore, culminating in the session of December 1932 (at which all three titles were recorded within fifty minutes, after Kirby, the last of many laggards, had turned up two and a half hours late). The activity was not confined to the obvious stars, to Stewart, ending his solo on *Underneath the Harlem moon* with a half-valve belch; to Higginbotham, gruff and excitingly repetitive in the *New King Porter stomp*; to Hawkins, nonchalantly brilliant in everything. It took in Stark, at his most sprightly, perhaps, when muted (he takes the opening solo on the *New King Porter stomp*), and the band's other trombonist, the vibrant Sandy Williams (who takes the first solo in this same piece, Higginbotham the second)

Allen plays adventurously on the next session, even if the final half of his solo in *King Porter stomp* does commence and conclude with quotations from the main theme of *Rhapsody in blue*: some day a thesis will be written on the fascination this particular work held for musicians of that period. But nobody dominated more awesomely than Hawkins. Just how confidently he could move around and against the beat is demonstrated by his solo in *Honeysuckle rose*, as daring as it is extravagant. Hawkins also composed *Queer notions*, which Horace Henderson arranged for the band: using the whole-tone scale may have been old-fashioned by the standards of European concert music, yet the piece remains intriguing when compared with contemporary jazz compositions (another version appears. on **122**). More importantly, it works as music, the framework giving resonance to the solos. And it is instructive to hear Allen and Hawkins improvising together in passages which anticipate something of the spaciousness of the modal jazz of the 1960s.

It was the partnership between another trumpeter, Eldridge, and another tenor saxophonist, Chew Berry, which gave substance and a characteristic ambience to the band of 1936, especially in *Christopher Columbus*, where Eldridge performs with an audacity that teeters on the edge of recklessness. *Stealing apples* begins, surprisingly enough, with Fletcher Henderson taking a thirty-two-bar piano solo: punctilious rather than inspiring, possibly intended as a genuflection to the piece's composer, Fats Waller. Horace Henderson's arrangement of *Blue Lou* now sounds mannered, yet once again Eldridge comes to the rescue with an agile, biting solo.

Later tracks are less fascinating. Emmett Berry takes spirited solos, but either in the style of Eldridge (*Rhythm of the tambourine*, *Back in your own backyard*, *Sing, you sinners*) or of Allen squeezing out his blue notes (*Chris and his gang*). Chew Berry sounds less thrusting without Eldridge to partner him, while Webster (*Sing, you sinners*) was still busy copying

Hawkins. Blake's clarinet playing is a distinct improvement upon Bailey's genteel correctness, its alternation between sweet and sour suggesting affinities with Edward Inge and Ed Hall. Blake plays the opening chorus of *Back in your own backyard*, helping to remind the listener that by this time Fletcher Henderson was writing scores for Benny Goodman (**141**); indeed, Goodman recorded a Henderson arrangement of this piece ten years later. But Henderson's own band never interpreted his scores with the attack or precision of Goodman's ensemble, so the period clichés are more noticeable. *Moten stomp*, incidentally, turns out to be the same tune as *Moten swing* (using the chords of *You're driving me crazy*), recorded more effectively by both the Benny Moten (**78**) and Count Basie (**135b**) bands.   C.F.

127 Fletcher Henderson 1934
Ace of Hearts (E) AH61, MCA (A) 1318

Fletcher Henderson and His Orchestra: Russell Smith, Irving Randolph, Henry Allen (tpt); Keg Johnson, Claude Jones (tbn); Buster Bailey (clt); Hilton Jefferson, Russell Procope (alt); Ben Webster (ten); Fletcher or Horace[1] Henderson (p); Lawrence Lucie (g); Elmer James (bs); Walter Johnson (d). Chicago, 11 September 1934.
Limehouse blues · *Shanghai shuffle*[1] · *Big John special* · *Happy as the day is long*[1]
Same personnel and location, 12 September 1934.
Tidal wave[1] · *Down south camp meeting* · *Wrapping it up*[1] · *Memphis blues*[1]
Benny Carter (alt) added. Chicago, 25 September 1934.
Wild party[1] · *Rug cutters' swing* · *Hotter than 'ell* · *Liza*

These important performances should be heard in conjunction with the Henderson sessions on **122** and **126** as showing the advance which his orchestral style was making in the early 1930s from the sometimes awkwardly eclectic arrangements which supplanted the work of Don Redman in the late 1920s — as demonstrated by **85** and **86**. Compared with the four tracks from 1933 included on **122**, these 1934 recordings, made within a space of fourteen days, show a significant improvement in terms of directness of purpose and relaxed execution. The personnel here is similar to that of the September 1933 session. Important changes are Webster for Hawkins, Keg Johnson for Dicky Wells, and Bailey essaying a far more ambitious clarinet role than Procope could have attempted.

The feeling of orchestral cohesion and purposeful yet relaxed musical swing is very satisfying in most tracks. It took time for

Henderson to draw together the lessons of his borrowings and to mature as an arranger, and now one hears, in some of its finest manifestations, the style which was to be one of the chief catalysts of the swing era big-band mode. If listened to with a technical ear, much of this orchestration — with its skilfully balanced interchanges between the brass and reed sections and the soloists — is in fact quite complicated; yet so freely does the performance flow, in most numbers, that the listener bent on simple enjoyment will not be distracted by the complexities. Only in *Tidal wave* does Henderson appear to edge backwards towards the brilliant bustle of a late-1920s Redman score, and though *Memphis blues*, which commits rapid mayhem upon an inherently polite tune, is melodically restless, its complication seems inspired by some other muse.

The convention of call-and-response is rather freely used in several of the pieces which later became identifying anthems of the swing craze — *Down south camp meeting*, *Big John special* and *Wrapping it up* being notable instances — but this had not yet become a stereotype. In these numbers, as in *Limehouse blues*, *Shanghai shuffle*, *Happy as the day is long*, *Rug cutters' swing* and *Hotter than 'ell* (the latter curiously more evocative of religious fervour than the camp meeting opus!), the variety and vividness of the orchestral vocabulary is admirable.

There is fine solo work on almost every track — expected excellence from Allen, especially rich in *Down south camp meeting* and *Wrapping it up*; Webster, slightly less volatile than Hawkins and frequently, as in *Happy as the day is long* and *Rug cutters' swing*, a languorous foil to the thrust of the ensemble; and Keg Johnson, contributing lightly-toned, floating solos in *Memphis blues* and *Liza*. High praise must be reserved for Bailey, whose ecstatic, reedy tone soars in numerous agile and expressive flights. He is undoubtedly the star of *Wild party*, and his solo on *Limehouse blues* might well be thought one of his best.   E.T.

128 **Spike Hughes and His All-American Orchestra**
Jasmine (E) JASM2012, London (A) LL1387

Shad Collins, Leonard Davies, Bill Dillard (tpt); Dicky Wells, Wilbur DeParis, George Washington (tbn); Benny Carter (alt, vcl[1]); Wayman Carver, Howard Johnson (alt); Coleman Hawkins (ten); Rod Rodriguez (p); Lawrence Lucie (g); Ernest Hill (bs); Kaiser Marshall (d). New York City, 18 April 1933.
Nocturne · *Someone stole Gabriel's horn*[1]

Sidney Catlett (d) replaces Marshall. Same date.
Pastorale · *Bugle call rag*

Henry Allen (tpt), Luis Russell (p) replace Collins, Rodriguez; Chew Berry (ten) added; Carver doubles on fl; Carter plays clt². New York City, 18 May 1933.
Arabesque · Fanfare² · Sweet sorrow blues · Music at midnight
Allen (tpt); Wells (tbn); Carver (fl); Carter (alt); Hawkins, Berry (ten); Rodriguez (p); Lucie (g); Hughes (bs); Catlett (d). Same date.
Sweet Sue
Allen, Howard Scott, Davies or Dillard (tpt); Carter (alt, sop³); Carver, Johnson (alt); Hawkins, Berry (ten); Rodriguez (p); Lucie (g); Hill (bs); Catlett (d). New York City, 19 May 1933.
Air in D flat · Donegal cradle song · Firebird³ · Music at sunrise
Allen (tpt, vcl); Wells (tbn); Carver (fl); Carter (alt); Hawkins, Berry (ten); Rodriguez (p); Lucie (g); Hughes (bs); Catlett (d). Same date
How come you do me like you do?

Hughes's earliest records were made in Britain with pickup groups, modelled at first on Red Nichols's Five Pennies, then playing arrangements like those Gene Gifford was writing for the Casa Loma Band. These earlier phases were followed by Hughes's discovery of Duke Ellington. The tracks on this LP resulted from a holiday spent in the United States, where his scores were performed by Carter's orchestra, augmented on two sessions by Allen and Hawkins. The pieces he wrote for that band made great use of sections of muted trumpets and trombones, creating the kind of textures that Ellington was also fond of deploying. But whereas in Britain Hughes had worked with musicians whose playing he knew at first hand, he was now faced by soloists he admired, even idolized, yet had heard only on gramophone records and by an ensemble unaccustomed to the kind of demands he was about to make on it. The latter circumstance explains the stilted playing on *Someone stole Gabriel's horn* and *Bugle call rag*. That situation improved later even if, according to Hughes, it took two and a half hours to achieve a satisfactory performance of a brass passage in *Donegal cradle song*[53]. Yet the presence of Catlett provided reassurance, momentum and, in *Sweet sorrow blues*, a hint of the elegiac.

What raised several of these pieces to the status of classic jazz recordings was the calibre of the solo playing by Hawkins and Wells. Hawkins already enjoyed a huge reputation among musicians and jazz *aficionados*, yet it could be argued that nothing he recorded elsewhere ever surpassed in delicacy his ornamentation of *Donegal cradle song* and *Arabesque*. Certainly it was these sessions that provided the evidence for considering Wells to be one of the most imaginative and daring of jazz trombonists. (Several of these solos, in fact, are cited by André Hodeir in his admirable analysis — and eulogy — of Wells's playing[54].) *Bugle call rag, Sweet sorrow blues* and *Arabesque* contain solos in which the trombonist contrives to be both poignant (his use of terminal vibrato, the shake at the end of a phrase, is comparable with Armstrong's) and a master of the unexpected. In contrast to the bizarreries of Wells and the sumptuousness of Hawkins, Carter's alto saxophone solos contribute a calm reasonableness. Carver plays what are among the earliest flute solos on jazz records, sounding competent but running no risks. Berry performs in a typically zestful fashion, yet the second chorus of *Firebird*, where he plays the first sixteen bars (very busily) and Hawkins the second sixteen (with characteristic nonchalance), illustrates the difference between the good and the great soloist. Allen is outstanding in two blues: *Sweet sorrow* and the faster, more disguised *Fanfare*. He also leads the two jam sessions, loosely but with authority.

To praise some of these solos so highly does not imply denigration of the orchestrations. A few fail to work (*Music at sunrise* never gets itself together); while some of the brass writing could have done with being less staccato. And, just like Ellington in those prewar years, Hughes was reluctant to entrust a main theme to the saxophone section (ironic, in view of the quality of Carter's team). Yet this composer did have the capacity, especially in slow pieces, to sustain tension, employing texture to enchance what are memorable, often Gaelic-sounding, melodies. Some of Hughes's most effective pieces (*Sirocco* and *Elegy*, for instance) were recorded by his British band. Nevertheless, items such as *Nocturne, Pastorale, Donegal cradle song* and, above all, *Arabesque*, with its alternating themes, show the heights to which he could rise.   C.F.

129 Earl Hines 1934–35
Ace of Hearts (E) AH159, MCA (A) 1311

Earl Hines and His Orchestra: Charlie Allen, George Dixon, Walter Fuller (tpt); Louis Taylor, Billy Franklin, Trummy Young (tbn); Darnell Howard (clt, alt, vln); Omer Simeon (clt, alt); Cecil Irwin, Jimmy Mundy (ten); Hines (p); Lawrence Dixon (g); Quinn Wilson (bs); Wallace Bishop (d); Fuller and Palmer Brothers Trio (vcl). Chicago, 12 September 1934.
That's a-plenty · Fat babes · Maple leaf rag · Rosetta · Sweet Georgia Brown

Same personnel and location, 13 September 1934.
Copenhagen · Angry · Wolverine blues · Rock and rye · Cavernism

Same personnel. New York City, 12 February 1935.
Rhythm lullaby · Japanese sandman · Bubbling over · Blue

Hines playing *Maple leaf rag* gives no hint of condescension towards a quaint ancestor, yet nowhere does his brilliant ardour permit mere pastiche. Here, piano solos and band arrangement draw out a vigour native to the Joplin original; and though the transformation carries the music well beyond ragtime's formalism, the rag remains the true in-formation of this performance. The strains are used in sequence and balance, and the spirit of this and of Morton's *Wolverine blues* testifies that this was a band in the great tradition. A pleasant lesson may be learnt from hearing how the swinging ensemble work in those two pieces fulfils the more urgent hints of riffs and syncopated chords — strong in Morton but by no means absent in Joplin — in a way that is as revealing about ragtime as it is about swing. (Fletcher Henderson's translation of *King Porter stomp* into orchestral language is a better-known instance of the same process — see **86**, **126** and **141**.)

The arrangement of *Maple leaf rag* appears to have been provided by Wilson. Most of the others were made by Mundy, whose arranging gifts, later developed with Benny Goodman (**142**) and Count Basie, were at a more flexible stage on these dates. His scoring for brass and reeds frequently shows the link between his writing and his own saxophone improvisations; and his purposeful solo on *Copenhagen* may be heard, along with his apt and unpretentious scored accompaniment, as a unified conception. Moments such as this say much about the adventurousness of the period, not yet stultified by the flatulent mannerism of later swing band arranging. Also, the presence of Simeon and Howard provides a link with styles associated with New Orleans — though it should be remembered that these were seasoned big band players. Howard's more limpid alto utterances grace *Wolverine blues* and *Bubbling over*, and his astringent, very Chicagoan, clarinet tone at the end of the former piece should be compared with Simeon's liquid enunciation during *Bubbling over*.

All the soloists turn out excellent work, though few reveal particularly individual voices. Young, a Jimmy Lunceford star from 1937, in his occasional solos makes interesting predictions, not only by his tentative harmonic searchings but also by the laggard phrasing seemingly at variance with the 'hot' impetus of most other soloists and the band as a unit.

Bubbling over, *Cavernism* and *Rock and rye* develop the kind of polyphonic complexity which soon was to become the peculiar mark of Lunceford's orchestra at its best. But, singular as Hines's band was in certain respects, its achievements would have been less memorable but for the enigmatic presence of its leader. He appears, at times, magistral as Prospero, at others like Ariel gleefully 'playing the jack' with his travelling companions. To appreciate his approach, it helps considerably to listen to his earlier recordings with Armstrong, particularly *Skip the gutter*, *Don't jive me* and the incomparable *Weatherbird* with its spinning vanes of melody (**48**); and then to hear *That's a-plenty*, *Maple leaf rag* and *Sweet Georgia Brown* carry Hines's love for musical dialogue over from that freer yet equally disciplined context into this rather more complicated one. His liberty and authority are everywhere apparent.

During those years, Hines's solo style was totally personal and remains virtually indescribable. The dizzying way in which one solo can swerve to and fro between the concise and the prolix, using hot rhythms as compulsive as Morton's together with impressionist cascades and rocket-tails of notes, daring shifts and suspensions of motion, and all within the unvarying tempo of a band which was there to be danced to, never ceases to sound amazing. It is hard to think of any other pianist-leader who has so successfully used his instrument as a countervoice to his band. His characteristic metallic shakes may well echo his crucial dalliance with Armstrong, and there are various other elements in these band performances (not to mention a brief vocal impersonation) which are affected by the immense popular standing of the great trumpeter at that time.   E.T.

Duke Ellington

130 Daybreak Express
RCA (A) LPV506, RCA (I) LPM34078

Duke Ellington and His Orchestra: Arthur Whetsol, Cootie Williams, Freddy Jenkins (tpt); Joe Nanton (tbn); Juan Tizol (v-tbn); Barney Bigard (clt, ten); Harry Carney (clt, bar); Johnny Hodges (sop, alt); Ellington (p); Fred Guy (bj, g); Wellman Braud (bs); Sonny Greer (d). Camden, New Jersey, 16 June 1931.
Limehouse blues · *Echoes of the jungle*

Same personnel and location, 17 June 1931.
It's a glory

Lawrence Brown (tbn) added; Williams[1], Greer[2] (vcl). New York City, 9 February 1932.
Dinah[1,2] · *Bugle call rag*

Louis Bacon (tpt, vcl[3]), Otto Hardwicke (alt, bs sx) added. Chicago, 26 April 1933.
Rude interlude[3] · *Dallas doings*

Tizol absent. Chicago, 4 December 1933.
Dear old Southland[3] · *Daybreak express*

Same personnel and location, 9 January 1934.
Delta serenade · *Stompy Jones*

Same personnel and location, 10 January 1934.
Solitude · Blue feeling

Bacon, Hardwicke absent; Ivie Anderson (vcl[4]) added. Hollywood, 12 April 1934.
Ebony rhapsody[4] *· Live and love tonight*

Jenkins absent; Tizol (v-tbn) added. Hollywood, 9 May 1934.
Troubled waters[4]

131a The Ellington Era Vol. 1 Part 2
CBS (E) BPG62179, Columbia (A) CL2047

Duke Ellington and His Famous Orchestra: Whetsol, Williams, Jenkins (tpt); Nanton, Brown (tbn); Tizol (v-tbn); Bigard (clt, ten); Hodges (sop, alt); Carney (alt, bar); Hardwicke (alt, bs sx); Ellington (p); Guy (g); Braud (bs); Greer (d). New York City, 18 May 1932.
Blue ramble

Same personnel and location, 19 September 1932.
Ducky wucky

Same personnel and location, 21 September 1932.
Lightning

Same personnel and location, 17 February 1933.
Slippery horn · Drop me off at Harlem

Same personnel and location, 16 May 1933.
Bundle of blues

Same personnel and location, 15 August 1933.
Harlem speaks

Carney also plays bs clt; Ellington (vcl[5]). New York City, 12 September 1934.
Solitude · Saddest tale[5]

Rex Stewart (cnt), Charlie Allen (tpt), Fred Avendorf (d) replace Whetsol, Jenkins, Greer. New York City, 30 April 1935.
Merry-go-round

Whetsol (tpt), Billy Taylor (bs), Greer (d) replace Allen, Braud, Avendorf; Hardwicke absent. New York City, 28 February 1936.
Clarinet lament · Echoes of Harlem

Hardwicke (alt, bs sx), Ben Webster (ten), Hayes Alvis (bs) added. New York City, 29 July 1936.
In a jam

Wallace Jones (tpt) replaces Whetsol; Webster absent. New York City, 14 May 1937.
Caravan

Tizol, Alvis absent. New York City, 20 September 1937.
Harmony in Harlem

Tizol (v-tbn), Anderson (vcl[4]) added. New York City, 7 June 1938.
Rose of the Rio Grande[4]

131b The Ellington Era Vol. II Part 2
CBS (E) BPG62612, Columbia (A) CL2364

Duke Ellington and His Famous Orchestra: Whetsol, Williams, Jenkins (tpt); Nanton, Brown (tbn); Tizol (v-tbn); Bigard (clt, ten); Hodges (sop, alt); Carney (alt, bar); Hardwicke (alt, bs sx); Ellington (p); Guy (g); Braud (bs); Greer (d). New York City, 15 August 1933.
I'm satisfied · Jive stomp · In the shade of the old apple tree

Same personnel and location, 12 September 1934.
Sump'n 'bout rhythm

Stewart (cnt), Allen (tpt) Avendorf (d) replace Whetsol, Jenkins, Greer. New York City, 30 April 1935.
In a sentimental mood · Showboat shuffle

Whetsol (tpt), Greer (d) replace Allen, Avendorf; Webster (ten), Taylor (bs), Anderson (vcl[4]) added. New York City, 19 August 1935.
Trucking[4]

Webster absent. New York City, 12 September 1935.
Reminiscing in tempo (4 parts)

Alvis (bs) replaces Braud, Taylor, New York City, 27 January 1936.
There is no greater love

Peter Clark (alt) replaces Hardwicke. New York City, 28 February 1936.
Kissing my baby goodnight[4]

Hardwicke (alt, bs sx) replaces Clark; Webster (ten) added. New York City, 29 July 1936.
Exposition swing · Uptown downbeat

Jones (tpt) replaces Whetsol; Webster absent. New York City, 14 May 1937.
Azure

Building on the compositional precedents of Jelly Roll Morton (**47**), which received so little understanding elsewhere, Ellington already had considerable achievements behind him when the oldest of the above recordings were made. But it was in the early 1930s that he first attained international recognition, first appeared in Europe, and the best of these performances illustrate the widening of his horizons, the growth of his powers. It is a long way, for example, from *Blue tune's* simple alternation of theme statements and solos to the relatively complex layout of *Reminiscing in tempo*, although perhaps it is a small indication of the wholeness of Ellington's output that the scoring of the former piece's main idea closely resembles that of one particular section of the 1935 extended work (bars 81–100).

Emphasis must be given to his inventiveness in terms of sheer sound and there are many passages that once heard remain for ever in the mind's ear, a good instance being provided by Williams at the beginning and end of *Bundle of blues*. Yet this invention is rarely the vehicle of mere self-indulgence, and

Echoes of the jungle, whose haunted atmosphere was beyond the reach of any other jazz musician at the time and which was the next of Ellington's seminal masterpieces after the October 1930 version of *Old man blues* (**91**), follows a quite rigorous design with each event placed to obtain maximum impact.

Not that he was always successful. *Lightning*, first of his train impressions, falls apart at the inappropriate 'stride' piano solo, and *Daybreak express* was a striking improvement, not least with a brilliant avoidance of repetitive figuration (a respect in which it might be contrasted with *Showboat shuffle*). However, it was only much later with his 1946 *Happy-go-lucky local* (Prestige (A) P24029) that he brought off this concept perfectly[55]. Again, we cannot well complain about the facile exoticism of *Caravan* when it gives rise to something as neatly abrasive as Williams's solo, but this theme hints at veins of expression Ellington completely mastered only with the *Far-Eastern Suite* of 1966 (RCA (A) LSP3782). Of course, not all subsequent changes were improvements, and this quietly atmospheric account of *Solitude*, in a style relating to *Mood indigo* (**91**), is superior to the sentimental ditty it became in later versions. And just occasionally things were done better elsewhere, a good example being Williams's own 1944 recording of *Echoes of Harlem* (Phoenix (A) LP1), which is slower, more intent, and dispenses with Ellington's bland saxophone passage in the middle. Also, the Blue Rhythm Band's version of *Trucking* (Jazz Archive (A) JA10) has a better tempo than the Ellington performance recorded eighteen days later.

A hint of his true relationship to the rest of jazz during this period is given, though, by such items as *In a jam* and *Uptown downbeat* (not to be confused with *Downtown uproar*) where, as if to amuse himself, he plays with the already conventionalized procedures of big band arranging. Already, however, his music's range of moods is far wider than swing would ever command, going as it does from *Delta serenade's* gentle wistfulness to the heavily satirical treatment *Dinah* receives, from the bright colours and knowing instrumental legerdemain of *Bugle call rag* to the somewhat ambiguous grace — exactly caught by Whetsol — *Drop me off at Harlem*. The methods of organization vary a great deal also, and the tightly-packed sequence of solos on *Exposition swing* (heard here in a different and slightly superior master to the original 78 rpm issue) may be contrasted with *Clarinet lament's* searching display of the scope of one performer and instrument. This latter, which should be heard in conjunction with *Boy meets horn* (**152a**) and *Concerto for Cootie* (**153**), may in part be considered a sophistication of *Basin Street blues*, and in it Bigard achieves one of the finest recorded expressions of

specifically jazz lyricism and virtuosity on the clarinet. Different
again is *Ebony rhapsody*, wherein the 'classical voodoo' of which
Miss Anderson sings is imaginatively recomposed, forming a
standing reproach to Ellington's much later manipulations of
Grieg and Tchaikovsky. It may be added, to contradict the lyrics,
that Liszt might, with his intense interest in Gypsy improvisation, have been more sympathetic to this piece, based on his
Hungarian Rhapsody No. 2, than is usually supposed.

It is the more outlandish moments which reveal Ellington best,
however, such as *Saddest tale*, with its extraordinary reconciliation of menace and resignation. This includes a pastel-toned
expression of sorrow from Whetsol and, from the ensemble, some
harmony very advanced for jazz at that time: this is another of the
band's masterpieces[56]. Amid the *Rude interlude* ensembles,
Bacon, with his vague and wordless vocal, sounds like the
proverbial ghost in the machine, and his similar obbligato to
Nanton's solo on *Dear old Southland* is another unusual case. The
latter is followed by Hodges, on soprano, who indicates the debt
Ellington's music owes to Sidney Bechet — a debt specifically
acknowledged much later (**224**). A more personal debt is
suggested by Stewart's fine solo on *Kissing my baby goodnight*
which, although an individual statement, clearly descends from
Beiderbecke; in fact it is instructive to listen to this while holding
Bix's *Singing the blues* improvisation (**64**) firmly in mind.

With *Reminiscing in tempo*, however, Ellington would seem to
owe very little to anyone. There were partial European precedents such as Spike Hughes's *Harlem symphony* and Fred
Elizalde's *Heart of a Nigger*, in four sections, yet it is, especially
in its structural ambitions, unlike any other American jazz of the
period and a notable demonstration of the independence of
Ellington's mind. A main point is the level of formal elaboration,
the simple frameworks that are suitable vehicles for improvisation being abandoned with a certainty of purpose, almost a
ruthlessness, that still seems remarkable. Most striking is his
freedom from symmetrical phrase-lengths. He essayed five-bar
phrases in *Creole rhapsody* (**88** and **90**), but here we find seven-,
ten- and fourteen-bar units. A few cases such as the ten-bar
phrase in the following year's *Echoes of Harlem* notwithstanding,
Ellington never took such procedures significantly further in
later works, and in some ways *Reminiscing in tempo* remains his
most adventurous piece, the furthest out that he went. (It is
unfortunate that, because of the exigencies of ten-inch 78 rpm
discs, it was recorded in four parts, because in fact it is in three,
corresponding to an exposition, development and modified
recapitulation[57].)

As in his other most balanced and satisfying extended pieces, especially *Crescendo and diminuendo in blue* (**152a**), *Harlem* and *Happy-go-lucky local*, there is little improvisation, and soloists are distinctly subservient to the personal expression of the composer. That is no way to keep a jazz band happy, and may well explain why this potentially most fruitful path was not pursued. The fact remains, however, that Ellington put some of the very best of himself into *Reminiscing in tempo*.   M.H.

Major Big Bands of the Swing Era

These recordings show the range of styles, the diversity of expression, which the big bands achieved at the various peaks of their development. At the same time, there is more discipline than hitherto and greater consistency of purpose.

Andy Kirk

132 **Walking and Swinging**
          Affinity (E) AFS1011, *Mainstream (A) MRL399

Andy Kirk and His Twelve Clouds of Joy: Harry 'Big Jim' Lawson, Paul King, Earl Thompson (tpt); Ted Donnelly (tbn); John Harrington (clt, alt); John Williams (alt); Dick Wilson (ten); Kirk (bar); Mary Lou Williams (p, arr[1]); Ted Brinson (g); Booker Collins (bs); Ben Thigpen (d). New York City, 2 March 1936.
Walking and swinging[1] · *Moten swing*[1] · *Lotta sax appeal*[1]
Pha Terrell (vcl[2]) added. New York City, 2 April 1936.
Until the real thing comes along[2]
Same personnel and location, 3 April 1936.
Cloudy[2]
Harry Mills (vcl[3]) replaces Terrell. New York City, 9 December 1936.
The lady who swings the band[3]
Henry Wells (tbn), Earl Miller (alt), Claude Hopkins (arr[4]) added; Harrington, John Williams also play bar; Kirk no longer plays; New York City, 15 February 1937.
Wednesday night hop[4]
Clarence Trice (tpt) replaces King. New York City, 8 February 1938.
Twinkling
Vcl by ensemble[5]. New York City, 10 February 1938.
Little Joe from Chicago[1,5]
Same personnel and location, 6 December 1938.
Mary's idea[1]
Don Byas (ten), Floyd Smith (g) replace John Williams, Brinson. New York City, 16 March 1939.
Floyd's guitar blues[1]

Same personnel and location, 15 November 1939.
Big Jim blues[1]
Harold Baker (tpt), Rudy Powell (clt, alt), Edward Inge (clt, ten) replace
Thompson, Miller, Byas. New York City, 7 November 1940.
Twelfth Street rag
Same personnel and location, 3 January 1941.
Ring dem bells[1]
Earl Miller (alt) replaces Powell; June Richmond (vcl[6]) added. New York
City, 17 July 1941.
47th Street jive[6]
Johnny Burris (tpt), Howard McGhee (tpt, arr[7]), Milton Robinson (tbn),
Ben Smith (alt), Al Sears (ten), Kenny Kersey (p) replace Baker, Trice,
Wells, Miller, Wilson, Mary Lou Williams. New York City, 14 July 1942.
McGhee special[7]

Anyone listening to this LP after hearing **77** will notice how
much more lightly the band moves — especially on the recordings
of 2 March 1936, a session that caught the orchestra at its
nimblest and best. Part of that new-found lissomness sprang from
the replacement of Kirk's tuba by Collins's string bass. Every bit
as important, though, was that Mary Lou Williams was writing
scores that were tailored very carefully to meet the needs of this
ensemble. The contrast between brass and reeds, Fletcher
Henderson's bequest to the swing era, continued to be stressed,
yet not so exclusively that broader harmonies could not be
achieved, as in the second chorus of *Walking and swinging*, by
putting a trumpet alongside the four saxophones. Later in her
career Miss Williams would develop into a much more adventurous composer (see **179**). Even within the time-span of this LP
there are indications of that happening: the languid entry by
saxophones during the opening chorus of *Ring dem bells* would
have seemed out of character five years earlier. Meanwhile, by
operating within a relatively simple framework she encouraged
this ensemble to make relaxed, worthwhile music.

Apart from *Wednesday night hop*, the work of Claude Hopkins,
and *McGhee special*, by Howard McGhee, most of the arrangements are presumably by Mary Lou Williams, including a piece of
harmless self-glorification, *The lady who swings the band*, composed by Sammy Cahn and Saul Chaplin. Harry Mills, one of the
then-famous Mills Brothers, sings the lyric with endearing
insouciance. Not quite so felicitous, although it brought the band
much commercial success, was Terrell's singing, heard at its
plummiest in *Until the real thing comes along* (another of Cahn
and Chaplin's efforts). *Twinkling*, agreeably melodic, is an
oblique reminder that both as a pianist and composer Miss

Williams had roots in ragtime (further evidence for which is provided by her *Corny rhythm* and *Swinging for joy* piano solos on Parlophone (E) PMC7156). When asked to name the biggest influences on her piano playing, she chose Jelly Roll Morton, Jack Howard and Earl Hines. Morton she encountered only on records, but the other two were active in Pittsburgh at the time she was growing up there. Howard played boogie woogie ('so forcefully that he used to break up all the pianos') but never made a name for himself. Miss Williams's approach to that idiom is typically graceful, almost lackadaisical, as can be heard in *Little Joe from Chicago*. Her arrangement, curiously enough, echoes the big band dixieland style of Bob Crosby's Orchestra (**236**).

With two exceptions, one of them being Mary Lou Williams herself, the soloists in Kirk's early band tended to be adequate rather than outstanding. Harrington's clarinet sounds neat enough inside the ensemble yet tentative when taking solos. On the other hand, Donnelly, whenever he gets the chance to play more than a middle-eight, comes across as a trombonist with possibilities. Lawson, always assuming it is he who takes the trumpet solos, has a forthright but not particularly inventive approach. (Anyone searching for a definitive example of Lawson's style will find *Big Jim blues* exceptionally frustrating, for it contains not a single bar of solo trumpet.) 1940 saw the arrival of Baker, a deliciously melodic trumpeter, his tone full of light and shade; he takes characteristic solos in *Twelfth Street rag* and *Ring dem bells*. By the time McGhee moved into the band, Mary Lou Williams had left and a new phase had begun. *McGhee special*, however, is a very engaging performance, full of the kind of dramatics that McGhee had learned from Roy Eldridge and was to channel into bop only a few years later. Another soloist who should be mentioned is Smith, perhaps the first electrically-amplified guitarist to attract attention in jazz. (Eddie Durham had recorded earlier — with Jimmy Lunceford as well as with the Kansas City Five and Six (**157**) — but Charlie Christian did not join Benny Goodman until the summer of 1939.) Nevertheless, *Floyd's guitar blues* remains an oddity, best summed up perhaps as Hawaiian Gothic. Smith is heard playing more successfully, if more conventionally, in *Ring dem bells*.

The other exceptional soloist in that early band was of course Wilson, whose death in 1941 proved a much greater loss to jazz than most people realized at the time. He could sound deceptively like Herschel Evans or a more *legato* Chew Berry, yet at other moments his playing hinted at the engrossing understatement of Lester Young. The overall effect, though, was less kaleidoscopic than those analogics might suggest: his tone, his way of phrasing, his lyrical stance were all very much his own. Wilson plays many solos on these tracks, but his final recording session was the one that produced *47th Street jive*, on which, paradoxically, he sounds unwontedly like Ben Webster. But he is featured at his very best in *Lotta sax appeal*, which mixes twelve- with sixteen-bar routines. He always played with the poise that reflects authority, frequently with brass riffing gently behind him. Perhaps nothing is more characteristic of Kirk's — and Mary Lou Williams's — music than the way that riffs were used. Another Kansas City band to become famous for its riffing went into a recording studio for the first time at the beginning of 1937. But where Count Basie's musicians used riffs hypnotically, transforming repetitiveness into a virtue, Kirk's band deployed them quietly, almost unobtrusively, creating a very controlled, almost dainty, species of excitement.   C.F.

Count Basie
133
The Count Swings Out
Coral (G) 97011LPCM, *2MCΛ (A) 4050E (2 LPs)

Count Basie and His Orchestra: Joe Keyes, Carl Smith, Buck Clayton (tpt); George Hunt, Dan Minor (tbn); Caughey Roberts (alt); Jack Washington (alt, bar); Lester Young, Herschel Evans (ten); Basie (p); Claude Williams (g); Walter Page (bs); Jo Jones (d); Jimmy Rushing (vcl[1]). New York City, 21 January 1937.
Pennies from Heaven[1] · *Roseland shuffle*

Ed Lewis, Bobby Moore (tpt), Freddy Greene (g) replace Keyes, Smith, Williams; Eddie Durham (tbn, g, arr) added. New York City, 26 March 1937.
Exactly like you[1]

Earle Warren (alt) replaces Roberts. New York City, 9 August 1937.
Time out · *Topsy*

Bobby Hicks (tpt) replaces Moore; Benny Morton (tbn) added. New York City, 13 October 1937.
Out of the window

Same personnel and location, 16 February 1938.
Every tub

Harry Edison (tpt) replaces Hicks. New York City, 6 June 1938.
Dogging around

Dickie Wells (tbn) replaces Durham. New York City, 22 August 1938.
Texas shuffle · *Jumping at the Woodside*

Basie (p); Greene (g); Page (bs); Jones (d). New York City, 26 January 1939.
Fare thee well, honey, fare thee well · *Red wagon*

Previous full band personnel except that Chew Berry (ten) replaces Evans; Shad Collins (tpt) added. New York City, 2 February 1939.
Cherokee

134 Swinging the Blues
Brunswick (G) 87036LPBM, *Affinity (E) AFS1010

Count Basie and His Orchestra: Keyes, Smith, Clayton (tpt); Hunt, Minor (tbn); Roberts (alt); Washington (alt, bar); Young, Evans (ten); Basie (p); Williams (g); Page (bs); Jones (d). New York City, 21 January 1937.
Honeysuckle rose · Swinging at the Daisy Chain

Lewis, Moore (tpt), Warren (alt), Greene (g) replace Keyes, Smith, Roberts, Williams; Durham (tbn, g, arr) added. New York City, 7 July 1937.
One o'clock jump · John's idea

Hicks (tpt) replaces Moore; Rushing (vcl[1]) added. New York City, 3 January 1938.
Blues in the dark[1]

Same personnel and location, 16 February 1938.
Sent for you yesterday[1] *· Swinging the blues*

Edison (tpt), Morton (tbn) replace Hicks, Hunt. New York City, 6 June 1938.
Blue and sentimental

Basie (p); Greene (g); Page (bs); Jones (d). New York City, 9 November 1938.
How long blues

Previous full band personnel except that Wells (tbn) replaces Durham. New York City, 16 November 1938.
Shorty George · Do you wanna jump, children?[1] *· Panassié stomp*

Berry (ten) replaces Evans; Collins (tpt) added. New York City, 2 February 1939.
Jive at five · Evil blues[1]

Although the loose, relaxed ensembles of standard fare such as *Pennies from Heaven* probably reflect the character of the best of the dancing for which this music was played, Basie's group achieved, on the finest of these its earliest recordings, a massive yet classic simplicity that offered a real alternative to the sophistication of Ellington, the virtuosity of Lunceford. Descended from Moten (**78**), though shorn of such inessentials as the accordion, this band nonetheless incorporated elements from elsewhere. Thus the main *One o'clock jump* riff is a simplification of one used on the Chocolate Dandies' 1929 *Six or seven times* (**84**), while the idea of juxtaposing two tenor soloists with different styles had been employed by Spike Hughes in 1933 (**128**). Again, *Jive at five* closely resembles *Barrelhouse*, a Tab Smith score recorded by the Blue Rhythm Band in 1936 (Jazz Archive (A) JA10). Even at this stage there were inconsistencies, like the final chord which spoils the effect of the pleasingly unexpected coda to *Topsy*, the banal eight bar interruption to Clayton's initial chorus, or Evans's ill-advised attempt in *Jumping at the Woodside* to improvise round the closing ensemble on his clarinet in the manner of Bigard with the Ellington band. There were always passages, too, which tried to conform to standardized swing band procedures, such as the ensemble statement of the *Exactly like you* melody, which anti-climactically follows Basie's far more subtle exposition in the previous chorus. Such conventionalisms are banished from the most creative of these performances, yet they were to return and eventually take over completely, leading, decades later, to the final ignominy of LPs such as *Basie's Beatle Bag* and *Basie Meets Bond*.

That lay far in the future, and the outline of such initial pieces as *Roseland shuffle* is almost austere, reflecting — unless it is the other way about — the daring simplicity of solos like the one Basie contributes to *Dogging around*. Equally remarkable are some keyboard passages of the quartet *Red wagon*, with their rejection of melody, use of silence and of musical space. *How long* is minimalist jazz, subverting the predictable cadences of the blues with wry understatement, and a similar instance is his second solo on *John's idea*, where each phrase is reduced to absolute essentials. Such tactics allow the plain yet forceful pulse of the rhythm section to assert itself to a hitherto unprecedented extent, and comparable relationships between solos and ensembles may be observed on more than one level. Thus Young's characteristic utterance on *Jumping at the Woodside*, marking a brave departure from established norms, is answered by the extraordinary momentum of the closing ensemble, while Edison's amazing entry in *Swinging the blues* seems to be born out of the ensemble riffs, later to be capped with massive phrases by the whole band.

There is another most striking entry by this trumpeter on *Sent for you yesterday* which leads to a dialogue with imposing ensemble riffs. His freely-inflected lines here and over the urging saxophones of *Every tub* can seem undisciplined, yet like the other leading soloists he is essaying (or assaying) new areas of expression which arose out of the original elements in the band's approach. The supreme instance of this is Young, whose contributions of a slightly later date are discussed under **135**. There are laconically expressive solos by him on *Jive at five* and, after four bars from Evans, on *Time out*; *Roseland shuffle* includes a dialogue between Young and Basie that is as beautiful for its demonstration of mutual understanding as for the quality of its musical ideas. The contrasts between Young and Evans are excellently deployed on *Dogging around* and *One o'clock jump*, but the latter's solo vehicle, *Blue and sentimental*, is aptly titled, although this track is notable for Young's clarinet. There are good solos by Morton on *Out of the window* and Wells on *Panassié stomp*, though both did better elsewhere. It was here that Clayton's quiet intensity first made its mark, however, and he has fine passages on *Time out* and *One o'clock jump*. His contribution to the close of *Swinging at the Daisy Chain* is also notable, for after the ensemble riffs he unexpectedly returns, backed with temple blocks and piano chimes, as the performance murmurs into silence.

Among the classics of recorded jazz are *Sent for you yesterday* and *Swinging the blues*, which perfectly integrate the band's chief innovations with one musical event growing out of another. In the former piece, for example, notice how the abrasive ensemble chords which answer the piano phrases become the background to Evans's solo, how the initial saxophone figure returns to introduce the vocal choruses, how Edison's solo line gradually emerges from behind Rushing's singing; and notice the conclusive effect of Basie's coda truncation of the theme heard from the brass at the outset. To these performances must be added *Evil blues*, again an exceptionally well unified and quite outlandish concept that marks a considerable step away from the usual climate of the band's work and is in its context comparable to the haunted *Saddest tale* (**131a**) in relation to Ellington's 1930s output. It is at the opposite pole to the irresistible momentum of the closing choruses of *Every tub* or *Panassié stomp*, taking much further the introversion glimpsed in a few passages such as the close of *Swinging at the Daisy Chain*. The sequence of events is outwardly simple: Lewis solos over the reeds and is followed by Rushing, who sounds less bland than usual. He receives a fascinatingly varied accompaniment in which Berry's tenor is the most active constituent; then ensemble chords that were another part of that accompaniment erupt with a violence that is astonishing even if we remember the growling brass behind Clayton on *Blues in the dark*. Lewis returns and, over the rolling, insinuating saxophone figures, his phrases are now discontinuous, as if fragmented by the preceding outburst. The music again murmurs into silence.

M.H.

135a
Lester Young Memorial Vol. 1
Fontana (E) TFL5064, Epic (A) LG3107

Jones–Smith Incorporated: Carl Smith (tpt); Young (ten); Count Basie (p); Walter Page (bs); Jo Jones (d); Jimmy Rushing (vcl[1]). Chicago, 9 October 1936.

Boogie woogie[1] · *Shoe shine boy*

Count Basie and His Orchestra: Ed Lewis, Harry Edison, Shad Collins, Buck Clayton (tpt); Dickie Wells, Dan Minor, Benny Morton (tbn); Earle Warren (alt); Jack Washington (alt, bar); Young, Buddy Tate (ten); Basie (p); Freddy Greene (g); Page (bs); Jones (d). New York City, 19 March 1939.

Rockabye Basie · *Taxi war dance*

Same personnel. Chicago, 19 May 1939.

Pound cake

Same personnel. New York City, 4 August 1939.

Clap hands, here comes Charlie

Kansas City Seven: Clayton (tpt); Wells (tbn); Young (ten); Basie (p); Greene (g); Page (bs); Jones (d). New York City, 5 September 1939.

Dickie's dream · *Lester leaps in*

Previous full band personnel. New York City, 6 November 1939.

Riff interlude

Same personnel and location, 7 November 1939.

Ham 'n' eggs

Al Killian (tpt), Vic Dickenson (tbn) replace Collins, Morton; Tab Smith (alt, arr) added. New York City, 31 May 1940.

Blow top

Smith absent. New York City, 19 November 1940.

Broadway

135b
Lester Young Memorial Vol. 2
Fontana (E) TFL5065, Epic (A) LN3168

Jones–Smith Incorporated: Smith (tpt); Young (ten); Basie (p); Page (bs); Jones (d). Chicago, 9 October 1936.

Lady, be good

Count Basie and His Orchestra: Lewis, Edison, Collins, Clayton (tpt); Wells, Minor, Morton (tbn); Warren (alt); Washington (alt, bar); Young, Tate (ten); Basie (p); Greene (g); Page (bs); Jones (d); Andy Gibson (arr[2]). New York City, 19 March 1939.

Jump for me[2]

Same personnel and location, 5 April 1939.

Twelfth Street rag

Same personnel and location, 4 August 1939.

Song of the islands

Rushing (vcl[1]) added. New York City, 6 November.

I left my baby[1,2]

Rushing absent. New York City, 7 November 1939.
Hollywood jump [2]
Killian (tpt), Dickenson (tbn) replace Collins, Morton. New York City, 19 March 1940.
I never knew [2] · *Tickle toe* [2] · *Louisiana* [2]
Jimmy Mundy (arr[3]) added. New York City, 20 March 1940.
Easy does it [3] · *Let me see* [2]
Same personnel. Chicago, 8 August 1940.
Moten swing

Though physically a child of the South with early years in New Orleans, Young showed little sign in later life of having heeded directly the musical traditions associated with that region. Formative years were lived at the other end of the Mississippi, in Minneapolis and in those Midwestern states which his family toured in pursuit of his father's employment with a minstrel troupe. Instruction on trumpet, violin, alto saxophone and drums came from his father, and he acknowledged the influence of Frankie Trumbauer upon his choice of the tenor saxophone and the development of his approach to jazz. Trumbauer played the utilitarian C-melody saxophone and it was, on his own admission[58], Young's attempt to replicate Trumbauer's singular tone on the tenor instrument that led to his peculiarly light, transparent sound in the middle and upper registers. 'I liked the way he slurred notes', he said of his early model; but to listen to Trumbauer's solo in *Singing the blues* (**64**) is to realize that there was more to his influence upon Young than these rather indulgent portamentos and the attraction of an instrumental sound. The slurs were part of a personal approach which produced a tone not simply that of an instrument, and an intonation as oblique in its own manner as Young's was to become.

By the time he was associated with Basie, other ideas were having their effect, especially the closely-linked solo and ensemble styles thriving in Kansas City and drawing upon the forthright blues tradition of the Southwest. The blues influence in Young's playing (on both tenor and clarinet) is hard to define, and he certainly retained that diatonicism and lightness of expression which made him appear such an unsuitable substitute for Coleman Hawkins with Fletcher Henderson in 1934 and which even lend a certain oddness to his celebrated and successful period with the Basie band.

His first records are those made in 1936 with a Basie group judiciously named (for reasons of contract) Jones–Smith Incorporated. Coming in for the second chorus of *Shoe shine boy*, Young impresses one first by a rhythmic strength earthed, particularly in the bridge passage, to the emphases of the rhythm section. Those emphases reflect, to some extent, a nascent swing jargon, and in his third chorus extension of the solo Young makes snatching references to what might be called the playparty songs of the jitterbug age. But the urbanity with which the entire statement is informed makes the most poignant impression, and the same wit shapes his parts in the split choruses with Basie and the vigorously lyrical Smith. A solo like that on *Lady, be good*, with its consistent linkage of lightly-jumping shapes, alternating symmetrical riff-like passages with extended looping melodies, reveals a style already confident in its maturity. A subdued but purposeful accompaniment to the trumpeter's muted solo shows his co-operative generosity, as does *Boogie woogie*, where he acts in call-and-response with Smith, posing as a one-man saxophone section and developing the boogie phrases in subsequent support of Rushing's attractive but melodically limited singing. When his solo comes in this latter number it is a piece of direct and reasoned improvisation on two sets of twelve bars, fully consistent with the mode of the piece yet with never a blue note in earshot.

As hinted, the blues imprint upon Young's playing is real but subtle. He seems to have taken the essential flexibility which, in the blues, is traditionally associated with the third and seventh degrees of the scale and not only applied it to different intervals but also incorporated it into his approach to virtually every note. And yet he does this with such finesse and avoidance of exaggeration that an illusion of legitimate tone is often strangely maintained.

The inclusion of the excitingly-scored *Rockabye Basie* and *Jump for me* is enigmatic in this context, since the tenor solos in them are almost certainly by Tate; so it is *Taxi war dance* that proves of greatest interest in this March 1939 date, especially as it seems to have been one of Young's own favourite recordings. He plays a puckish role throughout, emerging and re-emerging from the joyously chanting ensemble to indulge either in mock *ritardandos* or in half-comic motor horn blowings where the repeated notes seem positively chewed into shape. But perhaps the most delightful passage is at the beginning where he appears to guy the proceedings with an outrageous opening quotation from *Old man river* which is developed into a fresh and varied example of spontaneous melody-making. He sometimes took a perverse pleasure in sounding like a foghorn, and the gently honking entry of his solo in *Twelfth Street rag* with a distinctly oral quality in execution represents an element in his playing that was popularly exaggerated. In *Pound cake*, he twists and turns gently against brass crescendos, exhibiting a facet of his varied relation with the Basie ensemble in terms of dynamics. That he could produce a forceful countervoice is shown in the rapid vigour of *Clap hands, here comes Charlie*, and his playing there contains at least some suggestions of the less disciplined message which false disciples were later to transmit. The same day's detached rumination on *Song of the islands* is a contrasted piece of individualism, sardonically challenged from time to time by the startling macaw screechings of the trumpet section.

Riff interlude, Ham 'n' eggs, Hollywood jump and *I left my baby* complete this selection of 1939 big-band tracks. In the first three there are passages where Young's more fragile expatiations are set against ensemble accompaniments of varying degrees of exuberance and occasional violence. The tenorist contrives to remain gracefully poised amid some frantic goings-on in *Riff interlude*, and in *Ham 'n' eggs* tiptoes his elegant path through vast explosions of brass, conjuring an illusion of ease within extreme tension. Again, in the exciting *Hollywood jump* he shows his paradoxical skill in complementary detachment as he tumbles into a solo of agile introspectiveness which could, it seems, have been so easily overwhelmed by the flashing tide. The effect of the contrast of sounds is singular. One is tempted to see its greatest effectiveness in the recording studio. Did it work in public, or did Young project his rather forced wild goose *persona* in situations where the balance of threat weighed against him? Behind Rushing's singing of the only blues tune he ever seems to have learnt, Young plays instinctive tricks of temporal addition and subtraction, coming and going by unexpected doors and hinting, in the constant shift of tonal shade, at the deceptiveness of the power that lurked in his apparent gentleness.

During the 1940 performances he remains masterly even when jostled, as in *Louisiana*, which is extrovertly read, and in *Moten swing* where he sustains largeness of tone. In *Easy does it*, between lovely Clayton solos, he honks lazily in again and links sequences of melodic phrases, skilfully paced and placed. During *Let me see*, wherein Tate also solos, Young's phrasal development has an even more marked logic of inward dialogue; and on *Tickle toe*, where he sweeps ahead unpretentiously in the open, as in the brash swing-band jargon of *Blow top*, several kinds of insinuation are explored in fury's despite, and this ineffably vigorous yet dispassionate voice continually seeks to temper the atmosphere, to adapt the levels of strain. There is no more remarkable example in jazz than this of a soloist's contribution to the *total* sound of an orchestra.

But some believe that Young is best heard in a small group,

and it is hardly to be denied that the 1936 session and the 1939 Kansas City Seven performances give opportunities to judge his inventive gifts in freer surroundings. *Lester leaps in* and *Dickie's dream*, in addition to great work by Clayton, Wells, Basie, Greene, Page and Jones, have Young solos which are related, at one and the same time, to his interior thoughts and to the needs of the group. Long spiralling phrases alternate with terse and fiercely circumscribed tunes, and with simple rhythmic shapes which are sometimes taken up by the other horns or developed into momentary duets with the piano. The scalar bent of Young's improvising is evident, and he uses those slurs which he learnt from Trumbauer (upward slurs, frequently aimed at the sixth degree of the scale) as rhythmic punctuations and pivots of thought.

These small-band performances may be usefully compared with others in **157** and **196**. Meanwhile, it remains only to regret the lack of space accorded here to splendid soloists like Clayton, Edison, Wells, Tate, Warren, Tab Smith and the always delightful Basie. The importance of assessing Young dictates this niggardly treatment, but these other fine artists should be heard well.   E.T.

Al Cooper's Savoy Sultans

136 **Jump Steady**
Affinity (E) AFS1009, *MCA (A) 1345
Al Cooper's Savoy Sultans: Pat Jenkins, Sam Massenberg (tpt); Cooper (clt, alt, bar); Rudy Williams (alt); Ed McNeil (ten); Oliver Richardson (p); unidentified g; Grachan Moncur (bs); Alex Mitchell (d). New York City, 29 July 1938.
Jump steady · *Looney* · *Rhythm doctor man* · *Getting in the groove*
Same personnel and location, 19 August 1938.
Jeep's blues
Sam Simmons (ten), Cyril Haynes (p), Paul Chapman (g) replace McNeil, Richardson and unidentified; vcl by ens[1]; Jenkins (vcl[2]); Evelyn White (vcl[3]). New York City, 24 May 1939.
Stitches · *Jumping at the Savoy*[1] · *We'd rather jump than swing*[2] · *Dragging my heart around*[3]
Same personnel and location, 16 October 1939.
Little Sally Water[1] · *Jumping the blues*
Skinny Brown (ten) replaces Simmons. New York City, 29 March 1940.
Frenzy · *Sophisticated jump*
George Kelley (ten) replaces Brown. New York City, 28 February 1941.
Norfolk ferry · *Second balcony jump*

Playing at the Savoy Ballroom seems to have been rather like composing for the ballet, the music itself being only part of what was largely a piece of theatre, catering to — and being inspired by — those gyrating lindy hoppers. One result of this was that the two bands which flourished in those surroundings, Chick Webb's (**125** and **137**) and the Savoy Sultans, never really come across on record as they did in the flesh. All too few 'live' performances by Webb were captured on disc and none, apparently, by the Sultans. This means that the latter group has to be judged by studio recordings such as these, where its virtues — the rapport with the dancers, the highly functional swing — are minimized and its drawbacks — rough ensemble work, a certain over-obviousness in solos and riffs — are thrown into greater prominence. Nevertheless, the Savoy Sultans deserve to be listened to seriously as an example of the way quite a few jazz musicians operated in the 1930s — and for the playing of Williams, its one important soloist.

He was twenty-eight when he joined the Sultans in 1937, a musician whose earlier exploits seem to be completely undocumented. He was to die by drowning in 1954, by which time he had not so much faded into obscurity as been overtaken by history, in particular by the emergence of Charlie Parker. When these recordings were made, Williams was playing in a style obviously modelled upon Willie Smith's, yet he moved through chord changes in a way that foreshadowed some of the things that were to happen at Minton's and the Uptown House half a dozen years later. It is interesting that Parker liked to hear Williams play *Cherokee*, for the younger man presumably recognized in him a fellow explorer of what were then, by jazz standards, unfamiliar extensions of the chords. But Williams lacked Parker's rhythmic and imaginative audacity, so he remains a transitional figure — fascinating and exciting to listen to, but only venturing so far.

A handful of Williams's solos could almost be by Willie Smith, including, piquantly enough, a version of *Jeep's blues*, a Johnny Hodges theme which that master had recorded less than five months earlier. Most of his work, however, offers something that nobody else — in New York, anyway — was able to do in 1938. Certainly Williams stands out when in the company of musicians whose solo playing belongs within a genre and a period. Which does not mean that Massenberg is not a pleasure to hear, especially when blowing open, or that Jenkins's muted solos (he growls most convincingly in *Jeep's blues*) lack effectiveness. But the band's tenor saxophonists were cut very much to an end-of-the-decade pattern (Kelley sounds the best, his style quite obviously based on Lester Young's), while Cooper's clarinet playing rarely creates confidence. Haynes alternates between sounding like Basie, or — *vide* the first of his two choruses in *Jumping the blues* - like Billy Kyle. Not surprisingly, perhaps, Evelyn White sings like a less-energetic Ella Fitzgerald, although her efforts are sabotaged on the Affinity LP through being transferred from a 78 with a distressingly noisy surface.

The lyric which Jenkins sings on *We'd rather jump than swing* hints — 'swing's in a slump' — at the coming demise of the contemporary fashion. Nevertheless, most of the Sultans' repertoire was built around riffs that belonged very decidedly to the late 1930s, the band aiming, rather like a premature r & b group, for authenticity rather than originality. In a few pieces the saxophone section appears to aim at the kind of flatness of pitch which resurfaced thirty or so years later in the playing of South African kwela bands and of those jazz groups — Chris McGregor's Brotherhood of the Breath, for example — which drew upon that background. At the Savoy Ballroom and, as the present writer can vouch, on a pre-war broadcast in the BBC's *America Dances* series, the Sultans' saxophone players used to shuffle their feet on the floor, filling out the rhythm; Williams claimed that he wore out innumerable pairs of shoes that way. This homely touch, alas, is missing from the records. Otherwise the band's vigour and honesty still surge through, giving at least an inkling of what those dancers back in the 1930s found so intoxicating. C.F.

Chick Webb

137 **King of Swing 1937–39**

MCA (F) 510.020, Decca (A) DL9223, *Affinity (E) AFS1007
Chick Webb and His Orchestra: Mario Bauza, Bobby Stark, Taft Jordan (tpt); Sandy Williams, Nat Story (tbn); Pete Clark (clt, alt); Louis Jordan (alt); Teddy McRae (ten); Wayman Carver (ten, fl); Tommy Fulford (p); Beverley Peer (bs); Webb (d); Charlie Dixon (arr[1]). New York City, 24 March 1937.
Clap hands, here comes Charlie · *That naughty waltz*[1]
The Little Chicks: Chauncey Haughton (clt); Carver (fl); Fulford (p); Peer (bs); Webb (d). New York City, 21 September 1937.
I got rhythm
Chick Webb and His Orchestra: previous full band personnel except that Haughton (clt, alt) replaces Clark; Bobby Johnson (g) added. New York City, 1 November 1937.
Squeeze me · *Harlem Congo*[1]
Garvin Bushell (clt, alt) replaces Haughton; Ella Fitzgerald (vcl[2]) added. New York City, 17 December 1937.
The dipsy doodle[2] · *Hallelujah!*[2] · *Midnight in a madhouse*
George Matthews (tbn) added. New York City, 2 May 1938.
A-tisket a-tasket[2]

Benny Carter (arr[3]) added. New York City, 3 May 1938.
Spinning the Webb · *Liza*[3]
Hilton Jefferson (alt) replaces Jordan. New York City, 18 August 1938.
Who ya hunchin'?
Dick Vance (tpt) replaces Bauza. New York City, 17 February 1939.
Undecided[2] · *In the groove at the Grove*

For popularity, the obvious assets of the Webb orchestra at this time were its leader's own charismatic presence, the singing of Ella Fitzgerald, Taft Jordan's flamboyant romanticism and the idiosyncratic combination of Haughton (or Bushell) and Carver in the Little Chicks. And hardly inferior in ear-catching vigour was the work of Stark, Williams and McRae; but to say these things is not to make strictly musical judgments, and posterity may favour more fundamental ingredients.

Everything that made this ensemble so fervently loved of the Savoy dancers, the radio listeners and record buyers, blazes out in the heat and energy of *Clap hands, here comes Charlie* and *Harlem Congo*. The former may miss the magic of Basie's 1939 version (**135a**), but the controlled exaltation of its closing bars is still something to be wondered at; and Dixon's arrangement of *Congo* allows for and inspires some fine solos, notable among which are the piercing agilities of Haughton, grievously underrated as a clarinettist. The other acknowledged Dixon score, *That naughty waltz*, starts dully, but is lifted by Clark's fine piping and torrid cross-rhythms from Taft Jordan, and gains in liveliness at the close from enterprising temporal experiments in the writing. *Midnight in a madhouse* also suffers slightly from inconsistencies of mood, but has tough solos by Stark and Williams.

One of the conspicuous virtues of this instrumental ensemble is its achievement of a kind of quasi-choral proclamation, enlivening even conventional arrangements like *Squeeze me*, *Dipsy doodle* and *Spinning the Webb* with an almost Haydnesque jubilation. The provocative section enunciations of *Hallelujah!* and *Undecided* also bespeak something far more subtle than mere technical precision and have a puckishness which makes Miss Fitzgerald's singing appear a little sober by comparison. This confident and greatly talented young woman invests even the jejune lyrics of *The dipsy doodle* and *A-tisket a-tasket* with a sort of dignity, and it is worth emphasizing that the second of these — a nursery rhyme which is probably still her most famous hit — is, both in the singing and the playing, an episode of some jazz strength. Band and vocalist demonstrate the two ways of rendering the telescopic *Undecided* tune, and it is only here that Miss Fitzgerald gives much indication of the wit and subtlety which she was later to spin out of the rather basic stuff she was exhibiting at this stage, albeit with surprising authority.

That Webb as a drummer was almost peerless in his day is proved chiefly in his ensemble work, but also in rare but splendid solos. He is explosive on *Congo*, humorous in the Little Chicks' *I got rhythm*, and on the rumbustious hail and farewell that Carter asks of him in the fine arrangement of *Liza* there is something to be compared with earlier Webb–Carter collaborations (**125**) and later realization by Carter's own band (**149**). The polished gusto of the Chicks, though dominated by the admirable skills of the clarinettist and flautist, gains much of its effect from Webb's sensitive accompaniment. This sub-group was featured often, not just as a separate unit but also to insert contrasting interludes within a full band score. An example of this is *Hallelujah!*, Bushell having taken Haughton's chair.

There are occasional hints of fashions to come; perhaps especially in Taft Jordan's bravura, yet also in some of the more obvious band phraseology. *Spinning the Webb*, while showing zest, veers towards mere self-advertisement and one of its most pleasant features, even if it does echo ancestral voices, is Stark's cornet-like incisiveness, so well pitted against the grand swagger of Williams. Still, Webb was a driver and aimed for the future. One can think of no drummer who could exceed the verve with which he whips his team home at the end of *In the groove at the Grove*, showing no hint of the disease that would take his life, four months later almost to the day. E.T.

Jimmy Lunceford

138a Harlem Shout
MCA (A) 1305

Jimmy Lunceford and His Orchestra: Eddie Tompkins (tpt, vcl[1]); Paul Webster (tpt); Sy Oliver (tpt, arr, vcl[2]); Elmer Crumbley, Russell Bowles (tbn); Eddie Durham (tbn, g); Willie Smith (clt, alt, bar, vcl[3]); Laforet Dent (alt); Dan Grissom (alt, vcl[4]); Joe Thomas (ten); Earl Carruthers (bar); Ed Wilcox (p); Al Norris (g, vln); Moses Allen (bs); Jimmy Crawford (d); probably Tompkins, Thomas, Smith (vcl trio[5]).
New York City, 29 May 1935.
Four or five times[2]

Same personnel and location, 23 September 1935.
Swanee river · Oh boy

Same personnel and location, 30 September 1935.
I'll take the south[2,5] · *Avalon · Charmaine*[4] · *Hitting the bottle*

Same personnel and location, 23 December 1935.
My blue heaven[5] · *I'm nuts about screwy music*[3] · *The best things in life are free*[4]

Same personnel and location, 31 August 1936.
Organ grinder's swing
Same personnel and location, 1 September 1936
On the beach at Bali-Bali[5] · *Me and the moon*[5]

138b
For Dancers Only
MCA (A) 1307

Same personnel and location, 26 October 1936.
Running a temperature[2]
Same personnel and location, 20 January 1937.
I'll see you in my dreams[4]
Same personnel and location, 26 January 1937.
Linger awhile[4] · *Honest and truly*[4] · *Slumming on Park Avenue*[4]
Ed Brown (alt) replaces Dent. New York City, 15 June 1937.
Coquette[4] · *The merrygoround broke down*[2] · *Ragging the scale* · *For dancers only*
Same personnel and location, 8 July 1937.
Posing[2] · *Put on your old grey bonnet*[1]
Teddy Buckner (alt) replaces Brown; Trummy Young (tbn) added. Los Angeles, 5 November 1937.
Pigeon walk · *Annie Laurie* · *'Frisco fog*

A sense of style was, and is, important to the urban black American. How he dressed, the way he walked, his skill in keeping up with the latest slang: all were and are part of the image that black city-dwellers — the younger ones, at least — liked to project. Not surprisingly, that was reflected in black popular music, and nowhere more arrestingly than in the theatrically flamboyant big-band jazz for which Lunceford's orchestra became renowned during the late 1930s. Blues were in this band's repertoire, but treated glossily, boastful rather than lamenting. The ensemble's main singer, Grissom, used an exaggeratedly sentimental technique to put across some of the more lachrymose pop songs of the decade. Cleverness was rampant, often embarrassingly so; among the evidence are the rearrangements of Duke Ellington compositions, including a choppy *Mood indigo*, to be found on Vol. 1 of this series — *Rhythm is Our Business*, MCA (A) 1302. Yet that kind of shallowness represented only one side of the Lunceford band's policy of smartness at all costs. There were also abounding virtues.

The earliest Lunceford recordings reflected the influence of the Casa Loma Orchestra (**121**): Leon Carr's *'Frisco fog*, full of busily interlocking patterns, is a much later and, by then, rare example of that influence at work. Credit for recognizing the Lunceford band's own assets and building upon them must go to Sy Oliver and it may be worth noting that he claimed to be totally self-taught as an arranger, just like Morton, Ellington, Tadd Dameron, Gil Evans and Carla Bley. It was Oliver who persuaded Crawford to play only two beats to a bar at a moment when every other big band drummer, except Bob Crosby's Ray Bauduc (**236**), was using four. Oliver's arrangements habitually exploited the sounds of individual musicians, yet the solos, like those in Ellington's *Harlem airshaft* (**153**), would often be extremely brief, a matter of colouring rather than decoration. And Oliver's scores provided a musical counterpart to the mores of those audiences that went to hear Lunceford's band, elevating style above content, turning some of the most trivial pop songs into little masterpieces of orchestral jazz. All the more appropriate, then, that one of the band's most compelling performances, to be found on *Lunceford Special* (CBS Realm (E) 52567), should be titled *T'ain't what you do, it's the way that you do it.*

The ultimate, most distinguished proof of that axiom is Oliver's treatment of *Organ grinder's swing*, one of the most irritating hit songs of 1936. The arrangement is built around exquisite contrasts, constantly presenting new instrumental timbres, some surprisingly simple — the dialogue between guitar and saxophones, the woodblocks behind the celeste — yet effective just because of that. *For dancers only* works in an entirely different way. Almost the apotheosis of the riff number (using the chords of *Christopher Columbus*), this incorporates Webster's high-note spasms yet achieves its exciting ends with breathtaking economy.

This pair of LPs contains sixteen of Oliver's arrangements; one or two may be counted as failures, yet even those are splendidly uncluttered. Which was not always the case with those by other hands — usually Durham's, Wilcox's or Smith's. Durham's reliance upon riffs often causes his pieces to be too repetitive, *Harlem shout* being one example; he was to do better a bit later, after moving to Basie's band (see **133** and **134**). Incidentally, *Pigeon walk*, one of Durham's best scores for Lunceford, includes a brief sequence that appeared later in Basie's *Time out*, while the penultimate four bars of *Avalon* contain the riff which also provides a climax for *One o'clock jump.*

The success gained by Lunceford's orchestra probably owed more to the skills of its principal arranger than to those of its soloists. Nevertheless, those soloists did include an outstanding musician in Smith, a supremely confident performer, his solos marrying melodic with harmonic ingenuity. Plenty of his improvisations can be found on these LPs, but it is worth turning to the *Lunceford Special* LP for his outstanding performance on *Uptown blues*. On clarinet, he could be erratic, yet at his best he conveys that kind of lyrical pithiness that marks the work of some of the New Orleans clarinettists (he came, in fact, from Charleston, South Carolina). Thomas was, quite simply, superior to most tenor saxophone soloists in the big bands of the 1930s; his playing on *Me and the moon* is typically graceful. All three of the trumpeters took solos: Oliver specialized in resourceful, yet never vehement, growl work; Webster sailed through the upper register; while Tompkins, rather an underrated musician, takes most of the cheerful-sounding open solos. One merit of Lunceford's orchestra was its use of ideal, if sometimes rather surprising, tempos, a characteristic that called for an exemplary rhythm section. Allen often slapped his bass, like Wellman Braud with Ellington, but the really crucial chair was occupied by Crawford. Never a showy drummer, he was superbly reliable and unsurpassed — just listen to *For dancers only* — in his knowledge of what makes a big band swing. C.F.

139 Tommy Dorsey and His Orchestra
RCA (E) DPM2026 (2 LPs)

Tommy Dorsey and His Orchestra: Andy Ferretti, Sterling Bose, Bill Graham, Cliff Weston (tpt); Dorsey, Ben Pickering, Dave Jacobs (tbn); Sid Stoneburn , Noni Bernardi (clt, alt); Clyde Rounds (clt, alt, ten); Johnny van Eps (ten); Paul Mitchell (p); Mac Cheikes (g); Gene Traxler (bs); Sam Rosen (d). New York City, 18 October 1935.
I'm getting sentimental over you

Steve Lipkins, Joe Bauer, Max Kaminsky (tpt); Dorsey, Walter Mercurio, Les Jenkins (tbn); Joe Dixon, Rounds (clt, alt); Bud Freeman, Bob Bunch (clt, ten); Dick Jones (p); Carmen Mastren (g); Traxler (bs); Dave Tough (d). New York City, 18 October 1936.
Maple leaf rag

Bob Cusumano (tpt), Artie Foster (tbn), Fred Stulce (clt, alt, ten) replace Kaminsky, Mercurio, Bunch; Bunny Berigan (tpt) added. New York City, 19 January 1937.
Melody in F

Jimmy Welch (tpt), Red Bone (tbn) replace Lipkins, Foster; Jack Leonard (vcl[1]) added. New York City, 29 January 1937.
Marie[1] · *Song of India*

Ferretti (tpt), Slats Long (clt, alt) replace Cusumano, Dixon. New York City, 18 February 1937.
Liebestraum

Tommy Dorsey's Clambake Seven: Pee Wee Erwin (tpt); Dorsey (tbn); Johnny Mince (clt); Freeman (ten); Howard Smith (p); Mastren (g); Traxler (bs); Tough (d). New York City, 15 April 1937.
Twilight in Turkey

Tommy Dorsey and His Orchestra: Erwin, Bauer, Ferretti (tpt); Dorsey, Jenkins, Bone (tbn); Mike Doty, Stulce (clt, alt); Mince, Freeman (clt, ten); Smith (p); Mastren (g); Traxler (bs); Tough (d). Same date.
Stop, look and listen

Mercurio (tbn), Skeets Herfurt (clt, alt) replace Bone, Doty. New York City, 20 July 1937.
Smoke gets in your eyes

Tommy Dorsey's Clambake Seven: Erwin (tpt); Dorsey (tbn); Mince (clt); Freeman (ten); Smith (p); Mastren (g); Traxler (bs); Tough (d); Edythe Wright (vcl[2]). New York City, 11 September 1937.
The lady is a tramp[2]

Tommy Dorsey and His Orchestra: previous full band personnel except that Lee Castaldo (tpt), Earle Hagen (tbn) replace Bauer, Mercurio. New York City, 14 October 1937.
Who?[1]

Frank d'Annolfo (tbn), Artie Shapiro (bs), Maurice Purtill (d) replace Hagen, Traxler, Tough. New York City, 3 February 1938.
Shine on, harvest moon

Erwin, Castaldo, Ferretti (tpt); Dorsey, Jenkins, Hagen (tbn); Mince, Stulce, Hymie Schertzer (clt, alt); Herfurt (clt, ten); Dean Kincaide (ten); Smith (p); Mastren (g); Traxler (bs); Purtill (d). Hollywood, 11 July 1938.
Washboard blues

Tommy Dorsey's Clambake Seven: Erwin (tpt); Dorsey (tbn); Mince (clt); Herfurt (ten); Smith (p); Mastren (g); Traxler (bs); Purtill (d). Same date.
Chinatown, my Chinatown

Tommy Dorsey and His Orchestra: previous full band personnel. Hollywood, 25 July 1938.
Symphony in riffs

Charlie Spivak, Yank Lawson (tpt), Buddy Morrow (tbn) replace Erwin, Ferretti, Hagen. New York City, 16 September 1938.
Boogie woogie

Sam Shapiro (tpt), Babe Russin (clt, ten) replace Spivak, Herfurt; Elmer Smithers (tbn) added. New York City, 31 October 1938.
Tin roof blues

Spivak, Kaminsky (tpt), Jacobs (tbn), Herfurt (clt, ten) replace Shapiro, Castaldo, Jenkins, Kincaide. New York City, 29 November 1938.
Davenport blues · *Hawaiian war chant*

Ferretti, Castaldo, Lawson (tpt); Dorsey, Jacobs, Smithers, Ward Silloway (tbn); Mince, Stulce, Kincaide (clt, alt); Herfurt, Russin (clt, ten); Smith (p); Mastren (g); Traxler (bs); Tough (d). New York City, 19 January 1939.
Milneburg joys

Mickey Bloom (tpt), Schertzer (clt, alt), Cliff Leeman (d) replace Castaldo, Kincaide, Tough. New York City, 20 July 1939.
Stomp it off

Jimmy Blake (tpt) replaces Bloom; Herfurt absent. Chicago, 25 October 1939.

Easy does it

Ziggy Elman, Ray Linn, Chuck Peterson (tpt); Dorsey, Jenkins, George Arus, Lowell Martin (tbn); Mince, Stulce, Schertzer (clt, alt); Don Lodice, Heinie Beau (clt, ten); Joe Bushkin (p); Clark Yocum (g); Sid Weiss (bs); Buddy Rich (d). Hollywood, 16 October 1940.

Swanee river

Al Stearns (tpt), Jacobs (tbn), Manny Gershman (clt, alt), Bruce Snyder (clt, ten) replace Linn, Jenkins, Mince, Schertzer; Blake (tpt) added. New York City, 15 July 1941.

Loose lid special

Manny Klein (tpt), Jimmy Skiles (tbn), Milt Raskin (p), Phil Stevens (bs) replace Stearns, Martin, Bushkin, Weiss. Hollywood, 9 March 1942.

Well, git it!

Elman, Peterson, Blake, Jimmy Zito, Danny Vanelli (tpt); Dorsey, Arus, Skiles, Jacobs (tbn); Stulce, Harry Schuchman (clt, alt); Snyder, Beau, Lodice (clt, ten); Leonard Atkins, Seymour Maroff, William Ehrenkranz, Leonard Posner, Paul Poliakine, Sam Ross, Bernard Tinterow (vln); Harold Bemko (cel); Ruth Hill (hrp); Raskin (p); Yocum (g); Stevens (bs); Rich (d). New York City, 2 July 1942.

Blue blazes

George Seaberg, Vito Mangano, Dale Pierce, Roger Ellick (tpt); Dorsey, Nelson Riddle, Walter Benson, Colin Satterwhite (tbn); Buddy DeFranco, Sid Cooper (clt, alt); Gale Curtis, Al Klink (clt, ten); Bruce Branson (clt, bar); 9 unidentified strings; Milt Golden (p); Bob Bain (g); Sid Block (bs); Joe Park (tu); Rich (d); The Sentimentalists (vcl[3]). Hollywood, 14 November 1944.

On the sunny side of the street[3] · *Opus No. 1*

Seaberg, Mangano, Gerry Goff (tpt); Charlie Shavers (tpt, vcl[4]); Dorsey, Satterwhite, Karl de Karske, Dick Noel (tbn); Cooper, Gus Bivona (clt, alt); Branson (clt, alt, bar); Babe Fresk, Vido Musso (clt, ten); 13 unidentified strings; Duke Ellington (p); Bain (g), Block (bs); Rich (d). New York City, 14 May 1945.

The minor goes mugging

Bill Haller (tbn) DeFranco (clt, alt), Dave Harris (clt, ten), Johnny Potoker (p), Sam Herman (g) replace Noel, Bivona, Musso, Ellington, Bain. Hollywood, 20 September 1945.

At the fat man's[4] · *Chloe*

Once he separated from his brother Jimmy to lead a large group of his own, Tommy Dorsey was determined that it should be as versatile as possible, and this to facilitate commercial success in the intensely competitive world of the big swing bands. Yet those familiar with his earlier recordings, some of which are detailed in these pages, will not be surprised at the strong jazz content of most of these performances, the number of fine soloists he employed, or the inclusion of several uncompromising selections from the repertoire of the 1920s. Occasionally Dorsey was able to have it both ways: *Marie*, for example, selling in large quantities despite its containing a great solo from Berigan. The latter gains additional impact from contrast with the bland singing which precedes it (Erwin was not able to produce quite the same effect in similar circumstances on *Who?*), and this piece set the pattern for several other of the band's recordings included here. In the case of *Marie*, the antiphonal layout, supposedly derived from a group called the Sunset Royals, was also followed by Armstrong in his 1940 version with the Mills Brothers (MCA (F) 510.158). In each case, however, Dorsey's trombone, riding gently propulsive reed or brass figures and phrased with the smoothness of a french horn, was a potent element in the music's wide appeal, and his remarkable instrumental performances should not, as such, be underrated.

The relevant items, *Melody in F*, *Liebestraum*, *Song of India*, etc., also followed a tradition established in the 1920s by Paul Whiteman, who supposedly had so few links with the swing bands. There are, indeed, instructive lessons to be learnt about the development of the large jazz ensemble from setting Dorsey's *Song of India* beside the Whiteman versions of 1926 (RCA (E) DPM2027) and 1921 (Smithsonian (A) R028). In the former's hands this piece is a study in dynamic refinements, a score full of beautifully integrated variety, with an excellent Berigan solo, the whole borne aloft by Tough's drumming. Anton Rubinstein's *Melody* (here transposed into G) is drastically rephrased in its final presentation so that it turns completely into jazz, and a comparable service is rendered to *Smoke gets in your eyes* and other pieces; note also the intense dialogues between reeds and brass at the close of *Harvest moon* and *Tin roof blues*.

This last, together with *Davenport* and *Washboard blues*, *Milneburg joys* and *Maple leaf rag*, is treated quite without patronization, all undergoing a genuine modernization. Such convincing results owe much to the authority of the leader's unequivocal jazz improvising, for example on *Milneburg joys*, where he makes a very different impression from the tense and over-emphatic Lawson who precedes him. Kaminsky does better in *Davenport blues* (and also, muted, on *Hawaiian war chant*), yet the best treatment given to an old jazz standard is that received by *Washboard blues*, heard in a particularly sympathetic arrangement. This is one of the most satisfying performances here and underlines the band's high quality — a quality underrated because it also possessed many non-jazz virtues. *Swanee river*, full of varied yet well-ordered incident, is a miniature survey of the ensemble's diverse capabilities, as is the delightfully relaxed *Easy does it*; but *Symphony in riffs* can stand beside the Benny Carter recording of five years before (**122**), not least in its writing for saxophones. *Stomp it off* was scored by Sy Oliver in what is usually spoken of as the Lunceford manner yet this piece (recorded by Lunceford in 1934) is admirably suited to Dorsey's band: there was no question of Oliver imposing a new style.

After the imaginative octave-jump introduction, *On the sunny side of the street* becomes a dialogue between restrained and fiercely assertive elements, with some magnificent growl trumpet; even the vocal group phrases like a saxophone section. This is a perfect illustration of the band's power, tonal balance and of a warmth never achieved so consistently by Goodman or Shaw. Aside from Elman's mercifully brief contribution, the once-maligned *Loose lid special* is of similar quality. So is the ensemble performance of *The minor goes mugging*, and even if the association with Ellington was too brief and casual to be productive, it is of interest to hear him with a drummer as firmly propulsive as Rich, this looking forward to his encounters with Louis Bellson and Max Roach (**223**). *Opus No. 1* again demonstrates the ensemble's vehement precision and includes some well-integrated virtuoso clarinet by DeFranco. There is much good clarinet playing, too, by Mince, for instance on *Stop, look and listen*, *Twilight in Turkey* and *Chinatown* (although the Clambake Sevens lack the distinction of the Ellington, Goodman and Shaw small groups). There are characteristic statements, too, by Freeman on *Stop, look and listen*, *Harvest moon* and elsewhere, yet the main point is the singular nature of the ensemble, and this is epitomized by the kind of forthright solos its leader takes on *Stop, look and listen* or *Washboard blues* rather than on *I'm getting sentimental over you*.   M.H.

140 Charlie Barnet Vol. 1
RCA (E) RD7965, RCA (A) LPV551

Charlie Barnet and His Orchestra: Bob Burnet, Billy May, John Owens (tpt); Ben Hall, Don Ruppersberg, Bill Robertson (tbn); Don McCook (clt, alt); Barnet (sop, alt, ten); Gene Kinsey, James Lamare (alt); Kurt Bloom (ten); Bill Miller (p); Bus Etri (g); Phil Stevens (bs); Ray Michaels (d). New York City, 17 July 1939.
Cherokee

Skippy Martin (alt) replaces Lamare; Lyman Vunk (tpt) added. Hollywood, 10 September 1939.
The Duke's idea · The Count's idea

Same personnel and location, 9 October 1939.
The right idea

Spud Murphy (tbn), Cliff Leeman (d) replace Hall, Michaels; Mary Ann McCall (vcl[1]). New York City, 21 March 1940.
Wandering blues[1]
Same personnel and location, 8 May 1940.
Lament for May
Leo White (alt) replaces Martin. New York City, 19 June 1940.
Rocking in rhythm
Bernie Privin, Sam Skolnick (tpt) replace Burnet, Owen. New York City, 19 July 1940.
Pompton turnpike
Same personnel and location, 17 September 1940.
Night and day
Privin, May, Skolnick, Vunk (tpt); Murphy, Ruppersberg, Robertson, Ford Leary (tbn); Barnet (sop, alt, ten); White Lamare, Conn Humphreys (alt); Bloom (ten); Miller (p); Etri (g); Stevens (bs); Leeman (d). New York City, 14 October 1940.
Redskin rhumba
Burnet, George Esposito (tpt) replace Skolnick, May; Lena Horne (vcl[2]). New York City, 7 January 1941.
You're my thrill[2] · *Charleston Alley*
Burnet, Bob Price, Cy Baker, Mickey Bloom (tpt); Robertson, Tommy Reo, Claude Murphy, Leary (tbn); Barnet (sop, alt, ten); Humphreys, Lamare, Ray Hopfner (alt); Kurt Bloom (ten); Miller (p); Etri (g); Stevens (bs); Leeman (d); Bob Carroll (vcl[3]). Hollywood, 14 August 1941.
The heart you stole from me[3] · *Murder at Peyton Hall*
Jack LeMaire (g) replaces Etri. Hollywood, 11 September 1941.
Mother Fuzzy
Neal Hefti, Joseph Ferrante, Henry McQuinness, Burnet (tpt); Kahn Keene, Wally 'Blue' Barron, Robertson, Murphy (tbn); Barnet (sop, alt, ten); George Bohn, Humphreys, Lamare (alt); Bloom (ten); Miller (p); Edward Scalza (g); Stevens (bs); Jack Mills (d). New York City, 20 January 1942.
I can't get started

Bandleaders have seldom devoted much time to pondering on moral absolutes. Aesthetic absolutes, however, are another matter. Barnet, for instance, put his musical convictions on the line by recording *The right idea* and, though it is not included on this LP, *The wrong idea*. The latter parodied the sillier novelty bands of the 1930s; the former deployed Basie-style riffs and even had Burnet taking a trumpet solo which could pass muster for one by Harry Edison. Another piece, *The Count's idea*, did something very similar, although Barnet's tenor saxophone chorus has few links with either Lester Young or Herschel Evans. Barnet's commitment, in fact, was to the music of the large black bands: partially to Basie's, yet far more fundamentally to that of Ellington. Alone among the white swing bandleaders, Barnet modelled his orchestra upon the most inimitable of jazz ensembles, a difficult and paradoxical task.

If his orchestral style has to be called derivative, at least it displayed the imaginative skill of the pasticheur rather than the heavy hand of the imitator. His recording of *Rocking in rhythm*, for instance, is far from being a copy of any of Ellington's versions of this piece. What Barnet did was to encourage his arrangers — principally May — to use voicings and timbres that echoed many of Ellington's practices. These could turn up in contexts that were otherwise non-Ellingtonian — the seesawing riffs at the beginning and end of *Cherokee*, for instance. This piece also contains tenor saxophone playing which is typical of Barnet's approach to the instrument — skittish, staccato, rather trite rhythmically — but ends with an alto passage, one of many, in which his admiration for Johnny Hodges is apparent, just as it is in various solos on soprano saxophone.

Barnet's gifts, in fact, were not those of a jazz soloist, competent though he often sounded. Much more importantly, he was an inspiring leader, able to imprint his enthusiasm upon his bands. He also composed and arranged much better than he played. One of the finest scores on this LP, *Lament for May*, finds Barnet working within the Ellington style (just as Billy Strayhorn did) yet with a distinctive melodic flair that is all his own. Where Ellington's orchestra was unusual in moving around the string bass, Barnet conformed to more conventional attitudes of the time and, by 1940 at least, built his rhythm section upon the splendidly tight drumming of Leeman. The Ellington allegiance was reflected in the work of the brass section and in Burnet's command of plunger-muted solo playing — deftly executed but lacking the sting of Cootie Williams's. Perhaps Burnet's most engaging performance, however, can be heard in *Leaping at the Lincoln* (*Charlie Barnet Vol. 2*, RCA (E) RD8088), where he makes a Beiderbeckian use of *rubato*. *Charleston Alley* contains solos by Privin, at the beginning, and Burnet, at the end, which exploit the same kind of approach.

Miller, a useful if eclectic pianist, was adept at reproducing Ellington's characteristic left-hand thumps, though less successful in summoning up Basie's deceptive economy; in *Mother Fuzzy* he even contrived to sound like the inflexible Bob Zurke. Yet by far the most impressive of Barnet's soloists, apart from Burnet, was the guitarist, Etri. He can be heard in *Wandering blues* and the theatrically moody *Murder at Peyton Hall*; in both pieces his playing reflects the influence of Eddie Durham rather than Charlie Christian. Etri died in a car crash in 1941, otherwise he might have developed into an outstanding performer. But the virtues of Barnet's music reside mainly in the band as a whole rather than in particular individuals. The saxophone section was exceptionally strong and can be heard at its finest in a passage towards the end of *Charleston Alley*. And the music was never bland as, for example, Goodman's could sometimes be. Nothing illustrates this more vividly than *Redskin rhumba*, a head arrangement which begins where *Cherokee* ended, using the same chord sequence yet omitting the treacherous middle-eight. There are no solos of any significance, but the performance has an infectious looseness and swing to it.   C.F.

141 Benny Goodman: the Fletcher Henderson Arrangements
RCA (F) 741.044

Benny Goodman and His Orchestra: Nate Kazebier, Jerry Neary, Bunny Berigan (tpt); Red Ballard, Jack Lacey (tbn); Goodman (clt); Hymie Schertzer, Toots Mondello (alt); Dick Clark, Arthur Rollini (ten); Frank Froeba (p); George van Eps (g); Harry Goodman (bs); Gene Krupa (d); Fletcher Henderson (arr). New York City, 25 June 1935.
Blue skies

Ralph Muzillo (tpt) replaces Neary. New York City, 1 July 1935.
King Porter stomp · Sometimes I'm happy

Harry Geller (tpt), Joe Harris (tbn), Bill DePew (alt), Jess Stacy (p), Allan Reuss (g) replace Berigan, Lacey, Mondello, Froeba, van Eps. Chicago, 22 November 1935.
When Buddha smiles · If I could be with you one hour tonight

Same personnel and location, 20 March 1936.
Christopher Columbus · I know that you know

Pee Wee Erwin (tpt) replaces Muzillo. Chicago, 23 April 1936.
You forgot to remember

Chris Griffin (tpt), Murray McEachern (tbn) replace Geller, Harris. New York City, 27 May 1936.
I would do anything for you

Manny Klein (tpt) replaces Kazebier; Stacy absent. Hollywood, 13 August 1936.
Down south camp meeting

Sterling Bose (tpt) replaces Klein; Vido Musso (ten), Stacy (p) added. Hollywood, 21 August 1936.
Bugle call rag

Ziggy Elman, Harry James (tpt) replace Erwin, Bose; Clark absent. New York City, 14 January 1937.
I want to be happy · Chloe

George Koenig (alt) replaces DePew. Hollywood, 6 July 1937.
Can't we be friends?

Same personnel and location, 6 September 1937.
Sugar foot stomp
Vernon Brown (tbn), Noni Bernardi, Dave Matthews (alt), Bud Freeman
(ten), Ben Heller (g), Dave Tough (d) replace McEachern, Schertzer,
Koenig, Musso, Reuss, Krupa. New York City, 28 May 1938.
Big John special

Looking back, in 1939, upon his band's first fame[59], Goodman
acknowledged a debt to Fletcher Henderson, whose hard-won
skill as an arranger can be traced in **85, 86, 126** and **127**. The
1935 recordings of *King Porter stomp* and *Sometimes I'm happy*
won great public applause and helped to establish the band's
characteristic style. *Blue skies*, cut a few days previously, has
many of the elements of that style and, like *Sometimes I'm happy,
When Buddha smiles, If I could be with you, I know that you know,
You forgot to remember, I would do anything for you, I want to be
happy* and *Can't we be friends?*, shows the fruit of Goodman's
discovery that Henderson could bring to the treatment of popular
songs the orchestral techniques already applied to the jazz
classics and to original compositions. In 1934, at John Hammond's prompting, Goodman had bought jazz scores from a
somewhat needy Henderson. Some of these had been produced for
Henderson's own band, others were made to order; and Goodman
was persuaded to let Henderson loose on Tin Pan Alley ballads
which otherwise would have been treated with far less verve and
freedom. Once a hard-headed Goodman saw commercial possibilities in all this, contrary to earlier reservations on his part, a
famous and influential band style came into being — one that was
also, in the ensuing years, to utilize the arranging gifts of Edgar
Sampson and Jimmy Munday (**142**).

King Porter stomp catches much of the form and spirit of
Henderson's contribution to this phase of big band development.
It is also the culmination of a provocative sequence of interpretation wherein an earlier jazz genius was transmuted. By 1936, the
Goodman–Henderson *King Porter* was just one of those swing
standards for which the fans yelled at interminable one-night
stands. Two years later Jelly Roll Morton visited the Library of
Congress and cut two contrasting versions of the stomp, as if to
show the fickle world what magic still danced in the original
conception (**21**). But, back in March 1928, the Henderson band
had recorded a fine head arrangement of this Morton number
(**86**), notable not only because it successfully translated the
strains of the piano stomp into the language of orchestral
dialogue, but also because it achieved a simplicity of means and a
relaxation of performance which were unusual for the band at the
time

The arrangement recorded by Goodman is close relative to the co-operative interpretation of 1928. Its comparative smoothness results partly from the lighter rhythmic support, with guitar and bass replacing banjo and tuba, partly from the more sophisticated, not to say calculated, *rubato* with which a written score was being read. Tension is more subtly and dramatically handled, with the reed figures which had once accompanied Buster Bailey's solo adapted for the menacing bass notes of trombones beneath a long Goodman solo, and for the rather bland purposefulness of saxophones to abet Berigan and Ballard. In the final riff choruses, whose antiphonal hints had been realized by the Henderson band through intense exchanges of reed and brass, full of song-like expression, the Goodman sections play with a tough peremptoriness which may be a little closer to the bell-like chords of Morton's various piano versions but lacks some of their joyousness. A commonplace chromatic affirmation replaces the sombre coda which Henderson had originally added.

Perhaps comparisons with Morton are not too edifying. This is the music of a different world from his; different, too, in subtler ways, from the world of Henderson's own groups. A comparison of Goodman's *Down south camp meeting* and *Big John special* with Henderson's own 1934 renderings (**127**) may suggest that a certain ascendancy of form over feeling in the Goodmans was not just a consequence of Henderson's working — presumably at a remove — for a band not his own. He was a professional and knew what was required of him in such a relationship; so whilst one may find a more poetic satisfaction in the combination of his writing and the co-operation of musicians of his own choice, the work for Goodman deserves some assessment on its own terms. Henderson's writing for saxophones is often realized in languid voicings which rob it of some of its point. *Sometimes I'm happy* is typical of this tendency. *Bugle call rag* shows that the reeds' sound was to become more sinewy, but there is some doubt concerning Henderson's hand in this score, which has also been attributed to Dean Kincaide. Kincaide echoed Henderson's call-and-response device in Goodman's 1935 *The dixieland band* (RCA (F) 741.072) so could have been responsible for this 1936 number. *Down south camp meeting* may be the best-known example of the antiphonal mode learnt from the 'shout' tradition, but related passages are frequent, and Henderson's occasional use of a clarinet choir (*Blue skies, Down south camp meeting*) is another reminder of older habits, to be indulged in later by the Bob Crosby band (**236**). On the other hand, the incidental balance of voices within the band prompts Henderson to use effective contrasts of tension and relaxation. There are dramatic deployments of crescendos, key changes and melodic scoring for both brass and reeds which prove this arranger's gift for jazz variation. Weak, matter-of-fact endings mar some pieces, *Sugar foot stomp* and *Can't we be friends?* are examples; in the latter, loss of tension is due to an ill-advised reversion to the original key.

Solos, even Goodman's own, are generally brief, as suited the fashion; the memorable ones are Berigan's in the earliest numbers, James's recreation of the *Dippermouth* solo in *Sugar foot stomp*, and a splendid full chorus by Stacy in *Big John special* which seems like a belated reward for his zestful ensemble work earlier on. Goodman's Chicago origins are masked somewhat by his remarkable facility of execution, but they show through wryly in a solo on *I know that you know*, where Bud Freeman rather than Frank Teschemacher is echoed.   E.T.

142 **Benny Goodman: the Jimmy Mundy and Edgar Sampson Arrangements**
RCA (F) 741.084

Benny Goodman and His Orchestra: Nate Kazebier, Ralph Muzillo, Bunny Berigan (tpt); Red Ballard, Joe Harris (tbn); Goodman (clt); Hymie Schertzer, Bill DePew (alt); Arthur Rollini, Dick Clark (ten); Jess Stacy (p); Allan Reuss (g); Harry Goodman (bs); Gene Krupa (d). Hollywood, 27 September 1935.
Madhouse

Harry Geller (tpt) replaces Berigan. Chicago, 24 January 1936.
Stomping at the Savoy

Pee Wee Erwin, Chris Griffin (tpt), Murray McEachern (tbn) replace Geller, Muzillo, Harris; Helen Ward (vcl[1]). New York City, 15 June 1936.
In a sentimental mood · Swingtime in the Rockies · These foolish things[1]

Same personnel and location, 16 June 1936.
House hop · There's a small hotel[1]

Zeke Zarchey, Ziggy Elman (tpt), Vido Musso (ten) replace Kazebier, Erwin, Clark. New York City, 7 October 1936.
Organ grinder's swing

Same personnel and location, 5 November 1936.
Jam session

Irving Goodman (tpt) replaces Zarchey. New York City, 9 December 1936.
When you and I were young, Maggie · Swing low, sweet chariot

Harry James (tpt), George Koenig (alt) replace Irving Goodman, DePew. Hollywood, 6 July 1937.
Sing, sing, sing

Vernon Brown (tbn), Babe Russin (ten) replace McEachern, Musso. New York City, 16 February 1938.
Don't be that way
James, Elman, Griffin (tpt); Ballard, Brown (tbn); Goodman (clt); Dave Matthews, Milt Yaner (alt); Rollini, Bud Freeman (ten); Stacy (p); Ben Heller (g); Harry Goodman (bs); Dave Tough (d). New York City, 8 April 1938.
Lullaby in rhythm
Noni Bernardi (alt) replaces Yaner. New York City, 28 May 1938.
My melancholy baby

To what extent is the identity of a big band created by its leader, its sidemen or its arrangers? The answers vary, of course, depending on the individuals involved. Krupa's orchestra of the 1940s, for instance, never projected any consistent style, although the music was often excellent. The same was true of the Mills Blue Rhythm Band a decade earlier (**122**). In both cases, you might say, all three elements were lacking: the leader provided no particular musical policy, the sidemen were rarely quite distinguished enough to affect events, the arrangements were the work of too many, and too various, hands. Goodman's band invites a very different interpretation. The early success of Fletcher Henderson's scores, combined with the instinct of a strong-minded leader, resulted in the perpetuation of what was, at least until the arrival of Eddie Sauter in 1939, an orchestral pattern so precise that it almost amounted to a trademark.

Nobody was more assiduous or expert (the implications are both pejorative and admiring) at adhering to that formula than Jimmy Mundy. Previously best known for his work for Earl Hines (**129, 147**), he had no fewer than forty arrangements recorded by Goodman. Eleven can be found on this LP, commencing with the earliest, *Madhouse*. This was typical of what was to follow, especially in varying phrases rhythmically and establishing a fairly basic sort of counterpoint, yet rarely achieving any subtleties of texture, despite some useful writing for the saxophones. Performed by a lesser band, scores like these could take on a period flavour — always a risk run by arrangers as distinct from genuine jazz composers; indeed, *House hop* is a bit too humdrum for comfort. Most of the time, however, Mundy's arrangements were performed with a precision and crispness that could not be approached by any black bands of the day, apart from Jimmy Lunceford's (the ensembles of Ellington, Basie, Henderson and Redman possessed virtues that mitigated, sometimes justified, a certain incipient sloppiness). Characteristic of this executive sophistication is the work of Goodman's saxophone section, with vibratos matching, expertly led by Schertzer, in *Swing low, sweet chariot*.

The distinction between a skilful craftsman and a really imaginative writer can be seen by setting the above recording of *Organ grinder's swing* beside Lunceford's (**138a**). Sy Oliver's orchestration is virtually a recomposition of (and a vast improvement upon) fairly trite material, and done with much care for dynamics and surprisingly contrasted timbres. In comparison, Mundy's arrangement works, but in a far more obvious and predictable way. Nobody is quite sure who scored *My melancholy baby*, another routine affair in any case, but the remaining three pieces — *Stomping at the Savoy, Don't be that way* and *Lullaby in rhythm* — were the work of Edgar Sampson. In fact, he originally wrote the first two for Chick Webb's orchestra in 1934. Where Mundy is intent upon deploying riffs and even simplifying familiar themes into riff patterns, Sampson has a melodic instinct that always comes through. His tunes really are tunes, rhythmic but also lilting.

The same is true of the majority of Goodman's clarinet solos; even at its hottest — and the period term seems especially apt — his improvising stays close enough to the theme for even a lay listener to be able to grasp what he is up to. Understandably enough, he takes the bulk of the solos, since he not only led the band but also happened to be its outstanding instrumentalist. With the exception, that is, of Stacy, who was featured much too rarely on Goodman's records but is heard in a thirty-two-bar chorus on *Madhouse*. Brown contributes a few shortish trombone solos, James surfaces flamboyantly in *Sing, sing, sing*; and Freeman picks his elegant way through *Lullaby in rhythm*, the fastidiousness of his tenor playing in sharp contrast to Musso's declamatory manner. Time has been less kind to Krupa's rollicking performance in the two-part *Sing, sing, sing*: it was, after all, only Stacy's pellucid solo which turned the Carnegie Hall recording (CBS (E) 66202) into a minor classic. Elsewhere, though, Krupa compensates for the indifferent bass playing by holding the rhythm section neatly on course.   C.F.

Benny Goodman

143
Benny Goodman: Solid Gold Instrumental Hits

CBS (E) 88130 (2 LPs), 2-Columbia (A) PG33405 (2 LPs)

Benny Goodman and His Orchestra: Alec Fila, Jimmy Maxwell, Irving Goodman, Cootie Williams (tpt); Lou McGarity, Cutty Cutshall (tbn); Benny Goodman (clt); Gus Bivona, Skippy Martin, Bob Snyder (alt); George Auld, Jack Henderson (ten); Bernie Leighton (p); Mike Bryan (g); Artie Bernstein (bs); Harry Jaeger (d). New York City, 18 December 1940.

Superman · Moonlight on the Ganges

Teddy Wilson (p), Dave Tough (d) replace Leighton, Jaeger. New York City, 21 January 1941.

Time on my hands

Les Robinson (alt), Pete Mondello (ten), Johnny Guarnieri (p) replace Martin, Henderson, Wilson. New York City, 19 February 1941.

Scarecrow

Billy Butterfield (tpt), Martin (alt) replace Fila, Snyder. New York City, 27 March 1941.

Fiesta in blue

Jimmy Horvath (alt), Wilson (p), Jo Jones (d) replace Bivona, Guarnieri, Tough. New York City, 5 May 1941.

Something new · Airmail special

Al Davis (tpt), Clint Neagley (alt), Vido Musso, George Berg (ten), Mel Powell (p), Tom Morgan (g), John Simmons (bs), Sidney Catlett (d) replace Irving Goodman, Robinson, Auld, Mondello, Wilson, Bryan, Bernstein, Jones; Chuck Gentry (bar) added; Horvath absent. Chicago, 1 August 1941.

The Count · Pound Ridge

Same personnel and location, 15 August 1941.

The birth of the blues

Same personnel and location, 20 August 1941.

Clarinet à la king

Mart Blitz (bs) replaces Simmons; Catlett absent. New York City, 25 September 1941.

The Earl

Bernie Privin (tpt), Sol Kane (alt), Sid Weiss (bs) replace Butterfield, Martin, Blitz; Ralph Collier (d) added; Williams absent. New York City, 23 January 1942.

Jersey bounce

Art Ralston (bar) replaces Gentry; Peggy Lee (vcl[1]) added. New York City, 5 February 1942.

A string of pearls · My little cousin[1]

Williams, Tony Faso, Privin (tpt); McGarity, Charlie Castaldo (tbn); Goodman (clt); Hymie Schertzer, Bud Shiffman (alt); Jerry Jerome, Berg (ten); Johnny McAfee (bar); Powell (p); Dave Barbour (g); Weiss (bs); Alvin Stoller (d); Dick Haymes (vcl[2]). New York City, 17 June 1942.

Idaho[2]

Maxwell, Lawrence Stearns (tpt), Jan Walton (alt), Bob Poland, Neagley (ten), Leonard Sims (bar), Cliff Hills (bs), Howard Davies (d) replace Williams, Privin, Shiffman, Jerome, Berg, McAfee, Weiss, Stoller; Haymes absent. New York City, 27 July 1942.
Six flats unfurnished
Same personnel and location, 30 July 1942.
Mission to Moscow
Vincent Badale, Faso, Alex Cuozzo, Sonny Berman (tpt); Don Matthew, William Pritchard, Trummy Young (tbn); Goodman (clt), Stanley Kosow, Aaron Sachs (alt); Al Epstein, Bill Shine (ten); Danny Bank (bar); Charlie Queener (p); Bryan (g); Clyde Lombardi (bs); Morey Feld (d). New York City, 17 March 1945.
Clarinade · Love walked in

The band which made the RCA recordings discussed above is usually considered Goodman's best and most representative, although that judgment is the result of a nostalgic attitude towards its first great public impact in the mid-1930s. In fact, and as might have been expected from so exacting a leader, considerable further strides were made and many of the performances on this two-LP set gain an additional unity from being composed and scored by the same person, usually Eddie Sauter or Mel Powell. As *Moonlight on the Ganges* particularly well shows, Sauter's writing was far more imaginative and sophisticated than Henderson's, Mundy's or Sampson's, embodying a more creative attitude to ensemble texture and the varied blending of instrumental tone colours. At the same time, the band's heightened quality as an executive unit led to performances of greater assertiveness than hitherto, and not only of material by Sauter. Note, for example, the sheer drive of Buster Harding's *Scarecrow*, and air of spontaneity not easily achieved by a large ensemble, the cumulative vehemence. *Something new* and *The Count* are further instances of the band's vitality, and on *The Earl* not even the absence of a drummer lessens the music's impetus.

Just as striking are the precision and tonal fullness of each section: hear the lift and flexibility of the saxophones behind Haymes on *Idaho*, the support they give Williams in *Moonlight on the Ganges*, their phrases exactly complementing his. Powell's relaxed treatment of *Jersey bounce* completely alters the melody's character for the better; and it is no surprise that this *String of pearls* is so great an improvement on the famous Glenn Miller version set down three months before. Among jazz commentators, Goodman's reward for such things was the usual one, each advance being gleefully hailed as a further decline. During the period that these beautiful records were being made he was described, for example, as the 'magnificent monarch of fish cold swing'[60]. Yet his own playing continued to move forward; purely technical gains were scarcely possible and, though a strict jazz enthusiast would never believe it, the fairly subtle changes which occurred in Goodman's improvising may have been indirectly due to a broadening of horizons that came from his involvement at this time with the music of Mozart, Bartók, Copland, Hindemith and Milhaud. His solos here are more adventurous, departing further from the themes, and are longer than on 141 and 142; his consistency is remarkable, *Something new*, *Scarecrow*, *String of pearls* and *Airmail special* being just a few of these tracks which include brilliant clarinet extemporizations. A special case is *Clarinet à la king*, one of the finest miniature concertos in the jazz repertoire; Sauter may be said in this genre to surpass everybody except Ellington. The performance included here is less immaculate than the one chosen for the original 78 rpm issue, but probably the most satisfying version was that recorded on 23 October 1941 and intended for a twelve-inch 78 though not released at the time (Phontastic (Sd) NOST7617). *Clarinade* is Powell's entry in these particular stakes, and though a distinguished piece it is more conventional than Sauter's, its range of gesture smaller; but it elicits more superb clarinet work.

Another kind of pleasure arises from the quick-thinking exchanges between Goodman and Powell on *Mission to Moscow* and *The Earl*. The latter is an apt vehicle for the pianist's immaculate post-Teddy Wilson playing, and the band's participation is well varied. A companion piece to *The Count*, this rendering of *The Earl* should be compared with Earl Hines's version of two months later (RCA (F) FRM17000). That has a predictably more aggressive — though scarcely more inventive — keyboard part, but Goodman's is the better overall performance. A somewhat comparable instance is *Fiesta in blue*, initially named *Cootie growls*, wherein, both open and muted, Williams makes the most of the opportunities which Mundy's score provides. It has a high melodic content and is another *Concerto for Cootie* (see 153), though shaped with a much less knowing compositional craft. This reading is better than the widely-commended Basie recording of six months later which cast Buck Clayton in a somewhat uncharacteristic role and of which several different takes may be heard on CBS (F) 66102. But no doubt, as when the New Orleans Rhythm Kings were inconsiderate enough to record *Tin roof blues* (43) before King Oliver did *Jazzing babies blues* (44), we are required to believe that Goodman was somehow copying Basie. A still better vehicle for Williams is *Superman*, also intended for a twelve-inch 78 and of which the above is a previously unissued take. Excellently composed by Sauter, the music unfolds with much diversity of pace and emphasis, the soloist appearing in a number of distinct contexts. There are further outstanding contributions from Williams in *Pound Ridge* and *Moonlight on the Ganges*, and during this period he stood with Goodman and Powell as the band's most original soloist. The role of Butterfield in *Something new* and of McGarity in *Scarecrow, String of pearls* and *Jersey bounce* should not be missed, however.   M.H.

144 Harry James and His Orchestra 1936–38
The Old Masters (A) TOM36, *CBS (F) 88499 (2 LPs)

The Dean and His Kids: James (tpt, vcl[1]); Bruce Squires (tbn); Irving Fazola (clt); Dave Matthews (ten); Freddy Slack (p); Frank Frederico (g); Thurman Teague (bs); Ben Pollack (d). New York City, 16 September 1936.
Spreading knowledge around · Zoom, zoom, zoom[1]

Harry James and His Orchestra: James, Buck Clayton (tpt); Eddie Durham (tbn); Earle Warren (atl); Jack Washington (alt, bar); Herschel Evans (ten); Jess Stacy (p); Walter Page (bs); Jo Jones (d); Helen Humes (vcl[2]). New York City, 1 December 1937.
Jubilee[2] *· When we're alone · I can dream, can't I?*[2] *· Life goes to a party*

Vernon Brown (tbn) replaces Durham. New York City, 5 January 1938.
Texas chatter · Song of the wanderer[2] *· It's the dreamer in me*[2] *· One o/clock jump*

James, Ziggy Elman (tpt); Brown (tbn); Matthews (alt); Arthur Rollini (ten); Harry Carney (bar); Stacy (p); Teague (bs); Dave Tough (d). New York City, 27 April 1938.
Out of nowhere · Wrap your troubles in dreams · Lullaby in rhythm · Little white lies

The notion of bad taste is not a bourgeois shibboleth but an aesthetic reality. In jazz, for instance, there are performers who can, on occasion, deploy virtuosity to very unworthy ends and proffer *kitsch* instead of emotion. Charlie Shavers was a trumpeter of that sort. James is another, guilty of the pyrotechnical *Flight of the bumble bee* and the sugary platitudes of *You made me love you*, yet also capable of playing the music to be found on this LP. His style, paradoxically, reflects the influence of a cornettist generally thought of as being more sea-greenly incorruptible than most: Muggsy Spanier. James took over Spanier's trick of repeating phrases, neatly tucking them in after one another, as well as the habit of throwing in the occasional whoop; all performed, of course, with a superior technique and, in pieces such as *Life goes to a party*, absorbing the kind of harmonic and structural flexibility that Henry Allen and Roy Eldridge had introduced to jazz trumpeting. What James developed from this was a rolling, declamatory style, similar at times to Bunny Berigan's yet possessing a characteristic jauntiness.

James was only twenty and working with Pollack's band when he recorded the first two titles. *Zoom, zoom, zoom*, a tedious novelty number about string bass playing, operates rather along the lines of the Mike Riley–Eddie Farley version of *The music goes round and round*, which had just become something of a hit. *Spreading knowledge around* is much more worthwhile, not just because of James's enthusiastic playing but for Fazola's clarinet solos, deliciously poised, contrasting with the beefy dixieland surroundings.

John Hammond organized the sessions of December 1937 and January 1938, mostly using a contingent from Basie's orchestra. Hammond has recalled [61] that James did not like Lester Young's playing — which explains Herschel Evans's presence. Perhaps the trumpeter's fondness for Evans's work reflected a preference for richness of tone. Evans's high romanticism, as sensual as that of any jazz saxophonist, was maybe pushed to excess at the start of *I can dream, can't I?*, but elsewhere is kept excitingly in check. James's own ability to produce a ravishing trumpet sound comes across strongly in *Song of the wanderer*; this kind of playing has been compared to some of Joe Thomas's solos, especially that in Alex Hill's *Song of the plow* on Jazz Document (Sw) va-7999. Nevertheless, James concludes the piece with a chorus that would not be out of place in Spanier's *Relaxing at the Touro* (**235**).

When these recordings were made, Helen Humes had not yet joined Basie's orchestra. She possessed a freshness of phrasing, a kind of rhythmic alertness, that made her an exceptional and rather underrated singer of ballads, but which became coarsened and much less individual a decade or more later when she started specializing in blues. Clayton pops up behind her in *Song of the wanderer* and, again playing muted, during the middle-eight of *When we're alone*, his only solo contributions to these sessions. *One o/clock jump* might be called an example of *Hamlet* without the Prince of Denmark; not because Basie is absent — he was replaced by one of his peers — but because, after two choruses apiece from Stacy, Evans, Brown and James, the performance dies away without the final unforgettable riffs being heard.

Stacy's piano playing — crisply staccato, constantly inventive — is one of the delights of this LP, even when he is not taking a solo. There is, incidentally, a brief yet typical instance of the special rapport between him and Tough during the third chorus of

Lullaby in rhythm from a session where the band, except for Carney and Teague, was drawn from Goodman's orchestra. Just as James preferred to use Evans rather than Young, he chose, far more inexplicably, for his tenor saxophonist on this date, not Bud Freeman, who was with Goodman at the time, but Rollini, offering a watered-down version of Freeman's style. Matthews plays alto saxophone with more aplomb than he did tenor on the first session; indeed, he takes an airy solo, albeit one much indebted to Johnny Hodges, on *Wrap your troubles in dreams.* During this performance, unsurprisingly, James's playing reflects something of Armstrong's influence; not so much in its tone, for by now his timbre had become unmistakable, as in details of structure and phrasing. Even so, the coda might have come straight out of a Spanier solo. C.F.

145 Artie Shaw and His New Music 1936–37
Sunbeam (A) SB207

Artie Shaw and His Orchestra: Willie Kelly (tpt); Mark Bennett (tbn); Shaw (clt); Tony Zimmers (ten); Julie Schechter, Lou Klayman (vln); Sam Persoff (vla); Jimmy Oderich (cel); Fulton McGrath (p); Wes Vaughan (g); Hank Wayland (bs); Sammy Weiss (d). New York City, 11 June 1936.
Japanese sandman · A pretty girl is like a melody

Lee Castaldo, Zeke Zarchy (tpt); Buddy Morrow (tbn); Shaw (clt); Tony Pastor (ten); Jerry Gray, Frank Siegfield (vln); Persoff (vla); Bill Schuman (cel); Joe Lippman (p); Tony Gottuso (g); Ben Ginsberg (bs); George Wettling (d). New York City, 23 December 1936.
Sobbing blues · Copenhagen · Cream puff · My blue heaven

Artie Shaw and His Strings: Castaldo, Zarchy, Morrow, Pastor absent. Same date.
Streamline · Sweet Lorraine

Artie Shaw and His Orchestra: previous full band personnel; Peg LaCentra (vcl[1]) added. New York City, 15 February 1937.
Moonlight and shadows[1]

Artie Shaw and His New Music: John Best, Malcolm Crain, Tom di Carlo (tpt); Harry Rogers, George Arus (tbn); Shaw (clt); Les Robinson, Harry Freeman (alt); Pastor (ten, vcl[2]); Fred Petry (ten); Les Burness (p); Al Avola (g); Ben Ginsberg (bs); Cliff Leeman (d). New York City, 18 May 1937.
Someday, sweeheart

Same personnel and location, 22 July 1937.
How dry I am

Jules Rubin (ten) replaces Petry; Leo Watson (vcl[3]) added. New York City, 17 September 1937.
It's a long, long way to Tipperary · Nightmare · Shoot the likker to me, John, boy[3]

Nita Bradley (vcl[4]) added. New York City, 30 December 1937.
Whistle while you work[2,3] · *One song*[4]

By the tail-end of the 1930s, Shaw became one of the prime beneficiaries of the swing era, simultaneously rich and famous, the leader of a band that ranked alongside Goodman's and Tommy Dorsey's. Paradoxically, that very fashionableness probably resulted in Shaw's merits, both his playing and the quality of his various ensembles, being consistently underrated by the jazz community. This LP presents his earliest innovation, the forming of a band around a string quartet. Apart from some of Bill Challis's scores for Paul Whiteman (**65**), jazz arrangers habitually wrote for strings in a manner akin to Hollywood's filterings of nineteenth century romanticism, everything that *kitsch* implies. The string quartet ensured a drier sound. In addition, the writing, much of it by Lippman, the band's pianist, was successful in fusing the strings with clarinet or with the four, sometimes five, horns.

The former combination is heard at its most effective in *Streamline* and *Sweet Lorraine*. No doubt intended to evoke the image of a 1930s locomotive or propeller-driven aeroplane, *Streamline*, very fast, contains some of Shaw's most agile clarinet playing and also makes tactical use of contrast. *Sweet Lorraine* is a beautifully poised example of ballad playing, the leader's variations never lapsing into the sentimentality of Jimmy Noone's famous but excessively bedizened version (**41**). Some arrangements — those of *Copenhagen* and *Sobbing blues*, for instance — incorporate short passages in dixieland style, yet without upsetting the overall balance. The final sixteen bars of the latter title, incidentally, provide at least some evidence for the sleeve note writer's idea that Eddie Sauter may have scored this number. The solos, even those by Shaw, are generally brief and functional.

However kindly posterity may regard these experiments with strings, the contemporary American public preferred the louder, more obvious approach of conventional swing bands — which explains Shaw's *volte-face* early in 1937, reflected in the final seven tracks. Not surprisingly, quite a few of the scores follow the pattern established by Goodman's orchestra, alternating the brass and saxophone sections. Indeed, despite the fact that Jerry Gray was writing many of the arrangements, this period of Shaw's music lacks identity, a transitional phase which culminates in the performances on **146**. Like Goodman, Shaw takes nearly all the solos. Not that he had much competition. Best was a better than average trumpeter, Pastor no more than an amiable genre player. But Shaw always used good drummers, while in Leo

Watson he had one of the most beguiling and inventive of scat singers; alas, Watson performs far too briefly in *Shoot the likker to me, John, boy* and is only minimally present on *Whistle while you work*. *Nightmare*, which Shaw was to make his theme tune, deploys textures excitingly, while his clarinet playing is full of blue inflections; but then so it is, far more improbably, in *It's a long, long way to Tipperary*.   C.F.

146 Artie Shaw Bluebird Recordings Vol. 1
RCA (A) AXM2–5517 (2 LPs), *RCA (F) PM43175 (2 LPs)

Artie Shaw and His Orchestra: Chuck Peterson, John Best, Claude Bowen (tpt); Harry Rogers, George Arus, Ted Vesely (tbn); Shaw (clt); Les Robinson, Hank Freeman (alt); Tony Pastor (ten, vcl[1]); Ronnie Perry (ten); Les Burness (p); Al Avola (g); Sid Weiss (bs); Cliff Leeman (d); Billie Holiday (vcl[2]). New York City, 24 July 1938.
Begin the beguine · *Indian love call*[1] · *Coming on* · *Back Bay shuffle* · *Any old time*[2] · *I can't believe that you're in love with me*

Russell Brown (tbn), George Koenig (alt) replace Vesely, Robinson; Helen Forrest (vcl[3]) added. New York City, 27 September 1938.
Nightmare · *Nonstop flight* · *Yesterdays* · *What is this thing called love?* · *You're a sweet little headache*[3] · *I have eyes*[3]

Robinson (alt) replaces Koenig. New York City, 17 November 1938.
Between a kiss and a sigh[3] · *Thanks for everything*[3] · *Deep in a dream*[3] · *Day after day*[3] · *Softly, as in the morning sunrise* · *Copenhagen*

Bernie Privin (tpt), Les Jenkins (tbn), George Auld (ten), Bob Kitsis (p), George Wettling (d) replace Bowen, Brown, Perry, Burness, Leeman. New York City, 19 December 1938.
A room with a view[3] · *Say it with a kiss*[3] · *They say*[3] · *It took a million years*[3] · *Jungle drums* · *It had to be you*

Buddy Rich (d) replaces Wettling. New York City, 17 January 1939.
Lover, come back to me · *My heart stood still* · *Rosalie*[1] · *Suppertime*[3] · *Vilia*

Same personnel and location, 23 January 1939.
The man I love · *The donkey serenade* · *Bill*[3] · *Carioca* · *Zigeuner*

During its best fame, Shaw's band was regarded as more innovative and a little more sophisticated than Goodman's — the obvious comparison. Would these groups have been so compared had their leaders not both been clarinettists? In the 1930s, Goodman's solo work dominated his band's records less than Shaw's does in the work included here. There is hardly a number which does not get its sharpest flavour from Shaw's unmistakable sound. The popular songs and theatre tunes, and some of the swing standards, are scored in a manner which, though it is simple enough to be durable, adds nothing to the vision of men like Henderson, Sampson and Mundy (**141** and **142**), and takes few of their risks. Shaw sought variety of expression, and the work of his arrangers (best known among whom was Jerry Gray, of whose work *Begin the beguine* is typical, and who later became Glenn Miller's chief writer) maintains freshness and clarity most of the time. The embracing vision is Shaw's own. He is a tutelary spirit combining Prospero and Ariel in one, and his writers must often have been expressing his concepts at least as much as their own. As a player, his range of ideas is not wide but, with a tone squeezed from the blues into affective *chalumeau* sounds and an intense, almost harrowing, attenuation in upper registers, and with a facility of technique saved from glibness by the fine excitement in his constantly soaring melodies, he gives the band much of its distinction.

What is this thing called love?, *Any old time*, *I can't believe that you're in love with me*, *Lover, come back to me* and *The man I love* typify the arrangements of popular tunes. The last chorus of *Any old time* shows the relentless determination to ride out the journey which too often replaces any attempt at musical climax; yet this piece has as chief treasure a vocal chorus by Billie Holiday. Her rich tone and strong, flexible phrases make it difficult to listen to Helen Forrest later, who sings in twelve numbers, without unfair critical bias. Miss Forrest is a good, musicianly singer, serving a passing mode with unpretentious ability. 'Serviceable' may also describe the several brief solo appearances of Pastor, Auld, Jenkins, Arus, Best and Privin. In a broader context than this they suffer inevitably in comparison with future band members like Roy Eldridge and 'Hot Lips' Page who, like Miss Holiday, benefited from Shaw's defiance of racial mores and widened the band's jazz outlook. These earlier sidemen nonetheless perform with some flair. Pastor is featured more than most, and his singing in *Rosalie* and *Indian love call* suits that venerable tradition wherein humour partially conceals subtle jazz skill. *Rosalie* has the lift which quite often enlivens this band, a buoyancy more notable still in the earliest records of the Gramercy Five. Incidentally, a small prophecy of *Summit Ridge Drive*, so clear that one's ear strains for Guarnieri's harpsichord (see **160**), occurs in *Coming on* which, like other originals such as the springing *Nonstop flight* and the ultimately rather mechanical *Back Bay shuffle*, is more varied than the song arrangements.

Indian love call introduces one of Shaw's most famous trademarks, the duet between clarinet and tom-toms. This appears, not always aptly, in other places — *Coming on*, *What is this thing called love?*, *Softly, as in the morning sunrise* and, of course, *Jungle drums*. The last soon abandons its tropical fervours and reaches one of its nicer moments in a chorus shared by Pastor and the trombone trio. A deal of jazz spirit stirs in unlikely places such as *Carioca, Vilia, Zigeuner* and *The donkey serenade*, but is hindered amid the doom-laden atmospherics of *Nightmare*, a famous essay, laudable chiefly now for Shaw's expressive blues monologue (an earlier performance appears on **145**). The one hoary jazz standard, *Copenhagen*, also heard in an earlier version on **145**, is given a vivacious reading, and with the clarinet riding over richly-toned and melodic section scoring, lightly controlled eagerness in every part and some humour, too, this is probably the best track of all these. Its climax is swinging, compelling and musically well wrought.   E.T.

147 The Indispensable Earl Hines Vols. 1–2
RCA (F) PM42414 (2 LPs), *RCA (A) LPV512

Earl Hines and His Orchestra: Milton Fletcher, Edward Sims (tpt); Walter Fuller (tpt, vcl[1]); George Dixon (tpt, alt); Ed Burke, John Ewing, Joe McLewis (tbn); Omer Simeon (clt, bar); Leroy Harris (alt, vcl[2]); Budd Johnson (ten, arr[3]); Bob Crowder (ten, arr[4]); Hines (p, arr[5]); Claude Roberts (g); Quinn Wilson (bs); Alvin Burroughs (d); Horace Henderson (arr[6]); Skippy Williams (arr[7]). New York City, 12 July 1939.
Indiana[6] · *G.T. stomp*[5] (2 takes) · *Riding and jiving*[7] · *Grand Terrace shuffle*[3] · *Father steps in*[3] · *Piano man*[1,3]

Jimmy Mundy (arr[8]), Laura Rucker (vcl[9]) added. Chicago, 6 October 1939.
Riff medley[3] · *Me and Columbus*[9] · *XYZ*[3] · *'Gator swing* · *After all I've been to you*[1,8] · *Lightly and politely*[8]

Hines (p). New York City, 21 October 1939.
Rosetta

Earl Hines and His Orchestra: previous band personnel except that Mundy (ten) replaces Johnson; Billy Eckstine (vcl[10]) added. New York City, 13 February 1940.
Boogie woogie on St Louis blues[5] (2 takes) · *Deep forest*[4] · *My heart beats for you*[10] · *Number 19*[3]

Hines (Storytone p). New York City, 26 February 1940.
Body and soul · *Child of a disordered brain*

Earl Hines and His Orchestra: previous band personnel except that Shirley Clay (tpt), Johnson (ten, arr[3]) replace Fletcher, Mundy (ten); Buster Harding (arr[11]), Edgar Battle (arr[12]) added. New York City, 19 June 1940.
Wait till it happens to you[10] · *Call me happy*[11] · *Ann*[1] · *Topsy turvy*[1,12] · *Blue because of you*[2] · *You can depend on me*[10] (2 takes) · *Tantalising a Cuban*

Harry Jackson, Rostelle Reese, Leroy White (tpt); McLewis, Ewing, John Fant (tbn); Harris, Scoops Carry (alt); William Randall, Johnson, Franz Jackson (ten); Hines (p); Hurley Ramey (g); Truck Parham (bs); Burroughs (d); Madeleine Green (vcl[13]). Hollywood, 2 December 1940.
Easy rhythm[8] · *In swamplands*[8] · *I'm falling for you*[13]

As noted under **79**, Hines's orchestral achievements have always been neglected, and serious jazz commentary has underrated this ensemble almost as much as it has those of Goodman, Shaw or Tommy Dorsey. Contemporary assurance was given that its later performances 'show only too well the degenerate tendencies of the swing era'[62], yet 1939–41 was undoubtedly the peak of Hines's bandleading activities. That the problems he experienced in the mid-1930s in maintaining a stable personnel[63] were now behind him is confirmed by such powerful interpretations as *Call me happy* and *Easy rhythm*. Inventive scores by Harding and Mundy respectively, these, like most of the other performances, benefit from the relentless yet always flexible drive of Burroughs's drums. The ensemble builds impressively at the close of *G.T. stomp* and *Lightly and politely* (a title later to acquire odious journalistic associations), while the band's quiet entry behind its leader's fiercely stomping piano on *Grand Terrace shuffle* provides a moment notable in a different way. Perhaps this more insistent account of *Deep forest* is less in accord with Reginald Foresythe's unusual theme than Hines's 1932 recording (Tax (Sd) m-8007), but hear the surging accompaniment Sims receives from the saxophones on *Father steps in* and Williams's thoughtful scoring of *Riding and jiving*.

Much of the latter's strong character derives, however, from the contributions of Simeon, Harris and particularly Fuller, and the charge that Hines employed soloists inferior to those of his main rivals is often hard to understand. As on **129**, Simeon intelligently adapts New Orleans procedures, both to solo (*Indiana*) and ensemble (*'Gator swing*) passages, and it is worth recalling that half the tracks on **27** show he remained fluent in the parent style. Fuller's stingingly energetic contributions to *Riff medley*, *Topsy turvy* and *Call me happy*, among others, suggest that his reputation might have been larger if he had moved around more, instead of doing practically all his best recorded work with Hines. Separated with biting ensemble riffs, the solos of Johnson and Crowder on *Grand Terrace shuffle* signal that not all tendencies in swing tenor playing can be ascribed to Coleman Hawkins and Lester Young, the point being underlined by Johnson on *XYZ* and Crowder on *Number 19*.

Hines cuts through the ensemble textures to exhilarating effect in *Riff medley* and *Easy rhythm*, and produces a flow of vital solo ideas on *Piano man*, and especially *XYZ* and *'Gator swing*, where he is in explosive form. The absolute decisiveness with which broken rhythms and double-time are thrown off immediately establishes his authority in each case, though it can also have the slightly unfortunate effect of making the rhythm section appear superfluous. Wholly redundant on *Piano man* are the band's verbal exhortations, and if the first take of *Boogie woogie on St Louis blues* is preferable it is largely because it does without the second's 'entertaining' vocal interjections. That Hines can do without an accompaniment is emphasized by *Rosetta*, a masterpiece of recorded piano jazz. This is kaleidoscopic yet progressively concentrated, the invention finally being so tightly packed that it seems the music must burst apart. *Child of a disordered brain* and *Body and soul*, played on what evidently was an early form of electric piano, cannot be spoken of in the same terms, although the second of these intriguing essays reveals an unusual kind of sensibility.   M.H.

148   Sixteen Cab Calloway Classics
CBS (F) 62950, Epic (A) LN3265

Cab Calloway and His Orchestra: Doc Cheatham, Irving Randolph, Lamar Wright (tpt); Claude Jones, Keg Johnson, DePriest Wheeler (tbn); Chauncey Haughton (clt[1], alt); Andrew Brown (alt); Walter Thomas, Chew Berry (ten); Benny Payne (p); Morris White (g); Milt Hinton (bs); Cozy Cole (d). New York City, 20 February 1939.
Ratamacue

Calloway (vcl[2]) added. New York City, 17 July 1939.
Crescendo in drums[2]

Dizzy Gillespie (tpt) replaces Randolph. New York City, 20 November 1939.
Plucking the bass[1]

Mario Bauza, Gillespie, Wright (tpt); Johnson, Quentin Jackson (tbn); Tyree Glenn (tbn, vib[3], vcl[4]); Jerry Blake (clt[5], alt); Hilton Jefferson (alt); Brown (alt, bar); Thomas, Berry (ten); Payne (p); Danny Barker (g); Hinton (bs); Cole (d); Calloway (vcl[2]). Chicago, 8 March 1940.
Picking the cabbage · Paradiddle

Same personnel. New York City, 15 May 1940.
Calling all bars

Same personnel. Chicago, 27 June 1940.
A ghost of a chance · Bye bye blues[3]

Same personnel. New York City, 5 August 1940.
Boo-wah boo-wah[2]

Same personnel and location, 28 August 1940.
Lonesome nights

Same personnel. Chicago, 16 January 1941.
Willow weep for me
Jonah Jones (tpt) replaces Bauza. New York City, 5 March 1941.
Jonah joins the Cab[2]
Same personnel and location, 3 July 1941.
Take the 'A' train
Same personnel and location, 24 July 1941.
Hey, Doc[2,4]
Russell Smith (tpt), Teddy McRae (ten) replace Gillespie, Berry; Shad Collins (tpt) added. New York City, 3 November 1941.
Tapping off · A smo-o-o-oth one[5]

Calloway might be thought of as a latter-day Ted Lewis (**120**) who, despite immensely popular and inane vocal antics, usually employed fine musicians, above all in his 1939–41 bands. The section work is outstanding, the reeds especially, led by Jefferson, attained a mellow unanimity that was remarkable, as *Lonesome nights* shows. This selection provides a good idea of the sort of opportunities the players got when Calloway shut his mouth, though it could have been improved by the substitution of, say, *Come on with the come on*, which includes solos from Berry, Gillespie, Blake and Glenn, and *Special delivery*, which has Berry and Jonah Jones, for dull percussion displays such as *Ratamacue* and *Crescendo in drums*.

Jones and Berry were the major improvisers, and the former has never been accorded his true place in the tradition of jazz trumpet playing that leads from Oliver and Armstrong to Gillespie and Navarro. He is here far more independent of Armstrong's example than in his recordings with Stuff Smith (**198**), his virtuosity tempered by solid melodic invention, his warmth and rhythmic drive contained by a secure sense of form. Quite exceptional is the sustained fire of Jones's work on *Jonah joins the Cab*, where he is supported magnificently by the drumming of Cole, his associate in the Smith band; this partnership is also at work on *A smo-o-o-oth one*. *A ghost of a chance* was Berry's most celebrated feature with this band and it certainly demonstrates the urgent continuity of his best playing, and his beautifully rounded tone. Yet he never quite escapes the magnetic attraction of the original melody, and in this sense his reading of *Lonesome nights* is superior. He contributes with powerful conciseness to several other pieces also, such as *Take the 'A' train*, which is divested of what its composer, Billy Strayhorn, called 'the Ellington effect'. Jones is here greatly diminished by the mute, as he is on *Hey, Doc*.

Calloway also liked to have his bands play good scores. Benny

Carter arranged *Calling all bars*, a feather-brained theme, and *Lonesome nights*; his own version of this latter dates from 1933 (**122**), and Goodman recorded it the following year as *Take my word* (**117**). Andy Gibson's score of *Willow weep for me* provides a setting for Jefferson's elegantly decorative alto playing, while Buster Harding, besides arranging *A smo-o-o-oth one* effectively, also composed *Boo-wah* and *Tapping off*, which latter has splendidly propulsive writing behind McRae. Both are typical of the men who contributed imaginatively to the swing bands' libraries yet received little public credit.

Gillespie composed and arranged *Picking the cabbage*, which fitted in well enough with the expectations of the time yet contained enough unobtrusive originality to suggest that its creator would soon be making more drastic departures. This is, of course, underlined by his trumpet solos with their often still tentative use of altered harmonies, which show him escaping the influence of Roy Eldridge which so dominated his playing on, for instance, Teddy Hill's 1937 *King Porter stomp* (RCA (E) RD7827). In fact, Gillespie's solo on *Picking the cabbage* even if in it he plays major thirds over minor chords, appears sober indeed beside Eldridge's contemporaneous work (**184**), but his contributions to *Bye bye blues*, *Plucking the bass* and *Boo-wah* are points on a line which travels beyond the solo on Lucky Millinder's *Little John special* (**123**) to Chapter VIII and to the contents of this book's companion volume.   M.H.

149   Benny Carter and His Orchestra 1940–41
RCA (F) 741.073

Benny Carter and His Orchestra: Russell Smith, Sidney DeParis, Bobby Williams (tpt); Milton Robinson, Benny Morton, Madison Vaughan (tbn); Carter, Chauncey Haughton, George James, George Irish, Stafford Simon (saxes); Sonny White (p); Everett Barksdale (g); Hayes Alvis (bs); Keg Purnell (d); Roy Felton (vcl). New York City, 19 November 1940.
All of me · *The very thought of you* · *Cocktails for two* · *Taking my time*

Smith, DeParis, Jonah Jones (tpt); Vic Dickenson, James Archey, Joe Britton (tbn); Carter, George Dorsey, Bill White, Irish, Fred Mitchell (saxes); Sonny White (p); Herb Thomas (g); Ted Sturgis (bs); J. C. Heard (d); Felton (vcl). New York City, 21 January 1941.
Cuddle up, huddle up · *Babalu* · *There, I've said it again*

Doc Cheatham, Lincoln Mills, DeParis (tpt); Dickenson, Archey, Britton (tbn); Carter, Ernie Purce, Eddie Barefield, Fred Williams, Ernie Powell (saxes); White (p); Thomas (g); Charles Drayton (bs); Al Taylor (d); Maxine Sullivan (vcl[1]). New York City, 1 April 1941.
Midnight[1] · *My favourite blues* · *Lullaby to a dream* · *What a difference a day made*[1]

Nathaniel Williams, Emmett Berry, Rostelle Reese (tpt); Archey, Morton, John McConnell (tbn); Carter, Purce, James, Powell, Alfred Gibson (saxes); White (p); William Lewis (g); Drayton (bs); Berisford Shepherd (d). New York City, 16 October 1941.

Sunday · *Ill wind* · *Back Bay boogie* · *Tree of hope*

When Charlie Parker went to New York about 1939 he found few who cared to listen to him on his own still rather inchoate terms, but many who 'tried to get me to sound like Benny Carter'. Nothing as untroubled as Carter's utterance would have satisfied Parker's restless genius, yet the recollection testifies to the honour in which the older saxophonist was held. But not many soloists in jazz have thought fit to emulate Carter — not, surely, because he is inimitable, but perhaps because his approach is deceptively so simple and complete that people have fallen into the error of thinking it a cul-de-sac. What is generally admired is his consummate skill as a multi-instrumentalist and as a composer-arranger, and he has suffered the undesirable fate of being lauded widely, but neither loved nor hated with any degree of passion. Yet Carter is a jazz master precisely because he made craftsmanly elegance into a coherent, flexible and strangely timeless context for jazz artistry — his own and others'.

These 1940–1 recordings, typical of the music and musicians Carter directed in the years just following his lengthy association with Europe, are full of examples of his compact expertise as an orchestrator; the marvellous way in which he balances the different band sections in combination, separation and interaction. In many of the numbers the language is that of the swing age. Spiced with anything less than Carter's intellectual zest, much of it would sound distinctly tired now, but most of it actually does transcend its period and continues to please.

Writing unison variations for saxophones was a Carter speciality and there are good exemplars of this mode in *All of me, Cuddle up* and *Lullaby*. It is worth enduring Felton's bland singing in *The very thought of you* and *There, I've said it again* to hear the background scoring — perky in one, airy in the other. The brass writing is never less than firmly opportune and often is brilliant, as in the harmonized trombone passage in *Sunday*. Three of the tracks are rarities: *Lullaby*, introduced by Carter's trumpet playing, is a theme much in the class of his *Once upon a time* (**84**); *Tree of hope*, another original composition, in which he plays both trumpet and alto; and *Ill wind*, a Koehler–Arlen melody which becomes the vehicle for one of Carter's finest alto improvisations.

Satisfying as the leader's trumpet and clarinet (*All of me*) solos are, it is his alto playing which most reveals his creative gifts. The attractions of his suave 'legitimate' tone and rather haughty scoopings could soon pall, were it not for his consistent inventiveness. He has a way of slightly furbishing a theme and then extending the modest embellishments until, with disdainful legerdemain, he presents the melody's parts in aptly reshuffled patterns.

There are other brief soloists: Cheatham, Jones, Dickenson — but Carter takes the lion's share. Sonny White, the pianist on all four sessions, is an eclectic yet stimulating and, it seems, underrated performer, showing his great skill, if not his most typical mode, in the rapid choruses of *Back Bay boogie*. Maxine Sullivan's modest manner conceals a deceptive jazz skill. It is reported that Felton's singing was a chief reason for the band's contemporaneous popularity. For the jazz lover, it will surely be the only flaw in a sequence of very distinguished music.   E.T.

Louis Armstrong
150 Swing that Music
Coral (E) CP1, *MCA (A) 1304 and 1312

Louis Armstrong and His Orchestra: Armstrong (tpt, vcl); Leonard Davies, Gus Aitken, Louis Bacon (tpt); Henry White, James Archey (tbn); Bingie Madison (clt, ten); Henry Jones, Charlie Holmes (alt); Greely Walton (ten); Luis Russell (p); Lee Blair (g); Pops Foster (bs); Paul Barbarin (d). New York City, 19 December 1935.
Thanks a million

Same personnel and location, 18 May 1936.
Lying to myself · Ev'ntide · Swing that music · Thankful

Louis Armstrong with Jimmy Dorsey and His Orchestra: Armstrong (tpt, vcl); George Thow, Toots Camarata (tpt); Bobby Byrne, Joe Yukl, Don Mattison (tbn); Dorsey (clt, alt); Jack Stacy (alt); Fud Livingston, Skeets Herfurt (ten); Bobby van Eps (p); Roscoe Hillman (g); Jim Taft (bs); Ray McKinley (d). Los Angeles, 7 August 1936.
The skeleton in the closet

Louis Armstrong and His Orchestra: Armstrong (tpt, vcl), Shelton Hemphill, Bacon, Henry Allen (tpt); Wilbur DeParis, George Washington, J. C. Higginbotham (tbn); Albert Nicholas, Madison (clt, ten); Pete Clark, Charlie Holmes (alt); Russell (p); Blair (g); Foster (bs); Barbarin (d). Los Angeles, 12 January 1938.
Jubilee · Strutting with some barbecue

Armstrong (tpt, vcl); Higginbotham (tbn); Holmes (alt); Madison (ten); Russell (p); Blair (g); Red Callender (bs); Barbarin (d). Same date.
I double dare you

Previous full band personnel. New York City, 18 May 1938.
It's wonderful

Bernard Flood (tpt), Rupert Cole (alt), Joe Garland (ten), Sidney Catlett (d) replace Bacon, Clark, Nicholas, Barbarin. New York City, 18 December 1939.
You're a lucky guy

Louis Armstrong and His Hot Seven: Armstrong (tpt, vcl); Washington (tbn); Prince Robinson (clt, ten); Russell (p); Lawrence Lucie (g); John Williams (bs); Catlett (d). New York City, 10 March 1941.
Everything's been done before

Same personnel and location, 11 April 1941.
Hey lawdy mama

Louis Armstrong and His Orchestra: Armstrong (tpt, vcl); Jesse Brown, Thomas Grider, Andrew Ford, Lester Currant (tpt); Taswell Baird, Adam Martin, Larry Anderson (tbn); John Brown, Willard Brown (alt); Teddy McRae, Dexter Gordon (ten); Ernest Thompson (bar); Ed Swanston (p), Emmet Slay (g); Alfred Moore (bs); James Harris (d). Los Angeles, 9 August 1944.
Grooving

151 **Louis Armstrong Jazz Classics**
Ace of Hearts (E) AH7, Decca (A) DL8284

Louis Armstrong and His Orchestra: Armstrong, Davies, Aitken, Bacon (tpt); White, Archey (tbn); Jones, Holmes (alt); Madison, Walton (ten); Russell (p); Blair (g); Foster (bs); Barbarin (d). New York City, 18 May 1936.
Mahogany Hall stomp

Louis Armstrong with Jimmy Dorsey and His Orchestra: Armstrong, Thow, Camarata (tpt); Byrne, Yukl, Mattison (tbn); Dorsey (clt, alt); Stacy (alt); Livingston, Herfurt (ten); van Eps (p); Hillman (g); Taft (bs); McKinley (d). Los Angeles, 7 August 1936.
Dippermouth blues

Louis Armstrong and His Orchestra: Armstrong (tpt, vcl); Hemphill, Bacon, Allen (tpt); DeParis, Washington, Higginbotham (tbn); Nicholas, Madison (clt, ten); Clark, Holmes (alt); Russell (p); Blair (g); Foster (bs); Barbarin (d). New York City, 13 May 1938.
When the saints go marching in

Otis Johnson (tpt), Cole (alt), Garland (ten), Catlett (d) replace Bacon, Clark, Nicholas, Barbarin. New York City, 5 April 1939.
Hear me talking to you · *Save it, pretty mama* · *West End blues* ·
Savoy blues

Flood (tpt) replaces Johnson. New York City, 25 April 1939.
A Monday date

Same personnel and location, 18 December 1939.
Bye and bye

Same personnel and location, 14 March 1940.
Wolverine blues

Armstrong (tpt, vcl); Hemphill, Gene Prince, Frank Galbraith (tpt); Washington, Norman Greene, Henderson Chambers (tbn); Cole, Carl Frye (alt); Robinson, Garland (ten); Russell (p); Lucie (g); Hayes Alvis (bs); Catlett (d). Chicago, 16 November 1941.
Sleepy time down south · *You rascal, you*

Armstrong's small-group recordings of the 1920s (**48**) have nearly monopolized critical attention and this is understandable because he was then innovating almost constantly. During that period he was one of a tiny group of men who were drastically expanding the musical language of jazz: an exciting state of affairs. Later, innovation became unnecessary, because he had won all the territory he needed and his next task was that of discovering its full potentialities. Armstrong's solos on **52** draw together nearly all the implications of his work over the previous decade and their tendency is confirmed by the best of those on **80** and **113–115**. These latter, almost his first records with large ensembles, may therefore be said to represent a period of equipoise, yet the starkness of the riff climax of his 1929 *St Louis blues* (**52**) hints at a move towards refinement.

The process receives almost a formal demonstration in his four choruses on *Swing that music*, these progressively simplifying the solo's outline until it ends with a remarkable series of high, detached, repeated minim Gs. *I double dare you* may appear to move in the opposite direction, for here variety of phrase-shape seems to be his improvisation's main point. But Armstrong used diverse approaches, as the solos at the start of *Lying to myself* and at the close of *Ev'ntide* show. The effect of the changes he makes, however, is inexplicable: the melodies remain themselves yet are utterly transformed. Still more mysterious is *You rascal, you*, where verbal foolery and superb trumpeting coalesce in a way that nobody could emulate; his brief instrumental passages, indeed, combine fire and poise to an extent that is unique. The majestic *Savoy blues* includes three Armstrong solos of increasingly powerful impact, yet their design has an almost austere simplicity.

Such performances necessitate comparisons with his earlier and far more celebrated achievements, and sometimes a balance can be struck between gain and loss. *West End blues*, for example, largely follows the routine of the 1928 version, and if it lacks Earl Hines then Higginbotham answers the trumpeter's initial statement more eloquently than Fred Robinson did. Besides playing an extra chorus, Armstrong executes his familiar part with more subtlety than before. The ease of movement, a considerable advance on what was possible for him in the 1920s, never suggests mere facileness, partly because of the richness of his tone, now consistent across the whole register and inflected, as on *Jubilee* or *Monday date*, with a wide variety of nuance. With an inane and anonymous vocal interjection letting all the tension out of the peroration of an otherwise superlative *Hear me talking to you*, it is probably *Strutting with some barbecue* that most completely transcends the standards set by the Hot Five and Seven. Beyond this lies *Sleepy time down south*, which contains not a superfluous note and whose almost classical focusing on essentials distills all the qualities he brought to music. Surely no one could set this beside the 1931 version without grasping that Armstrong's musical growth continued right through ⁺he 1930s.

Although this 1941 *Sleepy time down south* is one of his very finest recordings, the accompanists sound like an altogether degenerate survival of the Luis Russell band which plays with such full-throated splendour on 50 and, with a younger Armstrong, on 52. Yet it might be argued that its neutral character provides the best possible backdrop to the individuality and expressiveness of his improvising. The writing is doggedly unimaginative, though, and while Chappie Willet's arrangements of *Jubilee* and *Strutting with some barbecue* are adequate, *Skeleton in the closet* is the only one among these twenty-six items whose scoring shows any thought. After the magical *Thanks a million* trumpet solo, the anti-climax of the full ensemble's entry is unmistakable.

These may be taken as no more than an equivalent to the weaknesses of a Lil Armstrong or Kid Ory on the earlier records, but the problem of integrating a great and creative virtuoso with a large ensemble was never properly faced. Certainly nothing was achieved comparable to Sauter's integration of Goodman's clarinet and band on 143. Only at the end of *Mahogany Hall stomp* does Armstrong's band add to the effect of his trumpet, although the previously unissued *Grooving* offers a hint of what might have been. Here there are passages of real musical interplay, the whole tenor of the ensemble's contribution being more astringent. It might be added that this personnel, like Dorsey's band on *Dippermouth blues* and *Skeleton in the closet*, plays with better attack and precision than Armstrong's regular group.

Other of his triumphs, such as the *Wolverine blues* solo, have not even been mentioned, and it perhaps scarcely needs saying that here is the best of all the countless recorded interpretations of Oliver's *Dippermouth blues* solo. Here, also, is almost the only bearable account of *The saints*. The perfect solo on *Skeleton in the closet*, its thought precisely fitted to its length, must be noted, if only because most of these performances are too short for the size of Armstrong's music, the grandeur of its conception. Aside from a number of Art Tatum's recordings (**181b**), one can think of little other jazz which, the passionate emotional expression of its truest moments notwithstanding, conveys a comparable feeling of being above the battle.   M.H.

152a The Ellington Era Vol. 1 Part 3
(CBS (E) BPG62180, Columbia (A) CL2048)

Duke Ellington and His Famous Orchestra: Wallace Jones, Cootie Williams (tpt); Rex Stewart (cnt); Joe Nanton, Lawrence Brown (tbn); Barney Bigard (clt, ten); Harry Carney (clt, bar); Johnny Hodges (sop, alt); Otto Hardwicke (alt, bs sx); Ellington (p); Fred Guy (g); Billy Taylor (bs); Sonny Greer (d). New York City, 20 September 1937.
Crescendo and diminuendo in blue

Harold Baker (tpt), Juan Tizol (v-tbn), Hayes Alvis (bs) added; Guy absent. New York City, 2 February 1938.
Riding on a blue note · The gal from Joe's

Guy (g) added. New York City, 3 March 1938.
I let a song go out of my heart

Baker, Alvis absent. New York City, 4 August 1938.
Prelude to a kiss

Same personnel and location, 19 December 1938.
Jazz potpourri · Battle of swing

Same personnel and location, 22 December 1938.
Boy meets horn · Slap happy

Same personnel and location, 20 March 1939.
Subtle lament

Same personnel and location, 21 March 1939.
Portrait of 'The Lion'

Same personnel and location, 28 August 1939.
The sergeant was shy

Jimmy Blanton (bs) replaces Taylor. New York City, 14 October 1939.
Grieving

Ben Webster (ten), Ivie Anderson (vcl[1]) added. New York City, 14 February 1940.
Stormy weather[1] *· Sophisticated lady*

152b The Ellington Era Vol. 2 Part 3
Columbia (A) CL2365, *CBS (E) BPG66302 (3 LPs)

Ivie Anderson and Her Boys from Dixie: Jones, Williams (tpt); Stewart (cnt); Nanton, Brown (tbn); Tizol (v-tbn); Bigard (clt, ten); Carney (clt, bar); Hodges (sop, alt); Hardwicke (alt, bs sx); Ellington (p); Guy (g); Alvis, Taylor (bs); Greer (d); Anderson (vcl). New York City, 8 June 1937.
All God's children got rhythm

Duke Ellington and His Famous Orchestra: previous personnel except that Tizol, Alvis, Anderson absent. New York City, 20 September 1937.
Dusk in the desert
Baker (tpt), Alvis (bs) added. New York City, 13 January 1938.
Stepping into swing society
Alvis absent. New York City, 11 April 1938.
Dinah's in a jam
Baker absent; Ellington plays hand d. New York City, 7 June 1938.
Pyramid
Same personnel and location, 20 June 1938.
A gypsy without a song
Same personnel and location, 4 August 1938.
Buffet flat
Same personnel and location, 22 December 1938.
Old King Dooji
Same personnel and location, 20 March 1939.
Pussy Willow
Billy Strayhorn (p) replaces Ellington; Jean Eldridge (vcl) added. New York City, 21 March 1939.
Something to live for
Ellington (p) replaces Strayhorn; Eldridge absent. New York City, 6 June 1939.
'Way low · *Serenade to Sweden*
Ivie Anderson (vcl) added. New York City, 12 June 1939.
I'm checking out go'om bye
Blanton (bs) replaces Taylor; Anderson absent. New York City, 14 October 1939.
Little Posey · *Tooting through the roof* · *Weely*

As is variously remarked under **87–91**, Ellington's first stimuli were New York 'stride' pianism (still evident here through his intelligent adaptation of some of its devices in *Riding on a blue note*) and the improvising of his best sidemen. Yet by the time the above performances were recorded, although the soloists were often given apparently free rein, the quickening development of his own innate powers had become overwhelmingly the main factor in deciding how the band's music should further change and grow. However, Ellington's dominance over his musicians had become more subtle than in former years. In *Riding on a blue note* the band sometimes supports Williams's phrases while at others his complement theirs; and it is the same in Carney's dialogue with the ensemble on *Slap happy* or the conversation between Hodges and *The gal from Joe's* muted trumpets. Likewise, the ensemble behind Nanton and Bigard in *Buffet flat* makes too much melodic sense to be regarded as mere accompaniment, while it provides an enhancing commentary on Hodge's *Grieving* ideas.

This integration of solo and collective voices paralleled a fusion of Ellington's many, separately forged techniques of orchestration and, as with any real composer, we often receive the impression that melody, harmony and orchestral garb were conceived simultaneously. Thus it is hard to believe *Stepping into swing society* began life as a song, so perfectly designed does it seem for the band's instrumentation. Further examples of Ellington's now more closely related skill and daring include *Dinah's in a jam*, a considerable advance on 1932's satirical assault on the tune itself (**130**), and the peppery *Boy meets horn*, a compositionally deft manoeuvring of the musical fabric so as to employ half-valve and other effects only available on a limited number of the notes of Stewart's cornet. Observe also the victory won in the *Battle of swing* with a wholly successful adaptation of concerto grosso texture to jazz needs, a *concertino* being formed by Stewart, Tizol, Bigard and Hardwicke, who play in harmony, a *ripieno* by the rest of the band who, for eloquent contrast, are confined to octave unison.

Again like other real composers, Ellington's output contains glances backwards and forwards at earlier and later productions. *'Way low*, for example, suggests a return to 'jungle' modes, with Bigard and Stewart responding especially well to the blue atmosphere, while most ensemble passages of *Buffet flat* anticipate the manner in which *Harlem airshaft* (**153**) always keeps two things happening at once. Occasionally the initiatives are such as to point beyond this music altogether, as in *Old King Dooji*, an unrecognized masterpiece. The continuous variation of the initial theme by the ensemble has implications that were not taken up until George Russell's Jazz Workshop recordings of 1956 (RCA (F) PL42187).

There is not much improvisation in the *Battle of swing*; the duet by Williams and Hodges is noticeably subordinated to *Old King Dooji's* overall design; and solos are virtually banished from the double-length *Crescendo and diminuendo in blue*, another brave venture, following on *Reminiscing in tempo* (**131b**), into pure jazz composition. Yet though so much is justifiably made of Ellington's individuality, he dwelt in no ivory tower and was influenced by swing, not least in the higher proportion of up-tempo items that he recorded in the late 1930s than hitherto. From such things as the tightly-interlocking riffs of the *Dinah's in a jam* ensembles or the dovetailing of brass and reed phrases as *Buffet flat* closes it might be argued that he could improve on anything the swing bands might do. Admittedly, the small-group version of

Pyramid recorded by Hodges in 1938 is superior to the one included here, but the imperturbable succession of solos heard on *Pussy willow* suggests a celebration of the current preoccupations of swing, as do the forthright ensembles of *Jazz potpourri* (also known as *Myrtle Avenue stomp*).

The equally buoyant, and more positively elegant, ensembles and keyboard passages of *Portrait of 'The Lion'* tell us something about aspects of the Harlem piano tradition, whereas Willie 'The Lion' Smith's *Portrait of the Duke* of ten years later (Jazz Reactivations (E) JR113) could say little about Ellington. This was largely because of his music's defiance — in these middle years of his life — of set patterns, of formulae, of easy ways out. This is manifest not only in an exuberant and musically sophisticated recomposition of *Bugle call rag* titled *The sergeant was shy*, but also in his own playing. Instances are his forward-looking contribution to *Subtle lament* and the brief, enigmatic solo, one of many such he later produced, at the close of *Crescendo and diminuendo in blue* where, partnered by Taylor, he anticipates the remarkable duets he was to record with Blanton (**153**).

Such playing was obviously in part a response to the extraordinary improvising which, his own waxing compositional powers notwithstanding, Ellington had going on around him. Examples include a Brown flatly contradicting his later reputation as a sentimentalist on *Dinah's in a jam* and *Little Posey* (a portrait of Freddy Jenkins), and Stewart's atmospheric contributions to the precisely titled *Subtle lament* and to *Weely*, where half-valving adds to the solo's melodic point. Yet perhaps it is better to end with *Dusk in the desert*, a beautiful instance of what might be termed 'imaginative geography'. Certainly the power of the imagination is the chief factor in all this music.

(**152b** was issued as a separate LP in the USA, but only as part of a boxed set in Britain; the record dealt with here is the third in that set.)   M.H.

153 Duke Ellington 1940
Smithsonian (A) RO13 (2 LPs), *RCA (E) 27133/4 (2 LPs)
Duke Ellington and His Famous Orchestra: Wallace Jones, Cootie Williams (tpt); Rex Stewart (cnt); Joe Nanton, Lawrence Brown (tbn); Juan Tizol (v-tbn); Johnny Hodges (clt, sop, alt); Barney Bigard (clt, ten); Harry Carney (clt, bar); Otto Hardwicke (alt); Ben Webster (ten); Ellington (p); Fred Guy (g); Jimmy Blanton (bs); Sonny Greer (d). Chicago, 6 March 1940.
Jack the bear · *Ko-ko* (2 takes) · *Morning glory*
Ivie Anderson (vcl[1]) added. Chicago, 15 March 1940.
Congo brava · *Concerto for Cootie* · *Me and you*[1]

Same personnel. Hollywood, 4 May 1940.
Cottontail · Never no lament
Same personnel. Chicago, 28 May 1940.
Dusk · Bojangles · A portrait of Bert Williams · Blue goose
Same personnel. New York City, 22 July 1940.
Harlem airshaft · At a Dixie roadside diner[1] *· All too soon · Rumpus in Richmond*
Same personnel and location, 24 July 1940.
Sepia panorama (2 takes)
Same personnel. Chicago, 5 September 1940.
In a mellotone · Warm valley (take 1)
Ellington (p); Blanton (bs). Chicago, 1 October 1940.
Pitter panther patter · Body and soul · Sophisticated lady · Mr J.B. Blues (2 takes)
Previous full band personnel. Chicago, 17 October 1940.
Warm valley (take 3) *· The flaming sword*
Herb Jeffries (vcl[2]) added. Chicago, 28 October 1940.
Across the track blues · Chloe · I never felt this way before[2]
Ray Nance (tpt) replaces Williams. Chicago, 28 December 1940.
Sidewalks of New York

It is always easy, aided by hindsight, to impose upon jazz history a symmetry of pattern, a simplifying design. Perhaps the commonest example is how musicians' careers can be seen to develop in a very orderly fashion, often a decade at a time. This species of generalizing can be dangerous, yet Ellington is certainly one artist for whom the process has the merit of clarifying what was going on. The 1920s had been largely a matter of giving support to the soloists. The 1930s witnessed Ellington the composer assuming much greater control, devising pieces in which soloists were decidedly subservient to a larger outline, conjuring up subtle textures as well as dramatic forays for, most especially, his three trumpets and three trombones. The next advance was to be partly rhythmic, partly structural, partly a matter of giving the saxophone section some sort of parity with those brasses. It is tempting, therefore, to cite particular dates. Blanton joined the band in December 1939; Webster did so only a few weeks later. Ellington himself was in his fortieth year and the century had just entered its fifth decade when a newly-invigorated orchestra recorded the music to be found on these two LPs.

In later years the Ellington band turned into a kind of living museum, the famous players doing little more than sounding like themselves, the new recruits chosen largely because they resembled earlier heroes. People who only became familiar with the orchestra during that long twilight may not realize how, in its heyday, the arrival of new musicians had a catalytic effect upon

Ellington's composing. True, there were always stock roles to be filled. Williams had taken over the trumpet growling from Bubber Miley just as, in November 1940, Nance took over from Williams; Stewart assumed Freddy Jenkins's responsibility — on stage, at least — for keeping the groundlings happy. The important thing about these recordings, however, is that Webster not only brought a new solo voice into the band (Ellington had never featured a tenor saxophonist before) but turned a four- into a five-piece reed section, while Blanton quite simply revolutionized the craft of jazz bass playing.

The way that the Ellington orchestra revolved around the string bass rather than around the drums has been mentioned on earlier pages. Blanton's arrival accentuated that dependence to an extraordinary degree. The difference he made is discernible during the opening bars of *Jack the bear*. As well as giving the rhythm section a new springiness, Blanton's sheer flexibility, the way he could phrase as melodically as a trumpeter or saxophonist, distinguishes his playing there and in *Ko-ko, Bojangles, In a mellotone, Sepia panorama, Chloe* and various other tracks. But the technical mastery comes across most spectacularly in the four duets, performances completely without parallel at the time they were recorded. Up to then the apogee had been represented first by the playing of Pops Foster, Al Morgan and Steve Brown, and afterwards by that of John Kirby and Milt Hinton. There were, indeed, few precedents for the dazzling virtuosity of Blanton's work, especially the *arco* playing that opens *Sophisticated lady*. The two versions of *Mr J.B. Blues* are revealing, the procedure differing (take 1 ends with *arco* playing, 2 with *pizzicato*) and with a fourth chorus in which Ellington's playing anticipates something of Thelonious Monk's jaggedness. Ellington performs with exceptional selflessness in these duets, content to fulfil an accompanying role on all tracks except *Pitter panther patter*, where his manner and his high spirits recall those nights in the 1920s when, escorted by Willie 'The Lion' Smith, he would do the rounds of Harlem rent parties.

Blanton's presence enabled the band to swing more consistently than it had done before, notably in pieces such as *Jack the bear* and *Cottontail*. Webster's swashbuckling solo in the latter is a counterpart to the truculent styles of Ellington's brass soloists. The structure is familiar (the chords are basically those of *I got rhythm*) and Webster has been credited with arranging the chorus for the saxophone section, in which the newly-found richness of the five-man team comes across. It is very probable that Webster suggested the outline, even if the voicing was left to Ellington; co-operation of that sort resulted in much grumbling by Ducal sidemen over the years. In fact, Webster's blend of pugnacity and tenderness was featured quite extensively: he roughs things up in *Bojangles*, is sensuous in *Blue goose*, is at his most gracious in *All too soon*, and displays a split personality in the separate takes of *Sepia panorama* (take 2, oddly enough, sounds less assured than take 1).

The established Ellingtonians were not neglected, of course. Indeed, one of the most perfect works from this period, *Concerto for Cootie*, focuses upon the virtues of Williams's sound and style, representing a considerable advance upon the earlier *Echoes of Harlem*, sometimes known as *Cootie's concerto* (**131a**). And Williams can rarely have played with greater ferocity than during *Rumpus in Richmond*, its theme ascending in semitones. Hodges takes a bubbling solo at the end of *In a mellotone*, yet it is the kind of thing he might have played ten years earlier, just as the composition itself — a paraphrase of *Rose room* — could easily have been recorded at the start of the 1930s, as, for that matter, could *The flaming sword*. The sleeve notes appear to err in identifying Hardwicke as the second saxophonist to be heard in the final chorus of *Sidewalks of New York*, where Hodges's phrasing seems unmistakable. The latter is featured in both takes of *Warm valley*, performances that just stop short of becoming too pretty. Ellington is credited with composing this, yet it has affinities with several items that Billy Strayhorn devised for Hodges and could be the first of Strayhorn's scores to be recorded by the full band. (The 1939 recording of his song, *Something to live for* (**152b**), was scored by Ellington.)

But more satisfying than that, or the beguiling *Never no lament*, is the two- and four-bar chase chorus between Hodges and Brown at the end of *Me and you* (on which Ivie Anderson sings deliciously), a collaboration almost as remarkable as that between Hodges and Williams on the 1936 *In a jam* (**131a**). With Webster now in the band, Brown's trombone playing no longer seemed quite so alien. His style would go on containing elements of *kitsch*, the emotional response predicated by the sentimental manner, yet Brown suited Ellington's 1940s romanticism better than he sometimes did the more lyrical concept of the 1930s. Stewart, used sparingly, was at his best when contributing a spiky jocisity. Although *Morning glory* can be viewed as a rather unenterprising 'Concerto for Rex', much superior to *Trumpet in spades* (1936, **64**) but inferior to *Boy meets horn* (1938, **152a**), both its theme and Stewart's playing are marred by a hint of unctuousness. But his cornet tone is remarkable and resemblances to Bix Beiderbecke (notably the *rubato* touches towards the end of the first chorus) still peep through.

There are solos, too, from three of the other senior musicians: Nanton, Bigard and Carney. Yet their inventiveness seems less important than the fact that they are present, contributing either to the ensemble texture or to what might be called the dramatic narrative. Bigard takes excellent solos in *Across the track blues*, *Jack the bear* and *A portrait of Bert Williams* (the most successful of Ellington's portraits, incidentally, evoking the laconic charm of that great entertainer); and he is heard swooping and curveting against a background of brass and reeds, just as he might, in his New Orleans days, have done against trumpet and trombone. Bigard remained the closest link that Ellington kept with his despised rival, Jelly Roll Morton. Carney provides *gravitas*, operating as a sort of musical keel; his solos frequently dawdle but his sound within the band is like a guarantee of authenticity. *Ko-ko*, for instance, begins and ends with pedal notes from Carney, and he remains intrinsic to the mood of that performance. Nanton is every bit as indispensable, vital to the preservation of Ellington's vigour as a composer, the very limitations of his style turning out to be part of its power. His playing in *Ko-ko* and *A portrait of Bert Williams* sounds both poignant and somehow essential to the validity of those compositions, yet the same is true of innumerable tracks on this and other albums. Of all Ellington's soloists, Nanton is the one who never lost his instinct for aptness, his feeling for the verities of his leader's music.

Ellington's prowess as a composer arose precisely because he was capable of pulling together these assorted individuals and aesthetic strands, turning them into elements within an orchestral entity. Yet, paradoxically enough, he had written very little during 1935 and 1936, while the sudden popularity of swing presented him with the problems that occur only when an art form is also a popular commercial entertainment, subject to shifts of fashion. Yet in 1940, Ellington was composing with the confidence of a man at the summit of his creative powers, maybe a 'petit maître'[64], but unequalled at deploying themes, instrumental colour and harmony within the three-minute dimensions of the ten-inch 78 rpm record. Some pieces perpetuate the deceptive simplicity of *Mood indigo* (**91**): *Dusk*, for instance, with Jones's pinched trumpet sound providing a substitute for Arthur Whetsol's fragility; or *All too soon* — just two choruses of a ballad yet carrying unexpected emotional weight. *Ko-ko*, another masterpiece, is mostly a minor blues, yet perfect in its proportions, moving from the exoticism of Tizol's valve trombone through Nanton's convulsive rawness to a dissonant and triumphant climax. Elsewhere, Ellington indulges his taste for what, by jazz standards, are unconventional groupings of bars: the alternation of twelve- and thirty-two-bar sequences in *Jack the bear*, for example, and the twenty-bar routines of *Congo brava*. And *Sepia panorama* is shaped rather like an arch, its first and eighth choruses each twelve bars long, the second sixteen and the seventh eight (this is the only break in the symmetry), the third and sixth eight each, the fourth and fifth — the middle choruses, in fact — both twelve bars long.

The structural innovations in these and other pieces, often taken for granted because the music has become so familiar, are emphasized by the helpful analyses provided for this album by Larry Gushee. Indeed, his breakdown of *Concerto for Cootie* is especially interesting because it conflicts quite drastically with the structure suggested by André Hodeir in what is generally accepted as a brilliant essay on this recording [65]. Musicological uncertainty of this sort is perhaps a tribute to the calculated overlapping within Ellington's composition, its capacity to be simultaneously ambiguous yet lucid. It also underlines an essential truth: that what really matters is how the music sounds, whether it works for the listener. And that, at least, is never in doubt.   C.F.

Recording Units from the Big Bands

Small bands within large ones were nothing new in the 1930s (see **15** and **34**) but, in and out of recording studios, they provided opportunities for more extensive improvisation, in more intimate settings, than was possible with the big formations.

154 Allen-Hawkins Orchestra 1933/Henry Allen's Orchestra 1934

Gaps (H) 070

Henry Allen, Coleman Hawkins and Their Orchestra: Allen (tpt); Dickie Wells (tbn); Russell Procope (clt, alt); Hawkins (ten); Don Kirkpatrick (p); Lawrence Lucie (g); John Kirby (bs); Walter Johnson (d). New York City, 27 March 1933.
Someday, sweetheart · *Sister Kate*

Hilton Jefferson (alt), Horace Henderson (p), Bernard Addison (bj, g) replace Procope, Kirkpatrick, Lucie; Kirby plays both bs and tu; Allen vcl[1]. New York City, 21 July 1933.
The river's taking care of me[1] · *Ain'tcha got music?*[1] · *Stringing along on a shoe string*[1] · *Shadows on the Swanee*

Allen (tpt, vcl[1]); Benny Morton (tbn); Edward Inge (clt, alt); Hawkins (ten); Henderson (p); Addison (bj, g); Bob Ysaguirre (bs); Manzie Johnson (d). New York City, 9 November 1933.
Hush my mouth[1] · *You're gonna lose your gal*[1] · *Dark clouds*[1] ·
My Galveston gal[1]

Henry Allen and His Orchestra: Allen (tpt, vcl[1]); possibly Claude Jones or Keg Johnson (tbn); Buster Bailey (clt, ten); Jefferson (alt); Henderson (p); Lucie (g); Kirby (bs, tu); Walter Johnson (d). New York City, 1 May 1934.
I wish I were twins[1] · *I never slept a wink last night*[1] · *Why don't you practice what you preach?*[1] · *Don't let your love go wrong*[1]

Romanticism has never flourished in jazz quite so vigorously as between the end of the 1920s and the middle of the 1930s, just before swing imposed its own hectic kind of formality. It began with Ellington's 'jungle' pieces and with Hawkins rhapsodizing — exploring a mood as much as a theme — on *One hour* (**166, 192**). But if Hawkins's sumptuous manner represented at least one triumph of that new phase in jazz, another could be discerned in the work of Allen. Not only did the latter ignore the symmetrical phrasing which gave Armstrong his particular, almost Miltonic, nobility; he also splayed his solos across the bar lines, as sophisticated rhythmically as Hawkins was harmonically.

Both men were working in Fletcher Henderson's orchestra when the first three of the above sessions were recorded. Their companions were also members of that band, apart from Kirkpatrick, Inge, Ysaguirre and Manzie Johnson, all with Don Redman's orchestra. Nearly every performance here depends for its success upon the quality of the solos, for the arrangements used range from the unambitious to the inadequate; the two-man saxophone section glimpsed in *The river's taking care of me* and *Hush my mouth* strikes a latter-day listener as especially perfunctory. Hawkins employs his grandest manner, with plenty of arpeggiation, in *Someday, sweetheart, Hush my mouth* and *Dark clouds*, and is boldly nimble elsewhere. In *Ain'tcha got music?* he even anticipates, if very discreetly, that repetition of phrases which was to become the basis of his style towards the end of the decade.

Wells takes trombone solos, nicely puckered and askew, on the first two tracks, while Morton is typically vibrant in *My Galveston gal*. Jefferson's alto saxophone solo in *Ain'tcha got music?* suggests something of Benny Carter's sleekness, and Inge plays the clarinet with the wilful elegance that one associates with a short story by Saki. Discographers allege that the trombonist on the 1934 session is Wells, but the shortish solos in *I never slept a wink last night* and *Don't let your love go wrong* (treated as a rhumba, incidentally) convey nothing of Wells's pungent style. It seems more probable that Allen used one of the trombonists working with Henderson at the time; Wells had departed at the very end of 1933.

The musician who dominates on all these tracks, however, is Allen. For once he could be said to have surpassed Hawkins. *Dark clouds* concludes with an Armstrong-like coda, but elsewhere the trumpet work could be that of nobody else but Allen, fragmented yet logical, allusive in a way that other trumpeters — Miles Davis for one — were to be a couple of decades later. And just as Armstrong's singing was another aspect of a total musical personality, so was Allen's. The lugubrious façade, deployed for even the most outrageously cheerful lyrics, was a counterpart to the sonority, the *gravitas*, of the trumpet playing, just as the scatted interjections, in *The river's taking care of me*, for example, communicate something of its zestfulness and tireless curiosity.   C.F.

155 Henry Allen
Collectors' Classics (D) CC13

Henry Allen and His Orchestra: Allen (tpt, vcl[1]); Keg Johnson (tbn); Buster Bailey (clt); Hilton Jefferson (alt); Horace Henderson (p); Lawrence Lucie (g); Elmer James (bs); Walter Johnson (d). New York City, 28 July 1934.
There's a house in Harlem for sale · *Pardon my southern accent*[1]
Claude Jones (tbn) replaces Keg Johnson. Same date.
Rug-cutter's swing · *How's about tomorrow night?*[1]
Allen (tpt, vcl[1]); Pee Wee Erwin (tpt); George Washington (tbn); Bailey (clt); Luis Russell (p); Danny Barker (g); Pops Foster (bs); Paul Barbarin (d). New York City, 23 January 1935.
Believe it, beloved[1] · *It's written all over your face* · *Smooth sailing*[1] · *Whose honey are you?*[1]
Allen (tpt, vcl[1]); Dickie Wells (tbn); Cecil Scott (clt); Chew Berry (ten); Horace Henderson (p, arr); Bernard Addison (g); John Kirby (bs); George Stafford (d). New York City, 29 April 1935.
Rosetta[1] · *Body and soul*[1] · *I'll never say 'Never again' again* · *Get rhythm in your feet*[1]
Allen (tpt, vcl[1]); J. C. Higginbotham (tbn); Albert Nicholas (clt); Scott (ten); Henderson (p, arr); Lucie (g); James (bs); Kaiser Marshall (d). New York City, 19 July 1935.
Dinah Lou[1] · *Roll along, prairie moon*[1] · *I wished on the moon*[1] · *Trucking*[1]

Allen broke out of the classic ensemble mould (he never really belonged to it for recording purposes) for different motives than those of Armstrong. Like the latter, he soon came to find the pattern restrictive to his aspirations as an improviser, but he always continued to find the co-operative group, large or small, congenial, and his gifts, though considerable, prompted no move towards monolithic stardom. He could be a strong, even a dominating, leader, yet his companions were never relegated to mere background support. These recording groups of 1934–5, with their close links to the Fletcher Henderson and Luis Russell bands, are nothing if not co-operative, and Allen thrives in them. His talents for lyricism and for musical humour may be taken sufficiently for granted for special attention to be paid to others' contributions.

Bailey's playing is exceptionally good, the drifting pathos he achieves on *House in Harlem*, the alternation between angular multiplications and sailing blues phrases in *Rug-cutter's swing*, the contrast between his low- and high-register melodies in *Believe it, beloved*, and his agile ensemble support, never concealing his debt to tradition but showing how contemporary his inspirations were. Berry's style is frequently bracketed with those of Hawkins and Webster, and he is related to them tonally; but his rhythmic discoveries are different and his energetic solos — as in *I'll never say 'Never again' again* and *Get rhythm in your feet* — developing simple livelier phrases within the middle register have a tough, jumping character which suits this sort of context well. Nicholas has a fuller, woodier tone than Bailey, and does not exhibit the same inventive flair in his July 1935 appearance, partly for lack of opportunity. Wells and Higginbotham are, as one might expect, equally forthright in declaration, and Wells's twisting, rolling phrases and tricks of rhythm in *Rosetta* and *I'll never say 'Never again' again* may be compared with Higginbotham's exuberant plainness in *Dinah Lou, Roll along, prairie moon* and *I wished on the moon*. Jefferson and Scott, and the two pianists, are little more than capable by comparison, though excellent in ensemble as are all four rhythm sections.

There is a strange tension in Allen's playing between urgent passion and rhythmic ease which, together with his astonishing range of expressive technical devices, gives his improvising its unmistakable quality. The lightly skilful tongue and valve effects in *Rug-cutter's swing* are evidence of his magnificent control over his instrument, and every statement, from the agitation of *House in Harlem* to the tuneful relaxation of *Trucking*, plainly refutes all critical accusations of 'vulgar declamation' [66], for even his seeming extravagances are always under control. His singing here seems less an extension of his playing than it was later to become (**207** shows how he went on enhancing his instrumental style), but his pokerfaced humour is versatile and acknowledges kindred spirits — as in *Believe it, beloved*, where even his playing pays wry homage to Fats Waller.

Most of the arrangements, and particularly those in which Horace Henderson has a hand, permit an illusion of immediate spontaneity which conveys much of the spirit of shared improvisation.   E.T.

156 Putney Dandridge Vol. 3
Rarities (D) 34

Putney Dandridge and His Orchestra: Henry Allen (tpt); Joe Marsala (clt, alt); James Sherman (p); Eddie Condon (g); Wilson Myers (bs); Cozy Cole (d); Dandridge (vcl). New York City, 3 August 1936.
A star fell out of Heaven · Mary had a little lamb · Here comes your pappy · If we never meet again

Clyde Hart (p), John Kirby (bs) replace Sherman, Myers. New York City, 1 September 1936.
Sing, baby, sing · You turned the tables on me · It's the gypsy in me · When a lady meets a gentleman down south

Myers (bs) replaces Kirby. New York City, 14 October 1936.
A high hat, a piccolo and a cane · Easy to love · You do the darndest things, baby · The skeleton in the closet

Doc Cheatham (tpt); Tom Macey (clt); Teddy Wilson (p); Allen Reuss (g); Ernest Hill (bs); Sidney Catlett (d); Dandridge (vcl). New York City, 10 December 1936.
I'm in a dancing mood · With plenty of money and you · That foolish feeling · Gee! but you're swell

Nothing illustrates more clearly than this LP the overlapping between jazz and Tin Pan Alley during the 1930s. Dandridge, like Bob Howard and Fats Waller, recorded some of the shoddier numbers of the day (the best had already been allotted to artists with bigger names) to an accompaniment of busked jazz. His singing reflects his period rather than himself: sentimental where it seemed appropriate, high-spirited when that was called for, and with even an occasional imitation thrown in (of Maurice Chevalier, for instance, during *You do the darndest things, baby*). Dandridge had worked as an accompanist for Bill 'Bojangles' Robinson, the dancer, before going out as a solo act. He played the piano on his first sessions (two tracks can be heard on **184**), but after that he preferred to use more talented outsiders.

The line-up on the first three sessions on this LP is deceptive, suggesting the band to have been more of an *ad hoc* group than it was. Marsala and Condon were, in fact, currently co-leading a band in 52nd Street — it was one of the earliest working groups to be racially mixed — that included Allen. So Allen and Marsala were accustomed to improvising together, which accounts for the rapport evident in most of these performances, the only really dull track being *You turned the tables on me*. Allen's merits are discussed elsewhere, and once again the listener will be struck by his boldness, what might be called his rhythmic impatience; also his instinct for varying textures as well as accents; the trumpet solo in *If we never meet again* perfectly incorporates all these virtues.

Marsala was not in Allen's class, but he was one of the best and most underrated clarinettists of the 1930s, a musician who learnt the right things from Jimmy Noone — how to stitch a solo together, for instance — while eschewing Noone's mawkishness. Marsala's Chicago associations also come through in the way he frequently chops up phrases to get the maximum rhythmic impact. He does something similar when playing alto saxophone, although on that instrument his influences are more various: Jimmy Dorsey as well as Teschemacher on *It's the gypsy in me*; Bud Freeman's nonchalance on *When a lady meets a gentleman down south*; three bars of Hodges-style smearing in *Here comes your pappy* (a vaudeville number rather than a pop song); even, in *Sing, baby, sing*, an anticipation of Pete Brown's huffing and puffing.

Little solo playing is heard from any of the pianists, except on the session of 14 October, where the performer alleged to be Clyde Hart takes eight- or sixteen-bar solos on every number. Intriguingly enough, this pianist sounds uncommonly like Teddy Wilson, more so, in fact, than Wilson does himself (if the discographers are to be believed) on the final session. That last date, in any case, represents a distinct falling away. Cheatham plays capably but without Allen's flair, while Macey has too much of Buster Bailey's sometimes pinched, over-correct manner. (A curious fact about Macey, an obscure musician if ever there was one, is that he packed his entire recording career — two sessions each with Wingy Manone and Tommy Dorsey's Clambake Seven, one apiece with Teddy Wilson and Dandridge — into the space of one year and one week: 3 December 1935 to 10 December 1936.) As if aware that his back-up was less exciting than usual, Dandridge warbles at even greater length. *Gee! but you're swell* suffers from having been transferred from a particularly noisy 78 rpm disc.   C.F.

157 Lester Young and the Kansas City Five
Stateside (E) SL10002, Mainstream (A) 56012

Kansas City Five: Buck Clayton (tpt); Eddie Durham, Freddy Green (g); Walter Page (bs); Jo Jones (d). New York City, 18 March 1938.

Laughing at life · *Good morning, blues* · *I know that you know*

Kansas City Six: Lester Young (clt, ten) added; Durham also plays tbn[1]; Greene also sings[2]. New York City, 8 September 1938.

Way down yonder in New Orleans · *Countless blues* · *Them there eyes*[2] · *I want a little girl* · *Paging the Devil*[1]

All-Star Sextet: Bill Coleman (tpt); Dickie Wells (tbn); Young (ten); Joe Bushkin (p); John Simmons (bs); Jones (d). New York City, March 1944.

I got rhythm · *Three little words* · *Four o/clock drag* · *Jo-jo*

The electric guitar's introduction as a jazz solo instrument owes most to three Southwesterners — the Missourian Floyd Smith (see **132**) and the Texans Durham and Charlie Christian. Durham's pioneering work, excellently represented with the Kansas City Five and Six, provides substantial hints of what inspired the more celebrated Christian, and the ensemble approach of these small Basie units is usefully compared with the music of the Goodman sextets which featured Christian (**159**). Durham's arranging skills were important in forming the character of the early Basie band, being the fruit of his desire to translate orchestrally what he heard happening in Kansas City jam sessions. The essence of Durham's garnerings is there in his own playing, and the success of the unusual combination of trumpet and electric guitar, in the three quintet performances, is substantially due to his linear and harmonic imagination. Clayton's indefinable amalgam of delicate sounds (whether his instrument is muted or open) and interior force complements Durham's conception beautifully, as their shared passages in *Laughing at life* well show. In *I know that you know* and *Good morning, blues*, wittily-timed guitar chords urge on the several swinging Clayton improvisations and a solo by Page.

With the support of the almost peerless Basie rhythm section (without the great pianist, as *Countless blues* acknowledges), each of these 1938 sessions achieves fine jazz. Some reservation may now be felt about the lightweight ensemble sound resulting from the combination of muted trumpet and guitar or clarinet, as in the theme statements of *Countless blues* and *Way down yonder in New Orleans*, for this sometimes seems rather at odds with the strength of the solos. Young's economically melodic tenor solo in the latter piece demonstrates both his dry but not attenuated sound and his ability to recreate thematic matter within a deliberately limited range of notes. His presence in the sextet tracks brings a different ensemble approach and Durham adopts a less prominent role, leaving the significant exchanges and harmonic passages to Young and Clayton — except in *Paging the Devil*, where his muted trombone is heard at the beginning and end. Young uses his clarinet most of the time, fashioning in *I want a little girl* and *Paging the Devil* two of the most beautiful jazz solos ever recorded on that instrument. Tonal purity and a firmly diatonic turn of thought mean that he employs overt blues phrases very sparingly but, in tune with the general nature of this music, he does draw deeply on the spirit of the blues. Tantalizing similarities to the style of Pee Wee Russell are due more to a kinship of introspection than to clear formal borrowings.

Led by the deeper tones of the tenor, the 1944 sextet session has more obvious vigour and a looser concept. Coleman's solos show rather less delicacy and variety than those typical of **102**, and their characteristic slight edge of indiscipline rubs uncomfortably against the urbanity of Young and another Basie sideman, Wells — though even the latter is sometimes tempted, as in *Four o/clock drag*, to expostulation. The riff themes, *Jo-jo* and the sardonically reshaped *Three little words*, are more ebulliently sounded than those of the Kansas City Six and are countered pleasantly by the filigree style of Bushkin, a pianist more suited to this scene than to that of his more famous appearance with Muggsy Spanier (**235**).

The dreamy retardations of his blues solo in *Four o/clock drag* may seem to confirm the popular image of Young as a cool, reclusive individualist, and even at faster tempo — *Three little words* and *Jo-jo* — an underlying nostalgia is often sensed; but the controlled energy with which he 'leaps in' at the very outset of *I got rhythm*, rapid phrases spinning up from copious depths, shows that he was as capable of extroversion as of more meditative moods.   E.T.

158 Benny Goodman Trio and Quartet
RCA (F) 730.629, *Quintessence (A) QJ25361
Benny Goodman Trio: Goodman (clt); Teddy Wilson (p); Gene Krupa (d). New York City, 13 July 1935.
After you've gone · Body and soul · Who?
Same personnel. Chicago, 27 April 1936.
Lady, be good
Lionel Hampton (vib, vcl[1]) added. Hollywood, 21 August 1936.
Moonglow
Same personnel and location, 26 August 1936.
Dinah · Exactly like you[1]

Hampton absent. New York City, 2 December 1936.
Tiger rag
Hampton added. Same date.
Whispering
Same personnel. Hollywood, 30 July 1937.
Avalon · The man I love
Dave Tough (d) replaces Krupa. New York City, 25 March 1938.
Blues in your flat[1]
Same personnel. Chicago, 12 October 1938.
Opus ½ · Sweet Georgia Brown

159 **Benny Goodman Sextet and Orchestra**
CBS Realm (E) 52538, Columbia (A) CL652

Benny Goodman Sextet: Goodman (clt); Fletcher Henderson (p); Charlie Christian (g); Artie Bernstein (bs); Nick Fatool (d); Hampton (vib). New York City, 2 October 1939.
Seven come eleven

Count Basie (p) replaces Henderson. New York City, 7 February 1940.
Till Tom special · Gone with what wind?

Dudley Brooks (p) replaces Basie. Hollywood, 11 June 1940.
Six appeal

Benny Goodman Septet: Cootie Williams (tpt); Goodman (clt); George Auld (ten); Basie (p); Christian (g); Bernstein (bs); Harry Jaeger (d). New York City, 7 November 1940.
Wholly cats

Jo Jones (d) replaces Jaeger. New York City, 15 January 1941.
Breakfast feud · Gone with what draft?

Benny Goodman and His Orchestra: Alex Fila, Irving Goodman, Jimmy Maxwell, Williams (tpt); Lou McGarity, Cutty Cutshall (tbn); Benny Goodman (clt); Gus Bivona, Skippy Martin, Bob Snyder (alt); Auld, Pete Mondello (ten); Johnny Guarnieri (p); Christian (g); Bernstein (bs); Tough (d); Jimmy Mundy (arr). New York City, 4 March 1941.
Solo flight

Benny Goodman Septet: Guarnieri (p), Tough (d) replace Basie, Jones. New York City, 13 March 1941.
Blues in B · Waiting for Benny · A smo-o-o-oth one · Airmail special

There were ample precedents for the sound of Goodman's Quartet in the vibraharp- or xylophone-laden textures of some of the earlier recordings on **119** and **199**, but turbulence was long caused in jazz commentary by the Trio. Those unable to see beyond the literal details of the instrumentation repeatedly said that he was copying Morton's 1927 initiative (**47a**), though if Goodman looked back at all in 1935 it was probably to his own *Clarinetitis* and *That's a-plenty* of 1928 (Vocalion (E) VLP2). The finest performances by the Trio remain, anyway, among his most satisfying records, their lucidity of outline relating to a lucidity of thought that necessarily found different outlets in the larger groups. One can so easily follow the intelligent progress of Wilson's left hand, and the informal counterpoint between clarinet and piano in, say, the first and last choruses of *After you've gone* or *Body and soul* is a source of great pleasure. So is the fresh response of both players to exceedingly familiar chord sequences like those of *Dinah* or *Tiger rag*; and one rejoices at the sheer musicality of Goodman's and Wilson's playing.

The addition of Hampton changed the balance of power and, though he was unable to support his leader's improvisations with anything that approached the level of the pianist's immaculate countermelodies, his chording sometimes intriguingly anticipates the invention of the electric piano. This is effective in *Moonglow*, where the melody is stated with much sensitivity by Goodman while the vibraharp shimmers in the background. Hampton's attack, the definition of his phrases, is not well caught on the Quartet performances; the Sextets are better, though not until the 1950s was his instrument recorded to satisfaction. He cannot sing and one is surprised that Goodman allowed him to try, although *Blues in your flat* affords us the rare opportunity of hearing the great clarinettist accompany in this idiom and doing so beautifully. Goodman's solos always contain surprises despite the urbanity of the Trio and Quartet music, and the cogency of the one that concludes *Sweet Georgia Brown* should especially be noted. *The man I love* may sound doleful, but it was recorded in the wake of Gershwin's death earlier that month. Tough's participation improves the rhythmic flow of the 1938 Quartet performances, particularly that of *Opus* ½, as does Basie's replacing Henderson in the Sextet.

This latter had two basic instrumentations, one arising out of the addition of Christian and a bassist to the Quartet. It yielded excellent results, as is shown by the drive of *Seven come eleven*, with the vibraharp figures dancing behind the guitarist's solo, but it placed a strain on the clarinet through it being the only wind instrument present. Maybe for this reason, Goodman tried another direction, which turned his group into a septet with a substantially different character (though it was usually still described as a sextet on the 78 rpm record labels). There is a considerable variety of figuration in the Trio and Quartet performances, but the Septet with, in the above instances, Auld's tenor and Williams's many-voiced trumpet places an emphasis on colour and texture. And though Hampton responds to the tightly organized frameworks of the Sextet head arrangements with some of his best recorded work, as on *Gone with what wind?*, it is the three-horn instrumentation of the Septet which gives rise to the best demonstrations of Goodman's leadership.

Several quite distinct personalities are reconciled in each of these pieces, as is suggested by the telling contrast between Basie's laconic contributions (or those by Guarnieri in a knowing variant of Basie's style) and the profuse clarinet, guitar and trumpet inventions. The chief link between them is a gift for consistently melodic improvisation, but out of their unity arise extreme contrasts. Notice, for example, the support given to solos by Williams, Goodman and Basie on *Breakfast feud*, in each case quite different yet perfectly apt. Beyond that is the exceptional variety of musical incident which makes up each piece; and beside this main current the textures, above all those of *A smo-o-o-oth one*, are rich in subsidiary detail.

Its leader aside, the common denominator of Sextet and Septet is Christian, who weaves a thread of the blues through all this music's fabric. There is a seeming paradox here in that his work is at the same time consistently modern, pointing towards bop at least as clearly as Gillespie on **123** and **148** or Parker on **246** and **250**. And despite their freedom of accentuation and sense of harmonic adventure, his best phrases have a logic, a simple inevitability, peculiarly their own. This is most apparent on the above version of *Airmail special*, where thirty-two extra bars of Christian and twenty-four of Goodman are spliced into a previously unissued take, with a repeat of the final eight bars from the latter. There is extra time also on *Breakfast feud*. The dynamic flow of such performances, or of *Gone with what draft?*, is highly impressive, and though Goodman's playing was soon to be grotesquely described as 'near-New Orleans (Bigard and water)' [67], his flow of ideas matches Christian's and covers a wide range of moods. As a vehicle for the guitarist, however, Mundy's *Solo flight* is inferior, especially in terms of interplay between soloist and band, to Sauter's *Clarinet à la king* for Goodman or *Superman* for Williams (**143**).

It may be noted that a figure used towards the close of *Gone with what draft?* is taken from Fletcher Henderson's arrangement of *Just like taking candy from a baby* (Nostalgia (A) CSM890–1) of the previous year, where it accompanies Fred Astaire's tap dancing.   M.H.

160

Artie Shaw and His Gramercy Five
RCA (E) LSA3087, *RCA (A) LPM1241

Artie Shaw and His Gramercy Five: Billy Butterfield (tpt); Shaw (clt); Johnny Guarnieri (hps); Al Hendrickson (g); Jud DeNaut (bs); Nick Fatool (d). Hollywood, 3 September 1940.
Special delivery stomp · Summit Ridge Drive · Keeping myself for you · Cross your heart

Same personnel and location, 5 December 1940.
Dr Livingstone, I presume? · When the quail come back to St Quentin · My blue heaven · Smoke gets in your eyes

Roy Eldridge (tpt); Shaw (clt); Dodo Marmarosa (p); Barney Kessel (g); Morris Rayman (bs); Lou Fromm (d). New York City, 9 January 1945.
The Grabtown grapple · The sad sack

Same personnel. Hollywood, 31 July 1945.
Scuttlebutt · The gentle grifter

Same personnel and location, 2 August 1945.
Mysterioso · Hop, skip and jump

This collection of all the RCA Gramercy Fives (the American LP omits *Mysterioso* and *Hop, skip and jump*) reminds us that Shaw, admittedly by restricting the number of titles he recorded, attained a consistency which eluded Goodman and was never approached by Hampton. The music, rather like that of Goodman's sextet and septet, is neat yet forceful and if, especially on the earlier dates, there are few sustained solos, the constant shifts of these tightly-patterned mosaics always sound purposeful, as on *When the quail come back to St Quentin* or the spruce, energetic *Special delivery stomp*, never merely restless. The instruments are juxtaposed in such a variety of ways, the range of colour, of differing emphasis, is so great that the ear is constantly engaged. Indeed, it is a tribute to Shaw's musical astuteness that, despite a few dated effects such as the pseudo boogie of *Cross your heart*, one can still listen with unflagging attention, even to the million-seller, *Summit Ridge Drive* — on which, in fact, the leader solos excellently over the easily-riding background figures.

A harpsichord adds a special slant to the first eight titles, and if this does not interfere with other aspects of the music that may well be because only a few of its resources are used. The instrument demands a quite different touch from the piano, and pianists tend at first to find this confusing as their sense of timing is upset — a point rather clearly demonstrated by Meade 'Lux' Lewis's contemporaneous and Erroll Garner's later brief encounters with it. But Guarnieri, an intelligently adaptable musician in so many ways, makes exactly the right adjustment and is excellent, for instance, on *Summit Ridge Drive*, both in solo and in dialogue with the horns, and with DeNaut's bass; note also the combination of clarinet and harpsichord on *Smoke gets in your eyes*. These two pieces, and also *Dr Livingstone, I presume?*, contain splendid playing from Butterfield which makes it easy, like his contributions to *The blues* and *Chantez les bas* with Shaw's full band (RCA (E) DPM2028), to forgive his much later World's Greatest Jazz Band nonsense.

There is finely abrasive work also from Eldridge on subsequent items like *The Grabtown grapple* and *The sad sack*, the latter being a Buster Harding blues of considerable distinction. The clarinet solos in *Scuttlebutt, The gentle grifter* and *Hop, skip and jump* are near Shaw's best, and Marmarosa is interesting on this last and also on *The Grabtown grapple*, his improvisations recalling, in their stylistic orientation rather than their pianistic detail, Bud Powell's recordings with Cootie Williams made during the previous year (Phoenix (A) LP1). One's final impression of these performances is of the high skill of all involved and, again, of a consistency rare in jazz.   M.H.

161a Lionel Hampton 1938–39
RCA (F) 730.641

Lionel Hampton and His Orchestra: Harry James (tpt); Benny Carter (clt, alt); Dave Matthews (alt); Herschel Evans, Babe Russin (ten); Billy Kyle (p); John Kirby (bs); Jo Jones (d); Hampton (vib). New York City, 21 July 1938.
Shoe shiner's drag · *I'm in the mood for swing* · *Muskrat ramble*

Walter Fuller (tpt); Omer Simeon (clt); George Oldham (alt); Budd Johnson, Bob Crowder (ten); Spencer Odun (p); Jesse Simpkins (bs); Alvin Burroughs (d); Hampton (vib, p[1]). Chicago, 11 October 1938.
Down home jump · *Rock Hill special*[1]

Irving Randolph (tpt); Hymie Schertzer (bs clt, alt); Russell Procope (alt); Jerry Jerome, Chew Berry (ten); Clyde Hart (p); Allen Reuss (g); Milt Hinton (bs); Cozy Cole (d); Hampton (vib). New York City, 3 April 1939.
High society

Randolph, Schertzer, Procope, Jerome absent; Hampton (vib, p[1], vcl[2]). New York City, 5 April 1939.
Sweethearts on parade[2] · *Shuffling at the Hollywood* (2 takes) · *Denison swing*[1] · *Wizzing the wizz*[1]

Ziggy Elman (tpt); Schertzer, Procope (alt); Jerome, Berry (ten); Hart (p); Danny Barker (g); Hinton (bs); Cole (d); Hampton (vib). New York City, 9 June 1939.
Ain't cha coming home?

Rex Stewart (cnt); Lawrence Brown (tbn); Harry Carney (bar); Hart (p); Billy Taylor (bs); Sonny Greer (d); Hampton (vib, p[1]). New York City, 13 June 1939.
Memories of you · *Twelfth Street rag*[1]

161b

Lionel Hampton 1939–40
RCA (F) 731.048

Lionel Hampton and His Orchestra: Elman (tpt); Schertzer, Procope (alt); Jerome, Berry (ten); Hart (p); Barker (g); Hinton (bs); Hampton (d). New York City, 9 June 1939.

Big wig in the wigwam

Dizzy Gillespie (tpt); Carter (alt); Coleman Hawkins, Ben Webster, Berry (ten); Hart (p); Charlie Christian (g); Hinton (bs); Cole (d); Hampton (vib, vcl²). New York City, 11 September 1939.

When lights are low · One sweet letter from you² · Hot mallets · Early session hop

Henry Allen (tpt); J. C. Higginbotham (tbn); Earl Bostic (alt); Hart (p); Christian (g); Artie Bernstein (bs); Sidney Catlett (d); Hampton (vib, vcl²). New York City, 12 October 1939.

I'm on my way from you² · Haven't named it yet

Elman (tpt); Toots Mondello (clt, alt); Webster, Jerome (ten); Hart (p); Al Casey (g); Bernstein (bs); Slick Jones (d); Hampton (vib, p¹, d³). New York City, 30 October 1939.

Munson Street breakdown¹ · I've found a new baby¹ · I can't get started · Gin for Christmas³

Carter (tpt); Ed Hall (clt); Hawkins (ten); Joe Sullivan (p); Freddy Greene (g); Bernstein (bs); Zutty Singleton (d); Hampton (vib). New York City, 21 December 1939.

Dinah · My buddy

Elman (tpt); Mondello, Buff Estes (alt); Jerome, Budd Johnson (ten); Odun (p); Ernest Ashley (g); Bernstein (bs); Nick Fatool (d); Hampton (vib). Chicago, 26 February 1940.

Till Tom special · Flying home · Tempo and swing

The vibraharp was a latecomer to jazz instrumentation, not really becoming familiar until halfway through the 1930s. True, there had already been xylophone and marimba playing by Red Norvo, using very subtle techniques (**199**) and, more obscurely by the percussionist Jimmy Bertrand, who performs an early and worthwhile solo on Blind Blake's 1928 *South bound rag* (London (E) AL3560). But, always excepting forays by that incorrigible all-rounder, Adrian Rollini, Hampton was the real pioneer of the vibraharp, the man who brought that instrument to the forefront of jazz. At first it must have seemed intractable; not accessible, for instance, to the gradations of touch that a sensitive pianist commands. Yet a succession of players, including Milt Jackson and Gary Burton as well as Norvo, have demonstrated the breadth of approach that is possible.

A drummer by upbringing, a romantic by disposition, Hampton accepted the percussive nature of the vibraharp — indeed, he revelled in it; yet he also exploited the instrument's overt vibrancy, adding sensuousness to his melodic ramblings. What might be called his unstoppable musical eloquence has sometimes relied upon his deployment of clichés, but at least they have usually been his own clichés, while even the most unenterprising of his solos generally possess a rhythmic zest, a tangential rather than an overt relationship to the beat.

His singing may have the dreariness of lukewarm water, his drumming — as represented on these LPs, anyway — stress the flashier aspects of that craft, his piano playing (the more conventional *Denison swing* apart) be a two-fingered replica of his work on the vibraharp; yet with mallets in his hands, Hampton acquires a curious kind of infallibility. And, as Max Harrison has pointed out, although his reputation has been that of 'a hard and insistent swinger' [68], his true merits are much subtler than that. Indeed, it is often on ballads that his finest improvising can be heard; his solos in *Memories of you* and *I can't get started* are sterling examples.

This pair of LPs contains a selection from the many recordings that Hampton made with pick-up groups between 1937 and 1941, years during which he was regularly working for Benny Goodman. When flanked by lesser talents, he tends to dominate: the session of 30 October 1939, for instance, features him at the piano in two numbers, drumming — and better than usual — in the far too hectic *Gin for Christmas* and outshining the other soloists on *I can't get started*. Yet when challenged successfully he could yield with good grace, as in *Sweethearts on parade*, where Berry, at his most impetuous and exciting, makes the going throughout the entire performance, tempering the tedium of Hampton's singing with a truculent obbligato and finally usurping what must originally have been planned as a vibraharp chorus.

Spontaneous uprisings of that sort, constituting what Harrison has called a rare form of collective improvisation for the 1930s, justify the casualness of Hampton's approach to routining and recruitment. The drawbacks can be seen in the extent to which inferior musicians such as Elman turn up again and again. Sometimes a likely-seeming combination fails to deliver, like the dull performances by the Ellingtonians in *Twelfth Street rag* and *Memories of you*, or the session of 12 October 1939, rescued only by Christian's solo and Catlett's drumming in *Haven't named it yet* and by Allen's marvellously oblique trumpet playing at the start of *I'm on my way from you*. At that time Allen was surely the most *avant/garde* trumpeter in jazz; more so than the fledgling Gillespie, whose solo on *Hot mallets* is mostly a reminder of the debt he owed to Roy Eldridge.

The *Hot mallets* session also serves to illustrate the fact that all-star ensembles do not necessarily guarantee performances of high quality. *Early session hop*, for instance, sounds decidedly ragged, with Webster's solo full of loose ends. Nevertheless, Hawkins is at his most majestic in *One sweet letter from you*, a track that concludes with some passages for saxophones that were obviously scored by Carter. Judicious arranging certainly helped to give an edge to many performances. For example, Johnson's writing for the session of 11 October 1938, where Hampton used musicians from Earl Hines's band, including Crowder, a promising tenor player who seldom realized his full potential (though see **147**).

It was Carter who was responsible for the most satisfying music of all, taking some of his finest alto saxophone solos (the one on *Shoe shiner's drag* — alias Morton's *London blues* — is particularly outstanding), chipping in a couple of times on clarinet, and his arrangements lending shape, and texture too in the case of *I'm in the mood for swing*, to all the tracks in which he is involved. Perhaps *Muskrat ramble* is a bit of an oddity, with Evans contributing some fleshy tenor playing, Matthews, a useful but undervalued musician, taking the second alto solo, and Hampton himself at his best. *High society* was an equally unlikely theme for sessions like these, the point being emphasized by the leader playing the traditional clarinet solo on his vibraharp.

An impressive feature of the July 1938 session is the rightness of all the tempos, with *Shoe shiner's drag* getting as close to perfection as possible. Jones's drumming on this occasion was exhilarating but on the whole, and certainly on the earlier dates, Hampton displayed shrewd taste in choosing drummers. As well as Jones, Burroughs, Cole and Catlett all bring the right kind of solidity to the music.   C.F.

Barney Bigard

162 Barney Going Easy
Tax (Sd) m-8023

Barney Bigard and His Jazzopators: Rex Stewart (cnt); Juan Tizol (v-tbn); Bigard (clt); Harry Carney (bar); Duke Ellington (p); Billy Taylor (bs); Sonny Greer (d). New York City, 29 April 1937.
Four and One-Half Street · Demi-tasse · Jazz à la carte

Fred Guy (g), Charlie Barnet (mar) added. New York City, 16 June 1937.
Moonlight fiesta

Barnet absent. New York City, 19 January 1938.
Drummer's delight · If I thought you cared

Same personnel and location, 8 June 1939.
Barney going easy · Just another dream

The Quintones (vcl gr) added. Same date.
Utt-da-zay · Chew, chew, chew your bubble gum

Jimmy Blanton (bs) replaces Taylor; Quintones absent. New York City, 16 October 1939.
Early morning
Billy Strayhorn (p) replaces Ellington. New York City, 22 November 1939.
Minuet in blues · Lost in two flats · Honey hush
Same personnel. Chicago, 14 February 1940.
Mardi Gras madness · Watch the birdie

Like the small combo recordings led by Stewart, Hodges and Williams, those under Bigard's name have a marked character of their own and this, likewise, arises out of the special qualities of the leader's improvising and technique. Here as in his performances with the full band, Bigard swoops and soars with an aerial freedom that few jazz clarinettists have approached, none surpassed: everything seems possible. One notes the consequent diversity of his phrases, the size and warmth of his tone, and all this is reflected in the Jazzopators' music. Considerable thought was evidently given to achieving variety of expression and, quite apart from the themes, there are strongly contrasting tempos and textures. This leads the sidemen into a fairly wide range of endeavours and, though Stewart makes characteristic statements on most tracks, he touches several distinct moods — sounding perky on *Mardi Gras madness*, for example, pensive on *If I thought you cared*.

The cornettist's battery of resources, with passages of tightly-choked ferocity, smears, half-valve effects and abrupt switches of tone colour, admirably balances Bigard's urbane convolutions, and their partnership closely relates to the crux of this music. A reconciliation of urgency and elegance was its aim, these being symbolized by, respectively, Greer's outbursts on *Four and One-Half Street* and the beautiful melodic statements which open and close *Just another dream*. Although the clarinettist plays with gentle intimacy on, say, *Barney going easy*, his virtuosity is always a positive factor, not least with respect to the rhythmic freedom it allows him, this being such as actually to have affinities with considerably later developments in jazz. In these relatively sophisticated settings, Bigard's inheritance from the Creole jazz clarinet tradition seems less important, though it in fact lies at the root of everything he does, even during *Minuet in blues*. A charming echo of Paul Whiteman's *Minuet in jazz* and Harold Arlen's orchestral *American minuet*, this Strayhorn score presumably typifies what soon were to be called 'his stereotyped, effeminate little swing arrangements for the Ellington small units' [69].

At the same time, and despite *Moonlight fiesta*, which owes most to Tizol, there is not much here of what on a later page is spoken of as Bigard's 'fine talent for romantic scene-painting' (**186**). For that one must, during his Ellington period, go to *Lament for Javanette. A lull at dawn* and *Ready Eddy*, surely the most evocative performances recorded under his leadership. These, along with other 1940–1 material of comparable standard, occur on RCA (E) RD8096, and it is regrettable that this LP's second side is occupied with inferior Albert Nicholas pieces. On RCA as on the later titles here, Blanton's work underlines the music's strong rhythmic fibre, as do the propulsive riffs which urge on many of the solos.

Honey hush is a slightly less original version of the *Solid old man* which Bigard and Stewart had recorded with Django Reinhardt earlier that year in Paris (**105b**). As their titles hint, the performances with the Quintones are jivey novelty numbers and the band does well to keep out of the way.   M.H.

163 Cootie Williams and the Boys from Harlem
Tax (Sd) m-8005

Cootie Williams and His Rug Cutters: Williams (tpt); Joe Nanton (tbn); Johnny Hodges (sop, alt); Harry Carney (bar); Duke Ellington (p); Hayes Alvis (bs); Sonny Greer (d). New York City, 8 March 1937.
Diga diga doo

The Gotham Stompers: Sandy Williams (tbn); Tommy Fulford (p), Billy Taylor (bs), Chick Webb (d) replace Nanton, Ellington, Alvis, Greer; Barney Bigard (clt), Bernard Addison (g), Ivie Anderson (vcl), Wayman Carver (arr) added. New York City, 25 March 1937.
Alabamy home · My honey's loving arms

Cootie Williams and His Rug Cutters: Juan Tizol (v-tbn), Otto Hardwicke (alt), Ellington (p), Greer (d), Jerry Kruger (vcl[1]) replace Sandy Williams, Hodges, Fulford, Webb, Anderson; Addison, Carver absent. New York City, 26 October 1937.
Watching[1] · Pigeons and peppers

Nanton (tbn), Hodges (sop, alt) replaces Tizol, Hardwicke; Fred Guy (g) added. New York City, 4 April 1938.
Swingtime in Honolulu[1] · Carnival in Caroline[1]

Hardwicke (alt, bs sx), Scat Powell (vcl[2]) added; Nanton, Guy, Kruger absent. New York City, 2 August 1938.
Sharpie[2]

Powell absent. New York City, 21 December 1938.
The boys from Harlem · Gal-avanting

Hardwicke absent; Williams (vcl[3]). New York City, 28 February 1939.
Beautiful romance · She's gone[3] · Boudoir Benny

Same personnel and location, 22 June 1939.
Night song · Black beauty
Jimmy Blanton (bs) replaces Taylor. New York City, 15 February 1940.
Toasted pickles

The mood, in general, is thoroughly Ellingtonian, particularly in the harmonic voicings, and the Duke himself frequently plays a virile instrumental role; but the dominant voice is that of Williams, the most widely celebrated of the 'jungle' trumpeters. In most numbers he lives up to his popular image, but manages to demonstrate a widely-ranging melodic ability and a far greater variety of textural nuance than that image has deigned to admit.

The Rug Cutters' *Diga diga doo* is well into the tropic thickets, with Greer's tom-toms and the characteristic plaint of Nanton setting the scene; but the impressionistic indulgence is dispelled by Williams's vivid configurations, Hodges's swirling alto lines, stomping piano from Ellington, and some very forthright swinging from Nanton and Carney. This is a typically variegated three minutes. The Gotham Stompers include some distinguished non-Ellingtonians, in particular the excellent Addison, whose agile, rich-toned guitar gives a special flavour to the ensemble, the exuberant Webb and one of his sidemen of the day, the trombonist Sandy Williams. *Alabamy home* has Cootie squealing like a train over urgent riffs and includes lovely work from Bigard and Carney. The trumpeter gives an open lead to the ensemble in *My honey's loving arms*, and the other Ellington men, in the absence of Duke, make typical donations to the common fund. Sandy Williams utters a telling break and Webb vents enthusiasms which make much of Greer's work elsewhere sound rather genteel.

All the other sessions use slightly varied permutations of Ellington employees. At the start of *Watching*, one recognizes in Tizol's haughty tone something just as evocative of that period as Nanton's wilder words. Cootie sounds here, as in *The boys from Harlem* and a few other places, very much like Rex Stewart in tonal effect. The other October 1937 piece, *Pigeons and peppers*, is greatly aided by fine rhythm section work with the able, underrated Taylor showing surprising hints of a Blanton yet unknown. In addition to fine sounds from Williams, there is what may be some of Bigard's best tenor playing on record, and a fair ration of his marvellous gliding and swooping clarinet.

Swingtime in Honolulu and *Carnival in Caroline* have Nanton and Hodges back, and in the former Nanton contrives a far more telling vocal than does the appointed singer, spinning the kind of super-realism that complements the leader's savagery so well.

The trouble with this session is the poor standard of its themes, yet there is good work from most of the instrumentalists involved.

Sharpie has great lift and amongst its most striking features is a series of vivacious clauses divided between Ellington and Hodges, with some peculiarly effective sounds from the piano. In *The boys from Harlem*, wherein Williams partially adopts another's *persona* (as already averred), Taylor's prominent beat reverts to an earlier period's slapping and there is some rather unpleasant unison scoring for the deeper saxophones — a temptation which ought to have been resisted; but there is redemption in the joyous, brilliant and intricate figurations of the leader's open horn. Open work again, in *Gal-avanting*, but some choked effects as the music proceeds over floating reed harmonies; then, before the trumpeter returns with beautifully-placed high-note tunes, there are some gentle obliquities from the clarinet.

She's gone is an outright blues with an abandoned, mocking and very well sustained vocal from Williams himself. He also ranges through his plunger effects with similar *élan* and no lack of art. *Boudoir Benny* and *Beautiful romance* have, among their several delights, examples of Ellington's inventive dialogic skill as he enters into warm musical debate, in the first with Hodges and in the second with Carney. There are rather heavy sounds in *Night song* and unpleasant echo for the ensemble; but *Black beauty*, from the same day, has Williams in deep-throated open tone interpreting the famous piano solo (91) and orchestration (87 and 90) in a manner that brings out a good deal of the nostalgia which the composer first put into it.

Finally, *Toasted pickles*, which has the newly-arrived Blanton bringing spring to the rhythm, and playing from the leader that ranges, in superb control, from the gentle to the impassioned. Bigard broods *sotto voce* in his solo and resumes unperturbed even after Williams has slammed in a sardonic middle eight. Gentleness has the last word, and all ends in lightness and quiet.   E.T.

164 Rex Stewart Memorial
CBS Realm (E) 52628

Rex Stewart and His Orchestra: Stewart (cnt, vcl[1]); George Stevenson (tbn); Rudy Powell (clt, alt); Bingie Madison (clt, ten); Ram Ramirez (p); Billy Taylor (bs); Jack Maisel (d). New York City, 12 December 1934.
Stingaree · Baby, ain't you satisfied?[1]

Duke Ellington and His Orchestra: Arthur Whetsol, Cootie Williams (tpt); Stewart (cnt); Joe Nanton, Lawrence Brown (tbn); Juan Tizol (v-tbn); Barney Bigard (clt, ten); Harry Carney (clt, bar);

Otto Hardwicke, Johnny Hodges (alt); Ellington (p); Fred Guy (g); Taylor, Hayes Alvis (bs); Sonny Greer (d). New York City, 17 July 1936.

Trumpet in spades

Rex Stewart and His 52nd Street Stompers: Stewart (cnt); Brown (tbn); Carney (clt, bar); Hodges (sop, alt); Ellington (p); Ceele Burke (g); Taylor (bs); Greer (d). New York City, 16 December 1936.

Rexatious · *Lazy man's shuffle* (2 takes)

Freddy Jenkins (tpt); Stewart (cnt); Hodges (alt); Carney (bar); Ellington (p); Brick Fleagle (g); Alvis (bs); Maisel (d). New York City, 7 July 1937.

Back room romp (2 takes) · *Love in my heart* · *Sugar Hill shim sham* (2 takes) · *Tea and trumpets* (2 takes)

Louis Bacon (tpt, vcl[2]); Stewart (cnt); Nanton (tbn); Bigard (clt); Ellington (p); Taylor (bs); Greer (d). New York City, 20 March 1939.

San Juan Hill · *I'll come back for more*[2] · *Fat stuff serenade*

Few musicians who worked in Ellington's orchestra for any length of time got over the experience, tending afterwards to pursue careers that encapsulated what they had learned within that intimate yet ebullient organization. Ben Webster was one player able to break loose. Another was Stewart, a performer of remarkable, if sometimes paradoxical, originality, combining jauntiness and a brassy gloss with the musical equivalent of a deadpan manner; following, at the outset anyway, in the footsteps of Armstrong, yet also reflecting, in solo after solo, *rubato* effects learnt from Beiderbecke — a fellow cornettist, significantly enough — as well as intervals, and sometimes timbres, that Bix was fond of using. And where trumpet players of Stewart's generation would frequently round things off with a flurry of high notes, he was just as likely to plumb the lower limits of his horn.

Armstrong's influence is audible on the 1934 session, recorded with a pick-up group just before Stewart joined Ellington for the first time; it is still detectable later on, particularly at the commencement of *I'll come back for more*. *Love in my heart* is perhaps the most Beiderbeckian of these performances. On *Trumpet in spades*, one of Ellington's earliest attempts at devising short concertos for his sidemen, Stewart's playing relies too much upon triple-tonguing and similar diversions, the solo never developing in any profounder sense. Much superior — indeed, a small masterpiece — is *Boy meets horn* (**152a**), recorded by the Ellington band in 1938 and featuring a technique that Stewart had just discovered and begun to develop. Often referred to as his half-valve style, it came about through the cornettist only partially depressing the valves. 'It caused me to produce a tone related to concert G instead of C', he later explained. 'This was for all intents and purposes the G sound on the horn, but it sounded like it was being heard through a fog!'[70] The results of this exploration had a kind of throttled eloquence to be descried at its most convincing, on this LP at any rate, in *Fat stuff serenade* ('Fat stuff' was Stewart's nickname, no doubt inspired by his portliness).

The two other sessions were also recorded by contingents from the Ellington orchestra, apart from Fleagle and Maisel, both lifelong friends of Stewart, and Burke, whose steel guitar playing in *Lazy man's shuffle* — processional, rather like a jollier version of *The mooche* — makes far more sense now that we associate this guitar style with southern blues rather than Hawaiian music. The tight, conspiratorial side of Stewart's playing surfaces here; he is perkier in *Rexatious* on which, incidentally, Hodges, in superb form, takes solos on both soprano and alto saxophones while Carney is heard playing clarinet as well as baritone saxophone. The label of the original American 78 rpm issue of *Back room romp* described the piece as 'A Contrapuntal Stomp', which is how it begins and ends. Differences between the two takes are minimal. Considerably more interesting is a comparison of the alternative versions of *Tea and trumpets*, where both Hodges's and Stewart's solos offer substantial variations of detail if not of outline, illustrating very usefully the way jazz musicians go about their business.   C.F.

Johnny Hodges/Rex Stewart

165 Things Ain't What They Used To Be
RCA (A) LPV533, RCA (G) LPM533

Johnny Hodges and His Orchestra: Cootie Williams (tpt); Lawrence Brown (tbn); Hodges (sop, alt); Harry Carney (bar); Duke Ellington (p); Jimmy Blanton (bs); Sonny Greer (d). Chicago, 2 November 1940.
Day dream · *Good Queen Bess* · *That's the blues, old man* · *Junior hop* · *Going out the back way*

Ray Nance (tpt) replaces Williams. Hollywood, 3 July 1941.
Squatty roo · *Passion flower* · *Things ain't what they used to be*

Rex Stewart and His Orchestra: Stewart (cnt); Brown (tbn); Carney (alt, bar); Ben Webster (ten); Ellington (p); Blanton (bs) Greer (d). Chicago, 2 November 1940.
Without a song · *My Sunday gal* · *Mobile bay*

Billy Strayhorn (p) replaces Ellington. Same date.
Linger awhile

Ellington (p) replaces Strayhorn. Hollywood, 3 July 1941.
Some Saturday · *Subtle slough* · *Menelik (The Lion of Judah)* · *Poor Bubber*

It is not only as vehicles for the creativeness of two very gifted Ellingtonian soloists that these recordings are so justly celebrated. They are also important documents of an artistic vision which had livelier implications for the progress of jazz than the talents of either Hodges or Stewart in themselves. Ellington was, at that crucial period, doing more than any other jazz figure to establish the truth that tradition is best honoured not by archaism or self-conscious revival, but by the constant rediscovery of what is timeless in one's heritage as a stimulus to originality. There are elements in these performances which are as firmly rooted in the traditions of early jazz and its attendant vocal forms as are, say, Spanier's lively genuflections to the past (235). But those elements are so brilliantly encompassed that they sound, decades later, not even slightly dated and are also alive with anticipations of the future.

In all their solos and leadings of the ensemble, Hodges and Stewart display inventive authority, and each certainly had a hand in shaping themes and routines, as did Ellington's *protégé* Strayhorn (*Day dream, Passion flower*). Yet the Ellington spirit pervades everything. The dry-edged harmonies of *That's the blues, old man, Things ain't what they used to be* and *Mobile bay* sound 'modern' still, but the chordal novelties flow from a distillation of the blues which can be heard in Ellington's piano solos — typically that on *Things ain't what they used to be.*

Gentleness and a subtle scheme of dynamics characterize most of this jazz, and yet its musical references are more varied than might appear. The Harlem dance tradition is there, not only in *Junior hop* and the swing-prompted *Good Queen Bess* but also in the programmatic *Subtle slough*, which was used to accompany the comic dancing of 'Pot, Pan and Skillet'. And there are constant hints of those cadences of song and rhythmic speech which have always enlivened jazz. These are especially pleasing in the ensemble figures of the Hodges blues numbers, and in Stewart's *Poor Bubber* (abetting Webster's high-register solo) and *Mobile bay*, wherein Williams and his 'preaching' forebears are honoured with snatches of call-and-response. The presence of Williams himself on the earlier of the two Hodges dates makes for more contrast (for example the Puckish interplay of alto and trumpet in *Good Queen Bess*) than does that of Nance, who simply matches the urbanity of Brown and Carney — though to suitable effect.

Hodges's acknowledged debt to Bechet is not over-obvious. A serious and workmanlike musician, he displays nothing of Bechet's flamboyance or will to dominate, and the romanticism of his arching and soaring *legato* seems entirely his own, prompted by the qualities of the alto rather than the soprano saxophone. Stewart pays tributes to Williams and to Bubber Miley but he, too, has his own immediately recognizable voice. It is well adapted to the goodtime spirit of *Some Saturday* and *Linger awhile*, and to the unexpectedly *Day dream*-like echoes in *My Sunday gal*. His fine plunger-muted passages in *Poor Bubber* are not merely imitative, yet they are scarcely as original as his atmospheric pedal notes in *Menelik*, a drama which requires Greer to forsake his ever-elegant brushes for tom-toms and timpani. Blanton, Greer's ill-fated rhythm companion, plays with unerring grace throughout. E.T.

52nd Street

Besides being an actual centre for jazz in New York, 52nd Street symbolizes all small-group activity at this time. A few of those represented here never actually performed at any of the 52nd Street clubs, yet they were part of the same movement in jazz.

166 From Chicago to New York: the Greatest of the Small Bands Vol. 4

RCA (F) 741.103

Mound City Blue Blowers: Glenn Miller (tbn); Pee Wee Russell (clt); Coleman Hawkins (ten); Jack Bland (g); Eddie Condon (bj); Al Morgan (bs); Gene Krupa (d); Red McKenzie (cap). New York City, 14 November 1929.
Hello, Lola · *One hour*

Gene Gifford and His Orchestra: Bunny Berigan (tpt); Morey Samuel (tbn); Matty Matlock (clt); Bud Freeman (ten); Claude Thornhill (p); Dick McDonough (g); Pete Peterson (bs); Ray Bauduc (d); Gifford (arr); Wingy Manone (vcl[1]). New York City, 13 May 1935.
Nothing but the blues[1] · *New Orleans twist* · *Squareface*[1] · *Dizzy glide*[1]

Adrian and His Tap Room Gang: Manone (tpt); Joe Marsala (clt); Adrian Rollini (bs sx, vib); Putney Dandridge (p, vcl[2]); Carmen Mastren (g); Sid Weiss (bs); Sammy Weiss (d). New York City, 14 June 1935.
Bouncing in rhythm · *Honeysuckle rose*[2]

Wingy Manone and His Orchestra: Manone (tpt, vcl[1]); Buster Bailey (clt); Chew Berry (ten); Conrad Lanque (p); Danny Barker (g); Jules Cassard (bs); Cozy Cole (d). New York City, 19 June 1939.
Royal Garden blues · *Fare thee my baby, fare thee well*[1]

Bud Freeman and His Summa Cum Laude Orchestra: Max Kaminsky (tpt); Brad Gowans (v-tbn); Russell (clt); Dave Bowman (p); Condon (g); Clyde Newcomb (bs); Danny Alvin (d). New York City, 19 July 1939.
I've found a new baby · *Easy to get* · *China boy* · *The eel*

Jess Stacy and His Orchestra: Billy Butterfield, Pee Wee Erwin, Nat Natoli (tpt); Will Bradley, Jack Satterfield (tbn); Sal Franzella (clt); Julius Bradley, Hymie Schertzer (clt, alt); Larry Binyon, Hank Ross (clt, ten); Stacy (p); Frank Worrell (g); Bob Haggart (bs); Mario Toscarelli (d); Lee Wiley (vcl[3]). New York City, 29 June 1945.
Daybreak serenade · It's only a paper moon[3]

This record collects together sessions that have few significant links yet which, the titles under Manone's name aside, usefully fill some gaps. All recorded in New York, they hint, too, at the diverse backgrounds of the music we have grouped under this heading. The Mound City Blue Blowers items also appear on **192** in a more suitable context, their main point being the sheer authority of Hawkins's strongly contrasted solos. He is on record as maintaining, reasonably enough, that jazz tenor saxophone playing did not start with him[71], yet very much came from the kind of improvising heard on *One hour*. Pushed hard by the pianoless accompaniment, his contribution to *Hello, Lola* is notable chiefly for his rhythmic energy, although this is of a somewhat retrogressive, on-the-beat sort. Only Russell's solos approach a comparable quality and he, too, is identifiable as a loner who worked things out for himself.

From the clarinettist's part in the Freeman date of ten years later one can deduce a wide range of musical experience, fully assimilated, although the chief point about these four performances is their demonstration of the leading role the tenor saxophone can assume in this type of ensemble. *The eel* offers a definitive mapping of a path utterly divergent from that of the romantic Hawkins; it should be compared with the two 1933 versions on **231** (in both of which Russell and Kaminsky also take part). Freeman's solos on the other titles sound tightly packed because of their clear organization, as do those of Kaminsky and, on *China boy*, Gowans.

Though his chief representation in this book is elsewhere — see **116, 189** and particularly **178** — the Stacy tracks embody another kind of individuality. Scored as dialogues for piano and large band, the latter's forceful yet anonymous interjections heighten the singularity of the leader's melodic ideas, touch and timing. Lee Wiley joins in to sensitive and charming effect on *It's only a paper moon*, but her partnership with Stacy gets a better chance on **178**.

Manone's is a curious assemblage and there is little teamwork by the front line, especially in *Royal Garden blues*. Bailey and Berry scarcely exert themselves in their solos, which in any case are spoilt by the leader's spoken interjections. If Rollini dominates his two items, it is for quite other reasons. The finest solo of the session is the one he takes, with bass saxophone, on *Bouncing in rhythm*, and he leads the ensemble strikingly on *Honeysuckle rose*, which may in this respect be compared with Red Nichols's 1927 *Ida, sweet as apple cider* (**70a**). *Honeysuckle rose* proves that Rollini was equally skilled with the vibraharp, and there are simple yet telling phrases from Marsala on both tracks. However, it was a mistake to allow Dandridge to sing.

Besides scoring them imaginatively, Gifford composed the four themes recorded under his name, and excellent they are. Berigan bites into them with particular appreciation, and the antiphonal nature of his phrases, implying two melodic lines, is especially clear on *Nothing but the blues*, one of his classic statements. More time is wasted on Manone, yet Berigan effortlessly dominates, his virtuosic ease of movement never lessening the expressive value of the notes. There are intelligent contributions from Matlock and Freeman, and there is an early sighting of Claude Thornhill. On *Dizzy glide*, Manone uses the phrase 'rock 'n' roll', but authoritatively slashing trumpet passages contradict the implications it was later to acquire.   M.H.

167a Swing Street Vol. 1
Tax (Sd) m-8026

The Three Peppers: Toy Wilson (p, vcl[1]); Bob Bell (g); Walter Williams (bs); Sally Gooding (vcl[2]). New York City, 27 February 1937.
Swinging at the Cotton Club[1,2]
Unidentified tpt, probably Prince Robinson (clt) added. New York City, 9 March 1937.
The midnight ride of Paul Revere[1,2]

Joe Marsala and His Chicagoans: Marty Marsala (tpt); Joe Marsala (clt); Ray Biondi (vln[3]); Joe Bushkin (p); Jack LeMaire (g, vcl[4]); Artie Shapiro (bs); Buddy Rich (d); Lou Hurst (vcl[5]). New York City, 16 March 1937.
Mighty like the blues[4] · *Woo-woo*[5] · *Hot string beans*[3] · *Jim jam stomp*[3]

Billy Kyle and His Swing Club Band: Charlie Shavers (tpt); Eddie Williams (clt); Tab Smith (alt); Harold Arnold (ten); Kyle (p); Danny Barker (g); John Williams (bs); O'Neill Spencer (d); Palmer Brothers (vcl[6]). New York City, 18 March 1937.
Sundays are reserved[6] · *Having a ball* · *Big boy blue*[6] · *Margie*

The Three Peppers: Wilson (p, vcl[1]); Bell (g, vcl[7]); Walter Williams (bs, vcl[8]). New York City, 27 May 1937.
Swing out, Uncle Wilson[1,7] · *The duck's yas yas yas*[1,7,8]

Gene Sedric and His Honey Bears: Herman Autrey (tpt); Sedric (clt, ten, vcl[9]); Jimmy Powell, Fred Kerritt (alt); Hank Duncan (p); Al Casey (g); Cedric Walker (bs); Slick Jones (d); Myra Johnson (vcl[10]).
New York City, 23 November 1938.
The joint is jumping[10] · *Off time*[10] · *Choo-choo*[9] · *The wail of the scromph*

167b Swing Street Vol. 2
Tax (Sd) m-8030

Fats Waller (p, vcl). New York City, 13 March 1931.
I'm crazy 'bout my baby · *Dragging my heart around*

The Five Spirits of Rhythm: Leo Watson, Wilbur Daniels (ten-string tipple, vcl); Douglas Daniels (four-string tipple, vcl); Teddy Bunn (g, vcl); Wilson Myers (bs); Virgil Scroggins (suitcase, whisk). New York City, 24 October 1933.
I got rhythm

Same personnel and location, 20 November 1933.
Rhythm

The Nephews: same personnel and location, 6 December 1933.
I'll be ready when the great day comes · *My old man*

Midge Williams and Her Jazz Jesters: Shavers (tpt); Buster Bailey (clt); Russell Procope (alt); Kyle (p); Barker (g); John Williams (bs); Spencer (d); Midge Williams (vcl); ensemble (vcl[11]). New York City, 10 June 1938.
Don't wake up my heart · *Where in the world* · *In any language* · *Rosie the Redskin*[11]

Clarence Profit Trio: Profit (p); Billy Moore (g); Ben Brown (bs).
New York City, 15 February 1939.
There'll be some changes made · *Tea for two* · *Don't leave me* · *I got rhythm*

Eddie South and His Orchestra: South (vln); Stan Facey (p); Gene Fields (g); Doles Dickens (bs); Specs Powell (d). New York City, 12 March 1941.
Lady, be good · *Stomping at the Savoy*

167c Swing Street Vol. 3
Tax (Sd) m-8034

The Three Peppers: Wilson (p, vcl[1]); Bell (g, vcl[7]); Walter Williams (bs).
New York City, 27 February 1937.
Get the gold[1,7] · *Alexander's ragtime band*[1,7]

Joe Marsala and His Chicagoans: Marty Marsala (tpt); Joe Marsala (clt); Ray Biondi (vln); Bushkin (p); Eddie Condon (g); John Williams (bs); Danny Alvin (d); Adèle Girard (hrp). New York City, 21 April 1937.
Wolverine blues · *Jazz me blues* · *Clarinet marmalade*

The Three Peppers: personnel as for 27 February 1937 except that unidentified d added. New York City, 27 May 1937.
If I had my way[1,7] · *Serenade in the night*[1,7]

Jimmy Johnson and His Orchestra: Henry Allen (tpt);
J. C. Higginbotham (tbn); Sedric (ten); James P. Johnson (p);
Casey (g); John Williams (bs); Sidney Catlett (d); Anna Robinson (vcl[12]);
Ruby Smith (vcl[13]). New York City, 9 March 1939.
Harlem woogie[12] · *Backwater blues*[13] · *He's mine, all mine*[13] · *After tonight*

Mary Lou Williams (p). New York City, 12 October 1939.
Little Joe from Chicago

Cootie Williams and His Orchestra: Williams (tpt); Lou McGarity (tbn);
Les Robinson (alt); Skippy Martin (bar); Johnny Guarnieri (p); Artie
Bernstein (bs); Jo Jones (d). New York City, 7 May 1941.
West End blues · *Ain't misbehaving* · *The blues in my condition* ·
G-men

Appropriately, the earliest of these performances are two songs
by Waller. The first recordings of his humorously affected, mildly
mocking voice had been made only days earlier, with Ted Lewis's
band (**120**). Here he sings, against his own gentle vamping, songs
from his co-operation with Alex Hill, and he develops a kind of
vocal improvisation, especially in *I'm crazy 'bout my baby*, not
scatting but fitting the words to reconstructions of the melody and
pepping up the rhythms with comic speech patterns. He makes
humorous capital out of Hill's rather maudlin *Dragging my heart
around* and, in his brief piano solo, 'pleads on the ivories' with
exaggerated tremolos, almost concealing the jazz demon which
gives this music its deceptive strength. Waller's insouciance ('I
feel so effervescent this morning!') is reflected in a good deal of the
music in this saga of the jazz associated with The Onyx, The
Famous Door and those other small ex-speakeasy clubs in the
Brownstone basements of 52nd Street.

It may be an overstatement that, after the exposure of his vocal
talent, 'Thomas Waller, organist and pianist extraordinary, was
destined to play a subordinate role to Fats Waller, entertainer
and buffoon'[72], but 'jazz as entertainment' seems very much to
have been the unwritten slogan of the times. Who would want to
make ponderous critical assessments of the lighthearted offerings
of Watson, Daniels and company as they scat and jive their way
through inconsequential ditties? Yet these Spirits of Rhythm,
using Bunn's exceptional gifts, enlivening the accompaniment
with the use of tipples (small relatives of the guitar) and revelling
in those vocal techniques which, for them as much as for Waller
and Armstrong, are of one character with instrumental jazz, are
as exciting today as at the time of their fame. Not quite so
relentless in their clowning are the Peppers, who have a lightweight 'stride' expert in Toy Wilson. The zestful routines of
Swinging at the Cotton Club and *Swing out, Uncle Wilson* have

much of the sort of skill that was to make the King Cole Trio even more popular.

Both the Kyle group and the band accompanying Midge Williams contain musicians who were otherwise associated with the newly-formed John Kirby Sextet, notably Shavers and Procope, who had followed Frank Newton and Pete Brown in the original Kirby group, Bailey, Kyle and Spencer. Looser, less stylized ensemble playing than Kirby was featuring places these bands in the same ambit as the Sedric Honey Bears. Comfortable celebrity gained with Fats Waller and His Rhythm was not to stretch the talents of Sedric, Autrey and Casey as more competitive company might have done and, even in an independent context, Sedric's jump tenor sounds rather prosaic, whilst Autrey falls short of Shavers' incisive wit, as exemplified in *Having a ball*. Casey, something of a pioneer in pre-electric guitar freedom, shows his mettle in *The wail of the scromph*.

Marsala's Chicagoans bring a reminder that groups led by Condon and McKenzie were active on 'The Street', and Condon himself joins Marsala for the second session. There are some famous numbers here, and moments both reminiscent and prophetic. A truncation of the *Dippermouth* introduction begins *Woo-woo*, and in *Hot string beans* both Spanier's *Relaxing at the Touro* (**235**) and Glenn Miller's *In the mood* are presaged. Joe Marsala's veiled clarinet tone is typical of the fairly gentle sense of the proceedings in the earlier session, varied chiefly by his brother Marty's virile trumpeting. When such dixieland standards as *Jazz me blues* and *Clarinet marmalade* are turned to, the ensemble accents gain toughness, with Biondi's hot violin making some amends for the politeness of the clarinettist's sound. As for Adèle Girard, once one has got beyond the impression of a stiff-keyed, aged piano, her harp solos are charming enough, if a little out of place.

The hedonism which coloured so much of the swing age's publicly acceptable creations is a thread running through many of these sessions too; partly the euphoria of liberation after the Depression and Prohibition years, partly response to the demands of the entertainment-loving patrons packing musical stamping grounds which had, of a sudden, become legitimate. An admirable ration of genuine jazz is mixed with the vaudeville hokum and Tin Pan Alley sentiment, yet the generative ferocity and joy which had fired the greatest periods of Oliver, Morton, Armstrong, Beiderbecke and the earlier Chicagoans is listened for in vain. To say this is not to deny the importance of the chronicle formed by this collection or the influential musical value of much that goes on here. 'Swing Street' was a scene of transition and, even in the early 1930s, strains were being discovered which would be followed through to the more startling changes that can be heard in Vol. 4 of this sequence (**249**). Bop, when it came, shaped its fierce angularities partly as a reaction to the tolerant amiability of Harlem swing, but it also drew upon the extended skills of groups and individuals such as those mentioned above.

All that having been said, there remain for consideration a few items of more self-contained value, and of a creative distinction which sets them outside any generalized assessment. The unassuming, withdrawn delicacy of Profit's work deserves special mention for its demonstration that a more reflective artistry had its place amid the general exuberance. His *I got rhythm* is exuberant enough, to be sure, and Moore adds some scintillating lines; yet here, too, the intimacy of mood is maintained.

Profit is now an almost forgotten figure, seldom mentioned in jazz histories. Not so Mary Lou Williams. She remained an honoured and musically vigorous pianist and composer until the end of her long life, and her well-known 1939 recording of *Little Joe from Chicago*, a tribute to Joe Sullivan, which she had earlier arranged for the Kirk band (**132**) and was to recreate many times, is a skilful and very personal interpretation of the barrelhouse piano tradition.

James P. Johnson's *Harlem woogie* introduces a session in which the mentor of Fats Waller is joined by other equally-celebrated friends together with men of somewhat lesser stature. This particular expression of the blues was (at least early in his career) less congenial to Johnson than the more solemn style heard in the revival of *Backwater blues* and in *He's mine, all mine*, in each of which Ruby Smith not too successfully imitates her great namesake, Bessie, adding histrionics of her own. Though the ensemble approach in these numbers is rather ordinary, there are notable solos from Allen and Higginbotham; and Sedric, particularly in *Harlem woogie*, improvises confidently. *After tonight* is yet another instance of the swinging grace which the pianist brought to the interpretation of his own tunes.

Cootie Williams, who had left Ellington for Goodman late in 1940, leads a well-organized septet in a genuflection to Armstrong, unafraid, for all his reverence, to add his personal accents to *West End blues* as he plays unmuted. He takes up the plunger elsewhere and rides the riffs of *Ain't misbehaving* and *G-men* in arrangements strongly reminiscent of the Goodman Sextet — although the latter theme is in fact derived from a phrase in his own solo on Ellington's *Harmony in Harlem* (**131a**). The excellence of Guarnieri's playing on *The blues in my condition* is characteristic of all his work here, and McGarity frequently shows himself to be a sturdy but unslavish disciple of Jack Teagarden.   E.T.

168 Café Society Swing and Boogie Woogie
Swingfan (G) 1013

Meade 'Lux' Lewis, Albert Ammons, Pete Johnson (p). New York City, 30 December 1938.
Boogie woogie prayer

Harry James and The Boogie Woogie Trio: James (tpt); Johnson (p); John Williams (bs); Eddie Dougherty (d). New York City, 1 February 1939.
Boo-woo · *Home, James*

Ammons (p) replaces Johnson. Same date.
Woo-woo · *Jesse*

Frank Newton and His Café Society Orchestra: Newton (tpt); Tab Smith (sop, alt); Stanley Payne (alt); Kenneth Hollon (ten); Kenny Kersey (p); Ulysses Livingston (g); Williams (bs); Dougherty (d). New York City, 12 April 1939.
Tab's blues · *Frankie's jump*

Lewis, Ammons, Johnson (p); probably Dougherty (d); Joe Turner (vcl). New York City, 30 June 1939.
Café Society rag

Pete Johnson and His Boogie Boys: 'Hot Lips' Page (tpt); Buster Smith (alt); Johnson (p); Lawrence Lucie (g); Abe Bolar (bs); Dougherty (d); Turner (vcl). Same location and date.
Loving mama blues

Joe Sullivan and His Café Society Orchestra: Ed Anderson (tpt); Benny Morton (tbn); Ed Hall (clt); Danny Polo (clt, ten) Sullivan (p); Freddy Greene (g); Henry Turner (bs); Johnny Wells (d); Joe Turner (vcl[1]). New York City, 9 February 1940.
Solitude · *Lady, be good* · *Low down dirty shame blues*[1] · *I can't give you anything but love*[1]

Barney Josephson's Café Society in Greenwich Village differed from most of the clubs where jazz could be heard in downtown New York at the end of the 1930s. For a start, there was no attempt to dissuade black patrons from attending. And the character of the music played there was often unlike that to be found in neighbouring establishments. It was at the Café Society, for example, that Lewis, Ammons and Johnson took up residence after appearing (on 23 December 1938) at the 'From Spirituals to Swing' concert in Carnegie Hall. They were to play a large part in popularizing boogie woogie, that style of piano blues playing that only a decade before had been confined to clubs in the black areas of Chicago, Kansas City and other mid- and Southwestern towns.

Ammons, the most accomplished pianist of the three, came from Chicago; so did Lewis, the most intense and rhythmically complex musician in the trio. Johnson was from Kansas City and, to some extent, his playing reflected the musical eclecticism to be found there.

Kingsley Amis once remarked, in a very different context, that 'more will mean worse'. It happened to be true when it came to putting these three pianists together, for example in the two-part *Boogie woogie prayer*. The possible gain in polyrhythms, not too evident here, and in energy had to be set against the loss of crispness and individual identity. Far more rewarding music was produced when Ammons worked with James. The dynamics of his piano playing come across handsomely in *Woo-woo*; *Jesse*, not boogie at all, presents the trumpeter using a slightly more gushing manner. Eyebrows may have been raised when this session was mooted, but James fits in well, his stylistic debt to Muggsy Spanier turning into a positive asset. Unlike Ammons, Johnson, in *Boo-woo*, relies too much upon repetition; but *Home, James* begins rather like an Armstrong–Hines duet and continues that way. In *Café Society rag* the three pianists are backed up, quite unnecessarily, by a drummer. The performance has nothing to do with boogie, but Turner obligingly explains which pianist is taking his turn.

Turner had come from Kansas City, where he worked regularly with Johnson. Indeed, all the musicians on *Loving mama blues*, apart from Lucie and Dougherty, were Kansas City men, including Buster Smith, Charlie Parker's tutor and perhaps his most crucial influence. The only soloist to be featured is Page, squeezing the notes out of his trumpet, a natural blues player. Otherwise this track is devoted to Turner, leaning back across the bar lines, bringing a Homeric spaciousness to his musings on the age-old theme of infidelity. He does the same in *Low down dirty shame* (his theme is poverty this time), and goes on to treat *I can't give you anything but love* rather as Bessie Smith used to handle a pop song, translating it into blues.

Sullivan's band used a mixture of black and white musicians, an uncommon practice in downtown New York clubs at the time, but typical of Josephson's policy. Polo, a fellow Chicagoan, not long back in America after spending the 1930s in Europe, plays tenor saxophone in a dry, slightly utilitarian fashion. Hall takes some palpitating clarinet solos, his style mixing a New Orleans upbringing with an understanding of the newer kinds of virtuosity introduced by Benny Goodman. Both Morton and Anderson are relatively subdued, although Anderson's muted solo in *I can't give you anything but love* could hardly fail to reflect something of

Armstrong's manner. Nobody manages to stretch out on *Solitude*, a piece which, rather like *Stardust*, defies an improviser to do much more than ornament the melody.

Perhaps the Newton *Tab's blues* owes something to *Jeep's blues*, which Johnny Hodges had recorded with an Ellington small group only eleven months earlier. At any rate, both performances feature soprano saxophone playing, in this case by Tab Smith. Newton's trumpet solo demonstrates how much can be done by using just a few notes, an awesome blending of adventurousness and sobriety. He is brisker and bolder, yet equally distinguished, in *Frankie's jump*, a faster piece built upon riffs. On this Tab Smith plays alto, his style airy and mobile, obviously influenced by Willie Smith. That he did not develop into a better-known soloist is probably a fate he shared with several enterprising alto saxophonists of the period, notably Rudy Williams (**136**). Their ambitions — and perhaps their confidence — were soon to be upset by the arrival of Charlie Parker.   C.F.

169 Cutting the Boogie: Piano Blues and Boogie Woogie

New World Records (A) NW259

Jimmy Blythe (p). Chicago, c. 1924–6.
Chicago stomp · *Mr Freddie blues*

Hersal Thomas (p). Chicago, c. February 1925.
Suitcase blues

Clarence 'Pinetop' Smith (p, spch). Chicago, 29 December 1928.
Pinetop's boogie woogie

Same personnel and location, 15 January 1929.
Jump steady blues

Meade 'Lux' Lewis (p). Chicago, 21 November 1935.
Honky tonk train blues

Same personnel and location, 11 January 1936.
Yancey special · *Mr Freddie blues*

Albert Ammons and His Rhythm Kings: Guy Kelly (tpt); Dalbert Bright (clt, alt); Ammons (p); Ike Perkins (g); Israel Crosby (bs); Jimmy Hoskins (d). Chicago, 13 February 1936.
Boogie woogie stomp

Ammons (p). New York City, 8 April 1939.
Bass gone crazy

Jimmy Yancey (p). Chicago, 25 October 1939.
The mellow blues · *Tell 'em about me*

Pete Johnson (p). New York City, 16 April 1939.
Climbing and screaming

Same personnel and location, 23 August 1940.
Blues on the downbeat · *Kaycee on my mind*
Ammons, Johnson (p); Hoskins (d). New York City, 7 May 1941.
Cutting the boogie

There is a *double-entendre* in the title. 'Cut' here embraces the process of sound-recording and also the performance of bodily antics; and the latter sense is a reminder that this music was dance music first. The term 'boogie woogie' is attributed to Smith, whose performance of that title, with its dance calls, conjures the atmosphere of the rent parties where this style was popular and the boogie was danced. However, by the time Ammons and Johnson recorded their duet, this species of piano blues had attracted devotees who were taken more by the music's own dramatic quality than by its terpsichorean associations.

Blythe's playing, in both of his pieces, has all the customary elements of a form that was to change little, and he shows sufficiently also how a sonorous rhythm permitted pianists to act surrogate for more expensive, space-consuming bands. Most of these musicians gained fame in Chicago. Thomas, who died after a very brief career, did not develop the celebrated boogie ostinato bass as fully as others. His accompaniments, in association with Armstrong and Dodds, of his sister, the singer Hociel Thomas, in the year of *Suitcase blues* reinforce the impression of a less complex blues technique (Biograph (A) BLP–C6). Smith's strong yet graceful phrases are taken up and given more muscular forthrightness by Ammons, whose *Stomp* is clearly based upon *Pinetop's boogie woogie* and, like Lewis's version of *Mr Freddie blues*, is an interesting reinterpretation of another's concept. (Ammons's piece is heard to best advantage, however, in his 1939 solo version, on Mosaic (A) MR3–103.)

A closely limited range of musical devices makes most boogie compositions seem like rehashings of a small common store of ingredients. Tedium and a sense of the uncreative easily result. Lewis, Ammons and Johnson were encouraged to ride the boogie cult in the late 1930s, and their marathon piano trios (**168**) were notable for their cumulative force rather than for real musical distinction. The duet included here sails close to the wind of similar criticism, but is mercifully two hands less heavy. Companion duets are found on RCA (F) 730.561, together with eight splendid recordings by the pianist honoured in Lewis's *Yancey special*. *Mellow blues* exemplifies the *habanera*-like bass figure which Lewis imitated and shows the greater flexibility of Yancey's use of it.

Johnson, a Kansas City musician, sometimes gives the impression that he could have shone in less circumscribed jazz modes. Like his partners, he favours the driving chordal ostinato basses of the 'rocks' type, and so one needs to hear other artists — Yancey in particular, but also notables omitted from this collection such as Clarence Lofton, Montana Taylor and Cow Cow Davenport — to discover the variety existent within boogie's admitted bounds.

Like ragtime, boogie had its shaping influence upon jazz ensemble styles. The Crosby band's idiosyncratic reworkings of Lewis's *Honky tonk train blues* and *Yancey special* (**236**) seem like a counterpart to the orchestrations of ragtime pieces heard on **10**; but a livelier spirit animates such things as the Basie band's 1946 *Hobnail boogie* (CBS (F) 54165). Echoes of the style reverberated on into interminable rock 'n' roll obsessions, and boogie itself only avoided stultification for so long as it drank at the freshets of the blues. Early blues guitarists influenced boogie much as banjo dance music affected piano rags. The spirit, rather than the form, of that influence is crucial. The miraculous fifth chorus of Yancey's march-like *Tell 'em about me* distills the essence of blues pathos in simple, luminous tone-clusters. A finely-wrought artistry aspires to undissembling emotion, and obligation to the inexorable bass is momentarily waived.　　　　　　　　　　　　　　E.T.

170 Swing Vol. 1
RCA (A) LPV578

Gene Krupa's Swing Band: Roy Eldridge (tpt); Benny Goodman (clt); Chew Berry (ten); Jess Stacy (p); Allen Reuss (g); Israel Crosby (bs); Krupa (d); Helen Ward (vcl[1]). Chicago, 29 February 1936.
I hope Gabriel likes my music · *Mutiny in the parlour*[1] · *I'm gonna clap my hands*[1] · *Swing is here*

A Jam Session at Victor: Bunny Berigan (tpt); Tommy Dorsey (tbn); Fats Waller (p); Dick McDonough (g); George Wettling (d). New York City, 31 March 1937.
Honeysuckle rose · *Blues*

Frank Newton and His Orchestra: Newton (tpt); Mezz Mezzrow (clt); Pete Brown (alt); James P. Johnson (p); Al Casey (g); John Kirby (bs); Cozy Cole (d). New York City, 13 January 1939.
Minor jive · *The blues my baby gave to me* · *Romping*

Una Mae Carlisle (vcl) acc Shad Collins (tpt); Lester Young (ten); Clyde Hart (p); John Collins (g); Nick Fenton (bs); Doc West (d). New York City, 10 March 1941.
Blitzkrieg baby · *Beautiful eyes* · *There'll be some changes made* · *It's sad but true*

Esquire All-Americans: Charlie Shavers (tpt); Jimmy Hamilton (clt); Johnny Hodges (alt); Don Byas (ten); Duke Ellington, Billy Strayhorn (p); Remo Palmieri (g); Chubby Jackson (bs); Sonny Greer (d); Red Norvo (vib). New York City, 11 January 1946.
The one that got away
Esquire All-American Award Winners: Shavers, Buck Clayton (tpt); J. J. Johnson (tbn); Coleman Hawkins (ten); Harry Carney (bar); Teddy Wilson (p); Collins (g); Jackson (bs, spch[2]); Shadow Wilson (d). New York City, 4 December 1946.
Blow me down · *Moldy fig stomp*[2]

Comparing the Krupa tracks with those from the final pair of sessions is enlightening. In 1936 Eldridge was, with the possible exception of Henry Allen, the most adventurous trumpet player in jazz, the audacity of his solos reflecting both his character and his technical command. If he used any clichés, and all jazz improvisers do from time to time, then they were his own, part of a unique musical *persona*. Shavers, on the other hand, frequently seems to offer nothing but clichés of the crasser sort. Alternatively schmaltzy and bombastic, his solos in *The one that got away* and *Blow me down* are an object lesson in the danger of relying upon effects rather than the thrust of aesthetic curiosity. Similarly, Hamilton offers a clinical counterpart to what Goodman was up to ten years before (and indeed was still up to), but without the older man's dramatic instinct and his ability to swing.

The Krupa tracks, as it happens, also contrast quite strikingly with a similar session recorded only three months earlier under his name (**116**). The difference lies in the presence of Eldridge and Berry, both with Fletcher Henderson's band at the time, both already being acclaimed for the tempestuousness of their playing. Though sounding less poised than Goodman in the hectic *Swing is here*, Berry performs on this session with characteristic panache but is, paradoxically, most impressive in the eight ruminative bars he contributes to *Mutiny in the parlour*. The catalyst, though, was Eldridge, perpetually inventive, flamboyant in the happiest sense — not only in his solos but also leading the riffs and giving all-in passages a glowing excitement comparable to that which Allen brought to the Billy Banks sessions (**56**).

The approaches of Berigan and Newton were very different from Eldridge's and from each other, but of equally high calibre. Nothing reveals this more than the way they set about a twelve-bar blues. Berigan's playing in *Blues* is passionate, optimistic, sometimes verging on the truculent; Newton's muted choruses in

The blues my baby gave to me contrive to be devious, even faintly subversive, as well as delicate. Yet both solos must be classed as small masterpieces. The Jam Session account of *Honeysuckle rose* is a jaunty affair (Waller, not surprisingly, excels in his own tune), but it is *Blues* that brings out the best in these musicians, from the guitar-and-moaning-trombone introduction to the triumphant climax. Perhaps the present writer is biased, for these two titles made up the first jazz record he ever bought; nevertheless, Berigan can rarely have sounded as good as he does here, particularly in the lower register.

Waller's mentor, Johnson, is outstanding on the Newton date: exuberant in *Romping*, blissfully reticent on the blues. Otherwise, apart obviously from the trumpeter himself and Casey's chording on the guitar, the solos are variable in quality. Brown performs with wheezy brashness, the apotheosis of 'jump' alto playing, while Mezzrow, as was his wont, keeps a low profile, deploying his limited technique mainly to tinge and sustain (he also wrote all the tunes).

Una Mae Carlisle was better known as a pianist immediately before World War II. Her singing turns out to be pleasant but undistinguished: *Blitzkrieg baby* is cheerfully topical (Josh White seems to have used the same melody later for his *Bon-bon, chocolate and chewing gum*); more striking, perhaps, is Miss Carlisle's work on the other pieces, where she appears to have been very much influenced by Billie Holiday, a resemblance accentuated by Young's presence. These four tracks would in fact be fairly inconsequential were it not for the latter's contributions: obbligatos in almost every number and, among other solos, a beautifully rounded sixteen bars on *Beautiful eyes*.

All-star bands arouse expectations that are rarely satisfied, and those assembled by the magazine *Esquire* were not exceptions. The shortcomings of Hamilton and Shavers have been commented upon, but there were better moments. Most of them were provided by Norvo, one of the music's great survivors, Hodges, with a fluttering solo that is intriguingly different from what he normally did with Ellington's band, and by the sumptuous playing of Byas, already in his mid-thirties yet a jazzman who had really only just made his mark. By now the music was becoming tinged with bop: Krupa's *Swing is here* used the chord sequence of *I got rhythm*; so does *Blow me down*, but with a significantly altered stance. Wilson, incidentally, sounds more than comfortable in this setting. *Moldy fig stomp* turns out to be that saddest of things, a musical joke which falls flat. Perhaps it should be explained that bop's early propagandists often referred to admirers of New Orleans and dixieland jazz as 'mouldy figs'.

The result is a bit of codding that is neither as blatantly populist as Pee Wee Hunt's *Twelfth Street rag* nor as affectionately perverse as Charles Mingus's *Jelly roll soul*. Shavers, aiming for once at simplicity, sounds much better than when he was showing off. (Incidentally, whatever the discographers may claim, it seems most unlikely that Ellington and Strayhorn both play the piano on *The one that got away*.)   C.F.

James P. Johnson
171 Father of Stride Piano
CBS (E) BPG62090, Columbia (A) CL1780

James P. Johnson (p). New York City, 18 October 1921.
Carolina shout

Same personnel and location, 28 June 1923.
Worried and lonesome blues · Weeping blues

Same personnel and location, 7 March 1927.
Snowy morning blues · All that I had is gone

Clarence Williams (p, vcl) added. New York City, 31 January 1930.
How could I be blue?

Williams absent. New York City, 14 June 1939.
If dreams come true · Fascination · The mule walk · Lonesome reverie · Blueberry rhyme

James P. Johnson and His Orchestra: Henry Allen (tpt); J. C. Higginbotham (tbn); Gene Sedric (ten); Johnson (p); Eugene Fields (g); Pops Foster (bs); Sidney Catlett (d); Anna Robinson (vcl[1]). New York City, 15 June 1939.
Memories of you · Old fashioned love · Swinging at the Lido · Having a ball · Hungry blues[1]

172 James P. Johnson: New York Jazz
Stinson (A) SLP21

James P. Johnson's New York Orchestra: Frank Newton (tpt); Johnson (p); Al Casey (g); Foster (bs); Eddie Dougherty (d). New York City, 12 June 1944.
Hesitation blues · The boogie dream · Four o/clock groove · The dream (Slow drag) · Hot Harlem

Johnson (p). Same date.
Euphonic sounds

173 Sidney DeParis/James P. Johnson
Blue Note (A) B6506

James P. Johnson's Blue Note Jazzmen: Sidney DeParis (tpt); Vic Dickenson (tbn); Ben Webster (ten); Johnson (p); James Shirley (g); John Simmons (bs); Catlett (d). New York City, 4 March 1944.
Blue mizz · Victory stride · Joy-menting · After you've gone

Sidney DeParis's Blue Note Jazzmen: Ed Hall (clt) replaces Webster.
New York City, 21 June 1944.
Everybody loves my baby (2 takes) · *Balling the jack* · *Who's sorry now?* · *The call of the blues*
James P. Johnson's Blue Note Jazzmen: Al Lucas (bs), Arthur Trappier
(d) replace Simmons, Catlett. New York City, 26 October 1944.
Tishomingo blues

Two 1921 versions of *Carolina shout* are usefully compared — the
Columbia gramophone recording here included and the QRS
piano roll made the preceding month (Biograph (A) BLP1003Q).
The QRS reproduction, though mechanical, preserves more than
a little of Johnson's characteristic accent and of the *joie de vivre* of
this famous composition. But what the roll cannot retain is the
relaxation, the continually varied dynamics, the lightness of
movement which come over in the Columbia performance despite
a certain deliberation. And though the rolls (one thinks of *Gypsy
blues* (Riverside (A) RLP151) and *Caprice rag* (Biograph (A)
BLP1009Q) leave one marvelling at Johnson's ease of melodic
invention and pianistic thinking, one needs the gramophone
recording — a new experience for him in 1921 — to receive the
subtleties of technique which turn simple animation into a
lyricism of the spirit.

James Price Johnson was a musician of remarkable range,
classically trained and perceptive, active upon the borderline
between jazz and symphonic music — and beyond it — and a
master of the popular theatrical music of his day. Yet the music
which emerges in his earliest recordings and persists in all the
performances by which he is now likely to be remembered is jazz,
and jazz of an unfailingly delightful kind. Diverse elements
inform it, but its overt character depends upon a refinement of the
rag and jazz devices which he learnt, early in his career, from
older pianists — Charlie Cherry, Jack the Bear, Fred Bryant,
Sam Gordon and so on. Ragtime formalism becomes fluid jazz in
Johnson's playing, seemingly by the heeding of vocal promptings.
Jelly Roll Morton transformed ragtime into jazz in a similar way,
but whereas he used the flexibility of the blues and brass band
strains (listen to the 1923 *Grandpa's spells* and *Wolverine blues*
on **45**), Johnson appears to be recalling a rural tradition in some
ways simpler and more naïve. The antiphonal elements in *Carolina
shout* are echoes of communal song, evocative of a religious form
(as the title confirms) not only in their melodic contrasts but in
their enthusiastic impetus too, so that they become augural of the
riffs of orchestral swing. *The mule walk* is like a swinging
panorama of country music, fiddle dances, playparty songs, gospel
tunes, and those transmit their own *élan* to his style.

Yet his response to the blues is more formal than Morton's, the effect of items like *Snowy morning blues, Weeping blues* and *Worried and lonesome blues* being of blues conventions interpreted from a ragtimer's viewpoint. The opening of *Worried and lonesome* suggests the influence of the player-piano, *Weeping blues* includes snatches of undoubted ragtime ornament, while the melodic forms in all of these so-called blues are clearly drawn from popular songs based upon the blues rather than from the blues themselves. This raises the question of how much of Johnson's knowledge of folk music forms was direct and how much of it came filtered through the nostalgia of ragtime and minstrelsy. Whatever the answer, the vigour and much of the intrinsic spirit of those forms is certainly persistent in Johnson's piano music, yet his translations of the blues are less convincing than his transmissions of the dancing and 'shouting' traditions. *Hungry blues* from the 1939 band session is taken from Johnson's opera *De Organiser* and adds to musical sophistication some stylish lyrics by the poet Langston Hughes: 'There's a brand new world, so clean and fine,/Nobody's hungry, and there ain't no colour line. . .'

Fascination, Lonesome reverie and *Blueberry rhyme* represent a rather different mutation of rag forms, a concentration upon the melodic and harmonic elements in a manner that could easily seem merely sentimental were it not for the wiry sense of wit with which they are interpreted. Such compositions allow for varied treatment. *Fascination*, played here at a slow-to-medium tempo, is of similar character to Johnson's *Daintyness rag*, which he recorded in both slow and rather fast versions. But this is not, for all its musical charm, the mode which has been his most potent gift to the growth of jazz. What that is will be more clearly understood from the superb treatment of *If dreams come true*, an almost perfect demonstration of all that is implied by that woefully inadequate label 'stride piano'. The elements could be analysed, the infinitely varied treble patterns imposed upon the basic striding beat, the use of subtle dynamics and missed steps to achieve swing, the rich and dexterous use of middle-register counter-melodies whilst treble and bass maintain their course — but, in the end, the effect is indefinable. It was not, like Morton's style, translated deliberately into orchestral jazz terms and, in this sense, Johnson's achievement as an orchestral composer belongs to an adjoining world and must presumably be assessed with different criteria.

Playing with the various groups included here, Johnson's role usually seems to be chiefly that of a brilliant accompanist and occasional soloist, but there is more to it than that. The ways in which Allen, Sedric and Higginbotham adapt themselves to his ringing lead in *Having a ball* and *Old fashioned love*, and respond to his clear but never obtrusive support, show what an inspiring presence he is. Not himself an improvisor of daring, he nevertheless provides just the right context in which the brilliant Allen and Higginbotham can stretch their imagination. (The items from this session should be compared with those cut three months earlier by a similar personnel on **167c**.)

The June 1944 session with Newton (recalling, perhaps, their association in the 1939 Panassié recordings on **170**) is more intimate and loosely contrived. Notice how those middle-register augmentations of Johnson's provide a countervoice to Newton's trumpet at the beginning of *The dream*, a piece in which most of the interest is found in the pianist's ranging variations. In *Boogie dream* Johnson, as if to confound judgments made upon his blues sympathies, demonstrates with some subtlety an ability to play in the barrelhouse style that was earlier hinted at in the 1927 *All that I had is gone*. But the most fascinating item from this session is certainly *Euphonic sounds* — Sedalia as viewed from Harlem, Johnson interpreting a Joplin composition of which he himself remarked, 'Even today, who understands it? It's really modern' [73]. Effortless in his grasp of the intricacies of this ambitious piece, he frequently extends the strains into stomping exuberance which may mock, just a little, the academic cast of Joplin's work but which also proves the free spirit of Johnson's approach to ragtime — an approach emulated in Hank Jones's 1964 recreations of rags by Joplin, Turpin, Lamb and Joseph Northrup (ABC–Paramount (A) ABC496). It is an exposition of one style in terms of another to be set beside Morton's *Maple leaf rag* (**21**) and it is marred only by a rather commonplace ending.

The sessions with DeParis produced music which, though not far removed from dixieland simplifications of the New Orleans ensemble style, achieves a concentration and a subtlety which allow for much more inventiveness in collective improvisation. The early 1940s may have been the last significant resurgence of this kind of shared freedom before revivalism began to impose its presumptuous orthodoxy, a freedom in which musicians of different backgrounds found a congenial framework. The concentration, breaking and remaking the classic counterpoint with its basis in a harmonic choral tradition, to create a relationship of parts closer to the antiphonal modes incorporated into Johnson's own keyboard style; so that it is tempting to suspect the influence of his own three-voiced (one had almost written 'three-handed') pianistic organizations upon the ensemble. But mutuality of influence is most probably the key, as it frequently has been in jazz. There is particularly good work in these sessions from Hall and Webster, and DeParis's lead is always strong. Whenever Johnson emerges from his rich rhythmic habitat to solo in his self-sufficient yet marvellously complementary fashion one wonders at the fitfulness of his fame in jazz circles, at his popular overshadowing by his greatest pupil, the far less reliable Fats Waller, who had died only a few months before these records were made. Numerous pianists based their styles on Johnson's and some may have exceeded him in harmonic imagination and improvisatory freedom, yet not one of them ever surpassed his superb joyousness or dramatic variety, none ever seemed as vigorously attuned as he was to the vital origins of jazz [74].   E.T.

174 Fats Waller Piano Solos
RCA–Bluebird (A) AXM2–5518 (2 LPs), *RCA (I) NL42444

Waller (p). New York City, 1 March 1929.
Handful of keys · *Numb fumbling*

Same personnel. Camden, New Jersey, 2 August 1929.
Ain't misbehaving · *Sweet Savannah Sue* · *I've got a feeling I'm falling* · *Love me or leave me* · *Gladyse* · *Valentine stomp*

Same personnel and location, 29 August 1929.
Waiting at the end of the road · *Baby, oh where can you be?*

Same personnel. New York City, 11 September 1929.
Going about · *My feeling are hurt*

Same personnel and location, 24 September 1929.
Smashing thirds

Same personnel and location, 4 December 1929.
My fate is in your hands · *Turn on the heat*

Benny Payne (p) added. New York City, 21 March 1930.
St Louis blues · *After you've gone*

Payne absent. New York City, 16 November 1934.
African ripples · *Clothes line ballet* · *Alligator crawl* · *Viper's drag*

Same personnel and location, 11 March 1935.
Russian fantasy · *E flat blues*

Same personnel and location, 11 June 1937.
Keeping out of mischief now · *Stardust* · *Basin Street blues* · *Tea for two* · *I ain't got nobody*

Same personnel and location, 13 May 1941.
Georgia on my mind · *Rocking chair* · *Carolina shout* · *Honeysuckle rose* · *Ring dem bells*

175

Fats Waller Vol. 6 (1930–35)
RCA (F) 741.112, *Bluebird (A) AXM2–5511

Waller, Payne (p). New York City, 21 March 1930.
St Louis blues · *After you've gone*

Fats Waller and His Rhythm: Herman Autrey (tpt); Ben Whittet (clt); Waller (p, vcl[1]); Al Casey (g); Billy Taylor (bs); Harry Dial (d, vib[2]). New York City, 16 May 1934.
A porter's love song to a chamber maid[1,2] · *I wish I were twins*[1] (2 takes) · *Armful o' sweetness*[1]

Gene Sedric (ten) replaces Whittet. New York City, 17 August 1934.
Georgia May[1] · *Then I'll be tired of you*[1]

Bill Coleman (tpt) replaces Autry; Sedric also plays clt. New York City, 7 November 1934.
Believe it, beloved[1] · *I'm growing fonder of you*[1] · *If it isn't love*[1] · *Breaking the ice*[1]

Charles Turner (bs) replaces Taylor; Waller also plays org[3]. Camden, New Jersey, 5 January 1935.
I'm a hundred per cent for you[1] (take 1) · *I'm a hundred per cent for you* (take 2) · *Baby brown* · *Night wind*[3]

It was Cyril Connolly, one of the plumper English book reviewers, who contended that inside every fat man was imprisoned a thin man, 'wildly signalling to be let out' [75]. Despite his nickname and unquestionable girth, Thomas Waller probably worried less about corporeal problems than about the way he became typecast in his later years. He was one of two outstandingly talented jazz players of his generation (the other being Louis Armstrong) who achieved widespread fame for reasons which had little to do with aesthetic excellence. Wiggling his eyebrows and scalp, tearing sentimental songs apart, keeping up a constant barrage of quips and cheeky insinuations, he became one of America's most popular entertainers, his musicianship more or less an appendage to his personality. Even the most insensitive of men — and Waller was far from that — would have experienced some sense of frustration in those circumstances.

The piano solos give an idea of his real quality, more than half of them recorded before he had even sung a note — on disc, anyway. They also demonstrate that, like other Harlem pianists such as James P. Johnson, he had a songwriter's respect for melodies. *Ain't misbehaving, Sweet Savannah Sue* and *I've got a feeling I'm falling*, just to pick three of his own compositions, are performed as if he were auditioning for a music publisher. There is embellishment, a degree of variation, some of it ingenious, but the themes are never tampered with too outrageously. The same was true when he got to grips with pieces by other men. Even when he elaborated upon his purely instrumental compositions

(*Handful of keys, Valentine stomp, Alligator crawl,* etc.), the listener is constantly aware of the material on which he is improvising. Very rarely does he set about the kind of harmonic transformation that Art Tatum or, later on, Bill Evans would have attempted.

Like most 'stride' pianists of the 1920s, Waller commanded a wide range of effects. And performing entirely solo encouraged an orchestral approach, the improvisor not being so interested in thematic or harmonic development as in the kind of textures and contrasts that an arranger might extract from a band. There are no *longueurs*; the listener is kept agog as rhythmic chording is succeeded by a shower of semiquavers or perhaps the melody is shifted to the left hand; there are alternations of tempo, much juxtaposing — rather as in ragtime, from which Harlem 'stride' style evolved — of different themes. Maybe not surprisingly, he performs relatively few abstract blues (*Numb fumbling, E flat blues* and — just about qualifying — *My feelings are hurt*) as distinct from the blues songs, notably Spencer Williams's *Basin Street blues*, or such stimulating artefacts as *Viper's drag*.

Several pieces — *Handful of keys*, for instance — evolve from fairly simple beginnings, the kind of thing Waller might spontaneously rattle off without premeditation, yet achieve a dazzling elaborateness. *Gladyse* might be classed as a 'novelty piano solo', and Waller invests it with great rhythmic *brio*. ('Novelty piano' was a 1920s genre descended from ragtime. Its more skilful composers, such as Willie Eckstein and Billy Mayerl, are mistakenly despised by jazz *aficionados*.) *Valentine stomp* and *Smashing thirds*, both exhibitionistic in intent, are like toys for adults, beautifully paced and controlled [76].

The four solos recorded in 1934 represent some kind of peak in Waller's use of the piano. As usual, one is never fully aware of how much was composed, how much improvised on the spot, and it seems a pity that he rarely went beyond a first take, denying us the chance to make comparisons. *African ripples* begins with the same descending triplets that are heard at the start of *Gladyse*, afterwards embarking upon a kind of impressionism which (as Mike Lipskin writes in his sleeve note) owes something to both Gershwin and Willie 'The Lion' Smith. And so, in parts at least, does *Clothes line ballet*, very delicate, very concise. *Alligator crawl* had been recorded seven years earlier by Armstrong's Hot Seven (**48**); Waller's version has much swing and exhilaration but never adds up to more than a succession of lively choruses. *Viper's drag*, as Richard Hadlock has pointed out [77], is a fascinating example of the pianist improvising with as well as within his own framework, perhaps one of his most ambitious forays into blues territory. *E flat blues* is simpler but still effective, while *Russian fantasy* complicates a strain from *Valentine stomp*, another instance of Waller's penchant for dipping into his past.

The 1937 and 1941 solos mostly make use of other people's tunes; *Honeysuckle rose*, which he perhaps had played too often, is treated rather perfunctorily. *Carolina shout*, a test piece for Harlem pianists of the 1920s, is performed boisterously yet respectfully as befits a composition by Waller's mentor, James P. Johnson. Ellington's *Ring dem bells*, taken at a very slow tempo, more or less collapses through inertia, but there is a subtle paraphrasing of *Stardust*, one which even expands the harmonies of that intractable melody. Best of all, however, is *I ain't got nobody*, a perfect illustration of Waller's virtues as an embellisher, its tempo leisurely, the approach witty but never frivolous.

Meanwhile, he had begun recording with the group he called his Rhythm. Apart from two erratic piano duets made in 1930, where Payne was apparently a last-minute replacement for Jelly Roll Morton, **175** is devoted to some of that band's early work. Later on, the mixture of second-rate material and Waller's relentless bonhomie resulted in many stereotyped performances. Yet these initial recordings project an unpretentious, wholly admirable vitality. And such facetiousness as Waller's guying of operatic singing in *If it isn't love* is derision well aimed. The solos tend to fit the context, inconsequential rather than distinguished. Casey's guitar, always a strength in the rhythm section, chords away pleasingly in *Georgia May* and the second take of *I'm a hundred per cent for you*; Sedric's tenor playing, deriving from Hawkins and Chew Berry, belongs ineluctably to the 1930s yet is rarely less than buoyant; Autrey's trumpet solos were to become more wayward, yet on the earliest sessions they usually possessed a fitful brilliance. But the man who comes across most strongly is Coleman, his vaulting lines sounding perpetually fresh. He is at his finest, perhaps, in *Believe it, beloved*, a track in which Waller's singing of the line 'Delicious, delightful delirium' sums up what was best about his popular *persona*.   C.F.

176   Teddy Wilson
CBS (E) 66274 (2 LPs), CBS (J) 66274 (2 LPs)

Teddy Wilson and His Orchestra: Roy Eldridge (tpt); Cecil Scott (clt); Hilton Jefferson (alt); Ben Webster (ten); Wilson (p); Lawrence Lucie (g); John Kirby (bs); Cozy Cole (d). New York City, 31 July 1935.
Sweet Lorraine

Dick Clark (tpt); Tom Macey (clt); Johnny Hodges (alt); Wilson (p); Dave
Barbour (g); Grachan Moncur (bs); Cole (d). New York City, 3 December
1935.
Sugar plum

Gordon Griffin (tpt); Rudy Powell (clt); Ted McRae (ten); Wilson (p); John
Truehart (g); Moncur (bs); Cole (d). New York City, 30 January 1936.
Rhythm in my nursery rhymes

Frank Newton (tpt); Benny Morton (tbn); Jerry Blake (clt, alt);
McRae (ten); Wilson (p); Truehart (g); Stan Fields (bs); Cole (d); Ella
Fitzgerald (vcl[1]). New York City, 17 March 1936.
Christopher Columbus · All my life[1]

Eldridge (tpt, vcl[2]); Buster Bailey (clt); Chew Berry (ten); Wilson (p); Bob
Lessey (g); Israel Crosby (bs); Sidney Catlett (d). Chicago, 14 May 1936.
Mary had a little lamb[2] *· Too good to be true · Warming up · Blues in
C sharp minor*

Jonah Jones (tpt); Harry Carney (clt, bar); Hodges (alt); Wilson (p);
Lucie (g); Kirby (bs); Cole (d); Billie Holiday (vcl[3]). New York City,
30 June 1936.
Why do I lie to myself about you? · Guess who?[3]

Griffin (tpt); Benny Goodman (clt); Vido Musso (ten); Wilson (p); Allen
Reuss (g); Harry Goodman (bs); Gene Krupa (d); Lionel Hampton (vib);
Helen Ward (vcl). Los Angeles, 24 August 1936.
Here's love in your eyes

Jones (tpt); Goodman (clt); Webster (ten); Wilson (p); Reuss (g); Kirby
(bs); Cole (d). New York City, 19 November 1936.
Sailing

Irving Randolph (tpt), Musso (clt) replace Jones, Goodman; Midge
Williams (vcl[4]) added. New York City, 16 December 1936.
Right or wrong[4] *· Tea for two · I'll see you in my dreams*

Buck Clayton (tpt); Goodman (clt); Lester Young (ten); Wilson (p);
Freddy Greene (g); Walter Page (bs); Jo Jones (d); Holiday (vcl). New
York City, 25 January 1937.
He ain't got rhythm

Cootie Williams (tpt); Carney (clt, bar); Hodges (alt); Wilson (p); Reuss
(g); Kirby (bs); Cole (d). New York City, 31 March 1937.
Fine and dandy

Harry James (tpt), Bailey (clt) replace Williams, Carney. New York City,
23 April 1937.
I'm coming, Virginia

Clayton (tpt); Young (clt, ten); Hodges (alt); Wilson (p);
Reuss (g); Artie Bernstein (bs); Cole (d); Holiday (vcl). New York City, 11
May 1937.
Yours and mine · I'll get by · Mean to me

Clayton (tpt); Bailey (clt); Young (ten); Wilson (p); Greene (g); Page (bs);
Jones (d). New York City, 1 June 1937.
I've found a new baby

James (tpt); Benny Goodman (clt); Musso (ten); Wilson (p); Reuss (g);
Harry Goodman (bs); Krupa (d). Los Angeles, 30 July 1937.
Coquette

Archie Rosatti (clt), John Simmons (bs), Cole (d) replace Benny and
Harry Goodman, Krupa. Los Angeles, 29 August 1937.
You can't stop me from dreaming

James (tpt); Wilson (p); Simmons (bs); Red Norvo (xylo). Los Angeles,
5 September 1937.
Ain't misbehaving · Just a mood · Honeysuckle rose

Clayton (tpt); Morton (tbn); Young (ten); Wilson (p); Greene (g);
Page (bs); Jones (d); Holiday (vcl). New York City, 6 January 1938.
When you're smiling

Bobby Hackett (cnt); Pee Wee Russell (clt); Willie Smith (alt); Gene
Sedric (ten); Wilson (p); Reuss (g); Al Hall (bs); Johnny Blowers (d). New
York City, 23 March 1938.
Don't be that way

Hacket (cnt); unidentified clt; Hodges (alt); unidentified ten; Wilson (p);
unidentified g, bs, d; Nan Wynn (vcl[5]). New York City, 29 April 1938.
If I were you[5] · Jungle love

177 Teddy Wilson, His Piano, His Orchestra
Tax (Sd) m-8032

Teddy Wilson and His Orchestra: Jones (tpt); Benny Carter (alt);
Webster (ten); Wilson (p); unidentified g; Kirby (bs); Cole (d); Wynn (vcl).
New York City, 29 July 1938.
*Now it can be told · Laugh and call it love · On the bumpy road to
love · A-tisket a-tasket*

Wilson (p). New York City, 11 August 1938.
I'll see you in my dreams · Alice blue gown

Same personnel and location, 27 January 1939.
Melody in F · When you and I were young, Maggie

Teddy Wilson and His Orchestra: Bill Coleman (tpt); Morton (tbn);
Jimmy Hamilton (clt); George James (bar); Wilson (p); Eddie Gibbs (g);
Hall (bs); Yank Porter (d); Helen Ward (vcl[6]). New York City,
9 December 1940.
I never knew · Embraceable you[6] · But not for me[6] · Lady, be good

Teddy Wilson Trio: Wilson (p); Hall (bs); J. C. Heard (d). Chicago, 7 April
1941.
Rosetta

Same personnel and location, 11 April 1941.
I know that you know · Them there eyes · China boy

Just as Eldridge has been reduced, in some popular misreadings
of jazz history, simply to a link between Louis Armstrong and
Dizzy Gillespie, so Wilson has often been seen as a mere step on
the road from Earl Hines to Bud Powell. This negligence can
almost be forgiven if we compare Wilson's 1935 recording of

Hines's theme *Rosetta* (CBS (F) 62876) with any of Hines's own versions (e.g. on **147**), then with Wilson's 1941 trio performance; and if we note the explicit Wilson influence on, say, Powell's 1953 *Jubilee* (Prestige (A) PR24024). Again, in early performances with Armstrong (**115**) and even later with Norvo (**199**), Wilson's musical personality is not at all clearly defined. Then, quite abruptly, so far as we can tell from records, it came into focus with his contributions to Benny Goodman's Trio (**158**) and his solo performances of October and November 1935 such as *Liza* and *It never dawned on me*.

One result was the series of recordings from which the above are selected. Their participants are *la crème de la crème* of the jazz musicians of that time, as on the best of Lionel Hampton's sessions (**161**); the outcome, however, is far more consistent. Indeed, aside from an occasional tear-up like *You can't stop me* (and the trio *China boy*), Wilson maintained remarkably high standards, considering that the personnel changed constantly and some of the material played was poor.

In relation to Hines's work, Wilson's style is a creative simplification of a rare kind. At the same time, on a piece like *Sweet Lorraine* he plays with exactly the right degree of elaboration in his solos and fills in delightfully between Eldridge's phrases. This performance, like many of the others, is essentially a sequence of improvisations and so almost everything depends on the quality of the invention. In these circumstances, Jefferson makes a better impression than Hodges who, on *Sugar plum*, for example, reverts to old-fashioned over-decorated saxophone display, though he does better with his sleek contribution to the well-integrated *Jungle love*. Carney achieves more, being very much himself on *Why do I lie to myself about you?*, but generally the Ellingtonians, out of their Ducal shell, create less impact than many of the other soloists. This particular track has, for instance, fine Jones trumpet — poised, dancing, unfailingly to the point.

That kind of expressive precision is best illustrated by the leader himself, though, and on a good many of these items he is the best soloist. A telling example is the unpromising *Rhythm in my nursery rhymes*, while on *All my life* his oblique treatment of the melody, dissolving it in fanciful keyboard figuration, is such as to make Ella Fitzgerald's chorus seem like a statement of the obvious. *Right or wrong* contains another quietly inventive piano solo, its effect somewhat mitigated by the rhythm section's heavy beat (which also spoils Webster's solo on *Tea for two*). This passage should be compared with the wholly successful sequences for piano and rhythm in *Fine and dandy* and *I'm coming,*

Virginia. The session of September 1937 is the only one with an even mildly experimental instrumentation, but as it is solos all the way, as usual, this counts for little in itself. However, just as Wilson's unaccompanied performances are generally preferable to his trios, so the absence of guitar and drums allows a fuller study of his always intelligent and musical ensemble parts. It is no exaggeration to say that every note counts here, and the general freedom of the occasion leads him to play with particular spirit. James and Norvo are consistently excellent: note the xylophone accompaniment to the trumpet on *Honeysuckle rose*, which urbanely flows into Norvo's graceful solo.

Goodman's presence on four of these sessions may be taken as a sign of his esteem for Wilson, and he comes off best among the participants in the fast *Sailing* with an excellently argued clarinet solo, packed with ideas. Morton's expressive contribution to *Christopher Columbus* should also be mentioned, its phrases so often taking an unexpected turn. *Don't be that way* is quite un-Goodman-like, with striking Hackett, Russell and Smith, *I'm coming, Virginia* wholly un-Beiderbeckian. James's vigour on the latter is engaging and he played, at this stage of his career, with enjoyable daring. Berry is preferable in the almost explosive *Warming up* to his oily *Too good to be true* mood. Eldridge and Wilson dominate here, though, with superbly concentrated offerings. Young's solos, also, tend to be the most notable events in nearly all the performances in which he takes part, above all *When you're smiling*. Billie Holiday's singing is discussed under **204–205**, but *Mean to me* boasts an exquisite tenor solo, very different in mood from that on the fast *New baby*; and *I'll get by* has some of Young's little-recorded clarinet.

Implausibly described as a foxtrot on the label of the original American 78 rpm issue — reproduced on the LP sleeve — *Blues in C sharp minor* is a sequence of deeply communing solos by Wilson, Eldridge, Bailey, Berry and again Eldridge. The sessions which produced this and *Just a mood* were the two most creative here, the latter piece being a double-length essay in the *C sharp minor* vein. Norvo's passage on *Just a mood*, another blues, is a triumph over his instrument's limitations; James plays one of his best recorded solos; Wilson plays one of his best ever and certainly his finest on this two-LP set, graceful yet always acutely expressive. Perhaps it was inevitable that such beautiful music should arouse hostility, particularly as the underrating of Wilson mentioned at the beginning is no recent phenomenon. Of *Blues in C sharp minor*, a worthy scribe wrote 'seldom have I heard a more nauseating noise', and Wilson had earlier been dismissed on the grounds that 'cooontially he is not a jazz pianist'. These dicta were dutifully echoed in a number of other places with descriptions of his playing as being, for example, 'chilled and dryly mechanical — cold, very cold' [78]. Such attacks on the more advanced masters of swing were frequently made by writers who subsequently were loud in their advocacy of this music and exactly prefigured the onslaught soon to be made on bop.

There might almost seem to be some justification for them in the band performances on 177, which follow on chronologically from those already dealt with yet are unmistakably more commercial in aim, the first session especially and the distinguished personnel notwithstanding. Though he admittedly shines more brightly on *A-tisket a-tasket*, Carter is obviously holding his inventive capacity in check on *Now it can be told*; and Nan Wynn is heavily featured on each track. The second band date here is better, with excellent solos from Coleman (as usual) and the leader, and the rhythm section generating a more flexible pulse than on many of the CBS dates. Helen Ward's singing is more musical than Miss Wynn's, and the trumpeter builds a melody of his own on the chords of *But not for me*.

But the main reason for this LP's presence here is that it carries several of Wilson's most characteristic solo and trio performances. Some of the material, as in the band recordings, is distinctly unpromising, yet the banal *Alice blue gown* and *I'll see you in my dreams* yield improvisations that are precise in expression and lucidly organized. Their urbanity can deceive, because although the textures are light and airy, the musical content is solid, the manner representing a highly resourceful utilization of some of the piano's capacities over its whole register. The solos are to be preferred, as noted above, because Wilson's well-varied left-hand progressions can be heard better, though *I know that you know* and *Them there eyes* offer brilliant trio jazz, as free of display for its own sake as the slow pieces are devoid of sentimentality.   M.H.

178 Jess Stacy and Friends
Commodore (A) XFL15358

Stacy (p). New York City, 30 April 1938.
Rambling

Same personnel and location, 18 January 1939.
Candlelights · Complaining · Ain't going nowhere

Bud Freeman (ten) added. New York City, 13 June 1939.
She's funny that way

Freeman absent. Same date.
You're driving me crazy · The sell-out · Ec-stacy

Muggsy Spanier (cnt); Stacy (p); Lee Wiley (vcl). New York City,
10 July 1940.
Down to Steamboat, Tennessee · Sugar
Stacy (p); Specs Powell (d). New York City, 25 November 1944.
*After you've gone · Old fashioned love · I ain't got nobody · Song of the
wanderer · Blue fives · Riding easy*

This pianist's lyricism often has a fugitive, Beiderbeckian quality, as *Candlelights*, one of Bix's own compositions and, on **116**,
Flashes and *In the dark* well show. Nobody has played these
pieces with deeper insight than Stacy, yet there are blues and
barrelhouse elements here too and, in such matters as the free
accentuation of *You're driving me crazy*, an Earl Hines influence.
The musical style and keyboard technique are, however, quite
singular; for one thing, Stacy draws an extremely individual
sound from the piano, this being partly a matter of touch, partly
of the voicing of chords, his feeling for keyboard texture. Such
features, allied to a characteristic sense of rhythm and of
harmonic nuance, make Stacy easy to recognize even in a large
band, whether led by Goodman (**141–2**) or himself (**166**). The
player's especially close relationship with his seemingly unre-
sponsive instrument is an important point though, and it is
notable that when *Complaining, Ain't going nowhere* and *Ec-
stacy* were later recorded by Bob Crosby's band the resulting
performances served only to demonstrate the essentially pianistic
nature of these themes. Indeed, everything about his music is
personal, reassuringly human.

One confirmation of this is its harmonic waywardness. Stacy
often is not much concerned with the accepted chord sequences for
popular melodies, although his account of *You're driving me crazy*
has little to do with the familiar tune and offers a diverse
invention on a variant of the orthodox harmonization. *Ain't going
nowhere* is based on a highly distinctive adaptation of the New
York 'stride' style, and it is of obvious significance that exactly
half the performances here use themes of Stacy's own. His sense
of structure is firm, yet as *Rambling* shows it operates in a
pleas ngly informal way, a fact reflected in the imaginative
departures from a decisive basic tempo. Essentially we have three
choruses, an introduction and a coda here, but he works, rather,
in eight-bar episodes, contrasting, blending. A further instance is
Complaining (a different piece from that recorded under the same
title by Willie 'The Lion' Smith on **237**), which boasts surprising
contrasts of mood and melodic material; and even at this business-
like tempo, a mellowness pervades.

The music's barrelhouse roots are echoed, but also transcended, in *The sell-out* and *Ec-stacy*, contrasting blues. These are brilliant improvisations, one bustling forward, the other cogently reflective; there is a distillation of much experience here, particularly in *Ec-stacy*. The blues usually sound through Miss Wiley's singing (see **202**), though nowhere with a more affecting plaintiveness than during *Steamboat, Tennessee* where, as in *Sugar*, vocal, piano and cornet phrases interlock memorably. A not dissimilar collaboration is that between Freeman and Stacy on *She's funny that way*, with its idiosyncratic textures and casually effective counterpoint; however, this also appears on **232** and is most advantageously heard in conjunction with the trio performances with George Wettling also found there.

Stacy's other duets, with Powell, were hitherto unissued. It might be thought that the drummer is not needed, yet he provides a percussive commentary which remains subtle during even the most vigorous episodes. With the pulse stated elsewhere, Stacy is freer than ever, but each piece leaves a strong impression of overall shape. He remained as steadily inventive of fresh keyboard layouts as of melody, one idea — and its treatment — seeming to arise spontaneously out of another, as in *After you've gone* and especially *Old fashioned love*. On *I ain't got nobody* he goes the opposite way from in *You're driving me crazy*, providing a true improvisation *on* the melody. He has the blues again in *Blue fives* and, far from *Riding easy*, the last performance, like *Song of the wanderer*, is a tough, hard-driven solo, packed with ideas that have Stacy's personal tone. And no matter how fiercely this music's arguments thresh around, its line and continuity hold. M.H.

179 Mary Lou Williams: the Asch Recordings
Folkways (A) FA2966 (2 LPs)

Mary Lou Williams and Her Chosen Five: Frank Newton (tpt); Vic Dickenson (tbn); Ed Hall (clt); Williams (p); Al Lucas (bs); Jack Parker (d); vcl by ensemble[1]; Edgar Sampson (arr[2]). New York City, 12 March 1944.
Lullaby of the leaves[2] · *Little Joe from Chicago*[1] · *Roll 'em* · *Satchelmouth baby*[1]

Newton, Dickenson, Parker absent. Same date.
Yesterday's kisses

Williams (p). New York City, 19 April 1944.
Mary's boogie · *Drag 'em* · *St Louis blues*

Nora Lee King (vcl) added. New York City, c. 1944.
Blues until my baby comes home

Mary Lou Williams and Her Orchestra: Dick Vance (tpt); Dickenson (tbn); Claude Greene (clt); Don Byas (ten); Williams (p); Lucas (bs); Parker (d). New York City, 5 June 1944.

Man o' mine · *Gjon Mili jam session* · *Stardust*

Mary Lou Williams Trio: Bill Coleman (tpt, vcl[3]); Williams (p); Al Hall (bs); vcl by ensemble[4]. New York City, 10 August 1944.

Russian lullaby[4] · *Blue skies* · *Persian rug* · *Night and day* · *You know, baby*[3] · *I've found a new baby*

Mary Lou Williams and Her Orchestra: Coleman (tpt); Williams (p); Jimmy Butts (bs); Eddie Dougherty (d); Josh White (vcl). New York City, 11 December 1944.

The minute man · *Froggy bottom*

Coleman (tpt); Williams (p); Eddie Robinson (bs). New York City, 15 December 1944.

Carcinoma

Coleman Hawkins (ten), Denzil Best (d) added. Same date.

Lady, be good

Greene (clt), Joe Evans (alt) added. Same date.

Song in my soul · *This and that*

Williams (p). New York City, 16 February 1946.

How high the moon? · *The man I love* · *Cloudy* · *What's your story, morning glory?* · *Blue skies* · *These foolish things* · *Lonely moments*

Milton Orent—Frank Roth Orchestra: Irving Kustin, Leon Schwartz, Edward Sadowski (tpt); Martin Glaser, Alan Feldman (alt); Maurice Lopez, Orlando Wright (ten); Williams (p[5]); Roth (p[6]); Orent (bs, arr); Parker (d); whistling by ensemble[7]. New York City, *c*. 1947.

Whistle blues[5,7] · *Lonely moments*[6]

Mary Lou Williams and Her Orchestra: Kinny Dorham (tpt); Williams (p); John Smith (g); Grachan Moncur (bs); vcl by ensemble[8]. New York City, *c*. 1947.

Kool · *Mary Lou*[8]

'You may see (and hear) the first "Lady Syncopators"', declared the London *Daily Telegraph* on 22 February 1927, 'cutting rhythm into jazz patterns with the best of mere male "syncopators"'. The subjects of that report (preserved in an entry on 'syncopator' in the Supplement to the *Oxford English Dictionary*) are forgotten, but it must have been at about that time that a midwestern vaudeville band, led by one John Williams and known as either his 'Syncopators' or his 'Synco-Jazzers', recruited a lady pianist, Mary Elfrieda Winn, who married the leader and later found fame as Mary Lou Williams — the most honoured 'lady syncopator' of them all. The Williams band made records — coincidentally in February 1927 (Riverside (A) RLP1040) — but it is the ones Mary Lou made with Andy Kirk between 1929 and the early 1940s (**77** and **132**) which preserve the emergence of one of the most sensitive and lively arrangers and instrumentalists in the development of jazz, middle-period and modern.

Somewhere in the midst of some very accomplished music-working may be found the reason why Miss Williams, for all her wit and skill, has never been numbered among the really great. It has something to do with the eclecticism of her style, her contentment in honouring others rather than shaping her own unmistakable *persona*, and something to do with her never quite deciding where her best strength lay — in performing, or in composing and arranging. Certainly she has not received her due; perhaps she failed to demand it resolutely enough. Still, the music is very fine indeed and these Asch recordings, though frequently marred by surface noise, contain many revelations.

The Chosen Five of 1944 are well chosen, and Newton and Hall excel in solo work and in the reading of scores by the leader and Edgar Sampson. The voicings which interpret the latter's arrangement of the unexpected *Lullaby of the leaves* lend it an appropriate airiness. Miss Williams's barrelhouse themes, *Little Joe from Chicago, Roll 'em* and *Satchelmouth baby*, determine their own less ambitious arrangements. *Little Joe* might be heard in conjunction with both the 1939 solo (**167c**), clearly scouting orchestral possibilities, and a heraldic 1979 version (Pablo (E) 2308 218), recorded when the pianist was approaching seventy. *Yesterday's kisses* turns the limelight upon Hall and, with some unusual figures in unison for clarinet and bass, is a singular exploitation of a slightly odd trio format.

Mary's boogie, Drag 'em and *St Louis blues* exhibit the style for which Miss Williams is still most widely remembered — an adaptation of boogie that allows for natural transition into more sophisticated rhythms and tone-clusters. The calculated dissonances and tricky descending runs of *Mary's boogie* look ahead rather shyly to the modernistic blues, *Joycie*, which she was to record twenty-one years later in her native Pittsburgh (RCA (E) RD7830). There are probing extensions of blues usage in accompaniment to Nora Lee King's unpretentious singing, also.

The piano tends to tether orchestral speculations to older forms in *Man o' mine, Gjon Mili jam session* and the splendid two-part *Stardust*; but the scoring, though superficially Ellingtonian, views uncharted regions. *Man o' mine* is an attractive collaboration between Miss Williams and Byas, a *précis* of fancies asking for lengthier expression. It is one of the most original creations in this body of recordings.

Coleman's dynamic presence is a substantial factor in the success of the August and December 1944 sessions. He plays beautifully during the brisk disquisition upon the interesting chord sequence of *Russian lullaby*, and is sprightly and searching by turns in this August set of six numbers which deserves a brighter fame for several reasons. The arrangements encourage relaxation and Miss Williams's solo playing is full of joys — brilliant flourishes and treble calligraphies in *Blue skies* and *Persian rug*, sardonic boogie in *You know, baby*. A readiness to vary the mood by changes of tempo bespeaks an artistic approach to arrangement and a bold challenge to the functional image of jazz to which few could rise in those days.

Minute man and *Froggy bottom* reduce Coleman and the leader to support of White's undistinguished singing of a patriotic ditty and a modish blues chant. They do, however, play with dedication, and Miss Williams has space in the second piece for some of her tougher blues ideas. The other December date brings a varied personnel. A trio with Coleman and Robinson achieves in *Carcinoma* (a title making Satie's *Embryons desséchés* seem quite genteel) strange, sombre wisdoms of linear concord; and when Hawkins joins in for *Lady, be good, Song in my soul* and *This and that*, he has the trumpeter to contend with as a rival in lyric expressiveness; though his own warm languors do predominate during *Song in my soul*. Miss Williams's writing is always thought-provoking, occasionally building on those 'screwy chords' (her term) which had presaged bop.

Then there are numerous forecasts and recastings in the lovely set of solos from 1946. The boogie image is abandoned and yet, not even in *How high the moon?*, does the lady strive noticeably after boppish effects, despite her known admiration for the new generation. Each of these treatments of standard and original themes has the feeling of exploration, but the vocabulary is tied to the previous decade and is even strongly nostalgic, as in *The man I love*, which suggests familiarity with Gershwin's own affective transcription (*cf.* William Bolcom on Nonesuch (A) H71284). The wedding of *Cloudy* to *What's your story, morning glory?* results in an exceptional meditation, rebuilding the dwelling from within. *These foolish things* is the most anticipatory performance, but it falls well short of the *volte-face* which admits a George Shearing influence to *Kool* and *Mary Lou*. The exact dates for the latter and the Roth–Orent session are not known, but the likeness of *Mary Lou* to *Happy birthday* may suggest 8 May 1947, the thirty-seventh anniversary of a Pennsylvanian birth!

The orchestral version of *Lonely moments* extends the questings of the piano solo and even echoes Miss Williams's time-keeping foot in the opening rhythm. But an air of detachment in this and in *Whistle blues* severs the form from the vital spirit even when, as in the blues, she is herself at the keyboard. That spirit is much better expressed in a moment of *Blue skies* when, out of an initial shepherding of rhythmic impulses, a gleeful upstroke liberates the music into swinging exultancy. And even when that improvisation lapses into cliché and quotation, it seems only to emphasize an *élan* which sometimes got lost in later flirtations with fashion and earnest expeditions along the borders of jazz.

E.T.

180 Nat 'King' Cole Meets the Master Saxes
Spotlite (E) SPJ136, Phoenix (A) LP5

Nat Cole Quintet: Shad Collins (tpt); Illinois Jacquet (ten); Cole (p); Gene Englund (bs); J. C. Heard (d). New York City, 1942.
Heads · Pro sky · It had to be you · I can't give you anything but love
Lester Young–Nat Cole Trio: Young (ten); Cole (p); Red Callender (bs). Los Angeles, 15 July 1942.
Indiana · I can't get started · Tea for two · Body and soul
Dexter Gordon Quintet: Harry Edison (tpt); Gordon (ten); Cole (p); possibly Johnny Miller (bs); unidentified d. Los Angeles, 1943.
I've found a new baby · Rosetta · Sweet Lorraine · I blowed and gone

An irony is implicit within the title of this LP. At the time of these recordings, Gordon and Jacquet, both members of Lionel Hampton's band, were twenty and twenty-one respectively. And although the pair of them could later be fairly described as master saxophonists, this early moment in their careers found them still deeply in thrall to Lester Young. Two or three years earlier and things might have been different, with Coleman Hawkins still a model for youthful jazzmen; a couple of years later and Charlie Parker's alto playing might have left its mark — as it certainly did on Gordon's subsequent work. Meanwhile, eight of these tracks provide a useful demonstration of how the jazz soloist learns his craft, first by copying, then by adapting, expanding and, if he has the ability, supplanting.

Jacquet possessed from the start a big, fleshy tone of the sort often associated with saxophonists from his home state of Texas. That is revealed clearly enough in the second of his solo appearances in *Heads*, while *Pro sky* presents what was to become Jacquet's particular musical persona, a swaggering style, making occasional use of what were then thought of as freak notes; what the serious-minded jazz fan of the 1940s regarded as vulgarities were, of course, to be given a very different aesthetic status by the *avant-garde* of two decades later. Elsewhere, Jacquet's phrasing is pure Lester Young. Some of the most original playing, in fact, is provided by the trumpeter, Collins, either muted and inquisitive or exploiting a broad, open tone. Heard sticks to brushes most of the time, his playing neatly functional.

Gordon's musical identity at this point may not have been as forceful as Jacquet's, yet he comes across as more inventive. The vocabulary may have been borrowed from Young (an exception is the furry tone, just like Ben Webster's, adopted for *Sweet Lorraine*), yet Gordon's always admirable playing already has the kind of dash and, from time to time, some of the phrasing that formed the basis of his mature style. Less pleasing are the solos taken by Edison, normally a reliable trumpeter but here revealing what can happen on an off-day; his second chorus in *Rosetta* might be called a practical definition of banality.

Cole is the common factor on all twelve tracks. Unfortunately his solo playing is not helped by the inadequate sound quality, and possibly balance, of the original recordings — which, incidentally, were all twelve-inch 78s. If Gordon and Jacquet display their admiration of Young, the piano playing reflects just as obviously the influence of Earl Hines. True, Cole never embarks on the elaborate rhythmic suspensions in which Hines delighted. Yet the essential springiness is there, and the clarity of those staccato treble lines. Diligent listeners might also like to try spotting other influences: touches of Tatum and Wilson; an Ellingtonian peremptoriness at the start of *I blowed and gone* — a theme suggestive, by the way, of Mel Powell's 1945 *My guy's come back*; and, a very up-to-date sound in 1942, the 'locked hands' style, using parallel chord patterns, then being popularized by Hampton's pianist, Milt Buckner. As against all this, even on one of Hines's own themes, *Rosetta*, Cole throws in chording that reflects his own harmonic thinking. And there are plenty of other instances of the originality and sprightliness which made it understandable why so many jazz *aficionados* grieved when, only a few years later, he found it more lucrative to sing than to play the piano.

The combination of Cole's resourcefulness and Callender's powerful bass playing makes it seem thoroughly reasonable for no drummer to have been present at the session of 15 July 1942. Young had left Basie's band about eighteen months earlier and his style was already showing signs of change, no longer quite so pale and reticent. A flakiness of tone is apparent at the very start of *Indiana*, while both of the ballads — *I can't get started* and *Body and soul* — find him producing a heavier sound than formerly. It is especially fascinating to compare this recording of *Body and soul* with Hawkins's celebrated version (**192**). The stance of the two improvisers is totally different. Where Hawkins's patterns emerge from within the chords, seeming almost a flowering of their possibilities, Young's solo lines are more oblique, almost creating the illusion of independence from the harmonic flow. That light, allusive manner is especially to the fore in *Tea for two*, where Young begins sternly yet in his second solo achieves a marvellous airiness. A pity the recording quality is so woolly — Cole's playing is frequently distorted — for these are genuinely masterful performances.   C.F.

181a Art Tatum Piano Solos Vol. 1
MCA (F) 510.081, *MCA (A) 2–4112 (2 LPs)

Tatum (p). New York City, 22 August 1934.
Moonglow · *Emaline*
Same personnel and location, 24 August 1934.
Ill wind · *The shout* · *Liza*
Same personnel and location, 9 October 1934.
I would do anything for you · *When a woman loves a man* · *Stardust* · *I ain't got nobody* · *Beautiful love* · *After you've gone* · *Liza*
Same personnel and location, 29 November 1937.
Gone with the wind · *Stormy weather* · *Chloe* · *The sheik of Araby*

181b Art Tatum Piano Solos Vol. 2
MCA (F) 510.082, *MCA (A) 2–4019 (2 LPs)

Tatum (p). Los Angeles, 12 April 1939.
Tea for two · *Deep purple*
Same personnel and location, 22 February 1940.
Elégie · *Humoresque* · *Sweet Lorraine* · *Get happy* · *Lullaby of the leaves* · *Tiger rag* · *Emaline* · *Moonglow* · *Love me tonight* · *Cocktails for two*
Same personnel and location, 26 July 1940.
St Louis blues · *Begin the beguine* · *Rosetta* · *Indiana*

From his earliest records, starting with a 1932 *Tiger rag* (Aircheck (A) 21), Tatum served notice that he would offer a virtuoso development of the New York 'stride' method, and he devoted his career to at once amplifying and refining this. A comparison between the 1934 and 1940 versions of *Moonglow* will quickly demonstrate what happened, for while in the first the melody is decorated, in the second it becomes part of a whole network of relationships which run through the fabric of a beautifully poised interpretation. The recurrent pianistic storms of *Ill wind* or the outburst which agitatedly obscures the *Stardust* melody are what the Victorians would have called 'fugues', flights from the 'reality' of the 4/4 beat, deliberately unleashed and then brought back into check. Yet one receives the impression from some of the 1934 solos that the young man was at times confused by being able to play everything that he could think of. Almost is there something of the 'sinister dexterity' about which a critic had a few years earlier complained in the young Horowitz[79]. This was gradually disciplined, and *Stormy weather* marked a notable step in that direction.

A theme of Tatum's own, *The shout*, later known as *Amethyst*, indicates his link with the 'novelty' pianists who are much underrated by most jazz commentators, but his main starting-point was the 'stride' school's adaptation of the centuries-old *cantus firmus* idea whereby a given melody is retained and a new texture, indeed a whole structure, is built around it. *After you've gone* is a clear illustration, *I ain't got nobody* one that includes some daring departures from the basic concept. By 1937 there was a more evident concern with emotional expression; the linear and harmonic elaborations were becoming integral, not something imposed, however brilliantly, from outside.

Other elements were present too, not least Tatum's humour. Whereas Fats Waller's jokes took the form of anarchic verbal asides, Tatum's, like Monk's, are *in* the music itself. Thus persistent virtuoso flourishes thoroughly undermine the hollow romantic pose of *Beautiful love*, as does a breakneck tempo like that of *I would do anything for you* (which, oddly enough, is a Claude Hopkins–Alex Hill piece: see **208**). Another case is the mischievous reference to Rachmaninov's gloomy Prelude in C sharp minor Op. 3 No. 2 at the close of *Get happy*, but sometimes he more simply contradicts our expectations. A good instance is *Indiana*, normally the subject of crude dixieland assaults, here accorded a thoughtful, lyrical treatment.

The 1937 date marks a point of equipoise, showing a complete mastery of everything thus far undertaken before scaling higher peaks. In fact, Tatum's musical growth in the late 1930s, in terms of his ability to generate, develop and shape material, was almost as extensive as that of Ellington. It is all summarized by the 1939 and, particularly, the 1940 sessions, that of 22 February being, despite the marathons which lay ahead (**217**), one of the great occasions in the history of jazz recording, with each piece except *Moonglow* brought off in a single take. *Tiger rag* marks the high-water level of Tatum's virtuosity at this time, yet more significant is the harmonically adventurous, rhythmically oblique introduction. *Elégie* and *Humoresque* are engaging examples of the normally trivial practice of 'jazzing' the classics; the latter should be heard in conjunction with Hines's good-humoured take-off of Tatum's approach to this piece (Real Time

(A) 105). On *Rosetta*, a Hines theme, we hear a beautiful translation of some of the earlier master's discoveries into Tatum's own idiom, but the point of *St Louis blues*, with its refinements of boogie, is not so much a response to Hines's version of several months before (**147**) as a resorting to the blues, in parallel with Barney Bigard — see **186** — 'to inform a freer vision'.

One thing about this music which sometimes confuses listeners is its feeling of a constantly shifting perspective, a notable instance being the sequence of brief, sharply contrasting yet resolutely unified episodes which make up *Elégie* — at one time reputedly Tatum's favourite among his own recordings and admired by Rachmaninov and Horowitz. Working through a multiple long-term interplay of tension and release, his method had become compositional, or recompositional, and a piece such as *Begin the beguine* undergoes a complete transmutation: it is almost impossible to believe that it was ever a song in a Broadway show. The 1940 *Emaline* has the same outward shape as the 1934 version but, in the later one, after an out-of-tempo introduction which shows how a cheap ditty can be transformed by highly personal brands of harmonic and rhythmic invention, Tatum in the sparkling stomp section deploys the standard devices of late-1930s jazz pianism with an ease so extreme as to suggest an ironic commentary on them.

The pensiveness which lies at the heart of the exuberant flourishes of *Deep purple* or *Lullaby of the leaves* implies that in Tatum's music things are rarely quite what they seem to be. Perhaps this is because these 1939–40 performances distill almost everything that had thus far happened in piano jazz, and they contain many echoes of this music's history, along with some anticipations of its future. Indeed, these are timeless performances by a musician soon to be dismissed as 'the carefully built-up sensation of the moment' [80]. Their almost classical balance of elements gives them an air, found elsewhere only in certain virtually contemporaneous recordings by Armstrong (**150–1**), of being above the battle.

(The American MCA issue listed above as a partial equivalent to Vol. 1 is a 2-LP set containing eight of the 1934 and 1937 solos, the 1937 Swingsters date, and material by James P. Johnson. For comments on the partial equivalent given for Vol. 2, see under **182**). M.H.

182 The Art of Tatum

MCA (F) 510.105, *MCA (A) 2–4019 (2 LPs)

Art Tatum and His Band: Joe Thomas (tpt); Ed Hall (clt); Tatum (p); John Collins (g); Billy Taylor (bs); Eddie Dougherty (d); Joe Turner (vcl[1]). New York City, 21 January 1941.

Wee baby blues[1] · *Stomping at the Savoy* · *Last goodbye blues*[1]
Battery bounce

Oscar Moore (g), Yank Porter (d) replace Collins, Dougherty; Hall absent. New York City, 13 June 1941.

Lucille[1] · *Rock me, mama*[1] · *Corrine Corrina*[1] · *Lonesome graveyard blues*

Art Tatum Trio: Tatum (p); Tiny Grimes (g); Slam Stewart (bs, vcl). New York City, 5 January 1944.

I got rhythm · *Cocktails for two* · *I ain't got nobody* · *After you've gone* · *Moonglow* · *Deep purple* · *I would do anything for you* · *Honeysuckle rose*

It was common opinion, when the recordings with Thomas, Hall and Turner first appeared, that Tatum had no business inserting his sophisticated talents into so straightforward a blues context. The pianist's reputation then rested upon the availability of a few solo performances all of which revealed a dazzling 'legitimate' technique, and a few of which, like his exuberant transformation of *Humoresque* (**181b**), encouraged the false notion that he really belonged somewhere in the no-man's-land between jazz and European concert music. The fact of the matter was, and is, that Tatum belongs totally to jazz, in his origins and aims, and furthermore that his instinct for the blues, among many other things, is deeply genuine and much more than a matter of form. Another misconception fed the adverse criticism, to wit that the music of Turner and Hall, in particular, sprang from a tougher soil and fitted ill with Tatum's apparent suavity.

With the purist blinkers off, listeners may still be aware, but gratefully, of sharp contrasts within these groups. The marvel is the cohesion that is achieved despite the different backgrounds of the players. It should also be recognized that there is more wit and sophistication in Turner's singing than the old 'earthy' label gave him credit for. Not only is he a fairly straight singer in relation to the melodic language of the blues; he is also one whose lyrics have marked elements of urbanity and irony which remove them from the simple image. 'Get your nightcap, baby', he invites in *Rock me, mama*, 'let's tip' off to bed!' And how well his approach is complemented by the tough lyricism of Hall and Thomas, whose styles are anything but doggedly traditional. That they are more than comfortably at home with Tatum is shown especially in the two wholly instrumental tracks, *Stomping at the Savoy* and *Battery bounce*.

The inspired lyrical construction of the trumpet solos in the two pieces just mentioned is telling evidence of the widely ignored jazz stature of Thomas. He is a superb melodist who has seldom been given his due in the histories, and that he retained and developed his gifts into the veteran years is well proved by 208.

His introductions and accompaniments for the six blues songs are ample proof of Tatum's artistic sensitiveness to this idiom. At this stage of his life it may be possible to pick out influences — the 'stride' pianists, certainly ('Fats, man — that's where I come from'), and the boogie pianists, too, a strong touch of Pete Johnson at the start of *Last goodbye blues*; also there are hints of Ellington in the chords of *Wee baby blues*, and even of Jess Stacy's Hines-based style in phrase-endings here and there. But surprisingly little is known of Tatum's early growth as a pianist or of the borrowings which he might have admitted to; and even his fantastic keyboard facility seems to have been the result of self-teaching. Overall, his expression is singular and inimitable, and his own influence, not only on other pianists, but also on the harmonic thought of much subsequent jazz can hardly be over-emphasized.

Though the heresy of his awkwardness as an ensemble companion needs to be exposed for what it is, undoubtedly it is in his solo work that the wonder of Tatum can best be contemplated. The trio tracks here give good opportunity for this. *I got rhythm* sets off to a cracking pace, and his daring exuberance is immediately evident in the freedom and equality which he is able to give to both right and left hands. Here, as in *After you've gone*, there are passages where walking (or running!) tenths, developed from 'stride' basses, take over an independent melodic role, and everywhere there are the dazzling treble runs and arpeggios which are so much the hallmark of his style that their function has frequently been misunderstood. No critical judgment could be more wrong-headed than André Hodeir's to the effect that Tatum's arpeggios have 'no other purpose' than to decorate[81]. Like the breathtaking, interweaving runs (*vide* the mid-tempo *Cocktails for two*), they have a multiple purpose — melodic, harmonic, yes, and rhythmic too, for a strategic Tatum run can be as rhythmically compelling as a single well-placed Basie chord. His aerobatic range in *Moonglow* and *I ain't got nobody*, and his successful search for the unsuspected back-flights of stairs in a theme, are not simply amazing in themselves; they are part of a conception of the joint importance of melody and harmony which moves far beyond anything achieved before. Almost every piece is a panorama of the possibilities of jazz language. Yet he can be simple, as in *Deep purple*, impishly humorous, as in *I would do anything for you*, and meditative, as in the blues accompaniments and, again, in *Deep purple*. And always there is total absorption in an act of creation. Music and living were one for him.

He gets fine rhythmic support on all sessions, and mention should be made of the splendid work of Moore and Grimes. Stewart's vocal-cum-instrumental showmanship is overdone, but his liveliness is apt, and Grimes occasionally 'pats juba' for him.

(The American MCA issue listed above as a partial equivalent to this record is a two-LP set which carries the eight 1941 band tracks together with some of the 1944 trios and a dozen of the solos found on **181b**.)   E.T.

Art Tatum

183 God is in the House
Polydor (E) 2344 043, Onyx (A) ORI205

Tatum (p). New York City, 11 November 1940.
Beautiful love · Laughing at life
Same personnel and location, 6 April 1941.
Georgia on my mind
Tatum (p); Reuben Harris (whiskbrooms). New York City, 7 May 1941.
Sweet Lorraine · Fine and dandy · Begin the beguine
Tatum (p, vcl[1]); Chocolate Williams (bs, vcl[2]). New York City, 26 July 1941.
Mighty like a rose · Knocking myself out[1,2] · Toledo blues[1] · Body and soul
Ollie Potter (vcl[3]) added. New York City, 27 July 1941.
There'll be some changes made[3]
Frank Newton (tpt); Tatum (p); Ebenezer Paul (bs). New York City, 16 September 1941.
Lady, be good · Sweet Georgia Brown

Tatum's reputation among his fellow pianists is reflected in the title given to this LP, a piece of hyperbole allegedly uttered by Fats Waller when Tatum dropped into a club where he was performing. Such hero-worship was based not so much upon the kind of playing to be heard on **181** and **182**, remarkable though this was, but upon personal and more informal encounters, usually late at night, often in quite small and unglamorous premises, frequently using a piano that was far from immaculate. This LP consists almost entirely of performances of that species, performances originally devised for the edification of Tatum himself and a cluster of friends or habitués. They are spontaneous and relaxed yet, significantly, exhibit at times even more technical bravura than Tatum's studio recordings did, *Sweet Lorraine* providing a memorable example of this.

The first two items were not recorded in a club but at the apartment, and on the portable machine, of Jerry Newman, an enthusiastic amateur. *Beautiful love* and *Laughing at life* are very brief — one minute forty-three seconds and one minute respectively — because these are edited versions of performances that originally included solos by the trombonist and alto saxophonist Murray McEachern. *Georgia on my mind*, taken from a Benny Goodman radio broadcast, is more substantial, ornate yet still functional. *Sweet Lorraine, Fine and dandy* and *Begin the beguine* are from Reuben's Club, whose owner was fond of playing along with the pianists who dropped in, using two whiskbrooms and a folded newspaper. These show how a virtuoso can cope with a fairly execrable instrument. Tatum's version of *Begin the beguine* was later to be simplified — and made famous — by Eddie Heywood jnr. This particular reading is suitably rococo, but then so is the dazzling final chorus of *Fine and dandy*, where characteristic runs alternate with subtle but dramatic chording and staccato single-note figures.

Repeatedly one is struck by Tatum's harmonic daring, a side of his playing that was less appreciated at the time — by non-musicians, at least -- than was the extravagance of his ornamentation. In retrospect, Tatum can be seen as foreshadowing, along with Coleman Hawkins and a few others, at least part of the harmonic vocabulary of bop. It is this aspect of his work that makes *Mighty like a rose* and *Body and soul* so satisfying. *Knocking myself out*, recorded by Lil Green earlier in 1941, is a hip blues, sung by the bassist Chocolate Williams (who sounds as if he had been listening to Louis Jordan) but with Tatum taking over for the final stanza. It is notable for its *joie de vivre* and for confirming that Tatum's luxuriant approach did not debar him from being a masterly blues player. This is underlined by *Toledo blues*, another track which has been abridged, incidentally — in this case by just over half a minute. It finds him singing traditional lyrics ('Mean ol' train, cruel ol' engineer'; 'When you see me comin', heist your window high'), his voice appropriately restrained and wistful, but with a concluding line which hints at the etiquette obtaining on these social occasions: 'My drinks are comin' too damn slow'.

What made Tatum much more than a technical nonpareil, of course, was his capacity to surprise, to be perpetually inventive even when traversing familiar terrain. It happens in *There'll be some changes made*, where Williams's bass solo and some rather run-of-the-mill singing become excuses for bold piano playing in the background. The final pair of tracks, taken down at Clark Monroe's Uptown House, are perhaps the most rewarding of all.

Newton keeps his mute in for *Lady, be good*, jogging along tidily, sounding rather as Harry Edison was to do a decade later. But where both Newton and Tatum really excelled themselves was in the eleven gripping choruses of *Sweet Georgia Brown*, the two musicians stretching out — the performance lasts for over seven minutes — in a way that was never possible on commercial recordings of the period. Tatum's rhythmic variations in the fourth chorus, followed by Newton's buoyant improvising above complex harmonic forays, are just two incidents within a performance that illustrates the exceptional rapport which existed between the pianist and trumpeter. That it concludes with laughter all round is a useful reminder of how the most serious music can still be played for fun.   C.F.

Roy Eldridge
184 Heckler's Hop
Tax (Sd) m-8020

Putney Dandridge and His Orchestra: Eldridge (tpt); Chew Berry (ten[1]); Dandridge (p[2], vcl); Harry Gray (p[3]); Nappy Lamare (g); Artie Bernstein (bs); Bill Beason (d). New York City, 25 June 1935.
Nagasaki[2,3] · *When I grow too old to dream*[1,2]

The Delta Four: Eldridge (tpt); Joe Marsala (clt); Carmen Mastren (g); Sid Weiss (bs). New York City, 20 December 1935.
Swinging on that famous door · *Farewell blues*

Mildred Bailey and Her Orchestra: Eldridge (tpt); Scoops Carry (alt); Herbie Haymer (ten); Teddy Cole (p); John Collins (g); Truck Parham (bs); Zutty Singleton (d); Bailey (vcl). Chicago, 19 January 1937.
My last affair · *Trust in me* · *Where are you?* · *You're laughing at me*

Roy Eldridge and His Orchestra: same personnel except that Dave Young (ten) replaces Haymer; Joe Eldridge (alt, arr) added; Bailey absent. Chicago, 23 January 1937.
Wabash stomp · *Florida stomp* · *Heckler's hop*

Gladys Palmer (vcl[4]) added. Chicago, 28 January 1937.
Where the lazy river goes by[4] · *That thing* · *After you've gone*[4]

Mildred Bailey and Her Orchestra: Eldridge (tpt, vcl); Eddie Powell (fl); Robert Burns, Jimmy Carroll (clt); Carl Prager (bs clt); Teddy Wilson (p); Collins (g); Pete Peterson (bs); Beason (d); Bailey (vcl); Eddie Sauter (arr). New York City, 15 January 1940.
Wham (Re-bop-boom-bam)

Irving Horowitz (bs clt), Kenny Clarke (d) replace Prager, Beason; Mitch Miller (ob) added. New York City, 15 May 1940.
Tennessee fish fry

Traces of Eldridge's early debt to Armstrong may be heard now and then in this collection, but his admiration for Henry Allen and Coleman Hawkins is more clearly evident. He later said that besides being influenced by Rex Stewart and Red Nichols, he was affected by Benny Carter and Hawkins, and got his first job through being able to play the latter's solo on Fletcher Henderson's *Stampede* [82]. Results of this can be heard chiefly in his handling of descending passages and, to some extent, in his tone.

After playing with Harlem bands during the 1930s, Eldridge was one of the first coloured players to be featured with popular white bands, travelling and recording with Krupa and Shaw, often in the face of hurtful prejudice. That big-band experience may have whetted, yet also effectively guarded, a taste for exhibitionism which was to mar some of his later small band work. Here, with these mid-1930s groups, he plays with cohesion and grace.

The Dandridge session is dominated by the bizarre humour of the leader, and Eldridge does little more than lead the supporters. It is in the two Delta Four titles that his creative gift begins to stretch itself, his questing imagination contrasting with Marsala's simple expression. Receding into the accompaniment again, he makes unobtrusive contributions to the first Bailey session, and one wishes that some of the solo time granted to Carry and Haymer had been his. However, when he takes over much the same group for *Wabash stomp, Florida stomp* and *Heckler's hop* he is heard to fine advantage, aided by the effective arranging of his brother Joe, an early musical mentor (and another saxophonist). *Heckler's hop*, containing some of Roy's most beautifully executed work urged by lively reed-section backing and the unfailing efforts of Parham and Singleton, is exceptionally good, and the passionate dialectic of the trumpet solo in *Wabash stomp* demonstrates how excitement can be achieved without strain. There is delightful, buoyant trumpeting in *After you've gone* in which, as in *Where the lazy river goes by*, the band is joined by the less than exciting Miss Palmer. *That thing* suffers from a rather leaden opening beat and a sombre ending, and only Roy's varied rhythms lend it life.

Mildred Bailey, who sings like a sophisticated child, has a good measure of that kind of ability which Billie Holiday had of transmuting Tin Pan Alley dross into jazz gold, and her skills are well represented in the four popular songs of her first session. Three years later, her voice sounds stronger, and the more emotive phrasing which partially emerged in *You're laughing at me* now serves the unsentimental humour of *Tennessee fish fry* and *Wham*. This last, an anthem to swing, has a lyric which, following several precedents including that of McKinney's Cotton

Pickers' *Four or five times* (**83**), makes a prophetic use of the syllables 're bop'. Eldridge himself has often been judged a prophet of the bop style and Dizzy Gillespie, who replaced him in the Teddy Hill band of 1937, began as his imitator.   E.T.

185   Frankie Newton at the Onyx Club
Tax (Sd) m-8017

Frankie Newton and His Uptown Serenaders: Newton (tpt); Ed Hall (clt); Pete Brown (alt); Cecil Scott (ten); Don Frye (p); John Smith (g); Richard Fullbright (bs); Cozy Cole (d); Clarence Palmer (vcl[1]). New York City, 5 March 1937.
You showed me the way[1] · *Who's sorry now?*

Frank Rice (g), John Kirby (bs), O'Neill Spencer (d) replace Smith, Fullbright, Cole; Gene Johnson (alt), Leon LaFell (vcl[2]) added; Newton, Brown (vcl[3]). New York City, 13 July 1937.
Easy living[2] · *The Onyx hop*[3] · *Where or when*[2]

Maxine Sullivan (vcl) acc Newton (tpt); Buster Bailey (clt); Brown (alt); Babe Russin (ten); Claude Thornhill (p); Kirby (bs); Spencer (d). New York City, 6 August 1937.
Loch Lomond · *I'm coming, Virginia* · *Annie Laurie* · *Blue skies*

Midge Williams and Her Jazz Jesters: Newton (tpt); Bailey (clt); Brown (alt); Billy Kyle (p); James McLin (g); Kirby (bs); Spencer (d); Williams (vcl). New York City, 1 October 1937.
The one rose · *The lady is a tramp* · *An old flame never dies* · *Fortune-telling man*

Frankie Newton and His Café Society Orchestra: Newton (tpt); Tab Smith (sop, alt); Stanley Payne (alt); Kenneth Hollon (ten); Kenny Kersey (p); Ulysses Livingston (g); John Williams (bs); Eddie Dougherty (d). New York City, 12 April 1939.
Tab's blues · *Frankie's jump* · *Jam fever*

Most jazz musicians can contrive to sound either exuberant or melancholy, but rarely within the same solo, Newton, though, was a trumpeter capable of making sudden shifts, able to justify switching from one emotional stance to another. He could sound as plaintive as Joe Smith, then display the kind of abandon commonly associated with Roy Eldridge or 'Hot Lips' Page. Yet the impetuousness was always controlled, the fieriness never imperilled a wider view. Indeed, his solos — rather like Bunny Berigan's — had a way of unfolding naturally, developing with the right sort of inevitability. Perhaps Newton was unlucky in having to cram all his recording career within about a decade and a half. He commenced in 1933, taking characteristically startling solos in Bessie Smith's final session; by halfway through the 1940s, however, illness had virtually brought his career to an end. That was, too, a period dominated by Armstrong, Eldridge and eventually by Dizzy Gillespie. Even as brilliant a trumpeter as Henry Allen found it impossible to win their kind of fame and Newton never came close to doing so.

Most of the items on this LP were recorded just before or during the few months that Newton spent in the John Kirby Sextet. That ensemble's urge to sound genteel (and matters grew worse after Newton was replaced by Charlie Shavers) is one reason why the four Maxine Sullivan tracks disappoint. In any case, the singer was more mannered then than during her later, more fruitful years; only in *Annie Laurie* does she loosen up, making the listener pay attention. Nevertheless, Newton displays his class in the eight solo bars that he contributes to *Blue skies*. It is worth noting, incidentally, that even a lesser-known drummer like Spencer could sound instantly recognizable: listen to the way his brush work stresses the off-beat in *Loch Lomond*. Midge Williams sang in a more animated style than Maxine Sullivan, even if her material included a couple of tear-jerkers that would not have been out of place among the bombazine and bead curtains of a late-Victorian drawing-room. Yet *An old flame never dies* contains delicious muted playing by Newton.

Much more substantial, though, are the performances with Newton's various bands. He probably wrote the arrangements himself, balancing the scored and the improvised neatly enough in *You showed me the way*, but making *The Onyx hop* sound far too busy. Hall's playing — skittish yet stylish — suggests the elegance to come, but Scott's tenor saxophone solos belong to an earlier epoch, while Brown bounces along with the regularity of a tennis ball, the repetitiveness sometimes offset by a wheezy charm. Many of Newton's solos attest to his liking for paradox. In *Who's sorry now?*, incidentally, his low-register work could be mistaken for a trombone. *Easy living* and *Where or when*, obviously aimed at more commercially-minded record buyers, feature LaFell, who imitates Bing Crosby more enterprisingly than most singers of that time and genre. The real delights surface in *Frankie's jump* and *Tab's blues*, already discussed under **168**. As was then indicated, Newton's playing is classic: sober on the blues, yet with crisp asides and concluding with an Armstrong-style coda, while in *Frankie's jump* he skips constantly and excitingly between lyricism and truculence.   C.F.

186 Barney Bigard 1944–45
Storyville (D) SLP807

Barney Bigard and His Orchestra: Joe Thomas (tpt); Bigard (clt); George Auld (alt, ten); Leonard Feather (p); Chuck Wayne (g); Billy Taylor (bs); Stan Levey (d); Etta Jones (vcl[1]). New York City, 29 December 1944.
Salty papa blues [1] · *Evil gal blues* [1] · *Blow top blues* [1] · *Long, long journey* [1] · *Blues before dawn*

Cyril Haynes (p) replaces Feather. Same date.
Poong-tang · *Nine o/clock beer* · *How long blues*

Barney Bigard Sextet: Joe Thomas (ten), Art Tatum (p) replace Auld, Haynes; Wayne absent. New York City, 5 January 1945.
Can't help loving that man · *Please don't talk about me when I'm gone* · *Sweet Marijuana Brown* · *Blues for Art's sake*

Late in 1944, Bigard was leading a band at the Onyx Club. This was one of his few essays as a leader. He had gained his well-deserved reputation as a member of more widely celebrated groups — King Oliver, Luis Russell and most notably Ellington, with whom he worked for the better part of fifteen years, leaving in 1942. It has been said that Bigard 'counted for little once he left the Ellington band' [83] but this, whilst true in general terms, has less to do with his real capabilities than with his subduing his gifts, in later years, to the constraints of ensembles which did not encourage his individualism as Ellington had. Though he was a clarinettist in the Creole strain, his extension of the Creole voice was different from that of, say, Bechet or Simeon. He was, at his best, no more typical of the New Orleans clarinet mode than was Tatum of the Harlem 'stride' tradition.

His solo in *Blues before dawn*, recalling many an Ellington contribution, shows his fine talent for romantic scene-painting, the virtuosic runs and soaring phrases combining to create a sense of imaginative space which is, paradoxically, markedly soliloquial. The dazzling and crackling figures in the fast *Poong-tang* still allow for that sense of exaltation by the interspersion of unexpected aerial hoverings, and in *Nine o/clock beer*, both in his reflective solo and in quiet final comments, he uses the blues characteristically to inform a freer vision. All this still counts for a great deal, and though his companions, the unfailing lyrical Thomas, the alternately rasping and shimmering Auld, and the adventurous Wayne, are all eloquent and also give life to rather functional ensemble passages, Bigard always seems to be inhabiting another conceptive sphere.

It is in the 1945 session, when Tatum joins the group and Auld is replaced by Thomas's namesake — a more even-toned tenorist — that a stronger feeling of imaginative kinship emerges. There are flashing exchanges between the two Thomases in *Please don't talk about me when I'm gone* and, after Tatum's solo in the same number, an all-too-brief liaison between clarinettist and pianist whets the appetite with its quiet and deceptively simple mutuality. There is a more vivid example of this in *Sweet Marijuana Brown*, and in *Blues for Art's sake* Bigard, in lower registers, swoops, glides and flutters, suggesting how similar his approach to the blues was to that of the great pianist. Would that we had more extended instances of such co-operation!

The trumpeter Thomas, Taylor and Levey were in Bigard's regular band. With Auld, Wayne and the aspirant Feather, they accompany Etta Jones, a capable band vocalist, in blues songs, the first three of which are more closely associated with Dinah Washington. It is worth listening to for Bigard's subdued comments, colouring the mood rather than paraphrasing the themes.   E.T.

Ed Hall

187 **Celestial Express**
Blue Note (A) B6505

Ed Hall Celeste Quartet: Hall (clt); Meade 'Lux' Lewis (cls); Charlie Christian (g); Israel Crosby (bs). New York City, 5 February 1941.
Jamming in four · *Edmond Hall blues* · *Profoundly blue* (2 takes) · *Celestial express*

Ed Hall's All-Star Quintet: Hall (clt); Teddy Wilson (p); Carl Kress (g); John Williams (bs); Red Norvo (vib). New York City, 25 January 1944.
Romping in 44 · *Blue interval* · *Smooth sailing* · *Seeing Red*

188 **Ed Hall 1941–47**
Queen (I) Q-020

Henry Allen and His Orchestra: Allen (tpt, vcl[1]); J. C. Higginbotham (tbn); Hall (clt); Kenny Kersey (p); Billy Taylor (bs); Jimmy Hoskins (d). New York City, 17 April 1941.
K.K. boogie · *Old man river*[1]

Same personnel and location, 22 July 1941.
A Sheridan square · *Indiana*

Ed Hall Swingtet: Benny Morton (tbn); Hall (clt); Harry Carney (bar); Don Frye (p); Everett Barksdale (g); Junior Raglin (bs); Sidney Catlett (d). New York City, 5 May 1944.
It's been so long · *I can't believe that you're in love with me* · *Big city blues* · *Steaming and beaming*

Teddy Wilson Sextet: Emmett Berry (tpt); Morton (tbn); Hall (clt); Wilson (p); unidentified bs; possibly Catlett (d). Presumably New York City, c. June 1944.
B flat swing · *Lady, be good*

James P. Johnson's Blue Note Jazzmen: Sidney DeParis (tpt); Vic
Dickenson (tbn); Hall (clt); Johnson (p); James Shirley (g); Al Lucas (bs);
Arthur Trappier (d). New York City, 26 October 1944.
At the ball · Walking the dog
Ed Hall Quintet: Hall (clt); Ralph Sutton (p); Danny Barker (g); Pops
Foster (bs); Baby Dodds (d). New York City, 13 September 1947.
The blues
Art Tatum and His Band: Roy Eldridge, Charlie Shavers (tpt); Morton,
Dickenson (tbn); Hall (clt); Ben Webster (ten); Tatum (p); Al Casey (g);
Slam Stewart (bs); Catlett (d). Probably New York City, date unknown.
Royal Garden blues · I got rhythm

Those of us who had begun writing about jazz by the early 1940s
were often guilty of naïvety. And never more so than in being
surprised because Hall — still using, like all the grand old men,
an Albert system clarinet — should have been so impressed by
Benny Goodman's playing that it affected his own. Slightly less
than a year younger than Albert Nicholas, but Omer Simeon's
senior by fourteen months and Barney Bigard's by five years,
Hall was, like them, a New Orleans clarinettist who got himself a
job in a big band. In his case it was that led by Claude Hopkins,
where — on records, anyway — he took solos that were brief yet
full of gurgling enthusiasm (**123**). By the time the above tracks
were recorded, however, he was working regularly in small
groups once more. The links with New Orleans were there for the
discerning listener to spot and even as late as 1947, on what
sounds like an airshot, Hall takes an opening chorus on *The blues*
that is at least reminiscent of George Lewis's careful arpeggia-
tions. A similar approach underlies his ensemble playing on
Indiana, as well as in many shorter solos that pop up elsewhere.

One merit of the Blue Note sessions is that the resulting music
was issued on twelve-inch rather than ten-inch 78s, giving the
players more time to stretch out. The 1941 tracks are especially
good; all are twelve-bar blues and represent, too, the meeting of a
couple of generations (Christian was around twenty-four at the
time) and of at least three major strands of jazz history. Hall came
from New Orleans, of course; Meade 'Lux' Lewis had earned his
reputation playing boogie woogie on Chicago's South Side, while
Christian epitomized the southwestern influence — plenty of
blues, plenty of riffs — that was revivifying swing. Christian
plays an acoustic guitar, but in roughly the same fashion as the
amplified instrument he was using with Goodman (**159**). Both
takes of *Profoundly blue*, in fact, begin with highly traditional
blues guitar playing: mostly single-string, a bit like Teddy Bunn.
These tracks also have some of Hall's simplest yet most reflective
work. Lewis reverts to boogie only in *Celestial express*; elsewhere

he deploys the celeste (on which he had recorded solos five years earlier) in a brisk, uncluttered way.

Hall always used illegitimate techniques — the rasp, the growl, even a kind of chuckle — sparingly, mainly to add texture to a line rather than, as Pee Wee Russell often did, as ends in themselves. And, of course, they turn up even more sparingly in Goodman's playing. The Blue Note session of 1944 shows how Hall had adapted some of Goodman's current mannerisms, including the slightly shrill blowing above the ensemble during final choruses. The presence of Norvo and Wilson heightens the resemblance; so do the neatly-arranged riff tunes; again every piece is a blues — except *Romping in 44*. But, despite the greater formality, the playing is sometimes too casual. In *Seeing Red*, Hall sounds very fallible, yet *Blue interval* comes off well, the badly boxed-in recording quality being the only drawback; the slow tempo paradoxically encourages the clarinettist to adopt a more economical manner. Indeed, the atmosphere created is akin to that on Wilson's *Just a mood* (**176**) — *Blue mood*, as it was called on the British 78 rpm label — or to the Goodman Quartet's *Blues in your/my flat* (**158**).

Tatum's group contained too many stars for any of them to come across effectively — apart from the pianist himself, who dazzles as usual. *I got rhythm* becomes a rowdy tear-up, but the conclusion of *Royal Garden blues* is the highspot of the session, with Eldridge suddenly taking command, spurred on by Catlett's drumming. James P. Johnson's musicians blend uncomfortably: what amounts to a New Orleans style front line, with DeParis, alas, sounding blander than he should, is juxtaposed with Shirley, who never really seems at ease with the amplified guitar. (*At the ball* proves to be more or less the same tune as *Down in honky tonk town*.) On *Walking the dog*, Hall plays one chorus in the low register, then, to provide contrast, moves up for the next, a device that Goodman, too, was fond of in his earlier years. The Wilson items, marred by poor sound quality, were recorded for the American Armed Forces Network 'Jubilee' radio show. *B flat swing* belies its title and also goes on for far too long, but *Lady, be good* bounces along cheerily, all the riffs pertinent and with a bright solo from Berry.

K.K. boogie and *Old man river* are both indifferent performances by Allen's standards; he even sings poorly on the latter track. Higginbotham is at his bluntest — he could even be said to bray on *K.K. boogie*, while Kersey imposes a remorseless eight-to-the-bar pattern on both tracks. *A Sheridan square*, another twelve-bar blues, is much better, especially Allen's glancing solo. Yet by far the finest music on this LP comes from Hall's Swingtet.

Each theme is stated by a different instrument, with Carney sounding especially tender and impressive in *I can't believe that you're in love with me*. Indeed, this session presents the baritone saxophonist taking what must be some of his finest solos on record; he is particularly good in *It's been so long* and *Steaming and beaming*. And once again Catlett's drumming gives muscle to the proceedings. These are, happily, tracks where Hall is again heard playing at slightly greater length — he was, after all, the leader— getting a chance to develop his ideas, as on *Steaming and beaming*, rather than, as in so many shorter outings, having to aim for instant sprightliness.   C.F.

189 Swinging Clarinets
London (E) HMC5005

All-Star Jam Band: Bobby Hackett (cnt); Joe Marsala (clt, ten); Pete Brown (alt); Joe Bushkin (p, cls[1]); Leonard Feather (p[2]); Ray Biondi (g); Artie Shapiro (bs); George Wettling (d); Leo Watson (vcl[3]). New York City, 10 March 1938.
For he's a jolly good fellow[2] · *Let's get happy*[1,3]

Joe Marsala and His Delta Four: Bill Coleman (tpt); Marsala (clt); Brown (alt); Carmen Mastren (g); Gene Traxler (bs); Dell St John (vcl[4]). New York City, 4 April 1940.
Three o/clock jump[4] · *Reunion in Harlem*

Mel Powell and His Orchestra: Billy Butterfield (tpt); Lou McGarity (tbn); Benny Goodman (clt); George Berg (ten); Powell (p); Al Morgan (bs); Kansas Fields (d). New York City, 4 February 1942.
When did you leave Heaven? · *The world is waiting for the sunrise* · *Blue skies* · *Mood at twilight*

Pee Wee Russell's Hot Four: Russell (clt); Jess Stacy (p); Sid Weiss (bs); Wettling (d). New York City, 30 September 1944.
Take me to the land of jazz · *D.A. blues* · *Rose of Washington Square* · *Keeping out of mischief now*

The role of the clarinet in jazz (up to the modernist movements from the later 1940s onwards, in which it had no significant place) was preordained by the use to which it was put in the earliest New Orleans ensembles. Made a far more flexible instrument by mid-nineteenth-century developments, the clarinet became an agile foil for the trumpet in the interplay of the early ensembles, and the tendency for the *clarino* register to dominate in collective improvising seems to find an echo in the orchestrally-accompanied flights of virtuosos such as Goodman (**141–3**) and Shaw (**145–6**). In the days when clarinet aerobatics were a cult, passages using the darker *chalumeau* register always came as something of a surprise, and it is notable that two of the three fine clarinettists heard here have a great liking for their instrument's lower ranges.

Marsala's gentle and unelaborate style seems to honour Jimmy Noone (**41, 229**), an influence upon players of the Chicagoan and swing modes not always sufficiently acknowledged. There are brief yet telling examples of Marsala's craftsmanship in *For he's a jolly good fellow* and *Let's get happy*, played by a band whose light-hearted motives are akin to those of another Feather group which had swung other traditional songs in London the previous May (**98**). Apart from Hackett's elegant leads and solos and Watson's genial scatting, these tracks are memorable for the contributions of Brown. That his bouncy style should have so quickly fallen out of favour is strange when one realizes its debt to the rhythmic idiosyncrasies of Noone. The stylistic relation between Marsala's very Noone-like solo in *Three o/clock jump* and Brown's which follows it is an even clearer revelation than the final ensemble of *I know that you know* (**229**) where Brown's attention to the staccato of Noone's preceding solos can be discerned. Brown's characteristic voice is well caught on *Reunion in Harlem*, and its subtleties, which vanquish the languorous perils of his instrument, may also be accounted for by the promptings of clarinet styles.

There is vivacious scoring for the three wind voices of the Marsala quintet, the third being that of Coleman, whose bright expression is well up to the standard of his fine Paris sessions on **102**. Mastren and Traxler provide exceptional support, the guitarist being so successful in his chordal underpinning that on *Reunion in Harlem* it is hard to believe that no piano is present.

Goodman's big band style is not significantly adapted when he appears in small groups, yet the dazzling ease of his improvisations betokens no attempt to upstage his companions. In any case, they would have been adequate to such a challenge. Powell especially, his lightness of touch brilliantly reproduced here, plays solos with a freshness of thought which rivals Goodman's own statements wherein facility occasionally masks lapses in melodic and harmonic inventiveness. The clarinettist's most thoughtful solo is on *Blue skies*. A slight edge of self-indulgence in his tone during *When did you leave heaven?* should be weighed against some blue-toned cadences in the same solo and by the cooler introspection he achieves in *Mood at twilight*.

Often Goodman seems to be guarding against emotional display, and this reserve may belie an oft-claimed Chicagoan inheritance. On the other hand, 'forthright introspection' could be the paradox to convey the disturbing poetry of Russell, whose Hot

Four session is the undeniable highlight of this collection. More is said under **209** about a style which developed the blues pathos of Roppolo (a very early associate) and the jagged intervals of Teschemacher towards expressions of sublime recklessness such as those which abound here, for these 1944 recordings preserve some of his finest work. The abandoned antics of *Take me to the land of jazz* and *Keeping out of mischief now* exemplify the paradox, for they never quite stray into extroversion. This is not Goodman's gentlemanliness, for within his private world Russell is always conjuring the liveliest of spirits. His blues playing is inimitable and *D.A. blues* bears comparison with his best elsewhere. Stacy's response to and support for all this is as suitable as all his other work would lead one to expect and, though known for his toughness, he can be meditative too, as in the splendid blues.   E.T.

190 Saxophones 1943–46
Mercury (E) SMWL21026

Lester Young Quartet: Young (ten); Johnny Guarnieri (p); Slam Stewart (bs); Sidney Catlett (d). New York City, 28 December 1943.
Sometimes I'm happy

The Keynoters: Charlie Shavers, Jonah Jones (tpt); Budd Johnson (ten); Guarnieri (p); Milt Hinton (bs); J. C. Heard (d). New York City, 7 June 1944.
You're driving me crazy · *I'm in the market for you*

Pete Brown All-Star Quintet: Joe Thomas (tpt); Brown (alt); Kenny Kersey (p); Hinton (bs); Heard (d). New York City, 19 July 1944.
It's the talk of the town · *That's my weakness now*

Charlie Shavers's All-American Five: Shavers (tpt); Coleman Hawkins (ten); Teddy Wilson (p); Billy Taylor (bs); Denzil Best (d). New York City, 18 October 1944.
Embraceable you

Cozy Cole and His Orchestra: Shorty Rogers (tpt); Vernon Brown (tbn); Aaron Sachs (clt); Don Byas (ten); Bill Rowland (p); Taylor (bs); Cole (d). New York City, 2 February 1945.
They didn't believe me

J. C. Heard Quintet: Buck Clayton (tpt); Flip Phillips (ten); Guarnieri (p); Hinton (bs); Heard (d). New York City, 6 July 1945.
All my life

Ted Nash Quintet: Thomas (tpt); Nash (ten); Geoff Clarkson (p); Trigger Alpert (bs); Heard (d). New York City, 25 January 1946.
Wicks kicks

The Keynoters: Willie Smith (alt); Nat 'King' Cole (p); Red Callender (bs); Jackie Mills (d). Los Angeles, 16 February 1946.
The way you look tonight · *Airiness à la Nat*

Herbie Haymer's Orchestra: Clyde Hurley (tpt); Heinie Beau (clt);
Haymer (ten); Tommy Todd (p); Dave Barbour (g); Phil Stephens (bs); Nick
Fatool (d). Los Angeles, 30 March 1946.
China boy

191 The Big Sounds of Coleman Hawkins and Chew Berry

London (E) HMC5006, *Mainstream (A) 6037, 6038

Chew Berry and His Little Jazz Ensemble: Roy Eldridge (tpt);
Berry (ten); Clyde Hart (p); Danny Barker (g); Artie Shapiro (bs);
Catlett (d). New York City, 10 November 1938.
Sitting in · Stardust · Body and soul · 46 West 52

Coleman Hawkins and The Chocolate Dandies: Eldridge (tpt); Benny
Carter (alt); p[1]); Hawkins (ten); Bernard Addison (g); John Kirby (bs);
Catlett (d). New York City, 25 May 1940.
Smack · I surrender, dear[1] · I can't believe that you're in love with me
Eldridge, Carter absent. Same date.
Dedication

Chew Berry and His Jazz Ensemble: 'Hot Lips' Page (tpt, vcl[2]);
Berry (ten); Hart (p); Al Casey (g); Al Morgan (bs); Harry Jaeger (d).
New York City, 28 August 1941.
*Blowing up a breeze · On the sunny side of the street · Monday at
Minton's · Gee, baby, ain't I good to you?[2]*

Coleman Hawkins with Leonard Feather's Esquire All-Stars: Cootie
Williams (tpt); Ed Hall (clt); Hawkins (ten); Art Tatum (p); Casey (g);
Oscar Pettiford (bs); Catlett (d). New York City, 4 December 1943.
Esquire bounce · Mop mop · My ideal · Esquire blues

Just as Irish poets during the first half of this century found it
impossible to avoid being influenced by W. B. Yeats, so the tenor
saxophonists of the 1930s recognized in Hawkins a model every
bit as inescapable. With the exceptions, naturally enough, of
Young and, to a lesser extent, Johnson, all the tenor players on
these two LPs share that common stylistic dependence. Young, of
course, was the heretic who in his turn became an admired
exemplar. *Sometimes I'm happy* reveals traces of the indolence
that later was to creep into his playing; things are not helped by
Stewart doing his party piece, humming as he bowed, yet the
overall effect is satisfying. As for Johnson, he mixes the two
stances, sometimes sounding, especially in *I'm in the market for
you*, a trifle like Young interpreting a Hawkins solo. Johnson is,
however, the outstanding player on the earlier of the Keynoters'
sessions, although Jones, using a mute most of the time, is a close
second.

The other tenor saxophonists mostly have gushing tones and
arpeggiate with varying degrees of fluency: predictably in the

case of Nash, or with the highly individual panache which earned Berry a status of his own. The Nash track, an adroit, slightly boppish rewriting of *Blue Lou*, contains a superb chorus by the trumpeter Joe Thomas; he also performs doughtily — indeed, he calmly appropriates *It's the talk of the town* — with Brown's Quintet. Berry's playing was never so orotund as Hawkins's; he relied, rather, upon the rapid juxtaposing — oscillation, almost — of brief phrases. That is illustrated to perfection on both the 1938 and 1941 recordings. Eldridge is in such lively form that he tends to dominate the earlier session, yet few things are more stimulating than the rapport between these two musicians in *46 West 52* (the address, incidentally, of the Commodore Music Shop at that time), using the chords of *Sweet Georgia Brown*. *Body and soul* is of special interest, for it was recorded exactly eleven months ahead of Hawkins's classic performance (**192**). The approach here is more conventional, the chord changes are negotiated less adventurously (Hawkins used to chuckle when he recalled how shocked his fellow tenor players were by some of the notes he used). Berry could not equal Hawkins's warmth of tone, his emotional presence, yet this is still a shapely and admirable piece of ballad playing. *Stardust*, not surprisingly, comes off less successfully, although Eldridge is at his best and boldest. On the later session Berry is, once again, better on the up-tempo numbers, notably *Monday at Minton's*, a twelve-bar blues; but Page, excellently though he plays and sings, cannot summon up Eldridge's anarchic lyricism.

Haymer based his style upon Berry's, a fact made obvious in *China boy*; an oddity of this track is the way Hurley starts off as if he were about to launch into *Strutting with some barbecue*. Byas's use of Hawkins's romanticism is noted under **197**; he decorates *They didn't believe me* quite lavishly, compensating for the curious way that genres become mixed; possibly Rogers wrote the score as well as playing the trumpet on this session. Phillips probably comes closest to sounding like Hawkins, although his tone is quite a bit lighter. *All my life* is turned almost into a duet for Phillips and Clayton, the latter phrasing with puckish jauntiness. Four of the other tracks on the Mercury LP feature the playing of alto saxophonists: Brown sounds trite when doubling the tempo in *It's the talk of the town*, yet is amiably idiosyncratic, even quite enterprising, on *That's my weakness now*. Smith starts badly by slurring too brazenly at the commencement of *The way you look tonight*, but edges close to Johnny Hodges's early buoyancy in *Airiness à la Nat*.

Hawkins is not, perhaps, at his most dazzling in *Embraceable you,* but the tracks recorded under his own direction are a different matter. *I can't believe that you're in love with me* opens with him leading the ensemble — pushing the others, rather as he was accustomed to doing a few years earlier with those recalcitrant Europeans — then embarking on a powerful solo, to be succeeded by Eldridge at his huskiest and most exciting, and by Carter, every phrase planted as carefully as an aside by one of Jane Austen's characters. Unfortunately, Carter plays the piano on *I surrender, dear* and his lack of flexibility within the rhythm section acts as a brake upon the soloists. On the other hand, *Dedication* would probably have been helped by having a pianist (not Carter) to fill out the harmonies. *Esquire bounce* offers the apotheosis of Hawkins's use of the riff as the basis for a solo. He is more melodically imaginative on the other tracks from that session, especially *Mop mop* (which uses the *I got rhythm* chord changes), where his solo ascends to heights of swerving recklessness. Williams plays as if he were on a date with the Benny Goodman Sextet — his solo on *Mop mop,* indeed, sounds alarmingly familiar — while Tatum adapts his virtuosity to the requirements of a seven-piece ensemble. A musician who contributes hugely to the success not only of the two Hawkins sessions but to various other tracks as well is Catlett, arguably the finest drummer of his generation. His cymbals shimmered more magically than those of anyone except Dave Tough, while he could swing an entire group, small or large, with just brushes and a side drum. C.F.

192 The Complete Coleman Hawkins Vol. 1
RCA (F) FMX17325

Mound City Blue Blowers: Glenn Miller (tbn); Pee Wee Russell (clt); Hawkins (ten); Jack Bland (g); Eddie Condon (bj); Al Morgan (bs); Gene Krupa (d); Red McKenzie (cap). New York City, 14 November 1929.
Hello, Lola · One hour

Coleman Hawkins and His Orchestra: Tommy Lindsay, Joe Guy (tpt); Earl Hardy (tbn); Jackie Fields, Eustis Moore (alt); Hawkins (ten); Gene Rodgers (p); William Smith (bs); Arthur Herbert (d); Thelma Carpenter (vcl[1]). New York City, 11 October 1939.
Meet Doctor Foo · Fine dinner · She's funny that way[1] *· Body and soul*

Coleman Hawkins's All-Star Octet: Benny Carter (tpt); J. C. Higginbotham (tbn); Danny Polo (clt); Hawkins (ten); Rodgers (p); Lawrence Lucie (g); John Williams (bs); Walter Johnson (d). New York City, 3 January 1940.
When day is done · The Sheik of Araby · My blue heaven · Bouncing with Bean

The Make-Believe Ballroom Jam Session: Roy Eldridge, Harry
James (tpt); Tommy Dorsey (tbn); Hawkins (ten); unidentified p, g, bs;
Lionel Hampton (d). Savoy Ballroom, New York City, spring 1940.
King Porter stomp

Coleman Hawkins and His Orchestra: Tommy Stevenson, Guy, Lindsay,
Nelson Bryant (tpt); William Cato, Sandy Williams, Claude Jones (tbn);
Ernie Powell (clt, alt); Fields, Moore (alt); Kermit Scott, Hawkins (ten);
Rodgers (p); Gene Fields (g); Billy Taylor (bs); J. C. Heard (d). Savoy
Ballroom, New York City, 19 July 1940.
California, here I come

Same personnel and location, early August 1940.
Chicago · The blue room

193 Coleman Hawkins: Swing
Fontana (E) FJL102

Coleman Hawkins's Quintet: Eldridge (tpt); Hawkins (ten); Teddy
Wilson (p); Taylor (bs); Cozy Cole (d). New York City, 31 January 1944.
*I only have eyes for you · 'Swonderful · I'm in the mood for love ·
Bean at the Met*

Coleman Hawkins and His Sax Ensemble: Tab Smith (alt); Don Byas,
Hawkins (ten); Harry Carney (bar); Johnny Guarnieri (p); Al Lucas (bs);
Sidney Catlett (d). New York City, 24 May 1944.
Three little words · The battle of the saxes

Coleman Hawkins's All-American Four: Hawkins (ten); Wilson (p); John
Kirby (bs); Catlett (d). New York City, 29 May 1944.
Make believe · Don't blame me · Just one of those things

Coleman Hawkins's Quintet: Slam Stewart (bs), Denzil Best (d) replaces
Kirby, Catlett; Buck Clayton (tpt) added. New York City, 17 October
1944.
*Under a blanket of blue · Beyond the blue horizon · A shanty in old
shanty town*

Charlie Shavers's All-American Five: Shavers (tpt), Taylor (bs) replace
Clayton, Stewart. New York City, 18 October 1944.
My man · El salon de gutbucket

The important Blue Blowers session is dealt with under **166** and
reference is also made to it under **101**, in both cases pointing out
the contrast between the old-style verve of Hawkins's solo in
Hello, Lola and the far more reflective essay on *One hour*. The
second solo, in Hawkins's own terms, has dated less than the first
and forecasts a style that was to make him such a towering
exemplar in the development of saxophone improvisation.

A leap forward of ten years to *Meet Doctor Foo* may not seem
very edifying in musical terms and his work of the 1930s with
Henderson and with European groups needs to be taken into
account; but his handling of faster themes, like this one, has
clearly become more flexible than it was in 1929. His response to

more modern scoring — scoring not a little indebted to his own rhythmic discoveries — is pleasingly instanced in *Doctor Foo* and in *Fine dinner* also. His introduction to *She's funny that way* has a thoughtfulness which is extended to his beautiful meditation after Miss Carpenter's singing, showing how the strength of both rhythmic and melodic thinking is sustained in a manner which saves the mode from mere airiness.

Body and soul is one of the most celebrated of all jazz improvisations, and justly so. That marvellous continuity of musical invention is even more evident here as he makes the tricky modulation in and out of the theme's bridge passage seem of insignificant difficulty, and as he uses not two separately considered refrains but the two regarded as one as the basis of his jazz transformation, achieving in the last eight bars climbing phrases which, in addition to being thrillingly climactic, are also of striking harmonic enterprise. The quiet accompaniment is perfectly judged. This session is one of Hawkins's very few essays as the leader of a sizeable band. The sixteen-piece group heard in *California, here I come, Chicago* and *The blue room*, only just adequately recorded at the Savoy, is one that he took on tour in 1940. This is a well-organized swing ensemble with good soloists, but it is the tenorist's tough solos which make the performances memorable.

In the 'Make-Believe Ballroom' recording, Hawkins makes of the second strain of *King Porter stomp* an ecstatic declaration, full of dancing clauses and self-reflected riffs. There is also some rather wildly developed work from Eldridge and Dorsey; and James improvises forthrightly. In spite of rough recording, the good things here can be well appreciated. But Hawkins was much more at home in smaller groups, and the most satisfying collective work in this album comes from the 1940 octet. Right at the start of *When day is done*, and at many other points throughout the four items played, the brilliance of Carter's trumpet work is evident; there are rousing statements from Higginbotham, particularly in the faster *Sheik of Araby* and *Bouncing with Bean*; and, though he is occasionally discountenanced by the faster tempos, Polo plays with both vigour and thoughtfulness.

Wilson, at the height of his powers in the 1940s, is the chief link connecting the groups with which Hawkins plays on the Fontana LP, and he is replaced only by Guarnieri, who serves the Sax Ensemble. Wilson has not been consistently regarded as a major jazz musician, but his contributions to these fine sessions, both as soloist and accompanist, are almost beyond praise. At the start of *I only have eyes for you* and *'Swonderful*, Hawkins dances round Eldridge's theme statements, creating skilful canonic effects and, on each of these occasions, Wilson follows on with swinging solos of a subtlety that seems to defy the law of gravity. The sympathetic comments beneath Eldridge's partially improvised rehearsal of *I'm in the mood for love* and the brief rococo development which follows are further proofs of this pianist's greatness. *Bean at the Met* — a unison riff theme based on the chords of *How high the moon?* — has agile muted work from the trumpeter and distinguished solos from Wilson and the ever-various Hawkins.

Three little words and *The battle of the saxes* bring together the differing talents of four saxophonists. Byas fares well in the company of his more charismatic leader providing, in fact, an interesting contrast with his harder, simpler phrasing. Smith, though he touches a languidness more typical of Hodges in the first number, shows that he has his own accent in a jumping solo during the second. Carney, a veteran insufficiently praised, makes his cumbersome instrument sound as agile as Byas's. Guarnieri, who often attains a bell-like brilliance of tone, develops a strain of utterance learned largely from Basie. There is no sense here that Hawkins is merely being paced by the other saxophonists. If the second event really had been a battle, and it does not seem it, he could certainly have triumphed; but he, one of the most respectful and encouraging of players, is obviously in no mood for such striving.

Don't blame me, Just one of those things and *Make believe* have Hawkins in the company of a rhythm section perfectly suited to his romantic spirit. There can be few more exhilarating moments in recorded jazz than Wilson's supremely buoyant take-off in the first chorus of *Just one of those things*, and the same irresistible swing enlivens each number. Hawkins, contemplative, disputative and sportive by turns, is a marvel, especially in those moments (*Don't blame me* has one) when he seems to combine without effort moods both of reflection and verve.

The quintets with Clayton and Shavers give opportunity for comparing these two trumpeters, and each of them with Eldridge. Shavers seems, at this time, rather less given to the perils of exuberance than Eldridge, although the latter was to capitulate more often in later years. The October 1944 All-American date was recorded under Shavers's name and he airs his lyrical gift in the free-timed and somewhat 'Yiddishe' minor-keyed introduction to *My man*. In *El salon de gutbucket*, after Hawkins has played one of his most remarkable sets of extravagant multiplications, Shavers appears to remove himself to a distant corner of the studio for a brilliant high-register announcement. (Another track from this session appears on **190**.)

Clayton normally avoids that kind of self-advertisement and is the most consistently pleasing of the trumpeters, his quieter emotions complementing Hawkins's moods rather than contrasting with them. Perhaps he corrects a little the feeling of indulgence which the saxophonist tries to introduce in *Under a blanket of blue* yet, with the individual vibrato which identifies his muted phrases, he is clearly a sympathetic ally. Best shows comparable sympathy as he suits his brushwork to Clayton's muted solo in *Beyond the blue horizon*, and there is the ubiquitous Wilson aiding and abetting everyone, everywhere. The excellence of Stewart's rhythm work here should not be overlooked, though his clever 'one-man duets' are likely to etch themselves more cheekily in the memory. But far more worthy of remembrance are Hawkins's solos like that in *A shanty in old shanty town* wherein he ranges through melodic and harmonic apartments, ferreting out amazing musical prey. Clayton approaches the *Shanty* theme more reverentially in a lovely open-toned variation.   E.T.

Coleman Hawkins/Lester Young
194 Classic Tenors
Stateside (E) SL10117, Contact (A) CM3

Coleman Hawkins and His Orchestra: Bill Coleman (tpt); Andy Fitzgerald (clt); Hawkins (ten); Ellis Larkins (p); Al Casey (g); Oscar Pettiford (bs); Shelley Manne (d). New York City; 8 December 1943.
Voodte · How deep is the ocean? · Hawkins barrelhouse · Stumpy

Dickie Wells and His Orchestra: Coleman (tpt); Wells (tbn); Lester Young (ten); Larkins (p); Freddy Greene (g); Al Hall (bs); Jo Jones (d). New York City, 21 December 1943.
I got rhythm · I'm fer it, too · Linger awhile · Hello, babe

Coleman Hawkins's Swing Four: Hawkins (ten); Eddie Heywood jnr (p); Pettiford (bs); Manne (d). New York City, 23 December 1943.
Crazy rhythm · Get happy · The man I love · Sweet Lorraine

Coleman Hawkins
195 Hollywood Stampede
Capitol (E) M11030, Capitol (A) M11030

Coleman Hawkins and His Orchestra: Howard McGhee (tpt); Hawkins (ten); 'Sir' Charles Thompson (p); Allen Reuss (g); Pettiford (bs); Denzil Best (d). Los Angeles, 23 February 1945.
April in Paris · Rifftide · Stardust · Stuffy

Vic Dickenson (tbn) added. Los Angeles, 2 March 1945.
Hollywood stampede · I'm through with love · What is there to say? · Wrap your troubles in dreams
John Simmons (bs) replaces Pettiford; Dickenson absent. Los Angeles, 9 March 1945.
Too much of a good thing · Bean soup · Someone to watch over me · It's the talk of the town

History used to be seen as a series of take-overs, one monarch giving place to another, this dynasty collapsing, another arising. Many people, particularly some writers, are tempted to view jazz in a similar way. But such assumptions are misleading. What might appear to be the supplanting of Hawkins by his later rival, Lester Young, for example, was never a simple matter of Hawkins's warm tone and arpeggiating manner being suddenly thrown out of date by Young's pale understatement and akimbo approach to chords; nor was it a choice between pushing the beat or lagging behind it. Both men operated within the harmonic conventions of 1930s jazz yet, though Young is often thought of as pointing the way ahead, it was actually Hawkins who seemed more at home with the emergent boppers. It was no accident that he became the first important musician of his generation to take younger players — Fats Navarro, Miles Davis, J. J. Johnson, Milt Jackson, Max Roach — into his groups. Perhaps Young's flexibility of phrasing had more in common with the new rhythmic practices, but Hawkins's harmonic sense, his grasp of chords, enabled him to operate alongside musicians nearly half his age.

That particular affinity was foreshadowed by *Stumpy*, using the chords of *Whispering*. Boppers were not the first people to erect fresh tunes above familiar harmonies: Sidney Bechet, after all, recorded *Shag* (**226**) less than two years after *I got rhythm* was first sung in the Gershwins' show, *Girl Crazy*. But they were so addicted to the practice, complicating the original chord changes in the process, that the procedure became especially identified with them. *Bean soup (Tea for two), Too much of a good thing (Fine and dandy), Hollywood stampede (Sweet Georgia Brown)* and *Rifftide (Lady, be good)* are all tilted towards bop, even if none of the players, apart from Pettiford, had very close links with the new movement. McGhee, for example, plays the trumpet — brassily, aggressively — in a style closer to Roy Eldridge than to Eldridge's disciple, Dizzy Gillespie.

The least successful of the 1945 sessions was the third, where Hawkins falls back upon arpeggiation as an end in itself, especially in *Bean soup*. He adopts a similar approach, but more understandably, in trying to avoid playing the melody of *Stardust*. The same session, however, inspired outstanding solos from him in *Rifftide* and *Stuffy* (where the front line exploits crisp unison riffs, paradoxically tight yet relaxed), while on 2 March he rambled imaginatively through *Wrap your troubles in dreams* and — meditative yet quizzical — *What is there to say?* Reuss's guitar is used in a quietly dramatic way, providing links, introductions and taking a couple of unflamboyant solos on *Stuffy* and *What is there to say?*

The real masterpiece, though, was created over two years earlier, on 23 December 1943. Hawkins's solo on *The man I love* ranks at least next to, if not alongside, his classic improvisation on *Body and soul* (**192**). The tune is taken at a surprisingly brisk tempo, Hawkins constantly shifting the interior rhythms, breaking up the regular accents, beginning with an exploratory first chorus before moving to a triumphant, attacking climax. Heywood's compact and harmonically stimulating piano playing, Pettiford's bass solo (it must have been the first time that anyone's breathing was captured on a record so meticulously) and Manne's drumming — heavily influenced by Dave Tough — all have their part in making this a superb performance. Almost as good are *Sweet Lorraine*, another demonstration of how to go about using arpeggios, and the fastish *Get happy* and *Crazy rhythm*.

A musician in common links the first two sessions: Coleman descends to blustering in *Hawkins barrelhouse* yet elsewhere he is typically restless and lyrical. Larkins, though a nonpareil accompanist to singers (as **203** well shows), takes dullish solos here, especially on *I got rhythm*, and deters the rhythm section from swinging to the full. But this does not put Young off. Perhaps Hawkins is too predictable on his four tracks, yet his rival plays with the kind of nonchalance he exhibited during the years with Basie. Maybe his routine on *I got rhythm* is a bit too familiar, but it can still exhilarate; and there is a fine edge to Young's work on the blues, *I'm fer it, too*. The musician who really excelled on this session, however, was Wells, displaying a confidence and audacity that invite comparison with his work for Spike Hughes's Orchestra (**128**) and in Paris during 1937 (**105a, 107a**). Repeatedly he takes over before the previous soloist has finished, eager to begin. The brusque, vibrant playing on *Linger awhile*, the way he uses a growling, dirty tone in *I'm fer it, too*, are both surpassed, though, by the pair of choruses he takes in *I got rhythm*, one building upon the other, an astonishing *tour de force*.   C.F.

196

Lester Young: the Complete Savoy Recordings
Savoy (A) SJL2202 (2 LPs)

Earle Warren and His Orchestra: Ed Lewis, Al Killian, Harry
Edison (tpt); Eli Robinson, Dickie Wells, Ted Donelly, Lou Taylor (tbn);
Warren (alt, vcl[1]); Jimmy Powell (alt); Young, Buddy Tate (ten); Rudy
Rutherford (bar); Clyde Hart (p); Freddy Greene (g); Rodney Richardson
(bs); Jo Jones or Shadow Wilson (d). New York City, 18 April 1944.
Circus in rhythm (3 takes) · *Poor little plaything*[1] (2 takes) · *Tush*
(2 takes)

Johnny Guarnieri and His All-Star Orchestra: Billy Butterfield (tpt);
Hank d'Amico (clt); Young (ten); Guarnieri (p); Dexter Hall (g); Billy
Taylor (bs); Cozy Cole (d). Same location and date.
These foolish things · *Exercise in swing* (4 takes) · *Salute to Fats*
(5 takes) · *Basie English* (2 takes)

Lester Young's Quintet: Young (ten); Count Basie (p); Greene (g);
Richardson (bs); Wilson (d). New York City, 1 May 1944.
Blue Lester · *Ghost of a chance* (2 takes) · *Indiana* (2 takes) ·
Jump, Lester, jump

Lester Young Sextet: Jesse Drakes (tpt); Jerry Elliott (tbn); Young (ten);
Junior Mance (p); Leroy Jackson (bs); Roy Haynes (d). New York City,
28 June 1949.
Crazy over J-Z (3 takes) · *Ding dong* (3 takes) · *Blues 'n' bells*
(3 takes) · *June bug*

In December 1943, Young rejoined the Basie orchestra after an
absence of three years. The band which plays the first three
numbers here (recorded the following April) is, in fact, Basie's,
with Hart at the piano, Warren leading. It utters vigorous,
jubilant music in *Circus in rhythm*; and Young, who had recorded
little between leaving and returning, plays with much of his old
disregard of the odds — not *pitting* his strength against the
ensemble rampages but letting his authority assert itself through
a species of indolent wonderworking. Each of his solos is different,
not in terms of development or improvement, but simply because
he approaches the task afresh in each take. Edison sounds almost
as effortless and enterprising, but he *is* bent upon improvement
and perhaps attempts a little too much in the third take. During
the second take, which was the one originally issued, there are
the clearest hints of deliberate correspondence of thought
between trumpeter and saxophonist. This is Warren's composition and, presumably, arrangement, and there are pointers in it
to stylistic change.

Poor little plaything, issued here for the first time, has gentle-
manly singing from Warren and brief musings by Young, but is
notable chiefly for a luminous orchestration by Tadd Dameron
(who had been developing his talents with Harlan Leonard and

would become an important figure in bop), colouring a trite melody with distinction. Wells makes exhilarating contributions to his own *Tush*, gambolling with his section colleagues; Young slithers and surges, relishing the theme's urgent motions, sparking his own brand of excitement with those oddly-placed ascending runs which seem to terminate nowhere in particular — yet with precision! Young was still a master of paradox.

The reflective *These foolish things* is first of four numbers recorded by the Guarnieri band on the same day as the Warren session. Once the impetus becomes more heated as, particularly, in the first take of *Exercise in swing*, what had still, in Young's tone, seemed vulnerable to a degree in a big band context, suddenly takes on unexpected power. Again, he regards each take as a different kind of challenge and it is fascinating to compare, for example, the oblique phrases of his third-take solo with the heraldic figures of the fourth. The other soloists respond to the spirit of adventure and do not repeat themselves unduly, though Butterfield and Guarnieri are sometimes carried away by their ability to impersonate others. That they do this very well is not to be denied. Not an authoritative clarinettist, d'Amico plays with exemplary thoughtfulness. In *Salute to Fats* he sounds, tonally at least, a little like Simeon. Then, in take 3 of the same piece, Young, who had broken off midway in take 2, finds new and expressive colours, inspiring Butterfield to greater personal certainty and d'Amico to new rhythmic daring. Guarnieri is pleasant and swinging always. He genuflects to Basie, Waller and Tatum by turns, and possibly has a surer devotion to the first which, in *Basie English*, tempers the glibness which sometimes bedevils his work.

After a tough declaration in the second take of *Basie English*, Young returns to his most reflective mode for a famous session featuring the relaxed simplicities of the Basie rhythm section. In *Blue Lester* he builds his mood out of long, curiously punctuated phrases, detached and dry. One has never heard this *Ghost of a chance* without marvelling at the way in which the rhythmic tension is maintained at so slow a tempo; and, again, there are expressive differences between takes, heavily-tongued accents in the second contrasting with the smooth ornamentation of the first. The darker spread of tone in the prancing *Indiana* is no new departure, but in *Jump, Lester, jump* he may be prodding after some less subtle gospel. The curiously measured phrases lose a little of the old poetic quality and there are new harsh outbursts.

Soon, Young was to undergo the trauma of his army service. If, as some aver, he emerged from it a 'broken man', there was still a good deal of vivid music to prove tenacity and more. In the late

1940s and early 1950s he gained popularity and commercial success; yet he was in a number of ways, or often sounded to be, a less delicate and discriminating artist than before. No doubt the choice of companions was his own but, with the marked exception of Haynes, the boppers who make up his sextet are hardly worthy supporters or particularly attuned to his aspiration. Sounding fairly independent, Young recovers, in his first entry on *Crazy over J-Z*, a gentleness and delicacy of construction which only the drumming matches for life. In the second take he is not above a little musical sarcasm, it seems — repeating stilted ensemble phrases and illuminating their drabness. The same blues theme is also worked over variously, with reshufflings of riffs and quotations, in *Blues 'n' bells* and *June bug*. Young's singular interpretation of the blues is expressed in various tones of voice, and he is the giant all through. Most worthy of preservation is his remarkable series of improvisations in *Ding dong* (*All of me*, disguised and accelerated) wherein his gifts for expansion and abbreviation, his many-dimensional sense of shape and his instinct for cross-calculation persist hardly diminished.   E.T.

197 Don Byas 1945
Black and Blue (F) BB33003

Don Byas All-Stars: Joe Thomas (tpt); Byas (ten); Johnny Guarnieri (p); Billy Taylor (bs); Cozy Cole (d). New York City, 23 January 1945.
Pennies from Heaven · Should I? · You call it madness · Jamboree jump
Buck Clayton (tpt); Byas (ten); Guarnieri (p); Eddie Safranski (bs); Denzil Best (d). New York City, 27 June 1945
Little white lies · Deep purple · Them there eyes · You came along
Byas (ten); Guarnieri (p, cls[1]); Safranski (bs); J. C. Heard (d). New York City, 3 October 1945.
Once in a while[1] · Avalon · Blue and sentimental · My melancholy baby

Although Byas worked with Dizzy Gillespie on New York's 52nd Street in 1944, he was much more a man of the 1930s than of the 1940s, his style based devotedly upon the romanticism that Coleman Hawkins brought to the tenor saxophone. Only nine months after the final session on this LP he was on his way to Europe with Don Redman's orchestra, and he did not leave that continent until the short forays to New York and Japan just before his death in Amsterdam during 1972. It was an oddly-proportioned career, and not without elements of paradox.

Despite the fact that Byas's harmonic expertise had made him, like Hawkins, one of the first swing players to consort, and to hold his own, with the boppers, the music and musicians on these sessions belong very much to the older tradition. Guarnieri, for instance, proffers a compendium of pre-1940s piano styles, mixing Teddy Wilson's nimble runs with Count Basie's minimalism and explosive single notes, and Fats Waller's two-handed solidity; though an exception occurs in *Them there eyes*, where the model appears to be Lionel Hampton's two-fingered style. Eclecticism of that sort rarely weathers well, yet Guarnieri operates efficiently within the ensembles, and on *You came along* (the title should really be *Out of nowhere*) he achieves a tidy sobriety, wedging his various influences together in a manner that works. The resemblance to Basie is emphasized, especially in *Little white lies*, by Best's frothing hi-hat sound. All three drummers, in fact, keep the rhythm tight, without too many showy asides. Safranski's occasional solos reveal, so far as the variable recording standards allow, a bassist aware of what had been happening to his instrument during the preceding years, even if he lacks Jimmy Blanton's *gravitas* or Oscar Pettiford's audacity.

Reputations in jazz history are often related to when and how often a musician gets into a recording studio. Thomas was among the unlucky ones, although it requires only a brief study of a few of his solos for their qualities to shine through. At first his style seems very simple and direct; yet the more he is listened to the more subtle does his playing appear. His solo in *Jamboree jump*, virtually an updated *Stomping at the Savoy*, shows how much can be achieved by shifting accents and varying tone; this is a doughty example of Thomas's narrow but genuine brand of virtuosity. Clayton was, and is, better-known; he had been, after all, like Byas, a featured musician with Basie's band. True, he starts his solo in *Them there eyes* with a quotation from *Twelfth Street rag*, then goes on to reveal further indebtedness to Louis Armstrong; yet his playing is always recognizably his own, and never more so than when he uses a mute. *Little white lies* is happily reminiscent of Clayton's delicate contributions to the Kansas City Five and Six (**157**).

Few tenor saxophonists could paraphrase a melody as deftly as Byas; few have been able to develop so skilfully a few basic riffs, not repeating but varying: listen to the solo in *Little white lies*. A musician from the Southwest, born in Oklahoma, he belonged roughly within the same tradition as Herschel Evans, who first endowed *Blue and sentimental* (a tune suspiciously like *Can't we talk it over?*, the old Bing Crosby hit) with romantic overtones when he recorded it with Basie (**134**). Nevertheless, Byas relies, more than Evans and far more than Ben Webster, upon ornamentation rather than on tone to make an emotional impact. At the same time he stays alert, phrasing lissomly, never a prisoner of his own arpeggios.   C.F.

198 Stuff Smith 1936
Collectors (Sw) 12-12

Stuff Smith and His Onyx Club Orchestra: Jonah Jones (tpt, vcl[1]); Smith (vln, vcl[2]); Raymond Smith (p); Bobby Bennett (g); Mack Walker (bs); John Washington (d). New York City, 11 February 1936.
I'se a mugging[2] · *I hope Gabriel likes my music*[2] · *I'm putting all my eggs in one basket*[2]

James Sherman (p), Cozy Cole (d) replace Raymond Smith, Washington. New York City, 13 March 1936.
I don't want to make history[2] · *Tain't no use*[2] · *If you'se a viper*[1] · *After you've gone*[2]

Vcl by ensemble[3]. New York City, 12 May 1936.
Robins and roses[2] · *I've got a heavy date*[2,3]

Same personnel and location, 1 July 1936.
It ain't right[2] · *Old Joe's hitting the jug*[2,3] · *Serenade for a wealthy widow*

Same personnel and location, 21 August 1936.
Knock, knock — who's there?[2,3] · *Bye bye, baby*[2,3] · *Here comes the man with the jive*[2,3]

It was possibly a puckish gift for comic invention which turned Hezekiah Leroy Gordon Smith into 'Stuff', for he was one of the most irrepressible of vocal humorists. Yet his fame, which flowered about the time of these recordings, rests properly upon his formidable violin playing — a style with an exciting range of effects and an instrumental voice in which lusty Negroid inflections overcame the temptations of tonal sweetness which other famous jazz fiddlers seem to have found it harder to resist.

After working in Dallas and Buffalo without much recognition, Smith took a sextet into the Onyx Club during 1935. His first popular hit was the two-part *I'se a mugging*, and much of this material is in similar vein. The musical routine varies but subtly — except in *Serenade for a wealthy widow*, a Reginald Foresythe theme and the only performance without singing, which has a more adventurous arrangement, and *Knock, knock — who's there?*, which is nearly all verbal shenanigans. Jones, who played with an earlier Smith group and had returned from McKinney's Cotton Pickers, sings *If you'se a viper*, radically adapting its tune, but the rest of the singing, apart from some raucous choral responses, is by Smith — a lively member of the large Armstrong Debtors Society.

As a trumpeter, Jones shows here skill and feeling, if not yet much originality, and it is usually he who leads the opening choruses with Smith's violin contributing wiry, acrobatic abetment. Jones's brilliant tone in *I've got a heavy date*, pugnacious clauses in *I don't want to make history* and untroubled negotiation of the provocative charleston stop-chords of *Old Joe's hitting the jug* are examples of a variety which, like Smith's own versatility, counters the threat of monotony in the accepted routines. The variety *within* Smith's solos is a marvel of unexpected juxtapositions and cross-beat multiplications, and the savage chordal effects, which are peculiarly his, emerge right at the start of *I hope Gabriel likes my music* and heighten the temperature of several already hot ensemble passages. (Hear the last chorus of *Tain't no use* — or 'juice', as Smith persists in singing.) He can also be subdued and romantic, as in *Robins and roses*, and though his livelier statements show the influence of saxophonists and trumpeters, he is by no means impervious to the glamorous possibilities of string tone. Against the breathless rhythms of *Old Joe* he traces lazily oblique lines of unusual thoughtfulness.

This record is yet another which shows how the best jazz comedy depends upon exceptional musical imagination. Those who have been unfamiliar with the music of a violinist who later strove with little success to regain his popularity, should find here what Smith, in *Knock, knock*, calls 'an Onyx-pected pleasure'. There is spirited rhythm-section accompaniment and the precise, clear, yet unobtrusive work of Cole is greatly to be admired.

(Earlier pressings of this LP did not include *I'se a mugging*.)

E.T.

199 **Red Norvo and His All-Stars**
Philips (E) BBL7077, Epic (A) EE22010

Jimmy Dorsey (clt); Fulton McGrath (p); Dick McDonough (g); Artie Bernstein (bs); Norvo (xylo). New York City, 8 April 1933. `
Knocking on wood · *Hole in the wall*

Benny Goodman (bs clt); McDonough (g); Bernstein (bs); Norvo (mrm). New York City, 21 November 1933.
In a mist · *Dance of the octopus*

Red Norvo and His Swing Septet: Jack Jenney (tbn); Artie Shaw (clt); Charlie Barnet (ten); Teddy Wilson (p); Bobby Johnson (g); Hank Wayland (bs); Bill Gussack (d); Norvo (xylo). New York City, 26 September 1934.
Old-fashioned love · *I surrender, dear*

Same personnel and location, 4 October 1934.
Tomboy · *The night is blue*

Red Norvo and His Swing Octet: Bunny Berigan (tpt); Jenney (tbn); Johnny Mince (clt); Chew Berry (ten); Wilson (p); George van Eps (g); Bernstein (bs); Gene Krupa (d); Norvo (xylo). New York City, 25 January 1935.
Honeysuckle rose · With all my heart and soul · Bughouse · Blues in E flat

Red Norvo and His Orchestra: Bill Hyland, Stew Pletcher, Eddie Myers (tpt); Leo Moran (tbn); Slats Long (clt); Frank Simeone (alt); Herbie Haymer (ten); Joe Liss (p); Dave Barbour (g); Pete Peterson (bs); Maurice Purtill (d); Norvo (xylo); Mildred Bailey (vcl); Eddie Sauter (arr). New York City, 26 August 1936.
A porter's love song to a chambermaid

Sauter (tpt, arr), Al Mastren (tbn), Hank d'Amico (clt) replace Myers, Moran, Long; Charlie Lamphere (alt) added. Chicago, 22 March 1937.
Remember

Mildred Bailey and Her Orchestra: Jimmy Blake, Zeke Zarchey, Barney Zudekoff (tpt); Wes Hein (tbn); d'Amico (clt); Leonard Goldstein, Lamphere (alt); Jerry Jerome (ten); Bill Miller (p); Allen Hanlon (g); Peterson (bs); George Wettling (d); Norvo (xylo); Bailey (vcl); Sauter (arr). New York City, 19 April 1938.
I let a song go out of my heart

Red Norvo and His Orchestra: Jack Owens, Jack Palmer, Zudekoff (tpt); Andy Russo, Al George (tbn); d'Amico (clt); Simeone, Maurice Kogan (alt); George Berg (ten); Miller (p); Hanlon (g); Peterson (bs); Wettling (d); Norvo (xylo); Sauter (arr). New York City, 26 July 1938.
Just you, just me

Much of the above material predates the 52nd Street scene, which is not surprising if we remember that Norvo's musical curiosity was still active when the recordings on **247** were made and at the Comet session with Charlie Parker and Dizzy Gillespie dealt with in this book's companion volume. True, there are elements of novelty ragtime in *Knocking on wood*, but they were part of the xylophone's tradition; and already *Hole in the wall* has a slightly wider range of expression. Serious business starts with *In a mist*, the strange instrumentation of which should be compared with that of Reginald Foresythe's 1935 New York recording session [84]. It is a sophisticated development of the sort of combination earlier used by Venuti and Lang (**67**, etc.), and Norvo displayed a precise aural imagination by here substituting the rounder-toned marimba for the xylophone. Prefiguring Goodman's own sort of chamber jazz, this is an oblique, subtle reading of the Beiderbecke piece, while *Dance of the octopus*, on which the bass clarinet is more active, evokes a gentle, subaqueous world.

In rather extreme contrast with this originality, the Septet items are notable chiefly for soloists nearly all of whom sound as if they are pretending to be someone else. Barnet, with his Mezzrow-like tone, is the worst, but Wilson is far from the delicacy he was soon to show with Goodman's Trio (**158**), Shaw is by no means his immaculate later self, and Jenney plays sub-Teagarden. *I surrender, dear* is the same, except that Wilson surprisingly invokes Jess Stacy rather than Earl Hines. In short, the band had no real character at this stage and probably only Norvo makes statements that he later would have wanted to acknowledge, the best instance being *The night is blue*, in which his playing is full of delicate nuances.

The Octet is better integrated, has a superior personnel and, although the emphasis is still on solos, these are better. *With all my heart* is notable for exultantly elaborate offerings from Berry and the leader, and there is an intriguing piano and xylophone duet on *Honeysuckle rose*. In the E flat piece, Norvo brings off the unlikely feat of playing convincing blues on the xylophone. He is tightly patterned, and logical too, in *Bughouse*, which has excellent lead playing fore and aft from Berigan, reminding us that this piece was recorded in memory of the veteran jazz trumpeter 'Bughouse' Jenkinson who had died the previous year.

Though he played trumpet and mellophone, Sauter's main contribution was to give the big band a strong individuality, a singular texture being evident from the first bar of *A porter's love song*. There is good singing by Miss Bailey, and Norvo's solo receives support which is an enhancement rather than mere accompaniment. The vocalist's and the arranger's responses to Ellington's *I let a song go out of my heart* are naturally of interest and there are some aptly warm, subdued orchestral colours here. There is fine Berg on *Just you, just me*, suggesting he was not given quite the chances elsewhere that he might have been, and Norvo dialogues with an ensemble whose power is restrained to impressive purpose. Sauter's treatment of *Remember* is particularly sensitive and a considerable departure from the conventions of the time. Not just a dressing-up of a popular song or a string of effects, this is conceived as a whole, and the solos of Norvo, Haymer and d'Amico are parts of a larger entity. A decided thrust into the future, *Remember* is cool big band jazz a decade before Gil Evans's work for Claude Thornhill.   M.H.

200 Mildred Bailey: Her Greatest Performances Vol. 1

CBS (E) BPG62098, CBS (A) JC3L-22

Eddie Lang and His Orchestra: Andy Secrest, Charlie Margulis (tpt); Bill Rank (tbn); Izzy Friedman (clt, ten); Bernard Daly, Charles Strickfadden (alt); Henry Whiteman (vln); Hoagy Carmichael (p, arr); Lang (g); Mike Trafficante (bs); George Marsh (d); Mildred Bailey (vcl). New York City, 5 October 1929.
What kind o' man is you?

Mildred Bailey (vcl) acc the Dorsey Brothers' Orchestra: Bunny Berigan
(tpt); Tommy Dorsey (tbn); Jimmy Dorsey (clt); Larry Binyon (ten);
Fulton McGrath (p); Dick McDonough (g); Artie Bernstein (bs); Stan
King (d). New York City, 8 April 1933.
Is that religion? · *Harlem lullaby*

Same personnel and location, 6 June 1933.
There's a cabin in the pines

Same personnel and location, 5 September 1933.
Shouting in that amen corner

Manny Klein (tpt) added. New York City, 17 October 1933.
Give me liberty or give me love

Benny Goodman and His Orchestra: Klein, Margulis (tpt); Sonny
Lee (tbn); Goodman (clt); Coleman Hawkins (ten); Arthur Schutt (p);
McDonough (g); Bernstein (bs); Gene Krupa (d); Bailey (vcl).
New York City, 2 February 1934.
Junk man · *Old Pappy* · *Emaline*

Mildred Bailey and Her Swing Band: Chris Griffin (tpt); Chew Berry
(ten); Teddy Wilson (p); McDonough (g); Bernstein (bs); Eddie Dougherty
(d); Red Norvo (vib[1]); Bailey (vcl). New York City, 20 September 1935.
Someday, sweetheart · *When day is done* [1]

Mildred Bailey and Her Alley Cats: Berigan (tpt); Johnny Hodges (alt);
Wilson (p); Grachan Moncur (bs); Bailey (vcl). New York City,
6 December 1935.
Willow tree · *Honeysuckle rose* · *Squeeze me* · *Down-hearted blues*

Mildred Bailey and Her Orchestra: Ziggy Elman (tpt); Artie Shaw (clt);
Francis Love (ten); Wilson (p); Dave Barbour (g); John Kirby (bs); Cozy
Cole (d); Bailey (vcl). New York City, 9 November 1936.
'Long about midnight

201 Connie Boswell and the Boswell Sisters
Jazum (A) 31

Boswell Sisters (Connie, Helvetia, Martha Boswell) (vcl) acc the Dorsey
Brothers' Orchestra: Berigan (tpt); Tommy Dorsey (tbn); Jimmy Dorsey
(clt); Martha Boswell (p); Lang (g); Bernstein (bs); King (d). New York
City, 9 January 1933.
Mood indigo

Connie Boswell (vcl) acc unidentified studio orchestra. New York City,
10 June 1933.
Under a blanket of blue

Boswell Sisters (vcl) acc the Dorsey Brothers' Orchestra: probably
Manny Klein (tpt); Tommy Dorsey (tbn); Jimmy Dorsey (clt); Martha
Boswell (p); Bernstein (bs); King (d). New York City, 15 June 1933.
Putting it on · *Swanee mammy*

Same personnel and location, 16 June 1933.
The river's taking care of me

Connie Boswell (vcl) acc unidentified studio orchestra. New York City,
14 August 1933.
It's the talk of the town · This time it's love

Connie Boswell (vcl) acc unidentified studio orchestra. New York City,
29 August 1933.
Dinner at eight · Emperor Jones

Boswell Sisters (vcl) acc Manny Weinstock (tpt); Charlie Butterfield
(tbn); Goodman (clt, alt); Chester Hazlett (alt); Harry Hoffman (vln);
Martha Boswell (p); Perry Botkin (g, bj); Dick Cherwin (bs); King (d).
New York City, 11 September 1933.
That's how rhythm was born

Connie Boswell (vcl) acc unidentified studio orchestra. New York City,
4 January 1934.
In other words, we're through

Boswell Sisters (vcl) acc Dorsey Brothers' Orchestra: Berigan, Klein
(tpt); Tommy Dorsey, Chuck Campbell (tbn); Jimmy Dorsey (clt, alt);
Binyon (ten, fl, possibly clt); McGrath or Martha Boswell (p); McDonough
(g); Bernstein (bs); King (d). New York City, 23 March 1934.
You ought to be in pictures · I hate myself

Boswell Sisters (vcl) acc unidentified studio group. New York City,
27 April 1934.
The lonesome road

202 Lee Wiley sings Rodgers and Hart and Harold Arlen

Ember (E) COS829, Monmouth-Evergreen (A) ME6807

Lee Wiley (vcl) acc Joe Bushkin's Orchestra: Max Kaminsky (tpt); Bud
Freeman (ten); Bushkin (p); Artie Shapiro (bs); George Wettling (d);
Brad Gowans (arr). New York City, June 1940.
*Baby's awake now · A little birdie told me so · I've got five
dollars · You took advantage of me*

Lee Wiley (vcl) acc Max Kaminsky's Orchestra: Paul Wetstein (arr)
replaces Gowans; Bushkin also plays cls. New York City, June 1940.
*A ship without a sail · As though you were there · Glad to be
unhappy · Here in my arms*

Lee Wiley (vcl) acc Eddie Condon's Sextet: Billy Butterfield (tpt); Ernie
Caceres (bar); Dave Bowman (p); Condon (g); Bob Haggart (bs); Wettling
(d). New York City, April 1943.
Down with love · Stormy weather
Caceres switches to clt; Butterfield absent. Same date.
Between the devil and the deep blue sea · I've got the world on a string

Lee Wiley (vcl) acc Eddie Condon and His Orchestra: Bobby Hackett
(tpt); Lou McGarity, Vernon Brown, Buddy Morrow (tbn); Caceres (bar);
Bowman (p, cls); Condon (g); Haggart (bs); Wettling (d). New York City,
April 1943.
*Fun to be fooled · You said it · Let's fall in love · Moaning in the
morning*

One of the fallacies to be encountered in jazz circles insists that the further a singer departs from the melody the more original, and better, the music is likely to be. The same belief is often held about instrumental jazz, yet where singers are concerned it seems to take on extra pungency, probably because singers frequently have to cope with banal lyrics. There are, of course, quite a few examples of an extravagant approach producing outstanding jazz: Sarah Vaughan's high-handed, sometimes icily abstract manner, and the witty syllabizing of Leo Watson. Other cases are the bizarreries of Betty Carter and Anita O'Day as well as, on a slightly different level, Billie Holiday's ability to dismantle a song and turn it into something of her own. Most jazz singers, however, have settled for a compromise — the term need not be pejorative — between the aims of the songwriter and their own ingenuity. Lester Young, after all, was happy enough to embellish as well as improvise more drastically, showing how placing and accenting can be every bit as creative as melodic variation. **202** actually revolves round the work of particular songwriters and treats their songs seriously, yet it also contains some of Lee Wiley's finest recorded performances. And if the other two LPs present a few songs that might be described as less than admirable, at least the singers still seem intent upon making every word count.

During the interwar years, Mildred Bailey, Connie Boswell and Lee Wiley were regarded as the foremost — indeed, practically the only — white girls singing jazz. That statement needs some qualifying, for both Miss Bailey and Miss Wiley were partly of American Indian extraction, while a rumour constantly circulated among British jazz buffs to the effect that Miss Boswell had what might be called a Creole tinge. She and her two sisters formed the most popular close-harmony group of the 1930s. Both Miss Wiley and Miss Bailey, however, worked with a succession of big bands.

When *What kind o' man is you?* (which also appears on **66**) was recorded, Miss Bailey was singing with Paul Whiteman's orchestra, which supplied all the musicians — except Carmichael — who perform under Lang's leadership. Her style was already shaping up, that small, sweet voice becoming pertly individual; yet there is a surprising lack of rapport between musicians and singer, a defect that is absent from almost every track that follows. Ironically enough for a singer noted for her friendship with and appreciation of many black performers, Mildred Bailey often recorded songs that celebrated the conjectured delights of life in the South — as glimpsed from the purlieus of Tin Pan

Alley. Typical of that genre is *There's a cabin in the pines*, while the fervour of black gospel meetings supplies the content of the lyrics of *Shouting in that amen corner* and *Is that religion?* — which latter contains some typically boisterous trumpet playing from Berigan. Yet far from seeming offensive, these songs take on, as it were, a period camouflage, even a kind of innocence. Many were composed for cabaret shows at the Cotton Club, Connie's Inn and other clubs featuring black performers, who also sang the songs with cheerful insouciance. So *Harlem lullaby* and the less specific *'Long about midnight* are reminiscent of many of the numbers that Ethel Waters (**95**) used to sing.

Although the accompaniments of the earlier tracks are the work of groups led by the Dorsey brothers, the jazz playing is relatively subdued. Much jauntier are the performances (which also appear on **117**) by Goodman's pick-up group, especially Hawkins's unashamedly decorative tenor saxophone solos. *Emaline* has notably relaxed singing by Miss Bailey, as well as a trombone chorus in which Lee sounds uncommonly like Jack Teagarden. (Both men had worked, though at different times, in Texas with the elusive Peck Kelley.) The session of September 1934 provides an example of how contiguous recordings can differ sharply in quality. *When day is done* is taken at an uncomfortable tempo, so far as the singer is concerned, for she rushes through the final chorus — yet *Someday, sweetheart* displays all the virtues of Mildred Bailey's style; it also contains one of Wilson's most elegant solos, beautifully proportioned. Equally distinguished, although indifferently recorded, are the tracks with the Alley Cats. *Willow tree* presents Berigan at his finest, simultaneously truculent and tender; and at least two of these pieces demonstrate Miss Bailey's ability to sing the blues. She was familiar with Bessie Smith's work, of course, yet instead of copying that singer's rich but rough authority she approaches a blues more winsomely, understating, keeping emotion slightly at a distance.

Although neither the Boswell Sisters nor Connie Boswell herself recorded all that many blues, what might be dubbed a blues ambience suffused nearly all their music. It is particularly evident in the slowish solo passages that Connie Boswell interpolates in many of the trio performances. All three sisters grew up in New Orleans, all played instruments in addition to singing. Connie (who subsequently changed the spelling to 'Connee') was born *c.* 1912 and contracted polio as a child; all her singing in public was done from a wheelchair. The cornettist Emmett Hardy, an even more elusive figure in jazz history than Peck Kelley, encouraged the girls' early attempts at close-harmony singing. Their mature style, which was perfectly voiced, very tight, but with the jazz musician's instinct for moving loosely round the beat, has never been surpassed; the Andrews Sisters and their many imitators now sound dated and synthetic by comparison. All this becomes apparent from the five above tracks by the Boswell Sisters, including a version of *Mood indigo* which underlines their familiarity with blues. But it is Connie Boswell who constantly occupies the foreground, imposing her stamp upon the performances, even bestowing a kind of validity on *Swanee mammy*, another of those songwriters' tributes to a paradisal South.

Both Tommy and Jimmy Dorsey make fleeting appearances on the Sisters' records, sounding amiable but rarely adventurous. However, Berigan takes a spirited solo in *I hate myself* and Goodman is briefly yet unmistakably himself in *That's how rhythm was born*. It is maybe paradoxical, although commercially understandable, that Connie Boswell's own sessions employed fewer jazz musicians. Nor were the tunes always the best. The record company probably saw her in the role of a 'torch singer', a period phrase most handily exemplified by the wistful, frustrated manner and repertoire of a performer such as Ruth Etting. *It's the talk of the town* is a song that fits the image exactly, yet before the end is reached Miss Boswell has embarked upon a rhythmic style of singing that was to reappear only a few years later in the work of Ella Fitzgerald. Another example of Connie Boswell's influence upon the very young Ella Fitzgerald (who officially was born in 1918 though Norman Granz thinks 1920 is nearer the truth) can be heard in *Emperor Jones*, a popular song that cashed in on the Broadway success of Eugene O'Neil's play (in which Paul Robeson took the lead). Quite apart from the singing, the orchestration here is interesting, using similar patterns and textures to those which Don Redman was devising for his band at that time.

Perhaps Lee Wiley (born in 1915) never possessed quite the same intensity of blues feeling as Mildred Bailey or Connie Boswell (though she does remarkably well in *Steamboat, Tennessee* on **178**). Her approach is, to fall back on an overworked adjective, cool, suggesting languor, even a nonchalance that comes close to seeming erotic; she might be called the jazz equivalent to Louise Brooks. She also wrote the lyrics to several songs, including *Got the South in my soul* and *Any time, any day, anywhere*, a fact that might go some way to explain why she became the first singer to record collections of the work of outstanding American songwriters. The earliest, recorded in November 1939, dealt with George Gershwin (Monmouth-Evergreen (a) ME7034, Halcyon (E) HAL6). Next came the sessions of June 1940 devoted to songs from Richard Rodgers's finest period, when he was in partnership with Lorenz Hart. Most of these contrive to be wry as well as melodic, a stance which makes them much better suited to jazz singers than most of his later output. The exquisite aloofness of Miss Wiley's singing is accentuated by the accompaniment, constantly jostling as Chicago-style jazz was wont to do. *You took advantage of me*, always one of Freeman's preferred numbers, presents the tenor saxophonist at his most staccato and audacious. Lee Wiley's liveliest performance, demonstrating her rhythmic skills, is of *I've got five dollars*, but perhaps the most sheerly satisfying music occurs in *A ship without a sail*, the voice concurring with the mood and quality of the song, with Kaminsky and Freeman noodling intelligently in the background.

The remaining pieces on **202** are all by Harold Arlen, whose songs have always been found congenial by jazz musicians; he did, after all, write many numbers for Cotton Club revues. *Let's fall in love* is taken at a more leisurely pace than usual, with Hackett sounding laconic and one of the trombonists, probably McGarity, taking a solo. There is, though, a disconcerting blandness about the overall context. Far more successful was Miss Wiley's collaboration with an Eddie Condon sextet (and quintet). Caceres, always undervalued as a clarinettist, plays with characteristic aplomb, seeming especially resourceful in *I've got the world on a string*.   C.F.

Ella Fitzgerald
203 Ella and Ellis
MCA (E) MCL1775, MCA (A) 215 and Decca (A) DL8068
Ella Fitzgerald (vcl); Ellis Larkins (p). New York City,
11 September 1950.
Looking for a boy · My one and only · How long has this been going on? · I've got a crush on you
Same personnel and location, 12 September 1950.
But not for me · Soon · Someone to watch over me · Maybe
Same personnel and location, 29 March 1954.
I'm glad there is you · Baby, what more can I do? · What is there to say? · Making whoopee · Until the real thing comes along · People will say we're in love

Same personnel and location, 30 March 1954.
Please be kind · *Imagination* · *My heart belongs to daddy* · *You leave me breathless* · *Nice work if you can get it* · *Stardust*

Ella Fitzgerald's voice, which was at its best at the time of these recordings, possessed a musical beauty rare among jazz singers, and her partnership with Larkins was more than merely apt. He was that extreme rarity in jazz, a great accompanist of the voice, apparently without independent ambitions of his own, though he did record some fine duets with the trumpeter Ruby Braff in 1955. Not much of a jazz soloist, as **194** confirms, his interludes, for example on *Making whoopee* and *My one and only*, nonetheless add something positive to these performances. Larkins stomps elegantly in *Nice work* and *Looking for a boy*, yet the main point is his multi-directional flexibility, which enables him to respond instantly to even the smallest of this imaginatively resourceful singer's nuances of rhythm, tonal shading, verbal stress. His figurations have an unobtrusive yet very considerable variety, and, in cases like *Stardust*, where Miss Fitzgerald is particularly adventurous, a complete, though rarely obvious, appropriateness that speaks of musical instincts as strong as the singer's own: the complementary currents in these interpretations run deeper than has usually been acknowledged.

The voice is excellently recorded, the piano less so, but it is hard to imagine more telling performances of between-the-wars popular songs than the best of these, above all of Gershwin's *My one and only*, *But not for me* and *How long has this been going on?* There is a considerable emphasis on the songs themselves rather than on the liberties of jazz improvisation — as Henry Pleasants has said, Miss Fitzgerald always had a sound instinct for knowing what not to do [85] — but there are very many subtle improvements to the written phrases, as at the very beginning of *I'm glad there is you*. As important is that the self-denying medium of voice and piano, which is remote from the palm court strings and the empty virtuosity of scat singing that characterise so many of this artist's other recordings, leads to a concentration on real musical expression. *Imagination* embodies an introspection which may seem untypical, yet related to this are the tenderness of *Someone to watch over me*, the wistfulness of *How long has this been going on?*

Such readings imply that Miss Fitzgerald had potentialities which her exceedingly active career did not allow to be properly developed, though it has been suggested that she learnt something about the blues from singers like those discussed under **200–202**, particularly Connie Boswell. In the event, her remarkably flexible voice led her to concentrate on phrasing that was fresh yet immaculate, fluent but always personal, informed by keen rhythmic and harmonic senses. She is well suited to sinuous melodies like that of Jimmy Dorsey's *I'm glad there is you*, and although Vernon Duke's *What is there to say?* is noted chiefly for its rhyming of 'wedlock' with 'deadlock', of greater moment is that the crotchet triplets which first appear in bars 5–6 of the chorus are here interpreted in a slightly different way each time. The singer takes full advantage of such features as the contrast between the smoothness of the first four bars of the *Nice work* chorus and the more demonstrative measures which follow — as does Larkins of Gershwin's striking harmonization of the main phrase of *How long has this been going on?* The only real weakness is a lack of humour. Miss Fitzgerald does not put over the cynicism of *Making whoopee* at all well, and at one point gets the words obviously wrong — 'well, can't you guess?' becoming 'well, you can't confess'. Also, she appears to imagine that the words of *My heart belongs to daddy* mean what they say.

The British record listed above brings together the contents of two complete and hitherto independent issues. The eight Gershwin songs from 1950 formed Miss Fitzgerald's first (ten-inch) LP, *Ella Sings Gershwin*, while the dozen 1954 items made up an LP called *Ella*. The American catalogue numbers refer to these two records in turn.   M.H.

204 **Billie Holiday: the Golden Years Vol.1**
CBS (E) BPG62037/9 (3 LPs), CBS (A) C3L-21 (3 LPs)

Benny Goodman and His Orchestra: Charlie Teagarden, Shirley Clay (tpt); Jack Teagarden (tbn); Goodman (clt); Art Karle (ten); Joe Sullivan (p); Dick McDonough (g); Artie Bernstein (bs); Gene Krupa (d); Arthur Schutt (arr); Billie Holiday (vcl). New York City, 27 November 1933.
Your mother's son-in-law

Dean Kincaide (arr) replaces Schutt. New York City, 18 December 1933.
Riffing the scotch

Billie Holiday (vcl) acc Teddy Wilson and His Orchestra: Jonah Jones (tpt); Harry Carney (clt, bar); Johnny Hodges (alt); Wilson (p); Lawrence Lucie (g); John Kirby (bs); Cozy Cole (d). New York City, 30 June 1936.
These foolish things

Billie Holiday and Her Orchestra: Bunny Berigan (tpt), Artie Shaw (clt), Joe Bushkin (p), McDonough (g), Pete Peterson (bs) replace Jones, Hodges, Wilson, Lucie, Kirby; Carney absent. New York City, 10 July 1936.
Did I remember? · *No regrets*

Irving Fazola (clt), Clyde Hart (p), Bernstein (bs) replace Shaw, Bushkin, Peterson. New York City, 29 September 1936.
A fine romance

Billie Holiday (vcl) acc Teddy Wilson and His Orchestra: Irving Randolph (tpt); Vido Musso (clt); Ben Webster (ten); Wilson (p); Allen Reuss (g); Kirby (bs); Cole (d). New York City, 21 October 1936.
Easy to love · The way you look tonight

Jones (tpt), Goodman (clt) replace Randolph, Musso. New York City, 19 November 1936.
Pennies from Heaven · That's life, I guess · I can't give you anything but love

Buck Clayton (tpt), Lester Young (ten), Freddy Greene (g), Walter Page (bs), Jo Jones (d) replace Jonah Jones, Webster, Reuss, Kirby, Cole. New York City, 25 January 1937.
This year's kisses · Why was I born?

Henry Allen (tpt), Cecil Scott (clt, alt, ten), Prince Robinson (ten), Jimmy McLin (g), Kirby (bs), Cole (d) replace Clayton, Goodman, Young, Greene, Page, Jones. New York City, 18 February 1937.
The mood I'm in

Billie Holiday (vcl) acc Teddy Wilson and His Orchestra: Clayton (tpt); Buster Bailey (clt); Young (ten); Wilson (p); Greene (g); Page (bs); Jones (d). New York City, 1 June 1937.
I'll never be the same

Billie Holiday and Her Orchestra: same personnel except that Ed Hall (clt), Jimmy Sherman (p) replace Bailey, Wilson. New York City, 15 June 1937.
Without your love

Count Basie and His Orchestra: Ed Lewis, Bobby Moore, Clayton (tpt); Dan Minor, George Hunt (tbn); Young (clt, ten); Earle Warren (alt); Jack Washington (alt, bar); Herschel Evans (ten); Basie (p); Greene (g); Page (bs); Jones (d); Holiday (vcl). Savoy Ballroom, New York City, 30 June 1937.
Swing, brother, swing! · They can't take that away from me

Billie Holiday and Her Orchestra: Clayton (tpt); Bailey (clt); Young (ten); Claude Thornhill (p); Greene (g); Page (bs); Jones (d); Holiday (vcl). New York City, 13 September 1937.
Getting some fun out of life · Travelling all alone

Count Basie and His Orchestra: same personnel as for 30 June 1937 except that Bobby Hicks (tpt), Benny Morton (tbn) replace Moore, Hunt; Eddie Durham (tbn, g) added. Meadowbrook, Cedar Grove, NJ, 3 November 1937.
I can't get started

Billie Holiday (vcl) acc Teddy Wilson and his Orchestra: Clayton (tpt); Morton (tbn); Young (ten); Wilson (p); Greene (g); Page (bs); Jones (d). New York City, 6 January 1938.
When you're smiling · If dreams come true

Billie Holiday and Her Orchestra: same personnel and location,
12 January 1938. ˙

*Back in your own backyard · On the sentimental side · When a woman
loves a man*

Charlie Shavers (tpt); Bailey (clt); Babe Russin (ten); Thornhill (p);
Kirby (bs); Cole (d); Holiday (vcl). New York City, 11 May 1938.

You go to my head

Clayton (tpt); Dickie Wells (tbn); Young (clt, ten); Margaret 'Countess'
Johnson (p); Greene (g); Page (bs); Jones (d); Holiday (vcl).
New York City, 15 September 1938.

The very thought of you

Charlie Shavers (tpt); Tyree Glenn (tbn); Chew Berry (ten); Sonny White
(p); Al Casey (g); John Williams (bs); Cole (d); Holiday (vcl). New York
City, 20 January 1939.

That's all I ask of you · Dream of life

'Hot Lips' Page (tpt); Tab Smith (sop, alt); Kenneth Hollon, Stanley
Payne (ten); Kenny Kersey (p); McLin (g); Williams (bs); Eddie
Dougherty (d); Holiday (vcl). New York City 21 March 1939.

Long gone blues

Shavers (tpt), White (p), Bernard Addison (g) replace Page, Kersey,
McLin. New York City, 5 July 1939.

Some other spring · Them there eyes

Clayton, Harry Edison (tpt); Warren (alt); Washington (alt, bar); Young
(ten); Joe Sullivan (p); Greene (g); Walter Page (bs); Jones (d); Holiday
(vcl). New York City, 13 December 1939.

The man I love

Roy Eldridge (tpt); Jimmy Powell, Carl Frye (alt); Kermit Scott (ten);
White (p); Lucie (g); Williams (bs); Doc West (d); Holiday (vcl). New
York City, 29 February 1940.

Ghost of yesterday · Body and soul

Roy Eldridge (tpt); Billy Bowen, Joe Eldridge (alt); Scott, Young (ten);
Wilson (p); Greene (g); Page (bs); J. C. Heard (d); Holiday (vcl).
New York City, 7 June 1940.

*I'm pulling through · Tell me more · Laughing at life · Time on
my hands*

Billie Holiday (vcl) acc Eddie Heywood and His Orchestra: Shad Collins (d);
(tpt); Eddie Barefield, Leslie Johnakins (alt); Young (ten); Heywood (p);
John Collins (g); Ted Sturgis (bs); Kenny Clarke (d). New York City,
21 March 1941.

Georgia on my mind · Romance in the dark · All of me

Eldridge (tpt); Jimmy Powell, Ernie Powell (alt); Lester Boone (ten);
Heywood (p); Paul Chapman (g); Grachan Moncur (bs); Herbert Cowans
(d); Holiday (vcl). New York City, 9 May 1941.

God bless the child · Am I blue?

Billie Holiday (vcl) acc Teddy Wilson and His Orchestra: Emmett Berry
(tpt); Jimmy Hamilton (clt, ten); Hymie Schertzer (alt); Russin (ten);
Wilson (p); Casey (g); Williams (bs); Heard (d). New York City,
7 August 1941.
I cover the waterfront · *Love me or leave me* · *Gloomy Sunday*

There is no more poignant instance of the jazz dilemma than the
singing of Billie Holiday as preserved here. The dilemma resides
in a conjunction of the ephemeral and the enduring, and is
to be discerned in every jazz performance of significance. The
ephemerality results partly from the weakness and modishness of
a good deal of the basic material chosen for transformation, partly
from the spontaneous manner of the transformation itself. The
enduring quality, retrieved by the ever-blessed mechanical memory of sound-recording, is the depth of intellectual and emotional
truth achieved by creative spirits with little self-conscious pretension to the thrones of Art.

The recordings which assure Miss Holiday's renown find jazz
at its apparently most insouciant, but elements of pathos emerge
in her voice, even in the first records made in 1933 with
Goodman. *Your mother's son-in-law* is the singing of a competent
band vocalist, little more. It is in the unlikely context of *Riffing
the scotch* that her claim to have heeded Bessie Smith receives its
first glancing confirmation in the blues irony of several musical
phrases. Already this rootless teenager's expression augurs the
future style of the greatest singer whom jazz has so far produced.
Already her jazz sense is equal to the challenge of companions
like Goodman and the Teagarden brothers. But it is in the
sessions with groups led by Wilson and with others of similar
character, recorded after the lapse of a couple of years or so, that
her real genius is revealed, suddenly complete in all its essential
qualities. The forty-six items from the 1936–41 period in this first
volume are almost uniformly delightful, and the singer has
consistently good, and often outstanding, support from a galaxy of
celebrated jazzmen. Many of the songs chosen bear out the
remark made above about trivial material, but some are made of
better stuff. Not a few of the wispier ones have undeserved
approval still, simply because they remain associated with this
singer.

The skill in phrasing that was to become characteristic is clear
in *These foolish things* and her mode is aptly served by Hodges's
obbligato. There is respect for the original melody, but also that
instinct to reshape that was soon to irritate the proprietors of the
songs she sang. Though the reshaping sounds spontaneous, there
is, at this stage, sufficient repetition to suggest a degree of

forethought. *Did I remember?* and *No regrets* have a remarkably mature authority and some toughness of delivery. There is a touch of theatre here, too, which is also evident in the zestful humour of *A fine romance*, and the unusually deep contralto delivery of *Easy to love* and *The way you look tonight. Pennies from Heaven* shows her rather curious habit of altering the first few bars of a tune and then returning to the melody, almost as if the challenge of improvisation could not be sustained. But even when she sings fairly straight, as in *That's life, I guess*, there is a constant information of feeling — resignation, petulance, sarcasm, amusement and so on, which has its effect upon tone and cadence. And the ways in which emotion expresses itself musically have obvious relation to the blues, and to the styles of musicians to whom she had listened or who happened to be playing alongside her. In *This year's kisses*, where she is wonderfully aided by Young, she shows how much she was learning from his dry and oblique approach. Yet her art differed from the instrumental in a number of ways, and this difference has everything to do with the fact that she was, in the last analysis, essentially a singer — however much she may have wanted, by her own claim, to sound like a saxophone or a trumpet. She frequently drew out whatever drama there might be in the lyrics she used and the clarity of her diction seldom lapses. One wonders, on listening to *The mood I'm in*, as she responds to Allen's peremptory flourishes, how much her public presentation depended upon the use of facial and bodily gesture. That she could wed all of that to a genuine gift for jazz improvisation is shown again in the superbly-managed variation upon *I'll never be the same*, through which Young threads his indolent phrases. Similarly, the tension of the partnership between voice and tenor saxophone in *Without your love* could hardly have been sustained without considerable dramatic flair.

Swing, brother, swing! and *They can't take that away from me* are well-recorded airchecks from the brief and awkward period during which Miss Holiday sang with the Basie band, as is the slightly later *I can't get started*. (These recordings were preserved by John Hammond.) The power and immediacy of the singing is well suited to the context, but there are hints, in the subtleness of some of the phrasing, as to why she preferred the backing of smaller groups. Somewhat later, she was featured with Artie Shaw's orchestra (see **146**) too, but there was a growing urge to develop her talents as a solo entertainer which made her impatient of any role as a featured vocalist.

As she sings again with her favourites, Young and Clayton, the effect of their lines can certainly be heard in hers, but once more the purely vocal spirit ascends as she hits the words precisely in *Getting some fun out of life*, throws away her airy questions in *Travelling all alone*, measures syllabic sustenance to the long phrases of *If dreams come true* and to the rapt *legato* of *Back in your own backyard*. Her mixture of haunted innocence and brazen challenge gives variety to *You go to my head*, certainly one of the better themes, and her 'city accent' is peculiarly effective in *The very thought of you*, which has some of Young's rare and gentle clarinet playing. Confidentiality and fine registral ease mark *Dream of life* and are brought to bear upon *Long gone blues* with an eccentric sophistication which does not, for all its singularity, make too unlikely the comparison of the latter with such Bessie Smith plaints as *Reckless blues* (**94**). These are also the very special qualities which make *Some other spring*, in which a very restrained accompaniment gives an illusion of strength to her woefulness, such a fine piece of music. Some of the tension goes out of her delivery in *Body and soul*, and there are verbal augmentations here which sound a little contrived; but after Eldridge's sensitive muted solo she recovers well, and ends with the kind of mock *rallentando* which she was to favour increasingly and which was a logical development of the laggard relation to the beat that characterized her singing almost from the start of her career. She also has good support from Eldridge in *Ghost of yesterday*, *I'm pulling through*, *Laughing at life*, *Tell me more* and *Time on my hands*, all of them songs which permit her to run the gamut of her effects. Yet she attains, especially in the last two, to a detached simplicity, sounding like the distillation of a score of songs sung many times before.

In some of the later sessions she does not receive the best of help from her accompanists, though Young appears from time to time to relieve the situation. Heywood's playing in *Georgia on my mind* has little interior wit, and the arranger does not really work with the singer on *Romance in the dark* or *All of me*. In such circumstances, and despite a marvellous chorus from Young in the latter, Miss Holiday sounds committed chiefly to her own declaration. The 'lost soul' cadences of her own *God bless the child* are nicely countered by Eldridge's incisiveness. In *Am I blue?* the voice's self-pity, even if contrived, threatens for a moment to overthrow art. Then in *I cover the waterfront* and *Love me or leave me*, in each of which she includes the song's verse, and especially in the portentous *Gloomy Sunday*, there emerges a tendency to indulge in voice production for its own sake and to choose themes which are self-consciously dramatic. Nevertheless, this singer, who had been so ready to receive and transmute gifts from instrumental jazz, was to go on being an inspiration in turn to a host of musicians.

It is not unusual for great art to come from the longings and resentments of personal insecurity, but in the case of Billie Holiday what Walter Pater called 'the flowering of the Aloe' — the spring of beauty in harshness — seems even more of a wonder. Her physical and mental tragedy is now well known, and it had grim years yet to run. If there was an allied musical decline, it may be to some extent due to her becoming ill-content to linger in those places where the alchemy of co-operative jazz made gold out of dross. Her admirers will be all the more grateful for the many recordings in which her unrepeatable mixture of joy and disquiet made passing jingles the basis of lasting and deeply affecting music.   E.T.

205 Billie Holiday: the Golden Years Vol. 2

CBS (E) BPG62814/6 (3 LPs), CBS (A) 66301 (3 LPs)

Billie Holiday (vcl) acc Teddy Wilson and His Orchestra: Roy Eldridge (tpt); Ben Webster (ten); Wilson (p); John Trueheart (g); John Kirby (bs); Cozy Cole (d). New York City, 2 July 1935.
A sunbonnet blue

Eldridge (tpt); Cecil Scott (clt); Hilton Jefferson (alt); Webster (ten); Wilson (p); Lawrence Lucie (g); Kirby (bs); Cole (d); Holiday (vcl).
New York City, 31 July 1935.
I'm painting the town red · What a night, what a moon, what a girl · It's too hot for words

Dick Clark (tpt); Tom Macey (clt); Johnny Hodges (alt); Wilson (p); Dave Barbour (g); Grachan Moncur (bs); Cole (d); Holiday (vcl).
New York City, 3 December 1935.
You let me down

Jonah Jones (tpt); Harry Carney (clt, bar); Hodges (alt); Wilson (p); Lucie (g); Kirby (bs); Cole (d); Holiday (vcl). New York City, 30 June 1936.
It's like reaching for the moon

Billie Holiday and Her Orchestra: Jones (tpt); Edgar Sampson (clt, alt); Webster (ten); Wilson (p); Allen Reuss (g); Kirby (bs); Cole (d); Holiday (vcl). New York City, 12 January 1937.
One never knows, does one? · I've got my love to keep me warm

Billie Holiday (vcl) acc Teddy Wilson and His Orchestra: Henry Allen (tpt); Scott (clt, alt, ten); Prince Robinson (ten); Wilson (p); Jimmy McLin (g); Kirby (bs); Cole (d).
You showed me the way · Sentimental and melancholy · My last affair

Cootie Williams (tpt); Carney (clt, bar); Hodges (alt); Wilson (p); Reuss (g); Kirby (bs); Cole (d); Holiday (vcl). New York City, 31 March 1937.
Carelessly · How could you? · Moaning low

Billie Holiday and Her Orchestra: Eddie Tompkins (tpt); Buster Bailey (clt); Joe Thomas (ten); Wilson (p); Carmen Mastren (g); Kirby (bs); Alphonse Steel (d); Holiday (vcl). New York City, 1 April 1937.
Where is the sun? · Let's call the whole thing off

Billie Holiday (vcl) acc Teddy Wilson and His Orchestra: Buck Clayton (tpt); Bailey (clt); Hodges (alt); Lester Young (ten); Wilson (p); Reuss (g); Artie Bernstein (bs); Cole (d). New York City, 11 May 1937.
Sun showers · I'll get by · Mean to me

Billie Holiday and Her Orchestra: Clayton (tpt); Bailey (clt); Young (ten); Claude Thornhill (p); Freddy Greene (g); Walter Page (bs); Jo Jones (d); Holliday (vcl). New York City, 13 September 1937.
He's funny that way

Billie Holiday (vcl) acc Teddy Wilson and His Orchestra: Clayton (tpt); Robinson (clt); Vido Musso (ten); Wilson (p); Reuss (g); Page (bs); Cole (d). New York City, 1 November 1937.
Nice work if you can get it · My man · Can't help lovin' dat man

Clayton (tpt); Benny Morton (tbn); Young (ten); Wilson (p); Greene (g); Page (bs); Jones (d); Holiday (vcl). New York City, 6 January 1938.
My first impression of you · I can't believe that you're in love with me

Billie Holiday and Her Orchestra: same personnel and location, 12 January 1938.
Now they call it swing

Charlie Shavers (tpt); Bailey (clt); Babe Russin (ten); Thornhill (p); Kirby (bs); Cole (d); Holiday (vcl). New York City, 11 May 1938.
If I were you

Unidentified g added. New York City, 23 June 1938.
I'm gonna lock my heart and throw away the key

Clayton (tpt); Dickie Wells (tbn); Young (clt, ten); Margaret 'Countess' Johnson (p); Greene (g); Page (bs); Jones (d); Holiday (vcl). New York City, 15 September 1938.
I've got a date with a dream · You can't be mine

Billie Holiday (vcl) acc Teddy Wilson and His Orchestra: Harry James (tpt); Morton (tbn); Benny Carter, Sampson (alt); Herschel Evans, Young (ten); Wilson (p); Al Casey (g); Page (bs); Jones (d). New York City, 9 November 1938.
Say it with a kiss · They say

Eldridge (tpt); Ernie Powell (clt, ten); Carter (alt); Wilson (p); Danny Barker (g); Milt Hinton (bs); Cole (d); Holiday (vcl). New York City, 30 January 1939.
More than you know · Sugar

Billie Holiday and Her Orchestra: 'Hot Lips' Page (tpt); Tab Smith (sop, alt); Kenneth Hollon, Stanley Payne (ten); Kenny Kersey (p); McLin (g); John Williams (bs); Eddie Dougherty (d); Holiday (vcl). New York City, 21 March 1939.
Why did I always depend on you?

Clayton, Harry Edison (tpt); Earle Warren (alt); Jack Washington (alt, bar); Young (ten); Joe Sullivan (p); Greene (g); Page (bs); Jones (d); Holiday (vcl). New York City, 13 December 1939.
Night and day · You're a lucky guy

Eldridge (tpt); Jimmy Powell, Carl Frye (alt); Kermit Scott (ten); Sonny White (p); Lucie (g); Williams (bs); Doc West (d); Holiday (vcl). New York City, 29 February 1940.
Falling in love again

Eldridge (tpt); Don Redman, George Auld (alt); Don Byas, Jimmy Hamilton (ten); Wilson (p); John Collins (g); Al Hall (bs); Kenny Clarke (d); Holiday (vcl). New York City, 12 September 1940.
I'm all for you · I hear music · It's the same old story · Practice makes perfect

Billie Holiday (vcl) acc Benny Carter and His All-Star Orchestra: Bill Coleman (tpt); Morton (tbn); Carter (clt, alt); Auld (ten); White (p); Ulysses Livingston (g); Wilson Myers (bs); Yank Porter (d). New York City, 15 October 1940.
St Louis blues

Billie Holiday (vcl) acc Eddie Heywood and His Orchestra: Shad Collins (tpt); Eddie Barefield, Leslie Johnakins (alt); Young (ten); Heywood (p); John Collins (g); Ted Sturgis (bs); Clarke (d). New York City, 21 March 1941.
Let's do it

Eldridge (tpt); Jimmy Powell, Ernie Powell (alt); Lester Boone (ten); Heywood (p); Paul Chapman (g); Moncur (bs); Herbert Cowans (d); Holiday (vcl). New York City, 9 May 1941.
I'm in a low-down groove · Solitude

Billie Holiday and Her Orchestra: Emmett Berry (tpt); Hamilton (clt, ten); Hymie Schertzer (alt); Russin (ten); Wilson (p); Casey (g); Williams (bs); J. C. Heard (d); Holiday (vcl). New York City, 10 February 1942.
Mandy is two · It's a sin to tell a lie

Because jazz is such an intimate art form, revolving around the activities of individual performers, occasional recordings have caught an instrumentalist or singer at a moment of personal tragedy or crisis, turning the listener into an involuntary *voyeur*. Charlie Parker's 1946 version of *Loverman* (Spotlite (E) 101) is just such a performance. So are many of the recordings that Billie Holiday made during the years leading up to her death in 1959, when her voice had become frayed, almost a ghost of its former self, and even her sense of pitch had grown unreliable. What she never lost, though, was her instinct for phrasing, her ability to enact a kind of lyrical drama. Those recordings have, too, the capacity for self-revelation — it might almost be dubbed *chanson-verité* — that was also present in the work of Edith Piaf, a singer who, like Miss Holiday, could both transform popular material and establish a bond, often a bond of disenchantment, with her audiences. Yet fascinating and, for some of us, horrifying as those later recordings could be, the real evidence for Billie Holiday's status as the greatest of jazz singers is provided by performances such as those in this album and in **204**.

The ill-informed sometimes call her a blues singer, an appellation actually encouraged by the title she gave to her autobiography. Yet no more than a couple of blues (*Long gone* and, in a much looser sense, *Riffing the scotch*) can be found on **204**, while out of the forty-eight titles presented here only *St Louis blues* falls within that category. That Miss Holiday should have been inspired, at least in part, by Bessie Smith, however, is perfectly compatible with that state of affairs, provided one takes into account the circumstances prevailing when she launched upon her career. A decade earlier, Ethel Waters (**95**) had already moved from blues to Broadway and Tin Pan Alley songs and, at the same time, became popular with white audiences, in Europe as well as America. Similarly, much of Billie Holiday's singing was done in night clubs — cosmopolitan, ostensibly sophisticated — rather than the vaudeville theatres where Bessie Smith had established her special rapport with working-class Negro audiences. Yet one of Miss Holiday's achievements was the way she conveyed the emotional climate of the blues through contemporary popular songs, an accomplishment all the more remarkable in view of the banality of many of their lyrics. It is true to say that for Bessie Smith a kind of poetry — often rough and jocose, yet profound as well — already existed in the blues she sang, while Billie Holiday had to create the equivalent by herself. This she did, stressing a syllable, lingering over a cadence, virtually translating a cardboard world into flesh and blood.

Not everything she put on record was a masterpiece. There are slightly fewer masterpieces here than in **204**. Yet all the performances are unmistakably the work of a musician who reshaped her material as drastically as anyone in jazz. The American critic Glenn Coulter has provided a percipient analysis of how she went about this. Not only was there the imposition of a modal feeling and a restructuring of the melody, but what Coulter calls 'incessant modifications of the pulse'; it meant that her songs took on 'a dramatic value not guessed at before'[86]. Yet the extreme fashion in which she would strip a melody down to just a few notes within a narrow compass could be deceiving, particularly as many of the songs are now remembered only because she recorded them. To hear a contemporaneous version by a commercial singer or dance band is often to realize the extent to which she took a song over. *One never knows, does one?*, for instance, was composed by Mack Gordon and Harry Revel for the 1936 film *Stowaway*. Yet today it exists only as a superb example of Miss Holiday's *gravitas*, of the sobriety, even philosophical dignity, she could coax from — if you concentrate merely upon the words — a very run-of-the-mill lyric.

Not that she did this from the very beginning. *A sunbonnet blue* is memorable more for a burst from Eldridge's trumpet than because of the singing. She performs buoyantly enough in *What a night*, yet generally speaking had not yet learnt how to cope with fastish tempos. Once again, Eldridge, sounding like Armstrong in *I'm painting the town red*, provides the liveliest music. *You let me down*, its ambience decidedly that of the torch song, allows her to operate on her own terms. Indeed, this is a fine example of her early style, with Hodges contributing one of his most effervescent solos. He is more restrained on *It's like reaching for the moon*, an indifferent song that Billie Holiday fails to rescue, although Jonah Jones livens things up towards the end. Just how good a trumpeter the latter could be is underlined in *One never knows*, where he sets up the right amount of activity behind and around the singing, animation contrasting with its processional quality. Allen, an even more oblique improviser, might have performed a similar role on the next session yet, eloquent though his solos are, no kind of partnership is established, Miss Holiday sings *This is my last affair* very movingly, but *You showed me the way* (of which Ella Fitzgerald was part-composer) and *Sentimental and melancholy* are less convincing.

That Coulter's 'incessant modifications of the pulse' did not always operate is demonstrated in *How could you?*, where the singer concentrates quite lengthily upon a single note, yet fails to provide sufficient rhythmic variation. On the other hand, she sounds masterly (if that adjective can be applied to a female) in *Moaning low* and *Carelessly*, both splendidly relaxed performances, the latter graced by a feathery solo from Hodges, who formed one third of an all-Ellingtonian front line. The next session was another of those under Billie Holiday's leadership, the principal difference being that she sang more than on Wilson's dates, taking the first chorus, then coming in again at the end. *Let's call the whole thing off* presents a rare example of her being outpointed by a songwriter; as usual, she reduces the melody to a minimum, but at the same time destroys the song's wit, its intrinsic gaiety. Far better is *Where is the sun?*, starkly moving, with pleasantly casual trumpet playing by Tompkins.

Lester Young turns up on the next session, as he does on several which follow. He and Clayton get *Mean to me* off to a good start, after which Miss Holiday rearranges the melody quite drastically, just as she pares down *I'll get by* to merely a few notes. Both performances rank as outstanding examples of her singing. Young's adroitly sympathetic obbligato playing helps to make *He's funny that way*, another of this singer's masterpieces. Clayton — muted, as he tended to be in those days — contributes an emotive middle chorus. He also brought strength to a nondescript personnel on the session that follows, on which Musso's tenor playing, especially in *Can't help lovin' dat man*, sounds far too soft-centred. Billie Holiday sings Jerome Kern's melody adequately, without hitting any peaks. And despite her being reunited with Young and having the Basie rhythm section (with Wilson replacing the Count) behind her, *My first impression of you* is another case of the singer being defeated by an unwieldly lyric and melody. (Neither she nor Wilson had any real control over the material the company expected them to record.) *I can't believe that you're in love with me*, in total contrast, has Young and Clayton sharing a deliciously varied opening chorus before the singer twists the melody to her own ends. The quartet of songwriters who cobbled together *Now they call it swing* were, in a way, saying something much wiser than they realized. Miss Holiday adds some furbelows to what could easily seem a period song, helped by Young, his phrases delightfully akimbo, and with Basie's guitar–bass–drums team at its most surging and insistent.

If I were you disappoints sadly, the accompanying group trying too hard to imitate the John Kirby Sextet (with Thornhill even contriving to sound like Billy Kyle), but *I'm gonna lock my heart and throw away the key* is redeemed by the singing. *I've got a date with a dream* presents Billie Holiday at her greatest, piquant as well as sensual, and once again using a line-up drawn almost totally from the Basie band; Young's admirably inquisitive clarinet solo deserves special praise. *You can't be mine* is less distinguished, although students of jazz minutiae may cherish the fact that it contains the only solo — eight bars long — ever put on record by Margaret 'Countess' Johnson, renowned in Kansas City but without any wider fame. *They say* is an example of Miss Holiday being outflanked by an arranger. Presumably it was Carter who wrote the involved counter-melody for saxophones that is heard behind the singer, and which may account for her sticking more tenaciously than usual to the tune. The arranger takes a shapely alto solo, James is glossy, yet becomes slightly more Berigan-like in *Say it with a kiss*, which also has Young demonstrating how much can be accomplished within eight bars.

The session of 30 January 1939 was the last on which Wilson used Billie Holiday as his singer. It can only be called a triumphant finale, for *More than you know* presents her excelling in a gravely decorous way, while *Sugar* communicates a kind of ecstatic happiness that becomes much rarer, indeed almost non-existent, as the singer's career moved into darker times. *Sugar*, in fact, comes as close to perfection as any recorded jazz performance, the voice being aided by characteristically melodic playing by Carter which forms an ideal illustration of the composer as soloist, and with Eldridge at his most passionately intense. One should never, of course, under-estimate Wilson's own contributions to these recordings. Apart from Young, he, more than anybody, provided Miss Holiday with the kind of support that brought out the best in her, as well as fashioning solos that combined rhythmic precision with the delicacy of filigree.

The remaining tracks, alas, represent a falling away. The bands get bigger, the arrangements are more noticeable, the solos — apart from a few outbursts by Eldridge — are mostly negligible. Worst of all, the singing often has a cloud over it. Nothing from the 1940–1 period, for instance, equals *God bless the child* or *Some other spring*, both found on **204**, although *Solitude* is surprisingly effective, with the voice set inside a sympathetic orchestration, while *Mandy is two* receives an animated and absorbing performance. There are, of course, minor pleasures on quite a few tracks: worthwhile singing in *I hear music*, where Clarke's drumming helped, as did a dryly-muted Eldridge solo, *It's a sin to tell a lie* and *I'm in a low-down groove*; while *St Louis blues* finds her singing against a succession of obbligatos, with Carter chipping in with a clarinet solo towards the end. She even copes bravely with *Let's do it*, exactly the kind of song that never was up her street — and almost makes it work. But the fallibility implied by some of these later recordings cannot detract from the greatness of her best work. Quite the reverse. Both as an artist and as a human being, Billie Holiday possessed an integrity that was, paradoxically, revealed by weakness. She never succeeded in faking a performance, as lesser singers do with ease. Her art was instinctive, concerned with feeling more than form. She lived on the edge of every song she sang, and if the feeling was missing she could only fall back on mannerisms. Delight could turn into dilemma.   C.F.

Swing Continues

Many figures prominent in the 1930s continued to grow musically well beyond the years of the swing period itself. The following recordings were contemporaneous with the postwar styles dealt with in Volume 2 of this work and they show that the vitality of many aspects of jazz was sustained far beyond the time of their greatest prominence.

Bobby Hackett–Jack Teagarden

206 Jazz Ultimate
Capitol (E) T933, Capitol (A) T933

Hackett (tpt); Teagarden (tbn); 'Peanuts' Hucko (clt[1], ten); Ernie Caceres (clt[2], bar); Gene Schroeder (p); Billy Bauer (g); Jack Lesberg (bs); Buzzy Drootin (d). Hollywood, 16 September 1957.
Indiana[2] · *It's wonderful* · *Way down yonder in New Orleans*[1] · *'Swonderful*[2] · *Baby, won't you please come home?* · *I've found a new baby*[1] · *Mama's gone, goodbye*[1]
Same personnel and location, 17 September 1957.
Oh, baby[1] · *Sunday*[2] · *Everybody loves my baby*[1] · *55th and Broadway*[2]

A handful of jazz musicians have been misguided enough to imagine, rather like the old breed of actor–managers, that the company of inferiors made them sound better. Yet experience proves that the meeting of equals or near-equals is likely both to produce superior music and to exhibit the musicians at their best. It was true of this coming together (not for the first time) of Hackett and Teagarden, two of the great melodists of jazz. Not that the partnership necessarily appeared ideal in theory. 'Hackett plays with sharp rhythmic agility', Whitney Balliett has written, 'but he invariably sounds as if he were loafing' [87]. Exactly the same was true of Teagarden, possibly — to use a piece of latter-day *argot* — the most laid-back of all jazz instrumentalists or singers. But instead of relaxation being compounded, the session turned out to be notable for the closeness of rapport that prevailed — illustrated, for instance, by the chorus of fours, followed by sixteen bars apiece, in *Way down yonder in New Orleans*.

Teagarden and Hackett first recorded together in 1938, soon after the latter, who played cornet in those days, had arrived in New York from Boston. Commentators, always eager to make comparisons, hailed him as 'the next Bix', although Hackett himself always seems to have felt that he owed more to Armstrong. Yet there was, and continued to be, a Beiderbeckian feel about both his timing and phrasing. The subtle use of *rubato*, and that relaxed approach, were characteristic. Listen to the way he moves into his solo on *It's wonderful* (not to be confused with Gershwin's *'Swonderful*, which turns up later), as beautifully considered a performance as he ever put on record, the tone pure but shining. That track also helps to explain the high regard in which Hackett's ballad playing was held by fellow trumpeters.

Luxuriant is the handiest word to describe Teagarden's playing here: typically rhetorical, rarely content to use one note where four can be squeezed in, yet with a warmth that rebuts any charge that his virtuosity was merely a question of technique. Although he had just entered his fifties, Teagarden was in better physical shape than for many years. He had, too, the self-confidence of a man who knows that none of his younger rivals could really outdo him; he preserved, in Richard Hadlock's phrase, 'something of the image of invincibility he first created in the 1920s' [88]. *Baby, won't you please come home?*, all too commonly an excuse for the brasher kind of dixieland routines, features Teagarden at his most deft, his tone light, his phrasing feathery. In *55th and Broadway*, a slow blues, he proffers once again some of his favourite musical ideas, yet without sounding stale; Hackett comes across as untypically quirky (even a bit like Rex Stewart) on this track, but obviously much more at home with the twelve bar blues than Beiderbecke ever was.

Apart from Caceres, imaginative as well as adroit on baritone saxophone (particularly in *Way down yonder in New Orleans*) and nearly as good on clarinet, the other musicians lack presence. Hucko plays the clarinet capably but is more interesting when he picks up the tenor saxophone, echoing a little of Eddie Miller's swivelling manner. Schroeder is a functional pianist, dull in solos but more than useful in what, despite Bauer's efforts, is otherwise an adequate rather than an inspiring rhythm section.   C.F.

207
The Very Great Henry 'Red' Allen Vol. 2
Rarities (D) 24, *RCA (E) RD27045

Allen (tpt, vcl[1]); J. C. Higginbotham (tbn); Buster Bailey (clt); Coleman Hawkins (ten); Marty Napoleon (p); Everett Barksdale (g); Lloyd Trotman (bs); Cozy Cole (d). New York City, 21 March 1957.
Let me miss you, baby[1] · *Ride, Red, ride!*[1] · *Love is just around the corner*

Same personnel and location, 27 March 1957.
'Swonderful · *I cover the waterfront* · *St James' Infirmary*[1] · *Algiers bounce*

Higginbotham absent[2]. New York City, 10 April 1957.
Sweet Lorraine · *Ain't she sweet?*[1,2] · *I've got the world on a string*

Let me miss you, baby is a blues song inviting the Jimmy Rushing treatment. Allen sings it with a flexibility and variety of phrasing which were, by this stage of his career, as much an extension of his improvising style as it is possible for vocal technique to become. He came rather later to the expressive unity of voice and horn which had been Armstrong's almost from the start. *St James' Infirmary* and *Ain't she sweet?* are other evidences that he contends for the highest rank among the true singers of *jazz*.

As for his playing, there are many moments of splendid inventive ease here, sufficient to prove that, with Armstrong no longer inhabiting quite the same musical world, Allen was now the peerless master of a style of trumpet playing which carried the first tradition through to challenge the virility of many a younger voice. Only he approaches artistic coherence in the reckless speed and gratuitous wildness of *Ride, Red, ride!*, and elsewhere his success in translating ranging imagination into music is matched consistently only by Hawkins. Allen's near-contemporary, Higginbotham, keeps his old strength of sound, but relates somewhat tired stories with an intonation occasionally suspect, while the rather older Bailey, though his freshness of thought is usually clear, seems to have lost some of his quickness of fingers and tongue. Barksdale, Trotman and Cole are fine, and Marty Napoleon (nephew to Phil) plays imaginatively according to his bop-kindled lights.

Hawkins suits his various personae to the requirements of each theme — feigning savagery in *Love is just around the corner*, nodding to the boppers in *Algiers bounce* (titled after Allen's Louisiana birthplace), combining toughness with pathos in *Let me miss you, baby*, and so on. But most of the elbow room is Allen's, and he uses it exuberantly. His combination of lightness and power in *Love is just around the corner* and *Ain't she sweet?* is close to being an epitome of his restless art, which maybe proves just a little too restless for the co-operative aims of *'Swonderful*, but can somehow also encompass the intense thoughtfulness of his final solo on *St James' Infirmary*, where his superb mastery of the trumpet's lowest register is displayed. His ability to relate separate solos to each other by developing similar ideas in different registers is shown on *Sweet Lorraine* and in *I cover the waterfront*, where the first solo weds faultless dexterity with generous lyrical wit and the second rehearses, with something like intellectual exultation, all those brilliant avowals which gave the trumpet for so long its pre-eminence in the jazz ensemble.

(The British RCA LP listed above lacks *Let me miss you, baby*.)   E.T.

Claude Hopkins

208 Let's Jam!
Fontana (E) 688405ZL, Swingsville (A) SVLP2020

Joe Thomas (tpt); Buddy Tate (clt[1], ten); Hopkins (p); Wendell Marshall (bs); J. C. Heard (d). New York City, 21 February 1961.
Offbeat blues · Safari stomp · Late evening[1] · The way you look tonight · I apologise · I surrender, dear · I would do anything for you

Not so much in the jam session manner as in that far more creative procedure by which groups associated with Basie had wedded spontaneity to co-operative order, this studio ensemble brings together musicians of wide and varied experience. Long and varied in the case of Hopkins, who began his career in the early 1920s, led one of the most popular big bands of the swing age (**123**) and had, in the two decades prior to this session, ranged through such a stylistic ragbag of associations that it is a little surprising to find him with so coherent and flexible a style. In this context, he favours Basie, yet the heeding of younger minds has given him a fresher store of ideas.

He introduces *Offbeat blues*, rejuvenating the piano blues over a bass figure which Marshall borrows from Jimmy Yancey, and the necessary tension of that rhythm, heightened by Heard's insistent cymbal, underlies the meditative economies of Tate and Thomas, each of whom is in excellent form. *Late evening* is another gentle blues, varying its rhythms more and featuring some pleasant clarinet playing of simple technique from Tate. Thomas plays muted over rolling piano chords and then Hopkins makes the piano converse indolently with itself. The springing beat of *Safari stomp* invites ebullient episodes from Thomas and Tate as they improvise, separately and jointly, in an intriguing sequence that owes a great deal to almost faultless rhythmic support. Hopkins inserts his own developing investigation, which gains its best effects through statements which are hinted at rather than uttered.

The other four numbers may be regarded as standards, though one of them, *I would do anything for you*, is a Hopkins–Alex Hill composition. *The way you look tonight* is introduced by Tate over a rather heavy beguine rhythm which modifies into something more amenable to the kinds of thoughtful variation at which Hopkins and Thomas, with his radiant tone, seem to excel. It is not easy to guess how seriously *I apologise* should be taken. Tate's saxophone sings this desperate sentimentality, evoking memories of gentler voices than that of Billy Eckstine as Thomas mutters dry comments and Hopkins lends trembling pathos. Such self-indulgence must have a vein of comedy in it, yet this is a very musical sending-up. Afterwards, Tate and Thomas sit out for *I surrender, dear* and leave Hopkins to demonstrate how another maudlin song may have its residue of genuine emotion refreshed by intellectual verve; and this he does in ruminative style, dividing, reshaping and multiplying both the rhythms of the theme and the patterns of his own variation.

He also leads a vivacious assault upon *I would do anything for you* — an item much requested when his band flourished (and undertaken by a different team on **209**, not to mention Art Tatum on **181a**) — and, from his entry to the declamatory ending, these youthful veterans celebrate both the song and its associations. Thomas struts elegantly, Tate jostles and snarls in mock aggression, and Hopkins, who must often have mused upon what might have been, skips like a man who bears no malice.   E.T.

209 Swinging with Pee Wee Russell
Fontana (E) 688403ZL, Swingsville (A) SVLP2008

Buck Clayton (tpt); Russell (clt); Tommy Flanagan (p); Wendell Marshall (bs); Osie Johnson (d). New York City, 29 March 1960.
What can I say, dear? · *Midnight blue* · *The very thought of you* · *Lulu's back in town* · *Wrap your troubles in dreams* · *I would do anything for you* · *Englewood*

Consulting those clarinettists who are supposed to have influenced it will not necessarily help in fathoming the unique musical mind of Charles Ellsworth Russell. Beiderbecke, heard at his most exploratory, might be a better mentor. 'Bix and I had the same feeling about chords', claimed Russell. 'We'd hear something and say, 'That chord just has to be there, whether it's according to Hoyle or not. You have to hear for yourself, and keep trying new ideas' [89]. Beiderbecke and Russell did some shared listening in early St Louis days, crossing town to hear Dewey Jackson, Charlie Creath, Thornton Blue and their like [90]. But theirs were independent minds which saw jazz as a game of musical self-discovery. It is a pity that so many of those who bewail Bix's lost maturity have consistently failed to recognize in Russell's work the unfolding of a similar imagination over several decades beyond the cornettist's death.

This lack of recognition may be partly Russell's fault. For a long time he allowed himself to be confined in the scanty spaces of dixieland ensembles and seemed, in addition, to cultivate the image of the croaky introvert. His eventual emergence into more roomy areas exposed an originality of invention which few records, other than his 1944 Hot Four session (**189**), had sufficiently honoured previously. The gift was there to be heard, even in his briefest earlier contributions, but the element of sharp contrast had, too often, caused him to be regarded as a mere eccentric — a curious judgment indeed, in the context of jazz music!

But Russell's strangeness was not attributable to what one writer miscalled his 'stark isolationism' [91]. Musically, in fact, he was quite a sociable character, with greater ensemble aptitudes than some have given him credit for. His determination to air his arcane discoveries without apology, and whatever the company, had nothing to do with any desire to be isolated; more to do with a genial obstinacy which insisted that jazz is, after all, an eccentric's art. His encounters with newer forms of jazz, as in the *New Groove* LP (CBS (E) SBPG62242), which finds him improvising with conviction on themes by Thelonious Monk, Tadd Dameron, John Coltrane and Billy Strayhorn, or in a teaming with Monk himself on CBS (E) SBPG62389, are intriguing. But he probably found an almost perfect balance of co-operation in the group here recorded. There are modernists in it, though Flanagan, who near that date was standing in for Bud Powell at Birdland, shows lines of continuity with an earlier style. Marshall, first cousin to Jimmy Blanton and, like Russell, from St Louis, and the musically versatile Johnson complete a smoothly riding session which enhances the freedom of the principals.

The pairing of Clayton with Russell invites comparison with the Clayton–Young tracks of 1938 (**157**) in which Young plays the clarinet; and, whilst Russell is a more angular draughtsman than

Young, there is a similarity of approach. The roughness and the tonal exaggerations with which Russell disguised the instrument's femininity may obscure for some listeners the real freshness of this thought. Like Young, if less subtly, he suffused the whole gamut of 'blueness', and there are splendid examples of the consequences of this in *Midnight blue* and *Englewood. The very thought of you* finds him drawing closer to a lyricism typical of Young and here, too, is intimacy of tone reminiscent of Ed Hall in similar mood. The faster pieces, such as *Lulu's back in town*, demonstrate Russell's odd rhythmic independence, which is not the sweeping cross-beat liberty of Clayton, but something closer to private footwork learned partly from a juba dancer, partly from Charlie Chaplin! There is a conquest of both tonality and rhythm in this music of his, which points ahead, not so clearly to the modality of Ornette Coleman as to Eric Dolphy's desire not to abandon tonality but to challenge it radically from within.

Following the warm serenity of Clayton in *What can I say, dear?*, Russell draws a sequence of those tangential lines which hint at esoteric chords 'not according to Hoyle'. He is up to comparable tricks in *Wrap your troubles in dreams*, but perhaps the quest is more comprehensively organized than it used to be and sounds rather less outlandish than it did when pitted against a neo-Chicagoan beat. It is not, however, that daring has given place to mellowness — *Englewood* will explode that idea — but rather that in such congenial and relaxed company gadfly tactics are hardly appropriate.　　　　　　　　　　　　　　　　E.T.

210　Jo Jones Special

Vanguard (E) PPL11002, Vanguard (A) VRS8503

Emmett Berry (tpt); Bennie Green (tbn); Lucky Thompson (ten); Count Basie (p); Freddy Greene (g); Walter Page (bs); Jones (d). New York City, 11 August 1955.
Shoe shine boy (2 takes)

Nat Pierce (p) replaces Basie. Same date.
Loverman · *Georgia Mae* · *Lincoln Heights* · *Embraceable you*

Lawrence Brown (tbn), Pete Johnson (p) replace Bennie Green, Pierce, Rudy Powell (clt) added. New York City, 16 August 1955.
Caravan

The veil of two decades falls away with the opening notes of *Shoe shine boy*, and the famous version with Lester Young is recalled (**135a**). That memory is not dishonoured, and it is not just that the Basie rhythm section — with the Count himself — is there, or that Berry's muted work strongly recalls the Buck Clayton of the

Kansas City Five and Six (**157**) but, in addition, that the traditionally rooted modernism of Bennie Green and Thompson brings in a proper spirit of musical advance. Both the latter sound accents learnt from the bop improvisers, but that their truer home is in company such as this is well shown by *Loverman* — a theme of the 'new age' if ever there was one — in which both tenor saxophonist and trombonist slip back into older, less cocky dialects, and it is Berry who discovers an uncharacteristic coolness of voice. The boundary between swing and bop is straddled by several of the solos in *Georgia Mae* (*Sweet Georgia Brown* in disguise). Pierce, who commits harmonic surprises at the start of *Loverman*, has a limiting reputation as a Basie impersonator; but, although he approaches that role — and falls short — in *Lincoln Heights* and one or two other spots, he is usually allowed to express his post-swing romanticism, which splendidly suits the musings of the soloists on *Loverman* and *Embraceable you*. His chordal support of Thompson in the latter is very effective, combined as it is with the clearly defined and perfectly balanced work of Freddy Greene and Page.

Throughout all this, the exuberance of Basie's erstwhile drummer, that timeless veteran Jonathan Jones, gives buoyancy and variety to the rhythmic context and bursts out, in *Caravan*, into solo playing of great character. Neither with Basie nor elsewhere has Jones been given to lengthy solos, but in this piece, which is very loosely constructed from a group point of view, he builds from the first peremptory rolls into vying and interracting patterns of marvellous skill and power. When he drops into the brisk beat that introduces the short and unsatisfying ensemble interludes, he shows, in his hi-hat and tom-tom work particularly, what younger drummers such as Art Blakey were learning from him.

Berry, Brown and Powell are allowed scant space in *Caravan*, and Johnson cannot really be heard at all. The second take of *Shoe shine boy*, which closes this LP, is of much the same fine quality as the first, though it may be that Thompson and Bennie Green find some added expressiveness. John Hammond, who supervised these sessions, decided that the takes of this number shared excellence sufficiently to be issued together. There should be thanksgiving for that, and many delighted echoes of the bright shout of laughter — Jones's? — with which the first take closes.

E.T.

211 Gene Krupa/Lionel Hampton/Teddy Wilson
Verve (F) 2304 482, Columbia (E) 33SX10027

Wilson (p); Red Callender (bs); Krupa (d); Hampton (vib). Los Angeles, 31 July 1955.

Avalon · Just you, just me · Moonglow · Blues for Benny · I got rhythm · Airmail special

212 Prez and Teddy
Verve (E) 2683 025 (2 LPs), *Verve (A) 2-2502 (2 LPs)

Jazz Giants 1956: Roy Eldridge (tpt); Vic Dickenson (tbn); Lester Young (ten); Wilson (p); Freddy Greene (g); Gene Ramey (bs); Jo Jones (d). New York City, 12 January 1956.

I guess I'll have to change my plan · I didn't know what time it was · Gigantic blues · This year's kisses · You can depend on me

Lester Young Quartet: Young (ten); Wilson (p); Ramey (bs); Jones (d). New York City, 13 January 1956.

Pres returns · Prisoner of love · Taking a chance on love · All of me · Louise · Our love is here to stay · Love me or leave me

Newcomers to jazz who get into conversation with the music's veterans are sometimes bewildered by the way in which a musician can dismiss his earlier playing — often the so-called 'classics' upon which his reputation rests — as if not exactly juvenilia then at least as mere 'prentice work. This attitude often derives from the fact that by his maturity the musician has generally achieved a better command of his instrument. What has frequently disappeared, however, is the overwhelming curiosity that lay behind, and gave excitement to, those early performances. Ezra Pound declared that a writer needs curiosity more than anything else; the same is true of every species of artist. For once curiosity has departed, blandness creeps in. It is a danger which threatened almost every musician on these three LPs, even back in the 1950s, when all of them except Callender were still in their forties. What makes these particular perform-ances outstanding is that the musicians were mostly able to summon up the kind of boldness which originally won them distinction.

Nothing can be more perilous, of course, than reinterpreting tunes very specifically associated with the past. For instance, the whole point of getting Krupa, Hampton and Wilson together in 1955, the year which saw the making of the film, *The Benny Goodman Story*, was to have them perform items they played two decades earlier with Goodman's Quartet. In the event it worked out marvellously. Wilson's presence no doubt had something to do with the ideal tempos that were struck (and the same is true of the two 1956 sessions, where the effect is heightened by a far more subtle rhythm section). Krupa's drumming, always a trifle extrovert compared with the finest of his contemporaries, comes across now as rather too obvious, yet it cannot be denied that the performances charge ahead with much fervour. Callender stays decidedly in the background — appropriately, perhaps, since the original Goodman Quartet never included a bassist. But the really felicitous playing comes from Hampton and Wilson, both jointly (towards the end of *Avalon*, for instance) and, most remarkably of all, individually.

Hampton can rarely have surpassed the eleven scampering choruses that he takes in *I got rhythm*, the solo developing with a logic that might be called remorseless if the whole exercise were not so light-hearted. The nearest comparison, perhaps, is with his extended version of *Stardust* recorded at a 1947 'Just Jazz' concert and once available on Ace of Hearts (E) AH19. *Blues for Benny* has moments when it might be called *Hamp's boogie woogie* with, at one point, Wilson backing the vibraharpist up in an uncharacteristic fashion. Elsewhere Wilson's delicate touch is very much to the fore, although the three choruses he takes in *Avalon* contrive to be taut as well as graceful, a summation of this pianist's approach to improvising. (Two more titles from this date — *The man I love* and *Body and soul* — were issued on an EP, Columbia (E) SEB10086, and are well worth seeking out.)

The five tracks by the band called Jazz Giants 1956 were originally greeted with exceptional enthusiasm, largely because they provided evidence that Young's postwar decline might not be as total as many people feared. Admittedly, his playing here is far removed from the airy nonchalance of his solos with the Basie band. The phrasing is warier, the tone heavier, even a bit leathery at times, the whole conception suffused with a sort of quizzical melancholy. Nevertheless, the stance is unmistakable and the playing — to advert to the opening paragraph — possesses something of the curiosity that Young was thought to have lost. It is certainly true of the solos on *I didn't know what time it was*, where he contrasts the note-values of his opening theme statement in a way more imaginative than the most extravagant flights of many lesser musicians; and *This year's kisses* is worth comparing with the version that Young recorded with Billie Holiday and Wilson in 1937 (**204**). Even more satisfying, perhaps, is Young's playing on the quartet session held a day later. In *Pres returns* (a title which may have its own significance) he settles down to work, at a relaxed, medium tempo, on a twelve-bar blues, taking eleven choruses altogether and ending with a reiterated blues riff. In *Our love is here to stay* he displays a beguiling warmth and even a breathiness reminiscent of Ben Webster. And notice how *Louise* is made to sound uncommonly like *Jumping with Symphony Sid*.

The concentration at the time of the recordings' first appearance on Young's return to excellence on the Jazz Giants session rather obscured the fact that really outstanding solos were taken by Eldridge, a musician who has never lacked curiosity; indeed, he has sometimes allowed it to take him along disastrous paths. He performs here, though, with an authority almost akin to Armstrong's, his tone either muted and dry (*I guess I'll have to change my plan*) or open and round (*I didn't know what time it was*). *This year's kisses* inspired a positively heroic solo, one which, to take a liberty with Mr Joyce's hero, appears to fit all three of Stephen Dedalus's categories of aesthetic form: lyrical, epical and dramatic. All of which unfortunately emphasizes the lack of inventiveness, and rhythmic diversity, in Dickenson's playing, which mostly does no more than establish the trombonist's presence, being full of characteristic effects but without much point or purpose.   C.F.

Mel Powell–Ruby Braff

213 **Thigamagig**
Vanguard (E) PPL11000, Vanguard (A) VRS8502

Mel Powell Trio: Braff (tpt); Powell (p); Bobby Donaldson (d). New York City, 24 August 1954.
Thigamagig · You're my thrill · Button up your overcoat · Don-que-dee · Bouquet · Ain't she sweet? · Take me in your arms · California, here I come

Braff (born 1927), though junior to some of the bop pioneers, gained surprising success as late as the 1950s playing a style not entirely untouched by postwar modernism but firmly in the line which led from Armstrong to trumpeters like Buck Clayton and Harry Edison. His rich vibrato and love of ornament are reminiscent of the style of Henry Allen's later years (**207**). Type-casting under the misleading 'mainstream' heading has often inhibited an attractively wayward gift for the romantic, and he achieves his most varied essays in sessions like the present one. However, a notable collaboration with Clayton in July 1954 (Vanguard (A) VRS8517) shows him in lyrical form, displaying both his kinship to and his independence of an admired senior partner.

Powell (born 1923), when he played this 1954 trio session, had but lately returned to jazz after some years studying composition with Hindemith. His early jazz expression, notably his playing and arranging with Goodman in the 1940s (**143**), was at first, like Johnny Guarnieri's, an amalgam of emulations. Waller, Tatum, Basie and Teddy Wilson were all evident mentors and, if it did not too strongly challenge the 'stride' heritage, the influence of Hines seems to have affected Powell in terms of touch and of readiness for adventure into the unusual. Even in the years preceding his Hindemith studies, Powell was exploring a jazz manner *à la* Debussy: hear his 1945 *Hommage à Debussy* (Esquire (E) 304). Yet in these performances for Vanguard he re-emerges with his gift for forthright improvisation greatly enhanced. He weds his new insights effortlessly to jazz thinking of great vivacity, and one can only regret that his renewed jazz career lasted only until about 1955. Subsequently he worked entirely as a 'straight' composer and teacher.

Thigamagig and *Bouquet* are Powell themes. After an angular and rapid statement by piano and trumpet, the former track passes into a stomping exchange between all members of the trio, and although this looks back in certain respects to the brilliant conversations between Armstrong and Hines (**48**), the piece is too short to allow any real development of ideas. *Bouquet*, a much slower affair, has hints, in the widely-spaced keyboard lines of aqueous Debussian episodes, as Braff traces ascending ninths in a wistful theme that is later exploited in a prolonged duet. A similar mood informs *You're my thrill*, which is one of the best items. Powell introduces the melody out of tempo with exploratory reharmonizations, lending it a character of airiness at variance with the sentimentality of the song itself, so that when Braff's warmly-committed serenade intervenes it makes for an unexpected contrast of colours. No such creative risks are evident in *Take me in your arms*, but a marvellous control of swing at medium tempo allows for the right tension of styles — Braff showing his ability to play in a manner that is tonally and rhythmically rather 'cool'.

Ain't she sweet?, *California, here I come* and *Button up your overcoat* are the numbers in which *un*buttoned enthusiasm breaks free. Powell indulges in a highly dramatic extension of the style that thrilled the 'parlours' of Harlem, made richer by bell-like Chicagoan echoes, whilst Braff creates exuberantly shaped melodies, whooping and smearing at the fringe of the upper register. Donaldson, a capable and interesting companion and supporter, has his best chance to shine in his own Latin American *Don-que-dee*. E.T.

Benny Carter

214 **Further Definitions**
Jasmine (E) JAS14, Impulse (A) S12

Benny Carter and His Orchestra: Carter, Phil Woods (alt); Coleman Hawkins, Charlie Rouse (ten); Dick Katz (p); John Collins (g); Jimmy Garrison (bs); Jo Jones (d). New York City, 13 November 1961.

Honeysuckle rose · The midnight sun will never set · Cherry · Crazy rhythm

Same personnel and location, 15 November 1961.

Doozy · Blue star · Cottontail · Body and soul

Among other things, this LP, like **220** and much of **239**, shows jazz reflecting on its own past. When it began recording in Paris during the 1930s, the Swing label tried several instrumentations that, for their time, were mildly experimental, and some of the results are discussed in Chapter 4. One such, in 1937, used pairs of altos, tenors and a rhythm section built round Django Reinhardt (**105a**), the other main proponents being Carter and Hawkins. Two dozen years further on, the latter returned to this format, not with Europeans but with fellow Americans, the other saxophonists and the pianist being of a younger generation. Nobody doubles on the clarinet, as Alix Combelle did in 1937, and no one picks up a trumpet, as Carter then did, but the earlier occasion is quite deliberately invoked. With slight modifications, Carter's original arrangements of *Honeysuckle rose* and *Crazy rhythm* are used (both recordings of the former piece should be compared with Combelle's *Onze heures vingt* on **107d**), and there are other references to the past. The initial *Body and soul* ensemble is Carter's scoring of the start of Hawkins's famous 1939 version (**192**), and he also reproduces the saxophone writing of Ellington's original account of *Cottontail* (**153**).

As much to the point as any of the above is that this simple instrumental combination produces exceptional results here, just as it did in 1937. A difference is that in the meantime Carter and Hawkins had emerged as two of the very few swing musicians who, without actually playing it, did properly come to terms with bop. The latter is dealt with elsewhere, but of the former it should be said that as he already thought in long, independent melodic lines it was not hard to adopt the more varied accentuation of postwar jazz, especially as this had already been hinted at by Hawkins, Tatum and several other of the most advanced swing players. Carter's solos on *Cottontail* and the new versions of *Crazy rhythm* and *Honeysuckle rose* illustrate the point and show that his adaptation of new rhythmic procedures relates interestingly to aspects of the music of Paul Desmond and Lee Konitz. Indeed, the LP should be heard along with *Additions to Further Definitions* (HMV (E) CLP3576, Impulse (A) S9116), a 1966 recording which uses the same instrumentation, plus a baritone saxophone, but, Carter aside, features exclusively musicians of the generation after his such as Bud Shank (alto) and Teddy Edwards (tenor). This highlights the organic changes in Carter's improvising as, in a different way, do his trio performances with Tatum and Louis Bellson (**219**).

Equally significant is that both *Definitions* and *Additions* convey a feeling of Carter's full involvement — something missing from many of his latter-day records. One senses this in the urgency of the *Honeysuckle rose* or *Doozy* ensembles, and there is a fine continuity between the solos of Rouse, Woods, Hawkins and Carter on the former. The latter is a blues, and Hawkins, more of a bluesman than in 1937, makes an especially powerful statement over Jones's deeply swinging beat. He is more abrasive on *Crazy rhythm* than he was in 1937, too, and despite having no doubt played it thousands of times, he finds fresh things in the, for him, inexhaustible vein of the *Body and soul* chord sequence. (Note, however, that on this last the bridge has a new harmonization, apparently suggested by Carter and Woods.) Woods is particularly striking after the opening ensemble's evocation of the classic 1939 reading: he speaks for a later time yet does so with a musical understanding of the past. Another interesting relationship occurs in *Cherry*, where Hawkins takes a quite complicated phrase from the end of Woods's solo — his best of the date — and multiplies its rhythmic complexity with relaxed self-assurance.

Carter's most characteristic writing here is in *The midnight sun will never set* and especially *Blue star*, his own theme. On the former he gets right to the melody's essential lyricism, and in both performances offers solos which reconcile grace, surprise and inevitability. He plays with more heat on *Cottontail*, where Rouse is particularly purposeful and Katz, an admirable accompanist throughout, plays his finest solo of these sessions. This piece is indelibly associated with Ben Webster, and it is a curious experience to hear an improvisation on it by Hawkins, the model whom Webster followed so assiduously. Considering its presumed origin, the distinction of the saxophone writing here needs no emphasis; yet, bereft of the individual tones of the Ducal bandsmen, it sounds oddly un-Ellingtonian. Perhaps this is an indirect confirmation of the rumour, noted under **153**, that the relevant passage was devised by Webster rather than Ellington.

A very different case is *Cherry*, where Carter dialogues with the ensemble, making it seem as if he is talking with his own reflection. And we get, in these eight performances, an unusually clear recording of his lead playing.   M.H.

Coleman Hawkins

215 Shelly Manne 2, 3, 4
HMV (E) CLP1625, Impulse (A) S20

Hawkins (ten, p); Manne (d). New York City, 5 February 1962.
Me and some drums
Hank Jones (p), George Duvivier (bs) added. Same date.
Take the 'A' train · Slowly · Cherokee
Eddie Costa (p, vib); Duvivier (bs); Manne (d). New York City, 8 February 1962.
The sicks of us · Lean on me

Jazz musicians tend either to die young and dissolute or to carry on playing until well into their sixties or seventies. Hawkins is a good example of a musician who never retired but kept performing until only a few weeks before his death in 1969. In the final years his breathing no longer kept up with his musical thinking in faster numbers, yet he could bring to slow ballads an astonishing emotional starkness and candour. The onset of that situation can be heard on what presumably was Hawkins's last, and very moving, LP, *Sirius* (Pablo (E) 2310 707), recorded in December 1966. Four years earlier, however, he had been totally in command, able to summon up aggressiveness as well as to sound contemplative. His tone was heavier, he tended to push the beat more persistently, but those characteristics were balanced by a fondness for the oblique phrase and for suddenly shifting from the majestic to the positively airy.

Nowhere is this more obvious than in the duet, *Me and some drums*. The sequence of chords at the start, bleak yet suggestive, allegedly represents Hawkins's debut on record as a pianist. That improvised passage sets the scene for what is in effect an exercise in free playing, although of course disciplined by the saxophonist's instinct for form, his flair for the dramatic. Every bit as remarkable are the pair of choruses that Hawkins plays in the middle of *Cherokee*, treating Ray Noble's tune as a ballad, almost as a blues. This is an emotional interpretation of a number which more normally is used to provide harmonic stimulus.

Slowly turns out to be not quite the leisurely performance its title promises. It is, in fact, not an 'original' but a song from the film *Fallen Angel*. Hawkins embellishes rather than improvises on it, a useful demonstration of the way a great jazz musician can take possession of a melody with the minimum of alteration. Jones's solo here contrasts the pliability of single-note lines with the chording he undertakes during the middle eight. In *Take the 'A' train* the pianist could almost be said to caricature Duke Ellington's more bravura manner. This version of Billy Strayhorn's tune begins and ends at a modest pace, with three brisk yet resonant choruses from Hawkins sandwiched in between.

By the time these tracks were recorded, Manne was no longer the ardent disciple of Dave Tough that he had been on some of Hawkins's 1943 sessions (**194**). Jazz drumming had undergone changes and Manne deploys the newer cymbal patterns and bass drum accenting as well as the techniques — press rolls, for instance — of earlier decades. There are moments in *The sicks of us* when he seems to be playing too loudly (it could be faulty recording balance, of course), rather like Krupa with Goodman. This is, though, a very tidy and cunningly integrated performance, the three musicians interweaving, sometimes in unexpected roles — an instance being the way, just before the end, that the vibraharp is used to create percussive rather than pitched sounds. Costa was always an outstanding vibraharpist; more invigorating on that instrument, in fact, than on the piano, which he plays, a bit portentously, in *Lean on me*. Nevertheless, it was the music recorded the day before, with Hawkins straddling events, that justifies this LP's inclusion in these pages.   C.F.

216 The Elegant Piano Stylings of Herman Chittison
88 Upright (Sw) 88UR-006, L'Elegant (A) LE1000
Chittison (p). New York City, 22 April 1962.
That's all · Little girl blues · It's easy to remember · Smoke gets in your eyes · Drop me off at Harlem · The touch of your lips · Tangerine · My funny valentine · Why? · Dancing on the ceiling

Chittison is almost the only jazz pianist who can realistically be compared with Tatum. Such reputation as he has is based on the Paris recordings of 1934 (Onyx (A) 213) and 1938 (**107c**), but the parallels between them are best observed in his 1944–5 trio and solo recordings (Musicraft (A) MVS506). Not that Chittison was an imitator. In the Musicraft *Where or when* and the initial rhapsodic explorations of *Little girl blue* or *Smoke gets in your eyes*, listed above, he proceeds quite differently from Tatum (although this is less true of *Dancing on the ceiling*). These 1962 performances are less free and flexible, are indeed somewhat heavier, than Chittison's work of the 1930s and 1940s, yet they contain plenty of surprises of their own and of a kind to make the LP's title misleading.

By this stage he was, it seems, less interested in diversification of texture than in previous decades, a consistently full sound being maintained with linear improvisation confined to the right hand over a left which lays down an absolutely solid progression of chords. What is most impressive is the constant stream of melodic ideas Chittison develops out of the original themes, a particularly good example being *That's all*. He indulges in little filigree bravura as such, yet, as *Why?* or *Dancing on the ceiling* show, it would be a mistake to underrate the right hand's degree of activity. Often he moves diametrically against the character of the original song, as the buoyant treatment accorded to *It's easy to remember* demonstrates; and *The touch of your lips*, of all things, is definitely a stomp. Again, one initially fears that *My funny valentine* is going to be melodramatic but, once a medium, bouncing tempo is struck, this proves to be far from the case. Another point to notice is the way the momentum is gradually withdrawn from *Dancing on the ceiling* so that the performance gently glides to a conclusion.

Completely un-Ellingtonian is the account of *Drop me off at Harlem*, though it is perhaps not unduly fanciful to suspect that the composer might have been intrigued by Chittison's oblique slant on his melody. The result is quite different from, say, Clare Fischer's remarkable pianistic evocation of the textures of the Ellington band in his 1973 *Moonmist* (Revelation (A) 31), or comparable earlier attempts in the 1930s, recorded and unrecorded, by Garland Wilson [92]. For another contrast, Chittison shows *Tangerine* to be an excellent jazz vehicle, although Martial Solal (MPS (G) 0068.221) appears to be the only other pianist who is aware of the fact; both draw an unrelenting flow of invention from it.   M.H.

217a The Tatum Solo Masterpieces Vol. 6
Pablo (E) 2310 791, Pablo (A) 2310 791

Art Tatum (p). Los Angeles, 28 December 1953.
I'm coming, Virginia · *Night and day*
Same personnel and location, 29 December 1953.
I've got a crush on you · *Ain't misbehaving*
Same personnel and location, 22 April 1954.
Small hotel · *The way you look tonight* · *Cherokee* · *You're blasé*
Same personnel and location, 19 January 1955.
Do nothing till you hear from me

217b The Tatum Solo Masterpieces Vol. 9
Pablo (E) 2310 808, Pablo (A) 2310 835

Tatum (p). Los Angeles, 29 December 1953.
You took advantage of me · *Embraceable you* · *Come rain or come shine*
Same personnel and location, 29 December 1953.
I'm in the mood for love · *Too marvellous for words* · *Tea for two* ·
Blue Lou
Same personnel and location, 22 April 1954.
Sophisticated lady · *I didn't know what time it was*
Same personnel and location, 19 January 1955.
Everything I have is yours

218 Art Tatum–Buddy DeFranco Quartet
Pablo (E) 2310 736, Pablo (A) 2310 736

Art Tatum–Buddy DeFranco Quartet: DeFranco (clt); Tatum (p); Red
Callender (bs); Bill Douglass (d). Los Angeles, 6 February 1956.
Deep night · *Once in a while* · *This can't be love* · *Memories of
you* · *You're mine, you* · *A foggy day* · *Loverman* · *Making whoopee*

The solo performances are from marathon sessions of a virtually
unique kind. On each of the first two of the occasions whose dates
appear above, Tatum recorded thirty-five items, twenty-seven at
each of the other two. Nearly all this material was originally
issued on fifteen LPs under the title *The Genius of Art Tatum* and
then reappeared on thirteen discs as *The Tatum Solo Masterpieces*. Both series were programmed in a completely random
fashion and with none too generous playing-time; a further
reduction in the number of records occupied could easily have
been managed. There was no logical way of choosing two LPs for
this book, and so considerations such as playing-time and the
non-duplication of repertoire with Tatum discs on other pages
were allowed to have an influence.

In fact, six of the solo performances and two of those with
DeFranco are his only known recordings of the melodies concerned, but even if more duplication had been unavoidable it
would not have concealed that his work had undergone dramatic
changes since he recorded the improvisations on **181**. There,
everything is conceived strictly in terms of the keyboard; here,
despite the music's superb pianistic effectiveness, the instrument
is transcended. As John Mehegan wrote in the shadow of Tatum's
early death, 'He adopted trombone, trumpet, saxophone, guitar
and drum sounds. . . . He was an orchestra — rhythm section,
brass, reeds, and even the vocalist'[93]. His voracious appetites
for performing and listening are symbolized by this later music's
almost constant use of the instrument's whole register, and the

consistency of his playing — the finest ever recorded by a jazz pianist — on these unparallelled sessions is a further indication of his protean gifts.

One duplication which could not be avoided was of *Tea for two*, a piece he recorded nearly as often as *Sweet Lorraine*. In comparison with the account on **181b**, a direct ancestor of Bud Powell's celebrated 1950 reading (Verve (E) 2632 051), Tatum's later version has, like the Hines performances on **220**, a freedom and spaciousness only in part explained by the LP format. His art was shaped by club and cabaret circumstances, and even in the special conditions of these sessions he did not go in for undue length. At 6 minutes 38 seconds, *The way you look tonight* is the longest solo track here, and the reason that such improvisations seem larger than his earlier ones is that they contain so much more. For some tastes the harmony is too consistently rich yet, as this dimension of his earlier music naturally impressed the boppers, it is interesting to listen to him at work on *Cherokee*, whose chord sequence was the foundation of Charlie Parker's *Koko*, Powell's *Serenade to a square*, Serge Chaloff's *Dial-ogue*, etc. Here, as elsewhere, the extravagance is always purposeful; behind it lies a remorseless attention to detail that is evidently beyond the scope of most jazzmen — is, indeed, contrary to their basic attitude. The scale and arpeggio runs always function with absolute precision on the rhythmic plane, as in *Night and day*, its flexible treatment of tempo notwithstanding, and the bravura phrases of *Come rain or come shine* all have melodic meaning. For all its grace, this latter indicates that Tatum's most unexpected ideas often came at the beginning or end of a performance: nobody could have anticipated that coda.

Yet just as surprising is the treatment accorded to Edgar Sampson's *Blue Lou*; this is the sort of jazz 'original' he did not much favour for recording purposes and one regrets the fact, as the ideas are here packed with especial closeness. However, *Do nothing till you hear from me*, Ellington's own diminishment of *Concerto for Cootie* (**153**), is expanded again, with a keyboard 'orchestration' on the lines implied by Mehegan; one hopes that the composer heard this recording, and that of *Sophisticated lady*. Perhaps, also, *Ain't misbehaving* gave rise to pianism of almost desolating brilliance because of its association with Fats Waller. In contrast, *Everything I have is yours* suffers from rather too grandiose bravura; yet the bluesy, hard-hit *I'm coming, Virginia* is a good answer to those who complain of the bland surface of Tatum's later work. Other highlights are the independent linear inventions of *I didn't know what time it was*, the chordal chemistry of *Small hotel*, the variety of emphasis in *You took advantage of me* — hard stomping one moment, gentle traceries the next.

Such music implies that there was no limit to the avenues open to Tatum yet, although we are supposed to find him 'sounding ridiculous in a small jazz group' [94], a major interest of his performances with others is that his vast resources had to be used with greater selectivity. Most of the items from the marathon solo dates were done in a single take, whereas nearly half of the performances with Benny Carter (**219**) needed a second take, and some of those with DeFranco required three. Players of lesser imagination found the going tough indeed, and Everett Barksdale, the Tatum Trio's latter-day guitarist, said, 'His ideas, melodically and harmonically, are so startling that sometimes you find yourself at a loss' [95]. Yet despite the obvious problems, and the simplifications, on some levels, which his style had to undergo in these circumstances, recordings on **182, 186** and **191** prove that Tatum could play most beautifully with others, and his sessions with Carter and DeFranco are his best attainments in this sphere. With the latter much was achieved that was just briefly hinted at in his exchanges with another clarinet virtuoso, Barney Bigard, on **186**, and this despite both Tatum and DeFranco being in poor health at the time. One's sole regret, although Callender, like Douglass, is a sympathetic accompanist, is that the precedent set by Morton (**47a**) and Goodman (**158**) was not followed and the bass omitted, thus making the pianist's left hand more audible.

In his way, DeFranco can think, and play, virtually as fast as Tatum, yet there is no feeling of mere competition here. He meets the challenge of the pianist's teeming notes with poise, unfailing invention and an apparent executive infallibility. Not much concerned with the vocalizations and tonal variety of earlier clarinettists, DeFranco's pure linearity edges Tatum in the same direction, as in the piano solos on *Deep night, Once in a while* and *Loverman*. At a deeper level there is a productive contrast in approaches here, as on *Memories of you*, where DeFranco has some particularly striking melodic ideas. His solos are always based on the chords, whereas those by Tatum, for all their harmonic intelligence, derive from the melody, and this divergence paradoxically results in a perfect matching of parts. *This can't be love* is a brilliant example, with a whirling conflagration of a piano solo which discomforts DeFranco not at all; he responds with superb, bop-inflected clarinet playing which leads to a marvellously complementary series of four-bar exchanges that sound like the work of a single mind. There is an amusing 'false recapitulation' effect too, with DeFranco dropping back to the melody so as to imply its final return — but then the fours go on. The bop elements here and in *Making whoopee* and *A foggy day* lead one to think wistfully of the projected Parker–Tatum session for this series.

As it was, the pianist audibly relished having a partner such as DeFranco, and several of his solos, such as the one in *Making whoopee*, have a special exuberance. On *Once in a while* the clarinettist shows that he can be just as unpredictable, with outlandish figures that are matched exactly and with seemingly complete spontaneity by Tatum (though see above regarding the number of takes). *Loverman* also draws a notable variety of phrase from DeFranco, and Tatum's solo is positively magisterial; yet their subsequent duet is one of the dates few weak passages. Repeatedly Tatum provides richly enhancing settings for DeFranco's initial melody statements, as on *Deep night*, and in some cases, like *Memories of you*, this amounts to real counterpoint. The contrasts resulting from their distinct melodic and harmonic approaches are especially productive in *You're mine, you*. Tatum weaves a sparkling web around the tune, then DeFranco sails in with something totally different yet audibly related to what has gone before. This divergence continues into their subsequent duet, where the effect is one of free, exhilarating flight.　　　　　　　　　　　　　　　　　　　　　　　　　　　　M.H.

219a Art Tatum–Benny Carter Trio Vol. 1
Pablo (E) 2310 732, Pablo (A) 2310 732

Art Tatum–Benny Carter Trio: Carter (alt); Tatum (p); Louis Bellson (d). Los Angeles, 25 June 1954.
Blues in B flat · *Street of dreams* · *'Swonderful* · *Blues in C* · *A foggy day* · *Undecided* · *Under a blanket of blue*

219b Art Tatum–Benny Carter Trio Vol. 2
Pablo (E) 2310 733, Pablo (A) 2310 733

Art Tatum–Benny Carter Trio: Carter (alt); Tatum (p); Bellson (d). Los Angeles, 25 June 1954.
Blues in my heart · *Idaho* · *Old-fashioned love* · *Hands across the table* · *You're mine, you* · *Making whoopee* · *My blue heaven*

Tatum's 1956 collaborations with the solo adepts DeFranco, Ben Webster and, two years earlier, Carter are supposed to have, like many of his partnerships, an air of the unlikely. DeFranco, less celebrated though not necessarily less able as an improvising voice, best matches the pianist in terms of instrumental skill and what might be termed 'linear endurance' (**218**). Webster and Carter, near-contemporaries of Tatum, might seem more set in their ways, less likely to adapt to this dominating genius of the keyboard. The facts are that men of such profound jazz experience have not the slightest difficulty in combining their vision with his, and that he is really anything but the rapt colossal introvert invented by partially deaf commentators. There is marvellous rapport in many of these performances, as well as an acceptance of fruitful contrast and difference of approach. Webster with Tatum (Pablo (E) 2310 737) is content to inhabit airier spaces, so the element of contrast is stronger and perhaps more exciting intellectually. The choice between Webster and Carter for this inclusion was a rather tormented one. The Carter session has won its place partly for the greater variety of themes and tempos, partly because Carter is less well represented in settings of this kind, and partly, too, because there is one jazz classic here — *Blues in C* — which would be inexcusably omitted from any compendium of essential jazz.

The opening piano choruses of *Blues in C* conduct a splendid exploration into basic jazz form, for Tatum was a master of the blues, and nothing in his style is inimical to the blues spirit — even the intricate hemidemisemiquaver embroideries are as much a part of the whole expression as is the expansive vibrato of a Bechet solo. The suaveness of Carter's first entry is deceptive, and the first few measures of the conversation dispel all thoughts of individualism as Tatum answers the saxophone phrases with a sensitiveness true to a tradition first given artistry in Armstrong's early blues accompaniments (**93** and **94**). Indeed, it is Tatum's commitment that steers Carter towards a more intense emotion to contrast with the more classically conceived intervals of the saxophone part in *Blues in B flat* (recorded immediately before the C major piece). This track is long and allows much variety. Towards the end, Carter affects a detached awareness which broadens the spaces again; whereas in the other blues it is he who challenges Tatum's sunny prologue with darker intimacies and urgent invasions. It may also call in question Carter's haughty image that he so vigorously matches Tatum's ability to stride at high speed in *Undecided, 'Swonderful* and *Idaho*, maintaining the flow of twisting and sweeping lines over the pianist's irresistible rhythms. And these swift excursions have one marvelling again at the distillation of so many rich pianistic substances which informs the Tatum style: the running basses so daringly harmonic, the staccato fingering, the tumblings of contrary motion which outstrip ragtime's most extravagant dreams, the stomping jubilation trailing its bright shadows in a spray of laughter. If anything is lacking, it may be that disconcerting readiness to chance all on some arhythmical leap into space which often marks the work of Hines. With Tatum there is never any risk involved, and even the atemporal false alarms in the slow *Hands across the table* and *Under a blanket of blue* set off no tremors.

In leisurely time, Carter's gift of controlled languor comes to the fore. Tatum's response to this in *Street of dreams* is, with mild perversity, to challenge the mood with sharply upsurging runs, and Carter is, in turn, drawn towards earthier emphases. In *Blues in my heart* the involuted alto phrases, shaped by Carter's unorthodox manner of tone-bending, are distinctly clarinet-like; but, although this great musician is an able trumpeter and clarinettist, he is usually one of the most 'saxophonic' of jazz saxophonists, and vocalization plays a negligible part in his work.

Contrapuntal discoveries are made in lightly swinging essays like the latter, and also in *Making whoopee, Old-fashioned love, My blue heaven* and *A foggy day*. It is here that Carter's formalism aids an unusual kind of music-building, though the range of expression is wide; and, in this respect, it is Carter's donation to the interchanges that is the more varied. When he builds melodies out of riff-like figures, as in *Idaho*, the relationship of thought between his improvising and his orchestrating gifts is clearly indicated. In *Blues in my heart* — to which Tatum gives several Gershwinian twists — Carter moulds distinguished tunes out of different layers of form, adapting the harmonic sense by subtle repetitions and transpositions.

A few months after the 218 session Carter acted as a pallbearer at Tatum's funeral, a fact which lends poignancy to the fortunate recollections sealed in these tracks. Yet these are zestful, life-affirming moments — timeless exchanges ably and unassumingly accompanied by Bellson, whose brushwork in the faster numbers is especially exciting. If it is Tatum's achievement that persists in the mind when all is done, that implies no detriment to his companions. They were undaunted by the expanse of his spirit and they were stimulated to some of their greatest work by his unceasing freshness of textural shift, his wonderful harmonic legerdemain, his love of ambiguity, and his determination, for all his dazzling skill, never to score points off anybody. If Tatum was not quite the greatest of jazz pianists, he was, without doubt, the most magnificently generous.						E.T.

Earl Hines

220 Quintessential Recording Session
Chiaroscuro (A) CR101

Hines (p). New York City, 1969.

A Monday date · Off time blues · Just too soon · Chimes in blues · Chicago high life · Blues in thirds · Stowaway · Panther rag

These are improvisations by Hines on the same eight themes, all his own, that he recorded forty-one years earlier for the QRS company (see **49**). From a comparison of the two sets of performances emerge lessons on the continuity and growth of styles in this music and an especially conclusive refutation of the weird notion that jazz is exclusively a young man's game. In fact, 'growth' is the key word, and in two senses. Firstly, the musical and pianistic devices heard on the QRS recordings were considerably extended in Hines's 1930s work but have attained here what might be termed a disciplined luxuriance. Secondly, notwithstanding the youthful fire of the pianist's 1928 playing, the earlier performances are distinctly episodic. The old *Monday date*, for example, made a rather deliberate use of first one sort of figuration then another, whereas each of the later solos conveys an impression of continuous organic growth, and on more than one level.

What most relevantly lies between the QRS and Chiaroscuro occasions is Hines's long period as a leader of large bands. Despite the soloistic brilliance of his playing, he latterly was in essence an ensemble man, his pianism not 'orchestral' in the Mortonian sense yet inherently multilinear. Elementary commentaries on his music always cite dramatic interruptions of the bass's continuity, and he still uses here many left-hand tenths and even the fundamental 'stride' bass pattern as points of departure, contradicting and sometimes nearly dissolving the metre. But this now happens in all strata of the texture, and if the overall configuration is less jagged, less abrupt, it is because usually several different things are happening at once.

With three exceptions, Hines's thematic ideas have proved to be dateless — an important factor in the success of this enterprise. He was probably wise in making an oblique approach to the *Monday date* melody, and is still more so when it returns near the close; but *Stowaway* is the only piece to embody an unequivocal 1920s ambience. It is played with greater delicacy than on QRS — the keyboard attack just as decisive yet less obviously hard — and in a more diverse setting. The improvisation which flows out of this reveals far more extensive resources of melodic, rhythmic and pianistic invention, there being a constant sense of discovery, nowhere more so than in the extended and wholly unpredictable coda. This music's bold outward discontinuity mocks the sleeve note's assurance that 'there was no risk' involved, for Hines takes risks all the time.

The pair of improvisations which have the closest links are those on *Chicago high life*, but the later one, despite its tightly-organized musical incident, has a spaciousness that is only in part explained by the larger amount of clock-time occupied. In any case, these solos are in no sense improvisations on improvisations — in the manner, say, of Duke Jordan's lovely variant on Charlie Parker's *Embraceable you* solos (Prestige (A) PR7849). The early *Panther rag* bore clear resemblances to the famous *57 varieties*, another of Hines's 1928 readings of the *Tiger rag* chord sequence, but that ghost is fully exorcised here. It may be significant, however, that this and *Chimes in blues* are much the shortest Chiaroscuro tracks. The basic 'chimes' idea of the latter may have been a fresh thought to the young man of the QRS session but could scarcely intrigue the vastly experienced musician of 1969.

In contrast, *Off time blues* and *Just too soon* are considerably more than twice the length of the originals, and their almost infinite variety demonstrates the engagement of profound imaginative resources. The essentially pianistic nature of this music is such that there is little direct, in any sense simple, melody here (much less than in Tatum's still more virtuosic late work). That is the principal difference between the old and new *Blues in thirds*. The former did not get far from the melody and even the left-hand part was simple. Here the pianist's invention describes a wide arch indeed, with one passage repeatedly giving way to another from which it is seemingly altogether different yet to which it bears a mysterious relationship, motivic or otherwise. The rising tide of musical intensity fully justifies *Blues in thirds* being this great LP's longest track.   M.H.

Earl Hines

221 **Tour de Force**
Black Lion (E) BLP30143, Black Lion (A) 2460 200
Hines (p). New York City, 22 November 1972.
When your lover has gone · *Mack the knife* · *Say it isn't so*
Same personnel and location, 29 November 1972.
Indian summer · *I never knew* · *Lonesome road*

Simpletons who imagine jazz to be just a matter of self-expression, a kind of emotional ragbag, are often puzzled, even annoyed, by the purity of Hines's exuberance. That delight in facing up to technical challenges was no doubt what caused some commentators of the 1930s, notably John Hammond, to dismiss Hines's work as flashy, prompted by a desire to overawe. On stage, Hines certainly displayed egotism. And, just as with Ellington, there was a theatrical dimension to both his personality and craft; in conversation he seemed as proud of planning the cabaret at the Grand Terrace as he was of his musical achievements. That influenced his approach to playing in the same way as the years he spent leading bands. For Hines, music was a construction, not a sequence of casual moods. He was, too, a dedicated improviser in a way that many jazz musicians are not. Ignoring such expected rituals as the prolonged trilling in *Boogie woogie on St Louis blues* (**147**), the tunes may have been the same but the interpretations were always different.

Artistry that is based upon craftsmanship rather than the lyrical spasms of youth rarely suffers because a musician grows older. Physical deterioration cannot be evaded; Hines, for instance, developed Parkinson's disease but died before it could affect his playing. Nevertheless, the pianist was still at his dazzling best when he made this LP at the age of 69 — according to the date of birth given by John Chilton; Hines himself claimed to be two years younger [96]. The musician who played with Lois Deppe in 1923 (**49**) is still audible, but the style has been magnified, made more tangible; the rhythmic vivacity is heightened, the harmonies are more subtle and assured, the melodic flights even more daring and confident. If you set aside a few sublime moments of historical discovery — Hines's duetting with Armstrong on *Weatherbird* (**48**), for instance — this is Hines in excelsis, sounding as good as at any time in his long career.

The melodies were not always the easiest on which to improvise. *Lonesome road* is intrinsically theatrical (and perhaps that is why Hines admired it), requiring a very strong personality to do some outflanking. Kurt Weill's *Mack the knife* (or *Moritat*) began, like the rest of *Die Dreigroschenoper*, as a kind of parody of 1920s jazz; later it was to be engulfed by Armstrong's charisma as well as treated bitonally by J. J. Johnson and André Previn (CBS (E) 61352). In Hines's version the piece is used, as Brian Priestley points out in the helpful sleeve note, to show off the variety of the pianist's left-hand playing. *Indian summer*, a Victor Herbert song, has ensnared many third-rate tenor saxophonists; Hines avoids the trap of lapsing into sumptuousness, keeping his lines taut and melodic. *Say it isn't so*, very popular with crooners of the 1930s but scarcely heard since then, has Hines tucking the theme neatly inside a performance that contrives to be spectacular without making too many detours. He alternates tempos in *I never knew*, deliberately injecting contrast. *When your lover has gone* is treated brightly (it seems unlikely that Hines paid any attention to the lyrics of the songs he played), introspection encroaching only with the coda's dying fall. This track is also a reminder that he could throw in quotations as wittily as anybody (*There's a small hotel* once, *Louise* twice), yet without ever allowing the practice to become a bore. 						C.F.

Duke Ellington

222 **Such Sweet Thunder**
CBS Realm (E) 52421, Columbia (A) JCL1033

Duke Ellington and His Orchestra: Cat Anderson, Clark Terry, Willie Cook (tpt); Ray Nance (cnt); John Sanders, Britt Woodman, Quentin Jackson (tbn); Russell Procope (clt, alt); Jimmy Hamilton (clt, ten); Harry Carney (clt, bar); Johnny Hodges (alt); Paul Gonsalves (ten); Ellington (p); Jimmy Woode (bs); Sam Woodyard (d). New York City, 7 August 1956.
Half the fun
Same personnel and location, 15 April 1957.
Sonnet for Caesar · *Sonnet in search of a Moor* · *Sonnet for Sister Kate*
Nance also plays vln[1]. New York City, 24 April 1957.
Up and down, up and down[1] · *Such sweet thunder* · *Lady Mac*
Same personnel and location, 3 May 1957.
Star-crossed lovers · *Madness in great ones* · *Sonnet for Hank Cinq* · *The telecasters* · *Circle of fourths*

Ellington's earliest attempts at moving beyond the limits of one side of a ten-inch 78 rpm disc, *Creole rhapsody* and *Reminiscing in tempo*, have been discussed already (**88** and **131b**). Their shortcomings were largely a matter of structure and development — which may be why his longer works during the following decades mostly took the form of suites, a number of short pieces united by a social, literary or more personal notion. *Black, Brown and Beige*, first performed in 1943, was Ellington's initial foray at a programmatic suite, yet the band never recorded a satisfactory complete version [97]. Other suites followed, sometimes marred by inconsistencies of style and content, until *Such Sweet Thunder* was composed and given its first complete performance on 28 April 1957. Built around characters or incidents in the plays of Shakespeare, the work is jointly credited to Ellington and Billy

Strayhorn, without any further indication of who wrote which passages. The musicians taking part seemed to be no more knowledgeable about that than we are; Clark Terry told the present writer that the individual parts provided no clues — all came from the band's copyist. Musicologists delving into jazz should give priority to this puzzle as well as to analysing Strayhorn's overall contribution to what has to be called Ellington's music; the vocabulary as well as the orchestra was Ellington's, even if Strayhorn adapted both for his own purposes. Meanwhile, all we have are theories and hunches.

The opening track, for instance, the eponymous *Such sweet thunder*, consists of elements so intrinsically Ellingtonian that one doubts if much collaboration went on. The opening theme is processional, rather like a variant of *The mooche* (**87, 91**), complete with snarling trumpets. What could never have happened in the 1930s, however, was the entrusting of an alternative theme to the saxophone section. Nance's cornet, lagging deliciously but riskily behind the beat, is the main solo voice. Old values are also reasserted in *Sonnet for Sister Kate*, with Jackson's trombone reproducing the kind of delicate robustness for which 'Tricky Sam' Nanton was renowned. The stance here is perhaps more forthright, more obvious, than in the three other sonnets. This term seems to have been taken over arbitrarily, with no more serious attempt at producing a musical equivalent to the literary discipline than T. S. Eliot made from the opposite direction when writing his *Four Quartets*. Each sonnet, however, is constructed around a single soloist. To that extent one might see the four earliest of Ellington's 'concertos' — *Clarinet lament, Echoes of Harlem* (**131a**), *Trumpet in spades* (**164**) and *Yearning for love*, all recorded in 1936 — as direct predecessors, even if they were never granted a collective identity.

This band was perhaps the last of Ellington's major orchestras. Soon he would be acquiring fresh musicians but not bothering to devise pieces around their particular talents; his ignoring of the trumpeter Johnny Coles was to be just one irritating example of that. Relative newcomers such as Terry, Woodman, Gonsalves and Woode, however, were featured in this suite. Woodman, for instance, was chosen to project the brazen heroics of Hank Cinq, an idea beautifully conceived and carried out. And although old admirers of the band considered that Hamilton's clarinet playing sounded antiseptic compared with Barney Bigard's Creole foibles, it brought exactly the right air of correctness to *Sonnet for Caesar*, contrasting with the deliberate unease of the background. (Woodyard's drumming on this track is typical of his resourcefulness throughout the entire LP, demonstrating that he was capable of much more than thwacking the off-beat, which often was all that Ellington encouraged him to do during the band's public appearances.) *Sonnet in search of a Moor* presents Woode's bass, lacking the *brio* of the young Blanton yet moving soberly and sensibly against a clarinet trio.

How seriously one should take the parallels with Shakespearean drama is almost a matter for the individual listener. The critic Burnett James has written an essay in which he relates text to music, and ponders as to whether Ellington could have translated Lear's agonizing into jazz [98]. The important point, though, is not whether the pieces reflect an acceptable view of Shakespeare's characters — Prince Hal, after all, is no more intrinsically worth celebrating than, say, Harlem worthies such as Bert Williams or 'Bojangles' Robinson, both subjects of earlier portraits by Ellington (**153**) — but whether the result is worth-while music. In many cases, individual movements appear to succeed on both counts, always assuming one appreciates the ironic tilt observable in much of Ellington's life and work. *Sonnet for Hank Cinq* [99] and *Sonnet for Caesar* are programmatic in the most overt way. Far more sidelong is the approach to *Lady Mac*. 'We suspect there was a little ragtime in her soul', Ellington said, at the same time setting this movement in triple time. The scoring is as witty as it is varied, culminating in ominous chords after Terry has revealed his skill at making a trumpet talk. He does it again, and in a literal fashion, at the very end of *Up and down, up and down*, where he makes a creditable attempt at uttering Puck's verdict on the human race. But this movement, inspired, of course, by *A Midsummer Night's Dream*, also makes adroit use of Nance's violin playing, almost as lacy as gossamer. In both pieces Terry was performing, though in a very individual fashion, roles that in the 1930s and 1940s might have gone to Rex Stewart, that master of the perky, strutting manner. Similarly, Anderson was now providing, but with a greater range and more musical panache, the showy antics in which Freddy Jenkins had specialized a quarter of a century earlier. That included the use of high notes — occasionally for functional, specifically aesthetic ends. Just as Jenkins imitated the applying of a railway train's brakes at the close of *Daybreak express* (**130**) so, in *Madness in great ones*, Anderson, somewhat more profoundly but no less spectacularly, uses freak techniques to suggest Hamlet's feigning of insanity — another brilliant musical conception.

The fact that *Half the fun* was recorded nine months before any of the other movements invites suspicion about whether Ellington (or more probably Strayhorn) originally had in mind Cleopatra floating down the Nile, especially as Strayhorn declared that he and Ellington took about six months to write the suite[100]. Nevertheless, no other composition could suggest more perfectly how 'The barge she sat in, like a burnished throne,/Burn'd on the water'. Hodges bubbles delightfully in this, but in *Star-crossed lovers* adopts his languishing manner, prevented from lapsing into sentimentality by self-restraint, by the dryness of the scoring behind him, and by occasional interjections from Carney, always a stout link with reality. *The telecasters* gives Carney a more prominent role, his baritone saxophone signifying Iago in a mixing of melodramas that has the trombone section deputizing for the three witches of *Macbeth*. This is a highly successful fusion, not least for the way it exploits the pregnant pause. At the time that the *Such Sweet Thunder* suite was initially released on record, its closing movement, *Circle of fourths*, during which Gonsalves's tenor saxophone hurries through every possible key, seemed highly inappropriate to most people, a tasteless descent into exhibitionism, not quite so boring as his marathon outing in the Newport Festival assault on *Crescendo and diminuendo in blue* but only because it was shorter. That flashy, thoroughly frivolous climax now seems to resemble the jokey, throwaway *envoi* with which writers of *canzones* were expected to conclude poems that were otherwise highly serious, even metaphysical. Such an attitude would be thoroughly in character for Ellington, never a man to allow too much solemnity to 'stink up the place'. For better or for worse, Gonsalves's sophisticated brand of rowdiness rounds off what must be ranked as one of the most satisfying of the longer works composed for the Ellington orchestra.   C.F.

Duke Ellington

223 Money Jungle
United Artists (E) ULP 1039, Blue Note (A) BNP25113

Ellington (p); Charles Mingus (bs); Max Roach (d). New York City, 17 September 1962.

Money jungle · *Les fleurs africaines* · *Very special* · *Warm valley* · *Wig wise* · *Caravan* · *Solitude*

Presumably because of his early concentration on orchestral composition, and perhaps, too, because of his sustained logical development in that sphere, Ellington's growth as an improvising pianist was markedly unsteady and, indeed, rather strange.

There are passages on quite early recordings which are remarkably advanced in both vision and musical language, yet he was capable, as on the 1940 *Cottontail* (**153**) of reverting to his 'stride' roots with disastrous stylistic incongruity. Consistency was finally achieved at a singularly late stage in his long career, and although there are several discs which set his playing in the foreground, the above can be taken as his crucial statement as a jazz pianist. Considering that he spent most of his life in a musical world that he had himself created, it is of exceptional interest that these recordings were made in quite other circumstances.

Ellington was briefly at liberty between two long-term contracts, and during this period made several LPs with musicians very different from those with whom he normally associated. These include a generally underrated set with Louis Armstrong, a discouragingly listless meeting with John Coltrane and Elvin Jones, and another with Coleman Hawkins which demanded too many compromises on all sides. Though it involved tensions — not across the generation gap but between Mingus and Roach[101] — this trio session of September 1962 had an altogether different character. In what might be called its post-Louis Bellson years, his orchestra employed a variety of inferior drummers, yet Ellington's response to Roach, a major innovator and master improviser in this field, was acute, as it had been to Jo Jones on other dates. Unfortunately, Roach is not well recorded, though he comes through fairly well on *Caravan* and the eponymous *Money jungle* track. Mingus's contributions excellently summarize his achievements as a bassist up to this time.

If account be taken of the unissued material from this session, which includes a *Slow blues* and a *Backward country blues*, there was a considerable emphasis on blues. The outstanding example is the turbulent, incantatory *Money jungle*, and it was right for the disc to take its title from this. One scarcely is aware of the twelve-bar structure, which is largely overlaid by the music's ongoing argument. Here as on the other tracks, Ellington's execution is unfailingly decisive, yet although he takes the lead, bass and drums are hardly less active and no less essential. In general, the freedom of Ellington's approach to keyboard texture here is amazing, and the description of *Wig wise* as 'Monkish'[102] is justified. This was a vein which surfaced repeatedly in his playing, another instance being the *New piano roll blues* of 1950, on which Roach was also present (Vogue (E) VJD525). Nor is it merely incidental that another unissued track from this 1962 date is a version of Monk's *Blue Monk*. (This equation may be sampled the other way round, of course, with Monk's recordings of Ellington compositions — Milestone (A) 47052.)

The third major new Ellington theme presented on this occasion, along with *Money jungle* and *Wig wise*, was *Very special* which, like the former, is another fast blues. Coming after the relative discontinuity of his playing on the other two pieces, this is easier to follow, though its originality is no less. Nor are its urgency and spontaneity — qualities which carry over into this treatment of *Caravan*, which began as a piece of rather facile exotica yet here sounds highly abrasive. Not that spontaneity is confined to the quick performances. *Les fleurs africaines* (also known as *La fleurette africaine*) had only been sketched out on the piano during a prior meeting at Ellington's office, but it was completed in one take with Mingus, especially, sounding, as the composer later said, as if he had been playing it all his life. On *Solitude*, Ellington rhapsodizes at length and does not quite abandon the melody even when bass and drums enter. In fact he reveals it in fresh lights in both sections of the performance, and this, no less than *Warm valley*, *Caravan* or the several blues, demonstrates Ellington's ability to renew himself on material that he had played countless times before. An extra edge is lent to the proceedings, however, by the full instrumental mastery he attained during these later years of his life.   M.H.

Duke Ellington
224
New Orleans Suite
Atlantic (E) 2400 135, Atlantic (A) 1580

Duke Ellington and His Orchestra: Cootie Williams (tpt); 'Money' Johnson, Mercer Ellington, Al Rubin, Fred Stone (tpt, fl h); 'Booty' Wood, Julian Priester (tbn); Dave Taylor (bs tbn); Russell Procope (clt, alt); Norris Turney (clt, alt, fl); Harold Ashby (clt, ten); Harry Carney (clt, bs clt, bar); Johnny Hodges (alt); Paul Gonsalves (ten); Duke Ellington (p); Joe Benjamin (bs); Rufus Jones (d). New York City, 27 April 1970.
Bourbon Street jingling jollies · Thanks for the beautiful land of the Delta · Second line · Aristocracy à la Jean Lafitte
'Wild' Bill Davis (org) added. Same date.
Blues for New Orleans
Cat Anderson (tpt), Chuck Connors (bs tbn) replace Johnson, Taylor; Hodges absent. New York City, 13 May 1970.
Portrait of Louis Armstrong · Portrait of Wellman Braud · Portrait of Sidney Bechet · Portrait of Mahalia Jackson

The strength of the Ellington unit as a self-perpetuating phenomenon is well instanced here. Four years prior to Ellington's death, there were in the orchestra players providing links with the beginnings and the middle period, and new men also who, like many who had come and gone, were borne up in the collective inspiration which had helped to make those veterans what they had become.

That Ellington had not simply moulded his artists to his own conception is exemplified by his acceptance of the personal strength of Hodges — always markedly his own man — and the newcomer Turney. The oft-rehearsed tale that Ellingtonians, once established, were worth little in separation is no more than minimally true; and though the tradition has required the assumption by individuals of others' *personae* — as in Williams's early succession to Miley, and Procope's imitation of Bigard here in *Second line* and *Portrait of Wellman Braud* — there has always been sufficient scope for personal inspiration, if not for marked self-assertion.

That non-Ellingtonians are honoured and even emulated here is part of the exercise. *Portrait of Louis Armstrong* gives a notably vocalized trumpet style the chance to capture the vocal and instrumental manners of a great jazz exemplar. Williams had heard Armstrong in the latter's Henderson days and was a lifelong admirer. Against chords which, alternating with Benjamin's octave pendulum, recall orchestral marvels of the 1940s, he celebrates the master's eternal youthfulness.

The other portraits of New Orleanians are similarly perceptive. Braud's bass authority is captured by Benjamin in skilful unison with sections of the band while Williams and the reed section evoke a mode which Braud himself did not remain to share. Bechet, for all that he joined the band briefly and left his trace, was no Ellingtonian, though profoundly admired; yet he receives a thoroughly Ellingtonian tribute which probably honours his influence rather than his direct personal achievements. The Duke had wanted Hodges to dust off his soprano saxophone for the eulogy of his chief mentor, but the great altoist died two days before the recording of this piece; and Gonsalves, playing tenor, makes no attempt at the physical evocation of either dead hero; yet he sings the best and most perceptive requiem to both of them — jazz without pretence.

Perhaps only Ellington could resume Mahalia Jackson's spirit and the character of her song orchestrally. There are moments when *Black and tan fantasy* could suddenly return, yet the harmonic recollections here are not those which the latter-day Negro Church has favoured the most. They sound closer to those instrumental dirges which reflect a culture hovering between black protestantism and Creole catholicism (2).

The work of the April session is kept for a conclusion, since it preserves the flavour of the first responses to George Wein's commission for the New Orleans Festival, and is the last Ellington recording to include Hodges. There is fine orchestral writing in *Blues for New Orleans* and thus greater cause for regret that such prominence is allowed to Davis's electronic shimmying. His 'voice' sounds rather like a grossly-distorted echo of the Ellingtonian shout, and its insidious glamour unfortunately spreads beneath part of Hodges's fine solo. The altoist's expression develops through the rather diffident blues phrases of its outset to the almost earthy declamations at its close.

Turney's ethereal flute roves across typically colouristic backdrops in *Bourbon Street jingling jollies*, aiding Ellington in his aim at 'overall pastel enchantment' and exploring a subcontinent in which Hodges long ago cultivated his passion-flowers, daydreams and moonmists. Gonsalves had learnt most of Ben Webster's solos by heart when he first joined the band, but the Websterian orthodoxy is extended, in *Thanks for the beautiful land of the Delta*, by Ashby, who sounds uninspired and is easily outshone by Procope and Turney, let alone Hodges. Procope's Bigard impersonation is the strongest Crescent City accent in *Second line*, for there is no orchestral attempt to recall the marching bands. The antics of the sidewalk supporters are effected by strutting brass figures.

Jean Lafitte, a reputedly magnanimous pirate, stands for the elegancies of a faintly mythical Louisiana past; and here, amid rhythms which nonchalantly mix slow two and fast three, Carney's staccato reverie, Stone's mellow flugel boppisms, Benjamin's lovely pattern and Ellington's own piano part not only create the desired effect but demonstrate the importance to this band's tradition of players who are outstanding craftsmen rather than great inspirational solo artists.

Ellington provides witty and apposite introductions at the piano for most of the numbers in this late addition to his long list of dance suites; but that is a small matter beside the Midas touch which makes invaluable this music, and so much which — over several decades — had preceded it. He was, after all, this urbane visionary from Washington D.C., the real self-perpetuating power within a remarkable, unforgettable jazz community which never lost its vivacity or its breadth of imagination so long as he lived.   E.T.

7

Against the Current
Traditional Survivals and Revivals

The older forms of jazz never entirely disappeared, but many of these recordings illustrate the quickening of interest in them during the later 1930s and beyond. They demonstrate a growing awareness that this music had a history, and confirm the coexistence — rather than linear succession — of jazz styles.

225 Bechet of New Orleans
RCA (E) RD7696, RCA (A) LPV510
The New Orleans Feetwarmers: Tommy Ladnier (tpt); Teddy Nixon (tbn); Sidney Bechet (clt, sop); Hank Duncan (p); Wilson Myers (bs); Morris Morland (d). New York City, 15 September 1932.
Sweetie dear · Maple leaf rag
Tommy Ladnier and His Orchestra: Ladnier (tpt); Bechet, Mezz Mezzrow (clt); Cliff Jackson (p); Teddy Bunn (g); Elmer James (bs); Manzie Johnson (d). New York City, 28 November 1938.
Weary blues
Jelly Roll Morton's New Orleans Jazzmen: Sidney DeParis (tpt); Claude Jones (tbn); Albert Nicholas (clt); Bechet (sop); Happy Cauldwell (ten); Morton (p, vcl); Lawrence Lucie (g); Wellman Braud (bs); Zutty Singleton (d). New York City, 14 September 1939.
I thought I heard Buddy Bolden say
Sidney Bechet and His New Orleans Feetwarmers: DeParis (tpt); Sandy Williams (tbn); Bechet (clt, sop); Jackson (p); Bernard Addison (g); Braud (bs); Sidney Catlett (d). New York City, 4 June 1940.
Shake it and break it · Wild man blues
Rex Stewart (cnt); Bechet (clt, sop); Earl Hines (p); John Lindsay (bs); 'Baby' Dodds (d). Chicago, 6 September 1940.
Save it, pretty mama

Professor Sidney Bechet with Dr Henry Levine and His Barefooted
Dixieland Philharmonic: Henry Levine (tpt); Jacques Epstein (tbn); Alfie
Evans (clt); Bechet (sop); Rudolph Alder (ten); Mario Janarro (p); Tony
Colucci (g); Henry Patent (bs); Nat Levine (d). New York City,
11 November 1940.
Muskrat ramble

Sidney Bechet and His New Orleans Feetwarmers: Henry Allen (tpt);
J. C. Higginbotham (tbn); Bechet (clt, sop); James Tolliver (p); Braud
(bs); J. C. Heard (d). 8 January 1941.
Egyptian fantasy · Baby, won't you please come home?

Sidney Bechet's One-Man Band: Bechet (clt, sop, ten, p, bs, d). New York
City, 18 April 1941.
The sheik of Araby

Sidney Bechet and His New Orleans Feetwarmers: Gus Aitken (tpt);
Williams (tbn); Bechet (clt, sop); Lem Davis (ten); Jackson (p); Myers
(bs); Kenny Clarke (d). New York City, 28 April 1941.
*When it's sleepy time down south · I ain't gonna give nobody none
of this jelly roll*

Charlie Shavers (tpt); Bechet (clt, sop); Willie 'The Lion' Smith (p);
Everett Barksdale (g); Braud (bs); Johnson (d). New York City,
13 September 1941.
Georgia cabin · Texas moaner

Catlett (d) replaces Johnson. New York City, 24 October 1941.
Twelfth Street rag

226 The Blue Bechet
RCA (E) RD7854, RCA (A) LPV535

The New Orleans Feetwarmers: Ladnier (tpt); Nixon (tbn); Bechet (clt,
sop); Duncan (p); Myers (bs); Morland (d); Billy Maxey (vcl[1]). New York
City, 15 September 1932.
I've found a new baby · Lay your racket[1] · Shag

Sidney Bechet and His New Orleans Feetwarmers: Bechet (clt, sop, vcl[2]);
Sonny White (p); Charlie Howard (g); Myers (bs); Clarke (d). New York
City, 5 February 1940.
Indian summer · One o'clock jump · Sidney's blues[2]

DeParis (tpt); Williams (tbn); Bechet (clt, sop); Jackson (p); Addison (g);
Braud (bs); Catlett (d). New York City, 4 June 1940.
Nobody knows the way I feel this morning · Old man blues

Stewart (cnt); Bechet (clt, sop); Hines (p); Lindsay (bs); Dodds (d).
Chicago, 6 September 1940.
Ain't misbehaving

Stewart, Lindsay absent. Same date.
Blues in thirds

Shavers (tpt); Bechet (clt, sop); Smith (p); Barksdale (g); Braud (bs);
Johnson (d). New York City, 13 September 1941.
I'm coming, Virginia · Limehouse blues

Shavers, Braud, Johnson absent. Same date.
Strange fruit
Sidney Bechet and His Orchestra: Henry Goodwin (tpt); Vic Dickenson
(tbn); Bechet (clt, sop); Don Donaldson (p); Ernest Williamson (bs);
Johnson (d). New York City, 14 October 1941.
Blues in the air · The mooche
Shavers (tpt); Bechet (clt, sop); Smith (p); Barksdale (g); Braud (bs);
Catlett (d). New York City, 24 October 1941.
Mood indigo

Bechet was a strange virtuoso, and it is reported by some who
knew and played with him that certain of the less savoury strains
of character which the demons of brilliance can encourage were
his to a sometimes painful degree. 'The most selfish, hard-to-get-
along-with guy I ever worked with' . . . 'all for himself' . . .
'jealous, don't want anybody to do nothing but him' . . . 'didn't
want nobody to tell him nothing'. But though arrogance may
accompany genius, the genius is never in the arrogance; and the
only aural evidence which might support these quoted complaints
is in those records where Bechet's dominance of a group seems
unreasonable. In fact, however, the strength of such evidence in
these two interlocking collections is less than might have been
expected.

It is Morland's drumming that sometimes threatens the 1932
session, sabotaging the brightness of *Sweetie dear's* mood with
savage thumps. The magnificent steering mastery of Bechet,
greedy dog or no, makes *I've found a new baby*, *Maple leaf rag*,
Shag and *Lay your racket* the classics they are. There is an oft-
repeated suggestion that Bechet fancied that he was playing a
trumpet with a reed in it, that he usurped the trumpet's rightful
ensemble lead, yet, even in the ensemble's astonishing translation of *I got rhythm* into *Shag*, the saxophone's heraldic dance
accepts the modest support of Ladnier and Nixon, and leads them
in whirling periods of synchronal improvising. The spirit is that
of New Orleans, but the form has developed beyond the more
fastidious balance of early Oliver and Armstrong groups to a
collective daring which is closer to the second-generation street
music of the 1958 Young Tuxedo Band (**18**). The original charm of
Maple leaf rag is swallowed by robust melodrama and loosely-
tethered wildness, a hazardous recipe for what turns out to be jazz
of great splendour.

In *Weary blues* (also found, with its session-mates, on **228**)
Ladnier's full tone and tough phrasing again prove an excellent
foil to Bechet's and the latter's respect for Mezzrow's simple gifts
is clear in the clarinet duet. The arranged passages show how the

older tunes could presage later style and, conversely, the experience of swing ensembles makes the attempt to recreate an older fashion, in the 1939 *Buddy Bolden*, rather less than successful on its chosen terms. The ecstatic dignity of Bechet's soprano solo overshadows the worthy but anachronistic statements of Morton's other companions.

The first 1940 session leaves all reminiscence of New Orleans behind. White's fine playing in *Sidney's blues* (not much helped by Myers's bowed figures) and *One o'clock jump* again raises the question of this pianist's critical neglect; and, in these as in *Indian summer*, Bechet lays claim, as so often elsewhere, to being one of jazz's most expressive singers — not in his ill-advised blues vocal, but by his affective work on both his instruments. In this Victor Herbert tune, he travels from entranced meditation to an extravagance of feeling which reunites mere music with its source in unalloyed vocal emotion.

Committed assistance from DeParis, Williams and a celebrated rhythm section reintroduces the communal spirit of the 1932 numbers. A Southern exhortation, *Shake it and break it* (and hang it on the wall), gives the theme for a performance almost matching *Shag* in its vivacity. *Wild man blues*, containing some of DeParis's strongest playing, and *Old man blues*, recalling Bechet's early link with Ellington, are fine re-creations. *Nobody knows the way I feel this morning* interprets in wholly instrumental terms the song which Alberta Hunter sang on one of Bechet's earliest recorded appearances, when the strikingly feminine character of the soprano saxophone was exploited in accompaniment. In the new version the blues song takes on characteristics of religious chant.

Stewart's personal tone and the graceful percussiveness of Hines bring additional distinction to *Save it, pretty mama* and *Ain't misbehaving*; and ambitious routines of interchange between cornet, piano and clarinet or soprano are nonchalantly managed. Brilliance of a different but equally satisfying sort is heard in *Egyptian fantasy* and *Baby, won't you please come home?* Allen's deep-throated trumpet complements the agile clarinet · wonderfully in the first piece, and there are fine two-chorus solos from Allen, Higginbotham and Bechet in the second. Bechet in full cry so powerfully concentrates the discoveries of the jazz ensemble in his solos that the lightweight superimpositions which produce *The sheik of Araby* appear superfluous, and restrictive as well.

When it's sleepy time down south and *I ain't gonna give nobody none of this jelly roll* are further partial genuflections towards the past. Aitken honours but does not ape Armstrong, and both

Williams and Jackson make ebullient statements. Bechet shows that his style, epitome of the Creole genius though it is, fits ably into a Harlem context; and when he is joined by Shavers, Smith and Barksdale for *Texas moaner, Georgia cabin, I'm coming, Virginia* and *Limehouse blues*, the difficulty of classifying his music according to style or period is re-emphasized. Furthermore, the fallacy of his constant musical egotism is dispelled by the restrained support he supplies from time to time, and by his evident respect for the skills of his *confrères*.

The repertoire for the October 1941 session is distinctly Ellingtonian, for even Bechet's own *Blues in the air* shows the Ducal influence in its preface. *The mooche* stays closer in pattern to the orchestral original than did *Old man blues*. Dickenson and Goodwin echo Nanton and Miley, and there are no extended solos. *Mood indigo* is more adventurously treated, with some splendid clarinet effects, expertly varied to suit the felicities of Shavers and Barksdale. In the fast and jovial *Twelfth Street rag*, where the tempo almost outwits 'The Lion' but spurs Shavers to lyrical agility, Bechet displays some of his finest clarinet work, completely recomposing the puerile theme. One regrets Bechet's gradual abandonment of the clarinet towards the end of his career, but rejoices that there are still several excellent instances of his use of the instrument in the later sessions contained in **242**.   E.T.

227 Sidney Bechet: in Memoriam
Ember (E) EMB3330, Riverside (A) RLP12-138
Bechet—Spanier Big Four: Muggsy Spanier (cnt); Bechet (clt, sop); Carmen Mastren (g); Wellman Braud (bs). New York City, 28 March 1940.
Four or five times · Sweet Lorraine · Lazy river · China boy
Same personnel and location, 6 April 1940.
If I could be with you one hour tonight · That's a-plenty · Squeeze me · Sweet Sue

This partnership might in theory have seemed impracticable, yet in fact it worked exceedingly well. Nor was this due to Bechet and Spanier making only simple music together, for the counterpoint on the last chorus of *Lazy river* is a striking achievement, comparable in its rightness and finish to Armstrong and Dodds on *Potato head blues* (**48**). Their lines also attain impressive independence in the closing ensembles of *China boy* and *Four or five times*, and there is a masterly avoidance of dixieland stereotypes in *That's a-plenty*. As Richard Hadlock said in the sleeve note to the American edition of this record, 'It is almost as though each spontaneous chorus were a structured composition', the detail and overall shape being exactly appropriate, seemingly inevitable.

Aside from Ladnier (**225–6** and **228**), no other trumpeter (or cornettist) adapted himself so well to Bechet on records as Spanier, Elsewhere, the former sometimes monopolizes the lead, thus casting doubt on the brassman's role, but here Bechet subordinates himself to Spanier at some points, as on *Sweet Lorraine* and *Lazy river*. This was partly due to the stage of development he then had reached. The Bechet *oeuvre* has many sides; the intensity of his early work reached a climax in *Maple leaf rag* (**225**), and during his final years in France he sometimes played with an unrelenting ferocity engendered by the abysmal quality of his accompanists, harsh accentuation and extreme vibrato obtruding on that wonderful flow of invention. But during the period of the above sessions, Bechet's improvising was often characterized by a mellifluousness, almost an inner tranquillity, which marks, too, such items as the RCA *Blues in thirds* (**226**) and Blue Note *Blue horizon* (**242a**). Perhaps this quality aided his accommodation of Spanier, and certainly it is beautifully demonstrated by the mellow lyricism of *Lazy river*, *Sweet Lorraine* and *If I could be with you*. It even brings out an unaccustomed warmth in Spanier, who has more ideas than usual on *Squeeze me* and the very fast *China boy*, and takes admirable muted solos in *Four or five times* and *That's a-plenty*.

Bechet's use of *rubato* on these performances is unusual in the jazz context, and he plays with notable freedom in, for example, his first *China boy* solo, at some points bearing down hard on the beat, at others appearing to lag behind it, at others again to race ahead. With such means of expression at his command, his playing naturally covers a wider variety of moods than Spanier's, and his exultant solos on *Lazy river* and *Sweet Sue* are among this record's highspots. The low points are furnished by the arid obviousness of the guitar, and even more the bass, solos. It should also be mentioned that although these performances originally appeared on twelve-inch 78 rpm discs the playing time is short, and it is a pity that the available alternative takes of *That's a-plenty* and *China boy* were not included in this memorial album. (They can be found on Swaggie (Au) S1392.) Bechet's playing here should be compared with his contribution to *Coal cart blues* with Armstrong (**230**), which uses the same instrumentation.

M.H.

Tommy Ladnier—Mezz Mezzrow/Frank Newton

228 **The Panassié Sessions**
RCA (E) RD7887, RCA (A) LPV542

Mezz Mezzrow and His Orchestra: Tommy Ladnier, Sidney DeParis (tpt); Mezzrow (clt); James P. Johnson (p); Teddy Bunn (g); Elmer James (bs); Zutty Singleton (d). New York City, 21 November 1938.

Revolutionary blues · Coming on with the come-on

Tommy Ladnier and His Orchestra: Ladnier (tpt); Sidney Bechet (clt, sop); Mezzrow (clt, ten); Cliff Jackson (p); Bunn (g); James (bs); Manzie Johnson (d). New York City, 28 November 1938.

Jada · Really the blues · When you and I were young, Maggie · Weary blues

Mezzrow—Ladnier Quintet: Ladnier (tpt); Mezzrow (clt); Bunn (g, vcl[1]); Pops Foster (bs); Manzie Johnson (d). New York City, 19 December 1938.

Royal Garden blues · Everybody loves my baby · I ain't gonna give nobody none of this jelly roll · If you see me coming[1] · Getting together (2 takes)

Frankie Newton and His Orchestra: Newton (tpt); Mezzrow (clt); Pete Brown (alt); James P. Johnson (p); Al Casey (g); John Kirby (bs); Cozy Cole (d). New York City, 13 January 1939.

Rosetta · The world is waiting for the sunrise · Who?

Reasserting the ethos and disciplines of New Orleans jazz at the end of the 1930s was by no means the romantic enterprise that it often became during the decades which followed. The heyday of that music, after all, lay not so very much earlier, and many of the major New Orleans players were only just into or approaching their forties. The great merit of the first three of the four sessions supervised by the French writer on jazz, Hugues Panassié, visiting the US for the first time, aided — indeed, counselled — by Mezzrow, was that they set out to recreate the spirit of New Orleans music instead of imitating past triumphs.

Mezzrow is an odd case: a jazz musician *manqué*; a white Chicagoan who aligned himself with black rather than white society; the leader or co-leader of several highly successful recording groups; a helpful teacher, capable of critical analysis of his own and other musicians' work (all these recordings are discussed in detail in the appendices of Mezzrow's autobiography, *Really the Blues*); a useful catalyst, in fact, yet a performer whose own playing consistently fell far short of his aims. His clarinet solo in *Royal Garden blues* is little more than trite arpeggiation, that in the brisker half of the two-part *Coming on with the come-on* an inadequate essay at Jimmy Noone's manner; nevertheless, *I ain't gonna give nobody none of this jelly roll* contains a solo where the intent is palpably original. The blues playing on *If you see me coming* contrives to be both authentic and effective also, though his feeling for blues perhaps had more in common with the approach of a folk rather than a jazz performer. There are ensemble passages in which Mezzrow sounds woefully incompetent, yet others where, despite faulty technique, his instinct makes the music work; good examples are the support he gives Bechet, and the tight partnership with Ladnier in *I ain't gonna give nobody none of this jelly roll*. His influence is audible in other directions, notably the passages for two clarinets (especially successful on *Weary blues*) and, as a composer, the reshaping of the blues formula in the thirty-two-bar *Revolutionary blues*.

The fact that Bechet specialized in the soprano saxophone tended to obscure the fact that he was also one of the great New Orleans clarinettists. He takes an acutely adventurous solo, warping the notes with abandon, on *Weary blues*, although even that is surpassed by his majestic soprano playing in *Really the blues*. Ladnier's reputation had dwindled by the time Panassié sought him out; he was only thirty-eight and died six months later. Illness and lack of regular work as a trumpeter probably account for the raggedness on certain tracks, such as *When you and I were young, Maggie*, but the concision of his lead playing fitted these groups and he takes an eloquently understated solo on *Really the blues*. Putting DeParis alongside him provided an interesting contrast in styles. DeParis does all the growling, and in the slow part of *Coming on with the come-on* he builds up tension when Mezzrow is allowing the music to sag. But as Mezzrow explains in his autobiography, an aesthetic clash between the trumpeters in the ninth and tenth choruses in the second part of this piece resulted in the performance's virtual collapse. All the rhythm sections operated efficiently, with Manzie Johnson using press rolls to particularly striking effect on *Really the blues*. In addition, Bunn takes guitar solos that communicate a playful elegance.

Different aims prevailed at the final session. The musicians were mostly younger and the emphasis was upon solos rather than ensemble interaction. Newton, who had been ill only a short time before, sounds slightly off form, while Mezzrow keeps a low profile. It is fortunate that he decided not to take any tenor saxophone solos — as he had, with embarrassing consequences, in *Jada* and *When you and I were young, Maggie*. Brown was always an enthusiastic musician, but his huffing and puffing resulted in solos that pushed rather than swung. Casey, chording throughout in contrast to Bunn's single-string manner, takes an exhilarating solo on *Who?*, a track which turned into something of a *tour de force* for the oldest player on the session, James P. Johnson, who was two years short of fifty at the time. Such playing, and again

in *Rosetta*, shares with Jack Teagarden's trombone solos elsewhere the capacity to sound familiar yet flexible. Johnson
emerges as the most impressive performer on this session.   C.F.

229   Jimmy Noone 1937–41
Swaggie (Au) S1226

Jimmy Noone's New Orleans Band: Guy Kelly (tpt, vcl[1]); Preston
Jackson (tbn); Noone (clt); Francis Whitby (ten); Gideon Honore (p);
Israel Crosby (bs); Tubby Hall (d). Chicago, 5 January 1936.

*He's a different type of guy · Way down yonder in New Orleans · The
blues jumped a rabbit*[1] *· Sweet Georgia Brown*

Jimmy Noone and His Orchestra: Charlie Shavers (tpt, vcl[2]); Noone (clt);
Pete Brown (sop, alt); Frank Smith (p); Teddy Bunn (g, vcl[3]); Wellman
Braud (bs); O'Neill Spencer (d, vcl[4]); Teddy Simmons (vcl[5]). New York
City, 1 December 1937.

Sweet Lorraine[4] *· I know that you know · Bump it · Four or five
times*[2,3,4] *· Hell in my heart*[5] *· Call me darling*[2,3,4] *· I'm walking this
town*[3] *· Japansy*[4]

Natty Dominique (tpt); Jackson (tbn); Noone (clt); Richard M. Jones (p);
Lonnie Johnson (g); John Lindsay (bs); Hall (d). Chicago, 5 June 1940.

New Orleans hop scop blues · Keystone blues

Noone (clt); Smith (p); John Frazier (bs); Walter Bishop (d). Yes Yes
Club, Chicago, 17 July 1941.

Body and soul

The forthright rhythm of *Sweet Georgia Brown* owes a lot to
Honore's tough, if incomplete, recollections of Hines with an
earlier Noone group (**41**). Other things differ from former preference. Noone liked saxophone support to set off his own peculiar
approach to improvisation and would happily, one guesses, have
dispensed with brass. Here he has Kelly, a hazardous timer but
lyrical in his way, Jackson, the brash antithesis of the leader's
elegance, and Whitby, who acts a role dissimilar to that of earlier
reed associates. Noone's popping ornamental solo shows the
impressive technique which may have been more influential than
his intrinsic jazz thought. The quiet, round-toned second solo
chorus of *Way down yonder in New Orleans* discloses another of
his faces, contrasting not only with Kelly's and Jackson's rough
expression but with their musical presuppositions, too. *He's a
different type of guy* exemplifies Noone's liking for a clear
statement of the theme while he weaves about it and embellishes
it, rather than searching into its possibilities for transformation.
This points to a formal spirit which finds a different embodiment
in the rather stilted riffing which backs his elevated second
chorus in *The blues jumped a rabbit*, which is otherwise a justly
famous sequence of blues solos.

Shavers, Brown, Smith and Bunn create a setting for the 1937 session which is closer to the 52nd Street scene; but Noone's determination to follow his own star remains — evident in the cloying accents in *Sweet Lorraine*, where swooping attack alternates with unassimilated trills, and the Chicagoan staccato of *I know that you know*. *Bump it* is a celebrated opus, known in both its A and B versions. This appears to be the latter, although the sleeve avers otherwise, and it contains some good blues work from all soloists, Shavers's modernism peeping through in bitonal hints here and there. Bunn's sliding introduction and assured solo in *Four or five times* are further proof of his pioneering guitar skill. Brown is more at home in his dry unison with Shavers in *Hell in my heart* and his mutual improvising with Noone behind Spencer's vocal in *Japansy* than with the Poston-like support asked of him in the former piece for Noone's pretty excursion. When this group falls naturally into collective freedom, as in *Call me darling*, Noone finds that ensemble role which somehow eludes him in the more self-consciously revivalist exercises of *New Orleans hop scop blues* and *Keystone blues* (which also appear in another, equally relevant, context on **230**). These are the only tracks here to reflect the 'traditional' manner to which he is so often and misleadingly linked. Primitive ruggedness is rather obviously striven for by Dominique and Jackson.

It is said that Noone's considerable reputation depends largely upon his playing outside the recording studio. That may be so, yet *Body and soul*, captured in a noisy nightclub, does not go very far towards proving the assertion. But, though it is no masterpiece, it is an exhibition of the craftsmanship which Goodman and Shaw seem to have emulated. In the lack of cohesion between its constituents, however, Noone's jazz style gives but small indication of what supposedly closer disciples — Simeon and Bigard, for example — might have learnt from him.   E.T.

Henry Allen/Louis Armstrong/Johnny Dodds
230 New Orleans Jazz
Brunswick (E) LAT8146

Louis Armstrong and His Orchestra: Armstrong (tpt, vcl[1]); Claude Jones (tbn); Sidney Bechet (clt, sop); Luis Russell (p); Bernard Addison (g); Wellman Braud (bs); Zutty Singleton (d). New York City, 27 May 1940.
Perdido Street blues · *2.19 blues*[1] · *Down in honky tonk town*
Jones, Russell, Singleton absent. Same date.
Coal cart blues[1]

Henry Allen and His Orchestra: Allen (tpt); Benny Morton (tbn);
Edmond Hall (clt); Lil Armstrong (p); Addison (g); Pops Foster (bs);
Singleton (d). New York City, 28 May 1940.
Down in Jungle Town · *Canal Street blues*
Zutty Singleton and His Orchestra: same personnel, location and date.
King Porter stomp · *Shimme-sha-wabble*
Jimmy Noone and His Orchestra: Natty Dominique (tpt); Preston
Jackson (tbn); Noone (clt); Richard M. Jones (p); Lonnie Johnson (g);
John Lindsay (bs); Tubby Hall (d). Chicago, 5 June 1940.
New Orleans hop scop blues · *Keystone blues*
Johnny Dodds and His Orchestra: Dodds (clt) replaces Noone. Same date.
Red Onion blues · *Gravier Street blues*

The sessions that Jelly Roll Morton recorded in September 1939
(one track from which appears on **225**) were aimed, however
Morton himself may have regarded them, at uncovering jazz
history, a procedure which involved the rediscovering of Sidney
Bechet. Hugues Panassié had set that process in motion a year
earlier: **228**. Frederic Ramsey and Charles Edward Smith's
Jazzmen, a seminal if overly romantic book, was also published in
1939 (Harcourt Brace, New York), inciting much preoccupation
with happenings at the start of the century, particularly in and
around New Orleans. A generation of purists and proselytisers
was born, a high proportion of which was far from happy with the
music recorded by American Decca in the spring of 1940. As those
zealots saw it, only the performances by Dodds and Noone
reflected jazz as it used to be, unfolding the past rather than, as
with Armstrong, Allen and Singleton, asserting the realities of
the present.

Even so, those recordings by Dodds and Noone really represented New Orleans music as it had been played in Chicago
(Preston Jackson, after all, had moved to Chicago in 1917 and
never actually blew his trombone in the Crescent City). This
music has a hardness that jazz acquired in Chicago, to which was
added a rigidity brought about by a further dozen years in exile.
Nevertheless, Dodds's session (which also appears on **38b**) is still
a curious affair, a mixture of the moving and the woeful. Much of
the trouble lay with the accompanying musicians, particularly
Dominique, seldom in full command of his instrument and
responsible for a good deal of the sour flavour. Dodds was in poor
health (he died only two months later), yet he contrives gritty
flourishes to *Red Onion blues* and even manages, at the very end
of *Gravier Street blues*, to float rather than scurry. But for most of
the time his natural acidity of tone and his spikiness of phrasing
are upstaged by the out-of-tune surroundings. Noone, whose pair
of titles also appears on **229**, comes off rather better, especially in

New Orleans hop scop blues, with its emphasis on solo rather than ensemble work. Indeed, Noone's climax to that piece demonstrates his talent for a kind of musical imperturbability. Not so in *Keystone blues*, however, where he sounds under-balanced and plays a brief solo which makes use of too many tricks and trills.

The musicians assembled under the leadership of Allen and Singleton may not all have hailed from New Orleans (Lil Armstrong, Benny Morton and Addison, for instance), but all had been working around New York for some time. And just as four years previously Singleton was drumming in a band led by Roy Eldridge (see **184** and **249**), then regarded as a bold young innovator, so Allen had gone on cultivating his instinct for the unexpected, a natural *avant-gardist* who was nevertheless always concerned about holding the public's attention. The latter task occasionally produced bouts of rabble-rousing, of trying too hard, the kind of thing that mars the later choruses of *Down in Jungle Town*, and — this time involving all the participants except Hall — in a far too frenzied *King Porter stomp*. The truth is that Allen shone most brightly within sterner surroundings, using a more sober style. That is proved by *Shimme-sha-wabble*, where he toys with the beat, stretching the melodic line to suit. Hall's palpitating approach sometimes becomes predictable, but Morton uses his furry sound intelligently, fitting very snugly inside *Canal Street blues*.

Whether Louis Armstrong and Bechet successfully recreated New Orleans jazz seems less important than the way they asserted their musical personalities. They had not played together since the sessions with Clarence Williams in 1924 (**36**). Meanwhile, Armstrong had moved through a phase of elaborate decoration and technical bravura, settling by the end of the 1930s for a manner that was taut and economical and which deployed his tone in more subtle ways, a manner far less simple than it seemed (see **150–151**). Bechet sounds in comparison positively florid, whether grizzling amiably on clarinet or sweeping majestically on soprano saxophone. It is a meeting of two great musicians, both at the height of their powers. Not surprisingly, the remainder of the group sound anonymous, overshadowed. *Coal cart blues*, by just a quartet, provides the tightest interplay between Armstrong and Bechet. Elsewhere one notes the ecstatic moments — Bechet's triumphant soprano solo on *Down in honky tonk town*, for instance — grateful that a concern with history resulted in the creation of such timeless music.   C.F.

Eddie Condon/Bud Freeman

231 Home Cooking
Tax (Sd) m-8019

Eddie Condon and His Orchestra: Max Kaminsky (tpt); Floyd O'Brien (tbn); Pee Wee Russell (clt); Bud Freeman (ten); Alex Hill (p, arr[1]); Condon (bj); Artie Bernstein (bs); Sidney Catlett (d). New York City, 21 October 1933.

The eel · Tennessee twilight[1] (2 takes) · *Madame Dynamite*[1] (2 takes) · *Home cooking*

Joe Sullivan (p) replaces Hill. New York City, 17 November 1933.

The eel · Home cooking

Bud Freeman and His Famous Chicagoans: Kaminsky (tpt); Jack Teagarden (tbn, vcl[2]); Russell (clt); Freeman (ten); Dave Bowman (p); Condon (g); Mort Stuhlmaker (bs); Dave Tough (d). New York City, 23 July 1940.

Jack hits the road[2] · *47th and State · Muskrat ramble · That da da strain · Shimme-sha-wabble · At the jazz band ball · After a while · Prince of wails*

232 The Commodore Years
Atlantic (A) SD2-309 (2 LPs), *London (E) DHMC1/2 (2 LPs)

Eddie Condon and His Windy City Seven: Bobby Hackett (cnt); George Brunies (tbn); Russell (clt); Freeman (ten); Jess Stacy (p); Condon (g); Artie Shapiro (bs); George Wettling (d). New York City, 17 January 1938.

Love is just around the corner · Beat to the socks · Jada

Hackett, Brunies, Russell, Condon, Shapiro absent. Same date.

You took advantage of me · Three's no crowd · I got rhythm

Bud Freeman Trio: Freeman (ten); Stacy (p); Wettling (d). New York City, 13 April 1938.

Keep smiling at trouble · At sundown · My honey's loving arms · I don't believe it

Eddie Condon and His Windy City Seven: Hackett (cnt); Teagarden (tbn); Russell (clt); Freeman (ten); Stacy (p); Condon (g); Shapiro (bs); Wettling (d). New York City, 30 April 1938.

Embraceable you · Meet me tonight in dreamland · Diane

Bud Freeman and His Gang: Hackett (cnt); Russell (clt); Dave Matthews (alt); Freeman (ten); Stacy (p); Condon (g); Shapiro (bs); Dave Tough (d). New York City, 12 July 1938.

Tapping the Commodore till · Memories of you

Marty Marsala (d) replaces Tough. Same date.

Life spears a jitterbug · What's the use?

Eddie Condon and His Band: Hackett (cnt); Vernon Brown (tbn); Russell (clt); Freeman (ten); Joe Bushkin (p); Condon (g); Shapiro (bs); Lionel Hampton (d). New York City, 12 November 1938.

Sunday · California, here I come

Bud Freeman Trio: Freeman (ten); Stacy (p); Wettling (d). New York City, 30 November 1938.
Three little words · *Swinging without Mezz* · *The blue room* · *Exactly like you*
Wettling absent. New York City, 13 June 1939.
She's funny that way

'Just like a *palais de danse* musician trying to improvise a jazz solo.' This assessment of Freeman's saxophone sound was ventured in a highly-regarded jazz study[103]. And in a later edition was quoted the damning assertion that 'when one has heard *The eel* one has heard all that Freeman has to offer' [104].

Well, to those with a taste for the terseness which is supposed to be the Chicagoans' chief mark, *The eel* may have sounded suspiciously like a novelty number; and Freeman *has* rehashed sections of it often enough elsewhere. But time has dealt mercifully, and in both the 1933 versions it sounds not only a sinuous but a wiry creature too, and it has an impetus which, aided by Hill's arrangement and a fine rhythm team, encourages apt solos from others; especially the hobbledehoy scrawkings of Russell, who achieves complement and contrast at once. In each rendering the slow, intense coda proves that no one's intentions are unduly sophisticated. (A 1939 version of this piece, in which Kaminsky, Russell and Condon again take part, is on **166**.)

The first session produced double takes of *Tennessee twilight* and *Madame Dynamite*. The former piece is akin to *Sleepy time down south*; the latter takes a phrase from *The eel* for its inspiration and, in turn, provides a figure later developed in Ellington's *Five o'clock whistle*. Hill's contribution to the development of swing arranging has been little noticed and he had the misfortune to have his reputation tied to a couple of unrepresentative boogie woogie solos. His skills are evident here, though his solos are less notable. There are pointed statements from Kaminsky, Freeman, O'Brien and Russell — the last sounding very much like a muted trumpet in his entry on the second take of *Tennessee twilight*.

The further performances of *The eel* and *Home cooking*, cut a month later, show no important changes of routine, but they benefit from the arrival of Sullivan, strewing recollections of the Hines of the Savoy Ballroom Five (**48**). The second *Home cooking* starts less dramatically than the first, but ends with more assurance, Russell echoing his own wonderful solo and ironing out the rumpled croak of his initial coda.

With *Love is just around the corner* we are ushered briskly into the world of the Commodore Music Shop, and given cause to praise the dedication of Milt Gabler, staunch friend, in the 1930s, of jazz student and jazz musician alike. A splendid rhythm eggs on one of Russell's most celebrated solos. Hackett, an emergent star, leads with deceptive elegance. Freeman's brief solo employs a vocabulary close to that of the clarinettist, but he sidesteps into his romantic mood for the slow reading of *Jada*, which again has fine tune-making from Hackett.

Stacy has already made his spirited presence felt, and he excels himself when introducing *Beat to the socks*, a blues which finds Brunies exploiting muted sounds unusual for him. Hackett here reveals his Beiderbeckian heritage more in his oblique turns than in his tone colour. But the best solo, in terms of sheer harmonic daring (and Bix may also take some credit for this — see **209**), is Russell's. How many, in prewar jazz, would have had the audacity to start a blues chorus on a note hesitating between the third and fourth of the scale, or would have shown the same cussed reluctance to abandon that note for any other throughout two-thirds of the solo? This is great jazz from a session also memorable because it made possible the first of three sets of trio explorations involving Freeman, Stacy and Wettling. And 'explorations' seems the right word, for although these trios spring from a familiar formation, their spontaneity and unpredictability increase as time goes on.

The unaccompanied introduction is a device much to Freeman's liking — as it was to the young Armstrong's. The tenor summons to *You took advantage of me* may have little of the spiralling vividness of *Cornet chop suey* (**48**), but it heralds a less tightly organized enterprise in any case; and out of the freedom come many gems of co-operative jazz. Stacy is, immediately, much more than an accompanist, and his solo is a genuine remaking. The way in which Freeman's staccato phrases are echoed and complemented by the pianist, and by Wettling's whirling attack on blocks, cowbells and crash cymbal, is typical of the participants' delight in the spontaneous. *Three's no crowd*, a bouncy blues, is, in creative terms, Stacy's track, whilst in *I got rhythm* Freeman improvises from the very first note, leading his associates into fine exhibitions of cut and thrust. It is, however, noticeable here as elsewhere that the tenorist has a tendency to run out of ideas in mid-chorus and to fall back on the theme.

After three months the trio reconvenes. *Keep smiling at trouble* gives Stacy an excuse for inner counterpoint, drawing upon both Hines and barrelhouse pianism for sustenance. Freeman is reflective here, though he is led to more dramatic gestures in *At sundown* which, in reproduction, vividly retains its music-of-the-moment air, the tenorist reaching atypically into his deeper instrumental resources. Wettling's power struts in *My honey's loving arms* — from November — an abandoned solo in the former leading to a headlong ride-out; and his awareness of his companions' thinking turns the witty *Three little words* into a stunning combination of the melodic and the percussive. The preamble to *Three little words* becomes suitaby adapted for a blues, *Swinging without Mezz*, and here the patterns of interchange grow in variety, so that at one point Freeman seems to be accompanying Stacy; and in *Blue room*, one of the best numbers, Chicago and Harlem coalesce in popping tenor expressions and silvery piano figures adapted from the Waller treasury. *Exactly like you* has Freeman rehearsing the essence of what Chicago gave to the swing style; and his *legato* treatment of the ballad *I don't believe it* is at the opposite end of a stylistic spectrum that is far richer in resource than glib commentary has allowed. The 1939 duet, which also appears on **178**, moves from celebration to reflection and back again, ending not only in a culmination of gathered experience but in surprising openness to the future.

The Windy City Seven, in spite of their name, do not depend only upon gathered experience either, and in the meeting of April 1938 Teagarden brings imaginations unguessed at by Brunies and an exalted sound which lends *Embraceable you* and *Diane* much of their buoyancy. Yet the trombonist can adapt to the excitement of *Meet me tonight in dreamland*, even if the Chicagoan demon lurks more purposefully in Russell's skittering, Stacy's eager surging and Freeman's eelishness. *Sans* trombone, the Freeman Gang seeks a slightly harsher voice, but in *Tapping the Commodore till* nobody quite reaches his best; and Hackett's gliding notions, better suited to *Memories of you*, are less appropriate than Russell's messages from outer space or Freeman's taut shapes. Hampton, an unusual visitor in *Sunday* and *California, here I come*, falls short of the versatility of Wettling, Catlett or Tough. It is contrasts which add spice, however: Russell and Hackett setting each other off nicely, and Bushkin's tripped rhythms vying with Freeman's dry-skinned sinuousness.

A leap to the summer of 1940 lands us in post-Ragtimers territory, and there is reason to speculate upon how much *Muskrat ramble, That da da strain, Shimme-sha-wabble* and *At the jazz band ball* owe to the successful routines of Spanier's group (**235**). *47th and State*, and maybe *Prince of wails*, celebrate Chicago more distinctly and have a different, looser character. *Jack hits the road* features Teagarden's totally personal manner of drawling the blues. *After a while* is a good tune, as readily associated with Freeman by his devotees (and no doubt by his detractors, too) as is *The eel*.

Finally, it should be remembered that none of these men was a watery-eyed survivor of some mythical golden age. Freeman played with the Tommy Dorsey band during this period (**139**), Stacy with Goodman (**141–2**), Teagarden, who formed his own big band in 1939, with Whiteman — and so on. Even the small bands of Hackett and Condon were regarded as part of the swing scene, and the music contained in these two records has a good deal more of the swing accent in it than promoters' talk would lead you to suppose.   E.T.

233 Louis Prima and His New Orleans Gang, Vol. 1
The Old Masters (A) TOM37

Louis Prima and His New Orleans Gang: Prima (tpt, vcl[1]); George Brunies (tbn); Sidney Arodin (clt); Claude Thornhill (p); George van Eps (g); Artie Shapiro (bs); Stan King (d). New York City, 27 September 1934.
That's where the South begins[1] · *Jamaica shout* · *'Long about midnight*[1] · *Stardust*[1]

Benny Pottle (bs) replaces Shapiro; Brunies (spch[2]). New York City, 1 November 1934.
Sing it 'way down low[1] · *Let's have a jubilee*[1,2] · *I still want you*[1] · *Breaking the ice*[1]

Same personnel and location, 30 November 1934.
Sing it 'way down low[1] · *Let's have a jubilee*[1,2]

Eddie Miller (clt, ten), Nappy Lamare (g) replace Arodin, van Eps. New York City, 26 December 1934.
House rent party day[1,2] · *It's the rhythm in me*[1] · *Worry blues*[1,2] · *Bright eyes*[1]

Prima (tpt, vcl[1]); Larry Altpeter (tbn); Miller (clt, ten); Frank Pinero (p); Garry McAdams (g); Jack Ryan (bs); Ray Bauduc (d). New York City, 3 April 1935.
Put on an old pair of shoes[1] · *Sugar is sweet and so are you*[1]

The wide popularity that Prima enjoyed during and immediately after World War II (his versions of *Robin Hood* and *Please no squeeze-a da banana* were once almost inescapable) has resulted in his bandleading achievements of a decade earlier being unfairly neglected. He sang and played the trumpet exuberantly, but what makes his early records really worth listening to is the work of the ensemble and at least one soloist: Arodin. Like most of his musicians, Prima came from New Orleans. And the overall style and sound of his group is that of a New Orleans band — flashy maybe, yet still authentic — rather than that of mass-produced 'tourist' dixieland.

Authenticity was almost guaranteed, of course, by the presence, on the earlier sessions, of Brunies, a veteran of the New

Orleans Rhythm Kings (**43**), his doughtiness unmarred even after long periods spent in Ted Lewis's orchestra (**120**). He was primarily an ensemble player, and his solos rarely involved more than drawing on a stock of reliable phrases that were, however always chosen to suit the context: forthright in *Breaking the ice*, growling with conviction on *Sing it 'way down low*, and even, muted, summoning up echoes of Tommy Dorsey's smoothness.

The account of **22** noted that Arodin, ostensibly a white clarinettist, recorded with the otherwise all-black Jones–Collins Astoria Hot Eight. Astute listeners to *Let's have a jubilee* may pick up a pointer to that unusual situation, for Prima addresses all the musicians by their nicknames, exhorting Arodin to 'Play it, Creole'. Yet as well as offering some aspects of the Creole clarinet tradition, Arodin's playing has quite an edge to it. There are even occasional flutters and croakings, a bit reminiscent of what Pee Wee Russell was getting up to, while the first half of Arodin's solo chorus on *Jamaica shout* has something in common with Frank Teschemacher's glossing of Jimmy Noone. This is really a way of suggesting that Arodin is difficult to categorize, his playing being a very personal blending of timbres and sudden, quirky forays. His replacement, Miller, worked much more from a formula and comes across as fleet but nowhere near as subtle. By May 1935, Miller's place had been taken by Russell, who helped to give the band a new identity; his arrival also coincided with the trombone being dropped. Russell's quixotic solos in such pieces as *The lady in red*, *Basin Street blues* and *Chasing shadows* make Vol. 2 (The Old Masters (A) TOM38) an equally indispensable LP.

Not surprisingly, Prima's trumpet playing was strongly influenced by Armstrong's. The same was true of much of his singing: *Stardust* contains what amounts to an Italian–American variant on the great man's singing of the same melody. But where Armstrong's best trumpet solos offer surprises as well as a rare kind of sublimity, Prima's playing seldom advances beyond a boisterous symmetry. He provided a rousing lead, however, sounding gaudier but no less reliable than Wingy Mannone. Sometime in the mid-1930s the American writer John Hammond accused Prima of playing the same solos night after night[105]. He could just as easily have cited the alternative versions of *Sing it 'way down low* and *Let's have a jubilee*, always assuming that these really do come from different masters. In both cases the playing, singing and ad lib remarks all sound identical.   C.F.

Eddie Condon/Jimmy McPartland/George Wettling
234
Chicago Jazz
Coral (E) CP38, Decca (A) DL8029

Eddie Condon and His Chicagoans: Max Kaminsky (tpt); Brad Gowans (v-tbn); Pee Wee Russell (clt); Bud Freeman (ten); Joe Sullivan (p); Condon (g); Clyde Newcombe (bs); Dave Tough (d). New York City, 11 August 1939.

Nobody's sweetheart · Friar's Point shuffle · There'll be some changes made · Someday, sweetheart

Jimmy McPartland and His Orchestra: Jimmy McPartland (cnt); Bud Jacobson (clt); Boyce Brown (alt); Floyd Bean (p); Dick McPartland (g); Jim Lannigan (bs); Hank Isaacs (d). New York City, 10 October 1939.

Jazz me blues · China boy · The world is waiting for the sunrise · Sugar

George Wettling's Chicago Rhythm Kings: Charlie Teagarden (tpt); Floyd O'Brien (tbn); Danny Polo (clt); Joe Marsala (ten); Jess Stacy (p); Jack Bland (g); Artie Shapiro (bs); Wettling (d). New York City, 16 January 1940.

Bugle call rag · Sister Kate · Darktown strutters' ball · I've found a new baby

These recordings were made only months before the parallel series celebrating New Orleans jazz (**230**), with an identical aim in mind but harking back to what was an even more recent past. Yet although only a dozen years had gone since the original Chicago sessions (see **53** and **54**), the mood had changed. Youthful toughness was replaced by gregariousness, even a tinge of nostalgia. And musical priorities shifted. The defining sound of Chicago jazz had been the spikey dissonance of Frank Teschemacher's clarinet. On the Condon tracks, Russell is much more capricious, brilliantly idiosyncratic yet not evoking any one limited style or period.

In any case, Russell was never a Chicagoan: he first arrived in Chicago on tour with Jean Goldkette's orchestra. Nor was Kaminsky, from Boston; a trumpeter whose expertise in leading small groups with incisive but joyous tenacity was more celebrated than his solo playing. Nevertheless, Kaminsky's blues choruses on *Friar's Point shuffle* illustrate his command of *morbidezza*. Except for the pianist, Sullivan, this band was actually Freeman's Summa Cum Laude Orchestra, as regular as any ensemble of its sort has ever been, the routines rehearsed, the musical collisions neatly calculated though still effective. *There'll be some changes made* has the right kind of forcefulness, with Freeman at his elliptical best. *Someday, sweetheart* has Russell slowly winding up a solo, increasing tension by unorthodox methods. The under-used musician seems to be Gowans, heard only in one solo.

But the outstanding music on this LP, apart from forays by Russell, Kaminsky and Tough's nonchalant drumming, is provided by Wettling's group. Their stance is Chicagoan but without any suggestion of the past taking over. Stacy demonstrates his harmonic sensitivity as well as his springy touch; he even takes a tersely exciting solo on *Darktown strutters' ball*, a number guaranteed to bring out the brashness in all but the most accomplished players. Apart from Stacy, the other participants have all been neglected by jazz commentators. Probably Polo spent too many years in Europe for his beautifully economical clarinet playing to make its mark on the American scene. Marsala, better known as a clarinettist, chose on this session to stick to the tenor saxophone. O'Brien, gruff but agile, plays a splendidly teasing muted solo on *Sister Kate*, taken at a slow, bluesy tempo. But the hero of that track, and of the entire LP, is Charlie Teagarden, copying nobody, using the jazz equivalent of a classic prose style, creating music that is clean-cut, subtle, timeless.

(The McPartland titles also appear on **239**, and are discussed there.)   C.F.

Muggsy Spanier
235 The Great Sixteen
RCA (E) RD27132, Quintessence (A) QJ25341

Muggsy Spanier's Ragtime Band: Spanier (cnt); George Brunies (tbn, vcl[1]); Rod Cless (clt); Ray McKinstry (ten); George Zack (p); Bob Casey (g); Pat Pattison (bs); Marty Greenberg (d). Chicago, 7 July 1939.
Big butter and egg man[1] · *Someday, sweetheart* · *Eccentric* · *That da da strain*

Bernie Billings (ten), Joe Bushkin (p), Don Carter (d) replace McKinstry, Zack, Greenberg; Casey switches to bs and replaces Pattison. New York City, 10 November 1939.
At the jazz band ball · *Sister Kate*[1] · *Dippermouth blues* · *Livery stable blues*

Nick Caiazza (ten) replaces Billings. New York City, 22 November 1939.
Riverboat shuffle · *Relaxing at the Touro* · *At sundown* · *Bluing the blues*

Al Sidell (d) replaces Carter. New York City, 12 December 1939.
Lonesome road · *Dinah* · *Black and blue* · *Mandy, make up your mind*

The music of this short-lived band — formed and dissolved within a year — has been so frequently praised (with or without faint damns from revivalist orthodoxy) that it may be useful to ask how it sailed 'against the current' of swing modernism. Commercial failure indicates that it was thought old-fashioned; and, unlike the Crosby Bobcats (**236**), it lacked the shelter of a popular parent group. Yet it was daring enough to aim for an identity which the variegated Greenwich Village and 52nd Street groups dodged. Simply to call it a dixieland band is inadequate, for there were other influences at play. The aim seems to have been not to recreate a style, for the collective genius had not lapsed — as witness the work of several Bechet and Condon groups — but to pay active tribute to a series of influential or personally significant performances of the past.

The session of 7 July begins with a genial bow towards Armstrong, whose Hot Five had recorded *Big butter and egg man* in 1926 (**48**). Vocal humour is largely dispensed with, although there are wild cheers from Brunies as Spanier fulfils Armstrong's promises to May Alix of musical altitude, his cornet phrases soaring in a manner perfected in early Chicagoan days. (As a boy, Spanier had played this tune with Armstrong at the Sunset Café.) *Someday, sweetheart* had been in the repertoire of the Bucktown Five, and there are obvious echoes of the 1924 recording (**53**), Volly DeFaut's plaintive solo being honoured in Cless's theme statement. But new impetus comes from Zack's surging figures and from a guiding authority to which Spanier at eighteen had not attained. *Eccentric* is modelled on the 1922 Friar's Society recording, and *That da da strain* is a sprightlier recollection of a New Orleans Rhythm Kings performance of 1923. Brunies had participated in both of these (**43**).

On 10 November came a version of *At the jazz band ball* owing more to the 1927 Bix Gang (**63**) than to the fast and totally collective Original Dixieland Jazz Band original of 1918 (**12**). *Sister Kate* celebrates the song rather than its two 1928 Charles Pierce treatments (**53**) and, whilst more ebullient, may be a little less musically adventurous than either of these. *Dippermouth blues* disdains other recreations and clearly goes back to source. Cless and Spanier reproduce the notes of Dodds's and Oliver's 1923 solos (**44**), with their own less fluid Chicagoan accent, urgency increased by a faster tempo. Considering Spanier's admiration for Oliver, one wonders that he did not include other Creole Band classics. *Livery stable blues*, with merry farmyard trio, looks back to the earliest ODJB creation (1917) and also heeds the originators' excellent 1936 re-creation (**12**).

On the 22 November session the Wolverines' (1924) and the Trumbauer orchestra's (1927) recordings (on **61** and **64**) nourish *Riverboat shuffle* (a title Beiderbecke urged upon Hoagy Carmichael as an improvement on *Free wheeling*). *Relaxing at the*

Touro, dedicated to the infirmary at which Spanier had recently recuperated, is a blues with authoritative solos and some dramatic trombone-led harmonies. The Bushkin signature at start and close had partially emerged in Marsala's 1937 *Hot string beans* (**167**). *At sundown* owes its character, in this version, to the band's own relaxed inventiveness. *Bluing the blues*, a sequence which mildly challenges the generalization that the blues were foreign to the ODJB, is another genuflection across the years, an important innovation being Bushkin's barrelhouse interjections.

Lonesome road and *Dinah*, from the December sitting, breathe the Armstrong spirit, but only an admirable daring could have risked the comparison of a version of *Black and blue* with Armstrong's sublime one of 1929 (**80**). Respect inspires proper modesty, yet this new conception of the Waller–Razaf tune is lyrical and strong. Which leaves the sunshine gambolling of *Mandy, make up your mind*. This, if it had been typical of the band's repertoire, would almost have justified a quaint name and a public uniform which included eye-threatening two-tone shoes. But even *Mandy* has a mind given to tougher thoughts, and benefits in numerous ways from the skills of men creatively rooted in the jazz they were remaking. They, in turn, were to inspire many others.   E.T.

Bob Crosby

236a Come on and Hear, Vol. 1
Coral (E) CP109, *MCA (A) 2-4083E (2 LPs)

Bob Crosby and His Orchestra: Phil Hart, Yank Lawson (tpt); Ward Silloway, Artie Foster (tbn); Matty Matlock (clt, alt); Eddie Miller (clt, ten); Noni Bernardi, Gil Rodin (alt); Deane Kincaide (ten); Gil Bowers (p); Nappy Lamare (g); Bob Haggart (bs); Ray Bauduc (d). New York City, 13 April 1936.
Dixieland shuffle

Zeke Zarchy (tpt), Warren Smith (tbn), Bob Zurke (p) replace Hart, Foster, Bowers. New York City, 16 June 1936.
Savoy blues

Same personnel and location, 19 August 1936.
Royal Garden blues

Andy Ferretti (tpt), Mark Bennett (tbn) replace Zarchy, Smith. New York City, 8 February 1937.
Gin mill blues

Zarchy, Lawson, Billy Butterfield (tpt); Silloway, Smith (tbn); Matlock (clt, alt); Miller (clt, ten); Joe Kearns (alt); Rodin (ten); Zurke (p); Lamare (g); Haggart (bs); Bauduc (d). Los Angeles, 5 November 1937.
Squeeze me

The Bobcats: Lawson (tpt); Smith (tbn); Matlock (clt); Miller (ten);
Zurke (p); Lamare (g); Haggart (bs); Bauduc (d). Los Angeles,
13 November 1937.
Who's sorry now? · *Coquette* · *Fidgety feet*
Previous full band personnel. Los Angeles, 16 November 1937.
South Rampart Street parade · *Dogtown blues*
Four of the Bobcats: Miller (ten); Zurke (p); Haggart (bs); Bauduc (d).
Chicago, 14 October 1938.
I hear you talking · *Call me a taxi*

236b   Come on and Hear, Vol. 2
Coral (E) CP110, *MCA (A) 2-4083E (2 LPs)
Bob Crosby and His Orchestra: Charlie Spivak, Lawson, Butterfield
(tpt); Silloway, Smith (tbn); Irving Fazola (clt); Matlock (clt, alt); Miller
(clt, ten); Kearns (alt); Rodin (ten); Zurke (p); Lamare (g); Haggart (bs);
Bauduc (d). New York City, 10 March 1938.
Yancey special · *Milk cow blues*
Haggart (bs); Bauduc (d). Chicago, 14 October 1938.
Big noise from Winnetka
Previous full band personnel except that Zarchy, Sterling Bose (tpt)
replace Spivak, Lawson. Chicago, 19 October 1938.
I'm praying humble · *Honky tonk train blues* · *Diga diga doo*
The Bobcats: Butterfield (tpt); Smith (tbn); Fazola (clt); Miller (ten);
Zurke (p); Lamare (g); Haggart (bs); Bauduc (d). New York City,
6 February 1939.
Mourning blues
Joe Sullivan (p) replaces Zurke. New York City, 18 September 1939.
Love nest · *Till we meet again*
Same personnel and location, 25 September 1939.
Feather your nest · *All by myself*
Jess Stacy (p) replaces Sullivan. New York City, 6 February 1940.
Jazz me blues

This item contends for inclusion in Chapter 6, but finds itself here
because of the Crosby band's popular association with the after-
math of New Orleans collectivism. It may well appear that the
matter is less simple. For example, it is complicated by Haggart's
arrangement of *South Rampart Street parade* which, whilst it is
as forthright an evocation of New Orleans as any the band
attempted, has remained, in endless recreations, a favourite with
swing band nostomaniacs. Interestingly enough, the number of
musicians involved in this piece exceeds that in the Young
Tuxedo Band — playing genuine parade music on **18** — by only
one; and this fact may underline the inadequacy of labels such as
'big band' and 'small group'.

The 1937 Crosby band is a well-drilled and tightly-scored group, but Haggart's enterprise in superimposing Matlock's free-wheeling clarinet over imitative section readings does achieve a lively evocation of a traditional form. The blues-imbued style of the Oliver Creole Band (**44**) is echoed, during the same session, in *Dogtown blues*, the effectiveness of which relies partly on rich harmonic drama, partly on the solo expression of Matlock and Lawson. *Dogtown* is in fact a finer distillation of the early band blues than *Dixieland shuffle*, recorded over a year earlier and unashamedly based on Oliver's marvellous *Riverside blues*. There harmonic resources are mostly ignored, in scoring terms, and the presentation sometimes lapses into an indulgent jokeyness. *Savoy blues* suffers from a similar lack of commitment; but, particularly in a passage where the trombone section effects Ory's *portamentos* and clarinet and muted trumpets evoke the thirds of Dodds and Armstrong, it does create interesting formalizations. At this stage the band fell between two stools, not sure whether to emphasize the looser small-group approach or to exploit big-band popularity to build an orchestral style out of skilful pastiche. Hints of the marshalled power of *South Rampart Street parade* are stronger in the 1936 *Come back, sweet papa* (MCA (E) MCFM2578) and the slightly later *Royal Garden blues*, whose ending persuades one that the big band's 'traditionalism' has greater musical durability than the often rather slick mobility of the Bobcats. (The MCA issue has twenty big-band performances and permits a review of development between the free-style novelty of *The dixieland band* — recorded shortly after Rodin had reconvened the Ben Pollack orchestra with Crosby as figurehead — and the sub-Ellingtonia of *Chain gang* in 1942.)

Gin mill blues is a good orchestral realization of Sullivan's piano composition (**116**) and would have been recorded with its originator but for the onset of his lengthy illness. The brilliant attack of Zurke, a pianist whose reputation is unbalanced by the fame of his later Meade 'Lux' Lewis impersonations (*Yancey special* and *Honky tonk train blues*), is commendable, and there are other instances of the excellence of a pianist singled out for praise by Jelly Roll Morton. *Who's sorry now?*, *Coquette* and *Fidgety feet* are from the Bobcats' first recording session, and there is splendid barrelhouse from Zurke in the first of these — to add to fine solos in all three from Matlock, Lawson, Smith and Miller. The pianist is heard to even better advantage in the quartet tracks, *I hear you talking* and *Call me a taxi*, each of which also exposes the enthusiasms of Haggart and Bauduc, whose famous collaboration, a duet recorded on the same day, enchanted devotees of swing world-wide. Bauduc's inordinate love of woodblock, cowbell and rimshot trivializes many an otherwise robust passage, which is a pity, because otherwise he shows himself to be a sensitive and versatile drummer.

Mourning blues, its sprightliness ribbing its title (as did the Original Dixieland Jazz Band performance of twenty-one years before — **12**), introduces Butterfield, a lighter-toned Spanier admirer than Lawson, and Fazola to the Bobcats' line-up. This group's dixieland devotion, which even runs to scored passages imported from the big band's style, is more consistent than that of the earlier personnel, which had strong Chicagoan tensions. With *Love nest, Till we meet again* and *All by myself*, with Sullivan replacing Zurke, and *Jazz me blues* with Stacy as pianist, the ensemble flares, and staccato swivellings return to challenge the 'Southron' voices of Smith and the delicately melodic Fazola.

The Bobcats were an important agency in the upkeep of 1920s styles, and were less eclectic than Spanier's most famous group (**235**). It is, however, in comparison not with Spanier but with their parent orchestra's best re-creations of tradition that they occasionally seem to lack musical substance. From the latest full band date represented here comes the fruity revivalism of *I'm praying humble*, the straightforward contemporary swing of *Diga diga doo* — with one of Fazola's most remarkable solos — and the second of the boogie adaptations, *Honky tonk train blues* which, like *Yancey special*, exemplifies another important source of sonorous inspiration for this singular and short-lived orchestra.

E.T.

237 Willie 'The Lion' Smith
Commodore (A) XFL15775

Smith (p, cls[1]); Joe Bushkin (p); Jess Stacy (p); George Wettling (d). New York City, 30 November 1938.
Three keyboards[1]

Stacy absent. Same date.
'The Lion' and the lamb

Smith (p). New York City, 10 January 1939.
Morning air · *Echoes of spring* · *Concentrating* · *Fading star* · *Passionette* · *Rippling waters* · *Sneakaway* · *What is there to say?* · *Between the Devil and the deep blue sea* · *The boy in the boat* · *Tea for two* · *I'll follow you* · *Finger buster* · *Stormy weather*

Luckey Roberts/Willie 'The Lion' Smith

238 Luckey and 'The Lion': Harlem Piano

Good Time Jazz (E) LAG12256, Good Time Jazz (A) S10035

Luckey Roberts (p). New York City, 18 March 1958.

Nothing · *Spanish fandango* · *Railroad blues* · *Complaining* · *Inner space* · *Outer space*

Willie 'The Lion' Smith (p). Same date.

Morning air · *Relaxing* · *Rippling waters* · *Between the Devil and the deep blue sea* · *Tango la caprice* · *Concentrating*

Smith's best work always was an independent line of endeavour, attractively so: he needed no revival of interest in earlier jazz styles to go 'against the current' because he had often done so. Yet at the same time he typifies the harmonic curiosity, rhythmic invention and to some extent the virtuosity of the Harlem 'stride' pianists, and in his finest moments is as original as James P. Johnson, Roberts, Waller or, we may be sure, any of the legendary unrecorded giants of this school. The combination of strength and delicacy is most impressive, the former quality being most evident in the bass (and one could wish the left hand to be less prominent in *Echoes of spring*). Smith had a smaller stretch than, in particular, Waller or Roberts, and so his sonority is rather less; this probably led to the use of ostinato basses, as in *Relaxing*.

However much they may have relished competitive after-hours piano sessions, the 'stride' men thought of themselves as composers, and the original Smith items heard on these two records are among the most enduring of the hundred or so that he copyrighted. Some of the titles were perhaps suggested by the harmony as much as by the character of themes or keyboard figurations, and several of the pieces are evidently responses to nature of a sort most unusual in jazz.

Essentially a latter-day sophistication of ragtime, with unexpected touches in the harmony, the Commodore *Morning air* is at two tempos, with a *rubato* transition between them. *Echoes of spring* is in the same mode, while *Concentrating* demonstrates Smith's concise management of sharply contrasting ideas. *Fading star*, too, has a variety of incident far beyond that of much piano jazz, while *Passionette* shows that no matter how abrupt this music's changes of direction, they are always relevant. As much applies to the surprise ending of *Finger buster* (not to be confused with Morton's piece of the same name on **46**). *Rippling waters* and *Sneakaway*, with its closely-packed textures, are almost explosive in their energy and in the rate at which things happen, and they point to Smith's unusual treatments of popular songs.

Sometimes he moves diametrically against the mood of the

original melody, this being an approach taken further by the latter-day Herman Chittison (**216**) and by Thelonious Monk who, in the next-to-last analysis, was related to the 'stride' school. Examples are Smith's toccata-like assaults on *Tea for two* and *Between the Devil and the deep blue sea*: there is no room for sentiment, let alone sentimentality, in these remarkably brusque performances. In a case such as *Stormy weather*, fine Harold Arlen song though it is, one must suspect a satirical intent (as with Monk's 1952 dressing-up of *These foolish things* with minor seconds). The ensemble pieces were an unsuccessful experiment, like the four- and six-handed boogie playing then going on elsewhere, and were not repeated.

It was *solo* performances like those heard on **237** that prompted Ellington's *Portrait of 'The Lion'* (**152a**). And it is a pity that Smith was unable to return the compliment effectively in his own *Portrait of the Duke* recorded in Paris during 1949 (Jazz Reactivations (E) JR113), which barely intersects any of the great man's styles. In fact, insensitivity, even carelessness, gradually became the rule in his playing, and the 1949 Paris account of *Echoes of spring*, for instance, is patently inferior, both musically and pianistically, to that of ten years before. Yet there were occasions when much of the relaxed precision of the Commodore performances was regained, and fortunately one of them was caught by Good Time Jazz. The explicit competition with Luckey Roberts, his presence in the recording studio, and the knowledge that their solos would appear on the same LP may have spurred Smith, but there is no doubt that, for example, this new *Relaxing* is greatly superior to the 1949 one recorded in Paris. Despite their grace, elegance and urbanity, the 1958 *Morning air* and *Rippling waters* are not on quite the level of the Commodores, though it is less easy to choose between the two versions of *Concentrating*. This more recent account of *Between the Devil and the deep blue sea* is considerably less peremptory than the 1939 one, yet still offers a most unexpected approach to another excellent Arlen melody. It is notable that Smith's only new piece at the Good Time session was *Tango la caprice*, a charming instance of jazz musicians' perennial fascination with Latin American rhythms.

Roberts's *Spanish fandango*, too, goes south of the border, finding trickier rhythms there than Smith's piece. And there is a virtuoso zest here, especially when the treble figurations scamper up and down above a left-hand melody. It is a serious loss that Roberts, one of the masters of the 'stride' idiom, was recorded so little. Several facets of his music are shown here, though. The unflatteringly-titled *Nothing* has an airy gaiety, but also an aggressive edge because of the eupeptic clarity of its textures and alacrity of execution. A tough, hard-bitten piece demonstrating the scope of Roberts's pianistic invention, *Railroad blues* is one of the best of all the many jazz train pieces. This is superior to the Circle recording of 1946 (Rent Party Piano (E) RPP1002). *Complaining* (not to be confused with the Jess Stacy piece on **178**) and *Outer space* are, again, quite different in thematic character and keyboard figuration.

Smith's pieces date mainly from the 1930s, but Roberts's go back further. *Nothing* and *Spanish fandango* were fifty years old at the time of recording, and although age is not intrinsically important, it is worth noting that *Inner space* is a jazz waltz written many years before more widely publicized ventures of this sort. (It should be compared with Johnson's *Eccentricity* on **17**.) All this music represents a beautiful utilization of some of the piano's resources. Smith's 1935 combo performances of *Echoes of spring* (three takes of which are on Gardenia (It) 4004), like Glenn Miller's adaptation of Roberts's *Ripples on the Nile* as *Moonlight cocktail*, do not really work.   M.H.

Jimmy McPartland/Bobby Hackett

239 Shades of Bix
MCA (A) 2-4110 (2 LPs)

Jimmy McPartland's Squirrels: Jimmy McPartland (cnt); Joe Harris (tbn); Rosy McHargue (clt); Dick Clark (ten); Jack Gardner (p); Dick McPartland (g); Country Washburn (tu); George Wettling (d). Chicago, 24 April 1936.
Eccentric · Original dixieland one-step

Same personnel and location, 25 April 1936.
I'm all bound 'round with the Mason–Dixon line · Panama

Jimmy McPartland and His Orchestra: Jimmy McPartland (cnt); Bud Jacobson (clt); Boyce Brown (alt); Floyd Bean (p); Dick McPartland (g); Jim Lannigan (bs); Hank Isaacs (d). Chicago, 11 October 1939.
Jazz me blues · China boy · The world is waiting for the sunrise · Sugar

Bobby Hackett and His Orchestra: Hackett (tpt); Ray Coniff (tbn); Bill Stegmeyer (clt); Nick Caiazza (ten); Frank Signorelli (p); Eddie Condon (g); Bob Casey (bs); Maurice Purtill (d). New York City, 23 December 1943.
When a woman loves a man · But not for me · Rose room

Hackett (tpt); Hank d'Amico (clt); Stegmeyer, Johnny Pepper (alt); Wolfe Tannenbaum, Hank Ross (ten); Johnny Guarnieri (p); Carl Kress (g); Bob Haggart (bs); Cozy Cole (d); Bill Challis (arr). New York City, 5 February 1946.
Soon · With a song in my heart

Arthur Rollini (ten), Joe Bushkin (p, cls[1]), unidentified d replace
Tannenbaum, Guarnieri, Cole. New York City, 15 February 1946.
Easy to love · What is there to say? · More than you know[1]
Jimmy McPartland and His Orchestra: McPartland (tpt);
Lou McGarity (tbn); Peanuts Hucko (clt); Ernie Caceres (bar); Dick
Cary (p, arr); Kress (g); Jack Lesberg (bs); Wettling (d). New York City,
16 March 1953.
Clarinet marmalade · Singing the blues
Cutty Cutshall (tbn), Stegmeyer (clt), George Barnes (g), Sandy
Block (bs) replace McGarity, Hucko, Kress, Lesberg. New York City,
7 April 1953.
Ostrich walk · Louisiana · Riverboat shuffle · I'm coming, Virginia
Paul Ricci (bar) replaces Caceres. New York City, 9 April 1953.
Davenport blues · Since my best girl turned me down
Bud Freeman (ten), Marian McPartland (p) replace Ricci, Cary; Barnes
absent. New York City, 2 February 1956.
Jazz me blues · Sorry · Way down yonder in New Orleans
Romeo Penque (ob), George Berg (bsn) added. Same date.
In a mist

Though his youthful exploits with the Austin High School Gang
have been recounted in numerous books, McPartland has slipped
through the critical net: despite worthy contributions to, for
example, records by Jack Teagarden (**73**), his playing is never
discussed. The worst thing he ever did was to replace Beiderbecke
in the Wolverines (**61**), as commentators have ever since been
lazily content to describe him as a Bix copyist. McPartland's
Squirrels date preceded the Original Dixieland Jazz Band's
return to the scene (**12**) by some months, the Mezzrow–Ladnier
recordings (**228**) and the Spanier Ragtimers (**235**) by some years.
This suggests a degree of independence on his part — and that the
current never turned completely against earlier jazz styles.

   The ensembles have a fairly individual texture on the Squirrels
session, and this relates to McPartland's quite personal phrasing,
although he is less confident during his *Panama* solo. Cornet,
trombone and clarinet interlock neatly, but Clark's tenor has
nowhere to go in the collective passages. This music has plenty of
rhythmic life, and the *Mason–Dixon* piece was an unusual choice,
suggested by McHargue, who solos with intent fluency here and
on *Panama*.

   It was enterprising to use Jacobson and Brown on the 1939
titles, which originally were done for a 'Chicago Jazz' album (of
78 rpm discs) that was reissued complete as **234**. The sleeve note
of the present set errs in saying that Brown 'never before featured
on a record' as he appeared on Paul Mares's 1935 Friars Society
Orchestra date. There he gave a somewhat better account of

himself — as he also did on the Wild Bill Davison Collectors' Item Cats session of 1940. A minor Chicagoan legend, he displays impressive mobility, and if he is not uninfluenced by Bud Freeman he still has an individual concept of jazz tone on his instrument. He dovetails tidily with McPartland, as on *Jazz me blues*, as does Jacobson, who is just as agile, produces a rather saxophonish tone and, despite echoes of Jimmy Noone, is also his own man. These two make the ensembles lighter and more melodious than the Squirrels', McPartland himself steps out more positively and Bean's barrelhouse piano playing contributes some telling contrasts. The original 1927 versions of *China boy* and *Sugar*, in which McPartland and Lannigan (on tuba) took part, are on **54**.

Neither the 1936 or 1939 performances are in any real sense re-creations, but the case of McPartland's 1953 titles (done as a Beiderbecke tribute) and 1956 additions (made to expand a ten-inch into a twelve-inch LP) is more complex, and we get here an early glimpse of the jazz repertoire movement. Eleven of these twelve interpretations follow, at least in outline, the routines of the 1927–8 versions (**63–4**) and are strongly informed with their spirit. A resourceful arranger, Cary intelligently adapted McPartland's instrumentation to the original conceptions of these pieces (rather than the other way round); but ensemble details are not much copied, nor are many solos. On *Singing the blues*, Hucko and his leader offer free readings of what Trumbauer and Beiderbecke played in 1927, and McPartland does so again on *I'm coming, Virginia*. It is pleasant to observe the similarities and differences, and though all these performances exist in their own right, they will always be most enjoyed by listeners who know the 1927–8 recordings thoroughly. This is jazz *about* jazz.

Naturally McPartland hews closer to Beiderbecke here than on the 1935 or 1939 items, but the individual authority of his smoothly-contoured playing on, say, *Riverboat shuffle* is clear. McGarity and Cutshall are great improvements on Bill Rank, who performed on the 1920s recordings, and take several excellent solos; Caceres plays as well as he does on **206** and **240**. The pieces originally done under Beiderbecke's name inspire more radical departures than those which appeared under Trumbauer's leadership. Essentially, *Davenport blues* is a 1950s distillation of Bixian ideas, and if *Sorry* is closer to the letter of the 1920s a more relaxed tempo leads to its notes meaning something rather different. *Jazz me blues* has few parallels with 1927 (or 1939), the sole literal Beiderbeckian echo being the trumpet solo's break, which is heard as it were between inverted commas.

Another matter is *In a mist* which, on the contrary, sounds very sure of itself. Lasting the greater part of five minutes, this is an arrangement by Cary along lines once discussed by Beiderbecke with the young McPartland, particularly with regard to its use of oboe and bassoon. The original piano solo is embedded in a rich fabric indeed, and here interpretation becomes a creative act on the parts of the arranger and all the performers.

Along with having been dismissed as possessing 'no real ability'[106], Hackett was at first, like McPartland, mislabelled as 'a new Bix', yet his attitude to harmony is freer than McPartland's (which is one reason that his work interested the boppers). These 1943 and 1946 pieces find him in respectively informal and formal situations, but his response is similar. He is on record as saying how difficult it is to play straight melody[107], yet on every track, and undeterred by a heavy rhythm section on the first date, he effortlessly extends the original tunes. *Soon* and *More than you know* are perhaps the most distinguished examples and, Hackett's consistency notwithstanding, Challis's quietly effective scoring does make a difference on the 1946 titles. It provides a sufficiently rich backdrop, heightening the feeling of leisured inevitability in the trumpeter's phrases. Other solos are mostly incidental, though Stegmeyer shines on alto during *Song in my heart*, on clarinet in *Rose room*, and the final ensemble of the latter is moderately rousing. However, there are few shades here of anyone except Hackett.

M.H.

Louis Armstrong–Jack Teagarden
240 Midnight at V-Disc
Pumpkin (A) 103

The V-Disc All-Stars: Louis Armstrong (tpt, vcl[1]); Billy Butterfield (tpt); Bobby Hackett (cnt); Jack Teagarden (tbn, vcl[2]); Lou McGarity (tbn, vcl[3]); Ernie Caceres (clt); Nick Caiazza (ten); Johnny Guarnieri (p); Herb Ellis (g); Al Hall (bs); Cozy Cole (d). New York City, 7 December 1944.
Play me the blues [2,3] (2 takes)

Butterfield, McGarity absent. Same date.
I'm confessing [1] (2 takes)

Bill Clifton (p), Sid Weiss (bs) replace Guarnieri, Hall; McGarity (tbn), Red McKenzie (vcl[4]) added; Armstrong absent. Same date.
Can't we talk it over? [4]

Felix Giobee (bs) replaces Weiss; McKenzie absent. Same date.
If I could be with you one hour tonight [2]

Guarnieri (p), Hall (bs), Specs Powell (d) replace Clifton, Giobee, Cole; 'Hot Lips' Page (tpt, vcl[5]) added. Same date.
The sheik of Araby [5]

Butterfield (tpt) added. Same date.
Miss Martingale[5]
Charlie Shavers (tpt); Trummy Young (tbn); Caceres (clt); Don Byas
(ten); Clifton (p); Ellis (g); Bob Haggart (bs); Powell (d). Same date.
Rosetta (2 takes)

241   Town Hall Concert Plus
RCA (E) RD7659, RCA (A) LPM1443

Leonard Feather's Esquire All-Americans: Armstrong (tpt, vcl[1]);
Shavers (tpt); Jimmy Hamilton (clt); Johnny Hodges (alt); Byas (ten);
Duke Ellington (p); Remo Palmieri (g); Chubby Jackson (bs); Sonny
Greer (d). New York City, 10 January 1946.
Long, long journey[1]
Neal Hefti (tpt), Billy Strayhorn (p) replace Shavers, Ellington. Same
date.
Snafu
Louis Armstrong and His Hot Seven: Armstrong (tpt, vcl); Vic Dickenson
(tbn); Barney Bigard (clt); Charlie Beal (p); Allan Reuss (g); Red
Callender (bs); Zutty Singleton (d). Los Angeles, 6 October 1946.
I want a little girl · Sugar
Louis Armstrong and His Dixieland Seven: Armstrong (tpt); Kid Ory
(tbn); Bigard (clt); Beal (p); Bud Scott (g); Callender (bs); Minor Hall (d).
Hollywood, 17 October 1946.
Mahogany Hall stomp
Louis Armstrong and His All-Stars: Armstrong (tpt, vcl[1]); Hackett (cnt);
Teagarden (tbn, vcl[2]); Peanuts Hucko (clt, ten); Dick Cary (p); Haggart
(bs); Sidney Catlett (d). Town Hall, New York City, 24 April 1947.
Ain't misbehaving[1] · *Rocking chair*[1,2] · *Back o' town blues*[1] · *Pennies
from Heaven*[1]
George Wettling (d) replaces Catlett; Hackett absent. Same date.
St James' Infirmary[2] · *Save it, pretty mama*[1]
Guarnieri (cls), Hall (bs), Cole (d) replace Cary, Haggart, Catlett;
Hackett (cnt), Caceres (bar), Al Casey (g) added. New York City, 10 June
1947.
Someday you'll be sorry[1]

A main point about these two LPs is that they demonstrate the
continuing vitality, indeed creativity, of Armstrong's playing in
the period following that covered by **150–151**. But in order to
produce improvisations of such electrifying authority it was now
essential for him to step outside what had long been his usual role
— that of a show business figure supported by a mediocre large
band. It was important, also, that Teagarden was at the centre of
the Pumpkin jam session for, as usual, he and Armstrong set each
other going. This started, however, with two accounts of *Rosetta*,
which include good solos from Young, Byas, Caceres and the
little-known Clifton. Shavers is quite sober, his facility not

running away with him. All except Young are better on the second take. Both *One hour* and *Can't we talk it over?* contain characteristic playing by Teagarden, and he is well matched by Hackett; it is a pity that McKenzie, instead of the trombonist, sings on the latter. Teagarden excellently accompanies Page's first vocal chorus on *Miss Martingale*, a blues, then takes a notable solo, as does Page. There is inventive work by Caceres here, too, and again on *The sheik of Araby*, which is a more substantial performance, with beautiful extemporisations from Hackett, Guarnieri and again Teagarden and Page.

It seems that Armstrong appeared at the session unexpectedly, and led two versions each of *Play me the blues* and *I'm confessing*. In 1947, together with Teagarden he recorded the former commercially as *Jack Armstrong blues*, but these earlier readings begin with well-argued exchanges between Teagarden and McGarity, and then, on take 1, there are two magnificent Armstrong solos, separated by a Teagarden interlude that is on a comparable level. These solos are not only among the best the trumpeter recorded during this period, but show that, in special circumstances, his playing had as much fire as at any time in his career. On take 2 of *Play me the blues*, Armstrong solos continuously from his first entry until the end, yet his contributions to take 1 have greater bite. On *I'm confessing*, sensitively accompanied by Guarnieri, he sings at the beginning and end, this framing a crackling trumpet solo and brief Teagarden passage. There is little to choose between the takes, except that in the second Armstrong improvises an even more striking conclusion to his solo than on the first.

If the above session, originally done for V-Disc, was a special occasion, it is difficult to know how to describe the 1947 New York Town Hall concert, beyond saying it was obviously one of the great events of that phase of his career, and luckily caught on disc. It is chastening to think of the countless other such nights whose music is lost for ever; in that perspective, indeed, one has a glimpse of just how much Armstrong gave. On *Back o' town blues*, preceded by superlative Teagarden, he plays with an intensity that remains astonishing after no matter how many hearings; there is lovely blues singing also, supported by Teagarden and Hackett. *Pennies from Heaven* is equally exceptional, and *St James' Infirmary* is in both instrumental and vocal terms quite simply one of the trombonist's greatest recordings, with an imaginative accompaniment from Cary. (It also appears, in a different but equally relevant context, on **74**.) These performances are completely informal yet nearly every detail is perfectly apposite. The exception is *Rocking chair* which, despite some majestic trumpet phrases, is too slow. The faster tempo demanded by ten-inch 78 rpm format gave the studio version (done two months later at the *Jack Armstrong* date) a heightened inner tension.

Although *Snafu* and *Long, long journey* arose from another of Feather's attempts to write himself into the history of jazz, the former illustrates the trumpeter's ability, not much reflected by his recordings, to respond to a disciplined, imaginative and well-played setting, to fit into a tightly-patterned sequence of musical events. (Among the few other instances are the 1928 *Beau koo Jack* and 1945 *Jodie man*.) On *Snafu*, marvellous trumpet phrases answer the ensemble, and then there is an intelligently backed solo which is on Armstrong's very best level. In its original form, *Long, long journey* was prefaced by an absurd announcement, written by Feather and read by Ellington, which has been excised here. That still leaves us with the former's lyric, and Armstrong does well to make some sense of it; a comparison between this and *Back o' town* should give an idea of the difference between false and true blues.

On *Someday you'll be sorry*, a personnel like that of the Town Hall concert is used to quite different ends, and a celeste's elfin tones mingle with the lines of Armstrong and Teagarden. *Sugar*, likewise, is more sophisticated, with clipped, poised trumpet phrases moving against sustained ensemble chords; the break with which Armstrong leads into the final half-chorus was described at the time as 'ridiculously pompous' [108]. This track should also be noted as one of the few postwar recordings on which the vastly overrated Dickenson plays in a responsible manner. Bigard's short but incisive contribution is the best feature of *Mahogany Hall stomp*, which has a rhythm section noticeably heavier than any of the others.

In fact, although this LP is indispensable because of the Town Hall items and *Snafu*, its selection of RCA studio recordings is not well chosen. *Please stop playing those blues, boys* and — Feather's presence at the keyboard notwithstanding — *Blues in the south* and *Blues for yesterday* would have been considerable improvements on the last three items mentioned. Beyond that there is, despite what was said at the beginning, the difficult question of to what extent these smallish informal groups any longer provided a suitable context for Armstrong. Even when he went back to fronting a small band regularly, he did not relearn the art of leading a collectively improvising front line. What he plays on the best of his latter-day All-Stars recordings is superb yet has little connection with the clarinet and trombone parts.

M.H.

242a
Sidney Bechet Jazz Classics, Vol. 1
Blue Note (A) BLP1201

Sidney Bechet Quintet: Bechet (sop); Meade 'Lux' Lewis (p); Teddy Bunn
(g); John Williams (bs); Sidney Catlett (d). New York City, 8 June 1939.
Summertime
Sidney Bechet's Blue Note Quartet: Pops Foster (bs) replaces Williams;
Lewis absent. New York City, 27 March 1940.
Dear old Southland
Sidney Bechet's Blue Note Jazzmen: Sidney DeParis (tpt); Vic Dickenson
(tbn); Bechet (clt, sop); Art Hodes (p); Foster (bs); Manzie Johnson (d).
New York City, 20 December 1944.
Blue horizon · *Muskrat ramble*
Max Kaminsky (tpt), George Lugg (tbn), Fred Moore (d, vcl[1]) replace
DeParis, Dickenson, Johnson. New York City, 29 January 1945.
Weary blues · *Salty dog*[1]
Bunk Johnson (tpt); Sandy Williams (tbn); Bechet (clt); Cliff Jackson (p);
Foster (bs); Manzie Johnson (d). New York City, 10 March 1945.
Milneburg joys · *Days beyond recall*
Bechet–Nicholas Blue Five: Bechet (clt, sop); Albert Nicholas (clt); Hodes
(p); Foster (bs); Danny Alvin (d). New York City, 12 February 1946.
Blame it on the blues · *Weary way blues*

242b
Sidney Bechet Jazz Classics, Vol. 2
Blue Note (A) BLP1202

Port of Harlem Seven: Frank Newton (tpt); J. C. Higginbotham (tbn);
Bechet (clt, sop); Lewis (p); Bunn (g); John Williams (bs); Catlett (d). New
York City, 8 June 1939.
Blues for Tommy Ladnier · *Pounding heart blues*
Sidney Bechet's Blue Note Jazzmen: DeParis (tpt); Dickenson (tbn);
Bechet (clt, sop); Hodes (p); Foster (bs); Manzie Johnson (d). New York
City, 20 December 1944.
St Louis blues · *Jazz me blues*
Kaminsky (tpt), Lugg (tbn), Moore (d) replace DeParis, Dickenson,
Manzie Johnson. New York City, 29 January 1945.
High society · *Salty dog*
Bunk Johnson (tpt); Sandy Williams (tbn); Bechet (clt); Jackson (p);
Foster (bs); Manzie Johnson (d). New York City, 10 March 1945.
Up in Sidney's flat · *Lord, let me in the lifeboat*
Bechet–Nicholas Blue Five: Bechet (clt, sop); Nicholas (clt); Hodes (p);
Foster (bs); Alvin (d). New York City, 12 February 1946.
Old Stack o' Lee blues
Sidney Bechet's Blue Note Jazzmen: DeParis (tpt); James Archey (tbn);
Bechet (sop); Don Kirkpatrick (p); Foster (bs); Manzie Johnson (d). New
York City, 5 November 1951.
There'll be some changes made

243 Really the Blues
Vogue (E) LAE12017

Mezzrow–Bechet Septet: 'Hot Lips' Page (tpt, vcl[2]); Mezz Mezzrow (clt); Bechet (sop); Sammy Price (p); Danny Barker (g); Foster (bs); Catlett (d). New York City, 30 July 1945.

House party · *Blood on the moon* [2]

Mezzrow–Bechet Quintet: Fitz Weston (p), Kaiser Marshall (d) replace Price, Catlett; Page, Barker absent. New York City, 29/30 August 1945.

I ain't gonna give nobody none of this jelly roll · *Gone away blues* · *Old school* · *Bowing the blues* · *De luxe stomp* · *Out of the gallion* · *Ole miss*

'Sox' Wilson (p), Wellman Braud (bs), 'Baby' Dodds (d) replace Weston, Foster, Marshall; Bechet also plays clt. New York City, 18 September 1946.

Really the blues

Price (p), Foster (bs), Marshall (d) replace Wilson, Braud, Dodds; spch by Mezzrow, Bechet[3]. New York City, 18 December 1947.

Funky butt · *I want some* · *Tommy's blues* [3]

There is a good deal of music here which aspires to 'traditional' expression, and some which has had the 'New Orleans jazz' label pasted upon it. But it should be emphasized in approaching it that Bechet was in no sense a dedicated revivalist. In this regard, Max Harrison has made the most apt judgment: 'Bechet's finest music is not New Orleans jazz, but a highly personal development out of it which is often truest to the spirit of that parent style when furthest from its letter' [109]. Here is a necessary *caveat* in assessing all musical revivalism, and its force is demonstrated by the earliest of these recordings, *Summertime*. In this, Bechet's Creole eloquence is unmistakable, yet entirely individual, and his choice of such a theme shows his independence of traditionalist presuppositions. Its emotional concentration made of this a popular success, but many hearers may have overlooked the subtler fusion of the feminine and masculine that was Bechet's response to the invitation of Gershwin's melody. It may be New Orleans in essence, yet who would call it a New Orleans performance? It has been described as 'florid' [110]. In fact, it is not; but its very intensity indicates a possible weakness in that linear consistency is occasionally set at risk by a passion for atmosphere. Less so here, however, than in the mewling solos on *Pounding heart blues* and *Blues for Tommy Ladnier*. Newton's exalted solo in the latter, like Higginbotham's rumbustious comments and the consistently apposite support of Lewis, Bunn, Williams and Catlett, is a clear sign that no bandwagons were being mounted at a session which ended Bechet's fortunately brief exile from professional music. *Dear old Southland, cast in the *Summertime* mould though *sans* piano, demonstrates again a certainty of vision which may well contain a strand of arrogance that borders upon undue earnestness; but the double-timed passage shows a spirit wide open to the humorous temper of jazz.

The year 1944 was alive with the excitements of rediscovery for men like Hodes, for whom enthusiasm could override discretion, and the stolid dixieland in *Jazz me blues* and *Muskrat ramble* is emphatically not Bechet's *milieu*. Still, there are some memorable solos in this session, notably Bechet's in *Muskrat ramble* and Hodes's on *St Louis blues*. Better ensemble spacing is achieved in this last number, doubtless because the principals' stylistic differences are more readily accepted. The date with Kaminsky, Lugg and the veteran Moore also suffers a little from Hodesian recklessness in ensemble; and with no one really capable of echoing Bechet's imagination, the mere relentlessness of *Weary blues* (formally indebted to Armstrong — **48**) does almost become wearisome. Bechet's vibrant accompaniment to Moore's singing of *Salty dog* may be too predictably affective, as also in *Jackass blues* a preoccupation with 'vocalism' bends the reed tone uncomfortably in the direction of Wilton Crawley and his mimic breed. The unduly extended *High society* is so fraught with forced excitement that rational ensemble control is nearly lost.

Yet the very first phrases of *Milneburg joys* announce a session of rare jazz distinction, and Johnson, edgy intonation and all, quickly reveals that he is magister of the occasion. Bechet had known Bunk in New Orleans and seems to have owed an early job to his advocacy; but the jazz conception of the two men was ostensibly quite different. How remarkable, then, that there should be such a warming reconciliation of utterance here — such fruitful rapport in the blues counterpoint of *Days beyond recall*, where the patterns of dialogue, with Williams's co-operation, shift and develop so richly. Bechet plays only clarinet, so the balance of timbres is kinder to the trumpeter than in many another Bechet group. Even so, there is brassy force to the *chalumeau* solo of *Up in Sidney's flat*, and the more Doddsian tracings around Johnson's lead on *Lord, let me in the lifeboat* are unusually restrained.

A partnership with Nicholas harks back to a 1939 liaison with Morton (**225**) which seems to have pleased Bechet. This later meeting is both more relaxed and more productive. However obvious the coloristic implications of combining Bechet's broad weave with Nicholas's slender, glistening threads, the result abounds in pleasant surprises. The range of contrast is hardly narrowed when Bechet switches to clarinet, as in *Weary way blues*, yet there is artistic subtlety in the choice. Nicholas's sensitive solo in *Old Stack o' Lee blues* depends upon another Creole instinct that recognizes the power of understatement.

There'll be some changes made rides and swings with much of the ease achieved in famous Bechet sessions of almost two decades before, with the saxophonist clearly feeling that he has no need to force the pace. Much is due to the gliding chordal support lent to fine solos from Bechet, Kirkpatrick (on a venerable piano), the exuberant Archey, and a DeParis whose assured classicism makes his later decline into nostalgic routine the more regrettable.

Admiration for Bechet had first possessed Mezzrow in the Chicago of the 1920s, and his opportunity to record with him on one of the Panassié sessions in 1938 (**228**) was a watershed for him, in terms both of fame and the concentration of his limited but undeniably dedicated abilities. Like Hodes, a similar case musically, Mezzrow was able to penetrate to the heart of the jazz reshaping of the blues, but since he had — for all his verbal bravado — none of the wild daring of, say, Pee Wee Russell, even his best solos seem craftsmanlike rather than imaginative. Bechet responds to his single-mindedness, however, and in the quintet recordings originally made for Mezzrow's King Jazz label, ease and mutual respect lead to unpretentious but justly lauded jazz. Without doubt, the quintets are of more particular interest than the spirited but conventional septet with Page, whose singing in *Blood on the moon* is more distinctive than his playing.

Mezzrow's skill is apparent as he and Bechet exchange the lead in *Jelly roll* from the productive sessions of August 1945, nodding to one another a little more calmly than they do in *Old school*, wherein the clarinettist's Chicagoan acerbity shows through. They find different ways of playing in duet, heeding harmony chiefly in *Bowing the blues* (a 'benefit' for the excellent Foster), and exulting in counterpoint during *De luxe stomp*, which has no solos. *Out of the gallion* starts indecisively and ends abruptly, but it contains one of Bechet's most entranced songs. *Ole miss* (later recorded as *Bugle blues*) releases an exciting sequence of contrasts and convergences dancing along merrily in spite of the rather heavy rhythm support which slightly mars this whole session.

Whilst it lacks the colour and sense of occasion marking the 1938 version (**228**), the two-part *Really the blues* is a worthy celebration. Bechet tends to be over-dominant as the exercise proceeds, and a splicing of irregular parts of the recording enables him to switch from clarinet to soprano without either moving or pausing for breath! Wilson's primitivism does not help matters greatly, and there is much deeper pleasure to be found in the rich, well-controlled piano playing of Price in 1947. Again, Mezzrow accepts a subdued role, deferring to Bechet in *Funky butt*, also the occasion for a *pizzicato* solo by Foster, but contributes a strong statement to *I want some*, whose theme is adapted from his 1939 solo on Rosetta Crawford's *I'm tired of fattening frogs for snakes*. *Tommy's blues* is another deserved tribute to Ladnier and the concentration of its emotions owes more than a little to Price's accompaniment.

Commentators' judgments have been kind to this collaboration, and not without good reason; yet, sometimes, kinder because of Mezzrow's picaresque reputation. Had he been a more urbane, cosmopolitan musician, these sessions might have been less coherent, or simply not have happened. They will endure, but if Bechet's duets with Nicholas have fallen short of such fame, it is hard to be persuaded that musical inferiority accounts for that.

E.T.

244 Refreshing Tracks, Vol. 2
Vogue (E) VJD552 (2 LPs)

Sidney Bechet and His All-Star Band: Bill Coleman (tpt); Bechet (sop); 'Big Boy' Goudie (ten); Charlie Lewis (p); Pierre Michelot (bs); Kenny Clarke (d). Paris, 20 October 1949.
Orphan Annie blues · Happy go lucky blues · Klook's blues · American rhythm

Coleman, Goudie absent. Same date.
Out of nowhere · Mon homme

Sidney Bechet Trio: Bechet (sop); Lil Armstrong (p, vcl[1]); Zutty Singleton (d). Paris, 7 October 1952.
Limehouse blues · Milneburg joys · Rocking chair · Big butter and egg man[1] · My melancholy baby · Black bottom · I've got a right to sing the blues · Blue room · Baby's prayer

Sidney Bechet and His Vogue Jazzmen: Jonah Jones (tpt); Bechet (sop); André Persiany (p); Benoit Quersin (bs); Marcel Blanche (d), Paris, 22 September 1954.
Crazy rhythm · Somebody stole my girl · Squeeze me · When you wore a tulip · Lonesome road · Chinatown, my Chinatown

Sidney Bechet with Sammy Price's Bluesicians: Emmett Berry (tpt); George Stevenson (tbn); Herbie Hall (clt); Bechet (sop); Price (p); Pops Foster (bs); Fred Moore (d). Paris, 16 May 1956.
St Louis blues · Tin roof blues · Darktown strutters' ball · Jazz me blues · Memphis blues · Dinah · Yes, we have no bananas · Back home

245 Sidney Bechet Has Young Ideas

Swing (F) LDM30065, Inner City (A) 7008

Sidney Bechet–Martial Solal Quartet: Bechet (sop); Solal (p); Lloyd
Thompson (bs); Al Levitt (d). Paris, 12 March 1957.
*The man I love · I only have eyes for you · Exactly like you · These
foolish things · Pennies from Heaven · Once in a while · Jeepers
creepers · I never knew*
Michelot (bs), Clarke (d) replace Thompson, Levitt. Paris, 17 June 1957.
*Embraceable you · All the things you are · Wrap your troubles in
dreams · All of me · Rose room · It don't mean a thing*

As noted under **206**, to consort with his peers is not an instinct
that every jazz musician possesses. Bechet, for example, was one
of a number of gifted soloists who imagined their talents shone all
the brighter in the company of inferior players. That attitude
came in handy, of course, when, rather like Odysseus returning to
Ithaca, he settled down triumphantly in Paris in 1951 (and
continued to live there until his death eight years later). Most of
his playing during that period was a matter of running through
the more familiar New Orleans classics accompanied by one of
several French revivalist bands, all of them simultaneously
mediocre, hero-worshipping and cowed — he was noted for the
short shrift he gave dissenters. Yet the fallacy behind Bechet's
thinking was exposed every time he found himself alongside
somebody of a stature close to his own. Devastating proof of that
was given by his collaborations with Louis Armstrong (**36** and
230). More can be gleaned on these LPs from those tracks where
he performs with at least three near-equals: the Americans
Clarke and Jones, and the Algerian-born Solal.

Klook's blues and *American rhythm* demonstrate that all
Bechet really needed was a first class drummer behind him.
Apart from its final four bars, the latter is a duet, Clarke's tom-
toms backing up the saxophonist's slashing phrases. In theory,
like the freest of free improvisers, Bechet could have played
whatever he chose to; very wisely, like Coleman Hawkins in *Me
and some drums* (**215**), in its way a comparable performance, he
stuck to a recurring pattern of bars and a familiar harmonic
framework. *Klook's blues* commences with pedestrian playing
from the band, then the tempo suddenly picks up and Bechet and
Clarke take off on their own. This is blues playing that puts one
in mind of Ornette Coleman, a musician, after all, of similar
melodic directness. The same sort of relaxed imperiousness
permeates Bechet's solo on *Out of nowhere*. Both *Happy go lucky*
and *Orphan Annie blues*, however, suffer from indifferent playing
by Goudie and Coleman (who was experiencing a loss of confidence brought about by the onset of bop).

The support Bechet received at the next session was simply inadequate. By the 1950s, Zutty Singleton was no longer the inspiring drummer of a couple of decades earlier. And Lil Armstrong, though musically knowledgeable (she was probably the most literate member of Oliver's Creole Band — **44**), had never been more than a competent ensemble pianist. She performs pleasantly enough in *Blue room* but does little elsewhere to encourage the saxophonist; *Big butter and egg man*, incidentally, is largely given over to her brash singing. Singleton works up some momentum towards the end of *Milneburg joys*, but mostly does no more than parade the superficial tricks of New Orleans drumming. A result of this was that Bechet set about arousing excitement with familiar, far too predictable routines. *I've got a right to sing the blues* is the only track on which, no doubt aided by the slow tempo, he properly takes command, his tone very broad, his phrases almost coiling around themselves.

Maybe Jones never possessed the touch of genius attributed to him by Hugues Panassié — 'His trumpet swings the most next to Louis Armstrong and Tommy Ladnier' [111]. Nevertheless, he had a powerful, attacking style, could shade his solos very cunningly and, most important in this context, was one of the very few trumpeters capable of standing up to Bechet, able at least to share the lead with him if not actually to assume it himself. They certainly tussled to good effect here, the quality of the partnership audible from the very first bars of *Crazy rhythm* and keeping up the same level throughout the session. Jones's only real descent into ineptness occurs during his solo on *Somebody stole my girl* (which is, though, a tune that hardly anybody except Bix Beiderbecke (**63**) managed to turn into jazz); in striking contrast is the delicate trumpet solo in *Squeeze me*. Persiany becomes tiresome, using the then-fashionable 'locked hands' style lately pioneered by Milt Buckner. Otherwise the music is consistently stimulating, with Bechet sounding both fresh and passionate. He deploys his tone feelingly in *Lonesome road*, achieving a kind of sublime sobriety.

Of the tracks he recorded with Price's Bluesicians, the most successful are those where the tunes — notably *Tin roof blues* and *Memphis blues* — impose formality upon the performances; the worst are those like *Darktown strutters' ball* where nearly everyone tries too hard and the effort shows, though Bechet, as might be expected, remains poised and abreast of events. The surprising thing is that *Yes, we have no bananas* turned out so well, a model of discreet playing until the final chorus. In most pieces, Bechet stays in the background, or even tacit, for uncharacteristically extended periods. Unfortunately, his intrusion into ensemble passages hindered rather than helped, the four-piece front line sounding much too crowded. Berry takes alert if unadventurous trumpet solos; Hall is a slightly blurred carbon copy of his brother Ed, lacking the exciting edge; Stevenson is inclined to growl too much. In fact, Price was the best soloist in his band, a genre player but an outstanding one, even converting a ballad such as *Back home* (alias *One sweet letter from you*) into a blues.

For the final pair of sessions, Bechet worked with what amounted to a modern jazz trio, playing tunes that in some instances were beyond the capabilities of most of the bands he then appeared with regularly. The change of context and material exerted what was both a chastening and beneficial effect upon his approach. His playing here is much terser, the flamboyancy trimmed, rhetorical devices abandoned, the impact somehow more functional but also more incisive. This compactness is heightened by the fact that all the performances are kept to well under four minutes. Those were early days for Solal, yet he already possessed originality, mixing aspects of Art Tatum and Bud Powell within a style that was neither florid nor cryptic. Levitt drums well but it is Clarke who once again proved ideal for Bechet. *These foolish things*, its tempo slightly faster than expected, presents a contrast between Solal's virtuosic understatement and Bechet's hinting at violent realities somewhere beyond earshot. *All the things you are* could have brought out Bechet's voluptuous side; in fact, Kern's melody is treated quite austerely, by Bechet's standards at any rate. These and the other tracks are intriguing performances, artistically satisfying in themselves but also arousing speculation about what Bechet might have achieved in these years had he worked more often in comparable surroundings, being challenged rather than hero-worshipped. C.F.

8

The Transition to Modern Jazz

This selection is necessarily incomplete and may even appear random, because it marks the beginning of a new phase in the music. On such occasions the early signs are isolated, seemingly inconclusive. Their coming together and the consequences of their doing so form the substance of Volume 2.

246 The Changing Face of Harlem, Vol. 1
Savoy (A) SJL2208 (2 LPs)

Ben Webster Quartet: Webster (ten); Johnny Guarnieri (p); Oscar Pettiford (bs); David Booth (d). New York City, 17 April 1944.
Honeysuckle rose · I surrender, dear · Blue skies

'Hot Lips' Page and His Hot Seven: Page (tpt, mel[1], vcl[2]); George Johnson, Floyd 'Horsecollar' Williams (alt); Don Byas (ten); Clyde Hart (p); John Simmons (bs); Sidney Catlett (d). New York City, 14 June 1944.
Dance of the tambourine[1,2] · Uncle Sam's blues[2] · Paging Mr Page[2] · I keep rolling on[1]

Miss Rhapsody (vcl) acc Emmett Berry (tpt); Walter 'Foots' Thomas (ten); Reuben 'June' Cole (p); Harold Underhill (g); Billy Taylor (bs); Cozy Cole (d). New York City, 6 July 1944.
Bye bye · My lucky day · Hey, lawdy mama · Grooving the blues

Pete Brown Quintet: Brown (alt); Kenny Watts (p); Al Casey (g); Al Matthews (bs); Eddie Nicholson (d). New York City, 11 July 1944.
Ooh-wee · Bellevue for you · Pete Brown's boogie · Mopping the blues

'Hot Lips' Page Band: Page (tpt, vcl[2]); Jesse Brown, Joe Keyes (tpt); Vic Dickenson (tbn); Earl Bostic, Williams (alt); Byas, Ike Quebec (ten); Hart (p, cls[3]); Tiny Grimes (g); Al Lucas (bs); Jack Parker (d). New York City, 12 September 1944.
I got what it takes[2] · Good for stomping · Lips' blues[2] · Blooey[3]

Tiny Grimes Quintet: Charlie Parker (alt); Hart (p); Grimes (g, vcl); Jimmy Butts (bs, vcl⁴); Harold 'Doc' West (d). New York City, 15 September 1944.
I'll always love you just the same · Romance without finance is a nuisance ⁴

Buck Ram All-Stars: Frank Newton, Shad Collins (tpt); Tyree Glenn (tbn); Bostic (alt); Byas (ten); Ernie Caceres (bar); Teddy Wilson (p); Remo Palmieri (g); Slam Stewart (bs); Cozy Cole (d); Red Norvo (vib). New York City, 18 September 1944.
Twilight in Teheran · Morning mist · Swing Street · Ram session

Tiny Grimes Quartet: Joe Springer (p); Grimes (g); Bass Robinson (bs); West (d). New York City, 3 November 1944.
Grooving with Grimes

Clyde Hart Band: Benny Harris (tpt); Herbie Fields (alt); Budd Johnson (ten); Hart (p, arr); Chuck Wayne (g); Pettiford (bs); Denzil Best (d); Joe Gregory (vcl⁵). New York City, 19 December 1944.
Smack that mess ⁵ · *Dee Dee's dance · Little Benny · Shoot the arrow to me, Cupid* ⁵

Herbie Fields Quartet: Fields (ten); Lionel Hampton (p); Casey (g); Stewart (bs). New York City, 4 May 1945.
Run down · Nuts to notes

Small-band jazz in Harlem during the late 1930s took on a lighter, more self-consciously springy rhythm. As indicated under **167**, the 'Swing Street' emphasis upon humour bent the music towards inconsequential material, and what came to be known briefly as 'jump style' had little staying power. At the same time, fast tempos and precise arrangements were encouraging players, especially saxophonists, to achieve greater linear dexterity. Considering the constant pressure for stylistic novelty, it is surprising that swing did not give way to something else sooner than it did. It was public self-fascination that enabled what was still essentially the style of the 1930s to persist during the period when the threat and then the advent of war extended the popular demand for the 'hepcat' and 'jitterbug' fancies of Slim and Slam, and Cab Calloway. What was to emerge in the name of 'rebop', 'bebop' and finally 'bop' and to move away from the musical conventions of swing had been forming its dialect in the work of a relatively small number of musicians, for some of whom the short-lived Charlie Christian (**159**) had been a catalyst.

Christian died early in 1942 when the inner movement which led to bop was at a very early stage. With the exception of Parker's, the music assessed hereunder does not — two years at least after Christian's death — show noticeable advances upon the guitarist's rhythmic innovations. Most of the leading players have well-formed styles in any case. Webster's firmly-controlled verve in *Honeysuckle rose* recalls that of his famous 1940 solo on Ellington's *Cottontail* (**153**), a performance which sounded scarcely less modern than the first codified bop creations. (*Cottontail*, like many a later 'original', was founded on the *I got rhythm* chords.) But Webster, less eclectic than Hawkins, remained little affected by novelties. Both his tenderness and his toughness are exhibited in *I surrender, dear* and *Blue skies*, and he is nicely supported by Guarnieri, whose emulations of Basie may prefigure the economies of later pianists, and Pettiford, who exults in the freedom which Jimmy Blanton — like Christian and Hart, an ephemerid — had won for the bass.

Little need be said, beyond broad commendation, about the seven Page items, which follow long-established patterns; though they are notable for the work of Hart, a pianist who was to be active in early bop before he died in 1945. Reuben Cole, one of the suitably lusty collaborators of Miss Rhapsody (Viola Wells Underhill), draws equally upon pianistic styles once associated with Harlem and the south side of Chicago. Every number here, saving *My lucky day*, celebrates the blues with an earthiness which became foreign to the sophistications of bop.

Brown's unsentimental use of the alto has a closer relation to things to come, though it still epitomizes Harlem's late swing manner: hear *Mopping the blues*. His light yet roughened tone is the opposite of the elegance of Hodges and Carter, so was probably more influential than the latter upon Parker and his followers. Brown, as the second chorus of *Pete Brown's boogie* shows, had the capacity for more daring. Casey's solos occasionally, as in *Ooh-wee*, hit unconventional intervals, but Grímes, whose singing is a paler version of Page's whine, is a stronger disciple of Christian.

Buck Ram's arranging for his eleven-piece assemblage is lively but of no originality, and therefore interest is attracted more to the eccentricities of Bostic on *Twilight in Teheran* and *Ram session*, and the skilled paradoxes of Newton, whose playing career was nearing its close. *Smack that mess* has reminders in its score that Hart had worked in the John Kirby Sextet, a touch of the same light intimacy. There are boppish turns and harmonic novelties in the solos of Harris, Fields and Wayne; also in Hart's own spots during *Dee Dee's dance* and *Little Benny*, each a straightforward unison bop theme. (In later bop recordings by several musicians, *Little Benny* was variously retitled *Bud's bubble, Crazeology* and *Ideology*.) Johnson is out of place in this search for astringency and sounds more comfortable in *Shoot the arrow to me, Cupid*, giving only rare hints of the fact that he was to become important in the development of bop composition, especially in the big band field, or that he had already organized the first significant bop recording session, in which the ubiquitous Coleman Hawkins was joined by the up-and-coming Dizzy Gillespie.

Nothing that happens elsewhere in this Savoy saga quite prepares the ear for Parker. There may still be elements of Lester Young in incidental phrases (as in his earlier work on **250**), but his dazzling shifts and multiplications of rhythm and mastery of melodic contrast are intensely personal, and beautifully encompassed even in these brief interpolations with Grimes, Hart and company. A certain formalism is put upon him by the brevity, and yet he is able to suggest the emotional range he was already reaching and which would flower abundantly in his recordings with Gillespie and Miles Davis in a few months' time. Parker is no handy criterion for the assessment of bop, since he seems, even in this, nearly his first small group recording, to have grasped almost wholly and shown signs of transcending the departures which the new style came to signify. It is almost incredible that a mere nineteen years separate the timelessly inspired utterance of his *Koko* (November 1945) from Armstrong's first truly virtuosic flight in *Cornet chop suey* (February 1926 — **48**). How different these statements are. Yet who will dare to say which of them sounds the more 'modern' from the aural vantage point of the 1980s? They share the immediacy of the highest inspiration — jazz beyond category.   E.T.

247 Red Norvo: the Savoy Sessions
Savoy (A) SJL2212 (2 LPs)

Red Norvo Trio: Tal Farlow (g); Charles Mingus (bs); Norvo (vib). Los Angeles, 3 May 1950.
Swedish pastry (2 takes) · *Cheek to cheek* · *Night and day* · *Time and tide*

Same personnel. Chicago, 31 October 1950.
September song · *Move* · *I've got you under my skin* · *I get a kick out of you* · *I'll remember April* · *I can't believe that you're in love with me* · *Little white lies* · *Have you met Miss Jones?* · *Zing! went the strings of my heart*

Same personnel. Los Angeles, 13 April 1951.
If I had you · *This can't be love* (3 takes) · *Godchild* (3 takes) · *I'm yours*

Same personnel. Location and date unknown.
Mood indigo · *Prelude to a kiss* · *Deed I do*

Norvo has always preferred subtlety to more emotive or more spectacular methods. At the end of the 1930s he led what was easily the quietest big band in America (**199**). Similarly, when he deserted the xylophone and marimba for the vibraharp he disdained, on the whole, to make use of that instrument's eponymous vibrato: 'I thought it sounded kind of corny', he confided to the present writer. A care for detail, almost a miniaturist's approach, had always come ahead of any preoccupation with larger or louder gestures. Which is why, right from the beginning and even including his career as a leader of a swing band, Norvo saw jazz as a species of chamber music.

At the start of the 1950s Norvo wished for personal reasons, to work on the West Coast. For that he needed a group that would be economical, able to get jobs in small clubs. It also happened to be a moment when a number of musicians were trying to make recent jazz innovations acceptable to a wider audience. Charlie Ventura, for instance, formed a group he called 'Bop for the People'; George Shearing was successful in what amounted to an adaptation of Lennie Tristano's harmonic strategy. Norvo's Trio shared certain similarities with Shearing's, using well-known tunes or the brighter bop 'originals'; although it seems unlikely that he intended any deliberate compromise. What he did fitted neatly alongside earlier achievements. He had, in any case, been one of the first swing musicians to work and record with bop players: the *Hallelujah!/Congo blues* date of 1945 (Spotlite (E) SPJ127) included Charlie Parker and Dizzy Gillespie as well as Teddy Wilson, Flip Phillips and Norvo himself.

Farlow was already in his mid-twenties when he moved from North Carolina to New York in 1944. He was enthusiastic about bop yet found himself working mostly in commercial dance orchestras, bands that, as he points out in the sleeve notes, had 'bad drummers, or no drummers at all'. He developed the habit of hitting the body of his guitar on the second and fourth beats of the bar, like a bongo player, and sometimes stroking the strings to produce an effect like brushes. Both devices were useful in supplementing the rhythmic resources of Norvo's Trio and can be heard at certain points on these LPs. Much more importantly, however, Farlow was a soloist with a broad-based style, making intelligent use of contrasting timbres and registers, adept at building long, self-sustaining lines, and also aware of what Max Harrison has called 'the guitar's potential for intimate nuance' [112].

When Norvo recruited Mingus for this trio, the bassist was relatively unknown, although he had played in Lionel Hampton's orchestra. Indeed, he had actually left music and in 1950 was working for the Los Angeles postal department. Now he was given a chance to operate on equal terms with the vibraharp and guitar. Brian Priestley has pointed out that it was in fact the first time that a regular jazz group used the bass other than in a rhythm section [113]. His tone was already totally individual, as the solo in *Swedish pastry* or the bowed double-stopping of *Time and tide* show. One wonders, too, if Mingus played a part in arranging the two Ellington tunes, both presented in uncommonly imaginative ways and making very effective use of the bassist's *arco* playing.

Norvo's concern with detail comes through in the Trio's approach to ballads. *I can't believe that you're in love with me*, for instance, demonstrates the close interdependence between these three musicians: fluttering guitar lines move above vibraharp chords and Mingus's bass; guitar and vibraharp present a paraphrase of the melody; guitar patterns are echoed by the vibraharp — all cohering within an overall shape that develops and also allows scope for individual solos. Something similar happens in *Little white lies*, the solos this time contriving to be ruminative while remaining far from leisurely. The bop pieces — *Swedish pastry*, *Move*, *Godchild* — are suitably lively, with *Godchild* offering substantial solo playing, especially by Mingus; it is instructive to compare the different versions. Glibness occasionally creeps in (*This can't be love*, for instance), where the approach suddenly hardens into a formula. Far more remarkable, though, is how this influential yet inimitable group displayed persistent inventiveness; as well as the way they satisfied a sizeable audience while preserving very high standards.   C.F.

248 Jazz of the 'Forties: Swing into Bop
Capitol (E) T20579

Benny Carter and His Orchestra: Claude Dunson, Jake Porter, Teddy Buckner, Freddy Webster (tpt); Carter (tpt, alt); Alton Moore, J. J. Johnson, Shorty Haughton (tbn); Porter Kilbert (alt); Willard Brown (alt, bar); Gene Porter, Bumps Myers (ten); Teddy Brannon (p); Ulysses Livingstone (g); Curly Russell (bs); Oscar Bradley (d). San Francisco, 25 October 1943.
Love for sale

Big Sid Catlett's Band: Joe Guy (tpt); 'Bull Moose' Jackson (alt); Myers, Illinois Jacquet (ten); Horace Henderson (p); Al Casey (g); John Simmons (bs); Catlett (d). Los Angeles, 19 January 1945.
I never knew · Just you, just me

Al Casey's Sextet: Gerald Wilson (tpt), Willie Smith (alt) replace Guy, Jackson. Same location and date.
Sometimes I'm happy · How high the moon?

Capitol International Jazzmen: Bill Coleman (tpt); Buster Bailey (clt); Carter (alt); Coleman Hawkins (ten); Nat 'King' Cole (p); Oscar Moore (g); John Kirby (bs); Max Roach (d); Kay Starr (vcl[1]). Los Angeles, 30 March 1945.
You can depend on me · Riffmarole · If I could be with you one hour tonight[1]

Red Norvo Ensemble: Ray Lin (tpt); Jimmy Giuffre (alt, ten); Dexter Gordon (ten); Dodo Marmarosa (p); Barney Kessel (g); Red Callender (bs); Jackie Mills (d); Norvo (vib). Los Angeles, 30 November 1947.
Bop!

Stan Hasselgard Sextet: Hasselgard (clt); Arnold Ross (p); Kessel (g); Rollo Garberg (bs); Frank Bode (d); Norvo (vib). Los Angeles, 18 December 1947.
Swedish pastry

Metronome All-Stars: Dizzy Gillespie (tpt); Bill Harris (tbn); Buddy DeFranco (clt); Flip Phillips (ten); Cole (p); Billy Bauer (g); Eddie Safranski (bs); Buddy Rich (d). New York City, 21 December 1947.
Leap here

Stan Kenton and His Orchestra with the Metronome All-Stars: Gillespie, Buddy Childers, Ken Hanna, Al Porcino, Ray Wetzel (tpt); Harris, Milt Bernhardt, Harry Betts, Harry Forbes, Bart Varsalona (tbn); DeFranco (clt); Art Pepper, George Weidler (alt); Phillips, Bob Cooper, Warren Weidler (ten); Bob Gioga (bar); Cole (p); Bauer (g); Safranski (bs); Rich, Shelly Manne (d); Kenton (arr). New York City, 21 December 1947.
Metronome riff

For 1943, Carter's orchestral dialogue was certainly not a style on the way out, and even though his arrangements took scant heed of the current ferment, his band was a congenial home for nascent boppers like Webster, Johnson (nineteen, and just emerging as a soloist) and Russell. The clipped swing classicism of *Love for sale*, with its clearly-defined interplay, demonstrates what would have appealed to men involved in what was a markedly unsentimental movement.

The smaller Catlett and Casey groups achieve a more even mixture of veterans and innovators. Henderson's over-prominent vamping in *Just you, just me* is an unfortunate tether, but he is more adaptable to the context than might have been expected. As for Catlett, he was surely one of the most versatile and thoughtful of drummers, and is as much at ease with the differing modernisms of Guy, Wilson and Jacquet as ever he was with companions of more traditional instincts. Jackson's rough-toned treatment of *I never knew* is only superficially more augural than Smith's deceptive romanticism. The riffs which both support and invade solos during these sessions teeter between swing and bop, yet lean mostly to the former mode.

Cole's riding style has an originality that makes one regret his subsequent neglect of the piano (see also **180**). The Capitol Jazzmen owe much to his presence and to the rest of an excellent rhythm section. Roach, a youth bringing new emphases, had replaced Bradley in Carter's band shortly after the 1943 session; and Carter is here also sounding affirmative in *You can depend on me*, in contrast to Bailey's gentle sweetness. Coleman, whose incipient modernism was mentioned in connection with **102**, has carried his varied accents and moulded tone a few steps forward, adapting them to simplicity in *One hour* and to complexity in *Riffmarole*. Compare the springy beat of *One hour* with the languor of that Mound City Blue Blowers session which featured a younger Hawkins (**166, 192**). The darting phrases of his solo here betoken widely-gathered skills and show why he could so readily consort with young lions.

Norvo, who is also heard with Buck Ram on **246** as well as on **199** and **247**, could adapt well to differing scenes, too, and was a keen supporter of new talents. It is rather surprising that his friends here lag some way behind the *avant garde* of the day. *Bop!* is a theme true to its name, but Norvo is no bopper, Kessel seems merely to be veering away from swing, and what Gordon and Marmarosa have garnered from Parker and Powell sounds but partially integrated. Callender's interpolation is, rhythmically at least, more adventurous. The clarinet–vibraphone unison of *Swedish pastry*, with the pianist, Ross, genuflecting to George Shearing, belongs to the more genteel regions of new style. Kessel's light-hearted assurance voices a necessary protest and is more successful, because more coherent, than Norvo's stabs at 'crazy' intervals.

Leap here starts with a rather disorganized statement of intent. After that, DeFranco, a clarinettist of great skill, plays pleasingly, as does the warmer Phillips. Not so Harris, who seems to imagine (as did some of its early detractors and supporters) that jazz has something to do with blowing raspberries at life. Gillespie, assured in his bop stardom, nevertheless has to contend at times with an unduly heavy beat; yet another symptom of the easy but often musically confusing way in which musicians of different backgrounds were thrown together for jam sessions and important recordings.

The so-called 'progressive jazz' of Kenton was amply to fulfil, in later times, the threats of megalomania that are present in the score of *Metronome riff*. The parts which accompany the *Leap here* All-Stars are not always unduly assertive, yet Bauer and Phillips have to row against the tide a little, and only the ludicrous Harris finds really apt comments to counter the pedal grunts and percussive explosions. Kenton's typical combination of lugubrious reeds and high, dissonantly scored *fortissimo* brass is either the ultimate raspberry or something which, more imaginatively handled, might have helped to achieve the big band bop which no one ever quite managed to create. As it is, most of the riff sounds boorish, and ends with the two drummers thundering and the brass section imitating 'the bellowing of mastodons at war' [114]. If polls conducted by the *Metronome* magazine are any guide, this is what the fans favoured at the end of 1947. It may seem to independent minds that real jazz, under whatever label, was making best headway elsewhere, and in less pretentious gatherings.   E.T.

249 Swing Street Vol. 4

Columbia (E) 33SX1521, Columbia (A) 4-JSN6042

Roy Eldridge and His Orchestra: Roy Eldridge (tpt); Scoops Carry (alt); Joe Eldridge (alt, arr); Dave Young (ten); Teddy Cole (p); John Collins (g); Truck Parham (bs); Zutty Singleton (d). Chicago, 28 January 1937.
That thing

Noble Sissle's Swingsters: Sidney Bechet (clt, sop); Jimmy Miller (g); Jimmy Jones (bs); Wilbert Kirk (d); Billy Banks (vcl[1]). New York City, 16 April 1937.
Okey-doke · Characteristic blues[1]

Pete Johnson and His Boogie Woogie Boys: 'Hot Lips' Page (tpt); Buster Smith (alt); Johnson (p); Lawrence Lucie (g); Abe Bolar (bs); Eddie Dougherty (d); Joe Turner (vcl). New York City, 30 June 1937.
Cherry red · Baby, look at you

Will Bradley and His Orchestra: Steve Lipkins, Joe Wiedman, Al Mitchell (tpt); Bradley, Jim Emert, Bill Corti (tbn); Artie Mendelssohn, Joe Huffman, Sam Sachalle (clt, alt); Nick Caiazza (ten); Freddie Slack (p); Steve Jordan (g); Doc Goldberg (bs); Ray McKinley (d, vcl). New York City, 21 May 1940.
Beat me daddy, eight to the bar

Coleman Hawkins and His Orchestra: Tommy Stevenson, Tommy Lindsay, Nelson Bryant, Joe Guy (tpt); Sandy Williams, Claude Jones, Billy Kato (tbn); Eustis Moore, Jackie Fields, Ernie Powell (alt); Kermit Scott, Hawkins (ten); Gene Rodgers (p); Gene Fields (g); Billy Taylor (bs); J. C. Heard (d). New York City, 9 August 1940.
Serenade to a sleeping beauty · Rocky comfort

Billie Holiday and Her Orchestra: Roy Eldridge (tpt); Don Redman, George Auld (alt); Don Byas, Jimmy Hamilton (ten); Teddy Wilson (p); Collins (g); Al Hall (bs); Kenny Clarke (d); Holiday (vcl). New York City, 12 September 1940.
I hear music · Practice makes perfect

Count Basie and His Orchestra: Ed Lewis, Harry Edison, Buck Clayton, Al Killian (tpt); Dan Minor, Vic Dickenson, Dickie Wells (tbn); Earle Warren (alt); Lester Young, Buddy Tate (ten); Jack Washington (bar); Basie (p); Freddy Greene (g); Walter Page (bs); Jo Jones (d). New York City, 19 November 1940.

Five o/clock whistle · Love jumped out

Dizzy Gillespie and His All-Star Quintet: Gillespie (tpt); Trummy Young (tbn); Don Byas (ten); Clyde Hart (p); Oscar Pettiford (bs); Shelly Manne (d). New York City, 9 January 1945.

I can't get started · Good bait

Woody Herman and His Orchestra: Conrad Gozzo, Cappy Lewis, Bob Peck, Chuck Peterson, Al Porcino (tpt); Bill Harris, Ed Kiefer, Ralph Pfeffner (tbn); Herman (clt); John LaPorta, Sam Marowitz (alt); Mickey Folus, Flip Phillips (ten); Sam Rubinowitch (bar); Jimmy Rowles (p); Chuck Wayne (g); Joe Mondragon (bs); Don Lamond (d). Chicago, 10 December 1946.

At the woodchoppers' ball

'Hot Lips' Page and His Orchestra: Page (tpt, vcl); Alfred Outcalt (tbn); Joe Evans (alt); 'Big Nick' Nicholas (ten); Bill Spencer (p); Carl Wilson (bs); Sticks Evans (d). New York City, 28 October 1947.

Walking in a daze

The LP's title refers, of course, to 52nd Street in mid-town Manhattan, and more particularly that block lying between Fifth and Sixth Avenues, lined with clubs from around 1935 to the late 1940s in which appeared most of the major jazz talent that found its way to New York City. Not all the tracks were recorded in New York, the Eldridge and Herman pieces being done in Chicago; the complete set of four LPs, however, aimed not so much at being scholarly as giving a general notion of the musical activity going on. Not surprisingly, all the ensembles, except for Gillespie's, have been mentioned already in these pages. A couple of items, by Billie Holiday, have been written about elsewhere (**205**), and Vols. 1–3 of this series are dealt with under **167**.

In 1937, Eldridge was the *enfant terrible* of trumpeters, rebellious, always taking risks, an exemplar of what jazz was then supposed to be about. *That thing* contains a typical solo by him, as ardent as it is adventurous. Nearly as interesting, however, is the first of the two alto solos, played by Carry and representing a slightly more daring use of harmony, comparable to what Rudy Williams then was doing with the Savoy Sultans (**136**). Another pointer to the future was Lester Young's playing with Basie's band — and, for that matter the work of Basie's classic rhythm section, with Jones's high-hat cymbal constantly frothing. Young could scarcely put a finger wrong in those early years and his calm, confident solo redeems what is otherwise an overblown performance of a third-rate popular song, *Five o/clock* *whistle. Love jumped out*, a riff number by Clayton, is more representative even if it lacks a solo by Young; the composer's muted work is as delicate as usual and there is a solo from Wells, tortuous but satisfying.

Perhaps the most tantalizing performances on the LP by a saxophonist, though, are the eight and twenty-four bars which Buster Smith plays in Johnson's *Cherry red* and *Baby, look at you.* Smith, who makes an even more fleeting appearance on **168**, was the alto saxophonist in Kansas City from whom Charlie Parker seems to have learnt most. Jay McShann even recalls hearing a broadcast in Kansas City during 1939 when he failed to realize he was listening to Parker and not to Smith; who had just left for New York. Hindsight can lead one to read more into short solos like these than they may deserve. No hindsight is required, however, to recognize the quality of Turner's singing, joyful and heroic, sexual boasting joined to an Homeric vision, or of Johnson's doggedly cheerful piano playing, both caught here at their very best. Johnson was an all-round blues player rather than a boogie woogie specialist like his companions on 52nd Street, Meade 'Lux' Lewis and Albert Ammons (**169**), even though he shifts to boogie patterns for part of *Baby, look at you.* Boogie scored for a big band and designed for mass consumption can be sampled in Bradley's *Beat me daddy, eight to the bar.* Despised by purists at the time and still sounding decidedly shallow, this has begun taking on the charm of a period piece; it features genial singing by McKinley and competent, if dispassionate, piano playing by Slack. Incidentally, this track is half of what originally was a double-sided 78 rpm performance.

The oddest inclusions are *Okey-doke* and *Characteristic blues*, on which Bechet plays the clarinet, warping his tone outrageously. *Characteristic blues*, ferociously eclectic, finds him launching into the standard *High society* clarinet solo and Banks yodelling as well as throwing in an excerpt from *Mean old bed bug blues* (**56**). Sissle's orchestra, with which Bechet was then working, supplied the rhythm section. Despite their eccentric moments, these tracks preserve some of Bechet's most intense playing. One could not say that for the two pieces by Hawkins's big band: his ornamenting of *Serenade to a sleeping beauty* sounds fairly off-handed, while in *Rocky comfort*, a straightforward riff number, he adopts an excessively hard-driving manner, playing right on top of the beat. Among the other solos is one by Guy, following very distinctly in the footsteps of Eldridge. Only a few years earlier, of course, that could have been said of Gillespie. By 1945, though, he was his own man, dominating *I can't get started* and in *Good bait* sharing the solos with two survivors of the swing era: Byas, a shapely soloist with a keen harmonic instinct, and Trummy Young, still alert and jaunty, not yet a prisoner of the rasping clichés he concocted for Armstrong's All-Stars. The former title is chiefly memorable for the chiselled perfection of Gillespie's carefully elaborate phrases, and though Tadd Dameron's *Good bait* is closer to swing practice, the other performances from this date, *Salt peanuts* and *Be bop*, not included here but each with a great trumpet improvisation, make it the first of several 1945–6 recording sessions that defined the full bop style.

The arrival of bop is audible not only in Gillespie's phrasing, but in some of the detail on the remaining tracks, even *Walking in a daze*. Page sings with hoarse fluency and plays the blues on his trumpet with an abrasive authenticity which Gillespie, despite his superb skills, was never to match. Nicholas, the tenor saxophonist, has the burly approach of an r & b sideman, but some of Page's other players reveal in small yet significant ways the fact that new musical practices were catching on. The same is true of Herman's remaking of *At the woodchoppers' ball* (originally recorded in 1939). Lamond drums with nonchalant vigour and the solos include one by Harris, not, perhaps, on top form yet, displaying himself as the true inheritor of Benny Morton's evasive but empirical trombone style.

(In its American issue this disc is available only as part of a four-LP set.)   C.F.

250 Charlie Parker: Early Bird
Spotlite (E) SPJ120, Onyx (A) OR1221

Jay McShann and His Orchestra: Orville Minor, Buddy Anderson (tpt); Bob Gould (tbn, vln[1]); Parker (alt); William Scott (ten); McShann (p); Gene Ramey (bs); Gus Johnson (d). Wichita, Kansas, 30 November 1940.
I've found a new baby · *Body and soul*

Bob Mabern (ten) replaces Scott. Wichita, Kansas, 2 December 1940.
Moten swing · *Coquette* · *Lady, be good* · *Blues* · *Honeysuckle rose*[1]

Parker (alt) with unidentified small group. Possibly Clark Monroe's Uptown House, New York City, c.1942.
Cherokee

Jay McShann and His Orchestra: Willie Cook, Jeepy Hickman, Jesse Jones, Bob Merrill, Dave Mitchell (tpt); Taswell Baird, Alfonso Fook, Rudy Morrison (tbn); John Jackson (alt); Rudolph Dennis (alt, bar); Flap Dungee, Paul Quinichette (ten); McShann (p); Ramey (bs); James Skinner (d); Walter Brown (vcl[2]). Possibly New York City, c.1943.
You say forward, I'll march · *Lonely boy blues*[2] · *Vine Street boogie* · *Jump the blues* · *One o/clock jump* (2 versions) · *Bottle it* · *Sweet Georgia Brown* · *Wrap your troubles in dreams*

Count Basie's band (**133–135**) had in Lester Young harboured one of the major evolutionary figures of jazz, and it is striking that an ensemble in the same Kansas City tradition, McShann's, should provide an early home for the next one, Charlie Parker. Actually, the later, 1943, performances, from which he is absent, give a better idea of the sort of blues and riff music for which this group was famous, but it is the 1940 pieces, played by a contingent from the main band, that have so much musical and historical value. These latter were recorded over a weekend (in the town of Stan Kenton's birth), during the course of a long tour. They were done without commercial intent, ostensibly for the use of the local radio station but really for the personal enjoyment of Fred Higginson, the station's jazz-loving manager, who knew McShann well. These transcriptions were rediscovered in the late 1960s by the pianist himself, and we should count ourselves extremely lucky that they survived.

The 1940 performances are the earliest unquestionable Parker recordings, rumours of items dating from his teens being no more than that at the time of this book's publication. Among the numerous points which demand attention is his obvious familiarity not just with Young's but with considerably earlier, even non-jazz, saxophone styles. As Ross Russell suggests in his exemplary sleeve note, the alto solo on *Coquette* is the one that looks farthest forward. The sound is creamy, the decorative phrases noticeably old-fashioned for 1940, yet there are slight bendings of notes, momentary discolourings of tone, which hint at quite another world. Indeed, two realities, one simple, one far more complex, briefly impinge upon one another; it is the sort of passage that only a budding genius could have played.

Elsewhere, Parker's future allegiances are more overt. True, on *Body and soul* he reminds us of Coleman Hawkins rather than Young and, despite the intelligent adaptations he makes, this approach does not really work on the alto. Yet there are suggestions of what was to come, not least in the use of implied double-time, and here is at any rate one of the elements that went into his great ballad improvisations of several years later. On *Honeysuckle rose*, Parker's tone does not have the expressive weight of his maturity, but this contains the outstanding solo of the set. His fluency is impressive on, say, *I've found a new baby*, yet in the former piece he shows himself to be more at ease at a rapid tempo than any other member of the band, his sense of time considerably more secure. Also, he feels the music's pulse in a more subtle way, and this is also evident on *Moten swing* and *Lady, be good.*

In the latter, Parker's debt to Young is especially apparent, yet he produces on both these pieces, as on *Honeysuckle rose*, improvisations that are logically ordered in a way that already is his own. *Lady, be good* and *Moten swing* also contain trumpet solos which indicate that Parker was not the only advanced jazzman in this band. These are by the unfortunate Buddy Anderson, who died in 1944 when he was well on the way to creating an individual manner. *Cherokee*, perhaps taken down at the Uptown House, a New York meeting place for progressively inclined young jazz musicians of the time, is incomplete and less self-confident than the best of the Wichita solos, yet it is unmistakably an early draft of his 1945 *Koko*, one of the masterpieces of recorded jazz.

On the full band's *Jump the blues*, John Jackson shows, as countless others would later, that it was not difficult to imitate Parker — in all except the essentials. The finest of the latter's work here indicates, as do several Dizzy Gillespie contributions which are scattered through these passages, not to mention the playing of the most advanced swing musicians, that jazz was in the process of taking on new qualities. Soon things would be different, sufficiently so to fill a second volume like this.   M.H.

Notes

[1]   A valuable account of this overlapping is given in Tony Russell: *Blacks, Whites and Blues* (Studio Vista, London, 1970).

[2]   See Edward Berlin: *Ragtime — a Musical and Cultural History* (California University Press, Berkeley, 1980), especially pp. 173–5.

[3]   However, see Berlin, op. cit. pages 98–122 for the relation between ragtime and immediately preceding forms such as the cakewalk.

[4]   The invention of this solo has usually been credited to Alphonse Picou, but according to Thornton Hagert's notes for the New Sunshine Jazz Band's *Old Rags* (Flying Dutchman (A) BDL1-0549) it was devised, as a piccolo counterpoint in the trio, by Robert Recker, a violinist who made the original orchestration. *High society* was popularized in New Orleans by the orchestra of John Robichaux, who, because of transposition problems, assigned the part to clarinet. The above Flying Dutchman LP includes a performance of Recker's orchestration.

[5]   Gunther Schuller: *Early Jazz* (Oxford University Press, New York, 1968), p. 184.

[6]   For example, Nat Hentoff: 'Jazz in the Twenties — Garvin Bushell' in *Jazz Review*, January 1959, especially p. 12.

[7]   Johnson claimed that he was born in 1879, but the correct date is approximately 1889. See Don Marquis: *In Search of Buddy Bolden* (Louisiana State University Press, Baton Rouge, 1978), pp. 4–6.

[8]   E.J. Bellocq: *Storyville Portraits* (Museum of Modern Art, New York, 1970).

[9]   Schuller: *Early Jazz*, op. cit. p. 75.

[10] Archey can be heard on Riverside (A) RLP12-211 in performances taken from 'This is jazz' broadcasts of June and October 1947.

[11] Incredibly, some commentators have imagined there is only one player here. Greatly daring, Humphrey Lyttelton in his notes for Fountain (E) FJ107 writes: 'One is tempted to think that two cornets are involved'!

[12]   Peter Bocage, for example, quoted in Marquis, op. cit., p. 105.

[13]   In the first edition of his *Jazz on Records 1897–1931* (Hatch End, 1961), B.A.L. Rust, like the sleeve of this LP, gives Dodds as the clarinettist. However, in a later edition (New Rochelle, N.Y., 1978) he lists Junie Cobb. This latter is more likely to be correct as the vibrato is noticeably tighter than that of Dodds.

[14]   Max Harrison: *Jazz on Record* (Hanover Books, London, 1968), p. 67.

[15]   Among several discographical problems arising from the Creole Band's output the most important musically concerns the identity of the clarinettist on the 5 October session. It is now usually assumed to be Dodds, simply because he was on most of the dates, yet the phrasing is quite different from his: more smoothly contoured and more facile in expression. He is indisputably present in the later *Working man blues* and a comparison makes the differences between the two players clearly apparent. Bailey has always been considered a doubtful possibility, yet the lines, especially in *Alligator hop*, where a curiously saxophonish tone is apparent, resemble those he produces with Clarence Williams (**57**), the Red Onion Jazz Babies (Fountain (E) FJ107) and particularly on his own 1925 *Squeeze me* (Historical (A) HLP25). Participants' testimony is not usually worth much in these circumstances — Noone, for example, having on different occasions both confirmed and denied his presence on the 15 and 16 October dates. But it should be mentioned that St. Cyr once claimed that the clarinettist on the 5 October session was Omer Simeon (*Jazzfinder*, December 1948, p. 7). When asked, Simeon denied his presence and said that it sounded like Bailey. St. Cyr's reply was that he had been thinking of another session, probably with Morton, and that 'it was quite possible Bailey was the clarinettist' (*Jazzfinder*, January 1949, pp. 5–6).

[16]   For a contrary view see William Russell: 'Zue Robertson — king of trombone' in *Jazz Miscellany*, edited by Albert McCarthy and Max Jones (Jazz Sociological Society, London, 1944), pp. 3–4.

[17]   Rex Harris and B.A.L. Rust: *Recorded Jazz: a Critical Guide* (Penguin Books, Harmondsworth, 1958), p. 19.

[18]   Reproduced in *The World of Earl Hines*, compiled by Stanley F. Dance (Scribner's, New York, 1977), pp. 20–21.

[19]   For further comment see Daniel Nevers: 'Les trompettistes fous — Jack Purvis' in *Jazz Hot*, February 1980, pp. 15–18.

[20]   In fact one is tempted to suggest that two of the best arguments in favour of this music are (i) that it is dismissed in *Early Jazz* with a single footnote, which speaks of 'commercial performances geared to a thriving mass market' (Schuller, op. cit., p. 194), and (ii) that none of these pieces is included in *The Smithsonian Collection of Classic Jazz* (Smithsonian (A) PG611891).

[21]   See Martin Williams's chapter on Morton in *Jazz*, edited by Nat Hentoff and Albert McCarthy (Rinehart, New York, 1958), p. 74.

[22] For further comments on this unusual piece see Alec Wilder: *American Popular Song* (Oxford University Press, New York, 1982), pp. 372–4.

[23] Eddie Condon and Thomas Sugrue: *We Called It Music* (Corgi Books, London, 1962), p. 94.

[24] Ralph Ellison: 'The Charlie Christian story' in *Jazz Journal*, May 1959, pp. 7–8.

[25] Quoted in Burt Korall: 'Coleman finally wins through' in *Melody Maker*, 6 August 1960, p. 30.

[26] Paul Oliver: *Jazz on Record*, op. cit., p. 158.

[27] Quoted in the programme book of the Bracknell Jazz Festival, 1981.

[28] *Journal of the International Association of Jazz Record Collectors*, April 1980, p. 21.

[29] 'My story, as told by Andy Kirk to Frank Driggs', in *Jazz Review*, February 1959, pp. 12–17.

[30] John Chilton: *McKinney's Music* (Bloomsbury Bookshop, London, 1978), p. 56.

[31] James Lincoln Collier: *The Making of Jazz* (Granada, London, 1978), p. 190.

[32] See section 5 of David Fuller's entry on Notes Inégales in *The New Grove Dictionary of Music and Musicians* (Macmillan, London, 1981), vol. 13, p. 425.

[33] Schuller, op. cit., p. 336.

[34] For a helpful analysis of the two versions see A.J. Bishop: 'Duke's Creole rhapsody', in *Jazz Monthly*, November 1963, pp. 12–13.

[35] Quoted in Nat Shapiro and Nat Hentoff (eds.): *Hear me Talking to You* (Rinehart, New York, 1955), p. 56.

[36] Bechet also toured New England with Ellington's band in May 1932, the month that they recorded a performance of *The Sheik of Araby* containing a Hodges solo whose close resemblance to later Bechet versions is noted under **36**.

[37] Ethel Waters: *His Eye is on the Sparrow* (W.H. Allen, London, 1951), p. 87.

[38] Henry Pleasants: *The Great American Popular Singers* (Gollancz, London, 1974), pp. 81–96.

[39] This is the band which prompted Ernest Ansermet's famous 1919 article on jazz, reprinted in *Frontiers of Jazz*, edited by Ralph de Toledano (Durrell, New York, 1947), pp. 115–22.

[40] Needless to say, according to Hines himself the influence was entirely in the opposite direction — see *The World of Earl Hines*, op. cit., p. 37; but Weatherford was insistent that he discovered and taught Hines — see *Jazz Forum*, April 1947, pp. 10–11. Little confidence can be placed in either of these assertions.

[41] Igor Stravinsky and Robert Craft: *Expositions and Developments* (Faber, London, 1962), p. 92.

[42] Alban Berg: *Letters to His Wife* (Faber, London, 1971), p. 275.

[43] The widely circulated story to the effect that the *Ebony concerto* was 'inspired' by Stravinsky hearing Herman's band on the wireless has been discredited. For a true account of the work's genesis see Vera Stravinsky and Robert Craft: *Stravinsky in Pictures and Documents* (Hutchinson, London, 1979), p. 377.

[44] However, Milhaud's score contains what sound like echoes of the Original Memphis Five's 1921 recording of *Aunt Hagar's children* (Fountain (E) FJ102). It has also pointed out by Jerome Shipman that one of *La création's* saxophone themes is close to a saxophone background figure on Collins and Harlan's *Casey Jones on the Robert E. Lee*, recorded by the Victor Military Band in 1912 (*Journal of the International Association of Jazz Record Collectors*, January 1979, pp. 18–19).

[45] Milhaud: *Notes without Music* (Knopf, New York, 1952), pp. 136–7; see also pp. 118–20.

[46] Ernst Křenek: *Horizons Circled* (California University Press, Berkeley, 1974), p. 79.

[47] For more extended comment on Lambert's *Concerto*, the longest and best-constructed work dealt with in this chapter, see Richard McGrady: 'The music of Constant Lambert', in *Music and Letters*, July 1970, pp. 242–58.

[48] Max Jones and John Chilton: *Louis* (Studio Vista, London, 1971), p. 237.

[49] It is worth giving more of this passage, which has for many years been a favourite of at least one of the authors of this book: 'Ted Lewis, the King of Jazz, is never tiresome. Those who have had the privilege of hearing him at the Apollo know that the man is worthy of his voice. This large and singularly elegant brigand leads a band of rogues who create rhythmic noise in an atmosphere of mystery. And Ted Lewis recited poetry . . .' Quoted in Robert Goffin: *Jazz — from Congo to Swing* (Musicians' Press, London, 1946), p. 158.

[50] Comments could be disinterred from the *Melody Maker* — for example by John Hammond in the March 1932 issue — to show that denigration of the Casa Loma Band has been going on for over half a century.

[51] For instance, 'Every year a new genius is hailed by the swing critics. The latest man to attract attention is Dizzy Gillespie. So far we can only hear him in this country on Lucky Millinder's *Mason flyer* and *Little John special*. His work here is mediocre, and apart from an ability to make piercing screams in the upper register he shows little hope of ever producing trumpet work of individuality' — Albert McCarthy: *The Trumpet in Jazz* (Citizen Press, London, 1945), p. 67. *Little John special* and *Mason flyer* have since reappeared on Affinity (E) AFS1004.

[52] 'The Jungle Band' was a name also used for Ellington and Henderson groups. *Dog bottom* and *Jungle mama* came out on a 78 rpm disc (Brunswick 6808) as by the Duke Ellington Orchestra.

[53] For Hughes's own account of these sessions, see his *Second Movement* (Museum Press, London, 1951), pp. 266–76.

[54] 'The romantic imagination of Dickie Wells', in André Hodeir: *Jazz: Its Evolution and Essence* (Secker & Warburg, London, 1956), pp. 63–76.

[55] The origin of such train pieces, within the jazz tradition, lies in items like the Yerkes Novelty Five's *Railroad blues*, recorded in 1920. And *Scratch*, a version of *Farewell blues* recorded by the Blue Ribbon Syncopators in 1927, sounds as if it might have been the immediate ancestor of *Lightning*.

[56] *Saddest tale*, along with *Ducky wucky* and *Merry-go-round*, was used in another form in Ellington's music for the 1935 film 'Symphony in black' (Biograph (A) BLPM-2). A new performance of the entire score for this Academy Award-winning film, by the Smithsonian Jazz Repertoire Ensemble under Gunther Schuller, can be heard on Smithsonian (A) NO24.

[57] For a helpful analysis see A.J. Bishop: 'Reminiscing in tempo', in *Jazz Journal*, February 1964, pp. 5–6.

[58] For example during an interview with François Postif in *Jazz Review*, September 1959, pp. 7–10; a fuller version of this interview appeared in *Jazz Hot*, June and July/August 1979.

[59] Benny Goodman and Irving Kolodin: *The Kingdom of Swing* (Stackpole, Harrisburg, Penn., 1939), pp. 156–7.

[60] Stanley F. Dance: 'Jazz on and off the track', in *Bulletin of the Jazz Sociological Society*, August 1943, pp. 2–4.

[61] John Hammond: *John Hammond on Record* (Ridge Press/Summit Books, New York, 1977), p. 196.

[62] Stanley F. Dance: 'Earl Hines' in *Jazz Piano 2*, edited by Max Jones and Albert McCarthy (Jazz Music Books, London, 1945), pp. 4–8. *Windy City jive, Water boy, Everything happens to me*, etc. are mentioned.

[63] See interview of Budd Johnson by Frank Driggs in *Jazz Review*, January 1961, p. 14.

[64] Constant Lambert: *Music Ho!* (Faber, London, 1934), p. 215.

[65] 'A masterpiece — *Concerto for Cootie*', in Hodeir, op. cit., pp. 77–98.

[66] 'He simply doesn't play well from any point of view. His tonal quality, which is more noisy than powerful, has no beauty. His vibrato has no sensitivity. His playing is a vulgar declamation. His ideas have no continuity and tend to be completely incoherent.' This typical early comment on the great trumpeter is from Hugues Panassié: *The Real Jazz* (Smith & Durrell, New York, 1942), p. 80.

[67] Jeff Aldam: 'Record miscellany' in *Jazz Forum*, April 1947, pp. 21–2.

[68] Max Harrison: *A Jazz Retrospect* (David & Charles, Newton Abbot, 1976), p. 34.

[69] Stanley F. Dance: 'Jazz on and off the track', op. cit. See also Charles Wilford: 'Current records' in *Jazz Music*, vol. 3 No. 6 (1947), pp. 28–31: 'The Ellington sub-units are always turned out hastily and carelessly', etc.

[70] Rex Stewart: *Jazz Masters of the 30s* (Macmillan, New York, 1972), p. 219.

[71] Nat Hentoff: 'The Hawk talks', in *Down Beat*, 14 November 1956, pp. 13, 50.

[72] Richard Hadlock: *Jazz Masters of the 20s* (Macmillan, New York, 1965), p. 160.

[73] Quoted in Rudi Blesh and Harriet Janis: *They All Played Ragtime* (Oak Publications, New York, 1971), p. 204.

[74] Although its composition is accredited to Johnson, *Victory stride* sounds like a more subtly accentuated version of Ellington's *Jubilee stomp*, the link certainly being closer than Leonard Feather's sleeve comment ('vague resemblance') would lead one to suppose. *Jubilee stomp* appears in 1928 versions under **87**, **89** and **91**, and to hear Ellington's markedly Johnsonian piano celebrations of the acrobatic theme is to be led into interesting speculations . . .

[75] Cyril Connolly: *The Unquiet Grave* (Grey Arrow, London, 1961), p. 58.

[76] For a detailed analysis of Waller's early solo recordings see Max Harrison: *A Jazz Retrospect*, op. cit., pp. 22–8.

[77] Richard Hadlock, op. cit., p. 162.

[78] These three quotations are by respectively Jeff Aldam: 'Mainly about records', in *Jazz Music*, November 1943, pp. 42–3; Hugues Panassié: *The Real Jazz*, op. cit., p. 131, Stanley F. Dance: 'Earl Hines', in *Jazz Piano 2*, op. cit.

[79] Pitts Sanborn on Horowitz: 'a sinister dexterity that was positively Schoenbergian', *New York World Telegram*, 21 February 1928, p. 17.

[80] Stanley F. Dance: 'Earl Hines', in *Piano Jazz 2*, op. cit. This writer claimed later that everyone, 'a few egoists excepted', recognized Tatum's ability as being 'outside the scope of their dusty arguments'. See 'The vanishing giant', in *Just Jazz*, edited by Percy Traill and the Hon. Gerald Lascelles (Peter Davies, London, 1957), pp. 97–117.

[81] André Hodeir, op. cit., p. 109. See also Hodeir's essay on Tatum in *Toward Jazz* (Grove Press, New York, 1962), pp. 127–34.

[82] See Nat Hentoff: 'Little Jazz', in *Down Beat*, 19 September 1956, pp. 13 14, 40.

[83] Max Harrison: *A Jazz Retrospect*, op. cit., p. 129.

[84] It was echoed decades later in Joseph Byrd's arrangement of *In a mist* for bass clarinet, alto saxophone, guitar, string bass and vibraharp for the pop musician Ry Cooder's *Jazz* LP (Warner (E) K56488).

[85] Henry Pleasants, op. cit., p. 172.

[86] Glenn Coulter: 'Billie Holiday', in *The Art of Jazz*, edited by Martin Williams (Oxford University Press, New York, 1959), pp. 162 and 163 respectively.

[87] Whitney Balliett: *Alec Wilder and His Friends* (Houghton Mifflin, Boston, 1974), p. 70.

[88] Richard Hadlock, op. cit., p. 192.

[89] From a conversation quoted in Nat Hentoff's sleeve note for this record.

[90] Richard Sudhalter and Philip Evans: *Bix: Man and Legend* (Quartet Books, London, 1974), p. 148.

[91] Barry McCrae: *The Jazz Cataclysm* (Dent, London, 1967), p. 7.

[92] For some remarks on Wilson's endeavours see Jeff Aldam: 'A portrait of Garland Wilson', in *Piano Jazz 1*, edited by Max Jones and Albert McCarthy (Jazz Music Books, London, 1944), pp. 13–15. This specifically mentions Wilson's performances of *Drop me off at Harlem* and *Black and tan fantasy*, in which he evidently attempted to transfer the orchestral arrangements to the keyboard.

[93] John Mehegan: 'Art Tatum — *in memoriam*', in *Down Beat*, 12 December 1956, pp. 15, 51.

[94] Stanley F. Dance: 'Earl Hines', in *Piano Jazz 2*, op. cit.

[95] Everett Barksdale talking to Max Jones, *Melody Maker*, 11 August 1956, p. 3.

[96] John Chilton: *Who's Who of Jazz* (Bloomsbury Bookshop, London, 1970), p. 178.

[97] The full score of *Black, Brown and Beige*, carefully restored by Alan Cohen and Brian Priestley, can, however, be heard from Cohen's band on Argo (E) ZDA159.

[98] Burnett James: *Essays on Jazz* (Sidgwick & Jackson, London, 1961), pp. 175–205.

[99] Titled *Sonnet* for *Hank Cinq* on the front of the sleeve of the original issue, *Sonnet* to *Hank Cinq* on the back.

[100] *The World of Duke Ellington*, compiled by Stanley F. Dance (Macmillan, London, 1970), p. 28.

[101] See Duke Ellington: *Music is My Mistress* (Doubleday, New York, 1973), p. 243.

[102] Martin Williams: 'The enduring Ellington', in *Saturday Review*, 16 March 1963, p. 96.

[103] Peter Gammond: *Jazz on Record* (Hutchinson, London, 1960), p. 134.

[104] Albert McCarthy: *Jazz on Record*, 1968 edition, op. cit., p. 103.

[105] Quoted in Arnold Shaw: *The Street that Never Slept* (Coward, McCann & Geoghegan, New York, 1971), p. 109. This was reprinted by DaCapo in 1977 as *52nd Street: the Street of Jazz*.

[106] Hugues Panassié: *The Real Jazz*, op. cit., p. 88.

[107] Nat Hentoff: 'Bobby', in *Down Beat*, 6 February 1957, pp. 15–16.

[108] Charles Wilford: 'Current records', in *Jazz Music*, op. cit.

[109] Max Harrison: *Jazz on Record*, 1968 edition, op. cit., p. 19.

[110] Peter Gammond: *Jazz on Record*, 1960 edition, op. cit., p. 38.

[111] Hugues Panassié: *The Real Jazz*, op. cit., p. 83.

[112] *Modern Jazz: the Essential Records 1945–70*, edited by Max Harrison (Aquarius Books, London, 1975), p. 45.

[113] Brian Priestley: *Mingus: a Critical Biography* (Quartet Books, London, 1982), p. 42.

[114] See Edith Sitwell: 'Three poems for the atomic age', in *Selected Poems* (Penguin Books, Harmondsworth, 1952).

Bibliography

Reference Books

General Discographies

Jorgen Grunet Jepsen: *Jazz Records 1942–62* (Knudsen, Copenhagen, 1963–70), 11 vols.

Tom Stagg and Charlie Crump: *New Orleans Revival* (Bashall Eaves, Dublin, 1973)

B.A.L. Rust: *Jazz Records 1897–1942*, 4th edn. (Arlington House, New Rochelle, N.Y., 1978)

Walter Bruyninckx: *60 Years of Recorded Jazz* (The Author, Brussels, 1978–81), 7 vols.

Critical Discographies

Charles Fox *et al.: Jazz on Record* (Hutchinson, London, 1960)

Albert McCarthy *et al.: Jazz on Record* (Hanover Books, London, 1968)

Biographical Dictionaries

John Chilton: *Who's Who of Jazz: Storyville to Swing Street* (Bloomsbury Bookshop, London, 1970)

Samuel Charters: *Jazz: New Orleans 1885–1963*, 2nd edn. (Oak Publications, New York, 1963)

Pictorial Histories

Orrin Keepnews and Bill Grauer: *A Pictorial History of Jazz*, 2nd edn. (Spring Books, London, 1968)

Franks Driggs and Harris Lewine: *Black Beauty, White Heat: a Pictorial History of Classic Jazz 1920–50* (Morrow, New York, 1982)

Afro-American Music

Marshall and Jean Stearns: *Jazz Dance: the Story of American Vernacular Dance* (Macmillan, London, 1968)
Paul Oliver: *The Story of the Blues* (Barrie & Rockcliff, London, 1969)
Tony Russell: *Blacks, Whites and Blues* (Studio Vista, London, 1970)
Paul Oliver: *Savannah Syncopators: African Retentions in the Blues* (Studio Vista, London, 1970)
James Storm Roberts: *Black Music of Two Worlds* (Allen Lane, London, 1973)

Ragtime

Rudi Blesh and Harriet Janis: *They All Played Ragtime*, 4th edn. (Oak Publications, New York, 1971)
William Schaefer and Johannes Riedel: *The Art of Ragtime* (Louisiana State University Press, Baton Rouge, 1973)
Edward Berlin: *Ragtime: a Musical and Cultural History* (California University Press, Berkeley, 1980)

Analytical–Historical Surveys

Sidney Finkelstein: *Jazz: a People's Music* (Citadel Press, New York, 1948)
André Hodeir: *Jazz: its Evolution and Essence* (Secker & Warburg, London, 1956)
Nat Hentoff and Albert McCarthy (eds.): *Jazz: New Perspectives on the History of Jazz* (Rinehart, New York, 1959)
Leroy Ostransky: *The Anatomy of Jazz* (University of Washington Press, Seattle, 1960)
Wilfrid Mellers: *Music in a New Found Land* (Barrie & Rockcliff, London, 1964)
Gunther Schuller: *Early Jazz* (Oxford University Press, New York, 1968)
Charles Fox: *Jazz in Perspective* (BBC, London, 1969)
Leroy Ostransky: *Understanding Jazz* (Prentice-Hall, Englewood Cliffs, N.J., 1977)
James Lincoln Collier: *The Making of Jazz* (Granada, London, 1978)
John Chilton: *Jazz* (Hodder & Stoughton, London, 1979)
Joachim Berendt: *The Jazz Book — from Ragtime to Fusion and Beyond* (Lawrence Hill, Westport, Conn., 1982)

Jazz Regions

Samuel Charters and Leonard Kunstadt: *Jazz: a History of the New York Scene* (Doubleday, New York, 1962)
Al Rose and Edmond Souchon: *New Orleans Jazz* (Louisiana State University Press, Baton Rouge, 1967)

Martin Williams: *Jazz Masters of New Orleans* (Macmillan, New York, 1967)
Ross Russell: *Jazz Style in Kansas City and the Southwest* (California University Press, Berkeley, 1971)
Duncan Schiedt: *The Jazz State of Indiana* (The Author, Pillsborough, Ind., 1977)
Leroy Ostransky: *Jazz City* (Prentice-Hall, Englewood Cliffs, N.J., 1978)

Critical Essays

Ralph de Toledano (ed.): *Frontiers of Jazz* (Durrell, New York, 1947)
Martin Williams (ed.): *The Art of Jazz* (Cassell, London, 1960)
Burnett James: *Essays on Jazz* (Sidgwick & Jackson, London, 1961)
Benny Green: *The Reluctant Art* (MacGibbon & Kee, London, 1962)
André Hodeir: *Toward Jazz* (Grove Press, New York, 1962)
Richard Hadlock: *Jazz Masters of the 20s* (Macmillan, London, 1965)
André Hodeir: *The Worlds of Jazz* (Grove Press, New York, 1972)
Max Harrison: *A Jazz Retrospect* (David & Charles, Newton Abbot, 1976)
Humphrey Lyttelton: *The Best of Jazz:* vol. 2, *Enter the Giants* (Robson Books, London, 1981)
Martin Williams: *The Jazz Tradition*, 2nd edn. (Oxford University Press, New York, 1983)

Musicians' Memoirs

Louis Armstrong: *Satchmo: My Life in New Orleans* (Prentice-Hall, Englewood Cliffs, N.J., 1954)
Sidney Bechet: *Treat It Gentle* (Cassell, London, 1960)
Cab Calloway: *Of Minnie the Moocher and Me* (Crowell, New York, 1976)
Hoagy Carmichael: *The Stardust Road* (Rinehart, New York, 1946)
Hoagy Carmichael: *Sometimes I Wonder* (Farrar, Strauss & Giroux, New York, 1965)
Lee Collins: *Oh, Didn't He Ramble?* (University of Illinois Press, Urbana, 1974)
Eddie Condon: *We Called It Music* (Corgi Books, London, 1962)
Baby Dodds: *The Baby Dodds Story* (Contemporary Press, Los Angeles, 1959)
Pops Foster: *Pops Foster: the Autobiography of a New Orleans Jazzman* (California University Press, Berkeley, 1971)
Max Kaminsky: *My Life in Jazz* (Harper & Row, New York, 1963)
Mezz Mezzrow: *Really the Blues* (Random House, New York, 1946)
Artie Shaw: *The Trouble with Cinderella* (Farrar, Strauss & Young, New York, 1952)
Willie 'The Lion' Smith: *Music on My Mind: the Memoirs of an American Pianist* (Doubleday, New York, 1964)
Nat Shapiro and Nat Hentoff (eds): *Hear Me Talking to You: the Story of Jazz by the Men Who Made It* (Rinehart, New York, 1955)

Biographies and Critical Studies of Musicians

Louis: the Louis Armstrong Story 1900–71, by Max Jones and John Chilton (Studio Vista, London, 1971)

Louis Armstrong: a Biography, by James Lincoln Collier (Michael Joseph, London, 1984)

Count Basie, by Alun Morgan (Spellmount, Tunbridge Wells, 1984)

Bix Beiderbecke, by Burnett James (Cassell, London, 1959)

Bix: Man and Legend, by Richard M. Sudhalter and Philip Evans (Quartet Books, London, 1974)

Eubie Blake, by Al Rose (Schirmer, New York, 1979)

In Search of Buddy Bolden, by Don Marquis (Louisiana State University Press, Baton Rouge, 1978)

Benny Carter: a Life in American Music, 2 vols., by Morroe Berger, Edward Berger and James Patrick (Scarecrow Press, Metuchen, N.J., 1982)

Stomp Off, Let's Go! — the Story of Bob Crosby's Bobcats and Big Band, by John Chilton (Jazz Book Service, London, 1983)

BG — Off the record: a Bio-Discography of Benny Goodman, by Donald Connor and Warren Hicks (Arlington House, New York, 1969)

Hendersoniana: the Music of Fletcher Henderson and His Musicians, by Walter Allen (the Author, Highland Park, N.J., 1973)

Billie's Blues: a Survey of Billie Holiday's Career 1933–59, by John Chilton (Quartet Books, London, 1975)

Billie Holiday, by Burnett James (Spellmount, Tunbridge Wells, 1984)

George Lewis, a Jazzman from New Orleans, by Tom Bethell (California University Press, Berkeley, 1977)

McKinney's Music: a Bio-Discography of McKinney's Cotton Pickers, by John Chilton (Bloomsbury Bookshop, London, 1978)

Mister Jelly Roll: the Fortunes of Jelly Roll Morton, New Orleans Creole and 'Inventor of Jazz', by Alan Lomax (Duell, New York, 1950)

Jelly Roll Morton, by Martin Williams (Cassell, London, 1962)

King Joe Oliver, by Walter Allen and B.A.L. Rust (Sidgwick & Jackson, London, 1958)

King Oliver, by Martin Williams (Cassell, London, 1960)

Django Reinhardt, by Charles Delaunay (Cassell, London, 1961)

The Book of Django, by Max Abrams (the Author, Los Angeles, 1973)

Bessie Smith, by Paul Oliver (Cassell, London, 1959)

Bessie Smith, by Chris Albertson (Barrie & Jenkins, London, 1972)

Jack Teagarden's Music: His Career and Recordings, by H.J. Waters (Allen, Stanhope, N.J., 1960)

Fats Waller, by Charles Fox (Cassell, London, 1960)

Ain't Misbehaving: the Story of Fats Waller, by W.T.E. Kirkeby (Peter Davies, London, 1966)

Clarence Williams, by Tom Lord (Storyville, London, 1976)

Lester Young, by Dave Gelly (Spellmount, Tunbridge Wells, 1984)

Some Periodical Essays

'The musical style of Louis Armstrong', by David Caffey, in *Journal of Jazz Studies*, autumn 1975, pp. 72–96

'Vintage Basie', by Edward Towler, in *Jazz Monthly*, June 1957, pp. 2–6

'The Blue Rhythm Band', by Frank Littler, in *Jazz Monthly*, September 1957, pp. 7–8

'Gray Jazz: a study of the Casa Loma Band', by Frank Littler, in *Jazz Monthly*, May 1961, pp. 8–12

'Johnny Dunn' by Harvey Pekar, in *Jazz Journal*, March 1971, pp. 28–30

'Roy Eldridge', by Michael James, in *Jazz Monthly*, February 1968, pp. 5–10

'Stomping at the Savoy with Fred Elizalde', by Peter Tanner, in *Jazz Monthly*, January 1971, pp. 26–30

'Un pianiste nommé Ellington', by Demètre Ioakimidis, in *Jazz Hot*, March, April, May, June 1961

'Ellington: a time of transition', by Demètre Ioakimidis, in *Jazz Monthly*, February 1973, pp. 5–7

'*Black, Brown and Beige* — an Analysis', by Alan Cohen and Brian Priestley, in *Composer*, spring, summer, winter 1974

'Volly de Faut', by Ralph Venables, in *Jazz Music*, vol. 3, No. 4 (1946), pp. 10–12

'Some Benny Goodman alternatives', by Max Harrison, in *Jazz Forum*, November 1983, pp. 48–52

'Brad Gowans', by Ralph Venables, in *Jazz Music*, vol. 3, No. 6 (1947), pp. 9–13

'Frank Guarente, a forgotten pioneer', by Giuseppe Barazzetta, in *Jazz Monthly*, December 1966, pp. 2–6

'Coleman Hawkins', by Charles Fox, in *Jazz Monthly*, October 1955, pp. 2–4, 32

'Coleman Hawkins today', by Michael James, in *Jazz Monthly*, March 1962, pp. 7–12

'Some Fletcher Henderson questions' by Jerome Shipman, in *Jazz Monthly*, March 1973, pp. 6–7

'Fletcher Henderson: naissance d'un style', by Daniel Nevers, in *Jazz Hot*, October 1974, pp. 8–11, 30

'Claude Hopkins', by Charles Fox, in *Jazz Forum*, January 1947, pp. 7–9

'Spike: an analytical study of Spike Hughes's British recordings 1930–33', by Peter Tanner, in *Jazz Monthly*, June/July 1971, pp. 8–10, and July/August 1971, pp. 13–16

'Bubber Miley', by Roger Pryor Dodge, in *Jazz Monthly*, May 1958, pp. 2–7, 32

'Benny Morton', by Richard Bolton, in *Jazz Journal*, February 1974, pp. 4–8, 70

'Structural aspects of King Oliver's 1923 OKeh recordings', by Lawrence Koch, in *Journal of Jazz Studies*, spring 1976, pp. 36–46

'Talking about King Oliver: an oral history excerpt', by Clyde Bernhardt, in *Annual Review of Jazz Studies I* (1982), edited by Dan Morgenstern *et al.*, pp. 32–38

'The achievement of ragtime', by Peter Dickinson, in *Proceedings of the Royal Musical Association*, vol. 105 (1978–79), pp. 63–76

'Don Redman', by Charles Fox, in *Jazz Monthly*, April 1962, pp. 8–12

'Adrian Rollini' by Tony Shoppee, in *Jazz Journal*, August 1970, pp. 20–2, and October 1970, p. 7

'Leon Roppolo', by Sally Ann Worsfold, in *Jazz Journal*, February 1980, pp. 21–2

'Artie Shaw and His Gramercy Five', by Vladimir Simosko, in *Journal of Jazz Studies*, October 1973, pp. 34–56

'Jabbo Smith: una grande tromba degli anni venti', by Aldo and Paolo Gianoli, in *Musica Jazz*, January 1981, pp. 2–7

'Frank Teschemacher: a reappraisal', by Vladimir Simosko, in *Journal of Jazz Studies*, autumn 1975, pp. 28–53

'Fats Waller: the outside insider', by Morroe Berger, in *Journal of Jazz Studies*, October 1973, pp. 3–20

'Leo Watson: a giant lost in time', by Martin Davidson, in *Jazz Monthly*, May 1973, pp. 14–20

'Juice Wilson', by Alec Boswell, in *Storyville*, February/March 1978, pp. 90–94

'Why so sad, Pres?', by Louis Gottlieb, in *Jazz*, spring 1959, pp. 185–96

Index of
LP Titles

References are to numbered LPs in the text, *not* to page numbers.

Index of
Tune Titles

All references are to numbered LPs in the text, *not* to page numbers. To facilitate comparisons this index includes tunes recorded two or more times by different performers.

Index of Musicians

and of other persons
mentioned in the text

All references are to numbered LPs in the text, *not* to page numbers. Both major references to records reviewed and minor references to incidental discussion are included. Where entries for a musician are either all major or all minor, the numbers are given in the ordinary type. When entries for a musician are both major and minor, the major are shown in bold type. For the most frequently cited musicians, the nature of the references is indicated more specifically.

Costa, Eddie, 215
Cottrell, Louis, 32
Coulter, Glenn, 205
Courance, Edgar, 102
Cox, Baby, 91
Cox, Ida, 32
Crawford, Jimmy, 138
Crawford, Rosetta, 243
Crawley, Wilton, 66, 242
Creath, Charlie, 44, **75**, 209
Crenshaw, Rev. R.C., **2**, 89/91
Crescent City Jazzers, 23
Crosby, Bing, 122, 124, 185, 197
Crosby, Bob, 12, 23/24, 118, 132, 138, 141, 169, 178, 235, **236**
Crowder, Bob, 147, 161
Cuffee, Ed, 30, 57
Curson, Ted, 56
Cutshall, Cutty, 239

d'Amato, Chappie, 97
Dameron, Tadd, 138, 196, 209, 249
d'Amico, Hank, 196, 199
Dandridge, Putney, 156, 166, 184
Daniels, Douglas & Wilbur, 167
Darby, Blind, 1
Davenport, Cow Cow, **17**, 169
Davenport, Jed, 4
Davis, Bobby, 69
Davis, Lew, 97, 98
Davis, Miles, 154, 194/195, 246
Davis, Wild Bill, 224
Davison, Wild Bill, 239
Debussy, Claude, 8/9, 67, 108, 118, 213
DeDroit, Johnny, 23
Deems, Barrett, 119
DeFaut, Volly, **45**, **53**, **54**, 235
DeFranco, Buddy, **139**, **218**, 219, **248**
Delaunay, Charles, 124
Delisle, Big Eye Louis Nelson, 25, 26
Delta Four, 184
DeNaut, Jud, 160
DeParis, Sidney, 81, 124, 173, 188, 225/226, 228, 242
Deppe, Lois, **49**, 221
DeReuver, Annie, 101
Desmond, Paul, 99/100, 214

Desnos, Robert, 120
Devonshire Restaurant Dance Band, 97
Dial, Harry, 59
Dickenson, Vic, 149, 212, 226, 241
Dickerson, Carroll, 48, 80
Dickerson, R.Q., 76
Dillard, Bill, 107
Dison, 49
Dixie Rhythm Kings, 59
Dixieland Jug Blowers, **1**, **39**, 58
Dixon, Charlie, 137
Dixon, George, 59
Dodds, Baby, 26, 28, 29, 31, 47
Dodds, Johnny, 4, 18, 22, 23/24, **34**, **35**, **37**, **38/40**, 42, **44**, **47**, **48**, 49, 53, 59, 60, 66, 82, 169, 227, **230**, 235, 236, 242
Dolphy, Eric, 56, 209
Dominique, Natty, 38/40, 229, 230
Donaldson, Bobby, 213
Donaldson, Jack, 97
Donaldson, Rev. W.A., 3
Donizetti, Gaetano, 21
Donnelly, Ted, 132
Dorsey, Jimmy, **66**, **67**, **69**, **70**, **71**, **72**, 83, 97, 119, **120**, 139, **150/151**, 156
Dorsey, Tommy, **56**, 98, 119, **139**, 145, 147, 156, **192**, 231/232, 233
Dorsey Brothers Orchestra, 84, 200, 201
Dougherty, Eddie, 168
Douglass, Bill, 218
Driggs, Frank, 77
Duffy, Al, 69
Dumaine, Louis, 22
Dunham, Sonny, 74
Dunn, Johnny, 46
Durham, Eddie, **78**, 132, **138**, **157**
Dutrey, Honoré, 12, **39**, 43, **44**

Eckstein, Willie, 17
Eckstine, Billy, 18, 208
Edegran, Lars Ivar, 10
Edison, Harry, **133/134**, **135**, 140, **180**, **196**, 213
Edwards, Eddie, 12
Edwards, Teddy, 214